T0328985

International Business Risk

A Handbook for the Asia-Pacific Region

International Business Risk is an attempt to help investors and students of contemporary Asian affairs navigate the risk environments of Asia. Using the most up-to-date information and analytical techniques, the volume analyses the political, economic, regulatory, and security environments of 12 Asian countries. Each country is assessed for its political and economic trends, investment risks, and opportunities in a way that is clear, concise and easily assessible. The handbook conveys forecast information through a series of charts, graphs, and boxed summaries of data, making it a handy reference guide for business professionals as well as teaching and research professionals engaged in international relations, international business and trade with Asia.

Darryl Jarvis is Director, Centre for International Risk, and Senior Lecturer, International Risk and International Relations, Faculty of Economics and Business, University of Sydney, Australia.

For My Grandparents
Irene and Leslie Allen
RIP

International Business Risk
A Handbook for the Asia-Pacific Region

Edited by
Darryl S.L. Jarvis
University of Sydney

CAMBRIDGE UNIVERSITY PRESS
Cambridge, New York, Melbourne, Madrid, Cape Town,
Singapore, São Paulo, Delhi, Tokyo, Mexico City

Cambridge University Press
The Edinburgh Building, Cambridge CB2 8RU, UK

Published in the United States of America by Cambridge University Press, New York

www.cambridge.org
Information on this title: www.cambridge.org/9780521175517

First published 2003
First paperback edition 2011

A catalogue record for this publication is available from the British Library

National Library of Australia Cataloguing in Publication data
Jarvis, D.S.L., 1963– .
International business risk: a handbook for the Asia–Pacific region.
Bibliography.
Includes index.
ISBN 0 521 82194 0.
1. Investments, Foreign – Asia. 2. Investments, Foreign –
Pacific Area. 3. Country risk – Asia. 4. Country risk –
Pacific Area. I. Title.
332.6730995

ISBN 978-0-521-82194-0 Hardback
ISBN 978-0-521-17551-7 Paperback

Contents

Acknowledgements

Volumes as extensive and far ranging as this one are the result of much effort, dedication, and countless hours of research and interviews, not to mention a wealth of personal experience and knowledge about the subject matter, business environment, and the countless number of factors that shape the risk climate for international business. As an editor, I have been blessed with a team of dedicated professionals who, without exception, have given far more than they were asked, obliged with deadlines, were good natured about critical suggestions, and produced insights and commentaries about their surveyed countries beyond my expectations. Each person deserves mention.

Colin Brown, Professor of Asian Studies at the Flinders University of South Australia, and long-time Indonesia observer, toiled under particularly stringent deadlines. His good humor in meeting these was inspirational and proved invaluable to the success of the project. Malcolm Cook set new standards for punctuality, and happily provided last minute modifications that would have tested the patience of any busy professional. William Case was first off the mark with his extremely insightful analysis of Malaysia, and his willingness to meet our onerous deadlines and suggestions. Likewise, S. Javed Maswood committed to the project with great enthusiasm and obliged with additional materials and on-going requests for still further information. To all concerned, I am profoundly grateful.

As with any research endeavor, a few individuals proved invaluable and instrumental to the successful completion of the project. Marcus Chadwick, of the Centre for International Risk in the Faculty of Economics and Business at the University of Sydney, gave both his time and expertise, as well as the wealth of experience from his professional life in risk insurance, and, prior to that, the development of strategic business information products. In no small measure, his contributions have shaped this volume for the better, for which I remain indebted.

By no means last, Jane Ford, a director and partner at the firm Alpha Risk International, and Terry O'Callaghan, co-director of the Centre for International Risk and resident of the School of International Studies, University of South Australia, were instrumental in discussions that led to the conception of the project, its design and realization. Their dedication to the project was time and again demonstrated, not least by the heavy research burden each assumed despite extensive professional commitments, and by the endless requests of Jane for assistance, input, and information – requests that I am sure she thought would never end! To both, my sincere thanks for a job well done.

Finally, thanks are due to the folks at Cambridge University Press, especially Peter Debus, whose belief in the project from the very beginning ensured its realization. Peter's great efforts in sticking with the project proved instrumental, as did the comments of the anonymous reviewers who generously provided a series of insightful suggestions and modifications, all of which have served to strengthen the volume for the better.

Darryl S.L. Jarvis

Risk and Country Risk Assessment: Methodology

This volume was developed for professionals who engage in cross-border investment and international business activities, as well as for corporate strategists, researchers and students of international economics and international relations.

The structure of the volume is based on a template formula, and was developed after wide consultation with fund managers, members of the international banking community, risk managers, corporate strategists, consulting houses and research professionals. Discussions and presentations were held throughout Asia, with numerous interviews conducted of leading investment professionals in the United States, United Kingdom, Australia and Canada.

The result was the formulation of a set of indices and qualitative assessments focusing on six major country risk areas:

Section A: Economy

Macroeconomic Overview

Section B: Risks and projections

Macroeconomic performance and risk indicators
Export performance
Currency movements and projections
Financial markets: Performance and developments

Private and public sector debt
Labor market trends
Consumer and business confidence
Stock market
Corporate tax
Residential and commercial property markets
Foreign direct investment

Section C: Politics

Corruption index
Corporate governance index
Political stability
Foreign investor risk index

Section D: Security

Section E: Economic and political risk forecasts

Section F: Country fact sheet

These were designed to be accessible to as wide an audience as possible, and to provide time series data as up-to-date as possible, while also using trend analysis and scenario generation to construct forecasts for 2003–04, and beyond.

The project has thus been devised with the explicit intention of looking forward, to appraise professionals of the risk environments they are likely to confront, examine major developments on the horizon, and the strategic trigger points that need to be factored into business and foreign investment planning decisions.

It is important to note that the project was not conceived as a purely economic forecast of the economies of Asia. On the contrary, after extensive discussions with business and investment professionals, time and again it was identified by them that much of the information they wanted to source was not always purely economic. Rather, they were interested in those political factors that would impact on markets; things like public policy developments or changes in government policy that would affect the operating parameters of enterprises or market segments; regulatory and prudential changes that might affect compliance issues for lawful operation and the implications for market depth and breadth; structural changes to market composition as a result of political interference, corruption, or nepotism; as well as strategic security developments that might impact on procurement practices, production and delivery schedules, foreign expatriate employees, and the viability of plant and equipment.

Indeed, what became overtly apparent was that, while there exists a wealth of economic forecasting instruments available to business, little strategic analysis of non-economic, and broadly political, regulatory, strategic and public policy areas is currently available to assist business professionals in corporate planning and investment placement decisions. It was thus decided to fill this void by providing a comprehensive and useful tool that surveyed the Asia-Pacific in ways contiguous with those needs identified in our varied conversations.

The problems in constructing such an analysis, however, have proven daunting, not least because of the multitude of factors that necessarily need to be considered, but also because standardized and well-recognized formulas for structuring such analyses, prioritizing issues, and connecting them in ways that provide insight to the holistic risk environment, are not yet evident. This project has thus been pioneering, inasmuch as we have been forced to engage with the blunt realities of issue identification, issue management, and issue prioritization and develop indices that measure the impact of these in ways that can be usefully mined by professionals.

It should be noted, however, that this process is far from complete: risk analysis – especially country risk analysis – is a constantly evolving profession. More generally, it should also be noted that the end result is far from satisfactory, if only because the twin objectives of the project have proven incongruous: the want to address the specifics of an investment environment in as detailed and richly informative way as possible, while also devising a country profile that speaks to a wider business community. This problem will be famously recognized by economists as the division between macroeconomics and microeconomics, with each speaking to the needs of different agendas and levels of analysis. No less a problem has been confronted in this volume; the need to speak to particular industry segments in order to make the information pertinent, juxtaposed against the need to be inclusive and speak to a wider international business community engaged in a multitude of industries and using numerous investment instruments.

Mindful of this, and the twin dangers of both particularism and generalism, this volume has sought to tread a fine line between the practical parameters of micro- and macro-political-cum-economic issues, where each country has been analyzed for its macroeconomic and macro-political indicators and environment, but then enriched by specific analyses of individual market and economic segments. Finally, each country analysis has then attempted to relate these factors to the macro-political and strategic environments, culminating in a series of risk indicators developed to measure the macro risks faced by business operations in terms of corporate governance and transparency, indices of the propensity to corporate restructuring, political stability, corruption, law and order, the capacity of authorities to govern effectively, and a broad measure of holistic risk in the operating environment in terms of generic risk to foreign investors.

As with any project of this nature, the utilization of disparate data series also posed problems, not least because of wide variance in terms of country reporting techniques, transparency, accounting procedures, and the frequency of reporting. To discount these variances, data was collected from internationally recognized sources like the World Bank, the International Monetary Fund, the Asian Development Bank, among others, and then supplemented with national data series and forecasts of the Economist Intelligence Unit.

Importantly, however, data collection was only partially useful as a medium to assess country risk, and qualitative assessment techniques have thus been developed in the construction of this volume, primarily through a reliance on the generation of scenarios.

These aim to give as full a picture as possible of likely future developments and their implications for each of the market and macroeconomic and political segments considered in each chapter.

Finally, some comment is warranted about the selection process in terms of the countries analyzed in this volume. This, in fact, turned out to be the easiest of the many issues confronted. The yardstick employed centered around flows of foreign direct investment (FDI), with countries registering only nominal FDI flows omitted from the volume. Thus, for example, Burma was judged well below the FDI levels of comparable countries in the region, as was Laos, Cambodia, and Papua New Guinea. Of perhaps greater controversy because of their omission were Bangladesh and Sri Lanka, whose FDI flows have increased considerably over the last decade, not least in terms of FDI associated with textile production for export. However, in the end it was decided that both these countries lacked the critical mass of foreign business presence to warrant inclusion; a decision that might well prove premature in the coming decade.

Figures

Figures

Contributors

Colin Brown is Professor of Asian Studies at Flinders University of South Australia. He has also taught at Griffith University, the University of Tasmania, and the Australian National University. His teaching and research interests are in the areas of modern Indonesian history, politics and economics. He is author of *Indonesia: Dealing with a Neighbour*, and has published articles in *Australia–Asia Survey* and *Emerging Economic Systems in Asia*.

William Case is senior lecturer in the School of International Business and Asian Studies at Griffith University, Brisbane. He has taught at the University of Texas, the MARA University of Technology in Shah Alam, Malaysia, the Australian National University, and the Australian Defence Force Academy. His most recent book is *Politics in Southeast Asia: Democracy or Less* (2002). He has also published many book chapters and journal articles on Malaysian and East Asian politics.

Marcus Chadwick gained a Bachelor of Science from City University, London before completing his Master of Science in international political economy at the London School of Economics and Political Science. As a former country-risk economist and political risk insurance broker, Marcus has worked with a range of Asia-Pacific multinationals, instituting risk management strategies throughout Southeast Asia. He has also lectured Asian business leaders in political risk management strategies, including institutional responses to financial risk. He is currently research fellow with the Centre for International Risk, Faculty of Economics and Business, at the University of Sydney.

Malcolm Cook is lecturer at the Ateneo de Manila University's Department of Political Science, where he teaches international political economy and Southeast Asian Studies. He is currently on study leave pursuing research on banking reform in the Asia–Pacific region at the Department of International Relations, Research School of Pacific and Asian Studies at the Australian National University, Canberra. Malcolm is a regular contributor to Oxford Analytica's Asia–Pacific briefings, has worked with the Philippine Institute of Development Studies at the APEC Studies Center, and has published articles in *Pilipinas*, and the *Asian Journal of Social Studies*.

Jane Ford received her PhD from the University of Sydney, before working for the Australian federal government in various advisory capacities. She specializes in the analysis of international institutions and the political economy of trade policy. She is also director and partner in the firm Alpha Risk International, a company specializing in risk advisory services for global business, where she heads the Asia–Pacific Investment Risk Division.

Darryl S. L. Jarvis is director of the Centre for International Risk and senior lecturer in international risk and international relations, in the Faculty of Economics and Business at the University of Sydney, Australia. His research interests include international risk analysis and methodology, risk assessment of the Asia–Pacific, and the globalization of money and finance. He has contributed articles to *Politics and Society* (USA), *Policy, Organization and Society* (Australia), and *Asian Survey* (Berkeley, USA), and is the author of a series of monographs and edited books on international relations. He is a frequent media commentator on international affairs, and regularly addresses business forums on international risk and regional developments in Asia. He is currently developing a book project for corporate professionals on international risk analysis and management.

S. Javed Maswood is associate professor in the School of International Business and Asian Studies, Griffith University. He has written several books on Japan and international political economy. His last two publications are *Japan in Crisis*, and *Japan: Continuity and Change*.

Terry O'Callaghan is lecturer in the School of International Studies at the University of South Australia. He teaches courses on international relations and international risk. He is co-author of *International Relations: The Key Concepts* and has published articles on international relations in the Asia–Pacific. His research interests focus on the relationship between international relations and international business, political risk analysis in the Asia–Pacific, and mining sector risk. He is co-director of the Centre for International Risk, a joint venture with the University of Sydney. He is currently writing a book on the principles of international investment risk with Darryl Jarvis.

Tianbiao Zhu is a Postdoctoral Fellow in the Research School of Pacific and Asian Studies at the Australian National University, Canberra, and a lecturer in the School of Public Policy and Management at Tsinghua University, China. He received his MPhil from the University of Cambridge and PhD from Cornell University. His main research interest is international and comparative political economy, and he is currently doing research on the political economy of development in Taiwan, South Korea, and China.

Abbreviations

Air Pollution	Convention on Long-Range Transboundary Air Pollution
Air Pollution–Nitrogen Oxides	Protocol to the 1979 Convention on Long-Range Transboundary Air Pollution Concerning the Control of Emissions of Nitrogen Oxides or Their Transboundary Fluxes
Air Pollution–Persistent Organic Pollutants	Protocol to the 1979 Convention on Long-Range Transboundary Air Pollution on Persistent Organic Pollutants
Air Pollution–Sulphur 85	Protocol to the 1979 Convention on Long-Range Transboundary Air Pollution on the Reduction of Sulphur Emissions or Their Transboundary Fluxes by at Least 30%
Air Pollution–Sulphur 94	Protocol to the 1979 Convention on Long-Range Transboundary Air Pollution on Further Reduction of Sulphur Emissions
Air Pollution–Volatile Organic Compounds	Protocol to the 1979 Convention on Long-Range Transboundary Air Pollution Concerning the Control of Emissions of Volatile Organic Compounds or Their Transboundary Fluxes
ANZUS	Australia–New Zealand–United States Security Treaty
APEC	Asia-Pacific Economic Cooperation
ARF	ASEAN Regional Forum
AsDB	Asian Development Bank
ASEAN	Association of Southeast Asian Nations
Autodin	Automatic Digital Network
Biodiversity	Convention on Biological Diversity
BIS	Bank for International Settlements
C	Commonwealth
Caricom	Caribbean Community and Common Market
CB	citizen's band mobile radio communications
CCC	Customs Cooperation Council
CE	Council of Europe
CEMA	Council for Mutual Economic Assistance; also known as CMEA or Comecon
CEMAC	Monetary and Economic Community of Central Africa
CEPGL	Economic Community of the Great Lakes Countries
CERN	European Organization for Nuclear Research
c.i.f.	cost, insurance, and freight
CIS	Commonwealth of Independent States
CITES	see Endangered Species
Climate Change	United Nations Framework Convention on Climate Change
Climate Change–Kyoto Protocol	Kyoto Protocol to the United Nations Framework Convention on Climate Change

COCOM	Coordinating Committee on Export Controls
Comsat	Communications Satellite Corporation
CP	Colombo Plan
CY	calendar year
DC	developed country
DSN	Defense Switched Network
DWT	deadweight ton
EBRD	European Bank for Reconstruction and Development
EC	European Community
ECO	Economic Cooperation Organization
ECOSOC	Economic and Social Council
EEC	European Economic Community
EFTA	European Free Trade Association
EIB	European Investment Bank
EMU	European Monetary Union
Endangered Species	Convention on the International Trade in Endangered Species of Wild Flora and Fauna (CITES)
Entente	Council of the Entente
Environmental Modification	Convention on the Prohibition of Military or Any Other Hostile Use of Environmental Modification Techniques
ESCAP	Economic and Social Commission for Asia and the Pacific
ESCWA	Economic and Social Commission for Western Asia
est.	estimate
EU	European Union
Ex-Im	Export-Import Bank of the United States
FAO	Food and Agriculture Organization
FAX	facsimile
f.o.b.	free on board
FLS	Front Line States
FY	fiscal year
G-2	Group of 2
G-3	Group of 3
G-5	Group of 5
G-6	Group of 6
G-7	Group of 7
G-8	Group of 8
G-9	Group of 9
G-10	Group of 10
G-11	Group of 11
G-15	Group of 15
G-19	Group of 19
G-24	Group of 24
G-30	Group of 30
G-33	Group of 33
G-77	Group of 77
GATT	General Agreement on Tariffs and Trade; now WTrO
GCC	Gulf Cooperation Council
GDP	gross domestic product
GNP	gross national product
GRT	gross register ton
GWP	gross world product
Hazardous Wastes	Basel Convention on the Control of Transboundary Movements of Hazardous Wastes and Their Disposal
HF	high-frequency
IADB	Inter-American Development Bank
IAEA	International Atomic Energy Agency
IBEC	International Bank for Economic Cooperation
IBRD	International Bank for Reconstruction and Development (World Bank)
ICAO	International Civil Aviation Organization

ICC	International Chamber of Commerce
ICJ	International Court of Justice (World Court)
ICRC	International Committee of the Red Cross
ICRM	International Red Cross and Red Crescent Movement
ICTR	International Criminal Tribunal for Rwanda
ICTY	International Criminal Tribunal for the former Yugoslavia
IDA	International Development Association
IDB	Islamic Development Bank
IEA	International Energy Agency
IFAD	International Fund for Agricultural Development
IFC	International Finance Corporation
IFCTU	International Federation of Christian Trade Unions
IFRCS	International Federation of Red Cross and Red Crescent Societies
IGAD	Inter-Governmental Authority on Development
IGADD	Inter-Governmental Authority on Drought and Development
IHO	International Hydrographic Organization
IIB	International Investment Bank
ILO	International Labor Organization
IMF	International Monetary Fund
IMO	International Maritime Organization
Inmarsat	International Mobile Satellite Organization
InOC	Indian Ocean Commission
Intelsat	International Telecommunications Satellite Organization
Interpol	International Criminal Police Organization
Intersputnik	International Organization of Space Communications
IOC	International Olympic Committee
IOM	International Organization for Migration
ISO	International Organization for Standardization
ITU	International Telecommunication Union
kHz	kilohertz
km	kilometer
kW	kilowatt
kWh	kilowatt-hour
Law of the Sea	United Nations Convention on the Law of the Sea (LOS)
LDC	less developed country
LLDC	least developed country
London Convention	see Marine Dumping
LOS	see Law of the Sea
m	meter
Marine Dumping	Convention on the Prevention of Marine Pollution by Dumping Wastes and Other Matter
Marine Life Conservation	Convention on Fishing and Conservation of Living Resources of the High Seas
Mercosur	Southern Cone Common Market
MHz	megahertz
NA	not available
NAM	Nonaligned Movement
NATO	North Atlantic Treaty Organization
NC	Nordic Council
NEA	Nuclear Energy Agency
NIC	newly industrializing country
NIE	newly industrializing economy
NIS	new independent states
NM	nautical mile
NSG	Nuclear Suppliers Group
Nuclear Test Ban	Treaty Banning Nuclear Weapons Tests in the Atmosphere, in Outer Space, and Under Water
NZ	New Zealand

OAPEC	Organization of Arab Petroleum Exporting Countries
ODA	official development assistance
OECD	Organization for Economic Cooperation and Development
OIC	Organization of the Islamic Conference
OOF	other official flows
OPCW	Organization for the Prohibition of Chemical Weapons
OPEC	Organization of Petroleum Exporting Countries
Ozone Layer Protection	Montreal Protocol on Substances That Deplete the Ozone Layer
PCA	Permanent Court of Arbitration
PFP	Partnership for Peace
SAARC	South Asian Association for Regional Cooperation
SHF	super-high-frequency
Ship Pollution	Protocol of 1978 Relating to the International Convention for the Prevention of Pollution From Ships, 1973 (MARPOL)
Sparteca	South Pacific Regional Trade and Economic Cooperation Agreement
SPC	South Pacific Commission
SPF	South Pacific Forum
sq km	square kilometer
sq mi	square mile
Tropical Timber 83	International Tropical Timber Agreement, 1983
Tropical Timber 94	International Tropical Timber Agreement, 1994
UAE	United Arab Emirates
UHF	ultra-high-frequency
UK	United Kingdom
UN	United Nations
UNCTAD	United Nations Conference on Trade and Development
UNDCP	United Nations Drug Control Program
UNDOF	United Nations Disengagement Observer Force
UNDP	United Nations Development Program
UNEP	United Nations Environment Program
UNESCO	United Nations Educational, Scientific, and Cultural Organization
UNHCR	United Nations High Commissioner for Refugees
UNHCRHR	United Nations High Commissioner for Human Rights
UNICRI	United Nations Interregional Crime and Justice Research Institute
UNIDIR	United Nations Disarmament Research
UNIDO	United Nations Industrial Development Organization
UNITAR	United Nations Institute for Training and Research
UNMOGIP	United Nations Military Observer Group in India and Pakistan
UNMOVIC	United Nations Monitoring and Verification Commission
UNRISD	United Nations Research Institute for Social Development
UNTAET	United Nations Transitional Administration in East Timor
UNTSO	United Nations Truce Supervision Organization
UNU	United Nations University
UPU	Universal Postal Union
US	United States
VHF	very-high-frequency
WCL	World Confederation of Labor
WEU	Western European Union
WFC	World Food Council
WFP	World Food Program
WFTU	World Federation of Trade Unions
WHO	World Health Organization
WIPO	World Intellectual Property Organization
WMO	World Meteorological Organization
WTO	see WToO for World Tourism Organization or WTrO for World Trade Organization
WToO	World Tourism Organization
WTrO	World Trade Organization
ZC	Zangger Committee

The Asia-Pacific region

1 Toward 2004: Asia-Pacific Outlook and Prospects

Darryl S.L. Jarvis

Introduction

The 1990s were both kind and cruel to Asia; kind inasmuch as growth in the first half of the decade was robust and expansive, development was widespread and rapid by historical standards, and markets were expanding in virtually every economic sector from consumer durables to infrastructure and construction. In response, investors from around the globe poured capital into the region, convinced of its future and stability. But even the Asian miracle proved fallible, bursting in 1997–98 in a series of cataclysmic financial sector meltdowns; the economic and social effects of which are still being widely felt today.

As Asia moves forward toward 2004, its markets, economies and political systems are viewed now in a more vexed and nuanced light by creditors and investors alike, who are acutely aware of the risk premium that all emerging markets carry. Risk has become the new benchmark by which to understand emerging markets, and its purview greatly expanded beyond purely economic quarters to include political, regulatory, social, indeed cultural risk. Understanding the rubric of risk and its multifarious dimensions as they apply to the leading economies of Asia in the coming years, comprises the principal concern of this volume.

Pain and suffering: Reform and restructuring

In large measure, the future of Asia and its composite risk profile is brighter today than it was before the financial crisis, thanks in large part to the painful but on-going series of public sector restructurings and private sector corporate reorganizations and rationalizations that have been taking place since 1998–99. These are far from finalized, but point the way toward the future, with an increasing emphasis on corporate transparency and governance, fiscal rectitude, anti-corruption crusades, and enhanced systems for public sector governance. Asia remains awash with international agencies attempting to engineer prudential and regulatory systems of governance to stabilize financial markets. Governments and populations too, have become more cognizant of the need for such measures as a means to longer-term stability and economic growth. Few would now suggest such measures unnecessary, and fewer still would want to turn the clock back to pre 1997.

In this light, and with the exception of Japan, Asia is experiencing great leaps forward, and a new-found confidence about its future. The movement toward democratization, greater electoral transparency, and popular participation in major national decisions, would have been thought largely impossible only a few short years ago. Corruption, nepotism and cronyism are all under the spotlight as antithetical to national interests, growth and political stability, and have touched nearly all the countries of the region in ways that have ushered in significant change. In the Philippines and Indonesia, these have changed governments and political systems, emblematic of a new mass consciousness of the dangers and forgone wealth that previous corrupt rule brought. Increasingly, democratic participation is now a requirement for governments to claim legitimacy, with widespread evidence of the rollback of undemocratic practices, graft and corruption. Nor should this trend be underestimated, representing a sea-change to forms of governance not imaginable in the mid 1990s.

All this bodes well for Asia's future, albeit that such reforms are far from complete. What it signals is a movement toward the formal organization of national polities along broadly concurrent liberal–democratic lines, and the formalization of markets and economies constructed along internationally recognized systems – broadly compliant with international standards in terms of capital provisions, prudential systems and regulatory norms. However, this said, great diversity remains in Asia, with some economies more advanced than others, as is evident by the diverse risk premiums attached to each country. This will continue to be the case beyond 2004, with dissimilar growth trajectories and reform processes taking place, although broadly situated amid overall regional progress.

Change and transformation: China and corporate reorganization

Of most significance to the region has been the about-face of foreign direct investment (FDI) flows, which, in the early to mid 1990s saw 50 percent of FDI into Asia locate itself in the economies of the Association of South East Asian Nations (ASEAN), with only around 16–20 percent destined for China. In 2002, this figure is virtually reversed, with approximately 55–60 percent of regional FDI locating in China and only around 16–19 percent locating in ASEAN.

The longer-term ramifications for ASEAN nations are profound, hastening them to better develop regulatory and prudential systems, and liberalize their economies more quickly in order to compete in the race for FDI, now drawn more than ever to the growth potential of the Chinese market. This is a trend that will only deepen in 2004, with China set to maintain its hold over the lion's share of regional FDI, with other Asian states forced to compete for the dwindling remainder.

In point of fact, however, there are benefits associated with this new found competition for FDI. ASEAN states, in particular, will doubtless have to stick with their reform programs or face the prospects of a growing disinterest from international investors, while international investors can increasingly expect better terms and conditions in order to attract them, with generally improved levels of corporate transparency and cleaner financial markets in which to invest.

To be sure, however, the process has been painful for both investor and ASEAN states alike – with little sign of relief before 2004–05. ASEAN states, for example, are witnessing closures of manufacturing plant and employment downsizings, depriving their governments of important revenue streams. Foreign multinational enterprises are likewise re-appraising their commitment to many ASEAN states, and generally closing their Southeast Asian country operations in preference for Chinese corporate forms of organization that are now regionally rather country focused.

This reorientation in corporate focus will deepen throughout 2004 and beyond, with the movement toward China set to gain greater momentum. Indeed, multinational enterprises have learned a harsh lesson after the initial exuberance for investing in ASEAN and Southeast Asian states, with these markets proving fickle and too small to sustain the level of FDI interest they initially generated in the early to mid 1990s. Consider, for example, the fact that the combined gross national product of Singapore, Thailand, Indonesia, and Malaysia, only just approaches the size of the GNP produced annually in the province of Ontario, Canada. Corporate strategists should thus be mindful of the fact that foreign investment allocations need to be proportional to market size and depth. By and large, emerging economies suffer a much lower capital saturation level than do more mature economies, compounded by generally underdeveloped financial markets lesser able to allocate financial resources in a way commensurate with investor risk expectations.

Likewise, market depth and GDP per capita in most ASEAN states remains small by comparison to the more mature markets of Western Europe and North America, indicating only limited stratums of middle-class consumers with both the taste preference for high-end consumer goods and the disposable incomes to enjoy them. The lessons being learnt now, then, are as much about poor corporate strategic planning and a less than familiar understanding of these markets, as they are about the apportionment of blame for poor governance, corruption, and the absence of regulatory transparency of financial markets. Corporate risk management practices and capital exposure levels will thus have to be reassessed in light of many of these failed ventures.

Unfortunately, it is not apparent that this is the case, with the deafening rush to China reminiscent of the rush to ASEAN and Southeast Asian states only a few decades earlier. Foreign venture failure rates in China, for example, hover at around 50 percent, and are probably much higher but for corporate face-saving exercises carried out to preserve share values and reputations. Indeed, the risk premium of investing in China is rarely appreciated; with corporate executives fond of suggesting that all is now well as a result of China's entry into the WTO.

Little could be further from the truth, however, with precious little evidence of regular or substantial profit remittance from China by leading foreign multinational enterprises. It

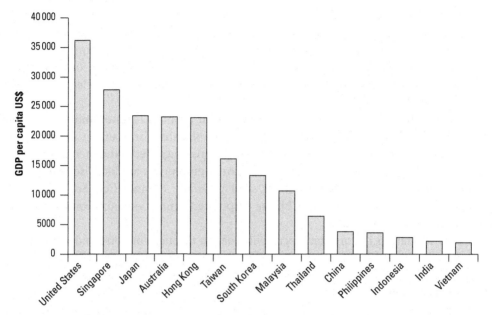

FIGURE 1.1 Rank of countries – GDP per capita US$ billion
Source: World Bank; International Monetary Fund

might well be the case that China could turn out to be the Vietnam of the new millennium, with corporate strategists wise to remember that fewer than 10 percent of the foreign multinational enterprises originally established in Vietnam in 1994 have turned a profit after 8 years of business activity. Most have now divested themselves of assets and returned home.

The bottom line: Beware of Chinese bearing gifts

If there is a lesson here it is one which suggests the need for corporate strategists to develop robust risk management practices; a better familiarity with the chosen investment destination(s); and a need to stand aside from the herd mentality of following the example of other organizations and assuming a fit with the risk profile and business strategy of one's own organization. In the case of China, the oft-quoted parable that it is a market of 1.3 billion people hides the fact that GDP per capita approaches only approximately US$3800, with this figure largely skewed by inclusion of income figures from the prosperous coastal cities. Indeed, if these are excluded, the GDP per capita of some 200 million Chinese is as low as US$2.00 per day. Consequently, the ability of the vast majority of China's population to absorb the increasing levels of FDI with commensurate consumption levels necessary to ensure foreign enterprise profitability, is vastly exaggerated by the 'China hype' currently working the corporate boardrooms.

Investors contemplating a move to China should therefore be acutely aware of the downsides, which, at this point in time, and well beyond 2004, will remain considerable.

External vulnerability: Risks ahead?

Asia's great success has rested largely on its ability to plug in to the demand structures of the Western economies, meeting the initially insatiable appetite for cheap, low-valued-added manufactured goods, labor-intensive production of consumer durables, and the provision of computer equipment and parts under the initial phase of the product cycle for personal and business computers.

This, of course, has also been Asia's great undoing, and responsible for the 'second regional crisis' of 2000–01 when the worldwide tech-meltdown occured. Particularly hard hit have been the economies of Singapore, Hong Kong, Taiwan and Thailand, with India and China relatively insulated due to the high level of protection enjoyed by India and the lower level of export reliance generally experienced by China.

The dislocation of the tech-meltdown has been tremendous, perhaps even greater in terms of longer-run implications than the crisis of 1997–98. The value of semi-conductor sales in September 2001, for example, was only half the equivalent of the levels in 2000, and only a nominal rebound was experienced in 2002. Income streams from exports in semi-conductors, otherwise extremely important to most of the Asian states, have therefore ushered in a period of profound restructuring and outright dislocation. Likewise, the end markets for these products have also suffered throughout Asia, with precipitous drops in valuations for telecom sectors in particular.

Unfortunately, little significant rebound can be expected in 2003–04, reflecting the ending of that phase in the product cycle that saw rapid demand expansion throughout the 1990s. What this signals for 2003–04 is a continuing high level of external vulnerability for

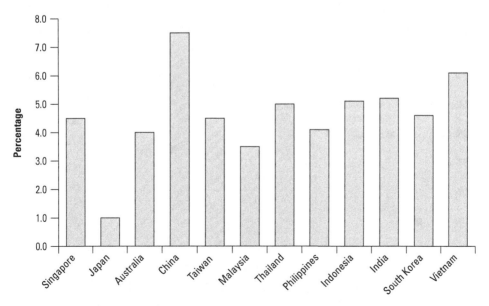

FIGURE 1.2 Growth forecasts for 2002–04
Source: World Bank Forward Estimates; Economist Intelligence Unit Forecasts

the Asian economies. In turn, much of their post-tech-sector meltdown recovery will be contingent on the fortunes of the main drivers of the global economy, principally the depth and continuity of the anticipated recovery in the United States in 2003–04, which, despite leading indicators, is still fragile.

Eyes on diversification

So too, much of the recovery in Asia will rest – especially in the longer term beyond 2004 – on the ability of governments to diversify the breadth of their economies beyond simply external demand drivers indicative of single product cycles, as with the technology sector. To a large extent, there is as yet little evidence to suggest much has been achieved, with most Asian economies, and especially those of ASEAN, currently in the midst of attempting to navigate the fallout of declining export revenues and rising unemployment levels. While this will moderate in 2003–04, astute investors should be looking for signs of economic diversification as a forward indicator of those economies that will be better placed to withstand future externals shocks.

Acknowledgement of this among regional governments is now well accepted, with a common mantra – although not always acted upon – to diversify into 'knowledge-based economies' and position themselves in readiness for the next product cycle likely to be driven by the anticipated bio-technology boom. Taiwan, South Korea, Thailand, Singapore, Malaysia and the Philippines have all indicated adoption of strategic plans to rapidly expand this sector of their economies, although some are better positioned than others to realize these ambitions. Singapore, in particular, is probably the regional leader, given both its

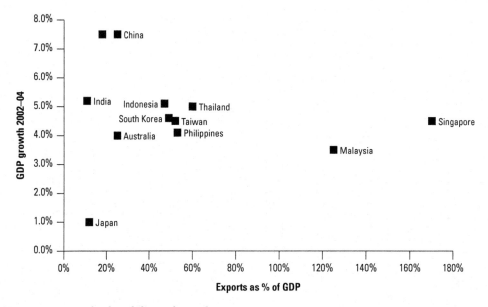

FIGURE 1.3 External vulnerability and growth prospects
Source: National Accounts; Economist Intelligence Unit Forecasts; Asian Development Bank

extensive educational infrastructure and well-developed levels of social capital. Thailand and the Philippines, by contrast, are less well positioned and likely will not realize significant FDI into bio-technology sectors.

Whatever the case, diversification will be the key to the longer-term game plans of Asian states beyond 2004, with those highly exposed and vulnerable economies already planning for such eventualities.

The Japan factor: Exporting deflation

Of equal concern to Asian states is not just the economic performance of the global and US economy, but also that of Japan. Japan remains a critical economy for Asia, being regionally predominant and the principal trading partner of most of Asia's economies. However, Japan's lackluster performance since the bursting of the bubble economy in the early 1990s, has not served Asia well, depressing Japanese consumption levels, import demand and asset prices, which, to some degree, have been exported to the rest of Asia in the form of lower demand levels and postponed consumption.

While reform of the banking and financial system is under way in Japan, as well as wide-ranging corporate sector reform, little meaningful resolution to this process can be expected in 2003–04. Consequently, as a demand source for Asian exports, Asia will remain dependent on the US and Western European economies if they are to achieve export-led growth. Again, this places greater emphasis on, and concentrates external vulnerability in, the US economy and its fortunes in 2003–04 and beyond.

This situation will likely continue for some time to come, not least because Japan is experiencing a rapid aging of its population, forestalling consumption expenditure by pushing up savings rates as a large segment of Japanese society prepares for retirement. So too, anticipation of deflation and continuing falling prices, while aggravating negative equity positions for investors in property markets and thus threatening savings and investments, is also stalling forward anticipated consumer expenditure with negative consequences for the region.

Unfortunately, there is little hope of any short-term solution to this conundrum in 2003–04; short of a deliberate government policy to re-inflate the economy, thereby eating away savings and forcing consumers to resume consumption expenditure for fear of seeing the longer-term value of their savings eroded. However, the current administration has steered away from any such policy, leaving the economy and the region to wait and watch for a slow, longer-term recovery.

Reform fatigue: The next great danger?

If there is perhaps a sleeping danger in Asia it resides in the onset of reform fatigue, already apparent in Thailand with creeping protectionism melded with political hubris and nationalism. The Thaksin administration, for example, has taken its foot off the reform accelerator, and shown a renewed disposition to dispense political favors through protectionist measures. In many senses, this harks back to the Asia of pre-1997, with thankfully few other economies following suit.

However, there are fears that if another round of crises were to hit the region, or the anticipated upturn in the US and global economy were less than hoped for, the reform agendas of many governments would necessarily be shelved for fear of domestic political backlash. While this looks like a worst-case and least likely scenario, it nonetheless underscores the fragility of the recovery process in Asia and its relationship to the reform process. Indeed, on the other side of the coin, exuberant growth, should it return to Asia post-2005, might also be reason for concern, with robust economic conditions tending to diminish the sense of urgency necessary to push through often unpalatable and politically sensitive reform agendas. Either way, both scenarios underscore that Asia has a limited window of opportunity with which to cement its commitment to the reform program and liberalization measures.

Regional security: Prospects and trigger points

Despite tumultuous changes in the region, stability has been more preponderant over the last few decades than at any time before. This bodes well for the immediate future, barring two on-going irritants.

First, the obvious great power rivalry between the United States and China, especially in terms of each wishing to exert a sphere of influence commensurate with its power capabilities, provides a backdrop to on-going regional tensions, demonstrated in 2001 with the downing of the US spy plane on Hainan Island.

There is every indication that these sporadic irritants will continue, with the Sino–US relationship likely to be underscored by a mutually suspicious, albeit congenial, relationship intermittently tested by diplomatic spats.

Importantly, however, there is no indication of the desire for hostile engagement, with the prospects for hot war rated as extremely low. Obviously, however, the trigger point

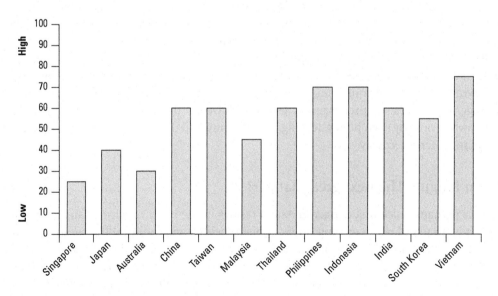

FIGURE 1.4 Risk rankings for Asian countries

leading to such outcomes lies in the alignment of US strategic interests with the protection of Taiwan's independence, something the United States under George W. Bush has been keen to reiterate, to the annoyance of Chinese authorities. Little is expected to change in 2003–04, with the issue of Taiwan remaining an on-going thorn in US–Sino relations.

Likewise, the War on Terror poses no overt security concerns for foreign investors in the region as a whole. While there are, to be sure, locally active militia and terrorist organizations, there is no discernible trend in the region toward Islamic militancy as a whole. The Philippines remains one exception to this, with a well-documented series of military skirmishes on the southern island of Mindanao requiring US troop deployment to help the Philippine administration secure its territorial integrity. However, there are few prospects of this spilling over into other countries and, for the most part, the security concerns are well contained.

Equally, the fear of resurgent Islamic fundamentalism in Indonesia is also contained, and represents a backlash against the breakdown of civil society and all forms of organized political expression that existed under Suharto. Much of the agitation currently in evidence in Indonesia, is thus better appreciated as the beginnings of organized political opposition, albeit using the instruments of Islam as a vehicle to mobilize mass political action. As such, it does not represent the beginnings of any nationally based fundamentalist movements with ambitions to terrorism and hostile engagement with the West or the United States.

In all, then, what can be observed about the region is inter-state stability in diplomatic and strategic affairs, and the continuance of this trend to at least 2004. What security concerns currently exist, are localized and are not tending to spill from one state to the next, as was often the case in the past. Foreign investors can thus approach Asia with few concerns about regional security stability in the coming decade.

Australia

2 Australia

Marcus Chadwick

Section A Economy

Overview

With as firm a grip as ever on the weathervane of Australian public sentiment and buoyed by rising living standards, the Howard-led conservative Coalition government confounded expectations by winning a third term in office in the November 2001 federal elections.

Fortunately for investors, growing protectionist sentiment toward illegal immigration is not reflected in the economic policy arena. Ostensibly, at least, the result paves the way for further reform of the Australian economy to complement deregulatory reforms undertaken in the previous two decades. The problem for the government is that a narrowly focused election campaign means only a narrow mandate to govern. The policy vacuum is all too readily apparent and will not serve Australia's international needs well in 2002–04.

Public policy reform slows

While this does not immediately detract from overall political and economic stability, it does undermine the administration's ability to push through electorally unpopular, industrial relations reform, as well as the proposed sale of remaining government assets – specifically, Telstra, the national telecommunications provider. It also reduces the likelihood that the federal government will tackle the issue of investment-distorting state-levied taxes. Other likely reform casualties include proposals to harmonize state electricity and gas pipeline regulations. Without the necessary government support, many of the proposed 'big-ticket' infrastructure projects such as the Queensland to PNG gas pipeline may also be stalled.

Paradoxically, the federal government's failure to engage the states may offer investors improved prospects of influencing the regulatory reform agenda. If investors are prepared to actively participate at the state level then reforms may be tailored more to the needs of existing and prospective investors than would otherwise be the case through engagement with the federal government, which tends to suffer as a result of its cumbersome size and thus insularity to the needs of individual investors.

To date, the current administration's failure to articulate a strategic vision for the Australian economy, preferring what may be labeled pragmatic – business-oriented – populist management, has been masked by the longest period of sustained postwar economic growth since the 1950s. Were the economy to slow below the current robust growth rates, the government's policy and reform shortcomings would not be so easily masked.

Fortunately, there are at present few signs that economic growth in the range of 3–4 percent cannot be sustained throughout 2003–04, if not beyond. Much, of course, will depend on the extent of the pick-up in business investment during late 2002–03 as a balancing weight to declining consumer spending because of rising interest rates. Consumer debt is at record levels and continuing to rise. Consequently, only marginal increases in borrowing costs will be needed to dampen consumer confidence, retail consumption, and curb Australia's ferocious appetite for residential property.

For the immediate future, market risk is stable and should remain so into 2003–04. For many companies operating in Australia, particularly in the newly privatized sectors of the economy, market risk will be outweighed by regulatory risks. Stalled regulatory reforms aimed at creating a national market for power generation and distribution, as well as failure to reform the transport sector, have cast a shadow over stronger than expected economic news.

The bottom line: Stable operating conditions and robust growth outlook

Meeting these challenges requires investors to adopt risk management strategies that contain flexible timetables for investment, including entry and exit strategies. Alternatively, investors may need to consider extending the time-frame of proposed investments to meet longer time horizons with regard to reform implementation and realization. Risk management strategies must also include – in addition to the more regular credit, market and regulatory risk appraisals – active monitoring of currency risk owing to a volatile Australian dollar, the behavior of which continues to baffle market analysts.

In general, investors will benefit from active engagement with policy-makers, and thus participation in the broader process of Australia's future economic development. Those that are prepared to do so can expect strong returns across all asset classes, underpinned by a healthy economy, robust consumer spending and sentiments, and an underlying commitment to real reform.

Section B Risks and projections

Macroeconomic performance and risk indicators

- The Australian economy continues to grow despite the slowdown in the global economy. Indeed, Australia has outperformed many of its OECD rivals at a time when concerns about the international environment have seen year-on-year economic contractions elsewhere. However, the concern for investors is that the current construction-sector-led growth will dissipate prior to recovery in business investment expenditure and/or key export markets. More generally, should world economic growth fail to match expectations in 2002–04, Australia's ability to buck global trends could be tested.[1] In the absence of lower than forecast global growth, the Australian economy will continue to outperform the OECD average, recording growth between 3–4 percent during 2002–04. Market risk is stable in the short term with strong consumer sentiment, spending and business confidence.

The Australian economy recorded its eleventh consecutive year of GDP growth in 2001–02. Output growth averaged more than 4 percent[2] per annum, buoyed by a stable macroeconomic environment – characterized by falling inflation and interest rates, rising asset prices, and significant trend growth in labor and multifactor productivity. The performance drew praise from the OECD and served to reinforce Australia's reputation as a safe haven for foreign investment in Southeast Asia.

Despite maintaining positive growth, Australia did not remain immune from growing economic uncertainty in the global economy in 2001– a trend discernible prior to September 11 but exacerbated in the aftermath of the attacks in the US. In particular, the labor market weakened sharply and consumer confidence fell, albeit only intermittently, before bouncing back in 2002.

The risk, though small, is that rising borrowing costs and/or labor market insecurity, as a result of a series of high-profile corporate collapses, will feed through to residential property spending, causing a sharp downturn in the construction and associated manufacturing sectors prior to a recovery in key export markets – forecast to kick-in in 2003–04. Were this to be coupled with an acceleration of prices growth, thereby reducing the latitude afforded to the central bank (Reserve Bank of Australia) to stimulate economic activity by keeping interest rates low, the Australian economy could slow markedly in 2002–04.

Thankfully for investors, this remains a worst-case scenario. In the medium term, the absence of any major economic imbalances, coupled with a supportive macroeconomic policy environment, should enable Australia to avoid a significant slowdown should the world economy, and the US economy in particular, fail to grow as quickly as expected in 2003–04.[3] Conversely, Australia remains well placed to exploit any unexpected upturn in the world economy.

Looking ahead to 2003–04, GDP growth will remain robust at between 3–4 percent, though much will depend on the rate of growth of the consumer price index (CPI). More immediately, the very growth otherwise propelling Australia's economy ahead, is also causing upward pressure on interest rates, causing some moderating of consumer expenditure. This will likely see increased pressure on margins and volumes for Australia's retailers and intermediate goods producers, and have negative implications for the commercial property market.

Indeed, the construction sector will experience contracting demand from late 2002–03, with a considerable knock-on effect for employment in the sector. Corporate and income tax revenues will decline as a result, placing pressure on the fiscal position of the federal treasury and threatening the viability of the administration's proposed tax cuts, forecast for the third year of the current term (2004).

The bottom line: Market risk is low

Beyond the current economic cycle there are a number of reasons for investors to be positive regarding Australia's future growth prospects. There has been a marked pick-up in trend labor and multifactor productivity as a result of comprehensive structural reforms undertaken during the late 1980s and throughout the 1990s. Key reforms include floating the Australian dollar, deregulating the financial services sector, decentralization of the labor market and, finally, implementation of a national competition policy. These developments took place in a low inflation environment, enabling export growth and thus reducing pressure on the Australian economy's Achilles heel – a reoccurring current account deficit. The combined impact has been a significant lowering of the risk premium attached to Australia by global investors.

Export performance

- Despite significant diversification of Australia's export markets and the export base, Australia's export performance is intimately linked to conditions in the world economy – specifically, the demand for commodities, the volatility of which shows no signs of waning. Declining demand will impact on manufacturers most acutely and lead to contraction in a number of sectors. Service exports will remain subdued in to 2003, driven by lower foreign-tourism-generated revenues. The reduced competitive position of Australia's exports is also likely to become apparent in 2003 if the rate of appreciation of valuations for the Australian currency continues – something that looks increasingly likely. This too will moderate export growth and place pressure on the currency account deficit.

Despite a decade of productivity-driven growth, the Australian manufacturing sector remains at risk, in part as a consequence of the global economic slowdown in 2000–01. For Australian manufacturers, the slowdown has been softened by a declining Australian dollar and increased export competitiveness. The problem ahead, however, concerns the ability of Australian manufacturers to recapture East Asian markets – the largest market for Australian manufacturers – after two years of regional import contraction between 2000 and 2002. This will prove difficult, not least because of increasing international competition and an appreciation in the Australia dollar that has been under way since mid 2002.[4]

These developments will likely force a comprehensive restructuring within the industry, felt first with a fall in labor demand and consequently employment in the sector. While the principal growth sector of the past decade, elaborately transformed manufactures (ETMS), including high speed ferries and vehicle exports, will see a short term decline in market share caused by increasing competition from abroad, low value-added manufactured exports are most at risk. Unless producers can establish high value-added niches, uncompetitive cost structures in the textile and footwear industry, in particular, could lead to manufacturers leaving Australia permanently.

> Australian producers must improve the development and application of R&D to manufactured exports if growth levels in the sector are to remain positive. Without a renewed commitment to R&D, and a reform process to reposition the industry vis-à-vis competitor states, the manufacturing export sector is in danger of long-term decline.

Falling demand, price weakness and an appreciating Australian dollar will also impact on commodity exporters in 2002–04. However, in the medium term the best practice standards adopted and initiated by Australian resource producers mean that the sector is well placed to exploit the expected upturn in world demand in late 2003–04.

By comparison, the Australian agricultural sector faces a more difficult future. The recent failure of the Australian delegation to have agricultural subsidies included as part of the next round of WTO trade talks is estimated to have cost Australian producers A$7 billion.[5] Likewise, the increasingly protectionist stance of the United States under George W. Bush, especially rulings on steel protectionism and agricultural subsidies, will have negative and long-lasting impacts on Australian steel and agricultural exports. The only prospects for salvation now appear to reside in the adoption of an Australian–US Free Trade Agreement, and a reversal of the United States' protectionist sentiments via collective European action through the WTO – or via an outright trade war. The latter, in particular, would be dangerous for Australia, risking collateral damage on Australian agricultural exports if the European Union moves to close down market access.

Foreign tourist arrivals – the largest single component of Australian service exports – fell by 12 percent in the year to September 2001.[6] In the wake of September 11, tourism operators also experienced further falls, compounded by the collapse of the second national airline in October 2001. Assuming some emergent international stability as the war on terror progresses and threats of terrorism diminish, there are signs that tourist arrivals should pick up in 2003–04, perhaps fuelled by increasing Asian tourism. More generally, the absence of serious terrorist threats to Australia, and the international perception of Australia as a safe environment, should also help restore US tourist interest in Australia in 2003–04.

Overall, the short-term outlook for Australian exporters is for reduced export growth during 2002–03 in the region of 5 percent per annum before picking up to 10 percent in 2004. In the longer term, the productivity gains made by Australian industry in the 1990s need to be complemented by on-going market reform to ensure world's best practice production standards. These developments will play a crucial role in determining the opportunities available to investors to diversify beyond the more traditional resource and financial services stocks.

The best prospects for investors lie in those areas of the economy that are able to utilize an abundance of skilled personnel, the price of which is low in Australia compared to other developed nations.

Currency movements and projections

• Leading indicators support the assertion that the Australian dollar has reached its floor after two years of trend depreciation. The traditional volatility of the Australian dollar will, however, continue for the foreseeable future. This presents investors with considerable foreign currency risk unless transactions are hedged. More generally, however, the Australian dollar continues to be undervalued, representing significant opportunities for asset acquisitions if these are acted on quickly. The Australian dollar should continue to trend slowly upward from late 2002–03.

The floating of the Australian dollar in 1983 signaled the beginning of a strategic reorientation of the Australian economy. From 1983–91 the Australian dollar trended downwards, driven by inflation differentials between Australia and its major trading partners.[7] The Australian dollar began to slide again in early 2000, driven by falling commodity prices and negative net equity investment.

A rising Australian dollar?

While investors, in the wake of the tech-sector downturn, appear to have rightly rejected the false old/new economy dichotomy that was seen to be holding back investment in Australia, significant increases in foreign capital flows have not yet materialized. Accordingly, the dollar has failed to recoup the losses posted during 2000–01. Until commodity prices rise or returns on Australian equities increase sufficiently to warrant bearing the additional risk posed by exposure to the currency itself – an attendant feature of equity investments – then it is unlikely that the dollar will return to previous highs – although it can expect to see modest improvements in its valuations into 2003.

A predominance of commodity exports – the price of which changes rapidly – makes the Australian dollar an attractive trading option and the seventh most traded currency in the world. Until this changes, investors should expect the Australian dollar's traditional volatility to continue in the future.

Most indicators support the assertion that the Australian dollar has bottomed in the current cycle and that it will begin to trend slowly upwards from mid-2002 as commodity prices begin to recover.[8] Other factors supporting the assertion include the current attractiveness of Australian resource producers, which will create considerable demand for Australian mining stocks and, by default, the dollar. Second, the Reserve Bank of Australia (RBA) has demonstrated a willingness to intervene in the currency markets to defend inflation targets in 2001–02 more than ever before.[9] Lastly, consistent and transparent policy aimed at controlling inflation means that inflation differentials are unlikely to exert further downward pressure on the dollar in the foreseeable future. The Australian dollar will likely trade in the 55–60 US cent range throughout 2002–03, with further slight rises possible in 2004.

The bottom line: Not much risk and some rich pickings

For those investors prepared to bear the current foreign exchange market's uncertainty toward the Australian dollar – with its limited downside risk – the current climate presents opportunities for attractive asset acquisitions with the prospect of significant currency gains in the medium term. Alternatively, existing investors will benefit from stabilizing asset values.

Financial markets: Performance and development

- The market for financial services in Australia has undergone radical reform since the 1980s. The result is a diversified and well-capitalized financial sector that is capable of supporting the full array of financing options for investors. Indeed, given Australia's strategic position in Southeast Asia, and the fact that it is the only fully developed, mature economy in the region, it provides an attractive locale and financial base from which to launch into the region. This is underscored by fully developed prudential systems and regulatory frameworks, something otherwise lacking throughout Asia, except for Singapore. While the global economic downturn has led to an increase in non-performing loans, these are well-provisioned for, with banking sector liquidity remaining excellent.

Australian financial markets have undergone extensive reform, including the floating of the Australian dollar, removal of controls on the movement of international capital, removal of restrictions on the operation of foreign banks, and the divestment of publicly-owned (state and federal) banks to the private market.

Accordingly, the market for financial services has deepened and the advent of international competition has resulted in decreased spreads and increased efficiency.[10]

Integral to broader structural reforms has been the introduction of a new regulatory framework. The new structure introduced in July 1998 is based on three independent statutory agencies, all of which have displayed sound prudential management.

Reform strengthens prudential regulation

Until recently, the RBA carried out the prudential regulation of Australian banks, not unlike the Federal Reserve in the US. Under the changes implemented in 1997, the RBA is now responsible for monetary policy and systemic stability and regulation of the payments system, while prudential regulation is now the responsibility of the Australian Prudential Regulation Authority (APRA). As a result, the stability of the Australian financial system has improved. Anecdotal evidence from investors also indicates that compliance costs have fallen.[11]

The Australian banking sector is also well capitalized and regulated. There are strict and well-enforced rules governing the transparency of transactions. Lending decisions are free of political interference and are thus solely commercial transactions. Moreover, there are strict requirements governing cross-ownership between banks and corporates to prevent the misuse of funds and thus protect the stability of the individual bank and the broader financial system itself. Accordingly, there have been no major bank collapses in Australia's recent history, nor do any look remotely likely in the medium to longer term.

However, the Australian banking sector has not managed to escape the current global economic downturn by virtue of its active participation in international markets, with approximately 50 percent of the profits of the four main banks being derived from overseas operations.[12] For instance, Australian banks are thought to have had more than A$100 million exposed to the US energy trading giant ENRON, which collapsed in late 2001. National Australia Bank has also lost upwards of A$4 billion as a result of poorly appreciated market conditions in the US mortgage market.

These international exposures come on the back of a number of high-profile Australian corporate collapses, such as that of mining giant Pasminco, as well as Ansett, HIH and One-Tel. More generally, insolvencies in Australia reached record levels in 2000–01 and are set to increase in the short term.[13] Accordingly, most Australian banks have increased their provisioning for non-performing loans (NPLs) during 2001–02, and are likely to be forced to do so again during 2003.

Project financing opportunities slow – but better prospects ahead in 2004

The sluggish international environment and, concomitantly, economic uncertainty will decrease the pool of funds available for 'big-ticket' project finance investments which, until now, have been well supported by Australian banks. Well-structured projects with strong cash flows will still go ahead, however, though investors may face increased borrowing costs owing to rising market risk premiums.

Potential investors, however, should not be overly concerned. Bank profits have continued to set new records in recent years, and in comparison with their Asian compatriots the sector is still extremely well capitalized and liquidity remains high.[14]

More generally, and in the longer term, investors can look forward to more attractive borrowing costs as competition in the Australian financial markets increases and conversely the spread between onshore and offshore borrowing decreases. For investors who previously borrowed offshore to finance Australian investments, this offers the opportunity to decrease foreign interest and currency risk on scheduled payments, though foreign remittances will still incur foreign exchange risks. Those corporates that have traditionally utilized the domestic market for financing will also benefit, as the greater stability in the Australian economy engendered by the RBA's handling of monetary policy reduces the risk premium attached to Australian corporates by the international capital markets.

Private and public debt: Risks ahead[15]

- Public sector debt has fallen rapidly since its peak in 1996 to just 7 percent of GDP. In contrast, private sector debt levels have continued to rise rapidly, with further increases forecast for the medium term. Credit risks on Australian corporates will increase accordingly, thereby necessitating increased due diligence by prospective investors.

In contrast with much of Australia's postwar history, the issue of public sector debt has receded in recent years as a result of falling public sector debt levels. The current administration returned the federal budget to surplus in 1998–99, a goal achieved through cuts to government spending and the sale of government assets rather than increases in taxation. Public sector debt now stands at 7 percent of GDP from a peak of 19 percent in 1995–96.[16] Indeed, the current administration has demonstrated its commitment to balanced budgets over the course of the business cycle, despite a strained international economic situation. The spread charged on Australian government debt has thus trended downwards since 1997.

Nonetheless, the spread between US and Australian government debt has widened since September 11, from an average of 72 bps to around 100 bps.[17] If the trend continues, investors can look forward to rising yields on new government debt issues that do not, in the short term, accurately reflect the stability of the budget position and thus the degree of sovereign risk.

Increased risk aversion by international capital markets will have a more significant impact on corporate Australia. The gap between Australian government and swap rates[18] moved out to more than 50 bps in October 2001.[19] The issue is an important one for investors, as private sector debt levels have almost doubled in five years to A$394 billion in 2000.[20] Rising spreads will make new financing more difficult, as well as increasing the existing debt burden and thereby further reducing the pool of monies available to companies for new investment.

The concern, although less pronounced than in previous cycles, is that the current pressure on profits and margins among Australian producers and retailers could coincide with rising interest rates abroad and/or a depreciation of the Australian dollar. If this occurs it could cause default on corporate debts. The mining sector, in particular, which has always been heavily geared, is at greatest risk if commodity prices fail to pick up as forecast in 2003–04. More generally, the mining sector is further weakened by poor hedging strategies, with a number of Australian miners holding considerable hedging exposures on their books.

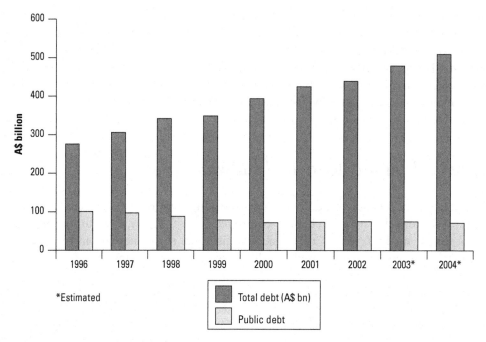

FIGURE 2.1 Total debt, Australia 1996–2004
Source: Australian Bureau of Statistics (ABS)

Widespread default, however, is unlikely. Not only is the total debt service ratio low, at around 10 percent of GDP, but Australian corporates, perhaps with the exception of the mining sector, have become more sophisticated in managing their foreign currency exposures than in previous business cycles. Stability should be the order of the day in 2002–04.

Labor market trends

• The Australian labor market softened in 2001, following five years of consistent employment growth across all sectors of the economy. In 2002, however, and after the initial concerns caused by the events of September 11, employment growth has returned with marginal falls in the unemployment rate. However, unemployment will remain stubbornly high relative to US benchmarks, even if current growth levels are maintained during 2002–04. This points to significant structural unemployment in the Australian economy, something that might be addressed via the government's proposed welfare reform program. Also notable has been the absence of significant labor disputation during the current business cycle. While labor market reforms have been crucial to the process, it is perhaps too early to herald a new and more consensual style of labor management relations compared to that which previously characterized Australian industrial relations.

The current administration has targeted labor market reform as integral to the broader reform of the Australian economy. A major step in this direction was taken in 1996 with the introduction of the Workplace Relations Act. The Act decisively shifted the focus of workplace relations from centralized wage fixing to enterprise (or company-wide) bargaining linked to productivity gains. The move also contributed to a lower inflation environment that, in turn, reduced expectations among the Australian workforce of year-on-year wage rises irrespective of productivity or profit performance. Previously, the system impeded economic and employment growth by imposing terms and conditions of employment that were not related to individual circumstances or general business conditions.

Employers favor decentralized wage bargaining

The new system offers investors considerable improvements by reducing the incidence of potentially destabilizing industrial disputes and the number of inappropriate wage claims. The combined impact has been a lowering of the operational risks faced by investors in the Australian market. Indeed, a recent Australian Chamber of Commerce and Industry (ACCI) survey found that 64 percent of employers favored the new system because it offered a more flexible wage system.[21] This sentiment has been echoed by foreign direct investors who had previously claimed that restrictive practices in wage negotiations had served to detract from the attractiveness of Australia as a destination for foreign direct investment (FDI).

For a number of investors, however, the reforms do not go far enough. They argue that Australian Workplace Agreements are still far more complicated compared to US employment contracts. Undoubtedly, though, the current administration will seek to push ahead with further reform; something that will see an improvement in Australia's international competitive position.

> The current wage pressure will dissipate as weaknesses in the labor market feed through into wage claims, thus ensuring a continuation of a trend that has seen productivity increases outpace wage growth in Australia for each of the past 15 years.

The advent of a more flexible and responsive industrial relations system was reflected in falling demand for labor in the last two quarters of 2001, before a moderate turnaround in early 2002. This caused unemployment to rise from 6.5 percent in the March quarter 2001 to 7.2 percent in the December quarter, before falling to 6.7 percent in 2002. Beyond this, however, the labor market can be expected to remain stagnant into 2003 as a sluggish international economy and domestic business investment expenditure continues to work its way through the Australian labor market.

Static labor demand should mean that recent wage pressures as indicated by the largest increases in the wage cost index for four years in the year to June 2001, are kept in check.[22] Wage costs rose by 3 percent during 2002, with a slight increase in the annual rate

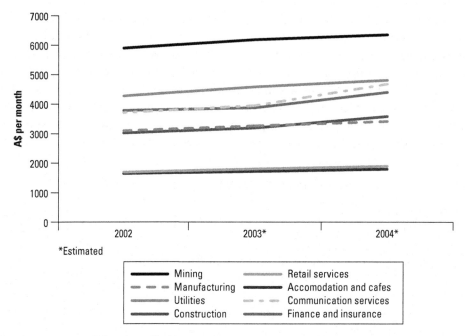

FIGURE 2.2 Wage cost index, Australia 2002–2004

of wages growth forecast for 2003 and 2004. Executive salary increases will outpace those for skilled and unskilled workers in the ratio of 2:1 through to 2004.

Labor market weakness will be most acute in the financial services and construction sectors after enjoying the most rapid gains during the recent economic upswing. This will lead to below-trend increases in wages growth in 2002–04, offering investors in the financial services sector the chance to capitalize on already low wages in comparison to those in the major international financial capitals.

Skilled labor shortages: A growing problem

Investors should be aware, however, that the abundance of skilled personnel in finance, as well as law and computing, will not last indefinitely. During the past three years net migration of university-educated 21–24-year-olds into Australia has been negative.[23] The trend will quicken if the Australian dollar continues to fall, as this will broaden the wage differential between Australia and other developed countries. Moreover, Australia is falling behind other developed countries with similarly aging populations who have taken the lead in reducing the impediments to skilled labor migration, thus making net emigration of professionals even more rapid. While the Australian government has recognized the issue and has committed itself to increasing the future intake of skilled professionals, the program will take a minimum of 18–24 months to feed through the system, with no discernible impacts anticipated until 2004–05.

Investors looking to procure skilled workers in certain sections of the engineering and manufacturing sector will face particular problems. The success of the sector, highlighted by increased sales of motor vehicles and fast ferries, has meant a shortage of suitably qualified personnel. Potential employers will need to factor in professional development and slow start-up times into their investment planning because of labor procurement problems. A recent Australian Chamber of Commerce and Industry survey of Australian producers, for example, found that qualified labor shortages, in particular a shortage of tradespeople, were considered the second largest constraint on business operations after corporate taxes.[24]

More generally, attitudes to work in Australia have changed in the past decade. The increasing prevalence of part-time employment and contract work, once considered demeaning in an Australian cultural context, means that the current labor market is less rigid than in the past. This has meant that large-scale downsizing now no longer attracts the degree of negative publicity for the firm concerned that it once did.

Consumer and business confidence: Mixed results

• Australian consumer confidence recouped almost all of the drastic falls witnessed post September 11. However, with lingering employment concerns, especially in the manufacturing and construction industry, some trepidation is evident, especially given the uncertainty about the anticipated US recovery, its depth and possible longevity. Rising interest rates, realized in May 2002, are strongly indicated as a future possibility by the RBA, which also harbors fears about the resilience of consumer sentiment and retail spending.

Surveys of Australian consumer sentiment reported a large fall in mid 2000, from the highs of 1999.[25] This was reflected in weaker retail sales. Shop sales recorded their worst result in 2000–01 since the recession of the early 1990s, before thankfully rebounding in 2002. Consumer confidence fell in the first part of 2001, then rebounded strongly in the mid part of the year and into early 2002, driven by a succession of mortgage rate falls (to their lowest level in a generation). Retail spending remained subdued throughout 2001, but rose strongly in 2002. Strong consumer spending is anticipated in 2002–03, with the RBA reiterating its desire to moderate consumer spending and reduce consumer debt levels. This will continue to be expressed via a series of small but significant interest rate rises.

Australia thus has two opposing forces operating on consumer and business confidence as it enters 2003. First, there is a continued strong level of consumer sentiment expressed in consumption levels, and especially expenditure associated with housing and construction. But this is matched by increasing apprehension and fears about interest rate hikes as the RBA sets about moderating consumer spending and bringing it off the boil for fear of starting inflationary pressures. These two forces can be expected to continue into 2003, although strongly influenced by the prospects for recovery in the US economy, as well as the knock-on effects this will have for Australia's Asian trading partners.

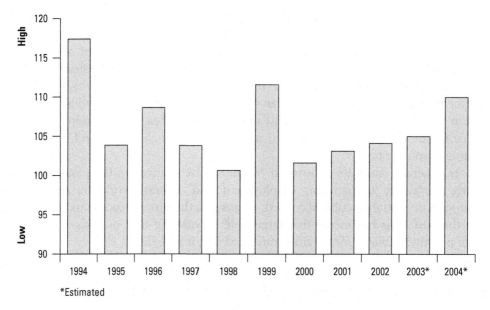

FIGURE 2.3 Business and consumer confidence, Australia 1994–2004
Source: Westpac Quarterly Consumer Confidence Index

Business sentiment: A mixed bag

Surveys of business sentiment fail to give a clear picture of operating conditions, though uncertainty has already fed through into investment planning, with an immediate fall occurring in non-essential expenditures such as training, R&D and IT equipment.[26]

The index has clearly been boosted by the low Australian dollar and record low interest rates. On the other hand, the sudden collapse of Ansett, HIH and One-Tel has damaged investor confidence. When questioned, most respondents answered that the outlook for their own business was slightly positive but almost all thought that the economic picture was vexed with uncertainty. What is noticeable, however, is a marginal upward trend with strong growth forecasts for 2003–04, and an increasing conviction among many Australian corporates that the business outlook in the US is tending stronger in 2003–04. Failing any about-face to this expectation, especially another bout of terrorist attacks, business confidence should remain cautiously optimistic into 2003–04.

The bottom line: Cautiously optimistic

Business confidence is likely to witness a rise in early 2003 and into 2004. Business sentiment is, however, fragile despite high levels of economic growth. In part, this is attributable to profit pressures creating a tough climate and causing business investment spending to be curtailed, at least until it becomes clearer where the international economy is tending and how potent its expected recovery will be.

Stock market

- In an environment of increasing economic uncertainty, the Australian Stock Exchange (ASX) All Ordinaries outperformed all the major international indexes, returning 5.1 percent in 2001–02. Looking to the future, investors can expect stable returns across a range of securities backed by a consistent regulatory environment and a growing economy.

The ASX was formed in 1987 by the amalgamation of six independent stock exchanges that formerly operated in the state capital cities. Total market capitalization increased from A$203 billion in 1988–89 to A$898 billion in 2000–01, placing the ASX thirteenth globally in terms of market capitalization. The number of tradable liquid securities have grown to 1461 in 2002, while daily trading volumes have increased by more than 500 percent, to 50,000 trades per day, equal to 60 percent of total market capitalization.[27]

Changes to the size of the market were accompanied by changes to the composition of the market – a trend that reflects broader developments within the Australian economy. Specifically, the sectoral composition moved away from resources and manufacturing by capitalization to services, with financial services and telecommunication companies enjoying the greatest gains. The pattern of domestic versus foreign equity ownership changed little after 1995, remaining steady at 28 percent of the market by capitalization into 2002.[28]

The market's increasing depth was also demonstrated by the success of initial public offerings (IPOs). Although smaller in number and size than the previous year's record (boosted by the government offering of shares in the partially privatized national telecommunications company, Telstra), the market's continued appetite for new equity issues, following three high-profile corporate collapses and the announcement of a number of company profit downgrades, coupled with a sluggish international economic environment, confounded expectations.[29]

> In the short term, investors can expect buoyant trading, boosted by the re-weighting of the MSCI index – which should increase offshore interest in the market. Larger corporates will be the primary beneficiaries of the re-weighting.

While the ASX did not witness the dramatic rises enjoyed by the major international bourses during 2000–01, by virtue of a lack of fashionable tech-sector start-ups that drove index gains elsewhere, the market has enjoyed consistent returns across the spectrum of stocks. In the year to June 2001, the ASX rose by 5.1 percent, outperforming all the major international indices. Average market returns for the 10 years to mid 2001 were 13.5 percent per annum.[30] Moreover, on a price to current earnings ratio (PE), Australian stocks are attractive trading in line with established trends and are far cheaper than US stocks on the same basis. Furthermore, the likely medium-term appreciation of the Australian dollar offers investors the chance to benefit from cross-currency movements.

In the medium term, manufacturing stocks will suffer as a result of falling export demand and reduced business confidence. This will generally delay investment in new infrastructure – including property. Construction sector stocks will face difficult trading conditions as the demand for residential and commercial property falls in line with rising interest rates in 2002–04, but also because forward consumption expenditure on residential property has now been exhausted. This sector is likely to under-perform the index during 2003. Conversely, strong growth in the bio-technology and pharmaceuticals sectors should see both outperform index trends. Banks have also shown a propensity to gain, regardless of the international economy, recording record profit levels in 2002. This should increase demand for their stock and higher valuations.

Investors considering Australian securities can look forward to a stable and consistent regulatory environment, and improved disclosure requirements for financial reporting, all of which will enhance transparency and thus the breadth and quality of information available to investors.

In the longer term, a solid economic backdrop should provide opportunities for growth and capital gain. This will be complemented by a growing pool of superannuation funds, thus increasing the pool of funds available for new equity issues and stock market investment generally.

Corporate tax

• Further major reform of the tax system is unlikely in the medium term, following the major overhaul of the corporate and personal tax system undertaken by the current government in 2000–01. Minor changes aimed at streamlining the new system are likely to be gradually introduced. Overall, however, investors can look forward to a stable and improving tax regime during 2002–04.

During 2000 Australia undertook a major overhaul of its business taxation rules with the first tranche of measures taking effect on 1 July 2000. The most significant measures included a lowering of the company tax rate from 36 percent to 34 percent, and to 30 percent on 1 July 2001, as well as the introduction of capital gains tax rollover relief for scrip-for-scrip exchanges.

As part of the taxation overhaul, the government also introduced a GST (a broad-based goods and services consumption tax, levied at 10 percent). There were also a series of significant amendments to existing arrangements relating to federal funding to state governments that should reduce the need, and therefore the propensity, of state governments to attempt to increase state-levied taxes to meet revenue shortfalls. This is good news for investors.

While Australia's overall share of tax revenue to GDP is not high by OECD standards, Australia's share of corporate taxes to GDP is the second highest in the developed world – and only behind Luxembourg.[31]

The re-election of the Coalition government means that much of the business tax reform agenda is once again back on track. While this may mean some pain up front for business in dealing with further changes, investors and Australian-owned business alike will reap significant gains in the longer term.

Among the areas showing the most promise is an improvement in the streamlining of tax compliance for corporate groups, an overhaul of the superannuation system, and a fairer deal for venture capital investors and expatriates.

Investors looking for an overhaul of the dividend withholding tax laws are likely to be disappointed, however, although proposed changes will reduce the punitive arrangements in place at the moment, thereby bringing Australia more in line with OECD norms. Investors looking for a guide to the proposed changes should examine recent changes introduced in the UK and Sweden.[32]

Another area of likely disappointment for investors will be the administration's failure to tackle the difficult issue of distorting state based indirect taxes that the OECD has stated are a major impediment to foreign firms considering locating in Australia.[33]

Finally, investors will need to closely monitor political developments with regard to the proposed introduction of environmental externalities taxation. This will likely affect the 'dirty' industries – manufacturing more so than others. Ratification of the Kyoto Protocol on greenhouse gas emissions, which Australia has not yet signed, will only increase the need to raise new taxes to better reflect environmental waste. Investors should watch this space and be prepared to respond accordingly.

Residential and commercial property markets

- With the exception of the hotels sector, which has been suffering from a sharp fall in demand since mid-2000, it is difficult to identify national and capital city sector trends with any confidence. This suggests that investors considering entering the market must do so on an asset-by-asset basis. For those prepared to bear the current uncertainty, asset acquisition offers the prospect of not only capital gain but also significant currency gains, if the dollar appreciates, as has been widely forecast.

The Australian residential property sector rebounded strongly in the second half of 2001, fuelled by a succession of mortgage rate declines and the increased incentives offered to first home buyers (the First Home Owners Grant [FHOG] was increased to a maximum of A$14,000).

A 70 percent increase in building approvals in the fourth quarter of 2001 compared to the lows witnessed just two quarters earlier was enough to add more than one-half of one percent to GDP for the year to June 2002.

Demand for new homes will, however, fall significantly from mid 2002 concomitant with the phasing out of the First Home Owners Grant (FHOG) and expected rises in borrowing costs in 2002–03. This will place pressure on margins in the construction sector. Rents will remain depressed and capital gains will be subdued due to oversupply, with the problem most acute in the inner-city markets where oversupply is greatest (Sydney and Melbourne in particular).

The office construction sector defied general economic sentiment for much of 2001–02, with building approvals up by 25 percent.[34] And while the events of September 11 have shaken investor confidence, in the absence of further shocks, sound economic fundamentals, including low interest rates and an expected rise in business investment toward the end of 2002, should see the sector regain momentum – notwithstanding some anecdotal evidence that points to significantly divergent performance across capital cities.

Building activity in the hotel/motel construction sector fell sharply in the period following the Olympics, recording a year-on-year fall in 2000–01 of 62 percent. This is symptomatic of excess capacity (particularly in the key Sydney market), which was reflected in five consecutive quarterly falls in occupancy rates prior to October 2001, to an all-time low of 66 percent.[35] International terrorism and associated fears relating to global travel, which caused the sudden drop-off in tourist arrivals post September 11, will further depress the market unless alternative markets can be sourced. High-end hotels are expected to suffer the worst downturns. Visitor arrivals are not forecast to improve until 2003, when normal air-travel arrivals should resume.

This aside, the sector has also witnessed some resilience, though it is continuing to slow. The purchase of BT's Hotel Fund portfolio by the US investor Colony Capital, for example, negotiated prior to September 11 and sold afterwards – albeit at a slight discount to the originally agreed sale price – suggests that a number of investors perceive the current weakness to be outweighed by the potential for longer-term capital growth and currency exposure gains.[36] The critical factor will be access to capital for prospective hotel investors, with lending institutions likely to demand higher debt service coverage ratios.

The bottom line: Healthy growth

More broadly, a healthy economic environment should see a return to trend growth in the Australian economy by 2003. There is no reason to suspect that such gains will not be equally shared by investors in the residential and commercial property sectors, hence the interest of counter-cyclical investors looking for discounted assets. The industrial property market is likely to continue its long-term decline owing to the long-term decline of heavy industry in Australia.

Foreign direct investment [37]

- Despite a welcoming legislative environment for foreign investors, there are still question marks regarding the current government's commitment to creating the necessary conditions to attract foreign capital. In part, this reflects a broader malaise affecting the current administration – a failure to articulate a vision of Australia's future that recognizes the opportunities and constraints imposed by globalization, and, more immediately, Australia's role in the Southeast Asian region/trading bloc. Foreign capital xenophobia, it is not! Unfortunately, in the current risk-averse international investment environment, political ambivalence toward foreign investors may prove equally damaging.

Despite its developed country status, Australia, in contrast with most of its OECD counterparts, is a net importer of capital.[38] Historically, Australia's late start in the development race gave rise to significant foreign investment as a means to exploit abundant natural resources spread over vast distances. Foreign capital has played a crucial role in propelling Australia's rapid economic development. In both regards, little has changed in the ensuing 200 years. Today, foreign capital is more vital than ever as a means to supplement a low savings ratio and consistently declining terms of trade.

Strong economy fails to attract new equity investment

Unfortunately for foreign investors, general recognition of this fact across the political spectrum at federal and state level has not translated into effective policy-making designed to facilitate foreign investment. Put simply, the rhetoric has not been matched by action. Uncertainty at the federal level is compounded by a multitude of state regulations that have led to uneven deregulation in key markets. In many cases, this has resulted in anti-competitive arrangements. Accordingly, aggregate equity flows have actually been negative into Australia during 2000–02.[39]

The Federal Department of Treasury regulates foreign investment in conjunction with the Foreign Investment Review Board (FIRB). The board screens investment proposals to ensure conformity with Australian law and policy. Takeovers of domestic firms by foreign investors, while occasionally generating nationalistic public sentiment, are rarely interfered with.[40] Notable exceptions include the current administration's decision to block Shell's proposed takeover of the Australian company Woodside Petroleum in 2001, citing contravention of ill-defined national interests.

A number of countries have protested about Australia's continued utilization of the FIRB as a screening mechanism for prospective foreign investment, including the US. However, there is little prospect of any meaningful reform in 2002–04.[41]

The current government's policy toward foreign investment was first outlined by the then Australian treasurer in 1992. The objective was to encourage FDI consistent with the needs of the Australian community. As a corollary to recognition of community concerns over foreign ownership of Australian assets, specific restrictions apply to sectors such as media, civil aviation and residential real estate ownership.[42] Accordingly, many of the risks

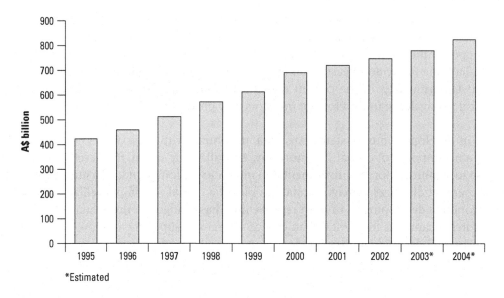

*Estimated

FIGURE 2.4 Foreign direct investment in Australia 1995–2004

to investors, both negative and positive, stem from the fluid (sector-specific) regulatory environment following the recent and only partial deregulation of key markets.

State-based regulatory regimes increase operational risks

Investor concerns regarding the regulatory regime have, for example, vexed natural gas pipeline operators, typified by the on-again off-again plan for the Queensland to PNG natural gas pipeline – something that highlights the costs of disparate state regulations to investors and the broader Australian economy alike. Indeed, with more than A$6 billion of new gas projects planned for completion by 2003, there should be no shortage of opportunities – on paper at least!

Of particular concern to investors is the current state-based system of regulating price increases.[43] Epic Energy, a US-based investor, recently mounted a legal challenge to the Western Australian government's decision to reduce gas transportation prices by 11–25 percent. The company went on to announce that it was considering exiting the Australian market, citing constant regulatory changes as the single most significant obstacle to success in the Australian market.

Electricity generators also face a high-risk regulatory regime. Successful investors will have to meet the challenges stemming from the absence of a fully competitive national electricity market and a lack of consistency in the approach of individual states to regulation and private ownership.[44]

In part, the difficulties reflect a psychological barrier to nationally competitive markets, necessitating, as it does, an attendant loss of strategic independence for state governments. European regulators, charged with creating a Europe-wide market fashioned out of national markets, would have recognized the Victorian media's angry reaction in 2001 to blackouts in Victoria while electricity was still being sold to NSW – Australia's two premier states and traditionally fierce rivals.

International energy generators have not, however, abandoned the Australian market, nor have investors in progressive state rail and waste management privatizations, despite facing similarly difficult operating environments. If these companies are to be successful, however, it will require genuine reform. At a minimum, this needs to entail harmonization, if not uniformity, of state-based regulations. Without these, the proclaimed goal of nationally competitive markets will remain little more than empty rhetoric. If it occurs, however, it promises investors substantial benefits over the existing arrangements.

Low political risks boost mining sector investment

If investment proposals can be used as a guide to foreign investors' perceptions of risk, one of the few sectors to experience improving prospects is the Australian mining sector. Investment in the Australian mining sector soared to its highest levels in 2001–02 since September 1999.[45] Attention has been driven by a number of distinct yet interrelated factors; the first is part of a broader trend toward global consolidation in the minerals sector, the second factor stems from increasing risk aversion in the wake of the terrorist attacks in the US. Political risks have proved no exception to the rule, and Australia is generally regarded as an extremely low political risk location in comparison with other major mineral-producing nations.

These trends have been amplified by reduced capacity and appetite among private insurers for non-recourse project political risk insurance. If the trend persists, investors can expect the current round of merger activity to continue well into 2002–03. Smaller miners will find capital raising increasingly difficult, thus making them takeover targets for larger miners for whom increased geographical diversity through acquisitions provides a natural hedge against country risks.

Integral to the upgrading of Australian risk perceptions among the international mining community has been the gradual weakening of the Native Title Legislation, promulgated in 1992. The federal Labor Party's decision in late August 2000 to vote with the current federal Coalition government to endorse the Queensland Labor government's state native title regime, suggests the emergence of a cross-party consensus. The interpretation of Mabo – as the Act was colloquially entitled – reduces the compliance costs faced by miners in establishing land title. Similar benefits will accrue to investors in the pastoral sector.[46]

Over the last five years Australia has been home to more public–private build-own-operate-transfer (BOOT) projects than anywhere else in the world.[47]

Significant opportunities, in addition to those accruing from the fluid gas and electricity regulatory environment and infrastructure projects, will arise for investors from the continued privatization of government assets, although the pace of disinvestment has slowed. In particular, the current government has signaled its intention to sell its remaining share of the national telecommunications operator, Telstra. This should be complemented by continued privatization of a number of assets currently in state hands.

However, attracting private interest in proposed new BOOT schemes for infrastructure projects will prove difficult without changes to the current punitive taxation arrangements governing private participants in private–public schemes.[48]

In conclusion, there is a general political consensus that in the long term Australia's growth performance rests heavily upon its ability to continue to attract international investment capital to supplement a low domestic savings ratio. Further, it is widely acknowledged that this will require the continuation of microeconomic market reforms as a necessary corollary to the long-term structural transformation of the Australian economy undertaken since 1983. On the other hand, recognition of the need for continuing investment flows has not, until now, translated into effective policy-making – if fostering competitive national markets is an accurate yardstick.

Section C Politics

- Market concerns over the potential cost of the opposition Labor Party's 'Knowledge Nation' were allayed by the Liberal–National Coalition's victory in the November 2001 elections. Despite this victory, it is of growing concern that the new administration's Cabinet selections have favored conservative factions within the party, a choice that confirms expectations the reform process will slow in 2002–04, in what will be the Prime Minister's third and final term. Any possible further reform will focus on continuing microeconomic reforms, broadly termed competition policy, though much will depend on the political will of the Prime Minister in the face of expected parliamentary opposition.

There are no major political issues that seriously detract from the business climate. All of Australia's major political parties seek to promote private-sector-led growth and encourage foreign investment. Furthermore, both the major parties support internal economic restructuring aimed at transforming the country into a globally competitive trading nation. Ideological difference is expressed only to the extent that the pace and scope of the desired reform agenda of the two main parties diverge. The issue is, perhaps, most easily identifiable in disputes concerning the optimum level of privatization of publicly controlled assets and services. However, with the political impetus for further privatization waning, the differences, though more than cosmetic, are not substantial. Accordingly, a change of government would not result in any significant divergence of economic policy.

Australia's political system – a hybrid of UK and US institutions

For British, US and European investors the Australian political system appears both foreign and familiar. In common with other liberal democracies, Australia has a written constitution, a bicameral parliament and an independent judicial system. The Australian model diverges, however, insofar as it has adopted a UK-style Lower House superimposed over a federal model, while incorporating an American-style Senate. The head of state is the Governor-General (the Queen's representative), although the role is now confined to a symbolic one. The real power is vested in the Prime Minister – the leader of the majority party in the Lower House. For investors looking to grasp the dynamics of Australian politics, the picture is further complicated by the existence of state parliaments, who exercise power over bread and butter issues.[49]

Leading risk indices: Corruption, stability, governance, risk

Capacity to govern: Institutional obstacles?

Traditionally, the government of the day does not control both Houses. Indeed, no government has had a majority in the Senate since 1981. As a result, legislation proposed by the government can be enacted only through negotiation with the opposition, or with minority parties such as the Democrats and the Greens. This makes the legislative process cumbersome, with the legislative parameters of Australian economic life being debated at the federal parliamentary House of Representatives, Senate and Committee levels, and often subjected to strong state legislative review, all harboring wide scope for debate and possible amendment or rejection.

> Most legislation originates in the Senate. For this reason, special interest and lobby groups tend to focus their attentions on this stage of the democratic process as the most effective means for influencing legislation.[50]

This multi-layered process is clearly reflected in the capacity-to-govern index, which is lower than might otherwise be expected of a developed country. Investors need be aware that the system of checks and balances actually improves political stability and rarely leads to policy paralysis. Once legislation is passed, and thus the political and economic agenda set, policy is ably implemented by well-functioning institutions. For instance, the RBA is widely credited with removing the inflation bias evident within the Australian economy through a well-articulated monetary policy free of political interference.

More generally, the index has risen slightly throughout the survey period. This is reflection of the success of the Coalition in maintaining high levels of economic growth.

The second component of the index, political stability, clearly indicates the absence of destabilizing shocks to the Australian political landscape in the recent past. Political continuity is the normal state of affairs, in terms of policy and practice. In many respects, this is a product of Australia's well-established party system of governance. Of all the countries in the region, Australia is the most stable in this regard; being one of few wholly formed liberal democratic states with a mature, highly developed, modern economy.

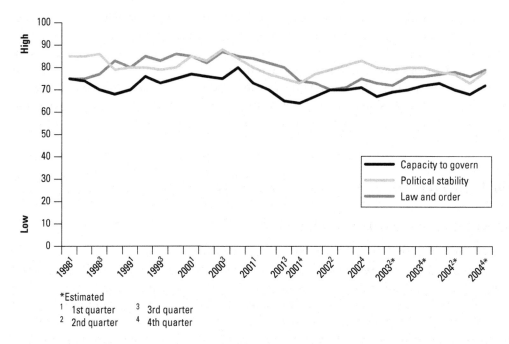

FIGURE 2.5 Political stability index, Australia 1998–2004

Political stability methodology
- The capacity-to-govern index is based upon the institutional reach of government, defined in terms of its ability to set the political and economic agenda and ensure its legislative program is enacted without significant compromise. This index is adversely affected by legislative opposition, lack of legislative implementation, failure to realize government policy and general political opposition.
- The political stability index measures violent opposition or organized demonstrations, terrorist activities, and popular discontent that adversely affect the institutional and electoral stability of the government.
- The law and order index measures the propensity to civil obedience, and the institutional reach of the rule of law in terms of regulatory compliance and enforcement.

Likewise, Australia enjoys a highly developed level of law enforcement and well-established judicial systems based on Common Law precepts. By international standards, Australia has a particularly low level of serious crime, benchmarked by countries of similar standing like Canada.

Corruption

The established nature of the party system, mature and highly legitimate parliamentary and legislative institutions, replete with the normal Western-style accoutrement of regulatory, prudential, and law and order institutions, make Australia a highly regarded climate in terms of corruption. Indeed, corruption is not considered a problem at all by foreign investors

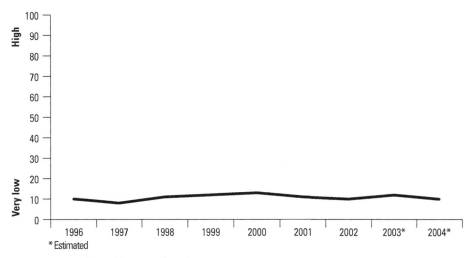

FIGURE 2.6 Corruption index, Australia 1996–2004

operating in Australia. Low levels of corruption by world standards contribute to Australia's strong ranking on the corruption index.

Corporate governance: Reform, speed and prospects

The success of John Howard's Coalition in the November 2001 elections has been portrayed as a Pyrrhic victory by sections of the media. There are two reasons for this, both of which suggest that the pace of microeconomic reform will slow in the medium term.[51]

First, the Coalition was elected on a narrow political mandate. For much of the election, campaigning was deliberately focused on the issue of 'immigration,' ably served and skillfully exploited by the Prime Minister's handling of the 'Tampa Crisis.' However, a narrow campaign does not provide the popular political mandate for change that the electoral success of the Coalition first indicates. More particularly, it suggests the current administration will choose the path of least resistance during 2002–04. In doing so, it paves the way for the promised succession of the current Treasurer, Peter Costello, to the prime ministership, possibly in 2003 or 2004. A staunchly orthodox free-marketeer, his selection will be welcomed by the markets and, importantly, will insure economic policy continuity well into the decade.

Second, and although benefiting from the largest swing to an incumbent government in the postwar period, the Coalition's majority in the House of Representatives is small and the Senate is controlled by the opposition in alliance with minority parties. Negotiating the passage of legislation will not be easy. The opposition has already signaled its intention to block further major industrial relations reform and the proposed changes to cross-media ownership laws.

In all, reform will continue, but its scope and pace will be slower than observed in the first two electoral terms of the current administration.

Regulatory and prudential reform: Risks ahead?

Despite the success of the RBA in implementing monetary policy and controlling inflation, the issue of prudential regulation has emerged as one of the key risk issues for investors. The issue has particular resonance in Australia, following a number of corporate collapses in 2001, including that of HIH, which is estimated to have left a A\$5 billion hole in the pockets of investors and creditors. These collapses have led a number of commentators to label the Australian Securities and Investment Commission (ASIC), charged with responsibility for Corporate Codes of Governance, a 'toothless tiger.'

Despite this criticism, investors should not be overly concerned. Australian companies consistently score highly in corporate governance surveys. Rules have been strengthened so that companies must provide investors with information on all fees, salaries, share options and benefits. In a recent survey on corporate governance in the Asia-Pacific region, Australian companies occupied 15 of the first 19 places, and no Australian corporate surveyed was ranked outside of the top half of the table.[52]

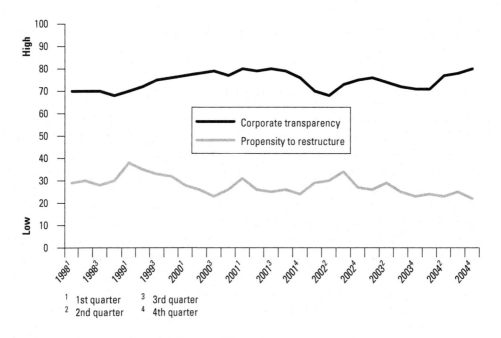

| 1 | 1st quarter | 3 | 3rd quarter |
| 2 | 2nd quarter | 4 | 4th quarter |

FIGURE 2.7 Corporate governance index, Australia 1998–2004

Corporate governance index methodology
- The corporate governance index is a composite index measuring the juridical requirements for corporate disclosure and financial reporting, prudential regime adequacy, prudential compliance enforcement, and the juridical reach of prudential authorities.
- The propensity-to-restructure index is a composite index based on media releases and reported corporate restructuring as a result of prudential regulation, financial incentives, loan restructuring/re-negotiation, or asset realignment. In the case of Thailand, it follows closely with the Financial Institutions Development Fund and bank rescheduling practices – and in the future with the newly created TAMC.

The corporate governance index demonstrates consistently high levels of prudential regulation by Australian authorities, as well as the stringent standards applied to financial information reporting by ASIC and the ASX. A stable framework for corporate governance has meant companies have rarely been forced to restructure operations or ownership structures to meet regulatory requirements.

Moreover, the promised review of the Trade Practices Act 1974 will likely reinforce the power of prudential regulators. Likely changes include strengthening of the powers of the Australian Competition and Consumer Commission (ACCC), to enable it to more proactively police violation of the laws governing anti-competitive behavior. So too, tougher sanctions for 'predatory' pricing will likely follow, which will have major implications for the newest entrant to the domestic aviation industry, Virgin Blue. In the past, a number of foreign investors have complained of the practice, citing it as a major impediment to successful investment in Australia.[53]

Foreign investor risk

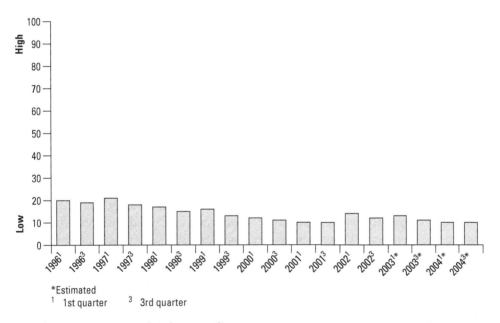

*Estimated
[1] 1st quarter   [3] 3rd quarter

FIGURE 2.8 Foreign investor risk index, Australia 1996–2004

Foreign investor risk index methodology:
- The foreign investor risk index is a composite index measuring tax burdens, discriminatory regulatory practices, adverse compliance regulations, government policy toward foreign enterprise, receptiveness to issuance of government contracts, foreign enterprise commercial restrictions, and official attitudinal changes to foreign direct investment and foreign commercial operations that impact on operational efficiency. The index also incorporates a nominal measure for market risk and market failure.

The combination of a stable party system, a well-functioning bureaucracy and a transparent political operating environment, mean that there is nothing in the Australian political landscape that should cause investors concern. A stable political system has, in recent years, been complemented by a healthy economy free of destabilizing shocks. For these reasons, the foreign investor risk index has been trending downwards since 1995, commensurate with sustained economic growth.

Conversely, the index began to trend slowly upwards toward the end of 2000, as growth levels began to tail off. The rise has also been supported by the concerns raised by a number of foreign investors stemming from the slow pace of market reforms in a number of newly deregulated markets that have acted to curtail opportunities and, in some cases, forced investors to exit the Australian market.

Section D Security

- The security environment is one of the most stable in the region, emblematic of a strong defense force, stable relationships with regional neighbors, albeit occasionally interspersed by recurrent diplomatic tensions. Most recently, this saw Australia undertake military action in support of East Timorese independence, where troop deployments as part of a UN effort are still in existence. However, as a middle power, and outside of Japan (the leading regional power), Australia operates from a position of strength with strong representation in second-track diplomacy forums. All this bodes well for the foreseeable future.

Companies operating in Australia enjoy the benefits of a stable operating environment, including a low-risk security climate. In short, few issues threaten the security of property or personnel.

As in all liberal democracies, political protests form an integral part of Australian cultural life, covering the whole spectrum of social issues from Aboriginal land rights to abortion and immigration. Few, it seems, are economically motivated, insofar as to involve a challenge to the operation of business and the market itself. Environmentally motivated protests are, however, the exception to the rule, though there is no indication to suggest that these are aimed at foreign producers any more so than local operators.

The number of industrial disputes leading to protests is falling and is likely to continue to do so in the future. Whether the issue is social or economic, the protests, while often vociferous, are rarely violent. Of more concern is the potential for industrial action to disrupt supply for downstream producers. For instance, a number of disputes between labor and management at vehicle parts' suppliers during 2001 and 2002 have threatened to halt automobile production.

The external security environment is equally secure with few discernible threats to Australia's borders. A number of Australian citizens have been linked with the Al Qaeda organization but as yet there are no credible reports to confirm that the terrorist network is operable within Australia's borders. Limited terrorist threats have been directed at laboratories by animal rights activists, but again these have so far amounted to little. Current government legislation designed to increase the powers available to law enforcement bodies to deal with potential terrorist threats in the wake of September 11 will further strengthen the environment, though the indications are that the full raft of proposals will be watered down before being passed by the Senate.

Section E Economic and political risk forecasts

- Ongoing economic reforms aimed at deregulating the Australian economy appear to have removed the structural impediments to growth that acted to curtail previous expansions. If Australia is to maintain its recent out-performance of the OECD average, it must continue to attract foreign investment and/or significantly increase its exports – most obviously to address a persistent current account deficit. For this to occur, Australian policy-makers must insure continued microeconomic reforms, aimed at creating truly competitive national markets in high-value adding sectors.

Short-term forecasts

- The short-term outlook for the Australian economy is for continued growth in the range of 3 percent. Inflation will remain within the target range of 2–3 percent (RBA target band) per annum. Unemployment will remain static before declining in 2003 – though only moderately. The outlook for exports is for reduced growth as the dollar appreciates, with manufacturing exports likely to experience the most difficult operating conditions.
- The Australian dollar will remain below appropriate valuations, with moderate appreciation likely in 2003–04. It will trade in the 55–60 US cent range for the duration of 2002–03.
- The receptiveness of the financial markets to new debt and equity financing for large infrastructure projects will deteriorate, which may stall a number of 'big-ticket' projects such as the proposed Queensland to PNG gas pipeline.
- Key regulatory reforms in the electricity generating and gas pipeline sectors will continue, although the pace of reform is likely to disappoint investors and thus retard foreign investor interest in the sector.
- Government procurement practices that currently favor Australian contractors over their foreign counterparts will not change in the short term. Opportunities for foreign contractors to participate in public service and infrastructure provision will continue to be limited in 2002–04.
- Proposed changes to the legislation governing mergers and acquisitions, as part of an announced review of the Trade Practices Act 1974, which would make it easy for investors to buy into and exploit opportunities for joint ventures with existing Australian companies, are also likely to be stalled in 2002–04.

Short-term opportunities

- The low value of the Australian dollar in historical terms suggests that for those investors prepared to bear the current uncertainty, now is a good time to consider asset acquisition, with the opportunity for dollar-play gains in the medium term.
- Opportunities for asset acquisition are likely to arise from the planned sale of a number of state-owned assets. This will be complemented by the sale of the federal government's remaining share of the national telecommunications provider Telstra, though the exact timing is unclear.
- With the demand for natural gas rising and alternative new supply sources around the globe subject to increasing political and economic risks, the Australian natural gas sector looks set to enjoy strong growth for the foreseeable future. Investors will face considerable regulatory challenges in the short term but can expect the regulatory environment to gradually improve.
- With a highly skilled workforce, low wages by world standards and rising sectoral labor market weakness, the Australian financial sector offers investors a low-risk, cost-efficient bridgehead into growing Asian markets.
- A world class bio-technology sector and medical research record, combined with immature alternative financing markets, likely to recede even further in the short to medium term as economic growth softens, offers significant opportunities for joint venture arrangements with foreign partners with access to long-term capital.

Medium to longer term

- The competitive position of the Australian economy has improved significantly during the past decade. This has enabled a degree of export diversification, with the proportion of manufactured exports rising comparative to more traditional resource-related exports. The benefits received from productivity improvements will continue to feed through into the Australian economy for some time yet.

Overall risk rating

The risk profile faced by foreign investors in Australia has improved significantly during the past decade. It will continue to do so, although with the bulk of macro-deregulatory reform already undertaken, the upside risk profile will, to a large extent, rest upon further sectoral reforms. Equally, however, downside risks are limited by a fundamentally sound economy, which should ensure continued growth and a transparent operating environment.

Australia must now complement on-going and to date largely successful domestic market reform with active political engagement with Southeast Asian trading partners if export opportunities are to keep increasing. The trend toward regional trading blocs such as the European Union and NAFTA, despite Australia's close cultural affiliations with the two regions, threatens to leave Australia internationally isolated. Unfortunately, the current administration has failed to recognize the importance of the issue and in doing so continues to squander the benefits of reform to date. Continued failure to do so will reduce the opportunities for investors by reducing the long-term growth potential of the Australian economy, and thus the ability of Australia to purchase goods and services, as well as reducing the opportunities available to export-oriented foreign investment.

Risk: Stable →
Risk Rating (0 = lowest risk, 10 highest risk) 3.0

Section F Australia fact sheet*

Geography

Capital
Canberra

Largest city (millions)
Sydney, 4.3

Location
27 00 S, 133 00 E

Adjacent countries
None

Terrain
Mostly low plateau with deserts; fertile plain in southeast

Land use
Arable land 6%, permanent crops 0%, permanent pastures 54%, forests and woodland 19%, other 21% (1993 est.)

Area (km²)
7,686,850

Economic statistics

Currency
Australian dollar (A$) = 100 cents

Exchange rate (January 2002)
US$1.00 = A$1.95

Gross Domestic Product (GDP)
US$395 billion + 3.8%

GDP per capita – PPP
US$25,285 (2000)

GDP composition by sector
Agriculture 3%, industry 26%, services 72% (2001)

* All figures are the latest available except where indicated. All figures are in US dollars. Figures are compiled from national, international and multilateral agencies (International Monetary Fund, World Bank, World Development Report, UNESCO Statistical Yearbook, International Labour Office, United Nations, Central Intelligence Agency World Fact Book). Gross domestic product (GDP) refers to the value of all goods and services produced in the preceding financial year. GDP per capita, Purchasing Power Parity (GDP per capita – PPP) refers to the indices developed by the World Bank to take account of price differences, cost of living differences, and relative purchasing power of a set basket of goods and services between countries so as to provide a more accurate measure of national wealth.

Percentage of the population earning less than US$2.00 per day
0

Inflation rate
2.8% (2000)[54]

Foreign debt (billions)
$220.6 (2000)

National unemployment rate
6.8% (2000)

Labor force
9,847,500 (November 2001)

Labor force by occupation
Services 82.3%, industry 12.6%, agriculture 4.9% (August 2001)

Budget (billions)
Revenues: $94
Expenditure: $103 (1999)

Industries
Mining, industrial and transportation, equipment, food processing, chemicals, steel

Major exports (billions)
$69 (f.o.b., 2000 est.)
Coal, metal and ores, petroleum products, gold, meat, wool and cotton, alumina, iron ore, cereals, machinery and transport equipment, natural gas, medical and pharmaceutical equipment

Major imports (billions)
$77 (f.o.b., 2000 est.)
Machinery and transport equipment, computers and office machines, telecommunications equipment and parts, crude oil and petroleum products

Major trading partners (exports)
Japan 19.7%, EU 11.7%, ASEAN 13.3%, US 9.7%, South Korea 7.7%, NZ 5.8%, Taiwan 4.9%, Hong Kong 3.3%, China 5.7% (2000–01)

Major trading partners (imports)
EU 24%, US 22%, Japan 14%, ASEAN 13% (1999)

Income/wealth distribution (household income or consumption by % share)
Lowest 10%: 2%
Highest 10%: 25.4% (1994)

Televisions
10.15 million (1997)

Telephone (lines in use)
9.58 million (1998)

Cellular phones
6.4 million (1998)

Internet users
10.6 million (2001)

Fiscal year
01 July – 30 June

Government and political statistics

Nature of government
Democratic, federal–state system recognizing the British monarch as sovereign

Constitution
9 July 1900, effective 1 January 1901

Structure of government
Executive branch and legislative branch

Executive branch
Chief of State: Queen Elizabeth II (since 6 February 1952), represented by Governor-General Rev. Peter Hollingworth (since 29 June 2001)

Head of government
Prime Minister John Winston Howard (since 11 March 1996); Deputy Prime Minister John Anderson

Legislative branch
Bicameral Federal Parliament consists of the Senate and House of Representatives.

Senate
(76 seats – 12 from each of the six states and two from each of the two territories; one-half of the members elected every three years by popular vote to serve six-year terms)

House of Representatives
(148 seats; members elected by popular vote on the basis of proportional representation to serve three-year terms; no state can have fewer than five representatives)

Cabinet members (as at January 2002)

Prime Minister
John Howard

Deputy Prime Minister
John Anderson

Treasurer
Peter Costello

Minister of Defence and Leader of the Government in the Senate
Robert Hill

Minister for Trade
Mark Vaile

Minister for Foreign Affairs
Alexander Downer

Minister for Communications, Information Technology and the Arts
Richard Alston

Minister for Employment and Workplace Relations
Tony Abbott

Minister for Immigration, Multicultural and Indigenous Affairs
Philip Ruddock

Minister for Environment and Heritage
Dr. David Kemp

Attorney-General
Darryl Williams

Minister for Finance and Administration
Nicholas Minchin

Minister for Agriculture, Fisheries and Forestry
Warren Truss

Minister for Family and Community Services
Amanda Vanstone

Minister for Education, Science and Training
Dr Brendan Nelson

Minister for Industry, Tourism and Resources
Ian Macfarlane

Minister for Justice and Customs
Christopher Ellison

Minister for Forestry and Conservation
Ian Macdonald

Minister for Arts and Sport
Rod Kemp

Minister for Small Business and Tourism
Joe Hockey

Minister for Science
Peter McGauran

Minister for Children and Youth Affairs
Larry Anthony

Minister for Employment Services
Mal Brough

Minister of State
Eric Abetz

Minister for Veterans' Affairs and Minister assisting Minister of Defence
Danna Vale

Administrative structure of government
Six states and two territories*;
Australian Capital Territory*, New
South Wales, Northern Territory*,
Queensland, South Australia, Tasmania,
Victoria, Western Australia

Main governing parties and ideological affiliation
Australian Democratic Party [Brian
Greig (interim)]; Australian Labor Party
[Simon Crean]; Green Party [Bob
Brown]; Liberal Party [John Winston
Howard]; National Party [John
Anderson]

Main opposition parties
Labor Party [Simon Crean]

International memberships
ANZUS, APEC, ARF (dialogue partner),
AsDB, ASEAN (dialogue partner),
Australia Group, BIS, C, CCC, CP, EBRD,
ESCAP, FAO, IAEA, IBRD, ICAO, ICC,
ICFTU, ICRM, IDA, IEA, IFAD, IFC, IFRCS,
IHO, ILO, IMF, IMO, Inmarsat, Intelsat,
Interpol, IOC, IOM, ISO, ITU, NAM
(guest), NEA, NSG, OECD, OPCW, PCA,
Sparteca, SPC, SPF, UN, UNCTAD,
UNESCO, UNHCR, UNMEE, UNTAET,
UNTSO, UNU, UPU, WFTU, WHO, WIPO,
WMO, WTrO, ZC

Business organizations
Australian Chamber of Commerce and
Industry (ACCI), Australian Commercial
Disputes Centre, Australian Industry
Group (AIG), Business Council of
Australia (BCA)

Date of UN membership
1948 (founding member)

Social statistics

Population size (millions)
19.3 (July 2001)

Fertility rate (average number of children born by women 15–49 years of age)
1.77 children born/woman (2001 est.)

Infant mortality rate
4.97 deaths/1000 live births (2001 est.)

Population growth
0.99% (2001 est.)

Life expectancy
Men 77.02 years
Women 82.87 years (2001 est.)

Ethnic composition
Caucasian 92%, Asian 7%, Aboriginal and other 1%

Religions
Anglican 26.1%, Roman Catholic 26%, other Christian 24.3%, non-Christian 11%

National languages spoken
English, native languages

Illiteracy rate (age 15+)
0%

By gender (ages 25+)
Male: 0%
Female: 0%

China

3 China

Marcus Chadwick and Tianbiao Zhu

Section A Economy

Overview

China's reform program is entering its most difficult phase. Social tensions are mounting, placing pressure on the government to boost already high levels of fiscal expenditure to stimulate economic growth and employment, and dampen opposition from those opposed to the reform process.

Recognition among China's leaders of the seriousness of the challenges that lie ahead has not translated into effective policy-making. For the present, the 'difficulties and severe challenges' ahead, and conceded by Prime Minister Zhu Rongji, have been overshadowed by the Communist Party's 16th National Congress in late 2002. More important to senior party elite officials is party politics, pushing to the side serious policy development and a delayed reform process.

Communist Party Congress: Eyes off the reform process

While the congress is important, and the basis for the accession of the next generation of party leaders, its obvious importance lies in the generational transition it hails, where the next spate of party elites will be the first not to have direct links with the founding of the party and the revolution. For example, the incumbent leader of the Chinese Communist Party (CCP), Hu Jintao, at 58, is the youngest member of the present seven-man Politburo

Standing Committee, and likely to remain a central player, but his reform credentials are questionable given both his ambition within the party and his pragmatic nature.

Indeed, few party members have been willing to risk alienating key factions in the run-up to the congress by adopting potentially controversial stances on issues of importance. As a result, the capacity of the party to sustain the reformist vigor of the past five years diminished during 2002. More importantly, this reform hiatus will likely extend into 2003 as the protégés of the current generation are maneuvered into position. Nor is it just economic reform that has slowed; Zhu's 2002 address to the CCP, for example, conspicuously steered clear of any mention of the 'road to democracy' that had comprised the bulk of his address to the party in 1999.

Looking ahead, the government's primary concern will be to maintain social stability through high levels of economic growth as a means to provide employment for former employees of state-owned enterprises (SOEs). Indeed, the scale of this challenge is staggering. For example, it is estimated that China will need to provide as many as 200 million new jobs during 2002–12 in the transition from a command economy to a market economy if unemployment is not to blow out and social instability gather pace.

More generally, the government's priority in the medium term is also guided by its fears about growing inequality, and again of the fears about possible instability this might cause, if some tangible measures are not developed for redistributing income toward the interior of China to help them keep pace with the dynamic provincial economies of the eastern seaboard. For investors, this will present opportunities to participate in a number of planned infrastructure projects, although the successful investor will need to tread warily. Despite all the hype, project financing in China, for example, remains in its infancy.

China continues to suffer from a murky regulatory environment that makes business risky and government regulations opaque. As one commentator notes, 'You don't know whether the government permits what you do or not.'[1]

For investors looking to enter the Chinese market in 2002–04, there are a few facts of which they should be aware. First, China, despite a formidable *national* Communist party lacks a consistent national legal framework to support free enterprise. More generally, and to borrow a familiar refrain, China best resembles a series of diverse economies, divided between private enterprise and a command economy (of roughly equal size), and complicated by economic regionalism where coastal regions prosper and interior regions struggle.

While two decades of reform, beginning in 1979, have removed many of the worst distortions of the command economy, and enabled China to fulfill a portion of its latent economic potential, internal problems continue to beset the economy. Equally important, it should not be assumed that these will eventually recede into distant memory, and that China is automatically modernizing its regulatory framework, infrastructure and judicial apparatus. Nothing is automatic in China, and many public regulatory institutions are not evolving as might typically be assumed in a Western setting.[2]

Importantly, then, reform continues to generate new challenges in the process of resolving old ones. This can be observed in the case of the closely intertwined SOE and financial sector, and the fiscal challenges they represent to Chinese authorities, and, in turn, of broader problems of reform in the economy generally as China attempts to address the social consequences of rapid modernization.[3] China's capacity to manage these challenges will shape the risk environment that foreign investors will have to confront in 2002–04 and beyond.

However, this should not cloud the massive progress that has been made by Chinese authorities in the last few decades, where China has been able to do more to reduce its domestic poverty than any other nation on earth. Equally, however, it is obvious that these reforms and advances have been less than sufficient, with more than 670 million people earning less than $2 a day, and of these there are some 200 million people who continue to earn less than $1 per day.[4] Such figures should alert all potential investors to the popular misnomer that China represents a market of 1.3 billion consumers. Its does not! Population size is no measurement of market size or economic consumption levels, with China continuing to rank as one of the world's poorest nations.

The challenges facing China are thus substantial, and more than any other nation on earth they are not readily solved by simple recourse to the making of public policy. Inside China there is no obvious or natural difference between public and private sectors, nor is there much evidence to suggest that after two decades of reform there has been a wholesale cognitive shift in the traditional Chinese view of the world founded on a conceptual unity between the state and the individual. Like it or not, the state's business will remain 'business' long after foreign investors attempting to impose Western ideas on China have packed their bags and gone home. Doing business in China will continue to be a cultural risk zone, with foreign investors well advised to prepare themselves for a culture shift if they are to be successful and navigate the unique cultural obstacles endemic to Chinese ways of business.

The bottom line: A unique operating environment

While generic platitudes such as these provide the investor into China with little in the way of day-to-day operational support, they must nevertheless be understood. Moreover, they point to the need for innovative risk management strategies built upon recognition of what are the salient realities of Chinese business practices. This is not to suggest that the prerequisites of contemporary business success can be deduced from a brief sojourn into Chinese history books, but rather that risk management strategies must be devised to capture the integrative nature of politics and economics in modern-day China. This calls for a 'holistic' operating and risk management strategy that eschews an artificial separation of business, public policy and Chinese societal norms, where business is as much a social practice as an economic one.

For those prepared to undertake such an approach, the rewards will be commensurate with the risks. For those investors unable or unwilling to countenance such divergence from traditional operating strategies, the potential benefits of operating in China will not be realized.

Section B Risks and projections

Macroeconomic performance and risk indicators

- Economic growth remains robust at 7 percent. The industrial sector led by foreign-invested enterprises (FIEs) continues to drive growth, buoyed by resilient consumer sentiment. High levels of public investment and retail spending will maintain strong growth levels into 2003–04. On the downside, rising public sector debt, coupled with an inadequate financial services sector and a poor selection of financial instruments, will constrain growth in the medium term.

China remained one of the best performing economies in the world in 2001–02, with GDP expanding by 7.7 percent. Quarterly figures reveal, however, that growth slowed significantly in the last two quarters of 2002 to 6.6 percent.[5] High levels of domestic investment, up by 12.1 percent, and stronger than forecast retail sales were the primary drivers of economic growth in 2001–02, contributing 58 percent and 43 percent respectively to GDP growth.[6]

The industrial sector was the best performing sector in 2001–02, with leading indicators suggesting this will continue to outperform other sectors of the economy in 2002–04. Growth in the sector was led by a robust performance from FIEs posting 11.9 percent growth for the year compared to 8.1 percent for SOEs.[7] Likewise, the services sector grew by 7.4 percent on the back of stronger than expected growth in transport and telecommunications, a trend that looks set to continue in 2003–04.

There is growing evidence to support critics of the government, who claim that growth figures are significantly exaggerated. There were more than 62,000 cases of statistical fraud in China in 2001–02. The pressure to meet SOE targets, please party officials, and gain the favor of superiors, seems to make for a strong case of fraudulent economic representations in all of China's economic data.

Although there is no cause to suspect a significant decline in economic growth in 2002–04, there is growing evidence to suggest that a moderation of recent growth levels is likely. In part, this stems from the fact that the present drivers of growth are unsustainable. First, for example, growth in fiscal expenditures has been high, reflecting the increased infrastructural needs of an economy expanding rapidly. Unfortunately, these have increased the budget deficit, that officially stood at 2.6 percent of GDP in 2001–02.[8] The real figure, however, is considerably higher, as debt figures fail to capture the impact of liabilities incurred through the issue of bonds by SOE management companies and state-owned banks, or state and SOE pension liabilities.

Further, there is growing evidence to suggest that public sector investment, due to requirements placed on state controlled and owned banks (SCOBs) to match public sector spending, is effectively crowding out private sector investment and creating sizable debt blowouts.

Second, the foreign component of investment spending – FDI – will likely tail off during 2002–04 as the proportion of capital flows accelerated to coincide with China's accession to the WTO begin to dry up. So too, reductions in the capital account surplus will be matched by a declining current account balance, as WTO entry will bring a greater increase in imports relative to export sales in 2003–04. All this will add pressure to the revenue streams of government.

> Inflationary pressures have all but disappeared. Consequently, monetary policy will remain accommodative to growth in 2002–04.

Third, China's recent growth has been achieved off the back of a low interest rate environment. While this strategy was initially successful in containing the fallout from the Asian crisis, it has left Chinese firms extremely susceptible to broader macroeconomic developments. China's SOE sector, for example, is largely unprofitable and illiquid, such that even the smallest rise in borrowing costs combined with a drop in sales would cause 40–60 percent of all company debt to become effectively unserviceable.[9]

Fourth, a high savings rate combined with a low interest rate environment has failed to supply adequate new investment capital for the private sector. In part, the problem has arisen due to the conditions under which private enterprise developed in China. Many firms were forced to adopt quasi public–private structures in order to meet the once draconian laws governing the conduct of private enterprise. Deliberately opaque ownership and operating structures mean that the four SCOBs (responsible for almost three-quarters of all lending) have been unable or unwilling to lend to the private sector. Consequently, more than 80 percent of private small and medium size enterprises (SMEs) considered their lack of access to finance to be a serious constraint in 2001–02.[10]

These four factors combined suggest a moderation in the growth rate for 2003–04, if not beyond; indeed perhaps a longer-term trend to lower, but more sustainable growth rates in the decade ahead.

Financial sector reforms: Important to continuing economic health in China

While the recent move to impose tighter financial risk regulations on banks is welcome, it signals problems ahead, especially if accounting practices fail to keep pace with financial sector prudential reforms. This is important since growth in the financial services sector has made it one of the most dynamic sectors in the Chinese economy, and overwhelmingly the primary source of new employment opportunities. The depth of reform must thus extend downwards to international standard accounting procedures if international confidence is to be maintained, growth in the financial services sector continued, and employment expansion assured.

The health of the financial services sector and improvements to its regulatory and prudential parameters is also important to insure the continued growth of adequate capital to service China's growing capital needs for infrastructure development and modernization. Indeed, this is magnified by the immaturity of equity markets, serving to inflate the liquidity premium attached to equity financing.

Further afield, if strong growth is to be maintained it is also obvious that there is need for widespread reform, not least in terms of improving the policy environment for supporting the private sector, and SMEs in particular. Priority areas include the simplification of market entry requirements, greater access to finance and enforcement of land and intellectual property rights. Growth in China in the coming years will increasingly rest on the operating environment for foreign and domestic enterprise, and unless this environment can show tangible and incremental improvements year-on-year, confidence will erode as will profits, investment and capital.

GDP growth moderating

In the absence of a significant rise in external demand, this combination of issues will tend to push economic growth down to around the 6–7 percent range in 2003–04. The industry and services sectors, albeit with massive firm level disparity, will once again outpace the moribund agricultural sector, recording growth of 7–9 percent and 2 percent respectively. If, however, the pace of global economic recovery in 2003–04 is less than forecast, the authorities will not hesitate to further strengthen already expansionary monetary and fiscal policies, adding considerable weight to the debt burden of SOEs and government budget deficits. Market risk can thus be expected to remain relatively high in 2003–04.

Export performance

- Export growth contracted during 2001–02 but has shown signs of an early recovery, highlighting the underlying strength of the sector. China's entry to the WTO will insure double digit export growth well into the decade but the short-term costs will be considerable, precipitating restructure in the agricultural, automobile, banking and insurance sectors. Opportunities abound for export-oriented FDI.

Amidst global economic slowdown, export growth declined sharply in 2001–02 to 6.8 percent from 27.9 percent in 2000. On the upside, import growth also fell from 35.4 percent in 2000 to 8.2 percent in 2001–02. The current account remained in surplus at $19.6 billion in 2001–02, due to lower import demand. This is likely to further decline in 2003–04, to less than half of one percent of GDP.

These trends will be exacerbated in the near term by China's entry into the WTO. The positive effects of the WTO accession will not be felt until 2005 when the Multi-Fibre Agreement (MFA) will be phased out. The immediate result will be an increase in imports. In particular, domestic automobile, banking and insurance companies will suffer most, due to uncompetitive production and regulatory structures. Resistance to WTO trade reform at the provincial level, principally in the form of non-tariff barriers, will likely worsen before it improves. Indeed, such barriers are currently considerable, as one executive of a foreign automobile producer noted recently, hidden barriers make operating in the market intolerably difficult. So much so, that disinvestment is being actively considered. The lesson is that an uncertain future faces all but the most efficient producers in these sectors of the economy.

> Export growth in the eastern and western provinces, such as Shangdong, Jiangsu, Zhejiang, Chongqing, Qinghai, and Gansu, outperformed north-eastern and southern provinces during 2001–02. In particular, Guangdong province, home to one-third of China's total exports by value, recorded export growth of just 2.9 percent in 2001–02.[11]

Service exports in the form of international tourism will increase gradually in the build-up to the 2008 Olympic Games. Opportunities for foreign investors to participate will occur primarily in the form of easier entry requirements for hoteliers and restaurant chains. Once again, the degree of ease of entry and official encouragement will depend on location.

Looking beyond 2005, low real wage costs and improving operating conditions should ensure strong export growth of 7–10 percent per annum for the next decade.[12] In particular, WTO entry means China's share of total world exports of apparel and electronics will likely double, from 18 percent to 40 percent, and 5–10 percent respectively.[13] Perhaps, more importantly, China's accession to the WTO should presage accelerated development of a framework for the private sector, including market entry, finance, land-use rights, and enforcement of private property rights. However, foreign investors should not underestimate the considerable provincial resistance toward the development of a private sector, rules-based regime for both intra-national and international trade. The WTO and its strictures will thus help mold China, but China can still expect to witness considerable resistance to such reforms in the majority of its provinces, making foreign investment establishment a tough call.

Currency movements and projections

• Fears that China will seek to devalue in the wake of currency depreciations elsewhere in the region are unfounded. Monetary policy has become more transparent, while still subservient to the goal of economic growth. More importantly, speculative pressure for a devaluation has subsided, reflecting China's continuing good fortunes in the export sector and its continuing strong growth. Pressure to float the currency will be resisted but a widening of the renminbi trading band will see limited but sustained appreciation during 2003–04.

Since the Asian financial crisis, the Chinese monetary authorities, which consist of a 12-member Monetary Policy Committee (MPC), have successfully maintained the narrow yuan dollar trading band at 8.3 yuan to the US dollar, and reduced speculative pressure on the currency.

Monetary policy has explicitly supported domestic investment and growth goals. Broad money (M2) increased by 14.4 percent in 2001–02, 2.1 percent higher than in 2000–01, with further marginal rises likely in 2002–03, provided inflation remains manageable – something that looks very likely.[14] Indeed, the expansionary monetary policy is supported by low underlying inflation that saw the consumer price index rise only slightly in 2000 at 0.4 percent, to 1.2 percent in 2001, and 1.9 percent in 2002. Inflation will continue to remain low throughout 2002–04, projected at rates of between 2.9 percent and 4.3 percent.

> The MPC's priority is social and political stability, not a competitive banking sector, convertibility and prudent monetary policy.

A declining current account surplus, expected to fall to less than one-half of one percent of GDP in 2003–04, will be offset by positive capital inflows for the foreseeable future. The stock of foreign reserves, excluding gold, will continue to rise and is expected to reach more than US$240 billion in 2003, equivalent to approximately 11 months import cover. Full convertibility will be maintained.

In general, the policy stance of the MPC has been supported by the markets. This is reflected in the reduction of pressures to devalue the exchange rate following real and nominal effective appreciation of the exchange rate against a basket of Asian currencies in the wake of the Asian financial crisis. With the tentative recovery of most Asian currencies, the real effective exchange rates of the yuan are now at pre-crisis levels.

More generally, a more transparent monetary policy has reduced speculation of a yuan devaluation. As a result, liquidity premiums on traded yuan dollar forwards have fallen from highs of almost 25 percent in 1997, equivalent to 10.5 yuan to the dollar, to negligible levels.

An appreciating exchange rate?

As yet, however, the PBC has resisted calls to allow market mechanisms to determine the exchange rate. There are signs, though, that this is beginning to change. The Chinese monetary authorities have recently turned a blind eye to narrow breaches of the band within which the renminbi trades against foreign currencies ($\pm$ 0.2 percent) – mainly the US dollar. There is evidence to suggest that the government is stealthily testing the water as a forerunner to a general widening of the trading bands in 2003–04. Market consensus remains divided on the scope of the planned broadening. What is clear, however, is that each time the authorities have permitted breaches, the renminbi has strengthened. Consequently, fears of a devaluation now appear outdated and remote. In the absence of a substantial decline in the external account balance, investors will need to factor in a gradual appreciation of the renminbi in 2003–05. Although volatile price movements are considered unlikely, there is no doubt that in the longer term the renminbi has the potential to appreciate substantially.

Financial markets: Performance and development

- NPLs exceed healthy limits at most banks, audit standards and transparency levels are low and control mechanisms, like asset liability analysis and credit management, are weak or non-existent. The result, unfortunately, is that private enterprise is starved of capital, and will continue to be so in 2003–04. Little change can be expected to prudential or regulatory parameters, with financial markets tending to remain mostly underdeveloped.

The problems facing China's financial sector are myriad and well documented. Estimates of non-performing loans (NPLs) as high as 50 percent are not uncommon – though accurate assessment remains impossible. Financial institutions are burdened by inadequate administrative and legal structures, political interference, excessive staffing levels, poor risk management skills, constrained investment horizons and, finally, a lack of incentive for profit-oriented lending. At a minimum, resolving these challenges will require a concerted overhaul of the prudential regulatory framework, continued economic growth and a massive injection of new capital from state and foreign sources.[15]

To date, the pace of reform has remained conditioned by concerns about social stability. The establishment of four asset management companies (AMCs) in 1999 to purchase the NPLs sector was a step in the right direction, but new NPLs are added to bank balance sheets constantly. For example, it is estimated that even after the purchase of 10 percent of the total SCOB loan portfolio, the level of NPLs in the banking system declined by only 4 percent, from 30 percent of total loans to 26 percent.[16] Added to this, existing prudential standards do not include loans as non-performing until the borrower has failed to meet principal repayments for 12 months rather than interest payments for three months as is the international standard. If the more stringent norms of loan delinquency are applied, the proportion of NPLs would rise as high as 50 percent.

> The Chinese government has a fundamental conflict of interest: it is both debtor as owner of SOEs and creditor as owner of state banks. This makes for poor regulatory practices, poor prudential systems, and a less than optimistic outlook for reform in this area in 2003–04.

Arcane accounting procedures: Investor beware

The desire to improve credit risk procedures is also thwarted by accounting procedures that distort the financial position of a firm, making it almost impossible to distinguish between good and bad risks in terms of asset acquisition and possible joint venture partners. In a nutshell, firms overstate profits and asset values, and understate debt. Likewise, all goods produced are valued at market prices, regardless of whether they are sold, paid for, or have outstanding calls on them through various financing arrangements. So too, under Chinese accounting procedures, unsold goods accumulate as inventories, while goods sold but not paid for accumulate as receivables. Both are then valued at market prices and classified as current assets. Finally, both inventories and receivables are then treated as revenues in the income statement and included as profits, even though neither generate cash income.[17]

Prospective investors looking to enter the market, or those in search of possible joint venture partners, must thus be cognizant of these accounting procedures and the risks they harbor. Indeed, it is also important to recognize the poor degree of protection afforded investors who have made investment decisions based on fraudulent accounting procedures. Typically, this is less than adequate, with little legal recourse to make financial redress. All too often, investors have found that the time elapsed during court proceedings has been used by the local partner to asset strip the joint venture, leaving only a worthless shell by the time the judgment is given.

One bright spot among the gloom appears in the form of smaller private banks that have sprung up to meet the needs of the private sector, and hence have loan portfolios weighted toward SMEs. These niche banks, with only a smaller proportion of burdensome SOE debt, offer investors the chance to implement improved risk-based lending and regulation practices, seek foreclosure should debts not be repaid, while also providing a chance to build up experience in the market prior to 2006 when all geographical limitations will be lifted in accordance with WTO rules. The International Finance Corporation (IFC), for example, the financing arm of the World Bank Group, has expressed interest in becoming a minority shareholder in such small banks, thereby offering investors a degree of additional protection. However, it remains to be seen whether such forays will reverse the checkered history of foreign minority stakes in Chinese ventures.[18]

Fixing the debt problem through AMCs: Progress and prospects in 2003–04

While the AMC initiative is to be welcomed as a necessary first step to addressing the NPL and bad debt problem, its success will need to insure that debt-equity swaps are accompanied by meaningful restructuring of debt-ridden and technically insolvent enterprises. This requires providing AMCs with sufficient legal powers, enabling them to force restructure, management changes, and improve business operations in the enterprises in which they hold equity. So too, it involves the enhancement of creditor rights by revising bankruptcy laws and establishing transparent procedures for the valuation and disposal of state assets. In large measure, of course, these problems are tied to the lack of legal frameworks to support the rudimentary needs of a functioning market economy, namely well-established property rights and enforcement of contractual obligations. While this problem is increasingly recognized, there is little optimism to assume strident achievements through reform in 2003–04.

A foreign consortium led by Morgan Stanley will try to recover what it can from a parcel of NPLs, comprising 254 debt-laden enterprises with a face value of US$1.3 billion. The deal could shape the future of China's banking reforms.[19]

As yet, the government has resisted calls for a complete revamp of the institutional structure governing the financial sector in China. To be sure, this is not possible without divorcing the administration from a source of its power and legitimacy – the control of capital. Investors should, as a result, expect a continuation of the piecemeal reforms to date rather than a radical change in state policy.

The bottom line: Don't bank on real reform

In concrete terms, this will likely manifest itself in the immediate future by resisting calls for liberalization of interest rates. The domestic banking sector will remain inefficient, characterized by high spreads and inadequate liquidity. Domestic financing options will remain limited.

Banking collapses will occur but will likely lead to enforced mergers rather than bankruptcy and closure. As a result, the government has signaled that banking sector reform aimed at attracting foreign investment into wholesale markets will be accelerated beyond that required by WTO accession during 2002–05. While this presents opportunities for foreign investors to enter the banking, insurance and asset management sectors, profitable ventures that yield returns commensurate with country risk will remain the exception to the rule for some time yet.

Private and public debt: A mounting problem[20]

- Official public debt figures are under-reported and will continue to rise during 2003–04, particularly in light of the overriding need to maintain deficit spending as a stimulus to growth. Despite anticipation of a further deterioration in public sector finances, the government's debt servicing capacity is adequate. However, downward pressure on China's sovereign rating will mount if current trends continue in 2003–04.

In the aftermath of the Asian financial crisis, the government followed an expansionary fiscal policy that now appears, in the absence of significant fiscal adjustment, to be structural in nature. The fiscal deficit rose to 2.6 percent of GDP in 2001, with a further rise of 19 percent to US$37 billion in 2002.[21] Total public debt is equivalent to 23 percent of GDP. While debt is moderate by international standards, at 14 percent of GDP the figures do not provide an accurate portrait of the potential fiscal vulnerability of China.

Indeed, the government budget for China gives only a partial picture of the actual revenue and expenditure position of the government due to the non-reporting of extra budgetary revenue and expenditure items. Estimates of the true debt position, accounting for quasi-fiscal expenditures, suggests the fiscal deficit for 2002 is probably closer to 8 percent of GDP, while the government debt stock is approximately 50 percent of GDP.[22]

More generally, the fiscal implications necessitated by the need to reform the social security system and resolve the legacy of NPLs suggest that annual fiscal deficits will continue to rise in 2003–05. Annual deficits in the range of 10 percent of GDP will see the

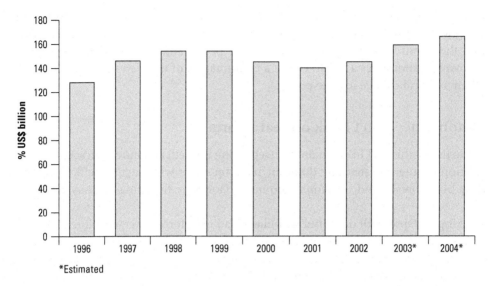

*Estimated

FIGURE 3.1 Debt, China 1996–2004

stock of public debt rise to 65 percent by 2003 and 90 percent by 2008. Should the portion of NPLs prove to be higher than the 20 percent of total loans on which the calculations are based – to, say, 30 percent – the ratio of debt stock to GDP would rise to more than 100 percent of GDP.[23] This means a realistic assessment of liabilities demands that the government increase revenue or decrease expenditures in the magnitude of 2 to 3 percent of GDP annually to limit the rise of the stock of public debt to 65 percent of GDP by 2008. Obviously this will require fundamental reform of the fiscal system, but the probability of this is not guaranteed. Investors should thus be prepared for changes to the level of taxation, directly or indirectly, through a phasing out of tax exemptions currently applied to non-export FIE earnings, or perhaps similar adjustments elsewhere in the tax regime as government authorities begin to re-engineer revenue streams in anticipation of a debt blowout.

Despite a worsening debt problem, the risk of sovereign default is low. Of more concern is that sovereign debt issues will prevent the development of the corporate debt market as funds are sucked into public sector deficit financing. In the absence of fiscal reform, the yield demanded by investors on government debt will rise thereby adding to the deteriorating debt position of the central authorities. For firms looking to raise long-term debt domestically through bond issues, the yield demanded will thus also rise, pricing firms with less than investment grade balance sheets out of the market, i.e. those in most need of financial restructuring.

Labor market trends

- China is in the midst of an industrial revolution. Nowhere is this more apparent than the labor market. The division between skilled coastal workers and unskilled rural workers is emblematic of China's dual development strategy. Unskilled labor is cheap and plentiful and will remain so for decades to come. Skilled professionals are in short supply and wages are rising. Labor laws that are liberal on paper are, in fact, restrictive in practice, forcing many firms to choose to close down rather than risk bureaucratic ire incurred through layoffs. Business operating conditions, and extensive latitude in terms of employment practices, are still well short of international standards.

The official estimate of urban unemployment stood at 5.5 percent in 2002, up from 3.6 percent at the end of 2001.[24] The figure takes into account only those who are registered with the Ministry of Labor and Social Security. It does not cover the Xiangang millions laid off as part of the SOE reforms. Nor does the figure account for an estimated 60–80 million floating workers from rural areas currently migrating to coastal regions in search of employment.

> If the current rate of SOE reform is maintained, an estimated 100–200 million new jobs must be found during the next decade to absorb displaced workers as a result of rural–urban migration.

Consequently, wage pressures are minimal in all but the most highly skilled jobs, where acute shortages of suitably qualified personnel combined with stringent immigration requirements for expatriates have led to significant wage pressures. Nonetheless, wage rates, even in these sectors, lag behind comparable wage rates throughout much of Asia.

Wages and productivity vary between provinces

There are considerable differences among the provinces in wage levels for comparable employment. Wages in coastal cities, for example, are considerably higher than those in the interior and the west. Indeed, large discrepancies also exist between coastal cities. For instance, wages in Suzhou, less than an hour inland from Shanghai, are 20–40 percent lower than comparable wage rates in Shanghai.[25] This trend is likely to increase in 2002–04, as significant differences between regional/provincial labor demand create discrete markets throughout China.

Historically, Chinese authorities have been remarkably effective in resisting wage demands, something that continues to this day. Unions must be registered with the central authorities, for example, and are strictly regulated, including a vetting process whereby all labor representatives must be approved by the state. Attempts to form non-state unions are dealt with severely; this includes support from home country unions for their Chinese counterparts. For this reason, wages in semi-skilled manufacturing operations remain low compared to regional standards, and will likely remain that way for some years to come.

The real challenge facing companies operating in China, however, is the lack of skilled workers. Recent moves to ease restrictions on expatriate personnel have helped alleviate this problem, but any further changes will be strongly opposed by domestic employees' groups. The good news for investors is that the Chinese authorities have begun to dismantle the system of *Hokou*, which barred people from seeking work outside of their places of residence. This should ease skills shortages in the coastal cities in 2002–04.[26]

Acute skilled labor shortages will continue in the financial services sector, including banking staff qualified in credit risk management and insurance professionals with actuarial qualifications. The scramble for Chinese citizens with Western MBAs will not disappear anytime soon. Prospective employers should thus factor this into any start-up process, with labor selection and recruitment being one of the most time consuming business activities for foreign investors in China.

Policies to reduce the shortage of skilled labor through an expansion of the secondary and tertiary education system are in place, but the impact will be only marginal during 2002–05, with such policies having a long lead time before they realize any practical results. More generally, however, without a radical overhaul of teaching and curriculum standards, particularly in rural areas, educational standards will remain below those required to meet the needs of the rapidly growing private sector. In the coming years, the lack of suitably qualified staff will be one of the primary obstacles to successful business operations in China.

Successful investors will thus need to factor in substantial costs for staff training and professional development. Enterprises undertaking training need also to be aware that the cost of doing so must be weighed against the fact that those with skills are more likely to move to higher paid jobs once they are trained. The rate of skilled employment turnover in coastal China is substantially higher than the norm.

Bureaucratic resistance to downsizing is considerable

Further problems faced by prospective foreign investors are the various obstacles to effective labor supply and demand management. While the ability of firms to adjust staffing levels to meet business conditions is improving, non-legislative requirements on employers are still onerous and downsizing remains politically unpopular. Anecdotal evidence suggests that the introduction of regulations that permit lay-offs has not changed a bureaucratic culture that once forbid such actions. Political pressure at the local government level against such a move by FIEs remains considerable, and can result in local backlashes with revenue stream implications.

More broadly, investors in the fast-growing manufacturing sector need to be aware that although generally proficient in terms of production techniques, the culture of local management is attuned to output – not profit! Decision-making has traditionally been channeled upwards, removing input from coal-face workers in terms of issues associated with quality control, production process improvements, and efficiency measures. Effective worker participation in decision-making processes, or creating a culture of worker responsibility for the products they produce is very often a new concept to many Chinese workers. This mindset, according to existing investors, is not easily overcome.

Dark clouds gathering?

Should China fail to meet the needs of an estimated 200 million new entrants to the job market through rural–urban migration in the next decade, the benefits of low wage costs will be grossly outweighed by the potential for social unrest. Already, the number of labor disputes is rising in 2001–02. This remains a worst-case scenario and one that will likely be avoided, but it remains indicative of the business risk environment in China.

Consumer and business confidence: Mixed results

- Business sentiment looking ahead to 2003–04 is mixed. Business confidence in the once booming southern port cities is muted. Firms in Shanghai are the most bullish about economic prospects in 2002–03. On the downside, the realities of China's WTO accession continue to depress sentiment among 'old' economy firms, with fears about competition and redundancy strong among many sectors. On the upside, however, consumer confidence, particularly reflected in high retail sales, shows no sign of weakening in the run-up to 2003–04.

Consumer confidence, buoyed by rising real incomes in urban areas, contributed to stronger than expected retail sales growth of 10.1 percent in 2001–02.[27] Lead indicators suggest that the sector will again record double digit growth in 2002–03, with marginally lower growth of 7–9 percent for 2003–04. However, much will depend on the government's handling of financial sector reform, the rate of liquidity expansion, and the trickle-down effects of China's entry into the WTO. So too, any severe external shocks to the global economy will have

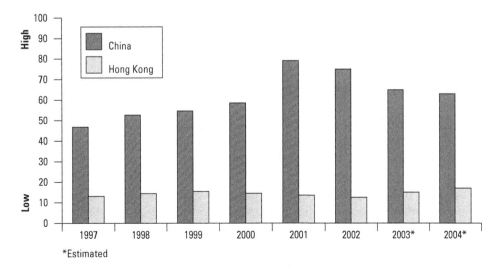

FIGURE 3.2 Consumer and business confidence, China and Hong Kong 1997–2004

negative knock-on effects for China's exports, depressing one of the most significant sectors in the economy. While this is not likely in 2003–04, save for another terrorist attack on the US, it nonetheless remains an area of vulnerability for China.

Generally, however, Chinese consumers continue to rank as the most confident in Asia, particularly with regard to the future macroeconomic environment.[28] Despite this, sharp divisions in confidence levels are emerging between regions and cities, such that it is increasingly difficult to talk about an integrated Chinese business or consumer confidence outlook. For example, residents of the southern provinces such as Guangzhou portrayed a far gloomier outlook than consumers in the northern cities of Beijing and Shanghai. More than 94 percent of respondents from Beijing believed that China's economy would grow steadily in 2002–03.[29] In part, these divisions are driven by the different regional sentiments regarding perceptions of the benefits that will accrue as a result of China's acceptance into the WTO.

Another reason for the regional division between consumer expectations is to be found in the balance sheets of local companies. In Guangzhou, 54 percent of companies saw profits remain static or fall in 2000–01, whereas 65 percent of residents in Beijing reported earnings growth.[30] Forward-looking estimates for 2002–03 suggest a similar pattern, with further falls forecast in profit growth from Guangzhou residents.

In general, business confidence lagged behind consumer confidence in 2000–01 and 2001–02, and is likely to do so again in 2003–04. More than 50 percent of companies in a recent survey expected profits to fall in 2002–03, with Beijing-based firms the most pessimistic. The trend has been reflected in private sector investment expenditures, which have lagged behind public sector investment. FIEs, in particular, have suspended capital investment projects where possible. More generally, there is a problem with over-capacity, especially in the consumer goods-producing and automobile sectors. There are few signs that this will change until the upswing in the world economy anticipated in 2003 helps boost business confidence levels.

Business confidence levels also show marked dissimilarity between various business segments. In particular, telecommunications executives expect prolonged growth in 2003 and beyond, while banking and insurance sector staff were the most gloomy.

Stock market: 'Caveat emptor'

- The fanfare that preceded the launch of the two stock exchanges in China should not disguise the market's poor performance since its establishment. Interest from foreign institutional investors is high but on-going concerns about corporate governance, including accounting practices, minimum disclosure standards and minority shareholder rights should deter all but the most experienced market operators. Signs that the government will delay further sales of state holdings in listed companies should provide a welcome boost to the struggling markets in 2003–04.

Stronger than expected consumer confidence and high levels of government expenditure contributed to above-forecast increases in the composite index, comprised of the two main stock exchanges, Shanghai and Shenzen, in 2001–02. Historically, the median return on equity has lagged below risk-comparable debt instruments, returning 4–7 percent between 1997 and 2000.[31]

The markets have risen consistently since late 1999, but have been plagued by destabilizing volatility and a lack of liquidity. The value of the composite index changed by 32 percent during the course of 2001–02, while liquidity fell in Shanghai and Shenzen by 11 percent and 47 percent respectively. Excess volatility reflects the predominance of small investors, numbering an estimated 50 million in 2001–02. This will not change until domestic institutional investors participate in a more substantial manner. Similarly, international portfolio flows will not be forthcoming until regulatory standards and liquidity improves. The exchanges remain poorly regulated and subject to price fixing.

The profitability of listed companies fell in 2001–02, and is likely to do so again in 2002–03. Further, the liquidity position of companies is weak due to the structure of pre-reform debt markets. Long-term debt accounts for only 6–8 percent of the total debt of domestically listed companies. The dominant share of short-term debt as a source of financing capital means that for market-listed companies current liabilities exceed current assets by a factor of three to one.[32] For those investors searching for value, a 30–50 percent discount over mainland share prices on a price earnings basis provides good reason to consider Chinese 'H' shares on the Hong Kong based Hang Seng Index. These stocks, in particular, are likely to benefit from strong domestic consumption during 2002–03.[33]

The stock market is illiquid and volatile

Unfortunately, it remains the case that the exchanges have not overcome entrenched attitudes among party power brokers, who tend to view the markets as vehicles via which to aid the reform of the SOEs, and only secondly as markets offering a means of raising equity liquidity through domestic and foreign investment. Despite this, significant reform has been occurring, and will assist the exchanges to mature in the coming years. These include the passage of the Securities Law, the establishment of the China Securities Regulatory Commission, and the China Insurance Regulatory Commission, all of which have helped introduce necessary reforms that largely conform to international prudential standards.

However, while these reforms mark an end to the inconsistent and cumbersome patchwork of regulations that existed before, they do not address the key structural issues; namely, government control of IPOs, the government's position as the majority shareholder in most firms, the inadequate rights of minority shareholders, as well as the disclosure and accounting standards imposed on listed companies. Consequently, despite the publicity that accompanied the abandonment of the A and B share lists for local and foreign investors in February 2001, this has not affected the ability of central authorities to manipulate its holdings of state-owned shareholdings by increasing the volume of shares on offer, or of restricting the banks from injecting new funds into the markets. The central authorities will thus be able to continue to meddle in a market that is only partially governed by market forces, and at the mercy of government whim and intervention.

Other problems also remain in the exchanges. Transaction costs for IPOs, for example, are costly by world standards and are likely to remain so for at least 2002–04. The volatility of equity prices too, makes raising debt more difficult, and has tended to force many formerly state-owned firms to list on international as opposed to domestic bourses – such as Singapore, London and New York. Likewise, the liquidity premium charged on equity raising is still well in excess of international norms, adding substantially to the costs of public floats. Unfortunately, there is no reason to suspect that the differential will be reduced in line with international norms in the near future.

In reality, stock markets in China are at least a decade away from being considered a viable source of finance for foreign investors. At present, there are few reasons for firms to choose a Shanghai or Shenzhen listing. Accordingly, few firms, other than near-insolvent SOEs, have chosen to do so.

Corporate tax

- Low rates of corporate tax are undermined by the high cost of regulatory compliance, owing to frequent amendments to the tax code. The penalties for failing to comply are punitive, including the cancellation of operating and export licenses, but these are rarely enforced where an alternative solution can be reached. Expect the same norms to dominate in 2002–04.

FIEs (to qualify for FIE tax status the minimum foreign ownership component is 25 percent), wholly-owned foreign enterprises and expatriate employees are subject to tax arrangements separate from those applicable to Chinese-owned businesses (private and publicly owned). The Foreign Investment Enterprise and Foreign Enterprise Income Tax Law (FEITL) sets a standard flat income tax rate of 33 percent. Of this, 3 percent is paid to local governments with the remainder going to the national government.

In practice, a wide range of tax exemptions act to significantly reduce the effective rate applied to the majority of FIEs. One estimate for actual income tax applied to FIEs is 11 percent.[34] Investors should note, however, that they will have to negotiate incentives directly with the relevant government authorities. More generally, many tax incentives are not automatically applied and require foreign enterprises to have specific knowledge before they can be claimed.

While China has a generally low rate of corporate taxation, this tends to be under-mined by the complexity of the tax system and a woeful lack of transparency. Anecdotal evidence from foreign enterprises operating in China, for example, suggests that consider-able time and resources are spent monitoring frequent tax changes and in dealing with cumbersome bureaucracies charged with collecting taxes.

Tax evasion accounts for as much as 50 percent of taxes due in the private economy. Total losses from tax evasion equal 100 billion renminbi ($12 billion) per year.[35]

This makes the tax and regulatory operating environment in 2003–04 particularly important to monitor, since a raft of changes to the current taxation arrangements are slated to be introduced to meet current WTO protocols. In particular, China will need to amend current arrangements applied to certain categories of imported goods – though exemptions on imported intermediate inputs for exporters will not be phased out.

These new measures will place further pressure on public spending by reducing tariff revenues that have already declined in 2001–02 to 7.7 percent compared with 20.9 percent in 2000–01. Much the same level of decline is also anticipated in 2003–04, again as a result of meeting WTO compliance protocols for tariffs on imported goods and services.

Tax evasion: Creating problems ahead for corporate tax levels

For central authorities, the greatest concern in 2002–04 will be on-going problems associated with tax evasion. Since 1997 tax revenues have grown from 11 percent of GDP to 14 percent, while expenditure has grown from 13 percent to 18 percent. If the current spending obligations are to be met, tax revenue will need to rise to 20 percent of GDP by 2003.

Meeting these expenditure obligations without proportional increases in public debt requires a fundamental overhaul of the tax system, including the mechanisms for enforcement, which are currently applied arbitrarily. In the first instance, this is likely to presage review of corporate tax applied to FDI, particularly in those sectors not considered vital to China's future development. This includes 'old' economy enterprises such as automobile producers and low value-added manufacturing operations. The indications are that this will mean a reduction in the standard profit 'holiday' afforded FIEs. To be sure, however, the current complexity will continue and may even worsen before it improves. Indirectly, the difficulties in enforcing legislative changes at the provincial and local level will likely lead to greater pressure on local government budgets, increasing the incentive of local governments to raise additional revenue by whatever means available – including increasing licensing requirements, indirect taxation on foreign enterprise, if not outright solicitations of bribery.

Residential and commercial property markets

- With stagnant demand for office space from multinational corporations, the property markets have slid. The Shanghai property market has been the hardest hit, with rents and prices falling. Excess supply in other coastal cities, as well as Shanghai, means that recovery in the commercial property market will lag behind the global economy by 12 months, with a significant turnaround unlikely before 2004. The residential property market has performed better but interest rate rises will dampen demand toward the end of 2003 and into 2004.

Excess supply of commercial property has acted to drive down rental and purchase prices in a number of coastal cities from the highs of 2000–01. The Shanghai commercial property market proved most sensitive to the downturn in the global economy due to the on-going freeze on staff numbers and capital expenditures by many multinational corporations. While the Beijing commercial property market will likely recover in 2002–03 it may take a further 12 months before the excess supply in Shanghai is worked through the system. However, it has been the Hong Kong commercial property market that has been hardest hit. Rentals in the 'Grade A' office market declined by 10 percent year-on-year in 2001, while vacancies rose to 8.6 percent. New supply in 2002 has further depressed prices, which, although likely to rise again in 2003, may not reach the precipitous heights of the late 1990s anytime soon.

In contrast with subdued commercial property markets, residential property prices in China rose by 4.7 percent during 2002. Similar increases should be expected in 2003–04.[36] However, once again disparities prevail, with the Beijing market in particular likely to grow faster than the national average.[37] A new supply of luxury serviced apartments in Beijing and Shanghai should, however, see an easing of property prices in this sector during 2003 and early 2004.

> Some 15–20 percent of spending on an average infrastructure or building project is lost to bribery, fraud, and poor-quality construction work.[38]

Also affecting commercial and residential property prices in China is the strong influence due to the nature of government regulation and centrally planned decrees, such as the establishment of housing and apartment quarters in China's fast-growing cities. In effect, then, supply and demand factors are filtered through a maze of provincial and local regulations that make forecasting a perilous task for even inveterate property market watchers. The successful property investor will need to keep abreast of the minutiae of provincial and local government policy changes. At a minimum, success will demand engagement with local authorities, as well as a degree of patience and flexibility. Perhaps the only meaningful national trend for investors to note is the inadequacy of the property rights as enshrined in law. Few changes to this system are anticipated during 2003–04.

For foreign construction companies the operating environment will remain extremely difficult. Foreign contractors must be prepared to deal with diverse provincial regulations and protectionism toward local operators. The chairman of China's largest construction company, Shanghai Construction Group, for example, reported that it is impossible even for Chinese nationals to operate outside of Shanghai because of local protectionism.[39] On top of this, construction contractors must also overcome the propensity of local government officials to view construction projects as opportunities for graft.

Finally, two on-going trends are worth noting. First, despite current government efforts to reduce provincial income disparities, the difference between the price of property in the growing commercial centers and interior provinces will increase. Recent government moves to abandon the long-held policy of limiting migration between regions for Chinese citizens (*hukou*), will further exacerbate the trend. This might provide better returns for contractors engaged in the provision of apartment dwellings in 2002–04. Second, interest rates will remain low by historical standards well into 2002, and possibly 2003, helping to increase demand for residential property year-on-year into 2002–04.

Foreign direct investment

- The excitement among foreign investors appears almost palpable. Visiting foreign business delegations are as common a sight on the streets of Shanghai and Beijing as in London or New York. Yet, most FIE's are not currently profitable, with estimations suggesting that upwards of 50 percent of FIE's remain unprofitable after three years. Excitement aside, China remains a high-risk business environment. Private enterprise operates in a still evolving legal and regulatory framework that makes long-term planning difficult and business failure rates high.

Despite widespread acknowledgement of high failure rates for foreign investors, investors continue to plough capital into China. China is now the second largest recipient of foreign investment in the world behind the United States, with a recorded 43 percent increase in FDI flows in the year to March 2001, following a 50 percent increase in 2000.[40]

Investors clambering aboard for fear of being left behind, however, should be aware that these figures are somewhat misleading. First, there is a large discrepancy between approved and actual or realized FDI. In this regard, officials and investors are equally complicit, insofar as provincial officials have an incentive to exaggerate their ability to attract FDI, while investors have an incentive to overstate actual investment in order to report lower taxable incomes. Second, the figures are inflated by capital 'round tripping' that sees a sizable portion of official FDI flows composed of domestic capital channeled out of China and back through Hong Kong in order to benefit from the tax exemptions afforded foreign capital.

> As many as 50 percent of all the contracts signed in China each year are thought to be unenforceable or fraudulent in various aspects.[41]

While the destination of FDI flows has changed little in the past decade (manufacturing concerns still attract the lion's share of FDI), the form of FDI has changed in accord with government policy. Early capital flows were primarily in the form of joint venture arrangements due to initial investor uncertainty and tight regulations governing inflows. Since the mid 1990s, equity and cooperative joint ventures have increased in importance relative to other forms of FDI. This trend is driven by the perception that joint venture enterprises are a lower-risk strategy to enter the market.

This is true in part, but investors would be wise to choose their partners carefully. Indeed, the role of the Chinese partner cannot be overemphasized. A good Chinese partner will have the connections to smooth through red tape and obstructive bureaucrats; a bad partner can make even the most promising venture turn sour. There are also numerous and legion complaints about Chinese joint partners. Common investor complaints include concern about conflict of interest (the partner setting up a rival business), and violations of confidentiality. Other common problems include breach of contractual payment obligations, irregularities in accounting practices, undisclosed debt and financial misman-agement. These problems can be minimized by investigating the financial standing and reputation of local companies and individuals before signing contracts – good quality and reliable due diligence procedures in other words. However, the best investigated partners can still go wrong, in which case arbitration may still be required.

As many as two-thirds of the biggest state firms are thought to produce false accounts.[42]

Although China is a member of the International Court for the Settlement of Invest-ment Disputes (ICSID), strong emphasis is placed on resolving disputes through informal conciliation and consultation. Foreign investors report that formal litigation should, if at all possible, be avoided as they have found it time consuming and unreliable. Enforcement of arbitral awards is sporadic. The good news for investors is that anecdotal evidence emerging from China suggests that court judgments are increasingly impartial, though rulings at the provincial level still favor local companies by a margin of two to one.[43]

More positively, China is in the process of moving from the rule of man to the rule of law. However, laws and regulations remain vague by OECD standards. As a result, Chinese courts are afforded flexibility at the cost of consistency. Companies and individuals face similar barriers to effective representation. In many cases it is difficult for companies to determine whether or not their activities contravene a particular regulation. Agencies at all levels of government have rule-making authority, producing regulations that are frequently contradictory. Finally, while there is no shortage of rules and regulations, there are few procedures in place to appeal regulatory decisions.

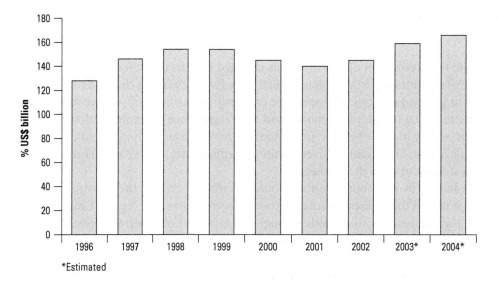

*Estimated

FIGURE 3.3 Foreign direct investment, China 1996–2004

Rule changes for foreign investors will evolve only slowly

The indications from Beijing are that legislative amendments, designed to reduce the obstacles to mergers and acquisitions (M&A), promulgated as a result of WTO accession, will not be rushed due to the complicated legal maze. In the carefully worded lexicon of FDI politics in China, this is a sure sign that officials will not be going out of their way to process the necessary permits for foreign investors undertaking M&A activity. At present only 5 percent of all FDI flows into China involve takeovers.[44] Foreign takeovers of telecommunications, petroleum and media organizations, in particular, are likely to incur the stiffest resistance from Beijing.

Investors also need to be aware of the considerable barriers to internal trade erected at the provincial level. A recent study found that goods crossing provincial borders in China faced the equivalent of a 46 percent tariff in 1997, up from 35 percent just a decade earlier.[45] China's reform has created an array of separate markets protected by non-tariff barriers such as licensing and 'buy local' rules. Service providers (domestic and foreign), for example, report higher than normal barriers to inter-provincial trade.

Unfortunately, internal barriers to trade will not disappear quickly while the CCP policy continues to judge the performance of provincial party cadres on the basis of provincial economic growth. For foreign companies wishing to exploit national markets the lessons are clear: the factory located on the outskirts of Shanghai may not be enough; regional diversification may be required if national markets are to be captured.

> Counterfeit and substandard goods account for 40 percent of all products made in China, with losses running at 200 billion renminbi a year.[46]

The very considerable barriers and challenges to foreign investors has not stopped foreign delegates from descending on China en masse. The challenge facing FDIs is that while the lure of China remains constant, for the time being, so too do the very real risks. In this regard, the reality does not match the hype. Experienced China investors talk of being 'cautiously optimistic' – business-speak that roughly translates two ways: 'We are making a little money but not enough to adequately compensate for the country risk and the additional hassles of doing business in such a cumbersome environment;' or 'We are losing money but are confident that it won't last forever!'[47]

In the same vein, a recent survey of US firms operating in China disclosed a little known reality – it is expensive, often more so than in Western countries, and considerably more than in other emerging markets. This contrasts sharply with the image of China as a cost competitive location in which to do business. Increasingly, then, the experience of foreign investors is considerably less than the hype would suggest, reinforcing the need to undertake comprehensive risk and pricing studies, extensive due diligence, and detailed feasibility studies before proceeding to invest.

Finally, firms should be prepared to actively monitor counterfeit products bearing their brand. This is as much a problem for Chinese as for foreign-owned firms. Microsoft, for example, admits frankly that it is losing money despite a dominant market share due to the fact it is forced to sell its products at low prices to head off piracy.[48]

The bottom line: Big carrot, big stick

Recent surveys suggest that in contrast to the often bullish public expressions of sentiment displayed by investment professionals, returns are still influenced more by government policies than by market conditions or the level of economic development. This was confirmed by the fact that 86 percent of respondents to one prominent survey of foreign enterprises in China concurred that the return on investment was below the normal corporate hurdle rate.[49] Investors cited restricted market access, high taxes, customs duties, high costs and slow market development as the major barriers to profitability.

At a minimum, investors considering prospective investment in China need to conduct an extremely thorough due diligence, carefully structure contracts and maintain on-site management so as to be able to monitor developments daily. Ultimately, however, until the legal system matures investors seeking dispute resolution will have to resort to the age-old technique of whispering in the correct ear. The task of cultivating relationships in China will remain the best way to get the job done for the foreseeable future.

Where to invest? Hong Kong or Shanghai?

Between them, Hong Kong SAR (Special Administrative Region) and Shanghai continue to attract a greater share of foreign capital than any other commercial city in China. As such, they are fierce rivals. While, undoubtedly, Hong Kong remains China's pre-eminent coastal city, and of great financial importance to the wellbeing of China as a whole, it also suffers from one major disadvantage – it is 1,500 km from the capital, Beijing. There is a danger that Hong Kong will be overlooked by the powerful Shanghai elite, whose members include President Xiang Jemin himself. The concern of Hong Kong's business community is tangible. In response, they have invested heavily in Pudong; so much so that they are now the largest outside investors in the city.

However, as the mainland economy liberalizes, doubts linger as to the future role of Hong Kong, for so long the stepping stone to China proper. Hong Kong is hamstrung by an ambiguous relationship with Beijing that inhibits the sort of innovative policy-making historically responsible for its success. Furthermore, recent trends suggest that as Taiwanese investors become more comfortable with doing business on the mainland they are increasingly choosing Shanghai over Hong Kong as the entrepôt for the island's trade with China. If this continues, the Yangtze River delta with its cheaper land and labor costs will become the hub of China's hi-tech economy. Furthermore, tight restrictions by the mainland on immigration to and from the SAR inhibit Hong Kong's ability to attract the sort of highly trained people that it will need if it is to build a knowledge-based economy.

The bottom line: Hong Kong is less risky but more costly than Shanghai

Despite this, for foreign investors Hong Kong continues to have real benefits over Shanghai. Not least of these is a far wealthier population with higher disposable incomes. For instance, it will take 15 years for Shanghai's GDP to match Hong Kong's at current growth rates, while it will take 20 years for its GDP per capita to catch up.[50] Moreover, Hong Kong benefits from a legal inheritance that better protects private enterprise. Hong Kong's courts, for example, have remained surprisingly independent from political coercion. This contrasts with Shanghai where lack of a legal framework for private business led one Western diplomat to lament that foreigners tend to be seduced by Shanghai's skyline while switching off their brains when making business location decisions. To be fair, of course, there are benefits to both locations, but, by and large, Hong Kong is more conducive to foreign enterprises with little Chinese experience, if only because its legal framework and business norms.[51]

Section C Politics

- The reformist faction within the CCP, while facing mounting criticism from those on the left, appears to have cemented the reform agenda. Emblematic of this has been the recent and highly controversial Politburo decision to grant 'capitalists' the right to join the party. This reflects the rising status of business people in China and of their centrality to the economic growth prospects of the Chinese economy. In the future, this decision may well prove to have been as vital to securing the long-term legitimacy of the CCP and its continued political stability as any other single decision. In the short term it will make it easier for foreign investors to find partners who are both business savvy and politically connected. Despite this leap forward, it does not indicate that China is ready to embrace the sort of political accountability that underpins free markets elsewhere.[52]

In contrast with the often internecine power struggles that have accompanied change at the top of the party in the past, a consensus appears to have emerged in the shape of the 58-year-old Hu Jintao as the successor to Jiang Zemin. The seven men elected to the Politburo Standing Committee in September or October 2002 will lead China, barring crisis, for the next decade.

To date, Hu has revealed little of his vision for China's future. The indications, however, are that he is less doctrinaire in his support for market-led reform than Jiang Zemin. Indeed, his only public appearance of note occurred in a highly unusual address to the nation following the bombing of the Chinese embassy in Belgrade in 1999, in which he called for mass demonstrations in the streets against the United States and NATO. Although an isolated incident, scenes of an angry mob in Chengdu setting fire to the residence of the US consul-general did much to damage the confidence of foreign investors, some of whom resorted to temporarily evacuating staff.

Hu's lack of experience in economic matters will mean that he is likely to consult regularly with his closest advisors, both of whom are known to be committed reformers. More generally, his real skill lies in his ability to maneuver between the party's factions on both the left and right. In this sense Hu is above all a pragmatist, like Jiang before him.[53]

Looking beyond the 16th Party Congress to 2003–04, the strongest opposition to the party's current reform agenda appears to be emerging from revitalized leftist factions within the party. Dismissed for much of the 1990s as reactionary Marxist ideologues, the party is increasingly concerned about the potential for popular dissent, primarily from mass movements appealing to egalitarian sentiment among disgruntled former employees of SOEs and rural workers.

Opposition from the left is likely to force the party to seek to bolster its power base by moving further toward the right. Jiang Zemin's highly publicized 'Three Represents' speech in July 2001 was evidence of this – though it should not be interpreted as a radical policy shift. Nonetheless, his declaration that 'most' people in the private sector are engaged in 'honest labor and work' and contribute to the economy (presented as a logical step in the development of Chinese Marxism, albeit with the usual deference to the unique virtues bequeathed by Confucianism), significantly raises the status of private business people in China.

Democracy: Not on the agenda

The party's main aim remains stability amidst social transformation. Democratic proclivities are not widely exercised in the party, and notions of Western democratic values are alien altogether. This, however, is different to the party's new found commitment to the private sector, at least insofar as private enterprise is judged the most effective vehicle to achieve the modernization and growth objectives of the Communist Party. In this sense, the CCP's attitude toward private enterprise might best be summed up as pragmatic ambivalence.

However, investors would be wise to note that a party that performs apparent ideological contortions with a degree of insouciance would not hesitate to perform equally an abrupt U-turn in the opposite direction – should the need arise.

Despite this, there are longer-term structural changes occurring in the party. Recently, for example, the party's move to accept membership from private business signaled a significant sea change, not least because it is estimated that more than 450,000 will seek to join the party as a result. This could have longer-term implications for the party's attitude to private enterprise, indeed reform as a whole.

At the same time, what was once thought to be a slow but cautious move to democracy under Jiang Zemin's widely heralded 'road to democracy' has fallen off the political agenda. Indeed, there are now few who call for it and even fewer who believe it a possibility. Political absolutism thus remains the norm. This is true in the case of the party's continuing efforts to maintain control over the media or, more generally, its non-negotiable policy stance with regard to more participatory forms of governance. This was also evident in the run-up to the congress where Jiang was more willing than ever to quell even carefully couched criticism when, for example, he closed down the left-leaning magazine *Zhenli de Zhuiqiu* in mid 2001.

Freedom of expression and Western-style democratic virtues will thus not be realized anytime soon in China.

> Economic corruption is thought to eat 13–17 percent of China's annual GDP. Much of this leaves China as capital flight.[54]

Leading risk indices: Corruption, stability, governance, risk

Corruption

There are signs, albeit small as yet, that developments are occurring that, while not intended to precipitate democratic reform, may improve the accountability of the party to provincial leaders. A number of provincial and local governments have adopted an increasingly belligerent stance toward party nominees. This practice has recently extended to disagreements over minor policy issues. At the very least the rejection of CCP appointees tainted by corruption scandals elsewhere should go some way to preventing the most glaring cases of corruption among public officials. To this end, the move has been quietly applauded by foreign business leaders. Ultimately, however, corruption will remain endemic until the party resolves a seemingly intractable contradiction, one that sees macro policy-making supported at the local level through patronage politics. This lack of progress is represented on the corruption index.

While the potential for corruption due to closer links between officials and business people is a real possibility, so too might it be the case that this will improve the channels of communication between business groups and the government. Until now, these have been retarded because of policies that officially discouraged the formation of business associations. In the long run this is likely to aid the development of policy more in tune with the needs of private enterprise. Nonetheless, corporate governance standards will be inadequate for some time to come.

Corporate governance

Many of the concerns with poor corporate governance stem from the failure to institutionalize capital management and business decision-making. Standard financial controls and supervision are usually weak; board chairmen often have too much personal power in making company decisions, and shareholders – especially small shareholders – do not have legal effective redress to force disclosure of accurate financial information. While there are punitive penalties for fraudulent accounting, they are not enforced. This applies as much to large SOEs as it does to private SMEs. As a result, the corporate governance index has remained static. Improvements in corporate governance will remain incremental rather than dramatic.

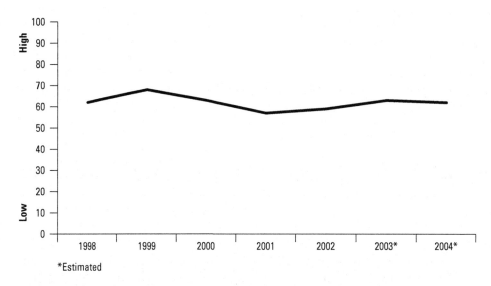

FIGURE 3.4 Corruption index, China 1998–2004
Source: Transparency International (http://www.transparency.org/)

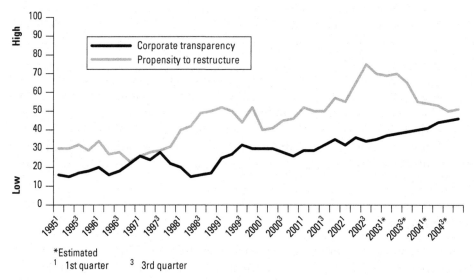

FIGURE 3.5 Corporate governance index, China 1995–2004

- The corporate governance index is a composite index measuring the juridical requirements for corporate disclosure and financial reporting, prudential regime adequacy, prudential compliance enforcement, and the juridical reach of prudential authorities.
- The propensity-to-restructure index is a composite index based on media releases and reported corporate restructuring as a result of prudential regulation, financial incentives, loan restructuring re-negotiation, or asset realignment.

Political stability

Despite the absence of effective political challengers to the central authorities, the CCP's capacity to govern continues to slide rapidly downwards and is likely to continue to do so for the foreseeable future. In the coming years, and to the obvious disappointment of investors, this will be most visibly expressed in a failure to implement WTO reforms at the provincial level. While this will not take the form of outright refusal, equally as effective will be the dragging of provincial feet, and a general failure to either comply with central party dictates or to enforce them. To this end, the recent proliferation of non-tariff barriers (NTBs) will likely accelerate in the medium term as provincial governors attempt to shield local producers from competition.

Nonetheless, political instability, while rising, need not overly concern investors. General protests among disgruntled agricultural workers and former employees of insolvent SOEs are increasingly frequent but there is nothing to suggest that this is directed toward FIEs, but rather wholly domestically-owned businesses. At the top, political stability remains firm. The smooth succession of Jiang's protégé represents a maturing of the political process, insofar as previous political transitions have resulted in varying degrees of turmoil.

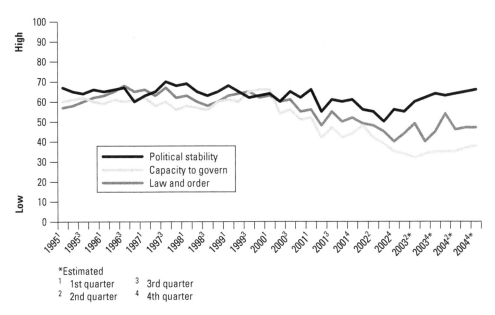

*Estimated
1 1st quarter   3 3rd quarter
2 2nd quarter   4 4th quarter

FIGURE 3.6 Political stability index, China 1995–2004

- The capacity-to-govern index is based upon the institutional reach of government defined in terms of its ability to set the political and economic agenda and ensure its legislative program is enacted without significant compromise. This index is adversely affected by legislative opposition, lack of legislative implementation, failure to realize government policy and general political opposition.
- The political stability index measures violent opposition or organized demonstrations, terrorist activities, and popular discontent that adversely affect the institutional and electoral stability of the government.
- The law and order index measures the propensity to civil obedience, and the institutional reach of the rule of law in terms of regulatory compliance and enforcement.

Ultimately, the CCP must resolve fundamental tensions between an autocratic system of political governance and an increasingly liberalized economy. While the problem is not new, there have as yet been no clear answers to suggest that this has been resolved.

The law and order index continues to decline in the face of growing petty crime, corruption and an inadequate legal framework.

Foreign investor risk index

Until the competing needs of an increasingly liberalized economy versus the persistence of an autocratic and non-transparent system of governance can be resolved, the economy will fail to meet the aspirations of China's population and the needs of all but the canniest investors. This problem, and the risk it gives rise to for investors, is reflected in the composite foreign investor risk index that continues to remain high, and indeed is rising.

The risk to foreign investors will continue to increase into 2003 before resuming its gradual downward slope, supported by a new leadership and high levels of economic growth.

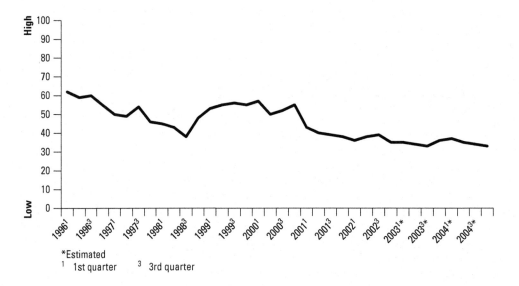

FIGURE 3.7 Foreign investor risk index, China 1996–2004

• The foreign investor risk index is a composite index measuring tax burdens, discriminatory regulatory practices, adverse compliance regulations, government policy toward foreign enterprise, receptiveness to issuance of government contracts, foreign enterprise commercial restrictions, and official attitudinal changes to foreign direct investment and foreign commercial operations that impact on operational efficiency. The index also incorporates a nominal measure for market risk and market failure.

Section D Security

- China's external security concerns remain relatively constant, albeit prone to recurrent crisis incidents with the US and Taiwan. These have been well publicized, and resolved diplomatically, albeit at great cost to the powers concerned in terms of the expenditure of much diplomatic and political capital. While in the longer term China will undoubtedly attempt to be expansionist, staking a claim to a great power sphere of influence in the region, and thus placing her at odds with the US and her interests in the Pacific, the immediate threat to investors is low.

The external security threat facing China has risen appreciably during the past 18 months, beginning with the much publicized 'spy plane' incident with the United States. Less high profile are a number of border disputes between China and her neighbors, including conflict over the resource-rich Spratly Islands with Vietnam. To the east, the issue of Diaoyu Island, claimed by Japan and China, is also unresolved. None of these should overly concern foreign investors – unless directly operating in these areas. Of more concern to investors is the simmering question of Taiwan's independence. Under President George W. Bush, the US has signaled that it is prepared to adopt a more aggressive stance and use force in defending Taiwan's independence; something that has distressed Chinese authorities and cooled relations somewhat.

Similarly, the new leadership's rhetoric toward US 'imperialism' will no longer be constrained by the need to smooth the way for WTO accession. There is, however, no appetite among China's leadership for conflict with the US over Taiwan; not least because of the more pressing concerns at home. Regardless, saber-rattling is likely to increase in frequency but the real diplomatic work will continue unhindered behind the scenes.

International security concerns

Internally, instances of violence perpetrated by a number of disparate ethnic separatist groups are increasing. To date, however, violence has largely been contained to the territories in dispute. These include border provinces and autonomous regions such as Neimenggu (Inner Mongolia), Xingjiang, Xizang (Tibet), Guangxi and Xingjiang. While there is a concern that China's harsh repression of these movements may one day inspire greater dissent, this should not obscure the fact that the greatest security threat faced by investors is closer to home, and concerns the growing income disparities between inland and coastal provinces, and between classes of Chinese workers and the new bourgeoisie. China's burgeoning economy has clearly benefited some regions and people more than others. Incomes in some rural areas have actually fallen in real terms. Accordingly, discontent has been expressed as protest, but these have been confined to local disputes.

Industrial disputes

Of more concern is the rising number of industrial disputes that have turned violent, though these have largely been confined to disgruntled employees of SOEs. Thus, and despite Hu's willingness to play to latent Chinese nationalism, nationalism is more likely to be expressed as a preference for Chinese-produced goods than attacks on property. It is this that should concern investors.

Section E Economic and political risk forecasts

- Investor risk in all its guises will rise in the short term. The current hiatus in the reform program is, however, only a temporary hiccup. The CCP remains committed to reform as the most effective means to insure economic growth and political legitimacy. Dissent within the party will continue, reflecting various concerns about the pace and depth of reform and its effect on social cohesion and political constituencies. Despite this, there are signs that policy-making is slowly becoming more inclusive, and addressing the needs and concerns of various stakeholders. Coalition building is replacing the destabilizing personality politics of the past.

Short-term forecasts

- The short-term outlook for the economy is positive. Robust growth of 6–7 percent will continue in the absence of significant increases in export demand. Growth will be driven by high levels of government and consumer spending, and a low interest rate environment.
- Financial sector reform will continue piecemeal. There are as yet no indications that the government is prepared to tackle the problem head on. Quite simply, the risk of social unrest is too great. Instead, the authorities will rely upon high levels of economic growth to reduce the size of bad debt relative to the economy as a whole.

Short-term opportunities

- The range of sectors in which foreign investors are permitted to operate will rise in the short term following China's accession to the WTO. In telecommunications, geographical restrictions on foreign firms will be gradually removed, ownership limits will be increased to 49 percent and the cost of imported inputs will fall. Foreign banks will be able to conduct local business with Chinese enterprises. So too, the short term should witness the extension of the same legal rights to foreign banks as those afforded domestic banks.
- Insurance companies will be able to offer increased lines of business, including large-scale nationwide risks, while geographic restrictions will be phased out. Growth in health and pension insurance will be fastest with double digit growth anticipated in 2002–06.

- Opportunities for consultancy work by foreign companies will continue to grow. Perhaps most importantly, China is committed to the removal of restrictions on trading and distribution rights on foreign firms, including wholesale and retail enterprises.

Medium to longer term

- Business risk will fall gradually. However, the risk environment will remain specific to the province and sector in which firms operate. Those expecting a wholesale improvement in the framework for private enterprise will be disappointed in 2002–04.
- The legal environment will never match the standards found in developed countries so long as the administrative, executive and judicial functions are controlled by the CCP alone. Nonetheless, the need for investment capital will strongly influence the direction of policy and the speed of change, giving investors a voice where previously they had none. Opportunities to participate in infrastructure development will increase in the form of BOOT schemes but the environment will remain high risk.
- More generally, the strength of Chinese culture dictates that for all the change that is likely to occur, the Chinese business environment will remain unique – the importance of personal business relationships will not diminish.

Overall risk rating

The risk environment in which private enterprise operates in China is high in absolute terms – and rising. However, this rise should be limited to a short-term phenomenon, driven by the current domestic political uncertainty. The current risks to business and government alike from the reform process are tangible but so are the rewards. China may one day become an economic powerhouse, but equally the potential for backsliding is real.

For the time being, investors will need to exercise caution and expect losses as well as wins. In the words of one China-watcher: 'Get on the bus but make sure you sit near the exit.'

Risk: Increasing in the short term before resuming a gradual downward slide. ↑ ↘
Risk Rating (0 = lowest, 10 highest risk) 6.0

Section F China fact sheet*

Geography

Capital
Beijing

Largest city (millions)
Shanghai, 11.8 (metro. area)

Location
35 00 N, 105 00 E

Adjacent countries
South to Mongolia, Russia and Kazakhstan, west to North Korea, north to Vietnam, Laos, Myanmar, India, Bhutan and Nepal, and east to India, Afghanistan, Pakistan, Tajikistan and Kyrgyzstan

Terrain
Cold-temperate north and tropical south; the Tibetan Plateau in the west, the desert or semi-desert areas of Xinjiang and Inner Mongolia in the northwest and north, the Sichuan Basin in the east of the Tibetan Plateau, the broad fertile Manchurian Plains in the northeast, and the southern plains along the east coast with rich and fertile soils; in general, upland hill, mountains and plateaux occupy over 66% of China

Land use (1993 est.)
Arable land 10%, permanent crops 0%, permanent pastures 43%, forests and woodland 14%, other 33%

Area (km²):
9.6 million

Economic statistics

Currency
Renminbi or yuan (Rmb), 1 yuan = 10 jiao = 100 fen

Exchange rate (October 2001)
US$1.00 = Rmb8.277

Gross Domestic Product (GDP)
US$1.1 trillion

GDP per capita
US$870

GDP per capita – PPP
US$4,700

GDP – Composition by sector
Agriculture 15%, industry 50%, services 35%

Percentage of the population who earn less than US$1.00 per day (1983–1999)
18.5

Inflation rate (2001, est.)
1%

Foreign debt (billions, by November 2001)
US$170.4

Current account balance (billions, 2001 est.)
US$14.9

* All figures are the latest available except where indicated. All figures are in US dollars. Figures are compiled from national, international and multilateral agencies (International Monetary Fund, World Bank, World Development Report, UNESCO Statistical Yearbook, International Labour Office, United Nations, Central Intelligence Agency World Fact Book). Gross domestic product (GDP) refers to the value of all goods and services produced in the preceding financial year. GDP per capita, Purchasing Power Parity (GDP per capita – PPP) refers to the indices developed by the World Bank to take account of price differences, cost of living differences, and relative purchasing power of a set basket of goods and services between countries so as to provide a more accurate measure of national wealth.

Officially registered unemployment rate
3.1% (estimated urban unemployment rate from other sources is roughly 10% in 2000 and even higher in rural areas)

Population below poverty line
10%

Labor force (millions, 1998)
700

Labor force by occupation (1998)
Agriculture 50%, industry 24%, services 26%

Budget (billions, 2001)
Revenues: US$190.4
Expenditure: US$225.4

Industries
Iron and steel, coal, machine building, armaments, textiles and apparel, petroleum, cement, chemical fertilizers, footwear, toys, food processing, automobiles, consumer electronics, telecommunications

Major exports (billions)
US$232
Machinery and equipment, textiles and clothing, footwear, toys and sporting goods, mineral fuels

Major imports (billions)
US$197
Machinery and equipment, mineral fuels, plastics, iron and steel, chemicals

Major trading partners (exports)
US 21%, Hong Kong 18%, Japan 17%, South Korea, Germany, Netherlands, UK, Singapore, Taiwan

Major trading partners (imports)
Japan 18%, Taiwan 11%, US 10%, South Korea 10%, Germany, Hong Kong, Russia, Malaysia

Income/wealth distribution (household income by % share, 1998)
Lowest 10% of population 2.4%
Highest 10% of population 30.4%

Televisions (millions, 1997)
400

Televisions per capita
0.3 (people per color television: 3.1)

Telephones (main lines in use, millions)
135

Telephones per capita
0.12 (people per telephone: 9.3)

Cellular phones (millions)
65

Cellular phones per capita
0.05 (people per cellular phone: 19.4)

Automobiles produced (millions, in 2000)
2.07

Internet users per 100,000 of population
1,746

Fiscal year
Calendar year

Government and political statistics

Nature of government
Socialist Republic

Constitution
Most recent promulgation 4 December 1982

President of the country
Mr. Jiang Zemin

Vice-president
Mr. Hu Jintao

Structure of government
Executive Branch and Legislative
Branch

Executive branch
The State Council, headed by Premier
Zhu Rongji

Legislative branch
The National People's Congress (2,979
seats; members serve five-year terms),
headed by the Chairman of the Standing
Committee Li Peng

**Key government leaders (as of
June 2002)**

Premier
Mr. Zhu Rongji

Vice Premiers
Mr. Li Lanqing, Mr. Qian Qichen, Mr. Wu
Bangguo, Mr. Wen Jiabao

State Councilors
Mr. Chi Haotian, Mr. Luo Gan, Ms. Wu
Yi, Mr. Simayi Aimaiti, Mr. Wang
Zhongyu

Secretary General of the State Council
Mr. Wang Zhongyu

Chief of Ministry of Foreign Affairs
Mr. Tang Jiaxuan

Chief of Ministry of National Defense
Mr. Chi Haotian

**Chief of National Development &
Planning Committee**
Mr. Zeng Peiyan

**Chief of National Economic & Trade
Committee**
Mr. Sheng Huaren

Chief of Ministry of Education
Ms. Chen Zhili

**Chief of Ministry of Science &
Technology**
Ms. Zhu Lilan

**Chief of Ministry of Foreign Trade and
Economic Cooperation**
Mr. Shi Guangsheng

Chief of Ministry of Culture
Mr. Sun Jiazheng

Chief of Ministry of Health
Mr. Zhang Wenkang

**Chief of National Family Planning
Committee**
Mr. Zhang Weiqing

Chief of National Auditing Agency
Mr. Li Jinhua

Chief of People's Bank of China
Mr. Dai Xianglong

**Chief of Scientific and Technological
Industry Committee of National
Defense**
Mr. Liu Jibin

**Chief of National Nationalities Affairs
Committee**
Mr. Li Demo

Chief of Ministry of Public Security
Mr. Jia Chunwang

Chief of Ministry of National Security
Mr. Xu Yongyue

Chief of Ministry of Supervisory
Mr. He Yong

Chief of Ministry of Justice
Mr. Zhang Fusen

Chief of Ministry of Finance
Mr. Xiang Huaicheng

Chief of Ministry of Personnel
Mr. Song Defu

Chief of Ministry of Labor and Social Security
Mr. Zhang Zuoyi

Chief of Ministry of National Land Resources
Mr. Zhou Yongkang

Chief of Ministry of Construction
Mr. Yu Zhengsheng

Chief of Ministry of Railways
Mr. Fu Zhihuan

Chief of Ministry of Transportation
Mr. Huang Zhendong

Chief of Ministry of Information Industry
Mr. Wu Jichuan

Chief of Ministry of Water Conservancy
Mr. Niu Maosheng

Chief of Ministry of Agriculture
Mr. Du Qinglin

Administrative structure of government
23 provinces, 5 autonomous regions, 4 municipalities, 2 special administrative regions

Governing party
The Communist Party of China

Key leaders, organizations, and ideology of the Communist Party

General Secretary of the Central Committee
Mr. Jiang Zemin

Members of Standing Committee of Political Bureau
Mr. Jiang Zemin, Mr. Li Peng, Mr. Zhu Rongji, Mr. Li Ruihuan, Mr. Hu Jintao, Mr. Wei Jianxing, Mr. Li Lanqing

The major organizations under Central Committee
Central Military Commission (Chief: Mr. Jiang Zemin); Central Commission for Discipline Inspection (Chief: Mr. Wei Jianxing); International Liaison Department (Chief: Mr. Dai Bingguo); United Front Work Department (Chief: Mr. Wang Zhaoguo); Organization Department (Chief: Mr. Zeng Qinghong); Propaganda Department (Chief: Mr. Ding Guangen)

Guiding ideology
Marxism-Leninism, Mao Zedong Thought, and Deng Xiaoping Theory

Other political parties
China Democratic League (Chairman: Mr. Ding Shisun), China Democratic National Construction Association (Chairman: Mr. Cheng Siwei), China Revolutionary Committee of the Kuomintang (Chairman: Mr. He Luli), China Zhi Gong Dang (Chairman: Mr. Luo Haocai), China Association for Promoting Democracy (Chairman: Mr. Xu Jialu), Jiu San Society (Chairman: Mr. Wu Jieping), Taiwan Democratic Self-Government League (Chairman: Zhang Kehui), China Peasants' and Workers' Democratic Party (Chairman: Jiang Zhenghua)

International memberships
African Development Bank (AfDB), Asia-Pacific Economic Cooperation (APEC), Asian Development Bank (AsDB), Bank for International

Settlements (BIS), Customs Cooperation Council (CCC), Economic and Social Commission for Asia and the Pacific (ESCAP), Food and Agriculture Organization (FAO), Group of 77 (G-77), International Atomic Energy Agency (IAEA), International Bank for Reconstruction and Development (World Bank), International Civil Aviation Organization (ICAO), International Chamber of Commerce (ICC), International Red Cross and Red Crescent Movement (ICRM), International Development Association (IDA), International Fund for Agricultural Development (IFAD), International Finance Corporation (IFC), International Federation of Red Cross and Red Crescent Societies (IFRCS), International Hydrographic Organization (IHO), International Labor Organization (ILO), International Monetary Fund (IMF), International Maritime Organization (IMO), International Mobile Satellite Organization (Inmarsat), International Telecommunications Satellite Organization (Intelsat), International Criminal Police Organization (Interpol), International Olympic Committee (IOC), International Organization for Standardization (ISO), International Telecommunications Union (ITU), Organization for the Prohibition of Chemical Weapons (OPCW), Permanent Court of Arbitration (PCA), United Nations (UN), United Nations Security Council, United Nations Conference on Trade and Development (UNCTAD), United Nations Educational, Scientific, and Cultural Organization (UNESCO), United Nations High Commissioner for Refugees (UNHCR), United Nations Industrial Development Organization (UNIDO), United Nations Institute for Training and Research (UNITAR), United Nations Truce Supervision Organization (UNTSO), United Nations University (UNU), Universal Postal Union (UPU), World Health Organization (WHO), World Intellectual Property Organization (WIPO), World Meteorological Organization (WMO), World Tourism Organization (WtoO), World Trade Organization (WTO), Zangger Committee (ZC)

Business organization
All China Federation of Industry and Commerce (Chairman: Mr. Jing Shuping)

Date of UN membership:
24 October 1945

Social statistics

Population size (billions)
1.26

Population density (per square km)
131

Fertility rate (per woman, 1995–2000)
1.8

Maternal mortality rate (per 100,000 births, 1980–99)
55

Infant mortality rate
(deaths per 1,000 births) 27.2

Population growth (2001 est.)
0.7%

Life expectancy (1999)
70.2
Men 68.3
Women: 72.5

Ethnic composition
Han Chinese 91.9%, Zhuang, Uygur, Hui,
Yi, Tibetan, Miao, Manchu, Mongol,
Buyi, Korean, and other nationalities
8.1%

Religions
(officially an atheist state)
Confucianism 20% of the population,
Taoism 2%, Buddhism 6%, Muslim 2%,
Christianity 1%

National languages spoken
Mandarin, and local dialects

Illiteracy rate (ages 15+, 1999)
16.5%

By gender
Male: 8.8%
Female: 25.4%

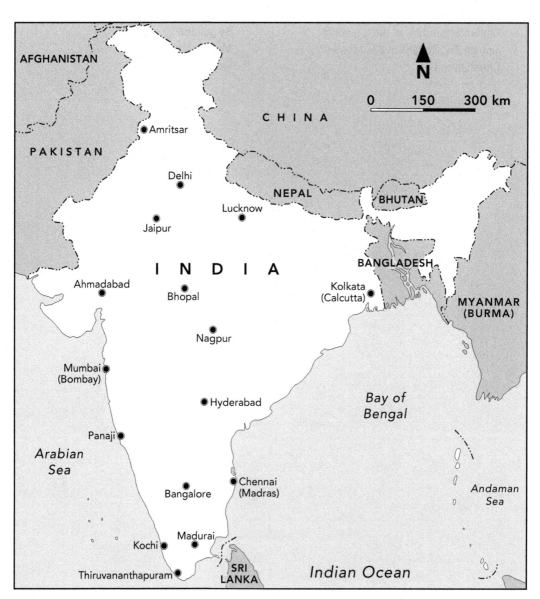

India

4 India

Jane Ford

Section A Economy

Overview

Escalating conflict and the prospects of all-out war with Pakistan overshadow India's steady economic liberalization and growth. Having hauled its economy out of the doldrums, India's reform program has lost some momentum. The economy looks to have slipped to a lower growth path of around 5 percent in 2002, from an average annual growth rate of 6.7 percent during the Eighth Five Year Plan (1992–97). While this remains a substantial improvement on the 3–3.5 percent average growth experienced in the previous 40 years, it is considerably below the 9 percent projected by the government for the first decade of the twenty-first century. It is also below the growth achieved by China over the past five years.

Having alienated itself from the international community with a series of nuclear tests in 1998, along with rising Hindu nationalism, the lead party of the ruling National Democratic Alliance – the Bharatiya Janata Party (BJP) – continued its rapprochement towards the US in 2001–02. However, a suicide bombing outside the Indian parliament in December 2001 by Pakistani militants working to achieve a Muslim state in Kashmir refocused the Indian government on saber-rattling rather than on economic reform. Equally, US overtures towards Pakistan following the September 2001 terrorist bombings in New York have threatened to undermine the recent improvements in the relationship between India and the United States.

The BJP's strong stance against Pakistan has relieved some of the political pressure that had built up following a rash of corruption scandals in 2001–02. This comes at an important time for the party, ahead of the state election in Uttar Pradesh. Nonetheless, the uncertainty comes at an inopportune time for the Indian economy, which is facing fierce trade competition from China. Indian export growth, for example, stalled slightly in 2001–02 due to uncertainty in the international economy, although India's economy is still relatively closed.

While the BJP has reiterated its commitment to continuing the reforms begun by the Rao government in 1991, this remains a complicated task. The economy is burdened by a morass of regulation, intransigent debt levels and a banking sector weighed down by non-performing loans (NPLs). Despite ambitions of fiscal responsibility, the state and central governments have been unable to ease the financial burden this has placed on taxpayers.

Risks remain for international investment

The Indian economy will slow further in 2002–03 due to domestic shocks and declining exports. The forecast for India's real growth as a percentage of Gross Domestic Product (GDP) is for 5.4 percent in 2003 and tending marginally upwards to 6.3 percent in 2004.[1]

While foreign ownership laws are gradually being liberalized, the regulatory system is cumbersome and established social practices make dealing with the bureaucracy difficult for those accustomed to Western government protocols. Customs and foreign investment rules, for example, are complex and cause expensive delays. Likewise, the lack of protection for intellectual property rights increases the risk of doing business in information technology sectors of the economy. Foreign investors will also be confronted by a throw-back socialist sentiment that is somewhat institutionalized and where international business is regarded with suspicion in many quarters, despite the government's attempts to court foreign investment.

With the government's attention focused on forthcoming state elections and conflict with Pakistan, few advances in economic reform are likely in the short to medium term. The conflict with Pakistan poses considerable difficulty in the development of important energy infrastructure, such as a much needed pipeline from central Asia. The ambitious privatization program is moving slowly, keeping infrastructure costs high.

The bottom line: Solid if unspectacular growth

The medium- to long-term prospects for investment in India are positive, but, in the meantime, difficulties remain. Investment rules are variable and restrictions remain in many key areas such as banking and professional services. Trade restrictions on many consumer goods and services remain. Internal political conflict, a lingering culture of bureaucratic corruption, impediments to liberalization and international economic downturn, are good reasons to be cautious about investing in India in 2002–05.

Section B Risks and projections

Macroeconomic performance and risk indicators

• The strong growth that has characterized the Indian economy for the past decade is waning, in part reflecting the global economic slowdown of 2000–02, but also the distraction of domestic and regional security concerns. Yet the medium-term prospects for the economy are brighter. On-going reforms should bring efficiency gains and help with productivity yields. Nonetheless, given that the country faces intensifying competition from Chinese exports through 2002–07, the Indian government will need to be firm in its resolve to reform the economy, foster innovation, and aggressively pursue export markets.

Growth was slower in 2001–02 (April–March financial year), thanks to a sluggish world economy and escalating tension with Pakistan. The IMF and ratings agencies have voiced concern about the government's commitment to economic reform, citing security issues as a distraction. Government finances are also cause for concern; the financial decline continues despite moves to broaden the tax base. The fiscal deficit seems intractable and the public sector is bloated. In 2001–02 the central government's net tax revenue reached only 48 percent of the budget estimate of US$33.5 billion.[2]

The government has reassured investors that it will continue a steady program of privatization and liberalization, and it is committed to reducing its fiscal deficit. Currently, growth is constrained by inadequate public sector investment, particularly at state level. While central authorities have attempted to boost investment in roads, railways and electricity stations in 2001–02, this has had only a modest effect on growth.[3] Nonetheless, the proposed reform programs have the potential to produce a growth dividend in 2002–05, as well as providing opportunities for investors.

The 2001–02 budget projected a 4.7 percent cut in the fiscal deficit, that was welcomed by financial markets. The combined government gross fiscal deficit improved slightly to 9.1 percent of GDP in 2001–02 from 9.4 percent in 1999–2000. However, tax revenues were lower year-on-year, reflecting the slowdown in economic activity and security concerns. Falling tax revenues were also due to the abolition of surcharges on direct taxes and customs, rate rationalization and a reduction in excise. Unfortunately, the taxation stimulus has not yet produced sufficient economic growth to boost tax revenue.[4] To this end, reforming taxation collection systems and broadening the tax-collection base remains a concern. For example, despite a growing share of services in the economy, only a small fraction is taxable due to the arcane legislative parameters currently in palace.

Inflation, that was running at around 7 percent at the beginning of 2001, declined to 4.3 percent in 2002. This represents a 10-year low and, perhaps more importantly, an end to systemic inflation in the Indian economy.[5] Consequently, the risk to the capital value of rupee-denominated assets in 2003–04 is low.

Looking ahead, monetary policy will remain accommodative to growth, with the government acutely aware of the need to grow the economy if inroads into poverty reduction are to be achieved. As a consequence, inflation will experience a nominal rise to around levels of 5.0–6.2 percent in 2003–04, and should then hold at this level into 2005. Wholesale prices will rise less rapidly than retail prices as the effects of previous industrial reforms begin to kick in and contribute to increased competition among domestic producers, exerting a moderating effect on price levels.

Industrial growth, sluggish during 2001–02 after steadily improving in the late 1990s, is likely to improve modestly throughout 2002–04, provided that recovery in the US economy can be sustained. However, not all is well in the Indian economy. While, for example, industrial growth increased by 2.5 percent in 2001–02, this was lower than the 5.9 percent growth experienced in the same period in 2000 and, on a cumulative basis, all sectors of industry showed either deceleration or decline in 2001–02. The slowdown was particularly apparent in mining, quarrying and manufacturing.[6]

While growth is unlikely to reach the desired rate of 7 percent in 2002–04, industrial growth forecasts are positive, with growth of around 5.5 percent likely in 2003–04.[7] Economic growth should continue its upward trend in 2003, reaching 6.0 percent with a further half percentage point increase forecast for 2004. Growth will be driven by growing exports and improved output among agricultural producers following a prolonged drought during 2001–02. This is good news for the economy generally because better rice and wheat crops usually translate into higher disposable income and greater demand for most domestic goods and services. While the share of the agricultural sector in GDP has declined from more than 40 percent of GDP to around 27 percent, the sector remains important.[8] Indeed, agriculture and agriculture-related activities still account for 60 percent of the workforce.[9]

Privatization and liberalization: On the reform agenda

The government is promising to push ahead with its privatization programs, despite opposition from unions and other groups. The telecommunications privatization program, for example, is being accelerated, with the government ending the telephone monopoly of Videsh Sandchar Nigam Limited (VSNL) early in 2002,[10] raising expectations of lower international call rates. However, international experience suggests that the market could be turbulent for some time to come. Other privatization projects are also progressing, including plans to privatize Air India and the Shipping Corporation, along with other state-run enterprises. Although the government has acknowledged the need to develop independent regulatory authorities in response to this new order, constructing an effective regulatory and prudential framework will be challenging.

While giving liberalization with one hand, the government is taking it away with the other; moving to insulate politically important sectors from competition. Anti-liberalization sentiment, particularly in the agricultural sector, is arousing significant political pressure given that about 50 million families are classified as rural poor. Consequently, the 2001–02 budget boosted customs duties on coffee, coconut and tea, limiting market access for foreign exporters.

The rural poor constituency can be expected to continue to exert significant political leverage in 2003–04, moderating the pace of reform otherwise seen as essential by the international business community. Indeed, rural poverty and low average incomes among the urban poor continue to constrain growth, although real average incomes have increased by 4.4 percent per annum between 1993–2001.[11]

While less dependent than many Asian countries on the international economy, India's economic development ultimately depends on capitalizing further on the gains from trade and foreign investment. Currently, many political parties promote populist anti-reform views and block or delay reforms.[12] India's greatest challenge will be to manage the liberalization program to ease the plight of those displaced in traditional industries.

Export performance

- Exports and imports were relatively flat in 2001–02 after strong growth in trade the previous year. While the government is actively promoting exports with the use of tax concessions, the economy remains comparatively closed and reliant on domestic consumption to propel growth. A weaker global economy and greater price competition from Chinese exports will put pressure on India's export growth in 2002–05. Nonetheless, China still has many quality control issues to solve and the outlook for Indian exports is for continued but unspectacular growth.

While the downturn in the United States and Japan has caused considerable hardship in Asian countries dependent on exports, India's comparatively closed economy has sheltered it from an otherwise sluggish international economy. Although the US receives more than 20 percent of India's total exports, exports are a comparatively small part of the Indian economy, accounting on average for 8.4 percent of GDP between 1992 and 2002. The ratio of exports and imports to GDP rose from an annual average of 13.2 percent during the decade to 1990–91 to 19.9 percent between 1992 and 2000.[13]

Export growth declined slightly year-on-year in 2002 to US$28.3 billion.[14] Nevertheless, the current account deficit improved, falling from US$2.87 billion in 2000 to US$938 million, as demand for imports also declined.[15] Growth in exports of consumer electronics equipment and electronic components declined to 12 percent in 2002 from 18 percent in 2001.

Tourist arrivals also experienced a fall of 6 percent in 2001–02, affected by the downturn in international tourism in the wake of the September 11 terrorist attacks in the US. In all, foreign tourist arrivals dropped to 2.4 million from 2.6 million in 2000–01, reversing a 6.4 percent increase in arrivals the previous year. Likewise, foreign exchange earnings from tourism also fell 3.6 percent to US$3.05 billion. This sector is unlikely to improve dramatically in 2002–04 given the tensions between India and Pakistan and fears of on-going regional instability due to terrorist activities and bombings.

Liberalization of the economy: Increasing, but slowly

In general, the Indian economy is far more liberal in 2002 than has otherwise been the case in the recent past. Liberalization policies since 1991 have virtually eliminated quantitative restrictions on imports of industrial raw materials, intermediate components and capital goods. The maximum tariff rate has declined from 355 percent in 1990 to 35 percent in 2002, and, from February 2000, the Indian government made approval automatic for all foreign direct investment – except for a small list of areas deemed inappropriate.[16]

> Despite increasing competition, Indian exports are predicted to grow steadily at 12–13 percent during 2002–03. It will be difficult to maintain double figure growth in 2003–04, however.

Special economic zones have also been created to provide an internationally competitive environment for export production. Import restrictions on 715 items were removed in 2001–02, including restrictions on textile, agricultural and manufactured products, including automobiles.[17] Nonetheless, controls do in fact remain on many industrial consumer goods because of the political sensitivity involved in removing them.[18] Indeed, while the government complied with WTO rulings and removed restrictions on hundreds of agricultural and consumer items in 2000–01, average rates of protection remain high. Agriculture, for example, which accounts for 25 percent of GDP, is especially protected and inefficiently distributed. The services sector too, also has substantial room for liberalization.

India's export sector is likely to come under increasing competition from Chinese exports following China's accession to the WTO. This will likely translate onto lower export growth for India until at least 2005, when the one-off effects of China's WTO entry should have worked through the international export system and begun to moderate, opening up space for renewed take-up of India's exports.[19] This will put pressure on profit levels in many export sectors of the economy, but should serve to help systematize innovation and re-invigorate competition leading to a restoration of international export competitiveness in 2004–05.

Currency movements and projections

- Interest rates are likely to fall another 25–50 basis points in 2002–03 and contribute to further weakness in the rupee. A deflating Indian economy and on-going security concerns will continue to depress rupee valuations into 2003 and possibly 2004. Indeed, there remains much scope for a deterioration in the security environment and knock-on effects for Indian exports, growth, and currency valuations. This has been observed in the Indian forex market, which continues to suffer the consequences of risk-averse investors moving to safe havens following September 11, and failing to return. Most of these negative sentiments should work themselves through the market by early 2004, assuming no further deterioration of the security environment. Until then, the continued weakness of the rupee will make asset acquisition cheaper, although India's foreign investment laws will limit opportunities on this front, particularly with respect to property development and the persistence of restrictive investment laws.

The rupee hit record lows against the US dollar in the wake of the September 11 attacks, and in response to concerns about public finances. While the currency had been stable throughout the first part of 2001, a credit ratings downgrade spooked investors. The rupee declined to all time lows of R48.18 against the US dollar on 17 September and has failed to recover, continuing downwards and trading around R49 against the US dollar throughout 2002. In all, since January 2000 the rupee has lost 11 percent of its value against the US dollar, before that losing 16 percent of its value between 1998 and 2000. This demonstrates a longer-term trend downward, as well as short-term selling in anticipation of further interest rate cuts. Regardless, little change to this trend is indicated for 2003–04.

Rating downgrades on Indian sovereign debt have also contributed to downward pressure on the rupee, as well as concerns over the current fiscal deficit and the long-term sustainability of public sector finances. This points to further weakness ahead and investors should hedge their transactions with a view to further currency weakness in 2003–04.

> The rupee will stay weak into 2003–04, driven by unsustainable fiscal expenditures at the state and federal level, and trade at levels of between R45 and R50 to the US dollar. However, a lower currency should help improve the competitiveness of Indian exports as well as help offset competition from China.

Financial markets: Performance and developments

- A true picture of India's financial sector debt is difficult to draw, given that reporting is only gradually becoming transparent and standard accounting procedures are only now being introduced across all of India's public sector agencies and services. India's banking system has a high exposure to economic and industry risk due to government-directed lending, often undertaken without regard to credit risk exposure levels or prudential regulatory systems being in place. While steps are being taken to shore up the system's capital adequacy and credit and prudential management systems, investors should be wary of further asset write-downs.

It is estimated that India's scheduled commercial banks need between US$11 billion and US$13 billion in new capital to offset losses associated with NPLs.[20] Indeed, the Indian banking system is close to insolvency, requiring massive capital infusion over the next five years equal to between 2 and 4 percent of the country's GDP, and between 50 and 90 percent of current bank capital. Up to 60 percent of this will be required to write off unrecoverable loans, 18 percent to finance productivity improvements and the rest to support growth.[21] The outlook is bleak.

The reform agenda: Will it be enough?

In order to meet these challenges, India has focused on adopting international financial standards and regulatory codes. Interest rates have been largely deregulated, statutory liquidity and reserve requirements have been reduced, and banks have been given considerable autonomy in operations. Concomitant with this deregulation, the Reserve Bank of India (RBI) and the government have sought to strengthen prudential standards, forming a Standing Committee on International Financial Standards and Codes in 1991 to align India's practices with international best practice. Codes are also being developed in corporate governance, accounting, auditing, bankruptcy, insurance and securities regulation, banking regulation, fiscal and monetary policy. The RBI now has jurisdiction over transactions in government securities, money market securities, gold-related securities and derivatives and forward contracts in debt securities.[22] Minimum capital requirements, loan classification and provisioning standards are currently being reviewed and risk-adjusted capital ratios have risen to 10 percent in 2002. Further, as of January 2002, the RBI asked commercial banks to transfer part of their profits on bond sales to a reserve account as a shield against unexpected price movements. Under this ruling, banks should have an Investment Fluctuation Reserve Account of at least 5 percent of the portfolio within a period of five years (2007).[23]

Realistically, however, it will be some time before risk in this sector is manageable. The local financial markets might not be able to raise sufficient capital to fund the recapitalization, something that would limit the government's plan to reduce its own stake in the banking system. Indeed, even partial privatization of the banking system could increase the risk of instability in the short term.

> The Indian savings rate has increased from an average of 17 percent of GDP in the 1970s to 20 percent of GDP in 2002. However, channeling these savings into productive investment remains a challenge. Creating a vibrant debt market to fund India's infrastructure and economic development must be assigned priority status.

Many of India's scheduled commercial banks are struggling to meet the strengthening prudential standards. While most banks are compliant to minimum regulatory capital requirements, they are significantly undercapitalized when tighter loan classification and provisioning standards are adopted. Only a small majority of India's 105 scheduled commercial banks have an absolute capital base of more than $US220 million. Furthermore, the Indian financial system has an organized and unorganized sector, and the latter remains outside the Reserve Bank's purview.[24]

The banking sector's significant NPL problem is largely due to the sector's traditional socialist lending practices, which do not reflect commercial imperatives. Scheduled commercial banks are required to lend a minimum 40 percent of their funds to priority sectors. Officially, gross NPLs in India's scheduled commercial banks stood at 12.85 percent of current loans in 2002, although this is based on a definition that does not accord with international standards. Unfortunately, loans in India are not classified as substandard until they become past due by 180 days, whereas the Western standard classifies a loan as substandard when it is overdue by 90 days. If international standards are applied, NPLs could account for 20–25 percent of currency loans.[25] On top of this, recovery of NPLs is complicated by India's weak legal system, and the Board for Industrial and Financial Restructuring has not been successful in expediting recovery.

The State Bank group and the nationalized banks' group have the lowest published capital ratios of all the scheduled commercial banks with adjusted total equity-to-total assets ratio between 4.61 percent and 4.68 percent in 2002. Their position is substantially weaker with a conservative asset appraisal. Equally, however, by this measure, while the nationalized banks have marginally higher published capital ratios, as a group they have negative equity of US$1.3 billion.[26]

Given the magnitude of the problem, debt restructuring will proceed slowly in India – as it has elsewhere in Asia. While demand for new bank lending has declined with the dip in the business cycle in 2001–02, credit growth will be limited by high NPL ratios. On the positive side, the process of financial restructuring will provide opportunities for investors in the financial services sector, but markets will first be looking for clear signs that the government is serious about shoring up the financial system before serious investors commit to this sector. Uncertainty on this score will add to volatility in capital markets in 2003–04, making debt financing in India unattractive.

Debt: Risks ahead

- While India's public and private net external indebtedness is improving, curtailing public debt continues to be a key problem. Debt service indicators showed sustained improvement in the 1990s. External debt as a percentage of GDP declined from 38.7 percent in March 1992 to 22.3 percent in 2001–02.[27] However, public sector debt is rising despite attempts to curtail state and central government debt. Bank lending rates remain comparatively high by international standards, at around 12 percent. Although a credit squeeze has been averted due to a decline in private sector activity, it remains a significant risk for investors in 2002–04.

Total debt to GDP is stabilizing and is expected to decline to 20.2 percent in 2002–03.[28] The decline is due partly to a concerted policy effort during the 1990s to finance productive investment with export receipts and to encourage non-debt finance. The government has encouraged foreign direct investment and portfolio investment since 1991–92, and liberalization in the financial sector has encouraged a range of new financial instruments.[29] Indian expatriates, in particular, have shown greater confidence in Indian markets and non-residents' deposits have generally increased throughout the decade.[30] Lower economic growth also reduced demand for foreign loans in 2001–02.

However, government finances remain a concern. While the Indian central government reaffirmed its commitment to curtailing the fiscal deficit, its finances continued to deteriorate

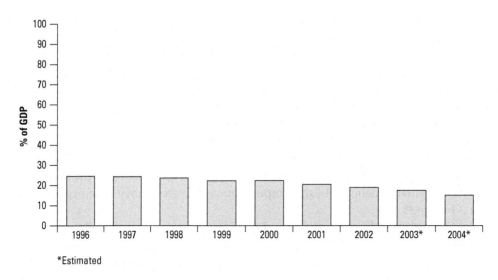

*Estimated

FIGURE 4.1 External debt as percentage of GDP, India 1996–2004

in 2001–02. Taxation revenue collection was well below the budget estimate of US$33.5 billion at US$17.5 billion. The central government's fiscal deficit increased by 37 percent year-on-year to US$18.3 billion, although this was less than the budget estimates of US$23.9 billion. The revenue deficit was up 63 percent on 2000–01 at US$13.7 billion, although this too was lower than the budgeted US$16.2 billion.[31] Furthermore, the combined central and state government gross fiscal deficit has risen to more than 9 percent of GDP, close to the levels experienced in the year before the 1991 fiscal crisis.

A worsening picture for 2002–04?

In reality, however, the position is actually worse than official figures suggest, as many government liabilities are maintained off-balance sheet and are not included in the consolidated fiscal deficit.[32] Indeed, this position is expected to weaken to a fiscal deficit of 10–11 percent in 2002–03, with few prospects for significant improvement in 2003–04.

Militant unionism will constrain the government's plans to boost efficiency and reduce public debt through privatization.

Privatization is a major platform of the government's current debt reduction program. Amid criticism that the privatization program was proceeding too slowly, the central government attempted to reduce its investment in a range of companies in 2001–02. The privatization schedule has included Hindustan Zinc, as well as VSNL, Maruti and Indian Petrochemicals Limited. Unfortunately, these efforts have not been met by contiguous efforts to reduce subsidies and widen the tax base in order to supplement the privatization program and bolster structural fiscal reform.

Indeed, the position is complicated by the need for government investment in infrastructure to support Indian economic development. Attempts by the central government to contain the deficit by reducing capital expenditure, for example, undermined growth in the late 1990s by depriving the private sector of the infrastructure necessary for productive investment. Consequently, the government has attempted to avoid cuts to capital expenditure in the current budget cycle, despite its deteriorating financial position. This will be an increasingly fine line to tread in 2003–04.

About 65 percent of the increasing fiscal deficit over the past five years has been due to the states. Combined state fiscal deficits have increased from 2.3 percent of GDP in 1993 to 4.6 percent of GDP in 2001–02. Most of this spending is non-developmental, encompassing interest, pension and administration payments. The growing stock of debt has created a heavy interest burden for the states, accounting for more than 20 percent of revenue receipts by 2001–02, and up from 15 percent in 1993.[33]

However, state governments expect their revenues to increase in 2002–03 by 14 percent and have announced a raft of measures to reform their respective budgetary positions.[34] Investors, nonetheless, should be skeptical of these expectations, as rhetoric traditionally has not translated into fiscal improvement. The public sector debt burden is thus likely to continue to place pressure on interest rates in 2003–04.

The budget will stay in deficit during 2003–04, albeit with small falls in borrowing anticipated. Total foreign debt will fall as a proportion of GDP to between 13 to 15 percent of GDP in 2004, while the debt/export ratio will improve to approximately 65 percent of GDP during 2003–04.

Labor market trends

- Unemployment is a major contributor to economic inequality in India. However, it is difficult to measure, given that around 90 percent of the Indian labor force is in the informal sector. The number of registered job seekers increased from 40.3 million in 1999–2000 to 41.2 million in 2001–02.[35] Despite labor laws that limit job reductions, employment prospects are likely to deteriorate in 2003–04. While this means reduced wage pressure, it also means less spending in the domestic economy.

India's restrictive labor laws are a considerable burden for business, counterbalancing the attraction of low wage rates. The Minimum Wages Act (1948) extends to anyone employing one or more persons. Furthermore, private enterprises above a certain size cannot close down without government permission – something that is rarely granted.[36] Companies have sought to circumvent this problem by outsourcing employment needs or by instituting early retirement schemes. However, restrictive labor laws ensure that employment growth in large-scale private sector entities is extremely slow. Not unnaturally, business is reluctant to take on staff for fear that they will not be able to downsize during periods of economic downturn. So too, mandated wage rates do not reflect productivity, further reducing the incentive to establish labor-intensive enterprises in India.

The formal employment sector aside, most of the Indian workforce remains in the informal sector, effectively excluding the majority of Indian workers from these employment provisions. The government estimates that more than a quarter of India's population earns a monthly income of less than US$9.47 per person, with most of these workers – some 52 percent of them – self-employed in 2002.[37] More generally, many of these workers operate outside of the cash economy, working on farms and in informal enterprises with their family, while others are artisans and traders. Productivity is particularly low, and productivity improvements will be critical in the coming decade if income levels are to rise and the cash economy extended.

Nonetheless, with a workforce of 390 million, India has one of the largest English-speaking labor pools in the world. In addition, India has a well-educated, urbanized middle class, whose skill levels are internationally accredited, specifically in software engineering and development. This has contributed to strong growth in the information technology sector, global data entry enterprise, and most recently in the contract call center market, which is expected to generate more than a million jobs by 2008.

> Labor market reform is likely to proceed incrementally as attempts to privatize public sector agencies and reduce public sector employment have generated considerable resistance.

Recognizing the economic gains to be made through encouraging foreign investment, the government has established a national taskforce to loosen the regulatory environment and attract multinational business. Measures include amendments in tax laws and changes to the Industrial Disputes Act, which would make it easier to institute layoffs and closures in specific industry sectors. These changes would also facilitate outsourcing and the use of contract employees.[38] The government hopes to implement a comprehensive single bill to make labor laws more flexible in 2003.

Yet general weakness in the economy in 2001–02 will make this program difficult to implement. In September 2001, for example, India's car giant Maruti, announced a voluntary redundancy program to shed 20 percent of its workforce.[39] Concerns over social dislocation caused by job losses have galvanized opposition to labor market reforms in the 2.2 million member central union movement.[40] Unions have vowed to take to the streets if existing protections are lifted. Protest activity, such as that surrounding the ill-fated Dabhol power plant in the 1990s, has already been politically disruptive and the government will be unwilling to confront it in the current climate. Thus, while reform of employment codes has been foreshadowed, in reality these will be hard to achieve, with foreign investors wise to consider the exit costs of employment downsizing should investment decisions fail to meet profit expectations.

Consumer and business confidence

- A stock market scandal in 2001, conflict with Pakistan and on-going security concerns throughout 2002, widespread risk aversion among foreign investors, as well as concern about the pace of Indian economic reform, all served to dampen business and consumer confidence in 2001–02. Little immediate change for 2003–04 is anticipated, at least not until the recovery in the United States is established and security concerns are addressed in the region. Much still hinges on how the war on terror is played out, and whether stability can be restored in the coming year.

Private consumption, which accounted for 64.7 percent of GDP in 2000, declined in 2001–02, contributing to the decline in GDP growth. Consumer confidence was affected by the global economic slump and heightened security concerns. However, despite the weaker short-term outlook, consumption is likely to continue to grow in the medium term, driven by an expanding middle class. India's middle class has tripled since 1985 but still accounts for less than 20 percent of the population. Nonetheless, it is estimated to grow to 50 percent between 2020 and 2040, and will make India one of the largest markets in the developing world.[41] Consequently, opportunities in the retail sector should present themselves in the medium term. Currently, the formal retail sector accounts for only a small part of total grocery sales, but this is expected to grow to 5 percent between 2002–06.[42] The Confederation of Indian Industry, for example, estimates that the retail industry will have a market size

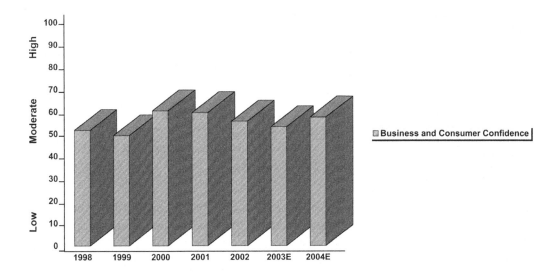

FIGURE 4.2 Business and consumer confidence, India 1998–2004

of US$300 billion by 2010 if it continues to grow at between 6 and 7 percent per annum – the rate of GDP growth.[43] As restrictions are gradually removed from consumer goods, there will be considerable opportunity for profitable investment in this sector.

Growing vehicle sales are further evidence of a growing middle class, with Westernized consumption habits and aspirations. Vehicle sales bucked the negative economic trend in 2001, indicating strengthening consumer sentiment. Sales rose 12 percent year-on-year, and continued to show strong returns throughout 2002, albeit suffering from fall-out from post September 11 jitters.[44] Indeed, 2001–02 displayed strong consumption trends with vehicle sales and motorcycle sales rising by 15 percent and 6 percent respectively.[45] Indicative of a generally high level of consumer confidence was the sale of luxury vehicles, where Mercedes sold more units in India in 2001–02 than ever before. So too, motorcycle sales were strong in rural areas where incomes grew modestly on the back of a recovery from drought that had depressed incomes previously. However, on a practical level, further growth in Indian vehicle sales is limited by India's dreadful road network and the generally inadequate level of investment necessary to improve the highway system.

Business confidence battered

In contrast to the trend in consumer confidence, business confidence fell to a two-year low in the wake of the September attacks in New York.[46] Weak business confidence has been reflected in the slowdown in industrial growth, with a lack of domestic demand for intermediate goods and low demand for capital goods. Business confidence fell 11 percent in the October quarter from the previous quarter as net sales and indices of new orders fell by more than 100 percent.[47] Pressure on wholesale margins during 2003 and 2004 will continue to dampen business confidence, although 2004 should witness a marginal recovery. Foreign investors should be wary of expecting a rapid turnaround in business profits, despite signs of improving sentiment in the US and hopes for an early international economic recovery.

Indian IT companies appear particularly gloomy. US IT companies have postponed outsourcing decisions and have been reluctant to travel to inspect Indian facilities for fear of attacks on expatriates. Work on developing new applications such as Internet-based portals, has decreased. While Indian companies are looking to Europe for new business, opportunities are limited, with European companies tending to be smaller and less experienced in outsourcing production.

Meanwhile, investment in local capital markets has been damaged by political and economic scandals in 2001. Investors abandoned the local bourse in March and April following a price-fixing scandal that landed one of the country's best-known share brokers in jail. An arms-trading scandal, which threatened to derail the ruling National Democratic Alliance, also undermined confidence. Finally, investors fear that prudential reforms have been merely cosmetic.

Stock market: Turbulent times

- The stock market has been hit by a series of political scandals that forced the resignation of government ministers and stock market bureaucrats over allegations of price fixing. So too, the fallout from September 11, as well as rising fears about the slow pace of reform, coupled with the general slowdown in the real economy, have tended to batter investor confidence in 2001–02. However, the market appears to have stabilized and reforms in reporting standards and further liberalization will create more opportunities for foreign investors in 2003–04. Unfortunately, with the global economic situation still uncertain and on-going hostility between India and Pakistan, further volatility is also possible in 2003–04.

The Indian stock market in 2001–02 was generally characterized by anxiety. Tapes of senior political officials taking bribes created panic selling in the stock market. This selling caused losses of 65 percent in new economy stocks in just one week of trading in March 2001. Market darling Infosys Technology, for example, lost 31 percent of its market capitalization in a horror week of trading.[48] The political controversy was compounded by a price-fixing scandal in the Mumbai stock market in April, which sparked fears about the country's regulatory standards.[49] Terrorist attacks in the US and outside the Indian parliament were the final straw, combining to produce a horror finish for local markets. The main Indian stock market index, the Sensex, touched an eight-year low of 2600 on 21 September 2001, falling 11 percent in one day. While it strengthened steadily into 2002, security concerns and general investor jitteriness will continue into 2003.[50]

> A declining stock market in 2001–02 was partly driven by falls in foreign portfolio capital flows, which declined from US$2.8 billion to US$1.3 billion in 2001–02.

While some major corporations in the software sector reported stronger than expected results in 2001–02, the fate of software exports remains uncertain. Further weakness in this sector will deprive the economy of a buffer against external shocks – particularly on-going concerns about the rising price of oil due to international security concerns associated with the war on terror. More generally, escalating military activity will also have implications for the Indian budget, something that could also spook markets.

There is also a general fallout as a result of changing taste preferences among international investors that previously saw Indian subsidiaries of multinational pharmaceutical companies highly favored, but which now appear to be on the sell list. Unfortunately, these companies have limited exports and growth in the domestic pharmaceutical market is down to single digits, with gloomy prospects for 2003–04. Consequently, demand for these stocks is stagnating and the situation is likely to be exacerbated by greater competition following liberalization as the sector is opened to international competition.

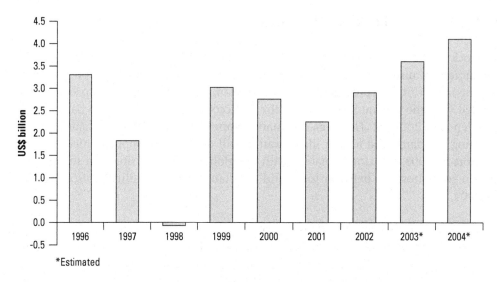

*Estimated

FIGURE 4.3 Portfolio investment, India 1996–2004

One bright spot has been demand for MNC stocks in the food manufacturing sector. These stocks have been buoyed by strong demand in the domestic market, pushing their price-earnings ratios higher than those of their parent companies. Companies such as Hindustan Lever, which managed to modify the European products of its parent company to appeal to the domestic market, are likely to benefit from further growth in the retail sector in 2003–04.

Overall, the value of India's stock market declined by 35 percent in the post-September melee, while other emerging markets lost 25 percent, making the Indian market one of the worst performers. In response, the government has moved to increase the foreign institutional investor limits in an attempt to encourage greater investment.[51] Until regulatory standards improve, however, the market will remain high risk with limited returns. This is not a market for the faint-of-heart foreign portfolio investor.

Corporate tax

• The tax base in India is extremely narrow and tax rates are high. While tax rates are declining, resistance to the removal of burdensome subsidies will impede reform. Foreign companies face particularly high rates of taxation along with copious bureaucratic burdens that tend to reduce significantly the incentive for foreign investment. There is little prospect of an across-the-board reduction in corporate tax levels in 2003–04, though the number of intermediate input items for exporters qualifying for tariff exemption will be increased in the 2003–04 budget.

While personal income tax rates have subsided from the highs of the 1970s, down to a top marginal rate of 30 percent, corporations are generally given a difficult run. Tax holidays for strategic industries and special economic zones are widely offered by state and central governments but the corporate tax rate is comparatively high at 35.7 percent. The corporate tax rate for foreign investors, at 48 percent, is particularly steep, and there is a further tax on distributed profits and a remittance tax also in operation.[52]

> State and central government tax burdens on foreign investment are substantial, despite sweeteners offered to strategic sectors. High taxes compound the burdens of bureaucratic restrictions, corruption and cumbersome labor laws. Corporate taxation is likely to be reduced as the tax base is broadened, but this will be incremental.

A raft of customs duties and indirect taxes add to the burden, although these taxes are gradually being reduced, with the government slowly beginning to recognize the disincentives they pose to foreign investors. Customs duty rates have been reduced from their peak of 38.5 percent to 35 percent in 2000–01 by discontinuing the 10 percent surcharge and streamlining excise duties. Industries, such as textiles and steel, have benefited from lower customs duties levied on inputs. However, other duties have been levied on consumer goods and agricultural products to compensate for the removal of quantitative restrictions and as a means of ensuring the viability of government revenue streams.[53] The four-rate import duty structure remains at 5 percent, 15 percent, 25 percent and 35 percent, although the government has announced plans to align the customs tariffs with other Asian tariffs by 2004 to a maximum rate of 20 percent.[54]

Despite the government's attempt to stimulate the economy with tax cuts in 2001–02, further taxation relief is constrained by the poor budgetary position of both state and central governments. Indeed, state taxes are also a significant burden, and likely to remain so with the poor budgetary situation of most state governments.

To offset expected budget shortfalls, a surcharge has been levied on cigarettes and tobacco to replenish the National Calamity Contingency Fund, and several services have been drawn into the taxation net to broaden the base. The government also announced in January 2002 that the Ministry of Finance will have authority to increase excise duties temporarily to make up for a shortfall in tax revenue.

Residential and commercial property markets

- Spooked investors fleeing the stock market in 2001, thrust their money into bricks and mortar in 2001–02. Interest rate cuts produced stronger demand for property, and improved rental returns also saw an increased interest in the sector. This has been a welcome boost to an otherwise dormant sector in the Indian economy, which, for the previous five years, has witnessed depressed property prices, relatively low capital returns, and flat rental returns. In 2003–04 capital growth should show more promise, as risk-averse investors look toward property and real estate. However, investors should be wary of a further cyclical downturn in the property market in the short term, as a lagged effect of declining equity values might have a negative knock-on wealth effect.[55]

Foreign investment in the Indian real estate market is a delicate business, with tight restrictions. Investment of up to 100 percent is permitted in some townships, resorts, hotels, as well as types of housing and commercial estates. However, there are also complete restrictions prohibiting foreign investment ownership of any type in many property category and specific regions.[56]

Residential real estate is showing a positive upturn in 2002 after being flat for much of 2001. Much of this growth is likely driven by the wealth effects flowing from a stronger stock market in 2000.[57] Lower prime lending rates, down to 11 percent in 2001–02 from 12.5 percent in 2000, have also helped.

Location, location, location: A mixed bag

While the residential property market in Delhi recovered slightly from its weak beginning in 2001, the market remains oversupplied. High-grade apartments have shown the greatest strength. In the medium term, however, the repeal of the Urban Land Ceiling Regulation Act should prompt the release of more land and see lower prices.

Overall, property prices in Mumbai, which grew by 17 percent in 2000, fell by 5 percent in 2001–02. However, the value of high-end residential property sales doubled to US$24.6 million in early 2001 and remained buoyant throughout 2002.[58] It is anticipated that the above-average performance of the luxury property sector will continue into 2003 before stock market weakness acts to reduce demand later in the same year.

Officially, the government has moved to permit 100 percent foreign investment in township projects. However, uncertainty continues to surround investment rules in this sector. Although devaluation of the rupee has contributed to buying opportunities for eligible foreign investors, further devaluation is expected in the short term with flow-on effects in the form of increased foreign sales due to lower foreign asset acquisition costs.

Commercial and retail property: Some ups, some downs

While investors can expect some improvement in the commercial property market, it is not an option for the faint-hearted. The prospect of another property slump in the wake of weakness in the stock market demands a high degree of risk tolerance from property market investors.

Lower interest rates and volatility in the share market have helped to boost the property market. However, further downward pressure on prices can be anticipated in 2002–03. With ambiguity in property taxes, foreign investors have few incentives to invest in the medium term.

Mumbai

Insurance companies dominated demand for commercial property in Mumbai in 2001–02. This provided a counterweight to depressed demand from the IT sector but, with the global insurance industry facing hardship in the latter part of the year, some buying activity is likely to dry up. Commercial rental rates are likely to rise following the introduction of property taxes based on the value of the property rather than the building's age.[59] However, the market is generally predicted to remain static for 2002–04, with moderate rental and sales increases as economic activity picks up.

The introduction of new international product brands in 2001–02 provided a fillip for retail property in Mumbai, where supply is limited. Organized retailing accounts for only 2 percent of the total economic activity and further growth in this sector is likely to occur. Chains such as Starbucks have grown in 2001–02, expanding into most commercial shopping centers. However, ambiguous property taxes and a 16 percent duty on lifestyle products and clothes will limit more robust growth in 2003–04.

Delhi

In Delhi, a rash of A-grade commercial property developments coming onto the market added further softness to a market already suffering from oversupply. Prices are expected to continue to fall. Rental prices in B-grade properties are even weaker. Demand for retail property was a bright spot, however, with retail rentals on the rise through increasing demand for multiplexes.[60] Further growth in retail sales forecast for 2003 will continue to drive growth in the sector leading to above-average rises in rental rates and prices on retail properties during 2003–04.

Foreign direct investment

- While the capital account has been substantially liberalized since 1991, attracting sufficient foreign investment for development remains a priority issue. The government is wooing foreign investors, promising to rationalize regulations, develop better regulatory and prudential systems, cut red tape to make business establishment and start-up easier, and generally provided better business environment than was otherwise the case for foreign investors in the past decade. Words are cheap, however, and the rhetoric is not always matched by the reality, which continues to witness foreign investment codes that hamper foreign business, particularly at the local level. Little substantive real change is anticipated in 2003–04.

Following several years of falling foreign direct investment (FDI), the government has moved to reassure foreign investors of its commitment to economic reform and to attracting international capital. The Indian government made significant overtures to foreign investors in 2001–02, reducing obstacles to investment in key sectors including IT and e-commerce, banking, insurance, pharmaceuticals and defense equipment. All FDI is now permitted under the automatic approval route – bar a few exceptions. Limits for FDI in projects relating to electricity generation, transmission and distribution (other than atomic reactor power plants) have been removed. So too, FDI limits in the oil-refining sector under the automatic route have also been raised from the existing 49 percent to 100 percent ownership allowance. Equally, the government has moved to improve access to overseas finance for local entities. External commercial borrowing (ECB) approvals have been expedited and any corporate legal entity is able to borrow up to US$50 million from an overseas lender without prior approval.

Increasing competition from Chinese exports will intensify the need for restructuring in India. This will pose risks to investments in sectors directly competing with Chinese products in export markets.

Liberalization measures such as these have been greeted warmly, with inflows of foreign direct investment showing some sign of improvement. Net foreign direct investment increased to US$2.4 billion between April and November 2001, and to US$4.25 billion in 2002.[61] The total stock of FDI is also set to rise, having shown gradual but consistent improvement since 1996, when it stood at US$7.95 billion, to US$26.67 billion. This too will continue to experience modest year-on-year increases though to 2004, and should round out at US$37.35 billion, as with net FDI that should hit US$5.0 billion by 2005.[62]

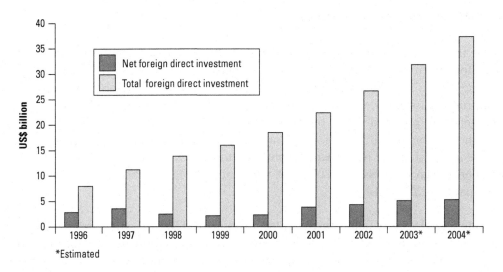

*Estimated

FIGURE 4.4 Foreign direct investment, India 1996–2004

The ill-fated Dabhol power plant investment by failed US energy company, Enron, should, however, stand as a warning of the difficulties involved in doing business in India. The joint-venture investment in the US$3 billion, 10-year liquefied natural gas project was to have been the largest direct foreign investment in India's history. However, the plant remains unfinished after a decade of conflict over prices and terms, and escalating public opposition to its environmental impact. Protestors took to the streets in the late 1990s to demand changes to the plant's design and to protest against the government's economic liberalization policies. The project finally stalled in June 2001, only 90 percent complete. In the weeks before Enron filed for Chapter 11 bankruptcy in November 2001, negotiations were under way to sell Enron's stake in the project, estimated to be between US$500 million and US$1 billion. The project, which was the focus of anti-globalization feeling in India, suggests the problems inherent in overlooking the financial realities of large-scale development projects, and relying too heavily on political contacts to sweep aside local criticism.[63] Investors should be wary of the political turbulence that frequently surrounds large-scale foreign investment projects, with a series of large-scale failures emblematic of the less than welcoming sentiments of many ordinary Indian citizens toward foreign investment.

Section C Politics

• Although political scandals have dogged the BJP in 2001–02, the government's strong stance against Pakistan in the wake of the December attack on India's parliament restored some credibility in the Indian electorate. This renewed support will be tested by state elections in 2002, and by domestic economic factors should the economy now make significant inroads into poverty reduction over the next few years.

Political volatility in the ruling National Democratic Alliance with in-fighting and corruption scandals has provided an unstable platform for foreign investment in India in 2002. While the senior partner in government, the BJP, intends to win back elector-confidence with a strong stance against Pakistan in Kashmir, its capacity to govern effectively has been significantly reduced by the perception of widespread internal corruption. Prime Minister Vajpayee survived attempts to claim his political scalp over a scandal that forced senior politicians to resign in March 2001, but the government's reform momentum has been severely damaged – perhaps crippled. Confidence in the government declined after an Internet news site showed images of senior government and military officials taking bribes from journalists posing as arms dealers. This has reduced the BJP's power in the ruling coalition.[64] Further problems arose when a regional party, facing state elections, pulled out of the coalition, citing the government's tardiness in responding to the allegations.[65] Railway Minister Mamata Banerjee and the Minister of State for External Affairs Ajit Panja also resigned in protest.

The corruption incident revealed conflict between the Prime Minister and the Hindu organization, the RSS, which took the opportunity to attack the Prime Minister, as two of his senior aides were implicated in the scandal. The Prime Minister's position with respect to the RSS will be further complicated by his response to rising religious violence, particularly since he is considered to be more moderate. Although the Prime Minister is a member of the RSS, the organization claims he has not implemented its Hindu agenda swiftly enough.[66] This could be a trigger point for further disharmony in the ruling coalition in 2003–04.

The government has thus far weathered the storm, backed by strong regional support. The BJP party is regarded as popular, in contrast to the main opposition Congress Party. Although the Congress Party, led by Sonia Gandhi, the wife of the late Prime Minister Rajiv Gandhi, ruled for 45 of the 54 years following Independence, the party is considered to be dominated by elites, and in increasing sectors of the public, seen as not representing their interests or needs.

Unfortunately, the corruption scandals are a significant distraction to the main game of economic reform – something that is threatening to stall. For example, the privatization program is likely to proceed, but now only intermittently, limiting the government's debt reduction and liberalization programs, as well as real financial reform. Likewise, state elections in May have also distracted attention from the reform agenda, with as yet little indication that this will be returned to center stage in 2003–04.

Corruption: An institutionalized way of life

The government is not alone in its connection to corruption. A senior aide to the main opposition leader, Sonia Gandhi, is being investigated for suspicious property acquisitions. Surveys on corruption in India suggest that it is broadly institutionalized. Low wages among officials and the comparatively low risk of prosecution combine to produce little incentive for reform. This makes foreign investment risky – particularly for those uninitiated into the Indian business environment.

Fortress India: Protectionist barricades

While trade has slowly been liberalized since 1991, India's trade regime is far from liberal. The government has replaced quantitative restrictions on many goods, such as agricultural and consumer products, with prohibitive tariffs. However, few sectors completely prohibit foreign ownership and many sectors allow 100 percent foreign ownership. Nonetheless, sectors in which foreign investment is forbidden or heavily restricted include some areas of real estate, print media and broadcasting, agriculture and plantations. The days of nationalization are apparently over, but further change is likely to continue at a moderate pace. Indeed, the culture in some of the state administrations, as well as many of the central government bureaucracies, continues to be informed by a socialist outlook; one not always disposed to assisting foreign investment.

Leading risk indices: Corruption, stability, governance, risk

Corruption

Leading risk indices suggest that while the trends of governance, corruption and prudential regulation are improving, and are forecast to continue to do so for 2003–04, volatility will continue.

Similarly, while the corruption index betrays some considerable improvement commencing in 1997–99, political and financial scandals early in 2001 have made a lasting impact. Despite attempts to reform, corruption remains prevalent at all levels of government, and the country consistently rates very poorly in corruption perception indices.

Political stability

The political stability index also shows signs of volatility, with much depending on the negotiating skills of Prime Minister Vajpayee and his ability to hold together the fragile coalition of 20 parties. The challenge of managing socio-economic inequality, as well as religious and caste-based conflict during 2003–04, will test the government's consensus-building powers. Consequently, political stability, while not deteriorating significantly during 2003–04, will remain fragile. Indeed, this will be especially so if external security threats begin to resurface and test the more militant elements in the governing coalition.

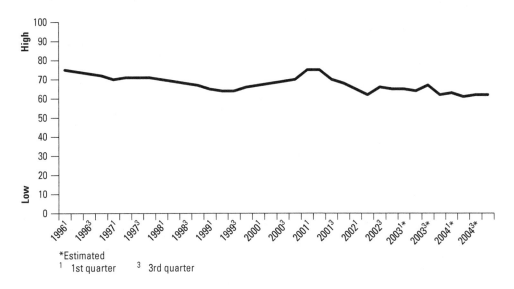

FIGURE 4.5 Corruption index, India 1996–2004

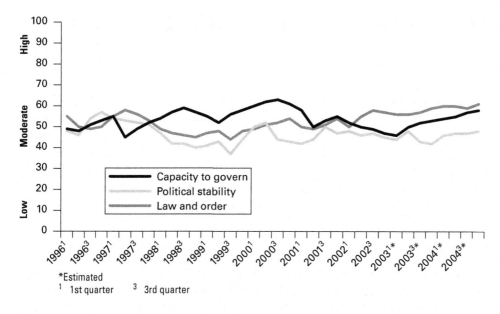

FIGURE 4.6 Political stability index, India 1996–2004

Political stability methodology
• The capacity-to-govern index is based upon the institutional reach of government, defined in terms of its ability to set the political and economic agenda and ensure its legislative program is enacted without significant compromise. This index is adversely affected by legislative opposition, lack of legislative implementation, failure to realize government policy and general political opposition.
• The political stability index measures violent opposition or organized demonstrations, terrorist activities, and popular discontent that adversely affect the institutional and electoral stability of the government.
• The law and order index measures the propensity to civil obedience, and the institutional reach of the rule of law in terms of regulatory compliance and enforcement.

Corporate governance

The corporate governance indices are improving but only gradually, reflecting the government's initiatives to introduce international reporting standards over the past few years. Corporate transparency has consequently improved slightly since 1998–99, albeit from a low base.

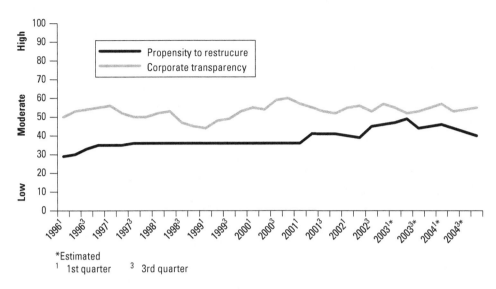

FIGURE 4.7 Corporate governance index, India 1996–2004

Corporate governance methodology
- The corporate governance index is a composite index measuring the juridical requirements for corporate disclosure and financial reporting, prudential regime adequacy, prudential compliance enforcement, and the juridical reach of prudential authorities.
- The propensity-to-restructure index is a composite index based on media releases and reported corporate restructuring as a result of prudential regulation, financial incentives, loan restructuring/re-negotiation, or asset realignment.

The propensity-to-restructure index has also been gaining momentum since 2001, although it has been moderating very recently. However, enforcement will continue to be an issue, given that widespread corruption exists in the bureaucracy, particularly at the local level. Expect some fluctuation in the short-to-medium term.

Foreign investor risk

While foreign investor risk has been declining in recent years, the risks are increasing as regional security issues have intensified. Nonetheless, continued structural reform in the medium term is likely to create greater incentives to invest in India. Expect the index to generally improve during 2003–05.

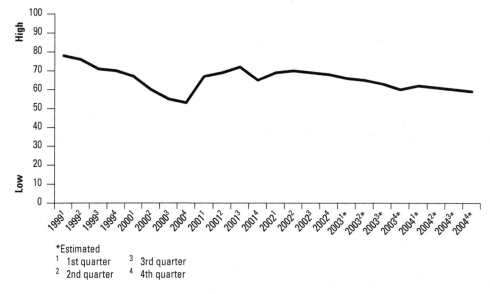

*Estimated
¹ 1st quarter   ³ 3rd quarter
² 2nd quarter   ⁴ 4th quarter

FIGURE 4.8 Foreign investor risk index, India 1999–2004

Foreign investor risk index methodology
• The foreign investor risk index is a composite index measuring tax burdens, discriminatory regulatory practices, adverse compliance regulations, government policy toward foreign enterprise, receptiveness to issuance of government contracts, foreign enterprise commercial restrictions, and official attitudinal changes to foreign direct investment and foreign commercial operations which impact on operational efficiency. The index also incorporates a nominal measure for market risk and market failure.

Section D Security

Major conflict with Pakistan over disputed territory in Kashmir sparked fears of nuclear warfare following a terrorist attack on the Indian parliament in December 2001. While this brinkmanship has subsided, security concerns are likely to dominate Indian politics in the immediate future. So too, the recent bombing outside the Indian parliament reiterated the often skittish security environment of India, something that is bound to spook foreign investors in an environment where the war on terror still dominates the international agenda. Tense times remain ahead for 2003–04, with the possibility of a sudden deterioration in the regional security environment.

Foreign investors have reason to be worried that the almost routine skirmishes between Pakistan and India will escalate into a major conflict. This is particularly concerning given their respective nuclear capabilities and previous indications that they would be prepared to use these weapons.[67] Both countries launched the largest military mobilization of their 54-year rivalry in December 2001, as Indian troops mobilized along the Pakistani border following the attack on the parliament. Prime Minister Vajpayee suggested that India would engage in a major war with Pakistan to force it to restrain militant groups seeking a Muslim state in Kashmir. This prompted international attempts to broker a peace between the historically hostile neighbors.

The incident has also threatened India's re-engagement with the US, as India has been critical of the latter's dealings with Pakistan in the war on terror in Afghanistan. India continues to maintain that the same rough justice that has applied to supporters of terrorism in Afghanistan should apply to Pakistan, which it claims supports militant groups such as Jaish-e-Mohammad and Lashkar-e-Toiba. For the moment the situation is calmer, but the conflict in Kashmir remains on a knife-edge. Even if this strife continues without escalating, it will destabilize the reform agenda and drain government coffers. Investors should therefore be cautious in their exposure, or adopt a long-term view on returns.

While relations with Pakistan remain strained, India's relations with China are the most positive they have been in recent history. China's Premier Zhu Rongji and a large business delegation visited India in January 2002 to enhance business relations.[68] There is every indication this relationship will continue to prosper in 2003–04.

Domestically, security is also intermittently threatened by ethnic conflict between the Hindu nationalists, Christians, Muslims and Sikhs, which makes an ambitious economic reform program difficult to sustain. Indeed, mob violence against a train carrying a group of Hindu nationalists in Gujarat forced the Prime Minister to cancel his trip to the Commonwealth Heads of Government Meeting in Australia in February 2002. Caste and inter-tribal violence has been increasing in the states, as has separatist activity, with groups such as the United Liberation Front of Assam seeking independence.

While not common, personal security concerns have emerged as an issue for foreign nationals and expatriate workers, especially those in north-eastern states and some of the remoter regions, where attacks, robberies and kidnappings have been reported. Caution is warranted.

Section E Economic and political risk forecasts

- Short-term risks are increasing in India as the government is diverted from its task of economic reform by security issues. At the moment, highly restrictive labor market rules and a bureaucratic business environment present difficulties, even for local investors. In addition, the traditional antipathy towards foreign investment, weak intellectual property protection and comparatively high taxes limit opportunities for foreign investment to predominantly niche markets. Although much of the workforce is comparatively well educated, greater flexibility is required for profitability in medium-to-large-scale enterprises. The winds of change are blowing but investors should expect more moderate growth in the economy as the pace of reform subsides.

Short-term forecasts

The short-term outlook for the economy is for further weakness as the international economy begins a slow recovery in late 2002–03. Positive growth is expected to continue at around 6 percent but this is well below the 8 percent required for any significant inroads into poverty reduction.

Opportunities for short-term foreign investment are gradually improving as restrictions are lifted, but changes in rules are frequently ambiguous thereby posing a significant challenge for foreign investors. Investors should also be wary of taxation changes in particular sectors, especially given the likely government revenue shortfalls. A high level of due diligence and expert local knowledge will be a prerequisite for the successful investor in the Indian market.

Protectionism is diminishing – but from a very high base. Significant impediments remain to trade and they will continue to do so, particularly in sectors such as agriculture. Equally, prudential and financial restructuring is under way but the banking sector will continue to be burdened by a high proportion of NPLs for many years to come.

Privatization is firmly on the agenda, as is government debt reduction, but India's fragmented democratic traditions frequently make political actions and intentions difficult to match. Opposition from unions will make the program highly fraught. This reform fatigue is likely to be matched in rural areas faced with reduced subsidies over the next five years (2003–07). Expect the unhealthy budgetary position to constrain further interest rate cuts, and to continue to cause weakness in the rupee's valuations in 2003–04.

Short-term opportunities

Considerable growth is expected in India's fledgling retail industry over the medium term as more foreign brands are introduced. Shopping malls, although popular, are in their infancy. India's emerging middle class is likely to provide a vibrant market for consumer goods as restrictions on the importation of these goods are dismantled. International brands with products tailored to local tastes will produce the greatest returns.

Continued strong growth is expected in the call center industry and in software development, particularly as the US economy revives. However, poor intellectual property protection will remain a real deterrent for many investors. Stronger competition from Chinese exports is likely to limit growth in the textiles and clothing industry particularly.

Medium to longer term

India's infrastructure requirements will continue to provide opportunities for foreign engineering companies and, increasingly, for telecommunications companies, as restrictions are removed. However, the battle over state government guarantees, as with the Dabhol Enron power generating facility, has spooked investors in infrastructure projects. This concern will constrain the government's privatization program, limiting potential demand from international investment partners.

Reform in the services sector will also provide opportunities for foreign professionals, particularly within the financial and legal services sectors, as the financial markets and banking industry continue to restructure.

India's high-technology and pharmaceuticals industries should continue to develop, particularly if intellectual property rights are enforced according to international standards set by the World Trade Organization. However, local profits in the pharmaceuticals industry could be curtailed by the trend of foreign MNCs creating wholly-owned subsidiaries in India. Investors should be prepared for regulatory changes as this trend has the potential to prompt the Indian government to attempt to capture a greater share of the profits in India.

Foreign investors should also recognize the importance of the cultural networks that underpin local business. Despite the prevalence of English in business circles, investors are wise to acknowledge cultural differences in business practices. Like elsewhere in Asia, personal connections are an important part of successful commerce. Profitable foreign investment often relies on cultivating local alliances and partnerships, and engaging with the community of policy-makers.

Overall risk rating

India's risk profile is increasing in the short term with reform fatigue, and international and domestic security concerns likely to create political instability. This will slow the pace of much-needed reforms in the financial markets, in agriculture, services and the labor market. The downturn and general sluggish growth in the world economy is also limiting export growth, although this will improve in 2003–04.

The signs are more positive in the medium term though, as there is a real commitment to economic reform and many have already reaped the benefits. India's software services industry has been carefully nurtured since the 1980s and the talent in Bangalore is highly regarded internationally. Other knowledge-intensive industries are likely to emerge from India's tertiary institutions in the medium term 2004–07, given the historical precedent for collaboration between public and private sector institutions. New economy sectors have averaged 9.1 percent growth between 1993–94 and 1999–2000, while old economy sectors averaged 5.3 percent. This trend is likely to continue for some time yet.

Risk: Increasing in the short term ↑
Risk Rating (0 = lowest, 10 highest risk) 6.0

Section F India fact sheet[69]*

Geography

Capital
Delhi

Largest city (millions, 2000 est.)
Bombay (Mumbai) 17.8

Location
Southern Asia, bordering the Arabian Sea and the Bay of Bengal, between Burma and Pakistan

Neighboring countries
Bangladesh 4,053 km, Bhutan 605 km, Burma 1,463 km, China 3,380 km, Nepal 1,690 km, Pakistan 2,912 km

Terrain
Upland plain (Deccan Plateau) in south, flat to rolling plain along the Ganges, deserts in west, Himalayas in north

Area
3,287,590 sq km

Economic statistics

Currency
Rupee

Exchange rate (February 2001)
US$1.00 = R48.53

Gross Domestic Product (GDP)
US$489 billion (2001)

GDP per capita
US$480

GDP per capita – PPP
US$2,200 (2000)

GDP – composition by sector
Agriculture 25%, industry 24%, services 51% (2000)

Inflation rate
3.1% (2001)

Gross total external debt (US$ 2001)
$100 billion

Current account balance (US$ million, 2001)
$938

National unemployment rate (1998)
n/a

Adult economic participation rate
(by gender): n/a

Population below poverty line
35% (1994 est.)

Labor force (millions, 2000)
390

Labor force by occupation
Agriculture 67%, services 18%, industry 15% (1995 est.)

* All figures are the latest available except where indicated. All figures are in US dollars. Figures are compiled from national, international and multilateral agencies (International Monetary Fund, World Bank, World Development Report, UNESCO Statistical Yearbook, International Labour Office, United Nations, Central Intelligence Agency World Fact Book). Gross domestic product (GDP) refers to the value of all goods and services produced in the preceding financial year. GDP per capita, Purchasing Power Parity (GDP per capita – PPP) refers to the indices developed by the World Bank to take account of price differences, cost of living differences, and relative purchasing power of a set basket of goods and services between countries so as to provide a more accurate measure of national wealth.

Budget (US$ billion, 2000–01)
Revenues: $44.3 billion
Expenditure: $73.6 billion

Combined gross fiscal deficit
% of GDP: 9.1

Industries
Textiles, chemicals, food processing,
steel, transportation equipment,
cement, mining, petroleum, machinery,
software

Major exports (billions)
US$36.3 (f.o.b., 1999)
Textile goods, gems and jewelry,
engineering goods, chemicals, leather
manufactures

Major imports (billions)
US$50.2 (f.o.b., 1999)
Crude oil and petroleum products,
machinery, gems, fertilizer, chemicals

Major trading partners (exports)
US 22%, Hong Kong 5.8%, Japan 5.4%,
UK 5.3%, Germany 4.6%

Major trading partners (imports 2001)
US 9%, Belgium 8%, Singapore 7.1%,
UK 7.1%, Japan 6%

**Income/wealth distribution
(household income or consumption
by % share)**
Lowest 10%: 3.5%
Highest 10%: 33.5% (1997)

Televisions (1997, millions)
63

Televisions per capita (1996, per 1000)
64

Telephones (2000 lines in use, millions)
27.7

Telephones per 1000 people
7

Cellular phones (2000, millions)
2.93

Cellular phones per capita
0.28

**Registered motor vehicles (1997
millions)**
36.3

Internet users (2000)
4.5 million

Fiscal year
1 April–31 March

Government and political statistics

Nature of government
Federal Republic

Constitution
1950

Structure of government

Executive branch
Chief of State: President Kicheril Raman
Narayanan (since 25 July 1997)
Vice-president Krishnan Kant (since
21 August 1997)

Head of government
Prime Minister Atal Behari Vajpayee
(since 19 March 1998)
Council of Ministers appointed by the
president on the recommendation of the
prime minister

President and vice-president

President elected by an electoral college consisting of elected members of both houses of Parliament and the legislatures of the states for a five-year term; election last held 14 July 1997; vice-president elected by both houses of Parliament for a five-year term; election last held 16 August 1997 (next to be held NA August 2002); prime minister elected by parliamentary members of the majority party following legislative elections; election last held NA October 1999 (next to be held NA October 2004)

Bicameral Parliament or Sansad

The Council of States or Rajya Sabha (a body consisting of not more than 250 members, up to 12 of whom are appointed by the president, the remainder are chosen by the elected members of the state and territorial assemblies; members serve six-year terms)

The People's Assembly or Lok Sabha (545 seats; 543 elected by popular vote, 2 appointed by the president; members serve five-year terms) *elections:* People's Assembly – last held 5 September through 3 October 1999 (next to be held NA 2004)

Council of Ministers (2001)

Prime Minister

Atal Behari Vajpayee
Also Minister for Personnel, Public Grievances and Pensions, Planning, Atomic Energy, Space

Ministers

Minister of Finance

Yashwant Sinha

Minister of Home Affairs

LK Advani

Minister of Urban Development and Poverty Alleviation

Ananth Kumar

Minister of State for Commerce and Industry

Murasoli Maran

Minister of Environment and Forests

TR Baalu

Minister of Chemicals and Fertilizers

Sukhdev Singh Dhindsa

Minister of Defence

George Fernandez

Minister of Shipping

Ved Prakash Goyal

Minister of Civil Aviation

Syed Shahnawaz Hussain

Minister of Tourism and Culture

Shri Jagmohan

Minister of Law, Justice and Company Affairs

Arun Jaitley

Minister of Social Justice

Satya Narayan Jatiya

Minister of Heavy Industries and Public Enterprises

Manohar Joshi

Minister of Human Resource Development; Science and Technology; Ocean Development

Murli Manohar Joshi

Minister of Parliamentary Affairs;
Communications and IT
Pramod Mahajan

Minister of Agro and Rural Industries
Kariya Munda

Minister of Rural Development
Venkaiah Naidu

Minister of Petroleum and Natural Gas
Ram Nai

Minister of Railways
Nitish Kumar

Minister of Tribal Affairs
Jual Oram

Minister of Coal and Mines
Ram Vilas Paswan

Minister of Power
Suresh Prabhu

Minister of Textiles
Kashiram Rana

Minister of Water Resources
Arjun Charan Sethi

Minister of Consumer Affairs, Food
Public Distribution
Shanta Kumar

Minister of Disinvestment;
Development of North Eastern Region
Arun Shourie

Minister of Agriculture
Ajit Singh

Minister of External Affairs
Jaswant Singh

Minister of Information and
Broadcasting
Sushma Swaraj

Minster of Health and Family Welfare
CP Thakur

Minister of Youth Affairs and Sport
Sushree Uma Bharti

Minister of Labour
Sharad Yadav

Main governing parties
All India Anna Dravida Munnetra
Kazhagam or AIADMK [C. Jayalalitha
JAYARAM]; All India Forward Bloc or
AIFB [Prem Dutta PALIWAL (chairman),
Chitta BASU (general secretary)]; Asom
Gana Parishad [Prafulla Kumar
MAHANTA]; Bahujan Samaj Party or
BSP [Kanshi RAM]; Bharatiya Janata
Party or BJP [Bangaru LAXMAN,
president]; Biju Janata Dal or BJD
[Naveen PATNAIK]; Communist Party of
India or CPI [Ardhendu Bhushan
BARDHAN]; Communist Party of
India/Marxist-Leninist or CPI/ML [Vinod
MISHRA]; Congress (I) Party [Sonia
GANDHI, president]; Dravida Munnetra
Kazagham or DMK (a regional party in
Tamil Nadu)
   [M. KARUNANIDHI]; Indian National
League [Suliaman SAIT]; Janata Dal
(Secular) [H. D. Deve GOWDA]; Janata
Dal (United) or JDU [Sharad YADAV,
president, I. K. GUJRAL]; Kerala
Congress (Mani faction) [K. M. MANI];
Marumalarchi Dravida Munnetra
Kazhagam or MDMK [VAIKO]; Muslim
League [G. M. BANATWALA]; Nationalist
Congress Party or NCP [Sharad
PAWAR]; National Democratic Alliance,
a 16-party alliance including BJP, DMK,
Janata Dal (U), SHS, Shiromani Akali
Dal, Telugu Desam, BJD, Rinamool
Congress]; Rashtriya Janata Dal or RJD

[Laloo Prasad YADAV]; Revolutionary Socialist Party or RSP [Tridip CHOWDHURY]; Samajwadi Party or SP [Mulayam Singh YADAV, president]; Shiromani Akali Dal [Prakash Singh BADAL]; Shiv Sena [Bal THACKERAY]; Tamil Maanila Congress [G. K. MOOPANAR]; Telugu Desam Party or TDP (a regional party in Andhra Pradesh) [Chandrababu NAIDU]; Trinamool Congress [Mamata BANERJEE]

Main opposition parties
Congress Party, Samajawadi

International memberships
AFDB, ARF (dialogue partner), AsDB, ASEAN (dialogue partner), BIS, C, CCC, CP, ESCAP, FAO, G-6, G-15, G-19, G-24, G-77, IAEA, IBRD, ICAO, ICC, ICFTU, ICRM, IDA, IEA (observer), IFAD, IFC, IFRCS, IHO, ILO, IMF, IMO, Inmarsat, Intelsat, Interpol, IOC, IOM (observer), ISO, ITU, MINURSO, MIPONUH, MONUC, NAM, OAS (observer), OPCW, PCA, SAARC, UN, UNCTAD, UNESCO, UNHCR, UNIDO, UNIFIL, UNIKOM, UNMEE, UNMIBH, UNMIK, UNU, UPU, WCL, WFTU, WHO, WIPO, WMO, WToO, WTrO

Business organizations
All India Plastic Manufacturers Association; All India Stainless Steel Association; American Quality Assessors; Chemical and Allied Producers Export Promotion; antipiracyindia.com; Coimbatore District Small Scale Industry Association; Confederation of Indian Industry; Cooperative Initiative Panel;

Electronic Component Industries Association; Federation of Indian Chambers of Commerce and Industry; Federation of Indian Export Organisations; Federation of Indian Micro and Small & Medium Enterprises; Gem and Jewelry Export Promotion Council of India; Tamilnadu Industrial Guidance and Export Promotion Bureau; The Institute of Cost and Works Accountants of India; Indian Institute of Interior Designers; India Business and Technology Consortium; India Automobile Industry Association; Kera Fed; Laghu Udyog Bharti; Madurai District Tiny and Small Scale Industries Association; Quality Circle Forum; Tea Board of India; Textile Association India; Fertilizer Association of India; Institute of Chartered Accountants; Trade and Technology Centre for India; US-India Business Council

Date of UN Membership
1945

Social statistics

Population
1,029,991,145 (average annual rate of natural increase: 1.6%)

Population density
811 people per square meter

Fertility rate
3.04 children born/woman (2001 est)

Maternal mortality rate (per 100,000 births)
445

Infant mortality rate (deaths per 1,000 births)
63.2 (2001 est.)

Population growth
1.55% (2001 est.)

Life expectancy
Men: 62.9% years
Women: 63.5 years (2001 est.)

Ethnic Composition
Indo-Aryan 72%, Dravidian 25%, Mongoloid and other 3%

Religions
Hindu 82.6%, Islam 11.3%, Christian 2.4%, Sikh 2%, Buddhists 0.71%, Jains 0.48%

National languages spoken
Hindi (official), English (official), Bengali, Gujarati, Kashmiri, Malayalam, Marathi, Oriya, Punjabi, Tamil, Telugu, Urdu, Kannada, Assamese, Sanskrit, Sindhi (all recognized by the constitution). Dialects, 1,652

Literacy rate (over 15 years can read and write, 1995 est.)
52%
Male: 65.5%
Female: 37.7%

Indonesia

5 Indonesia

Colin Brown

Section A Economy

Overview

Indonesia is suffering from a lack of any strong or clear economic leadership. The current Cabinet has some experienced and skilled ministers in the major economy-related ministries, but they have been unable to break the policy log-jam and take the initiatives all agree are necessary to pull Indonesia out of the economic morass it finds itself in. The major reason for this failure is not incompetence but corruption and vested interests.

The government's capacity to take action is also limited by the extent to which it is indebted to foreign lenders, especially the International Monetary Fund (IMF). Indonesia's total foreign indebtedness stands at approximately US$140 billion, of which more than half is owed by the government. The country's GNP is just under US$160 billion. These debts alone mean that the government's options for using fiscal policy to stimulate economic growth are greatly limited and will remain so in 2003–04.[1]

Virtually all the huge commercial concerns that dominated the economy before the fall of Suharto in 1998, including the conglomerates, usually headed by Sino-Indonesian business people, have either collapsed or are crippled by massive debt burdens. There are no signs that these conglomerates are making a comeback. Indeed, some of their bosses have been jailed for fraud, most notably former timber tycoon and Suharto-era Minister, Mohammad 'Bob' Hassan.

Economic structure changing slowly

The failure of so many of the large conglomerates and state-owned enterprises has opened the way for small- and medium-scale businesses to play a larger role in the economy. Most small enterprises are owned and run by indigenous Indonesian Muslims. It is therefore no coincidence that the post of Minister for Cooperatives, and Small and Medium Business is held by Alimarwan Hanan, Secretary General of the Muslim party, PPP. The Muslim parties have always been the most outspoken on the need to support small- and medium-sized enterprise, partly, perhaps, because this is the sector where most Muslim businesspeople are to be found, and partly also because big business has historically been dominated by non-Muslim ethnic Chinese entrepreneurs. For this reason alone, the Muslim-dominated business sector will likely see the availability of greater bank credit made available to it in 2003–04, and possibly be the recipient of preferential government contracts.

> Large-scale ethnic Chinese business concerns have increasingly found that the privi-leged access to government they enjoyed under Suharto has been lost – at least for the time being.

In some quarters, these developments are being viewed as anti ethnic Chinese, and to some extent they are, especially given the ethnic make-up of the Suharto-era conglomerates. But no future government is likely to allow policy to proceed very far in this direction, simply because the economy will never recover if ethnic Chinese business does not feel reasonably secure in Indonesia. Nonetheless, the ethno-religious composition of the Indonesian business community has changed and will continue to do so in the future, creating new challenges for foreign investors looking to establish business relations or possible joint venture partners. Consequently, the business environment has been trans-formed in Indonesia in 2002, and new strategic alliances will need to be formed and new cultural sensitivities addressed.

More immediately, foreign investment, having risen during 2000, fell again in 2001, and showed only a nominal increase in 2002 to US$63.05 billion, indicating a continuing degree of wariness about economic and political conditions in Indonesia. Some of the Sino–Indonesian capital that fled the country in 1997–98 may be returning via Malaysia and Singapore, and investment from China seems to be picking up. However, as yet there are few signs of other investors returning in any numbers, with fears about Indonesian stability, economic per-formance and corruption still acting as the main deterrents to international investors.

The bottom line: Wait and see

Whatever minor signs of stabilization – and eventual recovery – have appeared are likely to remain for 2002–03, after which time the country's next parliamentary and presidential elec-tions are due to be held in 2004.

While the elections of 1999 were remarkably peaceful, there will certainly be fears in the business community, especially the expatriate one, that the 2004 elections might revert to the violent practices of earlier Suharto-era elections. This fear will threaten the country's fragile recovery, and serve to keep foreign direct investment at depressed levels until a clearer picture of Indonesia's political situation emerges. Investors will need to exercise caution, as Indonesia's nascent recovery remains fragile and prone to continuing uncertainty. As a consequence, real stability is unlikely to return until after the 2004 elections. For the time being, reform is regarded as secondary to stability.

Section B Risks and projections
Macroeconomic performance and risk indicators

- The rate of economic growth declined in 2001–02 to around 3.3 percent, but is set to recover during 2002–03 to 4.2 percent in line with the pick-up in global economic activity. Inflation and interest rates also rose to post-1998 highs in 2001–02, but began to trend downwards in late 2002 and will continue doing so into 2003. Likewise, with continuing sluggish economic conditions, the cost of borrowing will continue to fall during 2003 as the government attempts to reinvigorate the economy through a stimulatory monetary policy – though much will depend on the government's ability to maintain inflation within manageable limits. In all, the economy is set to enjoy modest economic growth and recovery. However, economic conditions are still fragile and prone to recurrent problems in 2002–04.

Economic growth in 2001 was 3.3 percent, and toward the lower end of most analysts' predictions. The second half of 2001, in particular, saw a significant falling off in growth rates, as the downturn in the global economy hit home. This trend continued into early 2002, in part reflecting the fallout of post September 11 and contracting demand for Indonesian exports. Foreign and domestic investment also remained low. However, domestic private consumption was high: with a growth rate of 5.9 percent in 2002 – a rate comparable to that at any time since the onset of the Asian financial crisis in 1998.

Private domestic consumption rose 5.9 percent in 2001 as compared with 2000. However, it generally slowed during 2002, indicative of a slow global economy and fore-shadowing only modest economic recovery in 2002–03 in the absence of a surge in export demand. The current picture is, however, confused by still-strong consumer confidence and high demand for imports of consumer goods. Indeed, the Indonesian government's budget estimates are calling for a growth rate in 2002–03 of 4.2 percent. However, even assuming this growth target is achieved, it will do little to restore the economic fortunes of companies and consumers still suffering from the fallout of the financial crisis. The middle class has shrunk considerably, with no discernible reverse in this trend in 2003–04.

Renewed inflation

Inflation rates also showed substantial increases from 2000 to 2001, up from 3.7 percent to 11.1 percent, albeit moderating slightly in 2002 to 9.0 percent. While these continue to be relatively high by regional standards, they nonetheless are much improved from a high of 68 percent in 1998. In part, this inflation was due to rising demand in the economy and declining stocks. Government-determined rises in fuel and electricity prices were also a contributing factor. Not surprisingly, these price increases have been at considerable political cost to the government, but are clearly seen by the IMF as a test of the government's resolve to implement its agreements and to commence the reform process. Failure to increase these prices would have serious consequences for the government's capacity to attract IMF loans, and indirectly to negotiate re-scheduling of loans with the Paris Club of creditors.

One-off factors were also at work. The year-end inflation rates were driven up by the coincidence of the Islamic festival of Idul Fitri (marking the end of the fasting month of Ramadan) and Christmas in late December 2001. Both these festivals bring considerably increased demand for consumer goods, and are always marked by increased inflation. As the date of Idul Fitri moves back through the year by 11 days annually, these two festivals will be nearly a month apart in 2003, reducing their collective impact on the inflation rate. Nonetheless, the annual rate of price increases will reach 10 percent by end 2002–03, returning to the long-term trend average of the past decade at approximately 12–14 percent in 2003–04.

> Business confidence is likely to improve in 2002–03; not because of renewed confidence in the economy, but because business has simply become accustomed to new ways of dealing with an inefficient bureaucracy and new government – the new rules of the game are being learnt!

The failure of the Indonesian monetary authorities to reduce inflation continues to damage economic prospects and investor confidence. Bank Indonesia seems unwilling to limit the supply of new money and/or increase the cost of borrowing, for fear of harming growth prospects and the ability of indebted firms to service debt. There are few signs that the current government is prepared to meet these challenges by increasing interest rates and reducing money supply growth in order to restore healthy macroeconomic fundamentals. As a result, the outlook for the economy is for continued price instability in 2003 and 2004.

Export performance

• After rising strongly, export growth began to decline in 2001. In the short term the health of the export sector, in particular manufactures and commodities, will owe much to world demand returning in 2002–03. In the longer term, new markets, especially in China, will be more important in determining the fortunes of the Indonesian exporting sector. More immediately, there are few prospects of a return to real growth in 2002–03, with export growth of 5–7 percent likely in 2003–04.

After rising strongly after the Asian financial crisis, export growth began to decline from mid-2001 and continued at sluggish rates through 2002. In part, this was a result of the impact of slowing growth in the United States and Japan. But it was also a result of increasing concern on the part of foreign importers about Indonesian suppliers' capacities to meet agreed targets for the supply of goods. This development is notable, since until now, including the period during the crisis, most Indonesian firms have managed to maintain production and fill order books on time.

Commodity prices weakness has also damaged the fortunes of export-oriented producers due to the slowdown in world economic growth, especially with regard to soft and hard commodities.

> Indonesia has typically been an exporter of unprocessed or only partially processed raw materials. It is the world's second largest exporter of tin, and a significant exporter of natural gas and tropical hardwoods.

Tourism-generated export revenues have traditionally been a significant contributor to the Indonesian economy, accounting for 11–13 percent of GDP, although this is a considerable reduction on the 20–25 percent they were generating before the onset of the 1997 financial crisis. Total arrivals in 2001 were up slightly – by just under 1.8 percent – compared with 2000.[2] However, the average length of stay and the average expenditure per visit were both down on the previous year, causing total revenues from tourism to decline to only US$5.4 billion compared with US$5.7 billion in 2000.

Not surprisingly, the events of September 11 have compounded the impact on the tourism sector and revenues, especially since the US State Department issued a travel warning advisory urging Americans not to travel to Indonesia, and withdrawing all Embassy and Consulate non-essential personnel and dependants. The latter were permitted to return on 25 November 2001, but in April 2002 the Embassy was still warning US citizens to defer non-essential travel to Indonesia. Unfortunately, the impact of September 11, and the general downturn in US tourism to Indonesia, in particular, will have long-felt consequences for revenue well into 2004.

On the upside, Indonesia was not as affected in 2001–02 by declining exports of electronic goods to the US and Japan as some other Asian countries. In part, this reflects the fact that Indonesia has never been a substantial exporter of such goods, with the economy still relatively underdeveloped in this area with few investment opportunities. Consequently, Indonesia has had much less to lose than many of its regional neighbors.

Nonetheless, the decline in exports has been paralleled by a decline in imports during the corresponding period, leaving the current account in substantial surplus. Rising import demand from consumers will, however, reduce the surplus during 2003–04 to US$21.0 billion.

In the longer term, it is expected that Indonesia's export destinations will move away from the US and Japan to the region's emerging colossus – China. In recognition of this, President Megawati made a formal visit to China in March 2002, where trade was clearly on the agenda. Indeed, the visit was warmly received by the Chinese, although concerns were expressed by Chinese authorities about the treatment of Indonesia's ethnic Chinese business community. As one journalist noted: 'For China, the most important single country in ASEAN is Indonesia, because of its clout in the regional grouping, its size and its vast natural resources, particularly oil and gas.'[3] However, she went on to note that a limiting factor here is the recent history of the treatment of ethnic Chinese in Indonesia: 'News of the targeting of ethnic Chinese in 1998 riots in Indonesia did long-term damage to Indonesia's image in China. In its position paper on Indonesia, China's Foreign Ministry notes the issue 'remains sensitive'.'[4]

In fact, since the fall of Suharto in May 1998, there have been no significant outbursts of anti-Chinese sentiment, and many of the official restrictions on ethnic Chinese have been lifted or at least allowed to lapse.[5] However, discrimination against ethnic Chinese has not been wiped out altogether, with a continuing possibility of anti-Chinese movements re-emerging. On balance, however, this seems unlikely in 2003–04.

Currency movements and projections

- In April 2002 the rupiah was Rp9,500 to the US dollar. It is likely to strengthen slowly throughout 2002–03. While volatility has lessened, this is likely to be tested in the run-up to the 2004 general elections. If tensions are seen to escalate to unacceptable levels, it is likely that the currency will again depreciate up to the Rp10,000 mark and have far-reaching implications for the inflation rate as import prices of essential commodities increase.

The rupiah suffered much greater depreciation in the wake of the currency crisis than any other local currency. From Rp2,400 to the US dollar in mid 1997, it fell to Rp17,000 by early 1998. Early in 2002, the currency was trading at better than Rp9,800 to the US dollar.

The fluctuations in the exchange rate revealed here (see Figure 5.1) correlate closely to the changing political fortunes of government. Thus 2001 started with a steadily declining exchange rate, as disillusionment with the government of Abdurrahman Wahid (elected in November 2000) began to set in, to the point where parliament was contemplating his impeachment around the middle of the year. The selling rate for the US dollar peaked at around Rp12,000 per US dollar, and the buying rate at Rp11,000. When Wahid was succeeded by Megawati, in July, the rupiah strengthened to between Rp9,000 and Rp8,000 to the US dollar. The rate then worsened again until mid November, and then rose. By mid April, following the Paris Club agreement on the rescheduling of debt repayments, the rate was around Rp9,500 to the US dollar, the best it had been since Megawati's election to the presidency.

The bottom line: Stability into 2003

There may be some slight retreat from this position in the short term. However, the factors that strengthened the rupiah in late 2001 and 2002 – including stability in government,

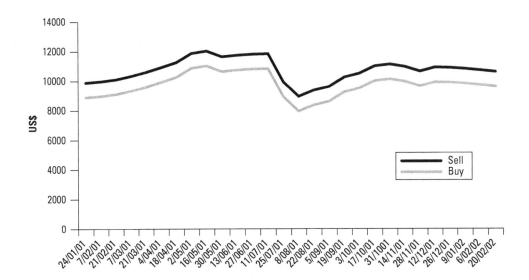

FIGURE 5.1 Exchange rate: Rupiah to US dollars

rescheduling of foreign debt, and some successes in the selling of government-owned assets to foreign buyers – are likely to continue through 2002–03. The prognosis for the future is, at worst, for the maintenance of an exchange rate just under the Rp10,000 level, and possibly for some continued slight strengthening into 2003–04.

Financial markets: Performance and developments

- The banking system remains in disarray, with no immediate prospect of a significant revival. The proportion of non-performing loans (NPLs) is, however, falling, and will continue to do so during 2002–03. Growing foreign investor interest, evident since 2000, will aid restructuring but interest will continue to be restricted to better managed, typically smaller Indonesian banks. On the downside, pseudo-nationalist opposition to such purchases will also continue, making it a high-risk environment for foreign investors.

The Indonesian banking system virtually collapsed following the onset of the financial crisis in 1997–98. In an attempt to rescue the system, Bank Indonesia provided emergency liquidity support (BLBI); the government established the Indonesian Banks Restructuring Agency (IBRA) to take over banks that could not otherwise be rescued, rather than allowing them to go bankrupt. In both cases, bank owners were required to lodge with the government assets sufficient to cover their debts.

However, this policy has largely failed. There is evidence of massive corruption of the BLBI funds, with many bankers diverting the money into their private companies.

One of the consequences of the government's chosen strategy of taking over failing banks and their obligations rather than allowing them to go bankrupt, is that the government is now the owner of a massive portfolio of under-performing and insolvent companies – a problem likely to drain large revenues in 2003–04, and one that can only be resolved through rationalization and declarations of bankruptcy.

Recapitalization of state banks was completed in 2000. Progress on operational restructuring and improving governance has been slow but positive. The rate of NPLs among the seven recapitalized banks (BII, Lippo, Universal, Patriot, Artamedia, Prima Express, Bukopin), fell to 13.41 percent in October 2001. Return on equity had risen to –3.87 percent during the corresponding period, up from –76.15 percent in December 2001.[6]

A recent sample survey by Bank Indonesia suggests that a significant portion of loans classified as normal or precautionary may need to be downgraded to non-performing status; there are concerns too about the quality of new lending and the pace of increase of new NPLs.[7]

Efforts to divest IBRA of these banks have not yet been very successful. In 2002, IBRA announced the sale to a consortium led by the US funds manager Farallon Investments of 51 percent of the shares in Bank Central Asia (BCA). BCA is by far the best-run of the major banks, and has a nation-wide branch network. The sale, as one observer put it, 'earns the government points with the International Monetary Fund and brings in 5.4 trillion rupiah (US$541 million) of sorely needed cash.'[8] But the sale caused considerable controversy in Indonesia and overseas: Farallon has no experience in running a retail bank; the return garnered by IBRA represented a low rate of return on its investment; members of BCA staff opposed the sale on the grounds that it would allow a vital national asset to fall into the hands of foreigners. The government has stood firm in stating that the sale is final and will not be reviewed, and that a smaller bank, Bank Niaga, would be next for divestment. However, quasi-nationalist opposition to the continuing purchase of these assets by foreigners will continue in 2003–04.

Private and public debt

- Government debts, though starting to decline, are still close to 100 percent of GDP. Negotiations with the Paris Club of creditors in April 2002 led to a rescheduling of $5.4 billion of repayments to the end of December 2003. Private sector debts are such that virtually all major firms in the country are technically insolvent. The outlook is bleak, with the bulk of corporate and public restructuring yet to be done.

In 1996, Indonesia's government debt was 23 percent of GDP; by the end of 2000, this had risen to nearly 100 percent. A major reason for the government's indebtedness is the costs it incurred in rescuing the nation's bankrupt banks following the onset of the financial crisis, together with energy subsidies and poorly designed fiscal decentralization reforms.[9] About half of this debt is owed to international creditors.

IBRA has acquired a massive portfolio of companies, pledged by their former owners against unpaid loans taken over by the government. The sale of these assets, and of government-owned companies, has reduced the extent of the repayment burden. In 2001–02, IBRA had a target of recovering Rp27 trillion in cash and Rp10 trillion in bond redemptions – it met (and in fact slightly exceeded) these targets. Targets for 2002–03 are Rp35.3 trillion in cash and Rp7.5 trillion in bond redemption.[10]

Asset sales have proceeded very slowly, and have been hampered by quasi-nationalist opposition to foreign investors. This anti-foreign sentiment is likely to remain for the foreseeable future, and may in fact become stronger as the 2004 elections approach and political leaders feel the need to demonstrate their nationalist credentials. Consequently, in 2002–03 it will be difficult for the government to maintain the rate of sales of assets achieved in 2001.

As part of its efforts to reduce the repayment burden, Jakarta has been negotiating with its major creditors in the Paris Club for a re-scheduling of at least part of this debt. In April 2002, agreement was reached on the re-scheduling of $5.4 billion, comprising both principal and interest debt for between April 2002 and December 2003. The deal reduced Indonesia's debt burden to instalments of $2.7 billion from $7.5 billion over the period.[11] Both the rupiah and the Jakarta Stock Exchange (JSX) index strengthened on news of the

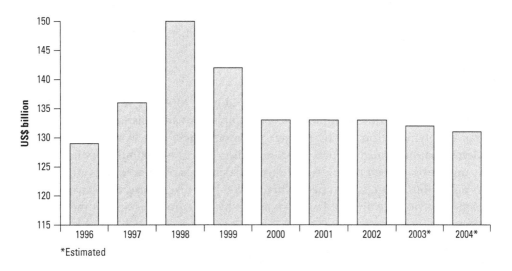

FIGURE 5.2 External debt (US$ billion), Indonesia 1996–2004

agreement, although at the same time Standard and Poors announced it was lowering Indonesia's sovereign rating to Selective Default.

In sum, the risk of sovereign default is ever present, although small. Likewise, Indonesian's corporates remain a high credit risk, with many failing to properly report debt on the books.

Labor market trends

• Wages will continue to rise slowly during 2002–03 in the order of 2–5 percent for unskilled workers. Underemployment levels, particularly in urban areas, will not decline significantly in the absence of any general recovery of the economy. Industrial activity will increase, but considerable slack needs to be worked through the system before employment gains match economic growth. The labor pool will increase by 3 percent per annum during the forecast period.

Both wages and employment levels have taken a severe hammering since the onset of the financial crisis. Official unemployment figures have usually been around the 10 percent level, but these are virtually meaningless in a society with no unemployment benefits available and thus no incentive to be recorded as unemployed – and the work test is so low as to render useless even the figures produced.

In any event, underemployment is a much greater problem. Estimates of the proportion of the workforce working less than full-time, and wishing and available to work full-time, range up to 40 percent. Levels of underemployment are higher in urban areas than in rural areas,[12] reflecting the relative scarcity in the cities of informal employment opportunities.

Wages paid to unskilled and semi-skilled workers fell significantly in real terms for much of 1998 and well into 2000. By late 2001, however, they had recovered the ground lost in the previous four years, and were above their pre-September 1997 levels.

Militant unions

Labor militancy has increased significantly. In mid-June 2001, for instance, labor unrest convinced the government to rethink its plans to implement administrative decrees relating to severance or termination pay by private employers. These decrees aimed to reverse an earlier decree that mandated payouts upon severance.[13] Most of the militancy has not been centrally organized; though there are now several federations of labor unions, none of them exercises tight control over its members. Where strikes have taken place, they have often been accompanied by violence, initiated as often as not by the employers and/or the state as by the employees.

Foreign enterprises and unions

Foreign firms have generally had a reasonably good record in industrial relations in Indonesia, although Korean – and, to some extent, Taiwanese – firms are often portrayed as treating their workers worse than their US and European counterparts.

Unfortunately, foreign firms have been an obvious target for labor activity because of their international vulnerability to charges of exploiting a wage force that is very lowly paid by almost any standards. Many firms also complain that the police are unwilling to protect them from illegal actions taken by strikers, including obstruction of access to work sites and damage or destruction of property.

There are few signs to suggest that these practices are improving. For foreign enterprises, in particular, the threat of industrial action turning violent remains a risk for a large number of organizations operating in Indonesia.

Although there have been complaints of Koreans mistreating their employees, there have been even louder complaints from Korean businessmen and women who claim that police do not arrest those who have obviously committed crimes and do not protect company property in times of labor unrest.

Consumer and business confidence

• Consumer confidence remains surprisingly high, and will remain high in 2002 and 2003. Beyond this, much will depend on the degree of instability in the run-up to the 2004 general elections. Business confidence, though, is much more difficult to read. It is low for major companies, but stable and perhaps rising for small- and medium-sized enterprises (SMEs).

While consumer confidence in Indonesia is relatively high at present, it is also usually very fragile and subject to substantial fluctuations over fairly short periods of time.

In large part, business and consumer sentiment have tended to be driven by domestic political developments more than economic data. When questioned on their perception of their personal prospects for the six months to June 2002, respondents reacted more positively than at any time since December 1999, following the country's first reasonably free general elections since 1955, and first ever free presidential election. The presidency of Abdurrahman Wahid, though, quickly soured, and confidence fell. But Wahid was replaced as president by Megawati Sukarnoputri in mid 2001: the relatively high level of consumer confidence expressed in December 2001 suggests that Indonesians were still satisfied that under Megawati the country was generally moving in the right direction.

This view, that despite the macroeconomic picture, consumer confidence is strong, is further supported by the level and rate of growth of consumer advertising expenditure in Indonesia. The annual rate of growth of advertising expenditure, at 27.5 percent, was the highest of 11 Asia–Pacific countries surveyed by AC Nielsen.[14] The main driver behind this

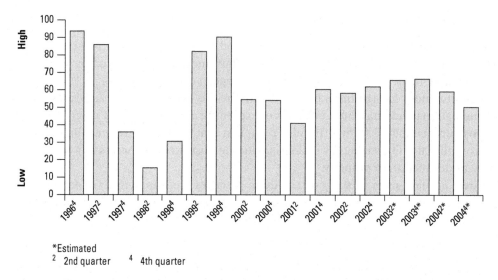

*Estimated
² 2nd quarter   ⁴ 4th quarter

FIGURE 5.3 Business and consumer confidence, Indonesia 1996–2004
Source: 'MasterCard International's MasterIndex Asia-Pacific Survey', 7 February 2002

growth in advertising was 'the unexpected resilience of consumer spending power, particularly in terms of sales of grocery products, and the highly competitive TV market with the entry of several new television stations.' 'I think everyone has been surprised,' the company's managing director remarked, 'by how well sales of fast-moving consumer goods (FMCG) have held up, despite the economic slow-down.'[15]

The one significant measure of consumer confidence that seems to be running the other way is vehicle sales, which after being in the 25,000 to 30,000 units per month range for most of 2001, fell to just under 16,000 units in December. The January 2002 figure was back up to nearly 23,000, however, suggesting that December might have been an aberrant month.[16] Maintaining this figure throughout 2002 and into 2003 will be difficult. Vehicle makers are bracing themselves for flat sales figures for 2002–03, as growth continues to be sluggish.

Business confidence, though, seems to be another matter altogether. The trend here is clearly downwards, with the election of Megawati represented by only a slight reduction in the rate of decline.

One of the reasons for the continuance of low business confidence levels is that the government has taken no effective steps to reform the country's notoriously corrupt legal system. Under considerable international pressure, in September 1998 the parliament adopted a Bankruptcy Law to replace a Dutch colonial law of 1905, and established a Commercial Court to administer that law. Progress in this area was seen by many business-people and other observers as crucial to the process of economic recovery: the government has thus far disappointed observers and those companies struggling to enforce opaque legislation on debtor companies.

'Several decisions to date demonstrate that the Commercial Court . . . appears not to fully understand the (Bankruptcy) law or the principles underlying it. Most decisions of the court have tended to favour the local applicant over the foreign creditor and the government as a creditor.'[17]

On the other hand, it should be recalled that during the 1980s and 1990s business confidence was high – even though the legal environment was, if anything, worse than today. Indeed, it was certainly even less transparent than it is now. The crucial point here is stability in the system, and business's familiarity with it. Most businesspeople can operate in a system with these characteristics, even though the legal environment is corrupt – they simply do not resort to the law in the case of contractual or similar disputes.

Stock market

- Trading values and volumes are likely to remain low for the foreseeable future, the JSX composite index will trend upwards but remain below 550 in 2002–03. Volatility will continue to be the order of the day, as will the lack of corporate transparency and suitable prudential supervision. The stock market should be avoided for all but the most risk-tolerant investors.

The stock market is largely open to foreign investment and to foreign participation more generally. Since 1987 foreign firms have been permitted to form partnerships with Indonesian interests to act as underwriters, broker-dealers, and investment managers.

Illiquid and volatile

The extent of the damage done to the JSX since mid-1997 is massive. Apart from the obvious factors, such as the massive devaluation in the rupiah, the equally debilitating debts owed by most of the major firms listed on the exchange and the flight of foreign capital from the exchange, stock prices were also badly hit by the withdrawal of domestic capital, much of it owned by Sino-Indonesian businesspeople. From 2000 to 2001, the dollar value market capitalization fell 35 percent; as a percentage of GDP, market capitalization fell 32 percent.[18] There is no immediate prospect of a return of this capital in 2002–04, nor of a substantial return of foreign investment, for that matter. Prospects are thus for a continuation of recent trends, which would see the composite index oscillating between the 450–550 levels.

Moreover, potential investors need be aware that the JSX is subject to fluctuations that sometimes challenge rationality. Relatively minor rumors can cause significant buying or selling activities. Predicting index levels is thus more than normally difficult. However, to the extent that rational forces predominate, the composite index is likely to rise slowly, boosted by improving economic growth and investment data. However, the rise will not be consistent, and will not exceed 550.

Corporate tax

- Corporate taxes are applied inconsistently. The major problem foreign companies face is the effect of the decentralization of most taxing functions to regional governments, which rarely have clearly stated and applied policies in the area. The risk of adverse changes to the taxation system during 2003 and 2004 is high. Investor caution is strongly warranted.

The major challenge facing business is not the level of corporate taxation as such, but rather the inconsistency of its application. The legal system is such that the level of taxation payable is a negotiable one, albeit that foreign firms tend to pay their taxes more than most Indonesian enterprises.

Further inconsistency has arisen as a result of the central government's efforts to decentralize political authority. Regional governments now have formal control over a wide range of taxation matters, formerly the sole preserve of the central government. And few of these governments have yet worked through what their positions on corporate taxation should be. The 2001 *Indonesian Human Development Report* noted that: 'Already districts anxious about their budgets have been introducing new taxes on local businesses.'[19] Foreign enterprises will obviously be the next target of these practices in 2002–04.

Indeed, foreign enterprises, in some areas at least, seem to have been singled out for particularly tough treatment.[20] Mining companies, in particular, have been hard hit. The vast bulk of these companies operate in regional or rural locations, and in many cases in regions subject to separatist movements, such as Aceh and Papua. Risk mitigation and management strategies should be the norm for any prospective investor operating in such regions.

But some regions have adapted more quickly to the new conditions, and recognized the value in trying to attract, rather than tax, foreign investors. For instance, one mining industry newsletter reported that many resource-rich provinces, such as West and South Kalimantan, are offering special incentives to attract investors, and many others appear to be preparing to do the same. It seems likely that, as time goes on, the competitive atmosphere currently developing between the provinces will result in more attractive opportunities.[21] However, this will not be apparent until after 2004–05.

In the short term investors should brace themselves for the tax climate to remain fluid for some time to come. The most that can be said with confidence is that foreign companies are unlikely to see the kind of taxation rules they were used to from the central government appearing in most of the regions in the foreseeable future. Uncertainty will be the norm.

Residential and commercial property markets

- The middle and upper levels of the commercial, retail and residential property markets have not yet recovered from the 1997–98 crisis. However, the lack of any significant new investment since 1998, and the slowly rising levels of demand in some sectors, means that property markets will strengthen slowly over the course of 2003–04.

There has been a steady recovery in the occupancy rates of leased and serviced apartments from the lows reached in the first two quarters of 2000, although occupancy rates for strata-titled apartments had, in fact, never fallen since before the crisis. The people who made the commitment to buy a strata-titled apartment – a legal possibility for foreigners only since 1996 – were predominantly long-term residents of Indonesia, and in some cases citizens.

The leased and serviced apartment market is more likely to attract transient tenants. The occupancy rate pattern confirms the view that the bulk of the flight from Indonesia in 1997–98 was of people with relatively short-term experience of the place, or whose employers were in this position. The rising occupancy rates for the latter type of apartment may well be accounted for by some return to Jakarta of short-term residents. Another reason, though, is that some strata-title apartment developers are converting their holdings to leased apartments, to meet the rising demand for that type of residence.[22] This is a trend that can be expected to accelerate in 2003, and possibly into 2004.

In the case of both types of apartments, though, some of the demand has come from expatriates, and wealthy Indonesians, who have moved out of rented or owned houses, attracted by the greater security apartment buildings offer. The recent major flooding in Jakarta will accelerate this trend in 2002–04.

Jakarta market is soft

Premium office space in the Jakarta CBD had suffered vacancy rates almost reaching 50 percent in late 1999 and early 2000. By July 2001, this had fallen to just above 15 percent. The market was dominated by tenants, with substantial pressure being exerted on building owners to reduce rentals. Lower grade office space had also suffered increases in vacancy rates in 1999–2001, but not to anything like the extent of premium office space.[23] The average rentals for premium office space in the Jakarta CBD in 2002 were in the order of US$10–16 per square meter per month.[24] Little appreciable increase is anticipated in 2002–03, with moderate increases anticipated in 2004–05.

The prognosis for 2002–03 is for some signs of revival in the market as the economy stabilizes and starts a mild improvement. With a major office development likely to enter the Jakarta market in 2002 and adding 28,000 square meters to the stock of just over 4 million square meters of office space, though, any increased demand is unlikely to produce substantially increased rentals to building owners.[25]

Retail property strong growth

The market for shopping mall space continues to outperform other sectors of the property market, reflecting the growth in consumer expenditure during 2001–02. Occupancy rates have been above 90 percent since the first quarter of 2000. In 2001–02, shopping malls in the greater Jakarta region recorded an occupancy rate of 97 percent, despite the addition during the year of a further 48,000 square meters of space bringing the total available space up to 1.67 million square meters.[26] Any visitor to Jakarta over the past three or four years will have noted that right through the depths of the financial crisis, upmarket shopping malls such as Pondok Indah, Taman Anggrek and Senayan Plaza remained well-stocked, with some turnover of shops but with the major international retailers maintaining a presence.

Rental rates have been rising, with premium space commanding monthly rentals of US$70 to US$80 per square meter. On average, rentals rose in 2001–02 by about 10 percent in Jakarta itself, and 5 percent in the surrounding regions.[27] Similar double digit increases are expected during 2002–03.

Foreigners remain forbidden to buy property. They can, however, secure a 25-year lease over property, which can be extended twice to a maximum of 70 years. However, as the Chair of Real Estate Indonesia, Yan Mogi, noted recently, Indonesia is suffering by comparison with neighboring countries in terms of the difficulties placed in the way of foreigners accessing land. If access was made easier, Indonesia would benefit economically, and the recovery of the property sector would be greatly accelerated. Mogi proposed making leases valid for 75 years in the first instance, permitting foreign purchases of land, and making bank credit available to foreigners wishing to purchase land. Unfortunately, there is no real urgency to enact the proposal in law, as is clearly indicated by later comments: 'The government has nothing to worry about . . . the property is in Indonesia, and is not going anywhere.'[28]

However, even if the government were inclined to alter the laws – and there is no sign that it is on its agenda – there would be a massive public backlash against what would be portrayed as a further selling off of vital national assets to foreigners.

Foreign direct investment

• There are no indications that foreign direct investment (FDI) from traditional sources – US, Japan, Western Europe, Australia – will return to pre-1997 levels in the immediate future. The mining sector, once the driving force behind high levels of FDI into Indonesia, is in a slump – new investment has stalled and most of the current investment relates to exploration expenditure required for companies to maintain operating licenses. There is no sign of a turnaround in 2003–04. Until the decentralization process is more certain this will not change.

Indonesia suffered major foreign disinvestment from 1997–98 as investors fled the economic meltdown and political crises. In 1997, foreign non-oil and gas investment totaled US$33.8 billion; in 2001, it was only just over US$9 billion.

One of the major causes of disinvestment has been the flow of ethnic Chinese-owned funds out of the country following the riots of May 1998. There is little evidence of any substantial quantity of this money coming back yet. However, it appears possible that some of these funds might actually be returning, having been laundered through other countries.

Chinese-owned companies made two major investments in Indonesia in early 2002. Chinese oil producer CNOOC Ltd. has agreed to pay US$585 million for the Indonesian oil

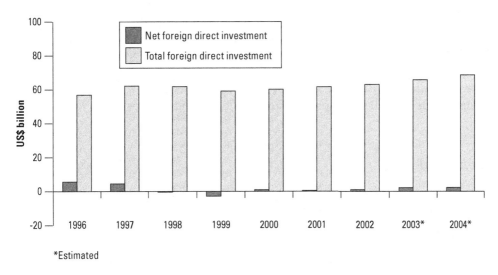

*Estimated

FIGURE 5.4 Foreign direct investment, Indonesia 1996–2004
Source: Bank Indonesia, Economist Intelligence Unit Forecasts

operations of Spanish company Repsol-YPF. The cash deal was the company's largest invest-ment outside China and made CNOOC the largest offshore oil producer in Indonesia.[29] In early April 2002, China's largest oil company, PetroChina, announced that it would buy Devon Energy Corp's Indonesian oil and gas operations for US$216 million.[30] Given that both the companies purchased were already foreign-owned, however, the Chinese invest-ment did not add to the total volume of foreign investment in Indonesia.

> Several mining companies have run into significant problems with local communi-ties, especially over the disposal of waste products from the mining process, and over ownership of and access to mining sites.

Mining FDI down: More risks to investors

For the mining industry – long a mainstay of the Indonesian economy – business activity has been trending downwards for some time. Foreign investment in the industry fell 35 percent in 2000–01 compared with the year before, which was itself down 50 percent from its peak in 1998.[31] The industry put forward a set of reasons for this decline, which was substantially greater than that experienced by the mining industry worldwide. These included: increased levels of labor unrest and associated illegal activities, fraudulent land-ownership claims, illegal mining and legal uncertainty following changes in the laws relating to mining and forestry.

Uncertainty among mining companies has been further compounded by the reluctance of political risk insurers to extend coverage for mining operators throughout the archipelago. Where cover has been available it has been expensive and for short tenures, making project financing difficult. There are few signs, particularly post September 11, that insurers are willing to reconsider the current position and extend much-needed cover. As a result, mining FDI levels will stay depressed well into 2004, and perhaps beyond.

FDI: Not all bad news

On the other hand, by no means all foreign companies have left the country. One observer has calculated that fewer than one in 10 of the 3,000 foreign companies operating in Indonesia in 1997 have left.[32] But to make a success out of staying, these firms have had to adjust their activities to the new economic and commercial realities: re-packaging their product, shifting production from domestic to export markets, changing their management styles and personnel.

These type of management innovations are evident in a number of large-scale foreign enterprises. For example, in order to maintain volumes and margins, Procter and Gamble Co. and Unilever Group now make smaller shampoo and detergent sachets that the newly poor can afford. For its part, L'Oreal of France has given up on trying to crack the domestic market and switched to an export strategy. Consequently, 70 percent of the cosmetics produced at L'Oreal's Jakarta plant now go overseas to Malaysia, Singapore, Thailand, Hong Kong, Taiwan and China.[33]

Perhaps of even greater significance is that a number of large multinational enterprises have recruited Indian managers to run their Indonesia operations. Indian managers are paid 60 percent less than Americans, and their experience in dealing with the vagaries of doing business in India is said to prepare them better to do the same in Indonesia.[34]

Finally, and optimistically, there has been some new investment. In January 2002, for example, Honda commenced construction of a new car manufacturing plant at Krawang near Jakarta. Representing an investment of US$30 million and scheduled to come online in April 2003, it will be capable of producing 40,000 automobiles annually.[35] However, the lack of new FDI into the manufacturing and mining sector has been the norm in Indonesia, and can be expected to continue into 2002–04.

The bottom line: High risk

Despite tentative signs of improvement, as represented by a limited amount of new FDI funds during 2002, Indonesia will remain a high-risk environment for investors throughout 2003–04 and beyond. The uncertainty caused by decentralization will not recede in the near future, though the initial indications are that it is not as bad as many feared in the period leading up to the promulgation of the law by parliament.

Section C Politics

- President Megawati's position is secure through to the 2004 presidential election, but the military will continue to wield political influence. Decentralization will remain the principal challenge facing the Jakarta government, as well as governments at the provincial and district/city levels. So too, this will be the principal operating difficulty for foreign investors, with the risk premiums increasing as the administrative divisions become blurred. This will pull foreign enterprise through a barrage of conflicting juridical environments, compliance regulations, and burgeoning provincial level taxes. Islam will continue to rise as a political force, though translating this into parliamentary power will be more difficult.

President Megawati is secure for the rest of her current term of office. In part, this reflects the fact that there is lacking any clear and widely acceptable successor. However, she will likely not seek a second term of office. The current vice-president, Hamzah Haz, from the Islamic-oriented Justice Party, is playing an increasingly prominent role in economic and political affairs, and positioning himself for a run for the presidency. However, given the small support base of his party at the 1999 elections, he will not be successful unless he is able to persuade a substantial portion of the supporters of other Islamic-oriented parties to back him. This is unlikely to happen.

The arrest and trial of Akbar Tanjung – Speaker of the People's Consultative Assembly (MPR) and Chair of the Golkar Party – on corruption charges, could cause a rift between Golkar and Megawati's PDIP, that might threaten their de facto coalition. If this coalition did break, then Megawati's administration, with its main party holding only one-third of the seats in parliament, might find it difficult to operate in 2003–04. However, this is probably an unlikely eventuality. Indeed, Golkar and PDIP need each other's support; neither wants to be manipulated by any of the smaller parties, especially those with an Islamic base. Thus, sheer political pragmatism is likely to keep the coalition in place, even if Tanjung is convicted and jailed – itself no means a foregone conclusion.

Powerful military but peaceful?

The political position of the military has eroded substantially since the fall of Suharto. Public trust in the military is probably at an all-time low. However, it has made something of a comeback under Megawati, whose particular form of nationalism resonates with several powerful military leaders. Yet, while elimination of all political activities by the military is unlikely, it is also unlikely that it will be able to re-assert anything like the influence it enjoyed in the 1970s and 1980s.

The commercial interests of the military, though, remain virtually untouched. Military companies are still prominent in industries such as transportation, hospitality, logging and plantations. These activities will not be curbed in 2003–04, if for no other reason than that such a move would confront the government with the dilemma of how to finance the military outside of its own commercial business base. Indeed, it is currently estimated that the military probably receives only 25 percent of the funds it needs for its operations from the state budget: the rest comes from sources such as its commercial enterprises.[36] Cutting out these enterprises would require a major increase in state funding for the military – or a substantial reduction in the size of the military budget, which, in effect, would mean a reduction in the size of the military. Neither of these options is likely to be attractive to any government coming to power in Jakarta in 2004.

Secessionist conflict

Jakarta is facing demands from the regions for greater autonomy, which in some cases might extend to demands for independence from the Indonesian state altogether. These demands are strongest in the resource-rich provinces, including Aceh in north Sumatra and Irian Jaya or West Papua in the east. Revenues derived from the provinces, such as royalties on mining and taxes on industrial production, have historically all gone to the central government in Jakarta, which has then disbursed small sums back to the provinces. This situation needs to be reversed, and virtually all the major parties acknowledge that this must happen.

Some progress has been made in starting to address these issues. In April 1999, the parliament passed laws on regional administration and finances relating to the devolution of political and financial power around the country.

Decentralization

New decentralization laws are still to be put fully into practice. It is hard to imagine that the national bureaucracy will readily give up much of the power it has acquired over the years. Nor is it likely that many public servants located in Jakarta will be willing to be transferred from the national public service to a regional public service – never to return to Jakarta again. Moreover, many political observers have been warning that the provinces face a variety of problems in exercising these new powers, including a lack of skilled human resources and inadequate administrative capability to capitalize on the advantages the new situation is supposed to offer.

> One of the major legacies of the Suharto era was the almost complete disintegration of civil society, independent of government. There are thus few, if any, institutions outside government that can act as a brake on its worst excesses.

If regional bureaucracies are strengthened sufficiently to handle the extra workload, this could cut time- and resource-consuming bureaucratic red tape considerably. However, little change is anticipated in the forthcoming two years. Change will be incremental, thereby necessitating close monitoring by foreign investors throughout 2002–04 and beyond.

On the other hand, devolution of authority to the regions is also likely to make operations of some foreign companies outside Jakarta, and certainly outside Java, more problematic. Local governments are likely to be much stricter than the central government in Jakarta ever was on a number of issues including, notably, the environment.

Unsolved environmental issues

In the past, Indonesian environmental legislation was rarely observed. Foreign companies tended to observe the legislation rather more than local companies, but even foreigners seem never to have been particularly worried about the environmental impact of their operations. However, regional governments are likely to want to enforce environmental protection legislation much more than Jakarta. The companies likely to be most affected are those in the mining industry and in the processing of agricultural and forest products – industries that typically impact very substantially on the local environment.

Mining companies have also had broader regulatory problems with regional authorities. The Rio Tinto-owned coal miner PT Kaltim Prima Coal (KPC), for instance, has had major problems with the government of the province of East Kalimantan over the company's efforts to divest itself of a proportion of its shares to local buyers. The provincial government has clearly decided it wants those shares for itself, and has embarked on a series of complicated legal – and not so legal – blocking maneuvers to prevent KPC selling the shares in the normal way. The central government seems unable to force or persuade the provincial government to honor the terms of the original contract signed with KPC.

Leading risk indices: Corruption, stability, governance, risk

Corruption

For decades Indonesia has had a reputation for high levels of corruption, in business, politics and the courts. The latest indexes suggest that corruption is at an all-time high, likely driven post-1997 as a result of continuing deteriorating economic conditions.

However, part of this apparent increase in corruption might also be accounted for by better reporting procedures. There is now a greater openness to identifying corruption, reporting it to authorities, and generally acknowledging that corruption is antithetic to the return of economic stability, foreign investment, and integration into the global trading system.

This development is not entirely new, of course. Even during the Suharto era, reports of corruption made the domestic press, and certainly the foreign media. But these reports were constrained by the need not to violate the implicit bounds of reporting established by the government and its allies – the principal beneficiaries of corruption.

Today, with the Indonesian news media being one of the freest in the region, reporting of corruption is virtually unlimited. Commentators feel able to report virtually any issue of corruption that comes to their attention. As the UNDP noted recently: 'Corruption may still be extensive but it is far less acceptable [than previously] – and no longer considered inevitable.'[37]

Unfortunately, while the press is much freer than it was in the past, it is not particularly skilled in using that freedom. Reporting is not of a high standard and there is no real way of knowing how accurate many of the reported incidents of corruption are.

Nevertheless, as President Megawati has acknowledged,[38] in a sense it is irrelevant whether the results of corruption surveys are correct or not: it is the perception that they measure that is of concern to those managing the Indonesian economy.

Top level corruption: still a problem

Top level corruption is still a major problem in Indonesia. More recently, one of the best known of these cases involved Syahril Sabirin, the Governor of Bank Indonesia (BI), and Akbar Tanjung. Sabirin was convicted in February 2002 of the misuse of BI funds made available to private banks, and was sentenced to three years' jail. Yet, at the time of writing he remains not merely free, but still holds the governorship of BI. Sabirin argues that the decision of the court is not final, since he is launching an appeal against his conviction, and thus there is no reason for him to step down from his post. His fellow directors of BI have supported him in this position. The reputation of BI for prudential management has never been particularly high; this puzzling interpretation of the law and of the principles of good governance have reduced it further. Likewise, Akbar Tanjung has been charged with embezzlement of state funds. After being kept in jail for two weeks he was conditionally released pending his trial. He retains the position of Speaker of the People's Consultative Assembly.

Both such cases serve to highlight the fact that while corruption might now be more freely acknowledged, it does not always lead to a curtailment of corrupt practices through

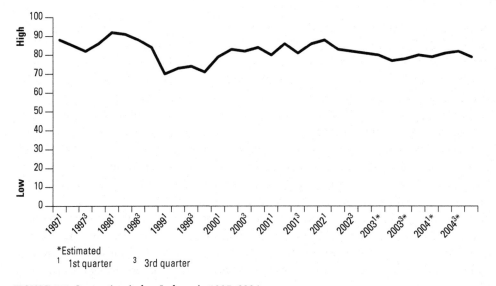

FIGURE 5.5 Corruption index, Indonesia 1997–2004

public sanction. International investors should thus continue to beware of the systemic nature of corruption in Indonesia, which will have a bearing on any business activity in the country.

Corporate governance

Despite the rhetoric about the need to improve corporate transparency, corporate governance levels have proven to be stubbornly low in Indonesia and will continue to be so in 2003–04. This problem threatens Indonesia's long-term economic health, and, more specifically, that of the financial sector, leaving the country highly vulnerable to future adverse economic events.[39] The absence of good corporate governance was one of the chief reasons why the crisis of 1997–98 has proven so prolonged and severe.

> The political parties are now free to take on virtually any ideology they wish – except communism, which remains banned. Despite this, no political party has taken up the cause of good governance with any great vigor, preferring, for the most part, to seek to share in the spoils of office and otherwise perpetuate the wrongs of the past.

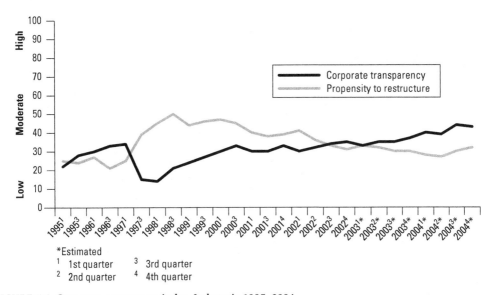

*Estimated
1   1st quarter   3   3rd quarter
2   2nd quarter   4   4th quarter

FIGURE 5.6 Corporate governance index, Indonesia 1995–2004

Corporate governance methodology:
- The corporate governance index is a composite index measuring the juridical requirements for corporate disclosure and financial reporting, prudential regime adequacy, prudential compliance enforcement, and the juridical reach of prudential authorities.
- The propensity-to-restructure index is a composite index based on media releases and reported corporate restructuring as a result of prudential regulation, financial incentives, loan restructuring/re-negotiation, or asset realignment.

However, achieving the good corporate governance ideal will be a difficult task in Indonesia, with no discernible signs of any strident advances to date. Having a largely free press is an important step, and some progress has been made along these lines in recent years. But the issue goes much further than that – albeit that not many of Indonesia's political elites are prepared to acknowledge this fact and act on it. Poor corporate governance will thus continue to dog Indonesia, keep foreign capital away, and perpetuate the poor state of economic development.

Political stability

The one element of civil society that has exercised very considerable autonomy from government is Islam – and in a variety of forms. Overtly Islamic mainstream political parties did poorly in the 1999 elections, securing a total of less than 10 percent of the popular vote. Nonetheless, representatives of these parties in the parliament continue to push for measures to recognize a more formal position for Islam in the Indonesian state: if not for the establishment of Islamic law as the law of the land, then at least for state support for the obligation on Muslims to obey Islamic law in their personal lives. There is little likelihood that they will succeed in these endeavors in the foreseeable future, but they are likely to continue to press the issue with ramifications for on-going political stability.

Islamic militants: On the rise?

Less mainstream Islamic organizations have acted more radically. Organizations such as the Islamic Defenders' Front (Front Pembela Islam: FPI) and the Indonesian Committee for International Islamic Solidarity (Komite Indonesia untuk Solidaritas Dunia Islam: KISDI) have been critical of the influence of the West in Indonesia – particularly of the role and influence of the United States, and by extension, the IMF. Indeed, there are certainly Islamic voices that call for cutting ties with the US and the IMF, and repudiating the foreign loans that Indonesia has contracted, on the grounds that these simply serve the interests of foreign capitalists and not Indonesians. Again, there is no real likelihood of these demands being met, but there is no real likelihood either that this will dampen the enthusiasm of those promoting them. Invariably, this could lead to sporadic and violent outbursts, especially if economic conditions worsen in Indonesia in 2003–04.

> FPI and like-minded organizations have taken the role of guardian of the morals of Indonesian society, organizing attacks on bars, discos and massage parlors. The security forces have done little to protect owners of businesses from these attacks. These problems will persist in 2003–04.

Further to the radical end of the religious–political spectrum, organizations like Laskar Jihad (Holy War Warriors) have taken part in inter-religious violence, especially in Maluku and Poso. They are not the only people to have done this. In Maluku at least, Christian militias have also been active, and arguably as brutal. But the leaders of Laskar Jihad have secured a degree of quasi-official recognition, suggesting that some government leaders either sympathize with their aims and methods, or else are afraid to confront them for fear of the political fallout. In most cases, it is likely to be the latter, even though this greatly exaggerates the degree of popular support groups such as these really have. These developments should serve to caution foreign investors about the longer-term stability of Indonesia as a destination for investment.

Foreign investor risk index

The events of September 11 both weakened and strengthened the Megawati government in its competition with radical Islam. It weakened it in the sense that Islamic groups were more adept than the government at playing on public disquiet about the way the United States reacted to these events, and in particular to their attacks on Afghanistan.

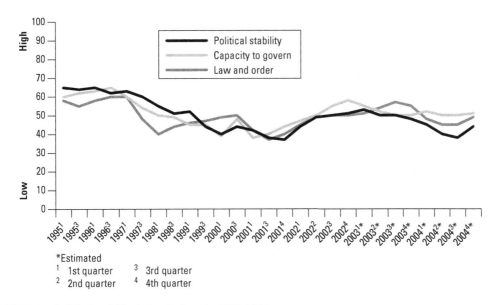

FIGURE 5.7 Political stability index, Indonesia 1995–2004

Political stability methodology:
- The capacity-to-govern index is based upon the institutional reach of government defined in terms of its ability to set the political and economic agenda and ensure its legislative program is enacted without significant compromise. This index is adversely affected by legislative opposition, lack of legislative implementation, failure to realize government policy and general political opposition.
- The political stability index measures violent opposition or organized demonstrations, terrorist activities, and popular discontent that adversely affect the institutional and electoral stability of the government.
- The law and order index measures the propensity to civil obedience, and the institutional reach of the rule of law in terms of regulatory compliance and enforcement.

However, in the longer term the government was probably strengthened, inasmuch as Washington now has little option but to support the Megawati administration and, significantly, its military allies. Military ties, broken following the violence in East Timor in 1999, are already being reviewed and have largely been reinstated, and US ties with the Indonesian National Police have also been resumed. So too, public support for demonstrations against the United States, never particularly great, faded dramatically after the rapid collapse of the Taliban regime.

Overall, the likelihood that civil society will strengthen sufficiently in the short to medium term to demand accountability by government is slight. Good governance will not be part of the Indonesian political scene in 2003–04, or indeed the foreseeable future.

For this reason, doing business in Indonesia will remain high risk. Investors will still make money but the number of those losing money may rise before it falls. It will take some time, likely after the 2004 elections and possibly into 2005, before the reform process will be taken seriously again; for now the main priority is stability and growth. Provided the two goals are met, business risk in Indonesia will remain static during 2002–03.

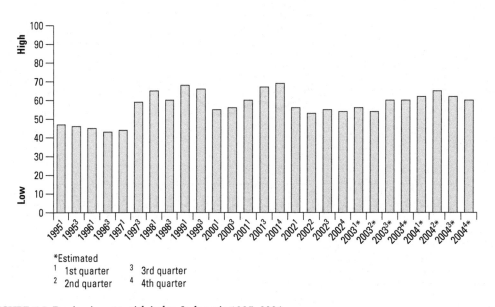

*Estimated
1 1st quarter   3 3rd quarter
2 2nd quarter   4 4th quarter

FIGURE 5.8 Foreign investor risk index, Indonesia 1995–2004

Foreign investor risk index methodology:
- The foreign investor risk index is a composite index measuring tax burdens, discriminatory regulatory practices, adverse compliance regulations, government policy toward foreign enterprise, receptiveness to issuance of government contracts, foreign enterprise commercial restrictions, and official attitudinal changes to foreign direct investment and foreign commercial operations which impact on operational efficiency. The index also incorporates a nominal measure for market risk and market failure.

Section D Security

- Separatist movements in Aceh and Papua continue to threaten national territorial integrity, but are unlikely to succeed in the foreseeable future. Communal violence is declining, but is still a threat to internal security. Crime is rising, and foreign business-people contemplating visiting Indonesia need to be aware of potential threats to their personal security.

Stability in Indonesia: Rising or falling?

The 1999 referendum in East Timor that saw the region vote overwhelmingly for independence from Indonesia has highlighted other separatist movements in Indonesia. Some foreign observers suggest the break-up of the state is imminent. This is most unlikely. There are a number of so-called separatist movements in several parts of the country, such as in Riau in Sumatra and Ambon in Maluku, but these are of little real consequence. The only meaningful separatist activities are being undertaken in Aceh and Papua.

The latter two separatist movements will continue to threaten national territorial unity, and directly challenge the prospects for foreign-owned mining companies operating in these two provinces, particularly the natural gas fields in Aceh centered on Lhokseumawe and the copper and gold mine at Tembagapura in Papua.

In the short term, the Aceh problem is the greater threat, with an armed separatist movement, the GAM, posing a major political and ethical challenge to Jakarta. However, the GAM is unlikely to secure any significant international support, especially in light of the aftermath of the events of September 11.

In the medium to long term, however, the situation in Papua will prove more difficult for Jakarta to deal with. The Free Papua Movement (OPM) though in the past splintered, shows signs of acquiring greater unity in 2002–05. It is also likely to secure increasing political and perhaps financial support from human rights and church groups overseas in Europe, the United States and Australia. This may not be sufficient to bring about success for the OPM, but it is likely to heighten the conflict, and to place further strain on Indonesia's relations with those foreign powers.

> Communal conflict has risen significantly since 1998, and while it does not threaten the continued existence of the Indonesian state, it does illustrate the powerlessness of central authorities to impose order on Indonesian society. Expect more of the same in 2003–05.

Major current conflicts

The major current conflicts are between Muslims and Christians in the Maluku islands – especially Ambon – and around Poso in Central Sulawesi. Central government-sponsored talks held in late 2001 and early 2002 at Malino in south Sulawesi, however, produced peace accords signed by most of the warring factions in both these locations. Though there are likely to be continued outbreaks of violence, the prognosis is for a gradual return to something approaching normalcy.

Since the resignation of Suharto in May 1998, there have been no outbursts of anti-ethnic Chinese violence. If this situation is maintained, which appears likely in 2003–04, it would augur well for Indonesia's social and economic future.

Crime

Common crime is on the increase. The police force, never a major deterrent to crime in Indonesia, and indeed a major participant in the crime of corruption, shows an increasing reluctance or incapacity to enforce the law. Almost daily, Jakarta newspapers report angry mobs catching alleged thieves, arsonists, kidnappers and other alleged offenders, and meting out their own rough justice to them, sometimes beating them to death. Unfortunately, unlawfulness will continue and likely worsen in 2003–04.

The major Western embassies in Jakarta now routinely warn their citizens to keep car doors locked when traveling, to vary their routes through the city, and to stay at home when demonstrations are planned. On the other hand, some of the threats of violence or intimidation against foreigners have not eventuated. The best examples are the threats to 'sweep' Americans out of Central Javanese cities such as Solo, issued by radical Islamic youth groups. Nothing came of these threats, although when they were issued in 2000 and 2001 the potential for them to cause real trouble was substantial.

Section E Economic and political risk forecasts

- Political stability will continue in Indonesia at least into 2003, albeit fragile. The economy will stabilize, and gradually improve. The run-up to the general and presidential elections in 2004 will, however, be a source of possible instability, with foreign investors well advised to prepare for disruptions to production and delivery schedules, and to take action to protect and insure property and plant.

There is general recognition among economic and political policy-makers in Jakarta that the country has run out of options. Although some political leaders and parties regularly call for breaking with the IMF and the repudiation of the country's foreign debts, they have little influence on policy-makers, and will not acquire such influence in the foreseeable future. Nonetheless, even among much less radical politicians there is concern, and resentment, at the degree to which the government has pushed Indonesia into the red in order to pay the debts of bankrupt – and largely ethnic-Chinese-owned – conglomerates. This resentment requires little for it to surface and break out into street protests. Investors should exercise caution in 2003–04.

Short-term forecasts

- Megawati's government will continue along the same general policy road it has followed thus far in 2003–04; a policy direction that, while it does not have the full support of the IMF, does at least have its tacit acceptance. There will, however, be no great reforms of the economic or political systems.
- Economic recovery will be slow in coming, and unlikely before 2003–04, but the economy will stabilize and strengthen to some extent. Economic growth in 2002–03 is likely to be between 3.8 percent and 4 percent.
- The JSX will continue to be characterized by weak demand and low trading volumes. The composite index will remain in the range 450–550 in 2002–04.
- Inflation and interest rates will trend downwards but remain around 10 percent; the rupiah will remain better than Rp10,000 to the US dollar, and will probably be around Rp9,500 by the end of 2002–03. In 2004 its valuations will improve, albeit nominally.
- The 2004 general and presidential elections have the capacity to disturb political stability and thus threaten a continuation of the fragile stability forecast above. If the elections produce a parliament and a president with fewer connections to the Suharto regime – and assuming that Suharto himself dies before the elections are held – the post-election period may see more economic and political reforms than in the years since 1998. This will increase instability in the short term, but lay a much stronger foundation for economic and political recovery in the long term, post-2007. There is a reasonable likelihood of this scenario eventuating.

Short-term opportunities

- Foreign enterprises operating in Indonesia face continuing uncertainty, but for those with the patience and foresight to stick it out, the longer-term prospects are favorable. Indonesia remains resource and labor-rich, and with a consumer-oriented middle class that, while it has taken some hits over the past four years, remains comparatively wealthy.
- A primary short-term opportunity lies in the supply of consumer goods to the urban, middle- and upper-class market catered for by hyper-supermarkets. Food – fresh, pre-packaged or prepared – is a major component of this demand, but it extends to juices, drinks, cosmetics and fashion items.
- Overseas education continues to be in high demand. Foreign universities are now permitted to establish joint venture campuses in Indonesia, and to offer twinning programs with Indonesian institutions. Indonesians still want to study overseas, though following the devaluation of the rupiah they have become more cost-sensitive, with the result that increasing numbers of students are going to regional centers in places such as Malaysia and Thailand.
- Professional services – accounting, legal, management and the like – are in high demand by companies wanting to restructure and re-position themselves in local and international markets. Some barriers to the employment of foreign professionals remain, but their removal – or at least reduction – is under way.

- The sale of government-owned assets offers opportunities for investment in banks, insurance companies, commercial property, plantations, mining and manufacturing. There will continue to be opposition to foreign takeovers of these assets, but for companies willing to factor this in to their cost calculations, and to forge politically and commercially valuable partnerships with local interests, there are profitable acquisitions to be made.
- The devaluation of the rupiah has seen growing demand for reconditioned motor vehicles and parts – especially the latter. The same is also true of reconditioned parts for machinery used in manufacturing. This trend will continue into 2002–04.
- Oil and gas exploration, despite the problems with regional governments, remains important and potentially profitable. However, investors need to be cognizant of the full ambit of politically centered problems they will encounter, and to undertake appropriate risk management and mitigation planning prior to investment.

Overall risk rating

Indonesia's short-term (2002–03) risk profile is fairly stable, albeit at levels high enough to frighten off many potential investors.

There will be no major challenges to the political leadership of Megawati during 2002–04, and no new challenges to the nation's security or territorial integrity. The major economic parameters, such as economic growth rates, inflation, interest rates and the exchange rate, are likely to improve slightly through to mid-late 2003. The political and economic risks involved in commercial dealings with Indonesia, evident in the past four years, will not increase and will probably decline.

However, the elections of 2004 loom as a major problem. The nine to 12 months prior to the elections – likely to be held in June – will see increased political tension as parties and politicians strive for advantage. Foreign investment or commercial activities in or with Indonesia will not be targeted by any of the mainstream political forces, but will inevitably suffer from a rising of the political temperature.

Risk: Medium to high, but stable, until mid to late 2003 when it will start to increase. → ↗
Risk Rating (0 = lowest, 10 highest risk) 7.0

Section F Indonesia fact sheet*

Geography

Capital
Jakarta

Largest city (millions, 2000 est.)
Jakarta, 9.7

Location
Southeast Asian archipelago between
the Indian Ocean and the Pacific Ocean

Adjacent countries
Malaysia, Singapore, Philippines,
Papua New Guinea, East Timor. Also
shares maritime boundaries with India
and Australia

Terrain
Mostly coastal lowlands; larger islands
have interior mountains

Land use
Arable land 10%, permanent crops 7%,
permanent pastures 7%, forests and
woodland 62%, other 14% (1993 est.)

Area (km²)
Total: 1,919,440
Land: 1,826,440
Water: 93,000

Miscellaneous
Population: 228,437,870 (July 2001 est.)

Economic statistics

Currency
Rupiah (Rp)

Exchange rate (April 2002)
US$1.00 = Rp9,350

Gross Domestic Product (GDP 2001)
3.3%

GDP per capita
$728

GDP per capita – PPP (2000)
$2,900

GDP – Composition by sector (2000)
Agriculture 17%; mining 13%;
manufacturing 26%; electricity, gas,
water 1%; construction 7%; trade 15%

Transport and communications
Finance 6%, public administration 5%,
other 4%

**Percentage of the population earning
less than US$2.00 per day (1998)**
20

Inflation rate (2001)
12.55%

Foreign debt (billions)
$140

* All figures are the latest available except where indicated. All figures are in US dollars. Figures are
compiled from national, international and multilateral agencies (International Monetary Fund, World
Bank, World Development Report, UNESCO Statistical Yearbook, International Labour Office, United
Nations, Central Intelligence Agency World Fact Book). Gross domestic product (GDP) refers to the value
of all goods and services produced in the preceding financial year. GDP per capita, Purchasing Power
Parity (GDP per capita – PPP) refers to the indices developed by the World Bank to take account of price
differences, cost of living differences, and relative purchasing power of a set basket of goods and services
between countries so as to provide a more accurate measure of national wealth.

**Current account balance
(2001, billions)**
$6.32

National unemployment rate (2000)
6.4

**Adult economic participation rate by
gender (2000)**
Female 41%
Male 59%

Labor force (2000, millions)
90

Labor force by occupation (2000)
Agriculture 45.3%, industry 13.5%,
service 41.2%

Budget (billions, 2000)
Revenues: $26
Expenditure: $30

Industries (2002)
Petroleum and natural gas, textiles,
mining, cement, chemical fertilizers,
plywood, food, rubber, tourism

Major exports (2000, US$ billions)
Animal oils and fats 17.7%, mineral
fuels 15.7%, basic manufactures 12.3%,
machinery 10.8%, petroleum and petrol
products 7.7%

Major imports (2000, US$ billions)
Machinery 9.2%, mineral fuels 6.7%,
chemicals 5.9%, basic manufactures 5%

Major trading partners (2000, exports)
Japan 21.4%, US 14.2%, Singapore
10.1%, South Korea 6.8%, Netherlands
3.2%

Major trading partners (2000, imports)
Japan 12.1%, US 11.8%, Singapore
10.5%, Australia 6.1%,Germany 5.8%

**Income/wealth distribution
(1996 household income or
consumption by % share)**
Lowest 10%: 3.6%
Highest 10%: 30.3%

Televisions (1997, per 1000 population)
60

**Telephones (1999, millions, lines in
use)**
29

**Cellular phones per 100 population
(2000)**
1.73

Internet users (2000, per 10,000)
94.3

Fiscal year (from 2001)
Calendar year

Government and political statistics

Nature of government
Republic

Constitution
August 1945, abrogated by Federal
Constitution of 1949 and Provisional
Constitution of 1950, restored 5 July 1959

Structure of government

Executive branch
The president is both the chief of state
and head of government. Cabinet is
appointed by the president, and the
president and vice president are elected
separately by the 700-member People's
Consultative Assembly or MPR for five-
year terms; election for president last held
23 July 2001 (next to be held NA 2006)

Election for vice president last held 26 July 2001 (next to be held NA 2006)

Legislative branch
Unicameral House of Representatives or Dewan Perwakilan Rakyat (DPR) (500 seats; 462 elected by popular vote, 38 are appointed military representatives; members serve five-year terms)

President
Megawati Sukarnoputri

Vice-president
Hamzah Haz

Ministers

Coordinating Minister for People's Economic Affairs
Dorodjatun Kuntjoro-Jakti

Coordinating Minister for People's Welfare
Yusuf Kalla

Coordinating Minister for Political and Security Affairs
Susilo Bambang Yudhoyono

Minister of Agriculture
Bungaran Saragih

Minister of Culture and Tourism
I Gede Ardika

Minister of Defense
Matori Abdul Djalil

Minister of Energy and Mineral Resources
Purnomo Yusgiantoro

Minister of Finance
Boediono

Minister of Fisheries and Maritime Affairs
Rokhmin Dahuri

Minister of Foreign Affairs
Noer Hasan Wirajuda

Minister of Forestry
M. Prakosa

Minister of Health
Ahmad Suyudi

Minister of Home Affairs
Hari Sabarno

Minister of Justice and Human Rights
Yusril Ihza Mahendra

Minister of Manpower and Transmigration
Jacob Nuwa Wea

Minister of National Education
Abdul Malik Fajar

Minister of Religious Affairs
Said Agil Munawar

Minister of Resettlement and Regional Infrastructure
Soenarno

Minister of Social Affairs
Bachtiar Chamsyah

Minister of Trade and Industry
Rini Suwandi

Minister of Transportation
Agum Gumelar

State Minister of Acceleration of Development in Eastern Indonesia
Manuel Kaisiepo

State Minister of Administrative Reform
Faisal Tamin

State Minister of Communication and Information
H. Syamsul Muarif

State Minister of Cooperatives and Small and Medium Enterprises
Alimarwan Hanan

State Minister of Culture and Tourism
I Gede Ardika

State Minister of Environment
Nabiel Makarim

State Minister of Research and Technology
M. Hatta Rajasa

State Minister of Revenues and State Companies
Laksamana Sukardi

State Minister of Women's Empowerment Affairs
Sri Redieki Soemarjoto

Head, National Development Board
Kwik Kian Gie

Attorney General
Muhammad Abdul Rachman

Main parties
Partai Demokrasi Indonesia Perjuangan (PDI-P, Indonesian Democratic Party of Struggle); Golkar; Partai Kebangkitan Bangsa (PKB, National Awakening Party); Partai Persatuan Pembangunan (PPP, Development Unity Party); Partai Amanat Nasional (PAN, National Mandate Party); Partai Bulan Bintang (PBB, Crescent Moon and Star Party); Partai Keadilan (PK, Justice Party)

International memberships
APEC, ARF, AsDB, ASEAN, CCC,CP, ESCAP, FAO, G-15, G-19, G-77, IAEA, IBRD, ICAO, ICC, ICFTU, ICRM, IDA, IDB, IFAD, IFC, IFRCS, IHO, ILO, IMF, IMO, Inmarsat, Intelsat, Interpol, IOC, IOM (observer), ISO, ITU, NAM, OIC, OPCW, OPEC, UN, UNCTAD, UNESCO, UNIDO, UNIKOM, UNMIBH, UNMOP, UNMOT, UNOMIG, UPU, WCL, WFTU, WHO, WIPO, WMO, WToO, WTO

Business organizations
KAPI, PAI, GAPENSI, KADIN, APIKRI, AREIBI, ASIN

Date of UN membership
1955

Social statistics

Population (2001, million)
228.4

Population density (2001, per square km)
119

Fertility rate (2000, average number of children per woman)
2.6

Maternal mortality rate (2000 est., per 100 000 births)
373

Infant mortality rate (2000 est.)
46/1,000 live births

Population growth (2000 est.)
1.6

Life expectancy (1998)
Men: 63.7, Women: 67.5

Ethnic composition:
Javanese 45%, Sundanese 14%,
Madurese 7.5%, coastal Malays 7.5%,
others 26%

Religions
Islam 87%, Protestant 6%,
Catholic 3%, Hindu 2%, Buddhist
and other 1%

National languages spoken
Bahasa Indonesia (official, modified
form of Malay), English, Dutch, local
dialects, the most widely spoken of
which is Javanese

**Literacy rate (% over 15 can read and
write, 2000 est.)**
Male: 90
Female: 78

Japan

6 Japan

S. Javed Maswood

Section A Economy

Overview

In early 2001, Junichiro Koizumi was appointed leader of the ruling Liberal Democratic Party (LDP) and became Japan's new Prime Minister. His rise to power is directly attributed to his personal charisma and popular support. If the selection had been entirely up to the parliamentary wing of the LDP, it is unlikely that Koizumi would have received the appointment because of his reputation as a maverick politician.

Not being the party's preferred leader, however, has added to his popular credibility and support. Unlike his predecessor, who had a popularity rating in the single digits, successive public opinion polls in 2001 showed Koizumi enjoying support among 80 percent of the electorate – an unprecedented level for any postwar Japanese politician. Koizumi has thus been regarded as a politician who can both help to restore popular trust in the highest political office and implement necessary structural reforms to lift the economy out of its stagnation and recession. Indeed, the Japanese electorate was generally disenchanted with a succession of politicians unable to resolve a decade-long economic crisis with traditional Keynesian fiscal measures.

Ordinary Japanese have invested a great deal of faith in Prime Minister Koizumi and his capacity to reform a moribund economy. Koizumi himself has stoked these expectations with promises of extensive structural reforms and deregulation to eliminate bottlenecks and inefficiencies in the regulatory framework and functioning of the Japanese economy that, traditionally, has resisted change and innovation.

The Japanese economic crisis remains a complex mix of periodic recession, deflation (prices have been falling at around 1 percent a year), relatively high levels of unemployment (5.5 percent during 2001–02), high levels of non-performing loans (NPLs) in the banking sector, and low business and consumer confidence. While the fall in price levels has been a boon to the few Japanese still spending, most Japanese continue to postpone their consumption in anticipation of lower prices. Moreover, for the large number of debtors, deflation has increased their debt repayment burdens.

Throughout 2001–02, Koizumi has promised structural reforms, privatization and deregulation, as well as administrative reforms to make the government more accountable. He has also promised a resolution of Japan's banking crisis that has starved even viable businesses of investment capital. While Japan has enjoyed a regime of cheap credit with low nominal interest rates, it remains the case that the increasing value of NPLs has made banks wary of adding to their loans portfolio for fear of running foul of Basle Capital Adequacy Requirements. Cheap credit has, in reality, then, not been available to Japanese consumers, with banks mostly reluctant to lend further given their precarious NPL levels.

As the first step toward achieving popular acceptance of the reform process, Koizumi has been candid in explaining to the electorate that the scale of the reforms envisioned will be both costly to the individual and society, but in the end necessary if Japan's economy is to be reinvigorated and returned to a high growth path in the decades to come. In doing so, Koizumi has convinced the vast majority of the importance of reforms and, in return, his popularity has remained strong, albeit experiencing declines toward the end of 2002.

> The Japanese economy has experienced negative growth for most of the 1990s, and is likely to experience only modest economic growth of around 1 percent in 2002–04. Ongoing structural problems, an aging population, and marginal international competitiveness are holding the Japanese economy back.

Despite popular support and the promise of structural reforms, actual achievements in 2001 have been nominal. Instead, most prime ministerial effort was invested in winning the Upper House elections, perhaps in the expectation that electoral victory would strengthen his position in the party and facilitate the reform process. While the elections were a resounding success for the LDP, the party elders refused to support the reform agenda – essentially stalling the reform efforts of the Prime Minister. Consequently, by the end of 2001 much of the reform momentum had been lost, with the popularity of Koizumi beginning to crumble in 2002. Koizumi has also had to confront the realization that the tenure enjoyed by Japanese prime ministers tends to be short, normally no longer than one or two years. For most observers, then, the lost reform momentum means that the game is pretty much up, and Koizumi's days are coming to an end.

It is now generally acknowledged that Koizumi has run out of steam although he continues to talk tough. The talk now has a hollow ring to it, confirming an assessment by political commentators that Koizumi is 'Mr. NATO' (No Action Talk Only).

Much of this was confirmed when in 2002 Koizumi's attention seemed to be absorbed with instability in the Cabinet rather than the task of structural reforms. In January, he was forced to dismiss his popular Foreign Minister, Makiko Tanaka, following a series of gaffes and administrative ineptitudes. More damaging to his credibility was the refusal of his first choice as replacement Foreign Minister, the very capable Sadako Ogata, former United Nations High Commissioner for Refugees, to accept a Cabinet appointment.

Tanaka had been in constant conflict with senior bureaucrats and politicians but she was an immensely popular politician and perceived as key to successful reforms. Following her dismissal, the approval rating of the Prime Minister fell to below 50 percent. This diminished Koizumi's strength and credibility in government and adversely affected the pace of structural reform. While Koizumi has continued to publicly proclaim his determination to push through major reforms, few now believe the rhetoric.

Given that crises, and their capacity to shock the system into action, have been a key to change in Japan, it now appears that the way forward for the Japanese economy lies in a new episode of sharp and painful crises to revitalize the reform agenda. Some of the latest indicators confirm that the economy has slipped back into recession; however, economic indicators are not nearly bad enough to provoke a determined attack on the various maladies. The Japanese political economy may be in need of another painful and sharp crisis to force political leaders to muster the political determination for structural reforms.

The bottom line: Opportunities and challenges

Bad as things are, current Japanese equity prices provide an opportunity for foreign investors prepared to take a long position on the Japanese economy. While there remain weaknesses in the economy, including sluggish consumer spending, there is also considerable latent potential and longer-term economic recovery is certain. Indeed, while 2002 began with a dismal economic outlook, the worst is now over. The stock market has recovered some lost ground, for example, and the slide in business confidence has moderated. Recovery, however, will be slow paced and Japan cannot be expected to replicate the strong growth performance of the 1980s any time soon.

> The Japanese economy is slowly opening up to foreign investment and becoming more welcoming of foreign business. However, starting from such a high level of protectionism, this process is far from complete and it will take a series of on-going reforms throughout the coming decade before the Japanese economy will be as transparent as other mature economies in North America and Western Europe.

Many foreign investors have successfully exploited opportunities presented by a crisis-stricken Japanese economy. In the period when Japan experienced economic prosperity and boom, foreign firms complained of not having access to the Japanese market. More recently, many foreign firms, such as The Gap, Carrefour, Starbucks, Gucci and Bulgari, have established a firm foothold in Japan. Others have acquired Japanese companies, such as the

Merrill Lynch acquisition of Yamaichi Securities and Ripplewood's acquisition of the Long Term Credit Bank of Japan (LTCB), which has subsequently resumed operations as Shinsei Bank. Foreign firms have also secured strategic alliances with Japanese corporations, such as the alliance between Renault and Nissan, Daimler Chrysler and Mitsubishi Motors, and that between Ford and Mazda. This reflects fundamental weaknesses in a Japanese auto industry that has suffered a loss of international competitiveness and low profits. The auto industry in Japan is ripe for significant restructuring, and foreign interest is an acknowledgement that outsiders are likely to be more successful in pushing through restructuring programs than their domestic counterparts. Two of the leading car manufacturers, Nissan and Mitsubishi Motors, for example, both have foreign chief executive officers. This trend is likely to continue.

The Japanese economy used to be inhospitable to foreign investors, and government policies were intended to protect local firms from foreign takeovers and competition. There is now, however, a more welcoming attitude toward foreign investment because of what it can contribute by way of improved management processes and streamlined operations. The example of the LTCB is especially noteworthy because the bank was initially nationalized before passing into foreign ownership and control.

Section B Risks and projections

Macroeconomic performance and risk indicators

- The Japanese economy has been in a long period of stagnation and intermittent recession since the collapse of the bubble economy in the early 1990s. In past economic crises, Japanese economic recovery was achieved through export-led economic growth. This might be the case again in 2003–04 as the US-led global economic recovery helps restore Japanese exports and boost GDP growth. At the same time, however, the government will have to tackle the problem of price deflation, a situation which has led to sluggish domestic demand. While there is no indication of a return to high economic growth rates, looking ahead, Japan can expect to avoid any further worsening of market conditions and, indeed, post a modest recovery on the back of export growth.

The 1990s was a decade of lost opportunities for the Japanese economy. After the economic bubble of the 1980s, growth ground to a halt in the early 1990s and the entire decade was marred by economic stagnation with only brief and intermittent periods of modest recovery.

Government efforts since the early 1990s to reflate the economy through extensive fiscal measures have produced little positive effect. Instead, fiscal measures have only added to the public sector debt burden. Likewise, a deepening fiscal crisis forced the government to introduce fiscal austerity as an official goal, declaring that it was unprepared to drive the fiscal position further into deficit.

As a result, the economy experienced a marginal contraction in 2001–02. In large measure, this reflected the fall in domestic personal spending, which accounts for 60 percent of GDP, and which continued to fall, down by 1.7 percent. In 2002, economic growth has run to around 0.5–0.6 percent. During 2003–04, Japanese government estimates predict a growth rate of around 1 percent per annum. While not robust, the growth projection is achievable, especially with the anticipated upturn in the US economy. Much will depend on the external environment and developments in the export sector, especially demand for electronic consumer equipment and vehicle exports, both of which should experience a strong uptake in the US economy in 2003–04.

Domestic sources of growth remain weak, however, due mainly to rising unemployment and projected cuts in public works spending. Consumer sentiment in Japan has been weak for several years and consumption demand is insufficient to engineer a domestic demand-led recovery. Japanese consumers are unprepared to commit to increased consumption at a time when prices are falling and are expected to fall further. Further dampening domestic demand is the still fragile employment market, with consumer sentiment reflecting on-going fears about job security. Little discernible change can be expected during 2003–04.

There have been a series of proposals for the government to adopt an inflation target and, essentially, induce domestic spending by eroding savings through higher inflation levels. While this is a popular policy with many economists, the Bank of Japan has not been prepared to adopt it for fear that it may trigger hyperinflation and create still further economic uncertainty. Instead, the Bank of Japan has preferred to keep nominal interest rates at near zero, hoping that cheap credit will induce consumer spending. It has also injected liquidity into the banking system in an attempt to pump-prime the economy and stimulate domestic demand. Despite both efforts, price deflation and contracting consumption have continued, seemingly unabated.

Export performance

- Japan's export performance in 2001–02 was sluggish. Some relief was delivered via a depreciating yen, which in the latter half of 2001 traded downwards against both the US dollar and euro. This provided a brief reprieve for Japanese exports in an otherwise harsh external environment. Much will now hinge on the anticipated recovery in the US, and its possible knock-on effects in Europe, two of Japan's primary markets. Assuming the US-led recovery gathers momentum in 2003–04, the export sector can be expected to enjoy stronger growth.

In all previous Japanese economic crises, exports assisted the recovery process. However, in the current post-bubble Japanese economic crisis, exports have not provided the same benefits. The problem is that many Japanese industries have lost their international competitive advantage. In the 1980s, the corporate sector in Western countries undertook large-scale reform and rationalization programs, successfully transforming their economies and their competitive position in the global economy. Unfortunately, this restructuring revolution completely bypassed Japan. More recently, Japanese corporations announced plans to rationalize their operations. The problem, however, remains the issue of timing, and the urgency with which to pursue corporate reform and restructuring. Recognition of this urgency is not universal in Japanese boardrooms, with reform plans spread out over a number of years, such that little positive result can be expected in 2003–04.

Corporate restructuring and international competitiveness

Despite this, there is growing recognition of the need to reform the economy, with emerging evidence that some Japanese firms are proceeding toward corporate restructuring to regain their international competitive position. Apart from mergers in the financial sector, Japanese steel companies have also shown strong movement toward rationalization and strategic mergers. NKK Steel Corp. and Kawasaki Steel, for example, have integrated their operations under a holding company as of late 2002, and are also negotiating a strategic alliance with foreign steel manufacturers in order to compete effectively with Nippon Steel. It remains the case, however, that the Japanese steel industry is struggling to cope with excess production capacity and falling prices, and, unlike the US, has no recourse to tariffs or other safeguards from foreign imports.

More generally, however, the Japanese export sector has experienced poor performance during 2001–02, reflecting a depressed international environment and overall sluggish economic conditions. In particular, Japanese technology exports were hard hit by the technology sector meltdown in 2001–02. This is of particular concern since there is growing evidence that the fall off in the technology sector represents a longer-term structural contraction and will not rebound any time soon. Reflecting this was the fall in Japan's trade surplus which registered its steepest fall in two decades, down 43.1 percent year-on-year. Combined with the general economic slowdown in the global economy, the export sector has thus tended to contract month-on-month throughout 2001 and early 2002. This has had knock-on effects for the current account surplus, which fell 12 percent in 2001 compared to 2000, and has recorded similar poor results for the first half of 2002. Better prospects lie ahead in 2003–04 as external demand recovers.

Signs of economic recovery in the US, Japan's major export market, have boosted export prospects. From mid to late 2002, for example, the export of cars, trucks and buses posted an increase of 6 percent month-on-month over the previous year. Likewise, electronics and information and communications technology (ICT) industries should also experience a modest pick-up in exports as a result of global economic recovery. By contrast, Japan's steel exports to the US have been affected by the new US tariffs introduced in 2002, ranging from 8–30 percent over different steel products. The steel industry in Japan could be affected further by similar safeguard tariffs by European countries if Japanese and East Asian steel exports are diverted from North America to Europe.

Export opportunities in China

The accession of China to the World Trade Organization in 2001 has important implications for the future of Japanese exports. Under the terms of accession, Chinese tariffs must decrease over time and this will help boost Japanese exports to the increasingly important

Chinese market. For example, Chinese tariffs on imported cars over 3,000cc were cut to 50.7 percent beginning in January 2002, down from 80 percent. The tariff on smaller cars has also been cut from 70 percent to 43.8 percent. More importantly, by July 2006 Chinese tariffs on imported cars will decline to 25 percent. China's accession to the WTO also means that it will no longer be free to take punitive action against foreign manufacturers, as it did during 2001 when it slapped 100 percent tariffs on Japanese cars, mobile phones, and air-conditioners. The Chinese action was in retaliation for Japanese safeguard import curbs on some Chinese farm products.

Currency movements and projections

- In 2001–02 the Japanese yen depreciated significantly, sliding to 127 yen to the US dollar. This has helped offset the effects on the Japanese export sector but will not prove sufficient to pull the economy out of its deflationary crisis. Expectations are that the government will try and stabilize rates at present levels and wait for these to feed through to the economy in the form of slight inflationary pressures.

Reflecting economic fundamentals, 2001–02 saw a significant shift in the value of the yen, depreciating to around ¥127 to the US dollar. In part, the yen was talked down by government officials, eager to help promote export growth and kick-start the economy and overall demand levels.

The lower value of the yen will have some effect on export growth but less than in past years. Indeed, a lower yen is not advantageous to all manufacturing exporters, many of whom relocated overseas when the value of the yen was high and foreign acquisitions and start-up costs were cheap. This made for a spate of offshore movement by many manufacturing and industrial entities, keen to take advantage of a yen which, in 1995, appreciated to ¥80 to the US dollar. This made offshore production attractive, indeed it increased the competitive position of many Japanese firms who were able to take advantage of lower foreign wage costs and avoid a relatively high Japanese tariff regime that made imports costly.

For such enterprises, the decline in the value of the yen has limited appeal; indeed it will pose serious problems for their cost structures in 2003–04, and will also represent diminished profit yields as capital is repatriated to corporate headquarters in Japan. However, for the Japanese economy as a whole the effect can be expected to be positive. The principal benefits of the lower yen will accrue to the electronics, automobile and ICT manufacturing sector.

Dangers of robust export sector recovery?

While not immediately anticipated, if improved international competitiveness leads to an export-led economic recovery, it could diminish the urgency for corporate structural reform and rationalization, with some negative longer-term impact on Japan's economic success. For foreign investors, however, the decline in the value of the yen and low equity prices,

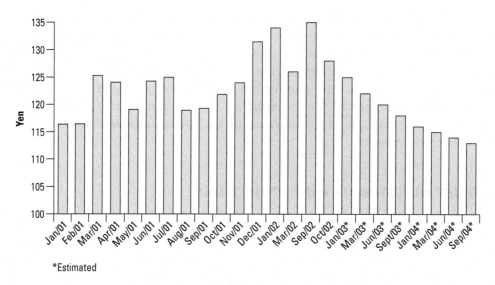

*Estimated

FIGURE 6.1 Exchange rate yen to US dollar 2001–2004
Source: Economist Intelligence Unit Estimates 2003–2004

present opportunities to take an equity stake in Japanese firms. This will be well suited to US venture capitalists, in particular, but should be viewed as a longer-term positioning strategy for entry and market share in the Japanese economy.

The yen averaged ¥121 in 2001, and ¥130 in 2002; a 13 percent depreciation compared with an average of ¥107 in 2000. Most market analysts expect the Japanese government to try and stabilize the exchange rate at around ¥130 to the US dollar. However, there is speculation that the yen could depreciate further to around ¥160, particularly if the interest rate differentials widen – a level that will generate considerable regional and global economic insecurity and instability.

> The yen averaged ¥121 in 2001 and ¥130 in 2002, a 13 percent depreciation compared with 2000. If interest rate differentials between Japan and the US continue, expect a further decline in the yen.

Further afield, a low yen has severe ramifications for regional economic recovery, as it will erode the export competitiveness of countries like South Korea, China, Singapore and Taiwan, each of which has an export-dependent economy. A Korean government official, for example, called the decline of the Japanese yen a 'dangerous' development. Indeed, there is widespread apprehension that further depreciation of the yen will have an adverse effect on regional exports and may, in the worst-case scenario, lead to a spate of competitive devaluations as countries like Korea and China try to recover their lost competitive advantage.

However, Japan is by far more sensitive to pressure from the United States and it is unlikely that the US government will countenance a yen–dollar exchange rate much below 135; a rate that will inevitably lead to further deterioration in their bilateral trade position and greater protectionist pressures in the US. For that same reason, the Bank of Japan, too, will not want the yen to continue its downward slide and spoil export markets in North America through a rise in protectionist sentiment. Market intervention and exchange rate management by Japanese authorities is thus firmly on the agenda during 2003–04.

Financial markets: The burden of non-performing loans

- During the bubble economy years, Japanese financial institutions lent large sums of money against inflated equity and real estate values. Collapse of the property and the stock market since then have left Japanese banks saddled with extensive NPLs with successive governments reluctant to invest public funds in bail-out packages for Japanese banks. However, a decisive and timely end to the NPL crisis is essential if Japanese economic recovery is to proceed. Unfortunately, little immediate action looks to be forthcoming.

Since the early 1990s and the collapse of the bubble economy, NPLs have become a growing problem for the Japanese economy. Unfortunately, the magnitude of the problem has only increased, despite intermittent but half-hearted attempts to provide relief to the banking sector. By 2001, the lowest available estimates of bad debt put the figure at ¥43 trillion, or 8 percent of GDP. The Bank of Japan, however, estimates total bad debt at about ¥83 trillion, or 16 percent of GDP. While since 1992 ¥72 trillion in bad debt has been cleared, the rate with which new bad debt accrues has not seen overall reduction in the NPL problem.

Japan's acute debt problem can be appreciated if one considers the capital base of Japanese financial institutions. The total reported capital base of Japanese banks, for example, stands at around ¥35 trillion according to official estimates – although this is probably overestimated. A more realistic figure is around ¥20 trillion; a position that is grossly insufficient to cover all the problem loans facing Japanese financial institutions, and exposing them to inadequate liquidity relative to NPL bad loan provisions.

As a consequence, Japanese banks have struggled since the early 1990s with mounting levels of NPLs, and with little discernible way out except for the injection of public liquidity. This problem partly reflects the highly protected and inefficient nature of increasing segments of Japanese industries, many situated in the real estate and services sector, and which account for 85 percent of all NPLs. It also reflects an old-fashioned banking culture, with Japanese banks reluctant to call in bad loans for fear of severing long-standing client relationships and losing market share.

The result has been a tendency to obscure the extent of the NPL problem. Indeed, Japanese banks have been reluctant to accurately assess NPLs for fear that they will be forced to set aside larger amounts in loan loss provisions. More generally, there is also an ongoing concern among Japanese financial institutions that many more firms otherwise currently classified as healthy are, in fact, technically risky. The problem facing the banking sector, however, is if they proceed with loan and asset reclassification it will inevitably force the collapse of many Japanese corporations, especially small- and medium-sized enterprises that have limited capacity to ride out a liquidity crunch. Thus 2003–04 is not likely to see a timely solution to the NPL problem, nor rectification of bank liquidity problems, unless the government immediately proceeds with intervention and reform.

On the positive side, Japan's major banks have begun to merge and restructure, hoping to create internationally viable and competitive banking institutions. April 2002, for example, marked a new phase in Japanese banking history with the launch of the world's biggest financial institution, the Mizuho Bank. Government policy has also shown signs of innovation, introducing changes to guarantees on all bank deposits. In particular, the government now guarantees only about 75 percent of bank deposits. Initially, this held out the prospects of a run on the banks, especially since the government also amended its policy of not permitting bank failures, creating what many perceived as increased depositor vulnerability. However, depositor fear did not materialize, allowing the government to reduce its exposure to NPL and bank deposit guarantees, both of which will help discipline the banking sector.

Opportunities for foreign investors

For foreign investors, cash-strapped small- and medium-sized enterprises represent a growing pool of possible acquisition targets during 2003–04, if not beyond. Indeed, combined with a declining yen, the rush for equity buyouts might well see increased foreign investor interest in the very near future.

Public debt: A growing problem?

- Japan's public sector debt is 130 percent of GDP, the highest among OECD countries. To deal with the fiscal crisis, the Koizumi administration introduced fiscal austerity measures, curtailing its public works program and overall expenditure levels. Alongside structural reforms, fiscal austerity will no doubt inflict considerable pain on Japanese producers and consumers in the immediate short term, and contract domestic demand.

In 1999 Japan's total public sector debt was 115 percent of GDP, blowing out to 130 percent by 2001, and continued to climb higher in 2002. Much of the public sector debt was accumulated in the 1990s in the many failed attempts to provide fiscal stimulus to the economy. The many large-scale public works programs that were implemented provided assistance to the LDP-aligned construction industry but failed to revive the economy. Instead, the government has been left with a large public sector debt at a time when aging baby boomers and growing numbers of elderly citizens are expected to impose a greater demand on welfare provisions in coming years. While household savings are sufficiently large to absorb the shock of extended unemployment, of increasing concern for the current administration is the rising cost of health-care provision and the possible drain on public expenditures this will cause throughout the next decade.

At ¥668 trillion, Japan's public sector debt is the highest among OECD countries. To finance this, Japanese authorities have relied extensively on bond issues (about 75 percent of total debt), which are risk rated at the same level as Italy's. In early 2002, falling prices for 10-year bonds pushed yields above 1.400 percent for the first time since April 2001.

While a 'Sell Japan' order will cause havoc in regional and Japanese financial bond markets, and considerable financial fallout for the wellbeing of the Japanese economy, there is little evidence that foreign institutional investors will be pushed in this direction in 2003–04. Japan is not considered a high-risk country likely to default, mainly due to the high individual savings rates and high levels of foreign currency reserves. Indeed, any immediate redemption of Japanese bond holdings by international investors could mostly be covered by domestic Japanese savings. Most Japanese, for example, hold their savings in the government-owned postal system – the largest financial institution in the country and the world. Collectively, these holdings amount to ¥1.4 quadrillion in financial assets, and backed up by the fact that Japan has the world's highest foreign reserves, currently amounting to US$400 billion. Further surety is also provided by the fact that Japan is a net international creditor, such that capital flight, while a theoretical possibility, is unlikely to be realized in what is expected to be an improving international environment in 2003–04.

Among OECD countries, Japan has the highest public sector debt, increasing from 115 percent of GDP in 1999 to 130 percent of GDP in 2002.

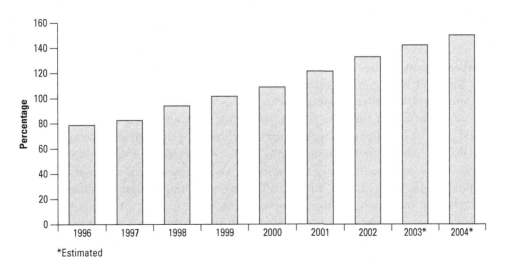

*Estimated

FIGURE 6.2 Debt as percentage of GDP, Japan 1996–2004

To restore fiscal health, the Koizumi administration has pushed ahead with fiscal austerity measures, even in the face of worsening economic conditions. Unfortunately, expenditure reductions so far have not matched the rhetoric of the Prime Minister. To lower health costs, for example, the administration attempted to increase salaried workers' co-payment from 20 percent to 30 percent of medical expenditures, but a strong political backlash saw the budget for 2002 back pedal, causing the PM to state simply that an increase will be implemented when necessary. Unfortunately, the political sensitivity of health-care funding means that the government will have to find other avenues for cost savings, including further cuts to public works spending.

The administration is also facing stiff resistance from within its own party to divert revenue from road taxes to the general account budget. At present, such revenue is quarantined for road construction purposes only. One possible revenue generating policy has been the decision to proceed with preparations to privatize most of the 163 public corporations that are currently a drain on the public purse. As a first step, Prime Minister Koizumi instructed the State Minister for Administrative Reforms to cut government subsidies to public corporations by ¥1 trillion beginning in 2002. However, it is expected that there will be significant resistance to anything more than token privatization from within the ruling party.

Labor market trends

- After decades of near full employment and high levels of job security, unemployment rates increased to a record percent in 2001–02. Unemployment rates for middle-aged men have risen sharply with significant social consequences, and there has been a rapid increase in part-time positions at the expense of full-time jobs. Between 1988 and 2002, the proportion of part-time positions increased from 12 percent to 25 percent. Industrial and corporate restructuring will add to the unemployment problems, as will government attempts to reduce fiscal expenditure.

When Koizumi became Prime Minister, he promised reforms and warned of potential costs and short-term pain. In the months since then, unemployment rates have risen sharply and Japanese workers have begun to feel the pain of an economy in crisis. In the first nine months of 2001, about 800,000 jobs disappeared, with similar figures for 2002. Unemployment levels are set to increase further once the government implements its reform agenda. Overall, the downward pressure on labor costs will continue into 2003–04. In 2001–02, average wages fell by more than 3 percent. Despite assumptions to the contrary, firms in Japan, both domestic and foreign, have considerable wage flexibility because a large portion of wages are paid as semi-annual bonuses that can vary with overall economic conditions and profitability.

In 2001–02, the number of unemployed reached 3.52 million, of whom 1.14 million had lost their jobs as a result of industrial restructuring. The rise in unemployment has affected, in particular, middle-aged men in their fifties, a development not witnessed before in Japanese society and one that is placing considerable stress on the administration to address the problem.

There is no clear evidence, however, that the so-called practice of lifetime employment, common among the big business sector, will be abandoned completely in the near future. Japanese firms are rationalizing their operations but have been reluctant to engage in significant labor-shedding practices, not because of institutional/legal obstacles to retrenchment but because of established norms of labor–management relations. Firms are cautious also because of anticipated future labor shortages as a result of demographic shifts. Taking a long-term perspective, firms are reluctant to introduce measures that may erode employee loyalty to the company and make it harder to retain employees in future.

Growing numbers of well-qualified graduates for foreign enterprises

Regardless, employee insecurity has increased – and much more than in the past, employees are prepared to move from one job to another. With fewer employment opportunities in the public service and major Japanese corporations, foreign firms have become particularly attractive to university graduates. In the past, prospects of lifetime employment in large Japanese corporations and a negative perception of foreign firms meant that they were handicapped in attracting the best and brightest Japanese graduates.

Unemployment in Japan is low by international standards, but historically high by Japanese standards, and likely to remain between 4 and 5 percent in 2002–05 before tending downwards as the reform process helps kick-start economic recovery.

Employment in foreign companies is attractive also because of greater work flexibility and the perception that foreign firms are more likely to reward individual merit than simply seniority, as is the rule in most Japanese companies. The attitudinal shift is significant for foreign firms operating in Japan.

Despite record high unemployment, by international standards unemployment in Japan is only slightly higher than in the US. However, official Japanese unemployment statistics may not reflect the true unemployment position. Many of the unemployed have chosen not to register for unemployment benefits because of the social stigma attached to receiving government welfare. Consequently, even a marked upturn in the economy in 2003–04 is not likely to see an immediate reduction in unemployment levels, as those currently out of the job market will begin to re-enter, adding to the pool of available labor.

One important development in Japan's labor market is the rapid shift in the country's demographics. Japan has a rapidly aging population as a result of declining birth rates and limited immigration programs. By 2020, 27 percent of all Japanese will be over the age of 65, compared to only 16 percent in the United States and 20 percent in Germany. This suggests future labor market shortages and a reversal of current decline in wage rates.

Rise in part-time employment

While full-time employment has declined, part-time and temporary employment have increased. In 2001, for example, part-time employment increased 640,000 to 13.77 million. This highlights moves by companies to lower their labor costs by hiring people on a temporary or part-time basis until economic conditions improve.

The shift in employment patterns has produced the new social phenomenon of *freeters*, or free workers, individuals who are employed on an irregular basis as full- or part-time employees. To some extent this reflects lifestyle choices by individual Japanese but it also reflects shifting employment patterns and some erosion of lifetime employment patterns. The number of *freeters* tripled to around 1.5 million between 1982 and 1997, adding flexibility to the work environment in Japan, especially as temporary and part-time employees do not expect to receive the generous semi-annual bonuses.

While the labor market can expect some improvement in 2003–04, principally through a pick-up in external demand and knock-on effect in the export sector, wage levels will generally remain depressed to stable. Unemployment levels will tend marginally downwards, with previously unemployed workers re-entering the labor market creating an increased participation rate.

Consumer and business confidence

- Falling consumer confidence has been very evident during 2001–02, with contracting consumer demand one of the main factors behind the deflationary conditions. Business confidence is also at low levels despite the fact that there was some increase in business investment activity in 2001–02. Continued fear about income and employment security, as well as general perceptions that prices will continue to deflate, is causing consumers to delay the purchase of consumer durables, especially big-ticket items. Nominal improvements in business sentiment and consumer confidence can be expected during 2003–04 as external conditions begin to improve.

Japan's high savings ratio has become the millstone around the neck of the Japanese economy. Most recently, reluctance to loosen purse strings and increase consumption demand has reflected consumer sentiment that economic conditions could deteriorate. The rapidly aging population also feels the imperative to add to savings for retirement purposes, especially in the context of worsening public sector debt and uncertainty that the state will be able to provide for the post-retirement years. Price deflation has added to the weakness of consumption demand, with consumption being postponed in anticipation of cheaper prices in the future.

In a year where there was a shortage of uplifting news, the birth of a royal princess in December 2001 initially raised hopes, especially among retail traders, that there might be a turnaround in consumer sentiment and a boost in consumer demand, especially with the approaching New Year's gift-giving season. However, by the end of 2002, there was little evidence that this optimism had infected consumers, with continued low sales volumes.

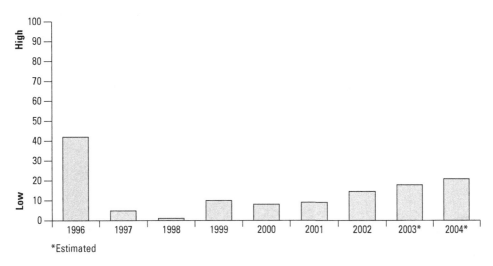

*Estimated

FIGURE 6.3 Consumer and business confidence, Japan 1996–2004

Business confidence has also been severely shaken by continued price deflation that has witnessed diminishing profit margins and falling volumes. Added to this, the technology sector meltdown and general global contraction have generally depressed business confidence with little prospects for dramatic improvement in 2003–04.

The Bank of Japan's *Tankan* business confidence surveys continue to find a gloomy consumer and business outlook for 2003–04. Unfortunately, the only optimistic finding is that consumer and business confidence levels tended to stabilize in 2002, suggesting that the worst is now over and a period of stability lies ahead. However, this comes on the back of a long and protracted period of year-on-year declining confidence, suggesting that the prospects for a return to more normal business and consumer confidence levels is some way off. This will likely take considerable time, however, and is obviously contingent on the pace and reality of meaningful reform – which itself could further destabilize confidence levels – and the rate at which a US-led recovery is able to reinvigorate global demand levels for Japanese exports.

Business confidence in Japan has also been affected by high and growing inventory levels; a combination of declining domestic and external demand for manufactured goods. Compared to previous years, inventory levels in 2001–02 have tended upwards, with no immediate sign of a turnaround in 2002–03. Adding to fears about growing inventories has also been the realization in the business community that no longer can they expect generous government bailout schemes as in the past. Indeed, there have been several examples of large-scale corporate failures, particularly in the banking sector, which, until recently, were considered too important to let fail.

In 2001–02, 14 listed companies were forced into bankruptcy. Unfortunately, it is likely that this trend will continue in 2002–03, as enterprises try to restructure their operations and banks try to recover questionable loans. Declining liquidity levels, in particular, could see a spate of bankruptcies, a prospect that will only add further to gloomy business sentiment.

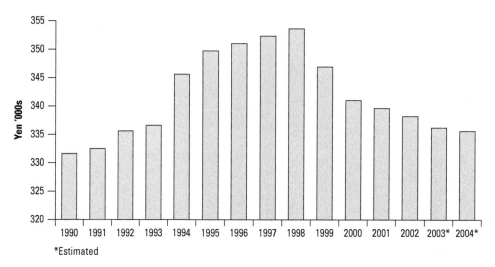

FIGURE 6.4 Household consumption expenditure, Japan 1990–2004
Source: Ministry of Public Management, Home Affairs, Posts and Telecommunications, *Statistical Handbook of Japan*, 2001

Stock market

- The 225-issue Nikkei stock average showed an upward trend in the first few months of 2001 but continued to trend down thereafter, breaking through the 10,000 mark in September. In 2002, the Nikkei has traded moderately upwards, to 11,500, in part reflecting foreign equity acquisitions and the attractiveness of Japanese equities to US fund managers due to the continuing low valuation of the yen. While initial public offerings (IPOs) have generally been few, in 2001–02 as a consequence of depressed economic conditions, there have been a few notable exceptions: Starbucks Japan, MacDonald's Corp. and Dentsu Inc, Japan's largest advertising agency. Corporate rationalization and restructuring, and ongoing, albeit slow movement toward restoring corporate Japan's competitive international position, should see continued interest in Japanese equities in 2003–04.

At its peak in the late 1980s, the Nikkei averaged around the 40,000 mark but collapse of the asset price bubble brought the share market average to very low levels. In 2001, the Nikkei average had opened above 13,000, but after strong initial growth performance lost about 2000 points during the course of the year. In early December 2001, about 150 of the listed companies had share prices below ¥100 (about US$0.80), a level that would have been unthinkable only a few years previously.

In 2001–02, the Nikkei looked for directions from the government and evidence of genuine structural reforms. In its absence, the market has been skittish, tending downwards below 10,000 in 2001 before tending upwards in 2002 to 11,500. In part, the regained

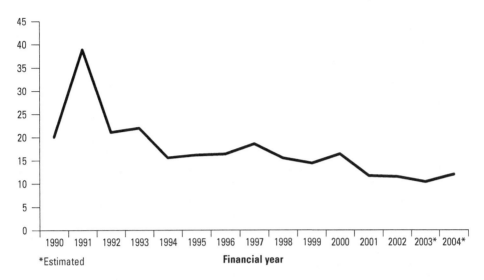

FIGURE 6.5 Nikkei stock market 1990–2004

confidence of the market reflects Prime Minister Koizumi's February 2002 statement in which he rededicated the government to its reformist agenda. So too, it reflects increased foreign portfolio investor interest due to low valuations of the Japanese yen that has made asset and equity acquisition attractive.

Ironically, the skittish nature of the Nikkei does not reflect public sentiment about testing economic times and depressed consumer sentiment. Unlike most other mature markets, the majority of equities on the Nikkei are held by the corporate sector in cross-shareholding deals. Individual share ownership is relatively small, such that the great fall in the Nikkei from its highs in the late 1990s has not had a deleterious effect on individual wealth perceptions. In fact, individual investments amount to ¥1.4 quadrillion or 5.3 percent of their financial assets, a figure that is about one-quarter of the amount invested by individual Americans in the US stock markets. While this has been a blessing in disguise – helping Japan avoid the fallout from what would have been a massive decline in the wealth effect as a result of rapid devaluation of the Nikkei since 1990 – by the same token, revaluation in the Nikkei will not have any discernible short-term wealth effect and help pump-prime consumer spending and aggregate demand.

Of immediate concern to Japanese policy-makers is the fall in equity prices combined with a depreciation of the yen, raising concerns of threats of foreign takeovers of Japanese corporations. Many Japanese firms are ripe for the picking, albeit that the massive spate of takeovers has not as yet materialized. This might not be the case in 2003–04, however, if foreign investors become less wary of Japan's economic prospects with a general pick-up in external economic activity. Assuming equities valuations remain low, and the yen suffers no dramatic appreciation, 2003–04 could well witness a flurry of foreign portfolio investment as well as foreign corporation acquisitions.

Segmented stock performance: What to buy, what to avoid?

During 2001–02, stock performance tended to be segmented. Depressed economic conditions tended to exacerbate declines in stocks associated with construction, housing and real estate. In part, this reflected postponed consumption of big-ticket items by Japanese consumers, but also the effects of declining government spending on public works programs as a result of fiscal austerity measures. This trend can be expected to continue in 2003–04.

By contrast, while the domestic corporate bond market has been in a lull as Japanese corporations focus on restructuring and postpone new investments, there has been a strong growth in the issuance of samurai bonds – yen-denominated bonds issued in Japan by overseas entities. The volume of samurai bonds in 1999 was ¥660 billion and increased to ¥2.5 trillion in 2002. Retail and institutional investors are receptive to samurai bonds, in particular, those issued by known foreign entities, which in recent years have included the South Korean steel manufacturer POSCO, the US insurance company AFLAC, Brazil, and several other Latin American countries. For foreign entities, yen-denominated bonds are a cheaper way of financing projects rather than dollar-denominated bonds, and their continued uptake by Japanese consumers is anticipated during 2003–04. This will likely have knock-on effects for Japanese government bond issues and the success of other capital-raising exercises, with risk-averse Japanese consumers seeking out options beyond traditional savings instruments.

Tax reform: Strategies to assist the corporate sector

- The government has repeatedly promised to introduce major tax reforms, including a consolidated tax structure for corporations in 2002–03, but is having difficulty meeting this commitment. Part of the problem stems from the increasing debt-to-GDP ratio and government concern about reducing revenue streams, especially without a discernible turnaround in the economy. The Japanese Federation of Economic Organisations (Keidanren) insists that tax reforms are needed urgently to restore corporate health and competitiveness. However, little substantial reform is anticipated during 2003–04, as the government sticks to its revenue targets and stringent budgetary measures.

Japanese industries have struggled to maintain their international competitive position and are now engaged in some, albeit modest, reform and rationalization strategies. They have also looked to the government to introduce tax changes that will benefit the corporate sector. In response to these demands, the Koizumi administration promised the introduction of a consolidated taxation system in 2002–03. Consolidated or group taxation will allow firms within a conglomerate to offset the losses of one unit against profits of another. This is intended to lower the corporate tax burden and provide a modicum of stimulation to corporate spending and thus overall demand in the Japanese economy. In the first two years of the plan, 2002–04, the government expects a revenue shortfall of ¥800 billion as a result of group taxation, part of which is expected to be recovered through a 2 per cent surtax on profits over the existing tax rate of 30 per cent.

With the government promising tax reforms, the initial corporate sector reaction was to prepare to take advantage of the promised changes, including mergers and consolidations. In the banking sector, for example, Daichi Kangyo Bank, Fuji Bank and the Industrial Bank of Japan (the Mizuho Group) were on track to complete their merger by April 2002. In the industrial sector, Kawasaki Steel planned to merge with NKK Corporation, and Mitsui Chemicals with Sumitomo Chemicals.

However, as with much of the promised reform agenda, the reality has proven much less than was anticipated. The promised surtax, for example, has in fact removed some of the attractions of group taxation, with a survey of 94 listed corporations in 2002 revealing that 80 percent were reluctant to introduce group reporting of their profit since the benefits were less than attractive.

More generally, the administration has announced its intentions to report on a major overhaul of the tax structure in 2002–03. The tax review by the Council on Economic and Fiscal Policy is part of an initiative to lower corporate taxes. The Tax Commission, however, has entered the debate with a call for reforms to be revenue neutral and for any lower tax ratios to be offset with a broadening of the tax base through a lowering of tax-free thresholds. Since the government wants to use tax reforms to stimulate the economy, it is likely that corporations will find an easing of their tax burden from 2003–04.

What is positive about these developments is the growing realization in the government sector that Japan needs wide-ranging tax reform. To attract individuals to invest in the stock market, for example, it will be necessary to offer them the same tax advantages currently available to personal investors in the postal system. Thus, the administration has tentatively signaled its intention to scope the prospects for offering tax exemption on capital gains in the stock market. If this comes into operation in 2003–04, then obviously the Nikkei will enjoy a strong injection of capital as personal investors shift out of postal savings bonds and deposits and into the stock market.

Unfortunately, it remains the case that tax reform might not be as wide-ranging as initially promised by the administration. To that end, Japan will retain a cumbersome tax regime, depressing otherwise important growth segments in the economy. For example, the Japanese construction industry remains severely depressed, in large measure due to a series of arcane tax laws. A recent study by the Japanese Construction and Transportation Ministry, for instance, estimated that if property taxes were abolished, the nation's GDP would be boosted by ¥6.9 trillion in five years through a combination of increased investment in real estate and construction activity. As presently structured, the prevailing tax system on commercial developments whittles away prospective profits through a plethora of taxes related to building registration, licensing, purchase, and business operation in the first year. Reform could thus re-engineer a robust industry segment with significant benefits for the Japanese economy. Unfortunately, it remains the case that the political road to reform tends to be obstructed by bureaucratic inertia, such that little change is anticipated during 2003–04.

Real estate and property market: A slow road to recovery

- In 2001–02 the property market has remained depressed. Poor business confidence, continuing high taxes and an absence of reform, will see little change in 2003–04, although a pick-up in economic activity might go some way to help stem deflationary prices. Of particular interest in this sector might be the proposed reforms to the tax structure of the property market, with several proposals made by LDP members to spur real estate activity by lowering taxes, including capital gains tax from 26 percent to 20 percent.

The property sector is expected to go through considerably more pain, brought on by a government decision to back away from past practices of large infrastructure and construction projects, a move that will hurt the property and construction industry in 2003–04.

This will continue a contraction in the construction sector that began in the first half of 2001, when the number of new housing construction starts fell more than 6 percent year-on-year. The decline was significantly more than the average for 2000, when housing construction had declined by only 1.1 percent. Again, few prospects for a positive turnaround are anticipated during 2003–04.

Part of the downturn stems from a combination of economic factors: bank reluctance to lend further against an already poorly performing sector which is responsible for a great proportion of the NPLs; deferred consumption due to a loss of consumer confidence and job security concerns; and a tax regime that is particularly high for commercial and residential construction – as well as continued deflation, which is also causing deferred purchases.

> Property markets and real estate have been the hardest hit by the busting of the bubble economy in the mid 1990s. Property markets have continued to deflate, experiencing falling prices year-on-year and contributing to negative wealth and equity effects. This is set to continue in 2003–04, albeit moderating.

In the case of the banking sector, the result has been a general movement away from banking practices based upon long-term client relationship banking in favor of more transparent arm's-length banking arrangements, and one now using better credit risk modeling to avoid taking on additional bad debt. Unfortunately, this is having knock-on effects in the construction industry, with the corporate bankruptcy rate among construction companies increasing significantly as banks withdraw financial support. For example, Aoki Corporation, one of the largest construction companies that had been bailed out by its creditor banks before, was forced to file for protection from its creditors in 2001. This trend can be expected to be repeated during 2002–03 as government construction contracts dry up and cash flows diminish.

Indeed, for prospective investors, the Japanese construction sector is likely to be the most unattractive, since it has been the real estate and property sectors that have been

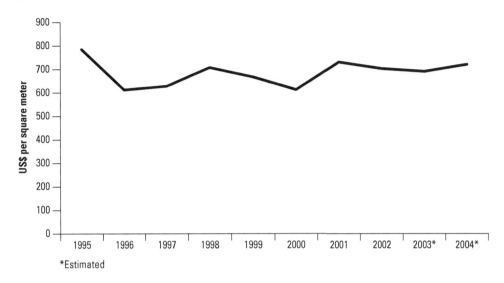

FIGURE 6.6 Tokyo CBD office rentals 1995–2004
Source: Jones Lang LaSalle

the main losers in the current economic downturn. Property prices across the board, for example, have fallen for the last 10 years in a row, the average fall being 5.9 per cent in 2001–02. The decline in commercial property was the greatest at 8.3 percent, while residential land values fell 5.2 percent.

Commercial office space has also registered a general downward movement, with falling revenues mirroring the economic downturn and downsizing endemic to many medium- to larger-size enterprises. This was reflected in the index of office building rents for Tokyo which stood at 250 in June 1993 but by 2002 had fallen close to 120. As a measurement of office space needs, rental returns, and prospects for future commercial demand, this is an ominous index for 2003–04. Indeed, Colliers International's assessment of Tokyo commercial office, retail, industrial, and luxury residential property indicates a continuing downward movement in values and returns for all categories during 2002–03.[1]

While the Japanese property sector was the backbone of the Japanese economic boom in the 1980s, it is unlikely that in the foreseeable future it will again enjoy much store with international investors, and could well repeat a continued net reduction in asset value. If there is a silver lining in the otherwise poorly performing sector, it is perhaps that the slump in property markets is helping reduce start-up and operating costs to business.

Foreign direct investment

- Foreign direct investment (FDI) has played an important role in the restructuring of Japan's corporate sector, growing from around US$29.9 billion in 1996, and increasing to US$64.7 billion in 2002. The amount of inward FDI is high in historical terms but is small relative to the size of the Japanese economy. Indeed, Japan has recently been bypassed as a destination for US and European investors, due to declining economic prospects and stagnant economic conditions. As the economy picks up and international conditions improve, the total stock of FDI can be expected to increase to around US$76 billion in 2004.

Japan is one of the most expensive operating environments in the world for foreign enterprises. Benchmarking costs (labor, land, tax, travel, etc.) for a foreign business in Japan at 100, the cost of doing business in the US is only 66.3 and in Germany 66. Still, foreign business penetration has increased dramatically in recent years because while costs are high, the potential for good returns is also high – albeit confined to specific sectors of the economy such as ICT.

More important have been changes in government and consumer attitudes to foreign investment, which have shifted markedly in the last few years, replacing the relatively closed mentality of Japanese business and government leaders to a now more welcoming attitude. Indeed, foreign investment is increasingly seen as a key element in domestic structural economic transformation and future development of international competitiveness – a process not dissimilar to past foreign diplomatic and political pressure that helped transform the Japanese polity and society.

It remains the case, however, that for foreign enterprise, the costs of establishing operations in Japan, including registration processes, are high relative to other advanced industrial economies. Japanese consumers are also very discerning and demanding. The Japanese market has a reputation for being extremely difficult and unforgiving to new entrants, whether domestic or foreign. Such internationally successful Japanese corporations as Sony and Honda, for example, had to struggle to establish brand reputations and to compete effectively against established Japanese enterprises. This tradition continues, with Japanese consumers wary of new market entrants, and fickle in terms of stringent demand regarding product quality, service, and follow-up client relations.

As a result, foreign firms have found it difficult to operate in Japan. This is reflected in the historically low levels of FDI. For example, Japan generates 13 percent of the world's GDP, provides 13 percent of the world's FDI, but receives less than 1 percent of the world's foreign investment in return. Some of this can be explained by an economy and society traditionally closed to much foreign investment and influence, but much of this is simply due to the peculiarly specific problems of effectively establishing and operating in Japan as a foreign market entrant.

The total stock of FDI has risen from US$27.1 billion in 1997 to US$64.7 in 2002. This is projected to increase to around US$76.3 billion in 2004. While initially impressive, much of the benefits from FDI inflows have been offset by FDI outflows, such that net FDI has actually been averaging around US$–18 billion in 2002, a trend set to continue in 2003–04.

Interestingly, increasing proportions of FDI inflows have been drawn to the Japanese stock market that in 2001–02 saw total FDI amount to ¥1.535 trillion, of which about 86 percent, or ¥1.326 trillion, was made up of foreign acquisition shares in Japanese firms. Again, this represents the effects of a depreciating yen and, since 1995, the precipitous fall in the value of Japanese equities, a trend set to continue assuming a continuing low yen and ongoing low equities valuations.

Foreign investor interest in Japan has thus been of the cherry-picking variety, affording foreign investors a unique and rarely seen ability to pick through blue-chip companies with bargain basement equity prices and an exchange rate further discounting equity acquisition costs. However, this should not be viewed as a shortcut into the Japanese market to establish brand presence and market share. Foreign investors should be prepared to ride out slow growth over the next few years in order to consolidate their presence and devise positions in the market so as to take advantage of future growth and market prospects.

Ironically, a strong and perhaps growing foreign interest in equity acquisition is not all bad for the Japanese economy. Attracting FDI inflows will be an important source of capital for helping stabilize sliding stock prices and returning stability to a stock market that, since 1995, has experienced one of the severest devaluations of any OECD country. Recognizing this, there has been a marked shift in attitudes toward foreign investment and many Japanese companies have welcomed foreign equity participation, using this as a strategic opportunity to advance corporate restructuring objectives and increase global competitiveness.

Outward FDI from Japan is also undergoing a reorientation, with traditional markets like Europe and the US still consuming the bulk of Japanese overseas investments, but with a discernible and increasing interest in Asia. In the coming years, this trend is set to continue, as the growth potential of Asian investments, especially in China, draw increasing funds away from Europe and the US.

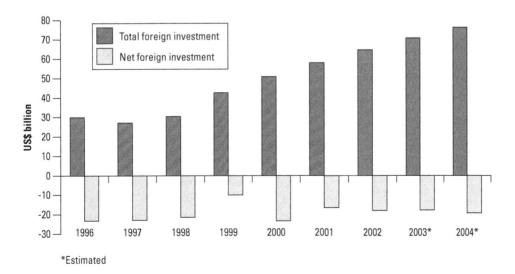

*Estimated

FIGURE 6.7 Foreign direct investment, Japan 1996–2004

Section C Politics

- Japan is one of the most stable countries in the region, with well-developed regulatory frameworks and a high degree of political transparency. Despite a series of well publicized scandals, the LDP has been in government for most of the postwar period, emblematic of its hold on power and integration in numerous facets of Japanese political life. While not a one-party state, Japan's opposition parties have failed to win popular support and, for the most part, have not managed to develop a rostrum of credible policy alternatives acceptable to the Japanese people. Little change in the composition of government can thus be expected in 2003–04, if not beyond. Indeed, Japan has a cautious and incremental approach to political change such that few dramatic policy shifts are anticipated any time soon. The only notable exception to this might be the replacement of Prime Minister Koizumi himself, with Japanese prime ministers normally only enjoying a short tenure of between one and three years.

In the mid 1990s, Japan's political and electoral system were overhauled to create a more representative democratic system. As a result, the LDP suffered its first major defeat, losing control of the Diet – although only for a short period of time and soon recovering its hold on power. It presently governs as the dominant party in a ruling coalition with smaller conservative political parties. While in 2001 there were important changes in the nature of Japanese domestic politics following the election of Koizumi as the new Prime Minister, by and large the structural composition of political life in Japan changed very little. Much as before, the institutional structure of Japan's political systems of governance have remained the same, with the spate of structural transformations that the Japanese braced themselves for with the election of Koizumi, going unrealized. This will remain the case during 2003–04.

This, then, is the great challenge and problem faced by the Japanese political system over the coming years: how to reposition the economy in a way that returns it to strong growth and international competitiveness, how to reform its systems of governance and restore confidence in an economy otherwise deflating?

What needs reforming?

The problems facing Japan are well recognized, culminating in a decade of economic stagnation, deflation, and the bursting of the bubble economy which has seen the evaporation of great swathes of wealth – especially that accumulated by the middle class. Land values continue to fall, property values have decreased, prices have generally fallen, consumption and domestic demand have contracted, savings have continued to increase, and the external demand for Japanese goods has declined, with a slowing in the global economy. More importantly, the international dominance enjoyed for so long by many Japanese enterprises has disappeared, leaving much of Japan's industrial, electronic, technological, auto and chemical sector in an uncompetitive international position.

Japan also faces a series of social changes, not least an aging population base and the increasing welfare and budgetary burdens this is placing on government. So too, these demographic shifts are causing a structural decline in state revenues as a result of a diminishing workforce relative to population size – something that cannot be addressed without a comprehensive reform of the taxation system.

Japan throughout the 1990s and into the twenty-first century has, in short, stood still, convinced of the rectitude of its ways and unconvinced of the need for institutional and political reform. Consequently, its economy, workforce, the fiscal position of government, and the regulatory structure that governs competitive policy, have all been found wanting.

Structural obstacles to reform

While the vast majority of Japanese now accept that a period of reform is necessary if Japan is to recover, less certain is it that this will be able to be implemented. In large measure, this problem stems from the various structural and institutional obstacles to reform, which are proving tenacious in their intransigence and otherwise stalling prospects for any turnaround in the economy during 2003–05.

Japan thus has to address, first and foremost, the nemesis of the 'Iron Triangle.' consisting of the bureaucracy, LDP party committees, and the various special interest groups whose stranglehold on high-level political decision-making and outcomes have effectively protected vested interests and derailed necessary change.

Unfortunately, looking ahead to 2003–04, we can only be pessimistic about significant government-led administrative and structural reform, although private sector reform will continue at a gradual and measured pace.

Political stability

For foreign investors, political stability in Japan is not a major risk factor. While Japan has experienced frequent changes of prime ministers for much of the postwar period, it has been continuously governed by the LDP and displays great regulatory, policy and political continuity. More generally, the LDP has tended to be a middle of the road to conservative coalition, with policies that have traditionally been pro-business – although its commitment to agriculture protectionism means also that it is unwilling to sacrifice that sector in order to enhance industrial competitiveness through large-scale deregulatory policies.

The opposition Democratic Party of Japan is largely an urban-based political party and has better reform credentials, but is considerably weaker in parliamentary representation. Should the unlikely event present itself where the Democratic Party formed government, it would obviously be more prone to pursue reformist policies that, in an ironic sense, would also be pro-business and provide an invigorated environment for Japanese enterprise to prosper and regain its international competitiveness. However, failing further significant economic turmoil, there is little prospect that the Democratic Party would be able to form government any time soon.

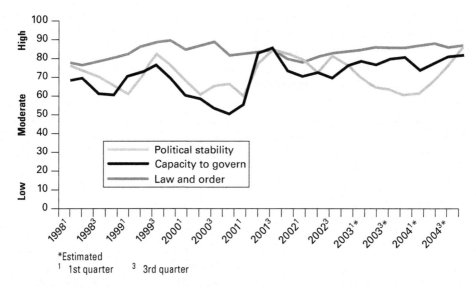

FIGURE 6.8 Political stability index, Japan 1998–2004

Political stability methodology:
- The capacity-to-govern index is based upon the institutional reach of government defined in terms of its ability to set the political and economic agenda and ensure its legislative program is enacted without significant compromise. This index is adversely affected by legislative opposition, lack of legislative implementation, failure to realize government policy and general political opposition.
- The political stability index measures violent opposition or organized demonstrations, terrorist activities, and popular discontent that adversely affect the institutional and electoral stability of the government.
- The law and order index measures the propensity to civil obedience, and the institutional reach of the rule of law in terms of regulatory compliance and enforcement.

Increasing role of Cabinet in political decision-making: greater transparency and better government?

Perhaps the only significant 'reform' under Koizumi's leadership has been the change in the nature of policy-making which has experienced a shift from a predominantly committee-dominated system of policy-making to one where the Cabinet has become a much more important institution. This has been accompanied by a loss in influence for the ruling LDP, and has had important effects in terms of restricting the influence of special interest lobby groups who previously had the ear of LDP committees and who could effectively influence policy outcomes. In all, this has been an extremely advantageous change, although the effects of this are yet to be fully realized but can be expected to start to materialize in 2003–04.

Indeed, there have been modest but important outcomes associated with Koizumi's appointment as Prime Minister, and his slow but unerring commitment to revitalize the institution of Cabinet, whereby ministers are now more in control of their respective portfolios than was the case before. Instead of intra-party coordination and a consensual style of leadership, the Koizumi administration is characterized by top-down leadership – much like that observed in the United Kingdom or United States. One of the great benefits of this is that there is now much more transparency in the political system – despite the fact that this has raised the ire of party elders, who feel isolated and diminished in importance, something that will undoubtedly come to haunt Koizumi in the near future when party support will be necessary to ensure his political survival.

Already there have been stirrings against Koizumi, when in 2001–02 about 50 hard-liners within the LDP formed an anti-Koizumi alliance; a faction generally opposed to both their loss of influence in policy-making through the previous dominance of committees, and more generally opposed to the reform and restructure agenda. Similarly, Koizumi has put other party members offside with his suggestions for numerous privatizations, not least because this would limit the ability of party members to engage in pork-barrel politics which, traditionally, have been the hallmark of the Japanese parliamentary system. In the end, of the many state-owned public corporations, the government was only able to announce the privatization of seven public corporations in 2000–02. Importantly, however, this number did include four politically sensitive highway corporations that all had a long history of association with the LDP.

Similar opposition to Koizumi was also displayed in 2001–02 when more than half the Upper House members joined together to campaign against the privatization of the postal services, comprising mail, banking and insurance services. The postal system is the largest financial institution in the world but far from competitive in terms of its international standing.

Koizumi has fought back, however, using US-style town meetings to bring government closer to the people and end the feeling of political alienation common among Japanese voters. In part this has been successful, in part a failure, especially since many of the well-publicized town meetings acted as magnets for the disaffected to criticize the government, making the tasks of the government and the reform agenda harder to implement.

Political corruption

Throughout the postwar period, most LDP and opposition politicians have engaged in corrupt electoral practices and extensive money politics. Japan is renowned for 'money politics' and LDP successes can be partly attributed to its close links to the business community, which has continued to supply it with large financial donations necessary to win (buy) popular electoral support. Although the legal spending limit for Lower House election campaigns was set at ¥16 million on average, in the 1990s LDP candidates exceeded the legal limit by at least six times and as much as 13 times. This tradition continues with no change in sight.

In order to control corrupt electoral practices, a non-LDP government reformed the electoral system in 1994, replacing multi-member constituencies with a combination of single-member electoral districts and proportional representation. Campaign financing rules were also changed to allow individual Diet members only one fund-raising organization to which donors could legally transfer ¥500,000 per year. In its place, Parliament approved public funding for political parties and campaign finance expenses.

In the elections since then, however, there has been little evidence to suggest that corrupt electoral practices have been significantly contained. In part, this reflects the fact that election campaigning in Japan remains very expensive by international standards.

Despite this, by regional standards Japan is a pillar of low corruption and transparency, and by far the best-ranked nation of all Asian states in 2001–02. Transparency International, for example, placed Japan at 21 out of 91 countries ranked, and only just behind Germany, a country also known for its transparency and low level of corruption. In terms of other OECD nations, however, Japan still ranks well behind the United Kingdom (13) and Canada (7), demonstrating that significant room for improvement exists.

Much Japanese corruption is comprised of soft-corruption practices, and stems from the close government–business relationship that inevitably engenders financial scandals and 'money politics.' However, with the change in attitudes toward foreign investment, and the strong lobbying foreign enterprise has exerted on the Japanese government to make more transparent its tendering and procurement practices, government procurement practices have been progressively liberalized, such that they no longer systemically disadvantage foreign corporations. This trend can be expected to continue in 2003–04.

Lending and investment risks: Low risks with opportunities ahead

While corrupt electoral practices extend to the corporate sector, they are, by regional standards, very minimal. For foreign investors contemplating greenfield or equity investments in Japan, the risks stem primarily from an inability of the Japanese government to effectively reform and deregulate the economy. The extensive state involvement in the Japanese economy adds to the costs of doing business in Japan and the Koizumi administration has made much rhetorical noise about its commitment to free up the business environment. However, given the many vested interests and opposition from within the ruling political party, the fate of reforms has to be viewed in the negative, at least in 2003–04.

More generally, Japan enjoys transparent corporate accounting practices, and has international standard accounting protocols in place. Importantly, in recent years Japan has also moved to reform corporate boardroom management structures, replacing what used to be the culture of stacking boardrooms with company insiders, such that there is now a more open and external representation on corporate boards. In 2002, for example, 40 percent of enterprises with capital in excess of ¥500 million have one or more directors recruited from outside the company, helping to ensure corporate board quality and management practices. This trend will continue to gain momentum as reform of the corporate sector gathers pace, to ensure a return of Japanese corporates to international competitiveness.

Crime and social disorder

Foreign investors should have few fears about the law and order situation in Japan. Among OECD countries, Japan has very low crime rates – indeed, in the region it is the safest of any country in terms of personal safety issues (assault, robbery, rape, and murder). However, while throughout the 1990s felony cases remained relatively stable, there was a marked

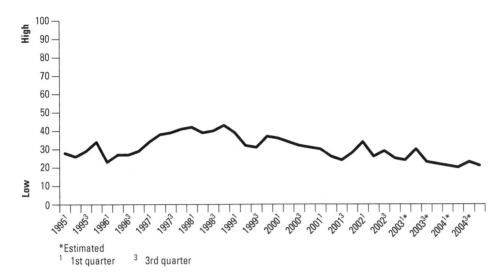

*Estimated
¹ 1st quarter   ³ 3rd quarter

FIGURE 6.9 Corruption index, Japan 1995–2004
Source: Transparency International; World Bank.

increase in robberies, growing from 1,653 cases in 1990 to 5,100 in 2002. This is largely accounted for by the increasing economic hardship faced by growing numbers of Japanese as the full weight of the economic downturn gathered momentum. Given that this has now stabilized, no further dramatic increases in crime are expected in 2003–04. Likewise, the murder rate also remained relatively stable throughout the 1990s, again reflecting the very orderly nature of Japanese society and displaying no inverse relationship to economic downturn.

Corporate governance and foreign investor risk index

The Japanese market continues to offer many opportunities for foreign investors, assuming they have a longer-term investment horizon. Although currently in a slump, Japan is still the second biggest economy in the world, with economic conditions set to improve in tandem with global economic projections.

Prospective investors should be wary of the financial sector, property and construction industries, which have experienced some of the greatest losses as a result of the fallout from the bust of the bubble economy and due to the continuance of the NPL problem. Better prospects lie in business technology and mobile telephones.

More generally, portfolio FDI in Japan reflects attractive equity prices, slow but coming regulatory reforms, and the significantly lower costs of establishing a market presence in Japan. There have also been significant improvements in corporate governance structures, as companies become more focused on profits and shareholder value and less on market share. The influx of foreign investment is bringing about a significant change, along the lines of

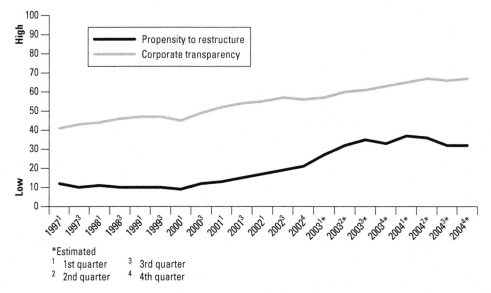

FIGURE 6.10 Corporate governance index, Japan 1997–2004

Corporate governance methodology
- The corporate governance index is a composite index measuring the juridical requirements for corporate disclosure and financial reporting, prudential regime adequacy, prudential compliance enforcement, and the juridical reach of prudential authorities.
- The propensity-to-restructure index is a composite index based on media releases and reported corporate restructuring as a result of prudential regulation, financial incentives, loan restructuring / re-negotiation, or asset realignment.

Western best practices, especially in corporate governance patterns. In the absence of a clearly discernible political commitment to structural reform, foreign investment is gradually eroding some of the uncompetitive practices within the Japanese economy. The government, too, recognizes the positive flow-on benefit of foreign investment and has encouraged greater foreign participation in the economy. It is worth emphasizing that the government sold the Long Term Credit Bank, following its privatization, not to Japanese interests but to foreign financial interests.

Section D Security

- There have been a number of high-profile criminal incidents in Japan in recent years but overall, Japan provides a very stable security environment for Japanese and foreign nationals. Japan's national security environment is also fairly stable, with the main threat stemming from instability in the Taiwan Straits, which could threaten trade routes in the event of hostilities. Neither internal nor national security concerns should be of major concern to potential investors. Little change is anticipated for 2003–04.

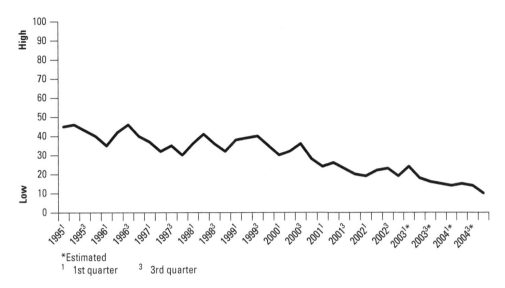

FIGURE 6.11 Foreign investor risk index, Japan 1995–2004

Foreign investor risk index methodology
- The foreign investor risk index is a composite index measuring tax burdens, discriminatory regulatory practices, adverse compliance regulations, government policy toward foreign enterprise, receptiveness to issuance of government contracts, foreign enterprise commercial restrictions, and official attitudinal changes to foreign direct investment and foreign commercial operations which impact on operational efficiency. The index also incorporates a nominal measure for market risk and market failure.

Japan is strategically dependent on the importation of nearly all raw materials and natural resources, as well as on the export of finished products for a great proportion of its national income. Its economic security rests on the security and stability of sea-lanes of communication, nominally defined by its trading relationships with Asian countries and, of course, its market dependence on the United States. Much of its security is thus gleaned from the strong presence of the US in the Pacific, and the guarantee this extends to Japan vis-à-vis China and North Korea. Obviously, given both the wartime activities of Japan, popular antipathy towards a large military establishment, and the constitutional limits placed on Japanese military spending, there are limits to what the Japanese government can do to secure its sea-lanes of communication.

Cognizant of this, successive Japanese administrations have maintained a low-profile defense posture despite large defense outlays, while fostering ongoing close defense relations with the United States and generally using its large foreign aid budget to foster good will among Asian states in the region. Indeed, Japan has invested considerable financial resources and a great deal of effort into second track diplomacy to insure good neighborly relations and to forestall the development of hostile trade and diplomatic actions. For the most part, Japan has been very successful in this capacity and will continue to be so in 2003–04.

Regional security and peacekeeping

Japan is a regional superpower but has avoided any regional security and peacekeeping obligations. In 2001–02, the government adopted a more forthcoming attitude toward its regional responsibilities. In particular, the Koizumi administration indicated its willingness to consider participation in UN peacekeeping operations in East Timor, for example, breaking with a postwar tradition of non-deployment in the region. The change of policy underscores Tokyo's recognition that its refusal to participate in UN peacekeeping operations hinders its ambition to secure a permanent seat in the UN Security Council, an ambition that is likely to see increasing involvement in the region throughout 2003–04 and beyond.

The September 11 terrorist attacks have also resulted in a further shift in popular and political attitudes. In the immediate aftermath of September 11, a poll showed that 87 percent of Japanese wanted the military to support the US with transport, supplies and medical services, although only 8 percent supported Japan's direct military involvement. Reflecting this shift in popular sentiment, the Japanese Diet passed new legislation to enable Japanese involvement in counter-terrorism activities, mainly in a non-combat logistic support role.

The on-going shifts and possibility of constitutional revision to allow Japan to resume a normal standing defense force may be welcome to its alliance partner and Western countries, but it has also caused concern among many southeast and northeast Asian states who retain fears of what a re-militarized Japan might mean for the longer-term stability of the region. The Japanese government thus has a difficult task ahead as it assumes more defense obligations while also attempting to placate domestic and regional opponents of military build-up.

External threats to Japanese security

The periodic spurts of antagonism between China and Taiwan across the Taiwan Straits has the greatest potential to undermine Japan's external security – as does the possibility of a cooling of Sino–US relations.

Added to this, there is concern about the security threat emanating from North Korea, which in the past has lobbed surface-to-surface missiles across Japan into the Pacific Ocean to demonstrate its military capacity and to intimidate the Japanese government.

Combined with the events of September 11 and the subsequent 'axis of evil' identification of North Korea as a threat to US and regional security, it is obvious that Japan's threat situation has increased. Indeed, this is likely to remain the case well into 2003–04, especially if the US pushes ahead with further activities designed to agitate against rogue state behavior.

While North Korea will not be as easy a target for the US as was Afghanistan – indeed it might be dealt with via nothing more than ongoing US denunciations and political rhetoric – it obviously remains of great concern to Tokyo that such denunciations serve only to destabilize regional affairs. The concern this has caused in Tokyo was demonstrated after Japan's Chief Cabinet Secretary, Yasuo Fukuda, denied that North Korea constituted a part of what President Bush had termed the 'axis of evil.' Obviously, Tokyo will have to follow a fine line if it wishes to maintain regional stability, placate the US, and be seen to support Asian allies fearful of US rhetoric and saber rattling. Thus 2003–04 could prove a tough period for Japanese defense and security interests with some fallout for market sentiment as regional security deteriorates.

Section E Economic and political risk forecasts

- The Japanese economy faces further short-to-medium term instability in 2003–04. However, this might be abated somewhat by the expected upturn in the US economy and a pick-up in external demand for Japanese exports. On the downside, the current administration has failed to exploit the opportunity to push ahead with the structural reforms otherwise needed if Japan's economic vitality is to be restored. Indeed, it bodes ill for the global economy if Japan, the second largest economy in the world, is not soon put back on the right economic track.

Short-term forecasts

- The short-term economic outlook for the Japanese economy is mildly encouraging, although slow reform and continuing low competitiveness is cause for concern.
- Projected real GDP growth for 2003–04 is estimated only at around 1.0 percent, which, while low, is achievable and sustainable. More importantly, if this can be preserved for 2003–04 it might go some way to breaking the deflationary cycle and laying the foundations for more robust growth in 2004–06.
- Corporate sector reform and restructuring will continue but not at an aggressive pace. This will only stall prospects for an earlier recovery from the economic crisis in 2003–04.
- Demand for labor will remain subdued and the number of unemployed will continue to increase throughout 2002. By international standards, however, unemployment in Japan is not very high. Some turnaround in the unemployment rate with a generally stronger labor market can be anticipated during 2003–04.
- Financial sector reform and resolution of NPLs are expected to have an adverse impact on the corporate sector, especially in the uncompetitive real estate, construction, wholesale distribution and service sectors. Expect continuing poor performance in these sectors during 2003–04.
- The government has promised an extensive agenda of privatization of state monopolies and public sector corporations but actual progress has been slow and unlikely to show a marked improvement in the immediate future. There are too many vested interests that will likely hinder and confound the government's reform plans. Little will change in 2003–04.
- The Prime Minister has declared 2002–03 to be the year of reforms but his own position is much diminished after the departure of his popular Foreign Minister from the Cabinet. He increasingly looks to be heading a lame-duck administration. Unfortunately, this will translate into little progress in terms of significant deregulation or privatization in 2003–04.

- The exchange rate will remain low with the Japanese yen tending downwards. This should help mitigate some of the export problems for Japan's manufacturers hurt by global economic downturn, and indeed might benefit them with an expected upturn in the global economy during 2003–04.

Short-term opportunities

- A depressed stock market and falling yen make Japanese assets very attractive to foreign investors. Foreign acquisition of Japanese equities has increased since the collapse of the bubble but foreign investors cannot expect an immediate return. The Japanese economy will remain depressed for some time, with positive growth rates only expected in the 0–1 percent range. While the costs of foreign investment in Japan are high, an increase in FDI can be expected in 2003–04, and will likely continue to increase thereafter in view of opportunities to selectively exploit existing weaknesses.
- The Japanese auto industry used to be the flagship for the economy but in recent years auto exports have slipped. In 1998, total export of passenger cars was around ¥6,550 billion but in 2001 it had slipped to around ¥6,123 billion. In 2002 with the backdrop of global economic stabilization, auto exports have increased. Some Japanese car manufacturers, however, remain weak, which has allowed foreign manufacturers, like Renault, to acquire a stake in Japanese car companies. The dominance of the Japanese auto industry globally is probably now over, with marginal improvement in competitiveness not likely to see a return to the halcyon days of the 1980s.

Medium-to-longer term

- The Japanese economy has been stagnant for an unusually long time but there should be no doubt as to its capacity to stage a strong comeback. In the past, after each setback the economy soared to new heights and the present economic difficulties do not suggest an entirely new pattern of economic growth.
- In recent years, the Japanese government has invested enormous sums in infrastructure development and these will stand the Japanese economy in good stead when recovery begins.
- The Japanese government is keen to enhance its international presence in the IT industry and this sector can be expected to perform strongly in the longer term.

Overall risk rating

The Japanese economy has been in a slump since 1990 and anything more than a modest recovery is not expected in 2003–04. However, on the upside, there is little likelihood of further deterioration in economic conditions, with the Japanese economy having weathered the worst. More generally, the longer-term resilience of the Japanese economy cannot be overlooked and should send a strong signal to prospective foreign investors to begin now to seek out longer-term investment strategies, so they will be ready to take advantage of economic recovery when it finally comes.

Current economic conditions provide foreign investors with an opportunity to enter the Japanese market, provided they are prepared to ride out short-term difficulties. Not all sectors of the Japanese economy, however, provide attractive opportunities, especially in the case of small- and medium-sized enterprises in electronics, ICT, and the auto industries.

Risk: Moderately decreasing ↓
Risk Rating (0 = lowest risk, 10 highest risk) 4.0 →

Section F Japan Fact Sheet*

Geography

Capital
Tokyo

Largest city (millions, 2000)
Tokyo, 34.75 (metro area)

Location
Eastern Asia, islands stretching between the North Pacific Ocean and the Sea of Japan, east of the Korean Peninsula

Terrain
Mountainous with limited availability of arable land

Land use (1993)
Arable land 11%, forests and woodlands 67%, permanent crops 1%, permanent pastures 2%, Other 19%

Area (miles²)
145,870

Economic statistics

Currency
Yen

Exchange rate (January 2002)
US$1.00 = ¥134

Gross Domestic Product (GDP, 2001 projection)
0.5%

GDP per capita
$23,257

GDP composition by sector
Agriculture 2%, industry 35%, services 63% (1999)

Inflation rate (1999)
−0.8%

Public sector debt
130% of GDP

Trade account balance (million yen)
22,342

* All figures are the latest available except where indicated. All sums are in US dollars. Figures are compiled from national, international and multilateral agencies (United Nations Development Assistance Program, International Monetary Fund, World Bank, World Development Report, UNESCO Statistical Yearbook, International Labour Office, United Nations, Central Intelligence Agency World Fact Book). Gross domestic product (GDP) refers to the value of all goods and services produced in the preceding financial year. GDP per capita, Purchasing Power Parity (GDP per capita – PPP) refers to the indices developed by the World Bank to take account of price differences, cost of living differences, and relative purchasing power of a set basket of goods and services between countries so as to provide a more accurate measure of national wealth.

National unemployment rate (Jan. 2002)
5.5%

Labor force
67,790,000

Labor force by occupation
Agriculture 4.5%, industry 40.5%,
services 50.5%

Budget (billions, 2001)
Revenues: ¥7,396
Expenditure: ¥7,661

Industries
Durable and non-durable consumer
goods, automobile, electrical machinery,
IT equipment, precision equipment,
transport machinery, capital goods

Major exports (billions)
¥47,548 (1999)
Electrical machinery and appliances,
transportation equipment, machinery
other than electrical, motor vehicles,
chemicals

Major imports (billions)
¥35,268 (1999)
Mineral fuels, machinery and
equipment, foodstuffs, petroleum,
textile and clothing

Major trading partners (exports)
United States 30.7%, Taiwan 6.9%,
Republic of Korea 5.4%, China 5.5%,
Hong Kong 5.4%, Germany 4.5%,
Malaysia 2.6%

Major trading partners (imports)
United States 21.6%, China 13.8%,
Republic of Korea 5.1%, Indonesia 4.0%,
Taiwan, 4.1%, Germany 3.7%,
Malaysia 3.5%

**Color television (1999, per 1,000
households)**
2,318

**Cellular phones (1999, per 1,000
households)**
1,061

**Automobiles in use (1999, per 1,000
households)**
83.6

Fiscal year
1 April–31 March

Government and political statistics

Nature of government
Parliamentary democracy

Constitution
New Constitution promulgated in 1947

Structure of government
Executive Branch and Legislative
Branch

Executive branch
Head of Government, Prime Minister
Junichiro Koizumi

Legislative branch
Bicameral Legislature (Diet)

House of councilors
252 members, 6-year term and
2 electoral cycles. 126 elected from
party list in multi-seat prefectural
constituencies, 24 elected from single
seat constituencies, and 100 elected
from national constituencies

House of representatives
480 members, 300 single seat districts
and 180 proportional representation

Cabinet members (as at February 2002)

Prime Minister
Mr Junichiro Koizumi

Minister of Finance
Mr Masajuro Shiokawa

Minister of Foreign Affairs
Ms Yoriko Kawaguchi

Defense Agency Director General
General Nakatani

Minister of Agriculture, Forestry and Fisheries
Mr Tsutomu Takabe

Minister of Land, Infrastructure and Transport
Ms Chikage Ogi

Minister of Economy, Trade and Industry
Mr Takeo Hiranuma

Minister of Public Management, Home Affairs, Posts and Telecommunications
Mr Toranosuke Katayama

Minister of Justice
Ms Mayumi Moriyama

Minister of Health, Labor and Welfare
Mr Chikara Sakaguchi

Minister of Education, Culture, Sports, Science and Technology
Ms Atsuko Toyama

Minister of Environment
Mr Hiroshi Ohki

Main governing parties and ideological affiliation
Liberal Democratic Party (conservative political party and ideologically pro-business)

Main opposition parties
Democratic Party of Japan, Social Democratic Party of Japan, Japan Communist Party

International memberships
Asia Pacific Economic Community, OECD, G-8, United Nations, World Trade Organization, International Monetary Fund, Asian Development Bank

Business organizations
Keidanren (Federation of Economic Organizations), Chamber of Commerce and Industry, *Keizai Doyukai.*

Social Statistics

Population size (millions)
126.549976

Population density
340 per square kilometer (1999)

Fertility rate (average number of children born by women 15–49 years of age)
1.4

Maternal mortality rate
9.5 per 100,000 births (2000)

Infant mortality rate (2001 est.)
3.88 deaths per 1000 births

Population growth
0.17% (2001)

Life expectancy
Men 77.62
Women 84.15 (2001 est.)

Ethnic composition
Japanese 99.4%

Religions
Both Shinto and Buddhist 84%, other 16% (including Christian 0.7%)

National languages spoken
Japanese

Illiteracy rate (age 15+)
n/a (by US standards 1%, by Japanese standards 15%)

By gender (ages 25+)
Male: n/a
Female: n/a

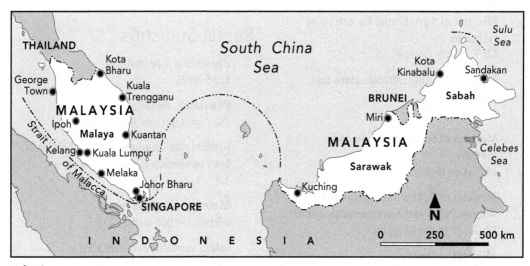

Malaysia

7 Malaysia

William Case

Section A Economy

Overview

During the year 2002, Malaysia's economic performance and the political standing of its government showed signs of recovery. During the previous year, the economy had slowed to around 1 percent growth, largely as a result of softening demand for electronics exports associated with the technology sector meltdown in the United States. In 2002, however, the economy expanded at 2.7 percent, ahead of what is expected to be better growth prospects in 2003–04. On the political front during 2001, the government, led by the modernizing United Malays National Organization (UMNO), appeared steadily to lose ground to an opposition party, the revivalist Pan-Islamic Party of Malaysia (PAS). But PAS's militant reaction to American retaliation in Afghanistan after September 11, contrasting with the UMNO's more measured response, appeared to reenergize support for the government throughout 2002.

Specifically, many urban middle class Malays, prime beneficiaries of Malaysia's rapid industrialization, drew back from the opposition. The country's ethnic Chinese also renewed their support for the government. Economic uncertainties and Islamic militancy, then, seemed to caution key social categories, thus restoring Malaysian politics to an earlier equilibrium. Indeed, Malaysia's prime minister Mahathir Mohamad, took full advantage of these new outlooks in order to crackdown on dissent. Meanwhile, the opposition, led by the PAS, but also including a party made up mostly of Chinese, fractured along religious lines. In this way, the UMNO regained an ascendancy that is expected to persist during 2003–04.

Gaining some breathing space, Mahathir announced his resignation in mid-2002, to take effect in October 2003. He thus prepared to transfer power to his deputy, Abdullah Badawi, who, while less politically forceful and technologically adept, possesses a more Islamic demeanor that may further increase support for the government. In this situation, it is expected that Mahathir will call an early general election before finally stepping down.

In the economy, growth had been driven during the first half of 2001 by significant restructuring and export markets. A recapitalization agency and consolidation exercise did much to revitalize the banking sector. An asset management agency greatly reduced the corporate sector's non-performing loans (NPLs). The removal of capital controls and restrictions on foreign ownership attracted some foreign investment, helping fuel exports. And local companies were exposed to new international standards of corporate governance, firmed by a civil service and legal system that by regional standards are regarded as effective, a trend that has continued throughout 2002.

Nonetheless, one must not overstate the extent to which Malaysia's corporate sector was reformed. Put simply, for several years after the 1997 crisis, much less restructuring took place among large politically connected conglomerates than in banking. During the second half of 2001, however, as foreign investment and exports again declined, several of the country's top tycoons were finally forced from their ownership and managerial positions, an outcome that was hailed by some analysts as marking the start of serious reform. In effect, the government used a variety of agencies to re-nationalize assets that had earlier been privatized on concessionary terms.

But even if this started Malaysia on the road to reform, the corporate sector will likely be of little help in the near term in coping with economic slowdown. Accordingly, the government has undertaken new levels of deficit spending. The benefits of the stimulus packages that have resulted, though, have mostly been confined to public construction projects, leaving other sectors to languish. It is thus difficult to foresee any overall improvement in conditions during 2003–04 without a significant revival of external demand for electronics.

Growing risks to foreign investment?

Malaysia's woes appear manageable, however, alongside those of most neighboring countries in Southeast Asia. Despite the government's sometimes harsh anti-globalization rhetoric and strident denunciations of multilateral agencies, it remains quietly pragmatic in practice. The country's capital controls, introduced amid much controversy during the economic crisis in 1998, have mostly been phased out, leaving only the currency peg in place. Furthermore, limits on foreign ownership of firms geared to domestic markets have been scaled back, while tariffs have been lowered. And though the government now provides stimulus spending and some social programs, it has not taken on anything like the populist commitments of neighboring Thailand, relying instead on labor flexibility, retraining, and job search assistance. Public debt thus remains at reasonable levels. Macroeconomic indicators mostly remain positive. In consequence, as other countries in the region now contemplate capital controls and protectionist measures, Malaysia's timelier use of these strategies enables it to retire them, providing a setting that, with improvement in the global economy in 2003–04, will again be congenial for foreign investors.

The bottom line: Improving fortunes ahead

Opportunities for foreign direct investors in Malaysia have traditionally been found in the production of electronics and electrical goods for export, as well as the infrastructure projects with which to facilitate this activity. But because the country's economy is relatively open and lacks the ballast provided by competitive local companies and a sizeable domestic market, its fortunes remain closely aligned with the global economy. In consequence, during 2003–04, investment opportunities in Malaysia must be assessed as modest.

Nonetheless, many positive features remain in place, albeit these are awaiting the revival of export markets anticipated in 2003–04. These include the government's generally pro-business attitudes, the relative capacity of the civil service, a sophisticated infrastructure base, moderately high levels of human capital, and a long record of political stability. What is more, despite the militancy displayed by the opposition PAS in the wake of September 11, the party's leaders are at the same time very receptive to foreign investment in the several states that they govern.

Section B Risks and projections

Macroeconomic performance and risk indicators

Malaysia's economy, heavily exposed to export markets, especially in the United States and Japan, contracted across most sectors during 2001 before experiencing modest recovery in 2002. Accordingly, foreign investment opportunities geared to electronics and electrical goods exports have generally declined. Other areas of domestic consumption grew, however, producing an ambiguous record overall. GDP growth will stay subdued during 2002 at around 2.7 percent, before rising to between 3 and 4 percent in 2002–03. Inflation remains low, with increases in the consumer price index of 1.5 percent forecast for 2002–03, and 3 percent forecast for 2003–04.

After growing rapidly in 2000, Malaysia's economy slowed during 2001. Initially, this was regarded as correcting the over-expansion that had taken place in the wake of the 1997–98 crisis, thus paving the way for a new round of growth. But with the worsening of conditions after September 11, the slowdown continued into 2002,[1] with manufacturing, agriculture, and tourism all seriously affected.

In these conditions, domestic investment and employment levels have been falling. Domestic investment declined by 4.1 percent in the first half of 2001, then a further 17.2 percent in the third quarter. After large-scale retrenchments, especially in electronics manufacturing, unemployment was projected to increase from 3.1 percent in 2000 to 3.9 percent in 2001, with an estimated total of 390,000 people out of work.[2] Further slight increases in unemployment can be expected throughout 2002 before beginning to gradually fall again in 2003.

As a result, the government remains committed to various forms of stimulus spending – and it possesses the necessary fiscal reserves. Thus, while increasing budget expenditures for 2002 by 10 percent, providing substantial salary bonuses to civil servants, yet cutting income taxes and import duties, the budget deficit remains at tolerable levels, an estimated 6.5 percent of GDP.[3] The revenue shortfall will decrease in 2002–03, falling to around 3.1 percent and then again to 0.5–1.0 percent in 2003–04 as economic conditions improve.

Further, domestic private consumption continued to display some areas of buoyancy, increasing by 2.1 percent in the third quarter of 2001, despite worsening external economic conditions. Improvement was most apparent in residential construction, automobiles and services, which were also boosted by low interest rates. Domestic public consumption thus grew from 5.9 percent in the second quarter to 14.6 percent in the third quarter of 2001, helping moderate the worsening external environment.

> The economy has slowed in 2001–02, recording growth rates of between 1 and 2.7 percent. Stronger economic activity will not resume until 2002–03, with growth anticipated at between 3–4 percent.

In sum, Malaysia's manufacturing, agriculture and tourism industries, heavily geared to global markets, declined during 2001 and early 2002, but are now showing signs of tentative recovery in line with international trends in late 2002. This will continue and gather momentum in 2002–03. Strong, discernible recovery, however, will not emerge until 2003, though tourism has shown signs of a slight improvement in 2002, albeit at the low end of the market only. It would appear that Malaysia's uncertain economic climate, characterized by export sector weakness and combined with mixed signals of consumer confidence, will prevail into 2003–04. Market risk is low by regional standards premised on sound macro-economic fundamentals but, at the same time, limited demand for tech-sector exports means that FDI opportunities will remain limited in the near term.

Export performance

- Exports from Malaysia, in recent years accounting for as much as 110 percent of GDP, contracted during 2001, largely as a result of diminishing US demand for electronics and electrical goods. The manufacturing sector has also been weakened in the longer term by rising labor costs relative to other countries in East Asia, especially China, and as a result of the fixed peg ringgit that has seen most other regional currency values fall, thus diminishing Malaysia's relative international competitiveness. While these effects will moderate in 2002–03, fuller recovery of the export sector will not be realized until 2003–04.

Malaysia's economy is characterized partly by commodities production, making it more diversified in some respects than its neighbor, Singapore. Petroleum, gas, palm oil, and rubber products are thus important earners of foreign exchange. So too is international tourism. Nonetheless, September 11 also caused most commodities markets and tourism to shrink. Hence, while the country's gross exports contracted by 8.8 percent in the second quarter of 2001, they declined by a more precipitous 19 percent in the third quarter. The rate of decline slowed somewhat in the year's final quarter. Malaysia's trade balance, an estimated $US17.5 billion in 2001, and falling again to US$14 billion in 2002, remains in surplus, but this is not regarded as altogether healthy, with declining exports offset by contracting imports of capital and intermediate goods.[4] Gross foreign exchange reserves have also declined in 2002 from a peak of $US35.5 billion in April 2000. In sum, these factors point to a continuance in the narrowing of the trade surplus during 2002–03. Rising export growth reaching 8–10 percent will, however, see an increase in the trade surplus to an estimated US$14.0 billion in 2004.

Malaysia has been involved in the production of electronics and electrical goods since the mid 1970s. It thus features a large manufacturing base in Penang, lesser nodes throughout the peninsula, and the Multimedia Super Corridor project south of Kuala Lumpur. Hardware product lines are diverse, including computers and peripherals, hard drives, integrated circuits, and memory chips. Together, electronics and electrical goods account for approximately 60 percent of Malaysia's total exports, nearly one-third of which go to the United States.[5] Hence, the economic recovery that took place in Malaysia from 1999 through the first half of 2001 depended heavily on a sustained US demand for information technology (IT) products. Conversely, Malaysia's stagnancy during the last half of 2001 and through 2002 can, in large measure, be attributed to reduced demand from US markets. What is more, with over-capacity in electronics production discouraging new investment, the erosion in this sector will probably be deep and prolonged – and continue well into 2003, if not 2004. Investment-led downturns, in contrast to ones produced by falling consumer demand, remain impervious to low currency valuations and interest rate cuts until excess capacity and inventories have been cleared.[6] Hence, more than any other country in Southeast Asia except Singapore, Malaysia's prospects for recovery are dimmed by the travails of the IT industry.

Some 60 percent of Malaysia's exports consist of electronics and electrical goods, rendering the country unusually vulnerable to competition from China, Vietnam, and Thailand, as well as cyclical downturns in US markets.

In other sectors, though, Malaysia's economy continued to perform reasonably well during 2001–02, to some extent buffering the impact of diminishing electronics markets, and showing moderate improvement in growth to around 2.7 percent in 2002. Most notably, prices for petroleum and palm oil remained buoyant. However, petroleum prices gradually flattened during the third quarter, but are now rising again, while the risks in servicing one of Malaysia's largest customers for palm oil, Pakistan, increased greatly after September 11. At the same time, Malaysia's international tourist market fell by 30 percent, prompting the government to make a bid for tourists from Muslim countries in order to take up the shortfall in Western visitors. Educational services also continued to make gains, though foreign enrolments appear not to have grown as rapidly as had been hoped.

Currency movements and projections

• Alone among the countries in Southeast Asia, Malaysia has opted for a fixed exchange rate, pegging its currency, the ringgit, at RM3.8 to US$1.00. The peg was introduced as part of the package of capital controls through which the government responded to the financial crisis of 1997–98. And while other elements of the package were subsequently phased out, including restrictions on foreigners repatriating capital gains, the currency peg remains. So too does a prohibition on the use of ringgit for offshore transactions, as well as limits on the amount of ringgit that travelers can transport out of the country.

Although the collective contribution of the capital controls to Malaysia's economic recovery during 1999–2000 remains a matter of much debate, the currency peg put an immediate halt to speculative short-selling, while restoring some certainty to the valuations involved in business dealings. The local business community thus welcomed the peg, and it showed new support for the government during the last election. In addition, the level at which the ringgit was valued, marking a 50 percent decline from its pre-crisis level, permitted the low interest rates that encouraged borrowing. But most importantly, the peg restored much of Malaysia's manufacturing competitiveness, facilitating IT exports to the United States.

> Malaysia's ringgit, pegged at 3.8 to US$1.00, came under pressure during early 2002 from other declining currencies, particularly the yen. The current exchange rate policy will only change, however, if the Chinese currency devalues.

Of course, the low currency peg also raised the cost of imports, which when affecting the capital and intermediate goods that are locally incorporated into re-exports, diminished foreign exchange earnings. The peg also carried other risks that became apparent during 2001–02. As the US dollar drifted upward relative to most Southeast Asian currencies it took the ringgit with it, attaining a level that compromised Malaysia's competitiveness in export manufactures. Speculation thus mounted that Malaysia's central bank, Bank Negara Malaysia, would adjust the peg downward, a move that would have been unpopular with local business. The bank thus avoided devaluation, but therein raised doubts over the peg's sustainability, recalling the fears over the ringgit in free-fall during the early months of the 1997–98 crisis.

In speculating about the ringgit's valuation during 2003–04 – whether the peg will be retained or whether an adjustment, even a float, might eventually take place – it is important to recognize the centrality of Mahathir's preferences. To be sure, the Prime Minister remains committed to globalizing Malaysia's trade activities and patterns of foreign direct investment. He remains suspicious, however, of floating exchange rates and, indeed, of highly mobile portfolio investment; forces he believes should be harnessed to production rather than risking their undermining it through the speculative abuses to which they lend themselves. In consequence, if the ringgit undergoes any movement during 2003–04 it will likely take place through a controlled adjustment followed by a prompt reapplication of the peg, rather than any return to the float. Based on current indicators, any movement in the currency will be downward during the forecast period. Market consensus suggests that the rate will then bottom out at approximately 4.5 to the dollar around mid 2004.

Financial markets: Performance and developments

- The banking sector's profitability, which rose during 2001, fell away again in 2002 as the previous year's weakness fed into the bottom line. Nonetheless, the stability of the sector is not threatened though the rate of NPLs has continued to rise, and will likely do so in 2003 before falling again. Major banking sector collapses are unlikely but restructuring will continue as the tail end of the reform measures started during 1998 is implemented in 2003–04.

Malaysia has done more than most among East Asia's crisis-ridden countries to reform its banking sector. Of course, Malaysia's recapitalization agency, Dandamodal, confronted a less onerous task than that facing authorities elsewhere in the region because lending had been better regulated from the start. Accordingly, less funding was required than initially feared, with 10 of the hardest hit financial institutions requiring RM7.6 billion. Danamodal has now been repaid by seven of the 10 institutions, and the agency is scheduled to be closed by 2003.

At the same time, a consolidation exercise was begun in 1998 in order to build larger banking institutions that would be able to withstand the opening of financial markets and increased foreign competition. This process was hampered by political and even ethnic rivalries, but was nearly completed by the end of 2000–01. In this way, 10 so-called anchor banks emerged, embracing 50 of the country's 54 institutions.[7] In early 2001, expectations mounted over a further round of consolidation, reducing the number of anchor banks to five.[8] Similar attempts at consolidation are under way in the stockbroking and insurance industries.

Regulation of the banking sector, assessed historically as good by regional standards, has been further improved since the crisis of 1997–98. To be sure, Bank Negara Malaysia has not been fully independent from political pressures. But it has nonetheless supervised the banking system with considerable effectiveness. In 2000, Bank Negara imposed new guidelines over the management of credit risk. It also increased the capital adequacy ratio, now exceeding the Basle norm of 8 percent by at least two percentage points. On the other hand, the statutory reserve requirement for banks has been lowered from 13.5 percent to 6 percent, while base lending rates for major commercial banks has been reduced to 11 percent. In 2001, a new Financial Sector Master Plan of 10 years' duration was released, designed to foster competition between domestic banks in preparation for their increasing exposure to foreign banking institutions.

NPLs declined through 2000, but began to rise again in 2001–02. Moreover, the totals were worse than the figures often revealed because many NPLs were merely transferred from bank balance sheets to the government's asset management company, Danaharta. Yet even in the aggregate, Malaysia's rate of total NPLs reached only 15–20 percent in 2001.[9] Further, though trending upward in 2002, much of the rise is attributable to previously extended loans that have been reclassified as non-performing in conformity with Bank Negara guidelines.[10] Still, as the country's economy continues to slow, the problem will worsen, with local business unable to repay much of the corporate debt raised prior to the 1997–98 financial crisis.

> In mid 2000, total NPLs amounted to RM86.84 billion. Out of this amount Danaharta acquired RM37 billion. The balance lay with financial institutions. RM46 billion worth of debt was referred to the Corporate Debt Restructuring Committee, with some 30 cases involving RM25.7 billion worked through and another 20 cases, amounting to RM16.3 billion, still to be resolved.

On the other hand, total deposits increased by 3.7 percent during the first half of 2001 over the previous June. And though deposits by statutory authorities and financial institutions fell toward the end of the year, they were offset by individual deposits. Bank lending also increased, facilitated by base lending rates that at the end of the year stood at 6.2 percent, the lowest in a decade. Much of the rise in lending has been for residential property and passenger cars, which produced a modest countervailing boom during the second half of 2001, and show signs of further improvement in 2003–04.[11]

The bottom line: Not a risk-free environment

Malaysia's banking system remains relatively well supervised and has undergone significant restructuring. Accordingly, bank profitability increased moderately during 2001–02. But profitability is regarded as a lagging, rather than a leading indicator.[12] As such, it will probably decline during 2002–03 as Malaysia's economic contraction persists. And it will not rise until after Malaysia's next recovery has been under way for some time, perhaps by early 2003.

Further, though regulation and restructuring may be regarded as sound, one is cautioned by the fact that this assessment is made in a regional context. Hence, in Malaysia, investors pondering investments in local institutions must remain vigilant about lending activities influenced by political and ethnic factors, as well as some speculative pursuits. Though the country's banks have been formally separated from state and party ownership, informal links remain, threatening recurrences of the ructions and scandals that have taken place over previous decades, even if on a smaller scale. Meanwhile, foreign banking institutions still confront limits on their financial activities and branch expansion.

In sum, foreign investors face a much more orderly banking sector in Malaysia than is to be found elsewhere in the region. One notes too that banking stocks rose in early 2002, fueled by speculation over a new round of consolidation. Nonetheless, investors in the banking sector should probably wait for clearer indications of economic recovery, likely in 2003–04.

Private and public debt: Risks ahead

- Malaysia's trend of deficit spending is quickening. Yet doubts persist over the effectiveness of stimulus packages. Still, the spending is modest relative to Thailand's undertakings. And Malaysia possesses the financial resources and bureaucratic capacity with which to fund and implement its programs. For this reason, though, the deficit spending may do little to bring about a broad-based recovery; neither will it cause undue stress.

Malaysia increased its budgetary expenditure in 2002 by 10 percent to around US$27 billion. This created the country's fifth consecutive budgetary deficit, perpetuating a trend that began with attempts to resolve the crisis of 1997–98. Yet, in current conditions, doubts persist about the effectiveness of stimulus packages, with many local analysts citing the failure of Japan's economy to recover, with a decade of deficit spending producing little more than a liquidity trap.[13]

However, as noted above, Malaysia has avoided the costly populist obligations that the government of neighboring Thailand has taken on. To the contrary, Malaysia has focused its spending on infrastructure development, thereby benefiting big contractors. In addition, in an effort to bolster private consumption, it has cut the income tax rates of high-level earners. To the extent that social spending increased in 2001–02, it was channeled toward education, with funding in this sector jumping by 50 percent.

Further, Malaysia's budgetary deficit, estimated at nearly 6.5 percent of GDP for 2001, 6.0 percent in 2002, and trending downwards to 3.1 percent in 2003, can be regarded as reasonable. Total public sector debt stood at 37.7 percent in 2001–02, only 2.5 percent higher than in 1996, the year before the crisis hit. Indeed, public sector debt has remained within a comparatively narrow band of 32–38 percent throughout the 1996–2002 period. Barring a sudden change in government and policy direction – which appear increasingly unlikely despite Mahathir announcing his resignation – there is no expectation, then, that Malaysia will experience the excessive fiscal pressures and public sector indebtedness that threaten debt-servicing obligations elsewhere in the region.

To be sure, Malaysia's total external debt has increased in the final quarter of 2001 to an estimated 50 percent of GDP, rising from 45–46 percent over the previous year and a half. But this remains well under the levels that were incurred in 1998 and 1999, standing at 59.4 percent and 54.3 percent respectively. Looking forward, the budget will remain in deficit during 2002–03 with borrowing equivalent to 4 percent of GDP. This will continue to fall in 2003–04 to approximately 2 percent of GDP driven by increased tax revenues.

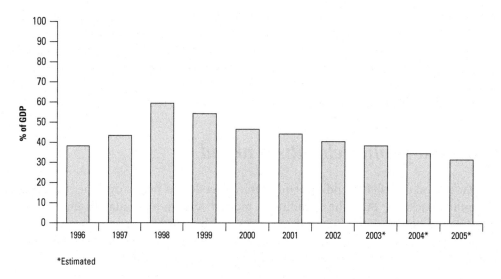

FIGURE 7.1 Government debt as percentage of GDP, Malaysia 1996–2005
Source: Asian Development Bank, Asia Recovery Report; Economist Intelligence Unit Forecasts.

In addition, short-term debt as a percentage of total external debt – with high levels having been so central in triggering the crisis of 1997–98 – is today quite low, suggesting that more stringent lending supervision is in place. To be sure, in the years prior to the crisis, Malaysia had incurred much less short-term debt than many other East Asian countries, standing at 22.8 percent of GDP in 1996. But it has since been reduced by nearly half, standing at 11.8 percent in the third quarter of 2001. In consequence, while Malaysian sovereign debt was punished with bond rating downgrades in 1998 after its adoption of capital controls, more positive ratings have lately been restored. The rise in investor sentiment was clearly expressed by the over-subscription to a recent bond issue totaling US$1 billion.[14]

Labor market trends

- As with many other countries in Southeast Asia, Malaysia's labor markets have been adversely affected by the current slowdown in global demand for electronics. In 2001, some 40,000 workers were retrenched, with a total of nearly 400,000 estimated to be out of work by the end of the year.[15] An unknown number of undocumented foreign workers have been repatriated. Official unemployment figures for 2001 stand at nearly 4 percent, for 2002 at 4.1 percent, both up from 3.1 percent in 2000. Further retrenchments are projected to take place in 2002–03 in the manufacturing, banking and airline industries.[16] A combination of higher export demand and economic growth from late 2003 should, however, presage increased labor demand, with the unemployment rate falling to 2.5 percent by end 2004.

Malaysia's education levels and English-language proficiency are far higher than in Thailand and Indonesia. Accordingly, a much greater proportion of the workforce has been incorporated into modern urban sectors. The government has also long paid attention to rural development, establishing land settlement schemes and agricultural support programs. Nonetheless, with greater policy preference given to urban industrialization since the 1970s, the disparities between urban and rural sectors have increased in 2002, and will continue to do so in 2003–04. Although Malaysia has attained the highest per capita income levels in Southeast Asia after Singapore and Brunei, while reducing the incidence of absolute poverty to very low levels, the country also displays some of the grossest socioeconomic inequalities. This unevenness is manifest in spatial terms between urban and rural areas. It also persists along ethnic lines, with Malay households still trailing behind Chinese ones, despite some 30 years of intensive government restructuring.

It is widely acknowledged that the solution for easing these inequalities lies in incorporating a still greater proportion of the workforce into the modern sector. It is also the case, though, that the skills of many workers already involved in industrial production, especially in electronics, must be upgraded beyond assembly line tasks. To be sure, Malaysia moved long ago beyond the labor-intensive production of consumer non-durables like textiles, footwear and homewares. But with its skills base nonetheless lagging behind wage increases, Malaysia has lost competitiveness to lower-wage electronics producers, especially China. Investors seeking to locate hi-technology plant in Malaysia, will thus suffer from a shortage of skilled workers.

> The labor force is well educated by regional standards, but greater training of the labor force will be needed if Malaysia is to realize its ambitions to become a knowledge-based economy. Skilled labor shortages will thus remain a problem for foreign investors beyond 2002–04.

The Malaysian government is hardly unaware of the need to increase labor productivity. Thus, in seeking to graduate from the assembly of IT hardware to more innovative products, the government created a vast development zone known as the Multimedia Super Corridor (MSC). Launched with much fanfare in the mid 1990s, the MSC was designed to attract technical expertise from the world's leading software producers. It was also linked backwards to a 'smart schools' program, encouraging the local development of software engineers and other sophisticated service workers able to sustain a broad-based 'knowledge economy.' However, there is as yet no clear evidence that the desire of government has met with reality, with software engineers, technical experts, and skilled labor shortages an endemic problem.

To help address this problem, Malaysia has invested far more in education than all other countries in Southeast Asia except Singapore, aspiring even to be an exporter of tertiary level training. The current secondary school enrolment rate, for example, stands at nearly 60 percent, with enrolment in public tertiary institutions recorded at 8.2 percent, though this figure overlooks a flourishing network of private technical institutes and business schools. Skill development of the labor force is thus actively under way.

> Malaysia is attempting to retrain its workforce to manufacture higher-value-added products, especially information and communication technologies and photonics.

Despite this, the MSC has failed to realize its aims fully.[17] Mahathir's acerbic reaction to the crisis of 1997–98, as well as his treatment of the former Deputy Prime Minister, Anwar Ibrahim, finally alienated many of the high-level US-based advisors that he had recruited. Much investment was also diverted to Singapore and India, then drained from the sector altogether by the decline of electronics markets. Thus, as the government continues to invest in the MSC, there is evidence that it is cannibalizing operations in Penang, even as Penang's free trade zone faces massive disinvestment by transnational corporations.

Labor laws and corporate downsizing

Malaysia possesses no state-sponsored labor front – on the order of Singapore's National Trades Union Congress – through which to incorporate and discipline labor. Instead, the peak labor organization, the Malaysian Trades Union Congress, retains autonomy from the government. Nonetheless, current labor legislation restricts organizing and strike activities. Further, in Malaysia's free trade zones, where much foreign investment in export manufacturing is concentrated, only in-house unions are permitted, effectively preempting effective mobilization of labor.

In this context, foreign enterprise has been able to shed staff in accordance with market contractions. While the government advises that retrenchment be treated as a last resort, of greater constraint on enterprise is the prevalence of social norms that militate against job termination and tend to favor job continuity.[18] Unfortunately, the rapidity with which many foreign enterprises have been closing down electronics production raises doubts about their intentions of returning, even when market conditions recover – the China card seems to be indicated here.

The weakness of organized labor will serve to reduce wage rises in 2003–04 as the economy picks up. There will, however, be some variation depending on the skill requirement of employers. Unskilled wages will remain stagnant beyond 2004, while labor costs for skilled workers will rise noticeably from mid 2003.

Skilled labor shortages

Much of the local labor utilized by foreign corporations remains geared to the assembly and testing of imported components. And though local personnel possessing medium to high levels of technical and managerial training are readily available in Malaysia, efficiencies are in some measure compromised by a continuing need to conform to ethnic guidelines and quotas. Likewise, educational infrastructure, though again far more advanced than in most neighboring countries, is ethnically fragmented, thereby eroding full synergies. In brief, at the primary level, many ethnic Chinese remain preoccupied with their defense of Mandarin-medium instruction. At the tertiary level, public institutions are dominated by ethnic Malays, often increasingly Islamicized. Meanwhile, Chinese students are sidetracked into 'twinning' programs, usually involving institutes and degree programs with foreign affiliation. Consequently, while Malaysia recognizes the need for education and invests much in proportional terms, there are impediments to its realizing returns. This situation imposes costs for investors as much as for the country as a whole.

Consumer and business confidence

• As Malaysian exports have fallen and job markets have tightened, business and consumer confidence have declined. Business investment has thus slowed. Consumer purchases have risen slightly in some key sectors like homes and automobiles, but have remained flat overall. And with only modest economic recovery projected for 2002–03, levels of confidence will remain flat before an anticipated upturn in 2003–04.

Business confidence eroded sharply during the second and third quarters of 2001. Malaysia's business conditions index (BCI), drawn from a sample of business leaders' expectations over sales, orders, inventory, capital utilization and other activities, fell 1.4 points between the second and third quarters to 42.6, the lowest rating since the third quarter of 1998 – a period of considerable political and economic turmoil. The country's leading economic think tank, the Malaysian Institute of Economic Research (MIER), thus warned in its quarterly report of continuing over-dependence on electronics exports and a high risk of recession. It also advised that the government's new stimulus package would not be enough to offset the fall in external demand.[19] As a result, business confidence will remain subdued well into 2002–03. Significant improvements will not occur until export demand strengthens, forecast for mid to late 2003.

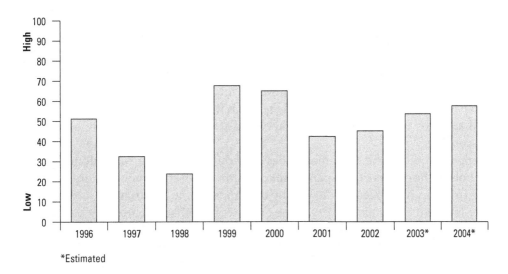

*Estimated

FIGURE 7.2 Business and consumer confidence, Malaysia 1996–2004

Business and consumer confidence remained flat during 2000, fell again in 2001, and has recovered only marginally in 2002. MasterCard International's MasterIndex biennial survey of consumer confidence revealed considerable 'anxiety' in consumer outlooks. The index dropped precipitously from a relatively robust score of 67.4 in December 2000 to 43.3 in June the following year, with a score of 50 points marking a critical benchmark of consumer optimism.[20] Consumer and business confidence will remain subdued well into 2002–03 in the absence of a recovery in the demand for tech-sector exports. However, 2003–04 should begin to see a discernible trend upwards as confidence levels fall in line with a pick-up in the international environment.

As noted above, home and automobile purchases rose, largely in response to low interest rates in 2001–02. Personal computer purchases also increased. MIER dampened any new optimism, however, alluding to the 126 point reading of the same quarter in the previous year.[21]

Stock market

- Along with some other stock markets in the region, the Kuala Lumpur Stock Exchange (KLSE) enjoyed a mild recovery in the third and fourth quarters of 2001, and has continued to trend upwards through 2002 reflecting increasing optimism about the regional and international outlook. This should continue to see the KLSE composite index trade around 800–860, with perhaps nominally higher valuations for 2003. However, while likely to be less volatile than 2001, the market is unlikely to record strong growth during 2002–03. It may be well into 2004 before the market reaches the highs of 2000, when investor confidence drove the market to 980.

In Malaysia's politicized business scene, investor sentiments have always been exaggerated, with politically well-connected companies attracting speculative money, while those out of favor have often languished, even in cases where they have been ably managed. The Securities Commission, while possessing some independence and enforcement capacity, does not possess final judicial authority through which to corporate compliance. Foreign investors have been cautioned, then, by the fact that the fortunes of local listed companies have had as much to do with political savvy and patronage as the quality of corporate decision-making.

It appears too that the stock market has sometimes been 'ramped' at election time in order to bolster the coffers of companies linked to the ruling coalition. In addition, foreign portfolio investors have been made wary by the limits on the repatriation of capital gains that were imposed at the end of 1998. They also recall Mahathir's arbitrary ban on short selling, however understandable at the time, as well as his proposals to prop up equity prices through a state-controlled strategic fund. The charters of many institutional investors prohibit their investing in the stock markets of countries where such interventions take place.

Reform: Cleaning house

Recently, however, several developments appeared to brighten the stock market scene. Malaysia's asset management company, Danaharta, continues to pursue its operations 'at a steady pace.' Thus, by 2001–02, Danaharta – through procedures characterized by the World Bank as 'clearly defined and executed'[22] – had successfully disposed of 85 percent of the loans that it had acquired. The agency is expected to be closed in 2005. Further, the Corporate Debt and Restructuring Committee, mediating voluntary workouts between creditors and corporate borrowers, had by 2001–02 resolved cases totaling RM28.2 billion, representing half of the disputes that had been referred to it.[23] Accordingly, NPLs, though again on the rise in 2002, have posed much less of a problem in Malaysia than in most neighboring countries.

Further, while Mahathir had earlier been critical of portfolio investment, a sentiment amply expressed through the introduction of capital controls, his government soon phased out most of the controls affecting foreigners, while launching sundry missions and road shows overseas through which to re-energize investor interest. These efforts appear to have been partly successful, with portfolio investment trickling back to Malaysia during 2000.

Finally, Mahathir retired his Finance Minister, Daim Zainuddin, during 2001, then took over the ministry himself. While Daim had been credited with advancing Malaysia's economic recovery, he was also associated with a select circle of favored business protégés. One of them, Halim Saad, was the controlling shareholder of Renong, a deeply indebted conglomerate with close links to the UMNO. Halim's refusal to engage his many creditors was described as exerting 'a depressing effect on the stock market.'[24] Another, Tajudin Ramli, held control over the loss-making Malaysian Airlines (MAS). Hence, Mahathir's assuming control of the finance ministry and his use of the government investment vehicle, Khazanah Holdings, and the Employees' Provident Fund effectively to re-nationalize some of the assets that had been privatized to Daim's favorites raised hopes among equities investors for greater transparency and corporate governance. To be sure, managers and owners were removed on terms that were vastly favorable to them. Tajudin, for example, was able to sell his controlling stake in MAS to the government at twice its market value. Nonetheless, the departure of Daim and his protégés was evaluated by many analysts as breaking the logjam in corporate reform.

As the Malaysian government comes to recognize debt restructuring as necessary for attracting foreign investment, its approach to MAS may provide a model for dealing with other insolvent firms.[25] Since acquiring most of MAS's stock, the government has announced plans to privatize the airline's profitable operations in international service and cargo by 2002–03. It will retain the assets in a special purpose vehicle (SPV), however, then lease planes and equipment back to the new company. Thus, with the prospects increasing for market-based reforms, MAS's stock prices have risen. MAS is now trying to recruit a strategic foreign partner, while the SPV will seek foreign investors. The government may soon take the same approach to several of Kuala Lumpur's highly indebted light-rail transit operators.

The bottom line: Not out of the woods, but looking brighter

Malaysia's deeply entrenched patterns of close business–government relations will not be fully dismantled. Nor will a 30-year-old policy be withdrawn by which 30 percent of new share issues and the non-foreign share of equity in joint ventures is reserved for 'indigenous' Malays. Indeed, the legitimacy of Mahathir and his UMNO-led government depends in some measure on these practices. Thus, some level of corrupt practices, inefficiencies, and the NPLs they give rise to will continue to impact on the KLSE into 2003–04. However, these issues are less pressing in Malaysia than elsewhere in Southeast Asia. As noted above, the country has gone far in terms of restructuring its financial sector. And there are new expectations of reform in the corporate sector.

Corporate tax

- The corporate tax rate for companies resident in Malaysia, whether foreign or locally owned, is 28 percent. However, the government provides a vast range of incentives that greatly reduce liabilities in order to encourage specified investment activities, especially capital intensive FDI in high technology production for export sectors. It is unlikely that there will be a rise in protectionist sentiments, made manifest in increased corporate tax rates or rollbacks of incentives. To the contrary, any changes to existing regulations will likely be in the opposite direction, a precedent perhaps set by the relaxation of foreign ownership requirements that took place in 1998.

Investment incentives that affect tax liabilities in the manufacturing sector take two principal forms, pioneer status and investment tax allowance (ITA). Companies may be granted pioneer status for a period of five years, entitling them to pay tax on only 30 percent of their statutory income. Companies that locate their activities in the east coast states of Kelantan, Terengganu, Pahang, and Mersing in Johor, forming the so-called 'Eastern Corridor', and in the East Malaysian territories of Sarawak, Sabah, and Labuan, enjoy a further reduction in their liability to 15 percent, a concession available on all applications received before the end of 2005.

The investment tax allowance forms an alternative to pioneer status. In this scheme, 60 percent of qualifying capital expenditure can be utilized for a period of five years to offset 70 percent of statutory income. Allowance that has not been utilized can be carried forward. The 30 percent balance of statutory income is taxed at the 28 percent corporate rate. Companies that locate their activities in the Eastern Corridor or East Malaysia can claim 80 percent of their capital expenditure to offset 85 percent of their income.

Investment in areas apart from manufacturing also attracts incentives, many of them involving pioneer status, ITA, or other kinds of tax exemptions, deductions, and duty drawbacks. Examples include investment in some agricultural activities, tourism, high technology, training, research and development, and the MSC.[26] Once again, these arrangements will, if anything, grow more liberal still during 2002–03, rather than less so.

Residential and commercial property markets

- Malaysia's property markets were hit by the economic crisis of 1997–98, causing construction to fall and NPLs to rise. However, they began to recover during the second half of 1998 through most of 2000. In 2001–02, though, they slowed once again, with the value of property transactions declining even more seriously than volume. Thus, the picture is mostly one of stagnancy today, though some sub-sectors and localities continue to perform reasonably well. Recovery is projected to resume in late 2002–03 led by demand for luxury residential property.

Residential markets

The residential market is the largest sub-sector in Malaysia's property market. Amid renewed economic downturn during 2001–02, however, transactions at the top and medium levels of the market slackened. The take-up of new properties in condominiums, townhouses, bungalow land, detached and semi-detached units averaged 40–60 percent. Existing homes in prime locations, however, retained their value.

Though economic uncertainty affected the top end of residential markets, low interest rates enabled one to two story terrace houses, about 30 percent of the market, to perform better. The take-up of new units that were launched during 2000–02 averaged between 62 and 77 percent, depending on size and locality, while supply is expected to increase by nearly 20 percent between 2002–05. Thus, in 2001–02, the residential market for properties valued at under $US50,000 performed reasonably well, especially in the southern areas of the Klang Valley.[27]

Commercial markets

In Kuala Lumpur and the surrounding Klang Valley during 2001–02, there was no appreciable change in office supply nor in rental prices. Though Malaysia's services sector has recovered somewhat from the crisis of 1997–98, gaps persist between the supply and demand of office space. The landmark Petronas twin towers building appears to be only half full. Transactions declined in terms of volume and value by 3 percent and 57 percent respectively over the previous year.

In the retail sector, floor space has steadily increased over the past decade, while, as noted above, consumer confidence has lately declined. Yet with many retailers resorting to sale promotions, shopping complexes in Kuala Lumpur have remained more than 90 percent occupied.

Finally, the hotel sector, like the residential market, has been weakened at the top end, with five-star hotels adversely affected by the diminishing arrivals of Western business travelers and tourists. Occupancy rates during the third quarter of 2001–02 thus slipped from an average of 75 percent to 65 percent from the previous year. The trend is likely to continue into 2002–03, driven by corporate cost cutting amid tight margins and weak export demand.

Three-star hotels, however, catering less to business than to medium-budget tourists from the region, have better maintained their occupancy rates. Further occupancy rate rises will occur during 2002–03 before peaking in late 2003 as new hotels come onto the market.

Property vacancy rates in Kuala Lumpur

	1998 %	1999 %	2000 %	2002 %
Office	13.5	17.0	17.7	18.1
Retail	–	14.0	13.3	12.5

Source: Asian Development Bank, Asian Recovery Report, Malaysia

The bottom line

While the global economy, on which Malaysia depends heavily, has grown only slowly during 2002, the country's property sector shows signs of recovering more rapidly in 2002–03. In Malaysia's politicized business scene, construction companies pose powerful lobbies. Thus, while nothing in Malaysia's 2002 budget targeted the property sector directly, increased allocations to state governments will probably find their way into low-cost housing. Heavy government promotion of the tourism and resort sector may also help to revitalize hotels and resorts. And the expansionary policy of low-interest rates will continue to bolster the market for terrace housing in 2002–03. Meanwhile, property markets in the rapidly industrializing southern city of Johor Baru, opposite Singapore, are expected to remain steady. Only in Penang, where production is geared closely to electronics production, are industrial property rents and prices expected to decline.

Foreign direct investment

- Malaysia, more than any other country in Southeast Asia except Singapore, has depended upon FDI to fuel its industrialization. As noted above, the government's pro-business attitudes and incentives, the state's administrative capacity, and the relative quality of the country's workforce, infrastructure, and resource base offer strong attractions. Of course, as in other countries in the region, official statistics regarding foreign applications for investment projects may be overstated in order to motivate investors. But there can be no doubt that Malaysia has long been a favored destination in the region, especially its west coast states of Selangor, Penang, and Johor. However, there are indications that the strong growth in FDI enjoyed in the past, may not be as rapid in 2002–04.

FDI in Malaysia failed to grow during the mid to late 1990s. The rising cost of labor, the small domestic market, and growing competition posed by China were all factors – as was the introduction of capital controls that served to further alienate many potential and existing investors alike. Thus, investor wariness, along with the lack of distressed assets relative to neighboring countries, kept FDI from rebounding sharply in 1999. The Malaysian

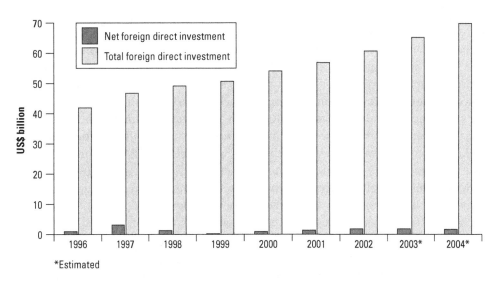

*Estimated

FIGURE 7.3 Foreign direct investment, Malaysia 1996–2004

Industrial Development Authority asserts that FDI in manufacturing recovered fully in 2000. However, external demand for Malaysia's electronics and electrical goods sector diminished the following year, again eroding investor interest.

Greater liberalization: Fewer restrictions on foreign access to market segments

Despite the most recent downturn, Malaysia has eschewed any policies of economic nationalism, even if the government's fierce criticisms of globalization might seem to suggest otherwise. Instead, it has responded by rolling back restrictions on foreign investors further, in particular the limits on foreign ownership of local ventures and land, as well as the tariffs on imported capital and intermediate goods. Foreigners can now buy residential or commercial properties valued above $US66,000.

> Foreign ownership in Malaysian ventures was long limited to 30 percent. Foreign investors can now hold majority control in telecommunications and new investments made in manufacturing. They can own up to 49 percent in the stockbroking and insurance industries.

Underscored by these developments, total FDI stood at around US$60.64 billion in 2002, up from US$56.84 billion in 2001, and is projected to increase to US$65.16 billion in 2003.[28]

Protectionism and nationalism: Foreign business as a political football?

While Mahathir is deeply nationalistic, and his criticisms of globalization and the West resonate deeply with large parts of the public, he recognizes that Malaysia has benefited greatly from globalized patterns of trade and investment. To be sure, his government has attempted to nurture some infant industries, seeking most prominently to protect the country's automobile industry. Import duties on cars thus remain around 100 percent. Further, the government has slowed the introduction of some tariff reductions associated with ASEAN Free Trade Area (AFTA), thereby irking some fellow ASEAN members.

But with Malaysia's deep dependence on trade and foreign direct investment well acknowledged among Malaysian business people, Mahathir has been encouraged to keep the economy open, if only to ensure continued economic growth and thus political stability. Indeed, while Thailand has lately reverted to new protectionism, a good indication of Malaysia's strategies lies in its further reductions in tariffs in an effort to encourage greater involvement and exposure to the international economy. There is speculation too that Mahathir is not averse to the national automobile company, Proton, being taken over by US interests, so long as production continues. In short, despite the shrill criticisms of the West and globalization, Malaysia's economic policies have generally remained pragmatic.

> Investor be warned: state contracts, licensing, procurement, and privatization are mediated by the UMNO in ways that cannot be understood as transparent.

FDI trends in 2002–04

The technology sector will again lead a year-on-year increase in FDI flows in 2002–03, with total FDI projected to reach US$4.7 billion in 2004. The capital account surplus will, however, be restricted by high levels of outward bound FDI, projected to stand at US$2.7 billion in 2003 and US$3 billion in 2004.

Electronics will remain the most targeted sector, followed by paper products, chemicals, non-metallic products, and food manufacturing. Natural gas and petroleum products fell from the top five industries in 2001, though FDI in these sectors should improve during the course of 2003–04.

Finally China replaced the United States as the single largest foreign investor in Malaysia during 2000–02, followed by the Netherlands, Japan, the US, and Singapore.[29] China's importance as a source of FDI for Malaysia will continue to increase in the medium term.

Section C Politics

- Malaysia's political system has long been one of the most stable in East Asia, an unexpected record given the country's geographic fragmentation, deep ethnic divisions, rapid industrialization, and Islamic resurgence. To be sure, it is a single-party dominant system, with the UMNO the keystone in a broad coalition of ethnic-based parties called the National Front. But elections, while regularly returning the National Front to power, permit much competition to take place, with the opposition typically capturing 40 percent of the popular vote and a significant share of seats in parliament. The opposition has thus been able to keep the government at least mildly accountable. Corrupt practices, however, known locally as money politics, remain a problem. All in all, then, it should be politics as usual in Malaysia in 2003–04, even if Mahathir steps down as he has promised, in late 2003.

Ethnic Malay support for the opposition continues to be galvanized by the way in which Mahathir warded off a perceived challenge from his deputy, Anwar Ibrahim, resulting in Anwar's receiving a lengthy prison sentence on charges that remain dubious. In these conditions, the country's opposition parties were re-energized, in particular, the PAS. Consequently, in the 1999 election the PAS cut deeply into the UMNO's Malay support base, earning it a greater presence in parliament and control of two state assemblies. And with its confidence bolstered, the party underscored its commitment to forming an Islamic state upon its coming to power at the federal level. Meanwhile, it attempted to introduce syariah law in the state of Terengganu whose assembly it controlled.

Mahathir fought back by trying to discredit the PAS as an extremist party, linking it to what were portrayed in the state-controlled media as terrorist groups. And using the Internal Security Act, his government arrested several top PAS officials in 2001.

Political tensions will thus remain in Malaysia, although they should be contained in the normal institutional mechanisms for political competition currently in place.

Leading risk indices: Stability, corruption, governance, risk

Political stability

After September 11, the PAS has reacted shrilly to US activities in Afghanistan, mounting large protests while declaring its support for holy war. In the view of much of the public, Mahathir's allegations of PAS links to terrorists suddenly appeared more credible and his use of the ISA quite justified.[30] At the same time, rising tensions over the Islamic state issue tested the PAS's most important partner, the largely Chinese-based Democratic Action Party, causing the coalition to finally fracture. In addition, with the country's economy threatened anew, consensus grew that only the National Front could be trusted to safeguard the country's prosperity. Speculation thus mounted over Mahathir's calling an early election, possibly in 2003, which his government is now expected to win easily. His announcing of his resignation in late 2003 may also have increased his party's popularity.

Nonetheless, despite Mahathir's re-equilibrating the political system, patterns of money politics will persist in Malaysia. Daim Zainuddin and his top protégés have been removed, and some assets returned from favored conglomerates to the state. But there is no assurance that market forces and transparency will prevail. Instead, in an on-going attempt to promote communal Malay interests, Danaharta may simply shift the assets it has acquired into the National Equity Corporation (which operates a massive unit trust on behalf of the Malays) and the Pilgrim's Fund Management Board.[31] Aspiring Malay business people will thus remain motivated to join the UMNO and scale its apparatus principally in order to gain access to state resources.

A dilemma thus appears, inasmuch as if Malaysia's political system is to remain stable, it must accommodate powerful business interests and ethnic aspirations. On the other hand, the social grievances that money politics arouse, especially amid economic recession, risk destabilizing the system much as they did in the late 1990s. Discontent will doubtless intensify as the memory of September 11 fades. Indeed, foreign investors also face a similar dilemma. While they gain from the stability that is derived, at least partly, through money politics, their returns are diminished by the accompanying distortions and inefficiencies.

The events of September 11 aside, political tensions have been a fact of life in Malaysia ever since the regional financial crisis of 1997–98, with popular discontent over government corruption finding organized form through Islamic resurgence. And government efforts to contain the challenges seemed only to deepen public cynicism. However, the government

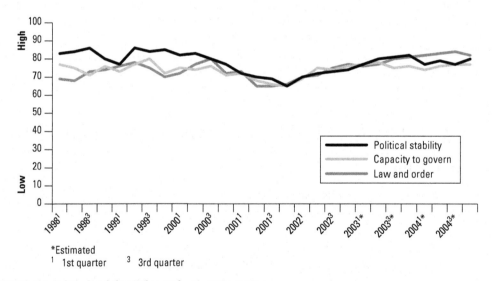

FIGURE 7.4 Political stability index, Malaysia 1998–2004

Political stability methodology:
- The capacity-to-govern index is based upon the institutional reach of government defined in terms of its ability to set the political and economic agenda and ensure its legislative program is enacted without significant compromise. This index is adversely affected by legislative opposition, lack of legislative implementation, failure to realize government policy and general political opposition.
- The political stability index measures violent opposition or organized demonstrations, terrorist activities, and popular discontent that adversely affect the institutional and electoral stability of the government.
- The law and order index measures the propensity to civil obedience, and the institutional reach of the rule of law in terms of regulatory compliance and enforcement.

retained the loyalty of the security forces. And, after September 11, the public appears to look more sympathetically upon the government's use of coercion. The slowing economy has also worked in the government's favor, at least in the short term, with many middle-class elements shaken by the renewed threats to their status. Public protests against the government have subsided. In these conditions one can expect that Malaysia's unique political synthesis of authoritarian controls and regular, reasonably competitive elections will persist.

Corruption

While Malaysia's distinctive brand of money politics lends itself inevitably to corrupt exchanges between politicians and business people, the problem is not so entrenched as in most other countries in Southeast Asia. Civil servants are reasonably compensated, while the military remains professional. Hence, after Singapore, Malaysia is assessed as the least corrupt country in the region, consistently earning a mid-level score of around 5 on Transparency International's scale of 0 to 10. Of the 90+ countries assessed, Malaysia usually ranks in the 30th percentile.[32]

However, corruption is perceived as serious in Malaysia. Mahathir, for example, has warned frequently of the dangers of corruption – its impact on the UMNO and public opinion – yet he has helped to fashion the mesh of business–government relations upon which his party depends. Malaysia's courts have gained a reputation for fairly resolving commercial disputes, but have also served as a tool of the executive in political cases. And though a new chief justice displaying integrity was appointed in 2001, this was matched by the government's changing attorney-generals in questionable ways.[33] Finally, while the country's Anti-Corruption Agency is staffed by 800 personnel and makes frequent arrests, it rarely investigates top-level officials,[34] unless they have fallen from favor.

Despite this, it remains the case that Malaysia has taken a comparatively restrained approach to corruption, leaving the vital production of tradable goods, largely the province of foreign investors, only mildly affected.[35] To be sure, expatriate managers of local production facilities are tapped for campaign contributions, thereby winning themselves additional tariff concessions or exemptions from some regulatory burdens.[36] But demands are not regarded as onerous, thus having little impact on the calculations of foreign investors.

More generally, corruption, while serious in Malaysia, is less distorting than in most other Southeast Asian countries. Only Singapore is assessed by Transparency International as less corrupt. Further, because of continuities in national leadership, corruption remains regulated at the center, thus not growing significantly worse in the wake of the crisis, as it has in some neighboring countries (refer to corruption index graphs in this book). Foreign investors are rarely harassed with large and extortionate demands.

Corporate governance and transparency

While Malaysia's civil service can be regarded as reasonably effective, governance in the corporate sector must be assessed as low. The government recognizes the problem, made even more pressing after the crisis. Hence, a new institute, the Malaysian Institute of Corporate Governance, has been set up. New guidelines have been produced by the High

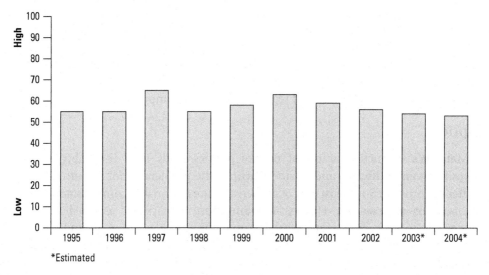

*Estimated

FIGURE 7.5 Corruption index, Malaysia 1995–2004

Level Finance Committee on Corporate Governance, and new regulations regarding stock market activities have been put in place. But the close links between politics and business, undergirded by ethnic restructuring, militate strongly against the effectiveness of reforms, with market discipline and minority shareholder rights remaining weak. Limited disclosure, political connections, sleeping partners, and interlocking directorships and shareholdings remain key features of Malaysia's corporate scene. Hence, a recent World Bank report ranked corporate governance in Malaysia as only slightly above that of Indonesia.[37]

Moreover, Malaysia, like most emerging markets, suffers much outright corporate fraud in the form of intellectual property theft. Counterfeit production of all manner of goods, ranging from IT products to automobile parts, is rampant. Perhaps as a function of its relative level of technological advancement, Malaysia has also earned a reputation in the region as the center for credit card fraud, with hologram technologies and number scanners having fallen into the hands of organized crime elements.

While corporate governance in Malaysia is low, the departure of the finance minister in 2001 and the re-nationalization of assets may enable standards to rise. Indeed, it is essential that greater transparency be introduced in terms of contract bidding, stock market listings, and corporate ownership, control, operations and returns. These have shown some indication of becoming reality, but there is no apparent haste to introduce them in 2002–04.

Corporate bankruptcy mechanisms in Malaysia are regarded as strong by regional standards. So too is the judiciary, at least in commercial disputes. Of course, large politically well-connected conglomerates historically have enjoyed immunity from bankruptcy rulings by the courts, with the government quickly qualifying them for bailouts rather than any serious restructuring. But the recent departure of the former finance minister and his protégés holds out the prospect of improvement.

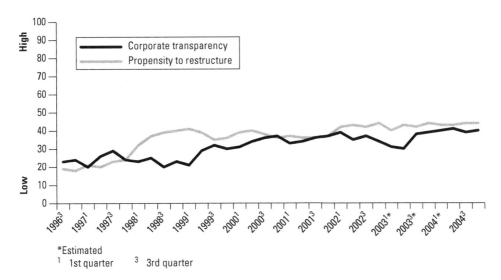

FIGURE 7.6 Corporate governance index, Malaysia 1996–2004

Corporate governance methodology
- The corporate governance index is a composite index measuring the juridical requirements for corporate disclosure and financial reporting, prudential regime adequacy, prudential compliance enforcement, and the juridical reach of prudential authorities.
- The propensity-to-restructure index is a composite index based on media releases and reported corporate restructuring as a result of prudential regulation, financial incentives, loan restructuring / re-negotiation, or asset realignment.

Foreign investor risk index

In general, foreign investor risk in Malaysia declined over 2001–02, and can be expected to decline further in 2003–04. The political equilibrium appears to have been restored, while tariffs and limits on foreign ownership have been eased. Restrictions on the repatriation of capital gains have been removed altogether. Corruption has ebbed and flowed since the crisis but is not discernibly worse, and corporate governance is set to improve, albeit marginally. But even if it can be shown that investor risk is declining, so too have external markets for Malaysia's exports. The domestic market, further, remains limited. The stock market is flat. Thus, while Malaysia has grown even more accommodating toward foreign investors, there are presently fewer reasons for them to take up the offer.

Section D Security

- Malaysia does not enjoy the full panoply of good diplomatic relations with most of its neighbors, with various on-going disputes still troubling the establishment of more normalized patterns of inter-state conduct. However, none of these diplomatic disputes

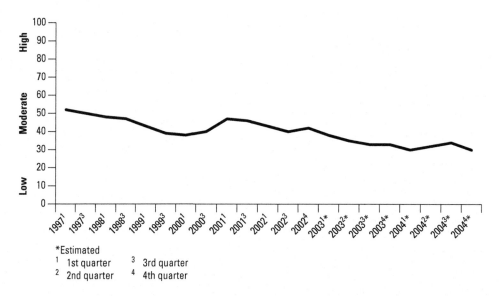

FIGURE 7.7 Foreign investor risk index, Malaysia 1997–2004

Foreign investor risk index methodology:
- The foreign investor risk index is a composite index measuring tax burdens, discriminatory regulatory practices, adverse compliance regulations, government policy toward foreign enterprise, receptiveness to issuance of government contracts, foreign enterprise commercial restrictions, and official attitudinal changes to foreign direct investment and foreign commercial operations which impact on operational efficiency. The index also incorporates a nominal measure for market risk and market failure.

approaches open hostility. Of more concern to foreign investors will be the resurgence of Islamic militancy and political movements whose antithetical attitude to the West is of growing concern in light of September 11. However, these groups are at this stage not considered a credible threat to foreign enterprise.

Border problems

Malaysia has longstanding border disputes with virtually all its neighbors – Thailand, Indonesia and the Philippines. There are also controversies over territory involving Singapore and Brunei. But none of these disputes is close to provoking any military response. More worrying have been the massive cross-border flows of undocumented workers from Indonesia, the Philippines, Burma and Bangladesh. While helping to fill the bottom end of the labor market during boom times, these workers are associated with unemployment, surging crime rates, and forced repatriation today. Large amounts of narcotics also filter into Malaysia from the Golden Triangle area. Cross-border automobile theft and smuggling into Thailand are endemic. Nonetheless, Malaysia experiences nothing like the loss of juridical control over its border regions, even in East Malaysia, that afflicts its northern neighbors.

Internal security

Since the late 1970s, Malaysia has been undergoing an Islamic resurgence. However, the PAS remains officially committed to democratic procedures and contesting elections, while defending civil liberties and transparency. More recently it has also governed the northeastern states it controls in pragmatic ways, making cultural concessions to Chinese populations. Meanwhile, it remains vague about the form that an Islamic state might take. Hence, the extent to which the PAS might be linked to a perceived rise in Islamic militancy on the peninsula is unclear. The government alleges that PAS members are part of the Al-Ma'unah group that, in early 2001, seized weapons from several military redoubts, killed two security personnel, and launched a grenade attack on the Carlsberg brewery near Kuala Lumpur. It has also arrested some top PAS officials, alleging that they had trained in Afghanistan and joined the shadowy KMM (Malaysian Militant Group) in order to carry out terrorist bombings. But whether the PAS is genuinely involved, or the government is merely seeking pretexts for a crackdown is unknown. In any event, the PAS appears to have lost some support after September 11.

Expatriate executives working in Malaysia seldom encounter nationalist resentments. Personal security is more regularly threatened by ordinary street crime, which, while still moderate by Western standards, has increased in the Klang Valley since the crisis.

Section E Economic and political risk forecasts

- Malaysia's dependence on foreign direct investment in low-to-medium technology export manufacturing has been made plain in the past few years. Most notably, its electronics sector remains vulnerable to competition from lower cost producers like China, Vietnam and Thailand, as well as cyclical downturns in US demand. However, Malaysia's economy is more diversified than neighboring Singapore's, with commodities like petroleum, gas, and palm oil remaining vital exports. In addition, the government has been active in attempting to upgrade its manufacturing base, initiating various technological development schemes and training programs in a quest to establish a 'knowledge economy.' Further, by regional standards, Malaysia's civil service capacity, infrastructural planning, and human capital remain good. The country's politics have also regained much of their earlier equilibrium. Prospects have improved in areas of corporate governance.

Short-term forecasts

- Malaysia's economy will slowly recover during the first half of 2002–03, gaining more momentum in 2003 as global markets for electronics begin to revive. Still, Malaysia will be squeezed in the short term by both lower-cost and higher technology producers. Growth for 2002–03 is projected at 2.7 percent. Unemployment and underemployment will continue to rise before leveling off toward the end of the year. Property markets will remain weak, especially as more office property comes on stream, though they should not decline precipitously.

- The government is currently committed to deficit spending to make up some of the short-fall in private investment, especially in construction and infrastructural development. But it shuns populist social programs, thus avoiding excessive debt increases. Macroeconomic conditions can be expected to remain reasonably sound. Bank Negara Malaysia will retain its currency peg, unless China devalues sharply.
- On the social front, foreign observers routinely argue that Malaysia's stability is threatened by ethnic tensions and Islamic resurgence. It appears, though, that after significant re-distribution during the past several decades, indigenous resentments over the relative prosperity of the Chinese have greatly abated. Further, while the country's Islamic resurgence has been under way for several decades, the PAS appears committed to demo-cratic politics and foreign investment. It has not been demonstrated that the party has any links to militant anti-system groups. Nonetheless, Mahathir's government has used popular suspicions to regain some of the ground it lost in the last general election.

Short-term opportunities

- Despite the resentments against Western domination and the inequities of globalization that are frequently given vent to by Mahathir, Malaysia's government remains quietly prag-matic and highly receptive to foreign investment. Indeed, the terms of approval, licensing, ownership, and operations have been relaxed. There is little likelihood of increased protectionism.
- Nonetheless, in the current conditions of global stagnation, short-term opportunities in Malaysia are quite limited. Foreign direct investors in electronics manufacturing continue to withdraw. However, because Malaysia was less affected by the crisis in 1997–98 than some other countries, it never underwent a sale of distressed assets. The current slowdown, then, may present new opportunities for acquisitions, especially as the government continues to invest heavily in necessary infrastructure and education.
- More speculative investors may explore the KLSE. Malaysia is currently regarded by some analysts as an under-held market, yet beginning to display some quality management teams.[38]

Medium to longer term

- The government's concerted efforts to deepen Malaysia's technological capacity and add value to manufactures may bear fruit in the medium to longer term. Hence, while Malaysia will lag behind neighboring Singapore in terms of knowledge-based services – notwithstanding the grand aspirations embodied in the Multimedia Super Corridor – it will forge ahead of other countries in Southeast Asia. Accordingly, Malaysia may carve out a niche as a reasonably sophisticated mid-level producer, therein establishing new complementarities with its neighbors.
- In addition, the government's having re-nationalized the assets of many once-promoted tycoons may bode well for corporate governance and efficiencies. Of course, Mahathir probably remains committed to creating an indigenous business class, one that can

participate effectively in otherwise free-market conditions. But there are reasons for thinking that in conducting this exercise a second time round, privatization and lending will be undertaken more prudently.

• As Malaysia's economy is restored to growth, investment opportunities will reappear in a variety of sectors, including port development and rail transport, power generation, industrial waste treatment, tertiary education, and health and aged care. Opportunities in these areas are probably contingent, however, upon the country's electronics industries advancing in the product cycle and gaining new international competitiveness.

Overall risk rating

Malaysia's risk profile is semi-stable. Political equilibrium, the government's pro-business attitudes, relative bureaucratic capacity, moderately high levels of human capital, and the prospect of improved corporate governance help to reduce risk. By contrast, the country's dependence upon electronic exports and its small domestic markets erode investment opportunities. Finally, Malaysia's Islamic resurgence, while until recently moderate in tone, and its location in what is increasingly regarded as a volatile region, may test the confidence of some foreign investors.

Risk: Mostly Stable →
Risk Rating (0 = lowest risk, 10 = highest risk) 4.5

Section F Malaysia fact sheet*

Geography

Capital
Kuala Lumpur

Largest city (millions)
Kuala Lumpur, 2 (est.)

Location
Southeastern Asia, peninsula and northern one-third of the island of

Borneo, bordering Indonesia and the South China Sea, south of Vietnam. Malaysia is geographically separated between Peninsular Malaysia and East Malaysia, comprising two states in northern Borneo.

Adjacent countries
Thailand, Singapore, Brunei, Indonesia, the Philippines

* All figures are the latest available except where indicated. All figures are in US dollars. Figures are compiled from national, international and multilateral agencies (Australian Bureau of Statistics, Central Intelligence Agency World Fact Book, International Monetary Fund). Gross Domestic Product (GDP) refers to the value of all goods and services produced in the preceding financial year. The Adult Economic Participation rate refers to the percentage of the population aged 15 and over (excluding military personnel) who are economically active. GDP per capita, Purchasing Power Parity (GDP per capita – PPP) refers to the indices developed by the World Bank to take account of price differences, cost of living differences, and relative purchasing power of a set basket of goods and services between countries so as to provide a more accurate measure of national wealth.

Terrain
Coastal plains rising to hills and mountains

Land use (1993)
Arable land 3%, permanent crops 12%, permanent pastures 0%, forests and woodland 68%, other 17%

Area (km²)
329,750

Economic statistics

Currency
Ringgit (RM) = 100 sen

Exchange rate (February 2002)
US$1.00 = RM3.8

Gross Domestic Product (GDP)
US$94.3 billion

GDP per capita (1999)
US$3,400

GDP per capita – PPP (1999)
US$10,700

GDP – composition by sector
Agriculture 14%, industry 44%, services 42%

Inflation rate
1.9%

Foreign debt (billions) (1999)
US$45.9

Current account balance (billions) (year to September 2001)
+7.41

National unemployment rate (2002)
3.4%

Population below poverty line
6.8%

Labor force (millions)
9.6

Labor force by occupation
Agriculture 16%, industry 27%, services 15%, government 10%, construction 9%, local trade and tourism 17%

Budget (billions)
US$27
Revenues: US$16.4
Expenditure (2000): 17.8, including capital expenditures of US$43

Industries
Electronics and electrical goods, light manufacturing, automobiles, steel, building materials, plastics, rubber and palm oil, logging, tin, petroleum and natural gas

Major exports (billions) (1999)
US$83.5
Electronics and electrical goods, petroleum, liquefied natural gas, chemicals, palm oil, rubber, textiles, wood and wood products

Major imports (billions) (1999)
US$61.5
Machinery and equipment, chemicals, food, fuel, lubricants, consumer goods

Major trading partners (exports)
United States, Singapore, Japan, Hong Kong, Netherlands, Taiwan, Thailand

Major trading partners (imports)
Japan, United States, Singapore, Taiwan, South Korea, Thailand, China

Televisions (1997, millions)
3.6

Televisions 1997, per 1000 people
486

Telephones (lines in use, millions, 1999)
4.5

Telephones per capita (2000, per 1000)
19.93

Cellular phones (1999, millions)
2.69

Cellular phones per 1000 (2000)
21.32

Automobiles in use (total vehicle registration 2001 millions)
3.87

Internet users (2000)
1.6 million

Fiscal year
Calendar year

Government and political statistics

Nature of government
Constitutional monarchy, parliamentary democracy, federalist system (de facto executive-centered limited democracy and unitary system)

Constitution
Adopted 1957

Structure of government

Head of state
Yang Di-pertuan Agong (King) Tuanku Syed Sirajuddin

Executive branch
Prime Minister Mahathir Mohamad

Legislative branch
Bi-cameral parliament

Senate (Dewan Negara)
69 senators appointed to a maximum of two consecutive three-year terms

House of Representatives (Dewan Rakyat)
192 representatives elected from single-member districts for maximum 5-year terms

Cabinet ministers (as of 14 February 2002)

Prime Minister
Dato' Seri Mahathir Mohamad

Deputy Prime Minister
Dato' Seri Abdullah Ahmad Badawi

Minister of Special Functions
Dato' Seri Mahathir Mohamad

Ministers in the Prime Minister's Office
Dato' Rais bin Yatim
Datuk Pandikar Amin Mulia
Tan Sri Datuk Seri Panglima Bernard Giluk Dompok
Brig. Gen. Senator Datuk Abdul Hamid bin Zainal Abidin

Minister of Finance
Dato' Seri Mahathir Mohamad

Minister of Home Affairs
Dato' Seri Abdullah Ahmad Badawi

Minister of Foreign Affairs
Datuk Seri Syed Hamid bin Syed Jaafar Albar

Minister of Defence
Dato' Sri Najib bin Tun Abdul Razak

Minister of Transport
Dato' Seri Dr. Ling Liong Sik

Minister of Works
Dato' Seri S. Samy Vellu

Minister of Primary Industries
Dato' Seri Lim Keng Yaik

Ministry of International Trade and Industry
Dato' Seri Rafidah binti Aziz

Minister of Energy, Communication and Multimedia
Datuk Leo Moggie Anak Irok

Minister of Information
Tan Sri Mohd Khalil bin Yaacob

Minister of Education
Tan Sri Musa bin Mohamad

Minister of Human Resources
Datuk Dr Fong Chan Onn

Minister of Domestic Trade and Consumer Affairs
Tan Sri Dato' Haji Muhyiddin bin Haji Mohd Yasin

Minister of Health
Dato' Chua Jui Meng

Minister of Housing and Local Government
Dato' Ong Ka Ting

Minister of Agriculture
Datuk Mohd Effendi bin Norwawi

Minister of Science, Technology and Environment
Datuk Law Hieng Ding

Minister of Land and Cooperative Development
Tan Sri Datuk Kasitah bin Gaddam

Minister of National Unity and Social Development
Dato' Dr Siti Zaharah binti Sulaiman

Minister of Entrepreneur Development
Datuk Mohamed Nazri bin Tan Sri Dato' Abdul Aziz

Minister of Rural Development
Dato' Azmi bin Khalid

Minister of Culture, Arts and Tourism
Datuk Abdul Kadir bin Haji Sheikh Fadzir

Minister of Youth and Sports
Dato' Hishamuddin bin Tun Hussein

Minister of Women and Family Development
Datuk Shahrizat binti Abdul Jalil

Administrative structure of government
13 states and 1 federal territory encompassing the capital of Kuala Lumpur and the offshore banking center of Labuan

Main governing parties and ideological affiliation
National Front (*Barisan Nasional*) coalition comprising United Malays National Organization (UMNO, centrist, modernizing, ethnic Malay constituencies), Malaysian Chinese Association (MCA, centrist, ethnic Chinese constituencies), Malaysian Indian Congress (MIC, centrist, ethnic Indian constituencies), People's Movement of Malaysia (*Gerakan Rakyat Malaysia*, nominally progressive and multiethnic, predominantly Penang-based constituencies), and 10 smaller parties, primarily ethnic, based in Peninsular Malaysia or East Malaysian states of Sabah and Sarawak.

Main opposition parties
Pan-Malaysian Islamic Party (PAS); Democratic Action Party (DAP);

National Justice Party (*Keadilan*); People's Party of Malaysia (PRM).

International memberships
APEC, ARF, AsDB, ASEAN, BIS, C, CCC, CP, ESCAP, FAO, G-15, G-77, IAEA, IBRD, ICAO, ICFTU, ICRM, IDA, IDB, IFAD, IFC, IFRCS, IHO, ILO, IMF, IMO, Inmarsat, Intelsat, Interpol, IOC, ISO, ITU, MINURSO, MONUC, NAM, OIC, OPCW, UN, UNCTAD, UNESCO, UNIDO, UNIKOM, UNMEE, UNMIBH, UNMIK, UNTAET, UPU, WCL, WFTU, WHO, WIPO, WMO, WToO, WTrO

Business organizations
Federation of Malaysian Manufacturers, Malaysia External Trade Development Corporation, Malaysia International Chamber of Commerce and Industry, Business Women's Organization in Malaysia, Association of Chinese Chamber of Commerce and Industry, Malaysia, Konsortium Industri Utara, National Association of Women Entrepreneurs in Malaysia, Malaysian Institute of Management, Women's Institute of Management, Malaysian Association of Certified Public Accountants, the Malaysian Agricultural Economics Association

Social statistics

Population size (millions)
21.8 (2000 est.)

Population density (per square km)
66.1

Fertility rate (average number of children born to women 15–49 years of age)
3.29

Maternal mortality rate (per 100,000 births, 2001)
39

Infant mortality rate (deaths per 1,000 births)
20.1

Population growth
2.01% (2000)

Life expectancy
71
Men: 68.22
Women: 73.63

Ethnic composition
Malay 58%, Chinese 26%, Indian 7%, Other 9%

Religions
Muslim 53%, Buddhism and other Chinese folk religions 30%, Hindu 7%, Christianity 6%

National languages spoken
Malay, Chinese (Mandarin and dialects), Tamil, English, East Malaysian languages and dialects

Illiteracy rate (age 15+)
83.5%

By gender (ages 25+)
Men: 89.1%
Women: 78.1%

Philippines

8 Philippines

Jane Ford

Section A Economy

Overview

The war on terror, with its ramifications for international consumer spending, ripped a hole in the Philippines' blueprint for a quick recovery from economic downturn in 2001, keeping GDP growth at a moderate 2 percent in 2002. Prior to the September 11 terrorist attacks in the US, many held high hopes for a reinvigorated economy in 2001–02. The new Macapagal Arroyo government had pledged to effect the regulatory change begun after the 1986 'People Power' revolution deposed the dictatorial Marcos regime. Many believed that the new order represented another chance for the country to revive incrementally its ailing political and economic structure and eventually shrug off the monikers of 'sick man' and the 'arm pit of Asia.' The 34 percent jump in the Philippine stock index in the opening minutes after Georgetown University-trained economist Dr Gloria Macapagal Arroyo took office was symbolic of the mood. The market's subsequent return to lower levels reflected widespread recognition that reform will be a slow process in light of the many problems the government faces. This will be ongoing in 2003–04.

War on terrorism: Economic battles ahead in 2003–04

Despite such pronouncements, with an economy highly reliant on US trade and a domestic Islamic insurgency to contend with, the Philippines is highly vulnerable to instability in both the US and in the global economy. A prolonged US 'war against terrorism' and ongoing distractions from kick-starting the world economy could have significant knock-on effects for the Philippines in 2003–04. More generally, the Philippines has felt the full force of what a war on terror means, with US troops deployed to the Philippines and helping combat domestic insurgency; a situation that can only add to investor fears and a fall in international investor confidence if domestic sources of terrorism continue into 2003–04.

Unfortunately, while Macapagal Arroyo has pledged support for the US campaign against Islamic terrorists, the Philippines' vulnerability to Islamic terrorists in the southern province of Mindanao is likely to continue, with deleterious consequences on the tourism industry, otherwise highly significant to the wellbeing of the Philippine economy. In addition, there has been domestic political fallout from the military cooperation between Manila and Washington to destroy the al-Qaeda network in the south of the Philippines. This has proven politically challenging to the administration, keen to placate secessionist fears on the south island and to smooth relations with Washington, which is eager to pursue the campaign against terror.

Consequently, investor confidence in the Philippines has been severely tested in 2001–02; indeed, there has also been a general aversion to emerging markets during this same period, compounding Philippine economic performance and future prospects. This is reflected by investor concerns about financial restructuring and the slim pickings in capital markets. Prospects of a US recovery, particularly in the electronics industries which are important to the Philippines, were cloudy even before the events of September 11, and will remain so for 2003–04.

While the Philippines survived the Asian currency crisis of 1997–98 with a comparatively mild reduction in foreign investment, significantly more damage has been caused by political turmoil, the spotlight on corruption and the lack of transparency in 2000–02. The share market lost 30 percent and the exchange rate depreciated by 11 percent in 2000, reflecting concerns with the Estrada presidency. Capital flight has continued until recently, despite initial optimism for the new government. In 2001–02 there was a net outflow of portfolio investments, although a net inflow in September 2001 propelled the account into a surplus of US$297 million.[1] Net portfolio investment finally improved to a surplus of US$1399 million in 2002.[2] This should now stabilize in 2003–04, with signs of tentative improvement in the Philippine Stock Exchange (PSE) – up 20 percent and showing modest improvement in 2002, albeit that the longer-term structural trend of the PSE has been downwards since 1997.

Reform: Lots of promises, But is there any action?

While the government has pledged to overhaul the nation's political and economic institutions, replacing the *utang na loob* system of obligation through favors with transparent governance, it remains less clear that the government can deliver on these promises.

One of the key questions for investors (and Filipinos) thus remains the government's capacity to effect change. Despite the optimism surrounding the Macapagal Arroyo government's reform agenda, the economic and political outlook for the Philippines remains uncertain. While the spirit of liberalizing reform is strong, the government faces real challenges to revive 'the sick man of Asia,' particularly if the global recession continues and the anticipated US-led recovery is longer in coming.

If such proves to be the case, then the economic growth and equity reforms touted by the new administration might well be side-lined from their otherwise prominent place in the government's reform agenda, one which has attempted to reposition itself in terms of attracting the interest of foreign investors by speaking directly of the benefits of (cautious) liberalization and market-oriented microeconomic reform. Assuming a modest pick-up in the external demand structure and better global economic performance, the administration should find it easier to persist with these announced reforms; indeed, they might well gain momentum in 2003–04 as the administration finds its feet and matures in terms of its hold on public administration.

> Economic indicators are mixed in the Philippines and the environment is perilous for investors without strong local connections. The economy continues to grow and the government almost met its fiscal deficit target of $US2.8 billion in 2001–02, posting a deficit of US$2.9 billion. Domestic consumption has remained buoyant. However, growth is limited by a low per capita income and high inequality. Exports posted a 9.2 percent year-on-year decline and the banking sector is also vulnerable. Continued weakness in the international economy will mean that the predicted economic recovery in the latter part of 2003–04 is likely to be subdued.

Investor beware: Wariness, watchfulness

Reform will inevitably produce opportunities for the astute investor as it progresses, but indirect impediments to investment remain. The Macapagal Arroyo government is actively courting foreign investors with trade missions throughout the region and a pro-foreign investment stance. The government has sought to develop a free-trade area with Malaysia to boost economic activity in the region. Tax incentives offered to the first mining project to come in under the Macapagal Arroyo administration are also representative of the pro-business stance. The pro-trade, pro-investment stance is likely to have a positive effect in the medium term – particularly in view of the protectionist trends in Thailand and Malaysia. In 2003–04 foreign investors can expect a warm welcome, innovative concessions, and a willingness to negotiate.

On the down side, in the short term the Philippines' image problem is likely to continue to create uncertainty in financial markets. Investors should proceed with extreme caution given the nation's ineffective and inefficient bureaucracy, a less than robust financial system, intransigent poverty and political violence, as well as an uncertain international environment.

Section B Risks and projections

Macroeconomic performance and risk indicators

- Unexpected strength in the agricultural sector has sheltered the economy from recession but it is far from healthy. The downturn in the US economy and general contraction in the global economy in 2001–02, combined with stagnation in the Japanese economy and slower demand for electronic equipment have all affected exports, down 15.6 percent in 2001–02. Although leading indicators suggested an upturn in 2003–04, international economic uncertainty will continue to limit external demand. While the mid 2001–02 inflation figure was the lowest in two years at 3.4 percent, fiscal reform and institutional change are needed. Given the difficulties experienced in effecting reform, uncertainty is likely to prevail in markets throughout 2003–04.

GDP growth has been modest, but resilient, at 3.3 percent in 2001 but contracted to 2 percent in 2002, and down from 3.9 percent in 2000. However, this is largely a respectable growth rate given the enormous obstacles the country has faced.[3] The overall weakening in GDP growth is due to the combined slowdown in the industry and services sectors, negating the accelerated 3 percent gain posted by the agriculture, fishery and forestry (AFF) sector in 2001–02, as well as contracting external factors. The industrial sector grew by only 2.7 percent in 2001, short of the 3.9 percent growth achieved in the same period in 2000, and has continued to contract, with industrial growth recording only modest growth of 1.7 percent in 2002. The services sector declined from 4.4 percent growth in 2000 to 2.8 percent growth in 2002.[4]

The good news, however, is that growth in services, industrial output and agriculture, should all experience better prospects in 2003–04, with forecasts of 3.5 percent for services, 5.4 percent for industrial growth, and 2 percent for agricultural growth.[5]

Most of the 3.3 percent GDP growth in 2001–02 was due to personal consumption expenditure, which grew by 3.4 percent and contributed 2.6 percent to GDP growth. The bulk of this spending was directed toward food, transportation, communication and miscellaneous expenditures. Transportation and communications expenditure increased by 8.5 percent, with a surge in the total volume of domestic and international calls.

Leading indicators suggest a pick-up in 2003–04, with projects of around 3.9–4.1 percent GDP growth. However, recovery is contingent on an improvement in the international economy, especially a US recovery, which remains fragile despite international pump-priming.

Investment growth and budget deficits: Good or bad prospects?

Investment began to grow cautiously after flooding out of the country throughout the final months of the Estrada presidency in 2000. Capital formation was up 4.3 percent in 2001–02 from 0.9 percent in 2000.[6] Year-on-year, the real value of production index (VAPI) grew by

11.4 percent in 2001–02. Manufacturing firms' average capacity utilization rose slightly to 79.7 percent in July 2002, from 77.7 percent in June 2001.

Yet further risk is not to be underestimated, with demand still weakening for electronics exports, which comprise 60 percent of total exports. Even a sudden end to the US slump will take some time to trickle through to the export sector of the Philippines.

> The outlook for 2003–04 is for continued uncertainty with gradual improvement in the macro economy. Much depends on an improvement in the US and Japanese economies and, in the longer term, on market diversification. The manufacturing sector, the largest of the industrial sector, is predominantly dependent on exports, and growth in 2003–04 is likely to be subdued.

The budget deficit will also continue to constrain the government's ability to stimulate the economy in the short term. As a proportion of GDP, this has blown out from 1.9 percent in 1998 to 4.1 percent in 2001, and has remained high at 3.9 percent in 2002. As a consequence, the IMF is monitoring the country's monetary and fiscal targets, with an agreement from the Macapagal Arroyo administration that all budget deficits should be eliminated by 2004 or 2006 at the latest.[7] Investors have focused on the budget deficit as a key indicator of government credibility after the blowout. The government has pledged to cut non-personnel expenses by up to 10 percent and it aims to rationalize government-owned motor vehicles, properties, luxury assets and corporate shares. This is proving difficult to achieve, however, with forward estimates suggesting a continuing and substantial budget deficit of around 2.1 percent of GDP in 2004 and still standing at 1.3 percent in 2005, albeit trending downwards.[8]

The central bank eased official interest rates by 800 basis points between December 2000 and May 2002, to 7.0 percent with the overnight lending rate at 9.25 percent. However, further downward movement will be difficult, given pressures on the currency, the budget, and, most of all, fears that inflationary pressures will persist in 2003–04.[9] Nonetheless, the Bangko Sentral ng Pilipinas (BSP) has bucked the protectionist trend in the region, reaffirmed its commitment to a free-floating exchange rate and ruled out capital controls.[10]

Export performance

- A weaker world economy has undermined the effects of a lower peso, producing poor export performance in 2001–02. International demand is likely to remain sluggish, given uncertainty surrounding economic recovery in the US, particularly the depth of the recovery and how sustainable this will be. The longer-term outlook for exports is stronger, and the government is attempting to diversify export markets. Export growth in 2003–04 should thus have a modest boost as the external environment improves and economic growth improves slightly.

After strong performance throughout most of 2000 with 17 percent growth in exports, 2001 was a disastrous year, seeing export growth contract by –1.7 percent. It was little better in

2002 with a modest pick-up in export growth of 2 percent, but still well down on its growth levels of 2000. Merchandise exports, in particular, have been hard hit, recording a 15.8 percent fall in 2001–02; the biggest year-on-year fall since 1975. So too, non-merchandise exports have fared badly, with negative growth of 11.5 percent in 2001–02.[11] The current account remained in surplus in 2001–02, standing at US$6.1 billion, and set to hover around US$5 billion to US$4 billion in 2003–04[12]

> With around 45 percent of exports going to the US and Japan, both experiencing economic difficulties, net foreign receipts in the coming year are likely to be constrained. Other major export markets including the Netherlands and Taiwan are also experiencing weakness.

Earnings sourced from the US accounted for over 30 percent of aggregate Philippine exports in 2000–01, with recession in the US in 2001 constraining growth in 2001–02. Export growth in 2003–04 hinges on reinvigorated US demand for the Philippines' main electronics exports, semiconductors, which account for 16.5 percent of merchandise exports. This is possible if the US recovers strongly in 2003–04.

Liberalization: Alive and well?

The Philippines economy is gradually liberalizing and diversifying. To this end, the government has pledged that information and communications technology (ICT) will play a key role in the country's development program. The Philippines has a comparative advantage in labor-intensive IT, with wages about half those of the main competition in India.[13] Under President Fidel Ramos in the 1990s, the Philippines unilaterally liberalized, stimulating the growth of non-traditional manufactured exports.[14] This has increased international competition and has placed some pressure on the traditional practices of cronyism. Economic zones, such as Subic Bay, are an increasingly important part of the Philippines' economic policies, providing access to infrastructure and incentives for foreign exporting companies. This is critical, given the inadequate infrastructure throughout the country, which has been frequently cited by investors as a great frustration.[15]

Indeed, the importance of private industrial estates to the export health of the Philippines was demonstrated in 2001–02, with exports from these estates increasing by 17 percent to US$7.9 billion. However, exports from state-run industrial estates declined 15.5 percent during the same period to around US$3.4 billion. Volatile currency markets and weaker demand from the US and Japan left new investments in special economic zones down 57 percent in 2001–02. This trend should be moderated by better economic conditions in 2003–04.

However, the bottom line is that the export outlook over the short term is grim given the global slowdown and the yet to be realized US-led recovery. Exports account for a third of the Philippines' national income and, although the government has predicted better times ahead after a 15 percent fall in exports in 2001–02, the budget forecasts are for zero export growth in 2002–03, with much depending on external recovery in the US economy and Japan – the latter highly unlikely.[16]

While the Doha ministerial meeting of the World Trade Organization (WTO) signaled an international intention for further trade liberalization in sectors important to the Philippines, it remains to be seen whether real reform can be achieved. In the short to medium term, the Philippines faces greater competition from Chinese exports, particularly in textiles, clothing and footwear. The year 2003–04 will not be easy for Philippine exports.

Currency movements and projections

• The peso has been under pressure since investors first took exception to the Estrada government in 2000 and began reassessing the Philippines' growth prospects. Little has changed, in part reflecting the continuing domestic machinations and general stability of the Philippines in light of domestic sources of terrorism and US troop deployment, continuing social inequality, general economic malaise, and a less than vigorous external environment in which to operate. The peso has thus continued to trend downward through 2001 and 2002. This makes assets cheap for foreign investors if they are willing to take a longer-term position and ride out the domestic machinations that undoubtedly lie ahead in 2003–04.

Investors withdrew from the Philippines in the latter part of the Estrada administration, as cronyism emerged on a major scale. For example, government attempts to restrict competition from Taiwanese airlines were perceived as a favor for Estrada-supporter Lucio Tan, the majority shareholder of Philippine Airlines. Tan also acquired the government's share options in a leading commercial bank in a secretive deal that left him as the sole bidder for the government's residual equity. A decision to abandon a multi-billion-peso tax evasion suit against Mr Tan compounded investor fears, as did numerous other similar examples of 'good fortune' for Estrada supporters.

Having lost 24 percent throughout 2000, the currency recovered early in 2001, based on investor enthusiasm for the Macapagal Arroyo government. Since then, though, the currency has been the target of intermittent speculation, with investors questioning the government's ability to achieve fiscal balance and fears about on-going recession. Regional risk factors, such as sustained selling of the Japanese yen and investor aversion to emerging economies, have contributed to weakness in the peso in 2002, something that looks set to continue in 2003. The Philippines' risk premium over US treasury papers increased to over 600 basis points in 2001 after falling to around 500 basis points in 2002. This prompted the BSP to increase its surveillance of the foreign exchange market and propose further measures to shore up the currency against speculation. The bank announced higher penalties for speculative behavior. It is also considering increasing the reserve requirement for commercial banks and limiting the amount of funds that banks are allowed to invest in the currency market.

The peso has traded downwards since 1998, experiencing accelerated depreciation in 2000 as a result of corruption and economic meltdown associated with the Estrada administration. While now stabilized, valuations will remain low, assisting the Philippines' export sector but providing some inflationary pressure.

Violent fluctuations in the peso have done little to assist the Philippines' economy in the face of generally weaker export demand. With foreign debt rising, the weaker currency could undermine the country's external position further in 2003–04.[17] Nonetheless, the level of foreign reserves is equivalent to 4.3 months' worth of import payments for services. This level of reserves is more than twice the amount of the country's short-term foreign liabilities, supporting the government's claims that restrictions on the capital account will not be necessary in 2003–04.

The peso is sitting at around P51.1 to the US dollar but is expected to track slightly stronger to P52 in 2003. The peso reflects concerns about structural weakness in the Philippine economy and the outlook for reduced profits. Nonetheless, *The Economist* Big Mac index suggests that the peso is undervalued by around 54 percent, affected by perceptions of regional risk.[18] Little dramatic turnaround in the peso's valuation can be expected in 2003–04.

Financial markets: Performance and developments

- Despite weathering the currency crisis comparatively well, the Philippines' financial sector is a millstone around the economy's neck. While the government is attempting to shore up the banking sector, non-performing loans (NPLs) continue to worsen and government deficits continue to crowd out private investment, starving key sectors of capital. With reform relatively slow compared to the obvious need for decisive action, the composition of financial markets will not change much in 2003–04. More generally, the health of the financial sector will remain at risk until substantial reform and addressing of the NPL problems are carried out.

Having recovered quite strongly after the Asian currency crisis, financial markets have taken a pounding since 2000, when investors voted with their feet against the profligate Estrada administration. Concerns about the Philippines' public debt and Asian financial systems more generally are limiting financing options. Commercial bank lending continued to grow in a subdued way in 2001–02, yet real interest rates remain comparatively high, despite cuts of more than 800 basis points in 2001–02. Nonetheless, the Bangko Sentral ng Pilipinas has cut interest rates in March 2002, lowering the overnight borrowing rate (for cash from commercial dealers) to 7 percent and the lending rate to 9.25 percent.[19]

Access to credit in the Philippines is a vexed issue as the country has one of the lowest degrees of financial intermediation in Asia.[20] Intermediation taxes are an impediment to business and private sector borrowing, and mainly restricted to short-term bank credit.

Currently, the national government is the principal issuer of debt securities in the Philippines. Local government and corporate debt securities are small with only about 40 local companies issuing such securities. US dollar-denominated Eurobonds have relatively high minimum transaction amounts, putting them out of reach for most funds.[21]

The General Banking Law has gone some way toward boosting confidence in the financial sector by ensuring Filipino banking rules meet global standards, although deposit secrecy remains an issue.[22] The law enhances the competitiveness of the banking sector and improves prudential standards in an attempt to meet the stipulations of the Basle Agreements. The General Banking Law also covers rules governing foreign stockholdings, outsourcing, micro-finance loans and the adoption of internationally accepted risk-based capital adequacy standards. The bank payment system has been upgraded into a Real Time Gross Settlement System, in an attempt to increase the reliability and timeliness of payment transactions and to help develop the capital market. General guidelines for banks planning to offer e-banking services also have been issued to ensure that their risk management systems meet international standards.[23]

Money laundering: A long way to go to meet international standards

However, while the Philippines' treatment of money laundering remains under intense international scrutiny, proposed laws giving the central bank greater scope to inquire into suspicious deposit accounts and to sanction banks with lax protocols have been watered down. The Philippines remains on the Financial Action Task Force's list of non-cooperative countries. This might come under increasing scrutiny in 2003–04, if only because US pressure to secure the banking system as part of its war on terror is likely to see Philippine authorities comply or face the animosity of Washington, something the current administration can ill afford given the precarious nature of the economy.

Prudential reform: Slowly happening

The new Financing Company Act has been enacted to boost confidence in the financial sector. Whereas there has been no law or rule setting a minimum paid-up capital for financing firms, new rules will require a minimum paid-up capital of P10 million (US$195,694) for financing companies based in Metro Manila and P5 million (US$97,847) for those outside Metro Manila. The SEC will also require that companies make a full disclosure of the true cost of credit or loans extended to a borrower.[24] Other key reforms have included progressively tightening prudential standards, reorganizing a more independent Philippine central bank, and allowing more competition from new domestic and foreign banks. Minimum capitalization requirements have been increased following the 1997–98 financial crisis and a mandatory 2 percent loans-loss provision has been introduced.

Yet plans to privatize the Philippine National Bank have stalled, creating nervousness about the government's commitment to reform. The National Bank was to be privatized, as part of the conditions of a US$600 million Banking Sector Reform Loan (BSRL) provided by the World Bank in 1998. However, the government was forced to admit that this could not be achieved and it forfeited US$400 million. The World Bank has subsequently renegotiated a US$200 million loan, anchored on improved tax administration.[25] Little forward movement is anticipated here in 2003–04.

Portfolio investment: Better times ahead in 2003–04

While the process of reform has begun in the financial sector, investor confidence remains fragile, and should rightly continue to be so in 2003–04. Portfolio investment ebbed throughout most of 2001–02, although a US$516 million net inflow reversed the trend.

Overall, portfolio investment has tended upwards in late 2001 and into 2002, restoring some degree of confidence to the Philippines but well down on historical norms.[26] Indeed, the relative improvement in portfolio investment commencing late 2001 and continuing throughout 2002, represented a dramatic turnaround on 2000, but was likely due principally to residents repatriating their investment funds, rather than a substantial rise in confidence levels from foreign investors. Net portfolio investment finished 2001–02 at US$1399 million.[27] By and large, 2003–04 should see positive portfolio investment as investors seek bargains on the Philippines' stock market, reflecting both some return of confidence and a continuing low peso.

Foreign investors: You should still be nervous

Banking sector weakness continues to be a cause for nervousness. Tough times associated with the downturn in exports and political turmoil have taken their toll on the banks throughout 2001–02, with little discernible change predicted for 2003–04. On top of this, each month brings further deterioration in the NPL ratio as borrowers struggle to repay their debts.[28] This too will not be a pretty story in 2003–04. Things will get worse before they get better.

> The NPL ratio is of concern at 19.76 percent. This is a particularly poor performance by the banking sector, given that the ratio was less than 4 percent prior to the Asian currency crisis. Unfortunately, worse is yet to come.

In short, while the new Philippines government is moving to clean up the country's image and its assets are undervalued, the risks associated with profit repatriation and further profit downgrades are high in the short to medium term. Caution is the catch phrase for potential investors in 2003–04.

Public debt: Risks ahead

- The ability of the Philippines government to pump-prime the economy during the recession has been limited, given investor concerns about its fiscal position. Equally, external debt is a concern. It accounted for 74.4 percent of GDP in 2001 – up from 67.4 percent the previous year.[29] Consequently, the debt service burden reached 9.5 percent of GDP by the third quarter of 2001, from 8.4 percent in the same period in 2000. While the government is committed to improving its position, this is a precarious balancing act. Austerity programs designed to reduce the debt to manageable levels in the short term risk undermining the longer-term goal of establishing a knowledge-based economy.

The Philippines was forced to enter a monitoring program (PPM) with the IMF in March 2001 after the country exceeded its $US1 billion borrowing quota with the IMF by US$770 million in 2000. The IMF will periodically review the country's fiscal and monetary policies, and has supported the Macapagal Arroyo administration's commitment to eliminate all budget deficits by 2006.

Fear over the Philippines' financial position has been compounded by financial difficulties in a range of public agencies. The social security system, for example, borrowed billions of dollars in 2000, after sustaining heavy losses from bad investments during the Estrada years. The pension fund for employees in the private sector drew a US$1.45 billion loan in the form of short-term credit lines and paid US$19.5 million in interest in 2000.

The government and the central bank fear that the country's financial options are becoming increasingly limited in the wake of the September bombings in the United States. Both announced plans in October to borrow ahead of a likely contraction in international credit markets for developing countries.

The government has begun its program of privatization in a bid to reduce the public debt, with privatization of the electricity sector a pillar of the policy. The National Power Corporation (Napocor) is wallowing in debts worth more than US$6 billion[30] and the

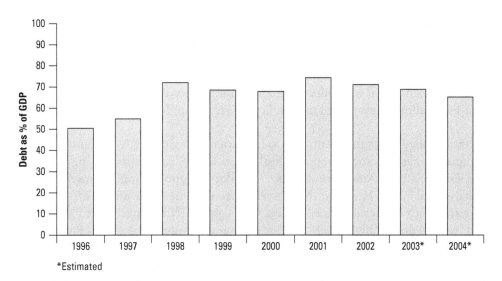

FIGURE 8.1 External debt as percentage of GDP, Philippines 1996–2004
Source: Bangko Sentral ng Pilipinas External Sector 3 April 2002

government will have to absorb the debts it cannot cover by selling the asset. Following the successful passage of the Omnibus Power Bill mid 2001, Credit Suisse Boston was appointed to manage the divestment and the first part of the sale was due to proceed in the first half of 2002. However, the economic slump has forced its postponement, adding to investor anxiety that the reform program is not credible.

Tax evasion is also a significant impediment to the project of stabilizing the budgetary position. The country has one of the lowest tax collection rates in Asia. Tax collection fell to 13 percent of GNP under Estrada, despite the comparatively high corporate tax rate of 35 percent. The Presidential Task Force on Tax and Tariff Reforms reported as early as 1994 that the government needed to reduce tax exemptions and broaden the tax base. However, reform on this front is understandably slow, given the power of vested interests. While asset-backed securitization of gambling and natural gas revenues have been considered as interim measures, most bankers doubt these instruments would be marketable to domestic or international investors.[31] Nonetheless, revenues for 2001 exceeded government expectations as collections by the Bureau of Internal Revenue and the Bureau of Treasury exceeded targets, although Bureau of Customs revenue declined due to a drop in trade.[32]

Much of the short-term debt reduction is likely to come from reduced government investment and privatization. While this is good news for private investors currently squeezed out of financial markets, these measures could have a long-term impact on the country's growth potential. Spending on primary education has been cut, posing a threat to long-term competitiveness. Even the army has announced plans for private fundraising – a move unlikely to improve the country's corrupt image and attract foreign investment.[33]

Labor market trends

- Unemployment has improved slightly year-on-year, down to 9.8 percent in October 2001 from 10.1 percent at the same time in 2000.[34] However, the downturn in the world economy and substantial wage increases mean the labor market will further soften, reducing aggregate demand. Nonetheless, this weakness could be good news for labor-intensive industries as it will reduce wage pressure. This could offset the effects of a daily cost-of-living allowance awarded to Manila workers to supplement minimum wages.

Cheap labor in the Philippines continues to be a source of comparative advantage in trade. The Philippines has become a popular destination for US call centers, as many English-speaking Filipinos have American accents.[35] Equally, Filipino computer programmers are increasingly in demand. However, this nascent success in new industries is threatened by declining standards in the education system. Although the Philippines' labor force is highly regarded, with generally high levels of education and a widespread use of English, some structural problems remain. Inadequate health care and effective illiteracy, symptomatic of great inequality, limit the supply of skilled labor needed for economic restructuring. This is exacerbated by the large number of workers who leave the country to work overseas, although most of these send money home.

While the number of IT graduates has been growing at a compound annual rate of 36 percent, the total number of college graduates has been declining. The situation is most alarming in the primary and secondary education sectors as tests put Filipino students near the bottom in maths and science skills, compared with their Asian neighbors.[36] The Philippines was ranked 36, near the bottom of the 38 countries studied in the third International Maths and Science Study of 1999. Although about 99 percent of children are enrolled in primary school and tertiary levels are relatively high, about one-third of primary school pupils do not complete their education. A report by the Congressional Commission on Labor (2001) found labor productivity in the Philippines grew by only 6 percent over a 12-year period from 1987.[37]

> The labor market remains soft, with unemployment standing at 13.7 percent in 2001, rising to 14.3 percent in 2002. Some relief is in sight with projections for 2003–04 suggesting the rate will drop to between 10.2 and 11.6 percent. Either way, labor is in abundant supply, albeit mostly unskilled.

The labor market remains soft and underemployment remains at around 17.5 percent, provoking concerns of a prolonged recession due to the combined forces of low domestic and international demand. The Employers Confederation of the Philippines warned of massive layoffs by export firms due to a projected fall in export earnings.[38] Consequently, the Macapagal Arroyo government announced a tripartite national employment summit in 2001 to address rising unemployment and underemployment, and to discuss appropriate public works programs.

Consumer and business confidence

- Consumer confidence has kept the domestic economy afloat in the stormy days since the presidential crisis. Consumer spending accounted for 2.6 percent of GNP growth in 2001 and remains the linchpin of the economy. However, recession overseas and further job losses are likely to be reflected in spending cuts. Business confidence, already weak following the debt blowout in 2000, has been further damaged by the downturn in the international economy in 2001–02. Further weakness is likely as recession in the US and Japan continues to bite.

Consumption was underpinned by favorable farming weather in 2001–02. Agriculture employs around 40 percent of the country's workforce, although the economy is gradually diversifying with the development of electronics industries.[39] Personal consumption expenditure remained robust, growing at 3.4 percent in 2001, only slightly down from 3.5 percent in 2000.[40] However, overall private consumption as a function of GDP has been declining in the last few years, down from 70.3 percent in 2000 to 68.5 percent in 2002, and forecast to be relatively stagnant at 69.8 percent in each of 2003 and 2004.[41]

Stable to stagnant consumer confidence outlook for 2003–04

This reflects the knock-on effects of declining external economic activity, the generally poor health of the domestic economy, and the deferral of private consumption scheduled for the 2003–04 period due to concerns about employment security. Much will hinge on the US-led recovery and the extent to which it is able to be sustained. Consumers will doubtless proceed with consumption expenditure, especially on large ticket items, if the external conditions begin to pick up and filter down to the Philippine economy. Consumer confidence, while relatively low at present, then, can be expected to improve throughout 2003–04 in line with the global economic recovery.

Business confidence is generally weaker, given the international downturn and contagion from the rest of Asia and the prospect of greater competition from China as a destination for FDI following its accession to the WTO. Nonetheless, there has been improvement in some sectors. Bank lending to the wholesale and retail trade; community, social and personal services; electricity, gas and water; agriculture, fisheries and forestry; and mining and quarrying sectors rose in 2001–02 from their previous year-on-year levels. This expansion, however, was counterbalanced by the decline in bank lending to the manufacturing; construction; transportation, storage and communication; and financial institutions, real estate and business services (FIREBS) sectors. Domestic liquidity or M3 growth has slightly eased from 13 percent in June to 11.7 percent in late 2001 and early 2002, showing signs of tentative recovery at year end and into 2003.

Automobile sales have improved markedly since 2000, but the growth forecasts are not especially robust. Sales fell 9.5 percent in the first 11 months of 2001 to 70,233 vehicles, although November sales rose 17 percent year-on-year.[42] Passenger vehicle sales were particularly flat, down 20 percent in the first 11 months of 2001, while commercial vehicle sales

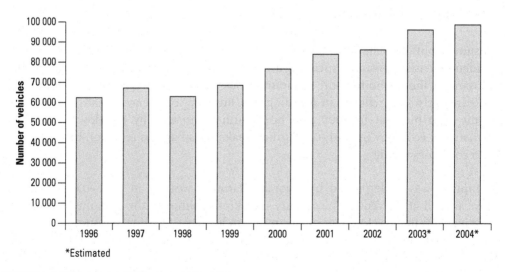

FIGURE 8.2 Vehicle sales, Philippines 1996–2004
Source: Chamber of Automotive Manufacturers, 2001

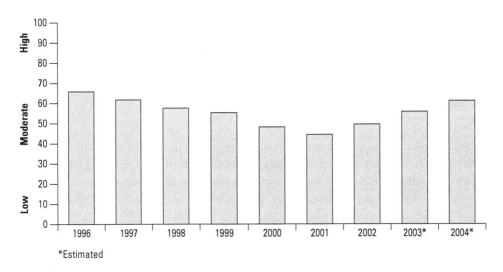

FIGURE 8.3 Consumer and business confidence, Philippines 1996–2004
Source: MasterCard Business and Consumer index

declined by 3 percent. Despite this weakness, overall, total vehicle sales finished stronger at 86,150 units in 2002, up from 76,670 units in 2000.

Leading indicators of demand and supply suggested improving economic activity prior to the September 11 attacks in the US, but then somewhat of a precipitous drop-off as the global economy suffered from the fallout. Unfortunately, Philippine consumers were not immune to this trend, suffering a drop in all indices in the wake of September 11. Fortunately, this trend has been mitigated throughout 2002, with confidence set to increase moderately in anticipation of better times ahead for the global economy.

Other factors have also helped consumer confidence. Manufacturing firms, for example, managed to increase their average capacity utilization slightly in real terms to 79.7 percent in 2001–02, suggesting some resilience in demand for manufactured goods despite the generally gloomy outlook reported in June. Nonetheless, like investors, consumers too are yet to be convinced that the worst is over in the Philippines. Certainly, though, strong investment in telecommunications is a good omen for economic recovery as the international economy strengthens.

Stock market: Slim pickings

- Having abandoned the local bourse in droves, investors are gradually returning. Investors have faced a barrage of bad news since the beginning of 2000, including corruption at the highest level, a doubling of the budget deficit, international recession, natural disasters, terrorism, and international war. However, the signs in early 2002–03 are that confidence is returning, with the local market gaining 20 percent in 2002.[43]

The exodus from the Philippines Stock Exchange (PSE) was determined in 2001–02. Market capitalization is low and investors have cited insufficient liquidity as an impediment to success in the domestic equity market. Officials of Nomura Securities Phils. and Securities 2000 Inc. told the Securities and Exchange Commission (SEC) that the market failed to produce sufficient trading volumes to break even. The officials blamed the country's uncertain economic and political situation.

> The Philippines' stock market was the worst performer in Asia in 2000–01. Unfortunately, throughout 2001 it suffered ongoing demise, prompting eight foreign brokerage houses, including Citicorp and Merrill Lynch to leave the Philippines in 2001–02. This follows the previous departure of more than 10 broking houses in 2000–01.[44] Few expect the PSE to experience a sudden turnaround of fortunes in 2003–04.

Bearish sentiment has dominated the PSE since 2000 as the political crisis and the country's fiscal position worsened. The PSE composite index, for example, has shrunk by around 50 percent from a high of 3,200 in 1998 to just on 1,450 in 2002. Other measurement indices tell a similar story. Stock market capitalization, for example, is down by 8 percent in 2001–02 to US$50 billion. Turnover, too, has dropped in total value from a high of US$17 billion in 1996 to US$5 billion in 2001–02.[45] The Bangko Sentral ng Pilipinas was forced to tighten its monetary stance toward the height of the political crisis in late 2000 to shore up the volatile currency markets. This pushed the benchmark 91-day T-bill rate (on which banks base their lending) up to 16.7 percent in November 2000 from an average of 9.9 percent throughout the year.

Monetary policy has since been eased dramatically, with the central bank borrowing rate down to 7 percent in 2002, down from 9 percent in October 2001 and 15.11 percent in November 2000.[46] The commercial lending rate was at 9.25 percent.

While the stock market posted its largest one-day gain of 17.6 percent following the first days of the Macapagal Arroyo government, 2001–02 produced only marginal joy with a slight rebound in 2002. By and large, however, the 'Gloria euphoria' has subsided and will not any longer provide a boost to equity values in 2003–04. More likely is the case that unless there is a sustained global recovery, Philippine equities investors will be left to digest the economic and political realities facing the new government – realities bound to induce unfavorable values and perhaps another spate of falls in the PSE index.

On the positive side, the market shows signs of rebounding in 2003. Much of this bounce might come from rising interest in electricity companies and IT companies backed by a strong traditional revenue base, as well as food and beverage companies, which probably represent the best long-term opportunities for investors.[47]

Corporate tax

- Reforming the taxation system to produce a fair and broad revenue base has been a priority issue for the Macapagal Arroyo government and the IMF. However, with powerful and entrenched interests this will be an extremely difficult task. Likewise, expanding the collection base of government will be a tough option to pursue in an economy where endemic poverty and high income inequality make paying tax a particularly hurtful experience. Revenue collection from the Philippines elite will continue to undermine economic development in the short to medium term. Few changes are expected in 2003–04.

While much of the initial improvement in the fiscal position has come from reduced spending, improving revenue collection is a key priority. Some progress on this front was made in 2001–02. Revenues totaled US$11 billion, beating the budget target by 1.1 percent and the government has projected an 11.8 percent increase in revenues for 2002–03.[48] Much of this will be dependent on increasing receipts as a result of increased economic activity, but with a projected GDP growth rate of 3.9 percent in 2003–04 these expectations might be a little high.

Indeed, adding pressure to the government revenues is the fact that government expenditure is also expected to rise to 18.5 percent of projected GNP in 2003–04, up from 18.2 percent of GNP in 2002.[49] Any possible increases in the government's revenue base will thus be largely offset by increased government expenditures. To address the situation, the Philippine Finance Department has begun monitoring local government remittances, intensifying audit and tax administration reforms, including computerization. A Tax Study Group has also been established to draft measures to improve collection. Foreign enterprise, as with everyone else in the economy, can thus expect closer scrutiny of their financial statements and less latitude from taxation authorities.

Nonetheless, the taxation system has proven to be somewhat of a tar baby for reformers. The Taxation Reform Committee suggested as early as 1991 that the system needed a dramatic overhaul. However, exemptions for the politically powerful remain an intransigent problem. Just 15 of the Philippines' estimated 15 million families control most of the nation's wealth, and about 200 families run its political life. Some of the rich evade taxes and bribe their way to concessions, contracts and franchises from the state. Continuity of this system, corrupt though it may be, will persist into 2003–04.

Corporate tax: Down, up, or the same?

Business opinion is divided on the Department of Finance plan to reform the tax system. The government proposes to change the corporate income tax from a 32 percent net income tax to a 20–26 percent gross income tax.[50] It also proposes a gradually increasing tax rate for people earning less than P60,000 (US$1170) annually. The IMF has opposed the changes, arguing that the new regime would be more complicated.[51]

> As much as 40 percent of state funds are estimated to be stolen by politicians and bureaucrats, depriving the country of much needed capital for public works and infrastructural development. Corruption is endemic with no change in sight.

The Philippines has 61 economic zones, industrial parks and estates, providing income tax breaks, duty- or tax-free entry of capital equipment and other financial incentives. Increasingly, these parks are dedicated to IT companies (as cyberparks), providing infrastructure and facilities conducive to these activities. Of these, Subic Freeport is the third largest export revenue earner in the country, contributing around US$1.5 billion in exports in 2002. Export processing zones and industrial estates are also being opened to agri-business ventures, providing tax and other incentives usually reserved for light industry and manufacturing firms.

Residential and commercial property markets

- Few would be brave enough to call a solid recovery in the commercial property sector given the limited prospects for employment and income growth in 2003. Public sector spending on construction is higher – up 15.1 percent year-on-year. However, with consumer and business confidence likely to remain relatively flat over 2003 and 2004, it is difficult to predict a substantial recovery in a market that has suffered a strong downturn after peaking in 1997–98.

Although the market appears to have bottomed, oversupply pressures remain. Licenses approved by the Housing and Land Use Regulatory Board, for example, fell 18.6 percent year-on-year in 2002 with little sign of an improvement.

> In the office sector, the weighted average rent in the Makati CBD has experienced a peak-to-trough dip of nearly 50 percent from its highs in 1997–98 and CBD capital values have declined by nearly 40 percent.

The vacancy rate in the office sector climbed to 16.2 percent in the second quarter of 2001, up from 14.9 percent in the first quarter, and showed a similar trend in 2002. This was particularly significant since supply was constant. Colliers Jardine predicted a vacancy rate of 16 percent by the end of 2002 and is looking for an upswing in the first quarter of 2003.[52]

The vacancy rate in the retail sector is also substantial at 12.7 percent in 2002. This is predicted to slide further with a decline in consumer confidence, poor industrial performance and a weak international economy. Rental rates are steady and forecast to grow just 3 percent in 2003.[53]

The residential sector has fared better, down only around 34 percent in the luxury end of the market, peak-to-trough in 2002. Overall, the vacancy rate is steady at 10 percent. Land values for prime lots are stabilizing after a drop of around 58 percent from their highs in

1997–98. Nonetheless, developers have been offering discounts of around 35 percent and demand for prime residential property is limited.

With uncertainty in the wind, developers have taken a softly-softly approach to prospective projects. Moving 12-month supply growth has diminished from 12 percent in 1999 to 8 percent in 2001–02, with supply growth likely to remain static in 2003–04.[54] Despite cheap asset prices due to a low peso, demand in the property sector is likely to remain weak in the near future, reflecting flat international activity.

Foreign direct investment

- Given the spate of internal political machinations, a fragile world economy, not to mention domestic terrorism and ongoing security fears in the south of the country, it is no great surprise that foreign direct investment (FDI) in the Philippines remains problematic. While FDI had been growing steadily following the currency crisis, corruption scandals in 2001–02 and the aftermath of September 11 have created new concerns and generally stalled strong FDI growth. In this light, investors should expect this pattern to continue in 2003–04 – or at least until there is a resolution in the security concerns of the Philippines and strong signs of reform in the financial sector. Unfortunately, the Philippines has a long way to go before foreign capital will be convinced of domestic stability, growth prospects, and opportunities.

The investment environment has changed dramatically over the past 10 years as exchange controls and controls on foreign investment have been substantially liberalized. The Foreign Investments Act of 1991 aimed to promote, attract and welcome productive investment from foreign individuals, partnerships, corporations and government. Successive governments have been particularly keen to attract foreign investment in infrastructure. The government is currently deregulating telecommunications, air services, mining, shipping and the oil industry, as well as the retail trade and energy sectors.[55] Indeed, in comparison to the hot-and-cold attitudes toward foreign investment prevailing in many Asian countries, the Philippines' environment is quite liberal. The government offers a range of incentives, including tax credits on imported inputs, and deductions on labor and infrastructure. Nonetheless, restrictions remain in areas such as media, licensed professions and retail trade. No change is anticipated in these sectors in 2003–04.

Uncertainty in 2001–02 was a significant deterrent to investment. By the end of June 2001, for example, total registered direct foreign investment had declined 81 percent year-on-year, to US$157 million.[56] Most investment was channeled into the manufacturing and mining sectors, with Australian and Japanese investors contributing 39 percent and 30 percent respectively.[57] Overall, FDI in 2001–02 finished stronger at US$15.54 billion, slightly up from US$14.02 billion in 2000–01.[58]

The prospects for FDI are likely to be somewhat brighter in the medium term as the effects of reforms such as the Banking Act and electricity reforms filter through the economy.

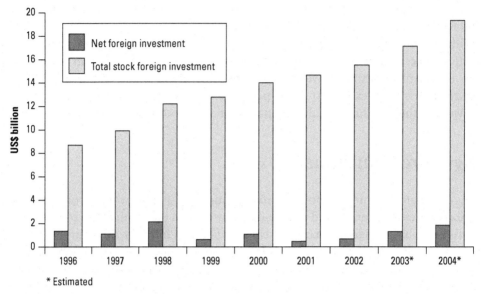

FIGURE 8.4 Net foreign direct investment, Philippines 1996–2004
Source: Bangko Sentral ng Pilipinas, External Sector, April 3, 2002

The planned development of new gas fields over 2002–07 should also provide some opportunities for foreign investors. Furthermore, whereas access to power has been patchy and expensive, the reforms are expected to have substantial benefits for manufacturers and consumers. The Power Bill stipulated a mandatory 5 percent cut in power rates and has created a spot market for electricity. This follows a decade of infrastructure improvements designed to overcome the regular 'brownouts' that have afflicted Manila for up to 12 hours a day.[59] Nonetheless, increasing investor wariness over the risks involved with build-own-operate projects for large infrastructure projects in developing countries will mean progress on this front is incremental.

Telecommunications deregulation is gradually increasing access to telephone lines and the Internet. This is expected to foster the development of e-commerce and its associated productivity improvements in 2003–04. The e-Commerce Act passed in 2000 to make electronic signatures legally binding and to promote universal use of electronic transactions is also a welcome addition. Nonetheless, effective enforcement, something often lacking in the Philippines remains an issue of concern to consumers and investors alike, with few prospects for prudential and regulatory reform any time soon.

Poor infrastructure continues to impede business, which is exacerbated by administrative inefficiencies – legendary among many foreign investors in the Philippines. Indeed, an estimated 25 percent of infrastructure projects funded by foreign aid fail to get off the ground due to poor administration, corruption and general inefficiency, a problem that continues to impede effective infrastructural development.

On the positive side, however, work has resumed on the US$46.8 million Light Rail Transit Project 2, after resolving right-of-way issues and it is expected to be running by

2003.[60] In the short term, a number of substantial, high profile direct foreign investments will help to restore confidence in the Philippines but, for the most part, the Philippines continues to suffer from a tarnished image.

Section C Politics

- While business initially hailed the reformist government of Gloria Macapagal Arroyo as a harbinger of better times to come, the difficulty of the tasks ahead have hit home. War in Mindanao, a sluggish international economy, and destabilizing opposition forces loyal to Estrada, combine to create a formidable challenge. While this opposition has subsided throughout 2001–02, Macapagal Arroyo's decision to invite US forces to help the Philippine army root out terrorist forces will test support. On the upside, there are signs that the government means business in addressing corruption and structural economic change. However, any real long-term solutions depend on curbing the influence of Philippines' dominant families and time-honored traditions of patronage. Despite signs that the government is serious about reform, a culture of transparency will not be introduced any time soon.

In its first few months of office, the new administration had to contend with a typhoon in northern Luzon, which, although considered comparatively mild, devastated farmland, killing 163, injuring 180 and displacing thousands. This was followed by volcanic activity in Mt Mayon. These natural disasters have been compounded by intransigent public debt, international recession and repeated terrorist attacks, which have undermined investment. The war against terrorism, with its effects on international confidence, has dealt the Philippines a blow at a critical time. While the economy and the political system had shown signs of recovery, the international burden has undermined progress and delayed whatever bounce back that might occur until 2003–04.

Although dogged by difficulty, the initial indications from the Macapagal Arroyo administration are relatively positive. Following more than seven months of legal wrangling over the impeachment and corruption trial of former President Estrada, Macapagal Arroyo was indirectly endorsed in elections in 2001. More importantly, the reform agenda will be greatly assisted by the fact that Macapagal Arroyo-endorsed candidates won eight of the 13 Senate seats. This was interpreted as a validation of her leadership, which began in January after the 'People Power II' demonstrations ousted Estrada over corruption charges and a failed impeachment trial. She will serve the remainder of Estrada's term to mid-2004 with a working majority in the Senate. This perceived electoral success is significant, given attempts to destabilize Macapagal Arroyo in the lead-up to the elections.

Business groups in the Philippines welcomed the election result, foreseeing a turn-around in international negative sentiment that caused investment to decline during Estrada's two-and-a-half-year rule. The Macapagal Arroyo government has repeatedly stated its commitment to reversing the Philippines' intransigent cronyism and corruption, which escalated to crisis levels during Estrada's rule. This is evidenced by Macapagal Arroyo's pledge to continue the economic liberalization started by President Fidel Ramos between 1992–98. Indeed, frequent statements have continued to commit her administration to transparency, a strong moral foundation and effective policy implementation. Government has also sought to reassure business that lower interest rates, fast-tracking banking reforms, improving competition, and enhancing investment will continue to form part of the economic agenda in 2004 and the next election cycle.

Projects to diversify the economy are being introduced, although the pace of reform is less than was originally anticipated. These are aimed at alleviating the country's reliance on electronic equipment exports to the US and Japan, which account for around 45 percent of its export market. The government, as with others in the region, is especially keen to develop its knowledge-based industries. This has resulted in the Philippines-based Smart Communications Inc., for example, investing US$332.3 million in 2002–03 to expand its cellular network. Likewise, the administration has vigorously promoted the country as a competitive IT investment site, managing to secure US$380 million worth of investment in the IT sector in 2001 alone.[61] Special economic zones such as Subic Bay have also attracted foreign companies such as Taiwan's Acer Information Products, with infrastructure and taxation benefits, as well as cheap labor. Accenture and Barnes and Noble also have opened back-office operations, complementing the ICT push.[62] While a positive start, it remains to be seen how viable a high-level ICT sector can be, especially given the widespread skills shortages and the less than stellar communications infrastructure that dogs the Philippines.

Leading by example

The government has made much of its commitment to 'lead by example', with Cabinet members appointed on the basis of their proven integrity. The USAID project, Accelerating Growth, Investment, and Liberalization with Equity (AGILE), began an extensive push to reduce graft and corruption within the first few months of the government's incumbency. The AGILE team and a Department of Budget and Management (DBM) team prepared legislation aimed to eliminate major sources of corruption in government procurement.[63] While a long road remains ahead, this is the first sign in years of a strong and meaningful intention to clean up public administration in the Philippines and set the country on a better developmental path.

Open for business: Come one, call all?

Reflecting its cleaner, meaner government approach to public administration, the government has been aggressive in leading various delegations to promote investment and court international business, affirming its commitment to globalization, free trade and liberalization. Delegations to trading partners have emphasized the reform agenda, promising transparency and infrastructure development. The government has highlighted its privatization program, pushing the controversial Power Bill through Congress within the first six months of office, as well as the anti-money laundering Bill. Deregulation in the agricultural sector is high on the agenda, with evidence that movement is afoot here and will continue to take hold in 2003–04. Micro-finance for poor businesses will also play an important role in raising incomes and consumption, something the government has targeted in particular as a means of improving access to capital from an otherwise disenfranchised low-income sector. This should have a dramatic impact on small enterprise and help push up consumption in the years to come.

Patronage politics: Dividing up the pie

Nonetheless, the domination of 15 wealthy families in business and politics is indicative of a political system that thrives on connections and shady deals.

> The top 15 families own 55 percent of the Philippines' wealth – a concentration that ranks second only to Indonesia with 61.7 percent. This makes the Philippines one of the most unequal societies in Asia, with most of the population cut off from asset ownership.

Reducing corruption is likely to prove extremely difficult given the Philippines' history of clan-based rule. Political clans are likely to continue to dominate politics, despite moves to give local government more economic and political power throughout the 1990s. While traditional wisdom suggests that higher national income leads to a decline in clan power, the evidence in the Philippines shows no sign of this group waning. Of the top 20 wealthiest provinces, 65 percent have both congressmen and governors coming from one political family. Eight of the provinces, or 40 percent, have either a congressman or a governor representing a political clan. Of the 20 provinces with the lowest human development index, only five, or 20 percent, have leaders from political clans.[64] There will be no change in the composition of political representation in 2003–04, as wealthy families continue to use money as a means of buying representation and ensuring policy outcomes.

The World Bank has been working on a project to address corruption issues in the Philippines since 1999 after the Estrada government enlisted the bank's assistance. The bank's director in the Philippines noted that the country was increasingly cited by business surveys, media and corruption watchdogs as a country where corruption inhibits foreign investment and development.[65] Similarly, the Philippines has low judicial efficiency.[66] This makes the tasks of taxation reform and institution-building incredibly difficult. Taxation exemptions and opaque business dealings are crippling the country's development prospects. The kinds of deals highlighted in the Estrada case are well established in Filipino political culture.

Indicative of her commitment to reform, Macapagal Arroyo has promised to pursue Estrada for his theft of between US$200 million and US$300 million in secret accounts. However, the political reality is that he is likely to escape scot-free, as there is a precedent of not convicting politicians and prominent citizens. Certainly, the Supreme Court has ruled against Estrada's challenge, determining the trial should proceed. If convicted, Estrada could face life imprisonment or the death penalty. However, the Philippines' record of punishing corruption is poor. It has been 15 years since the last Philippine president accused of corruption, the late Ferdinand Marcos, was deposed, and the authorities failed to prove in court that he committed any crime. Expect the same to prove true of Estrada.

Corruption: A booming business

The Philippines also continues to rank high on the international 'shame files' of countries soft on fraud. The Philippine Department of Justice, for example, recently dismissed, for lack of evidence, criminal complaints filed by the Securities and Exchange Commission against 21 firms and 14 individuals allegedly involved in the operation of a multimillion-dollar stock fraud syndicate. Such lax enforcement and easy criminal evasion is emblematic of the Philippines' poor regulatory and prudential systems. Indeed, the Philippines remains on the Group of Seven Financial Advisory Task Force list of 15 'non-cooperative' countries in money laundering.[67] Similarly, despite IMF urgings to relax the bank secrecy law to facilitate the identification of tax delinquents, new legislation recently introduced is less than convincing and likely to have no real effect.

Bureaucratic reform: Lacking?

Despite this, there is pressure for reform. The head of strategy and economics at the Hong Kong regional headquarters of securities firm Nomura International, has pushed strongly to get recognition for the fact that stable political institutions are crucial to economic recovery in the Philippines.[68] Increasingly, there is recognition among the majority of Filipinos that the country desperately needs reform both to kick-start the economy and return it to a developmental trajectory, and to ensure what limited international aid the Philippines receives is used effectively and not pocketed by corrupt officials. This is important, since the Philippines is in receipt of US$10.3 billion in multilateral loans but is unable to access this money due to red tape and corrupt practices. Moreover, the government estimates that a third of all projects drag on for an average two years longer than scheduled, causing a blow-out of costs and inefficient project delivery.[69]

Uncertainty and opposition: Tough times ahead in 2003–04

As well as the possibility of an on-going stagnant international economic climate and economic torpor in Japan, intermittent political resistance to the Macapagal Arroyo government continues to shroud the country in uncertainty. In 2002–04 the government will have to navigate a political minefield in pursuing the Estrada case, balancing the residual populist support for the leader against pressures to establish strong and transparent institutions, and managing a fledgling economy whose performance could falter if international recovery is slow in coming. Failure on any one of these fronts will undermine support for the government at home and with foreign investors.

Likewise, 2003–04 will see the administration judged on its commitment to address poverty and equity issues to equip the country to meet the challenges of globalization, something that, given the hold on power and patronage politics enjoyed by the elite families, will be less than easy to achieve – if at all.

Likewise, the government will likely stand or fall in terms of its ability to begin the process of infrastructural development, desperately needed if the economy is to work toward a turnaround in 2004. Currently, for example, and despite significant expenditure and subsidies to public monopolies, only 4 percent of the population is connected to the power grid and only 6 percent of the population has access to water.[70] The challenge is to regulate utilities effectively and to create 'fiscal space' by relieving pressure on public budgets and thus to address what is at present massive underdevelopment of the Philippines infrastructure.

Leading risk indices: Corruption, stability, governance, risk

Political stability

Having trended sharply downward during the Estrada regime, the indices of political stability and governance have plateaued and now shows signs of tentative upward movement and a return to stability. Not unexpectedly, the political stability index reveals a turbulent pattern of opposition, indicative of the deep divisions over the Estrada presidency, and over the conflict with Muslim rebels. It also suggests that destabilizing forces will continue as the reform agenda breeds discontent in some quarters and international economic sluggishness causes further hardship. Nonetheless, the reform agenda has sufficient support to permit its continuation into the medium term. As the economy improves, the political stability index is likely to improve throughout 2003–04 with orderly election cycles anticipated in 2004.

Corruption

While the corruption index was higher in 2000, it stabilized in 2001 and continued downward in 2002, reflecting the tentative move toward reform of government procurement practices and tendering processes by the new administration. More generally, the new administration has made loud noises about rubbing out corruption and this has likely had some dampening effect on corrupt practices by various officials. While this is to be welcomed, the resurgence of issues associated with economic hardship and the central function of corruption as a means of supplementing meager state salaries for government workers, will still see a relatively high corruption index throughout 2002–04.

Corporate governance

The corporate governance indices are improving as reforms in the banking sector and international accounting standards begin to have effect. While transparency remains poor, this is likely to show some improvement in the medium term. The propensity-to-restructure index is showing considerable improvement. Expect further improvement in the index in 2003–04.

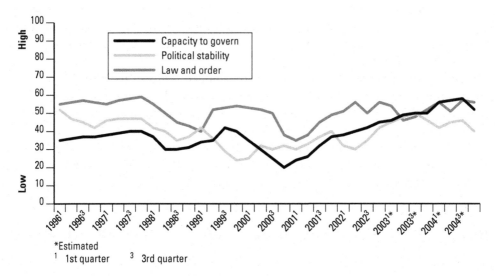

FIGURE 8.5 Political stability index, Philippines 1996–2004

Political stability methodology:
- The capacity-to-govern index is based upon the institutional reach of government defined in terms of its ability to set the political and economic agenda and ensure its legislative program is enacted without significant compromise. This index is adversely affected by legislative opposition, lack of legislative implementation, failure to realize government policy and general political opposition.
- The political stability index measures violent opposition or organized demonstrations, terrorist activities, and popular discontent that adversely affect the institutional and electoral stability of the government.
- The law and order index measures the propensity to civil obedience, and the institutional reach of the rule of law in terms of regulatory compliance and enforcement.

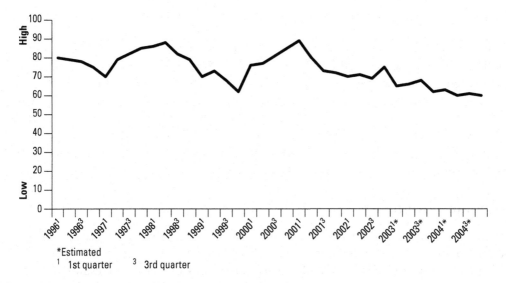

FIGURE 8.6 Corruption index, Philippines 1996–2004

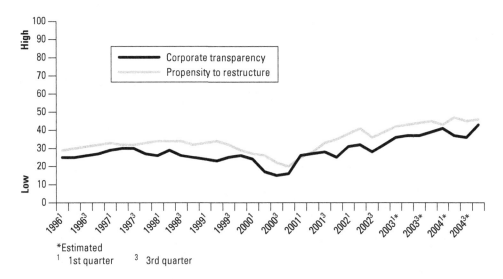

FIGURE 8.7 Corporate governance index, Philippines 1996–2004

Corporate governance index methodology
- The corporate governance index is a composite index measuring the juridical requirements for corporate disclosure and financial reporting, prudential regime adequacy, prudential compliance enforcement, and the juridical reach of prudential authorities.
- The propensity-to-restructure index is a composite index based on media releases and reported corporate restructuring as a result of prudential regulation, financial incentives, loan restructuring / re-negotiation, or asset realignment.

Foreign investor risk index

The foreign investor risk index shows continuing upward movement as the effects of the international economic downturn bite and government policy continues to be weighed down by debt and the slow pace of reform amid mounting domestic economic problems and the continuation of domestic terrorist and security issues. Investors should expect an improvement as economic growth improves – principally from an improvement in the external global environment – and as microeconomic reform begins to kick in and help productivity. So too, improvement should be discernible on the domestic security front as concerns associated with terrorism are addressed by military action supported by the United States.

Section D Security

- Internal security issues in the Philippines are the main concern for investors and tourists alike. Armed skirmishes continue in Mindanao where Muslim separatists have been waging war for decades. Foreign tourists are increasingly taken hostage for ransom by the rebel Abu Sayyaf group. Links between the Abu Sayyaf and the al-Qaeda network have also

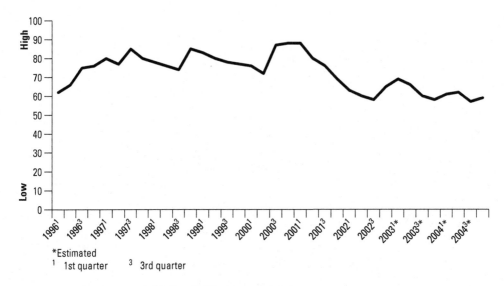

FIGURE 8.8 Foreign investor risk index, Philippines 1996–2004

Foreign investor risk index methodology:
* The foreign investor risk index is a composite index measuring tax burdens, discriminatory regulatory practices, adverse compliance regulations, government policy toward foreign enterprise, receptiveness to issuance of government contracts, foreign enterprise commercial restrictions, and official attitudinal changes to foreign direct investment and foreign commercial operations which impact on operational efficiency. The index also incorporates a nominal measure for market risk and market failure.

raised concerns about escalating terrorism. Security concerns will likely persist well into 2003 and 2004. No quick resolution to this problem is anticipated despite active US involvement.

Although the Ramos government signed a peace agreement with the Moro National Liberation Front (MNLF) in 1996, conflict continued with the Moro Islamic Liberation Front (MILF) and with the Communist Party (CPP) and New People's Army (NPA).

The government has no agreement with the rebel group, the Abu Sayyaf and sporadic attacks from that quarter seem likely to continue – particularly if there is a deepening of the ideological divide between the 'Islamic' and 'Christian' worlds. The Abu Sayyaf has direct links to the al-Qaeda network and Osama bin Laden. Kidnapping and the occasional execution of foreign tourists has provided the Abu Sayyaf with considerable leverage. Indeed, the organization held a group of foreign tourists hostage for most of 2001, beheading two people, and reports of ongoing kidnappings during 2002 do not look promising.

While the government is increasingly hardening its stance and refusing to negotiate with the group, military attempts to weaken the organization have been largely ineffectual, with suggestions that some members of the military have colluded with rebels. The US has sent 600 troops to help fight the Abu Sayyaf, arousing some opposition to the Macapagal Arroyo government's alliance with the US. While the Filipino government is conducting talks with the intransigent groups, few observers believe that the government can resolve overnight the issues that have left 120,000 people dead over the past 25 years. Meanwhile, the conflict continues to undermine international confidence and the tourism industry. It also continues to sap government resources. In early 2002, even the negotiated peace with the MNLF was in doubt as rebels attacked an army camp in the southern Philippines, killing 55 people.

Internationally, the security risks are substantially less significant. Like many in the region, the Philippines has struggled to balance its relations with the People's Republic of China and Taiwan. While the Philippines remains in a low-level dispute with China, Vietnam, Malaysia and Taiwan over the resource-rich Spratly Islands, this has simmered without boiling over for many years. The government has taken a pragmatic approach to improving relations with neighbors in the interests of trade and economic growth. This approach will continue during 2003–04.

The Macapagal Arroyo government has made much of its attempts to build multi-lateral, bilateral and regional relationships. The President has highlighted her family's historical ties with the family of Indonesian president, Megawati Sukarnoputri during a visit to that country. High-level delegations have also traveled the Asia–Pacific region in a bid to develop commerce and the government has reaffirmed its commitment to multilateral forums such as the World Trade Organization and APEC. This determination to engage with the international sphere will benefit international investors in 2003–04.

Section E Economic and political risk forecasts

- Despite high hopes for a turnaround in the Philippines' political and economic fortunes in 2002, the short-term risks for foreign investors are significant. Institutional reforms are just beginning and the potential for further shocks remains. Entrenched vested interests will make government attempts to restructure the economy into a knowledge-based regional hub all the more difficult. Equally, the fiscal deficit and the persistence of NPLs in the banking sector, will limit growth and policy options. The short to medium term is still laden with vexed issues that make failure equally as likely as success. Trepidation, caution, and a wait-and-see policy should inform the strategic assessments of foreign investors as they approach the Philippines as a possible investment destination.

Short-term forecasts

- Short-term risk indicators for foreign direct investment in the Philippines suggest further turbulence ahead. While GDP has continued to grow at around 2 percent despite the downturn in the US, the economy continues to be sluggish, reform slow, corruption high, and infrastructural bottlenecks of particular concern. As a consequence, the real economy has suffered and there is considerable surplus capacity and unemployment at more than 13 percent. Housing approval rates and bank lending are flat. International demand for exports is likely to remain flat until the end of 2002–03, creating higher unemployment in the short term.

- Macapagal Arroyo aims to foster the country's high-tech industries, yet public investment in education is declining due to the fiscal squeeze. Investment in high-value industries is only likely to occur if there is an appropriate labor supply. While the government is a strong advocate of further economic liberalization and has demonstrated a commitment to multilateralism, there is rising domestic pressure to 'go slow' on WTO commitments due by 2004. Business is struggling to compete and still hampered by the high cost of infrastructure and a lack of long-term finance. The cost of shipping goods from Luzon to Mindanao, for example, is higher than shipping the same from Luzon to Thailand.[71]
- Experience in the region and good commercial contacts are essential for any successful deal. A culture of corruption has existed at the highest levels for decades and will not be overturned in one presidential term. More generally, with on-going hardship due to the weight of NPLs and banking reform, combined with the fiscal burden and a slump in international demand, reform fatigue might well set in during 2004, adding further risk to foreign investors and diminish prospective market opportunities. This will also be compounded by fear generated through the Abu Sayyaf and the international war against terrorism. This will be tough, and could well get tougher before there is improvement.
- The ongoing crisis in Japan, general weakness in Southeast Asia, and growing competition – particularly from Chinese exports – combine to create a difficult investment environment in 2003–04.

Short-term opportunities

- Government spending on infrastructure during 2003–06 will provide considerable opportunities for foreign investment. Changes to investment laws have provided scope for investment in major projects, particularly in the energy sector, with investment opportunities in liquefied natural gas and electricity.
- Opportunities also exist in the service sector in areas such as legal services and accountancy to develop corporate infrastructure, sound accounting practices, and suitable corporate governance protocols. However, many international consultancy houses have recently closed down their Philippine operations, indicating a still tight and less than expansive market.
- With the peso low, assets are at bargain prices. However, with demand likely to be constrained by the international situation and substantial debt, investors must be selective.

Medium to longer term

- The outlook is rosier in the medium term if Macapagal Arroyo can continue to institute fundamental reforms and infrastructure development continues.
- Comparatively low wages and a predominance of English-speakers provide opportunities for the creation of support services for high-tech industries (call center services for example). Telecommunications industries are also likely to experience good growth levels during 2003–05, supported by government initiatives to encourage the formation of a knowledge-based economy.

Overall risk rating

The risk profile of the Philippines is declining but from a high base. Incremental improvements are being made in corporate governance, the development of financial instruments and bureaucratic transparency. However, substantial impediments to this reform process remain.

Risk: Decreasing – but slowly ↓
Risk Rating (0 = lowest, 10 highest risk) 7

Section F Philippines fact sheet*

Geography

Capital
Manila

Largest city (millions, 2000)
Manila, 10.492

Location
Southeastern Asia, archipelago
between the Philippine Sea and the
South China Sea, east of Vietnam

Neighboring countries
Archipelago but close to Indonesia,
Malaysia, Taiwan and China

Terrain
Mostly mountains with narrow to
extensive coastal lowlands

Land use
Arable land 34 %, forests and woodland
49% (although only 21% is under forest
cover)

Area
300,179 sq km

Economic statistics

Currency
Peso (P) = 100 centavos

Exchange rate (February 2002)
US$1.00 = P 51.41

Gross Domestic Product (GDP)
3.3%

GDP per capita (2000)
US$960

GDP per capita – PPP (2000 est.)
US$3,800

GDP – composition by sector (2001)
Agriculture, fishing and forestry 18.2 %,
industry 32.3%, services 43.4%

* All figures are the latest available except where indicated. All figures are in US dollars. Figures are compiled from national, international and multilateral agencies (United Nations Development Assistance Program, International Monetary Fund, World Bank, World Development Report, UNESCO Statistical Yearbook, International Labour Office, United Nations, Central Intelligence Agency World Fact Book). Gross domestic product (GDP) refers to the value of all goods and services produced in the preceding financial year. GDP per capita, Purchasing Power Parity (GDP per capita – PPP) refers to the indices developed by the World Bank to take account of price differences, cost of living differences, and relative purchasing power of a set basket of goods and services between countries so as to provide a more accurate measure of national wealth.

Inflation rate (January 2002)
3.8%

Total external debt (US$ millions, 2001)
$52,426

Current account balance (US$ millions, 2000)
$9,349

National unemployment rate (1998)
13.3%

Population below poverty line
41%

Labor force (millions, 2000)
41.1

Labor force by occupation (2001)
Agriculture and fishery 34%, mining and quarrying 0.002%, manufacturing 9%, electricity, gas and water 0.36%, construction 4.7%

Budget (peso billions, 2000)
Revenues: P506
Expenditure: P642
Deficit: P136 or 4.1% of GDP

Industries
Textiles, pharmaceuticals, chemicals, wood products, food processing, electronics assembly, petroleum refining, fishing

Major exports (US$ millions, July 2001)
Electronics and components $1331, articles of apparel and clothing accessories $194 million, Coconut oil $41

Major imports (US$ millions, July 2001)
Electronics and components $554, telecommunications equipment and electrical machinery $287, mineral fuels, lubricants and related materials $274

Major trading partners (exports, 2001)
United States 29.5%, Japan 16.1%, Netherlands 9.01%, Singapore 6%

Major trading partners (imports, 2001)
Japan 20.3%, US 17%, Singapore 7.1%, Indonesia 8.46%, South Korea 6.4%

Income/wealth distribution (household income or consumption by % share)
Lowest 10% of population 1.5%
Highest 10% of population 39.3% (1998)

Televisions (1997, millions)
3.7

Televisions per capita (people per color television, 1996)
4.1

Telephones (lines in use, millions, 1997)
1.9

Telephones per capita (people per telephone, 2000)
4

Cellular phones (millions, 1998)
1.959

Cellular phones per capita (people per cellular phone, 2000)
8.44

Registered motor vehicles (millions, 1999)
3.534

Internet users (2000)
500,000

Fiscal year
Calendar year

Government and political statistics

Nature of government
Pluralist presidential democracy

Constitution
1987 Constitution establishes the Philippines as a democratic and republican state

Structure of government
Executive presidency, bicameral congress

Executive branch

Head of Government (*Pangulo*) and Chief of State
President Gloria Macapagal Arroyo. Cabinet appointed by the President President and Vice President elected by popular vote on separate tickets for 6-year terms

Senate (*Senado*):
24 seats. One-half elected every three years. Members elected for six year terms

House of Representatives (*Kapulungan Ng Mga Kinatawan*):
204 seats. Members elected for three-year terms. Additional members may be appointed by the president but the constitution prohibits the House of Representatives from having more than 250 members

Cabinet members (2001)

President
Gloria Macapagal Arroyo

Vice president
Teofisto Guingona

Ministers

Minister of Finance
Jose Isidro Camacho

Minister of Health
Manuel Dayrit

Minister of Budget
Emilia Boncodin

Minister of Economic Planning
Dante Canlas

Minister of Foreign Affairs
Teofisto Guingona

Minister of Defence
Angelo Reyes

Minister of Agrarian Reform
Hernani Braganza

Minister of Agriculture
Leonardo Montemayor

Minister of Interior
Joey Lina

Minister of Justice
Hernando Perez

Minister of Labour
Patricia Santo Tomas

Minister of Education and Culture
Raul Roco

Minister of Energy
Vincente Perez

Minister of Public works
Simeon Datumanong

Minister of Tourism
Richard Gordon

Minister of Trade and Industry
Manuel Roxas

Minister of Transport and Communications
Pantaleon Alvarez

Executive secretary
Alberto Romulo

Main governing parties and ideological affiliation
Parties and ideologies are significantly less important than personalities in the Philippines. Generally, congress supports existing political and social structures.
Lakas ng Edsa-National Union of Christian Democrats (pro-business, formed in 1992 to support Fidel Ramos). Appeals to ruling elites. Joined with Reporma, Probynsya Muna Development Initiative, Aksyon Demokratiko, the Liberal Party (LP) and Partido Demokratiko Sosyalista ng Pilipinas in the Peope's Power Coalition behind Macapagal Arroyo in 2001

Main opposition parties
Broadly populist coalition. Puwersa ng Masa (Force of the Masses) includes: Laban Ng Demokratikong Pilipino (Struggle of Filipino Democrats) or LDP; Laban Ng Masang Pilipino or LAMP (Struggle of the Filipino Masses) and People's Reform Party or PRP; Kilusang Bagong Lipunan (New Society Movement); Nacionalista Party; National People's Coalition or NPC Outside of Congress, the Maoist National Democratic Front (NDP) provides strong opposition.

International memberships
APEC, ARF, AsDB, ASEAN, CCC, CP, ESCAP, FAO, G-24, G-77, IAEA, IBRD, ICAO, ICC, ICFTU, ICRM, IDA, IFAD, IFC, IFRCS, IHO, ILO, IMF, IMO, Inmarsat, Intelsat, Interpol, IOC, IOM, ISO, ITU, NAM, OAS (observer), OPCW, UN, UNCTAD, UNESCO, UNHCR, UNIDO, UNMIK, UNTAET, UNU, UPU, WCL, WFTU, WHO, WIPO, WMO, WTO

Business organizations
Philippine Chamber of Commerce and Industry, Makati Business Club, Mindanao Business Council, American Chamber of Commerce in the Philippines, Australia-Philippine Business Council, Management Association of the Philippines, Australia New Zealand Chamber of Commerce (Philippines), Bosconian Chamber of Commerce, Bulacan Chamber of Commerce, Camara Official Espanola de Comercio Industria Y Navagacion en Filipinas, Canadian Chamber of Commerce of the Philippines, Cavite Chamber of Commerce and Industry, Federation of Philippine Industries, Subic Bay Freeport Chamber of Commerce

Date of UN membership
1945

Social statistics

Population
75.35 (millions, 2000)

Population density (per square km)
255

Fertility rate (average number of children per woman, 2001 est)
3.42

Maternal mortality rate (per 100 000 births, 2002 est.)
170

Infant mortality rate (deaths per 1000 births, 2002 est.)
30

Population growth (2001 est.)
2.03%

Life expectancy (2001 est)
Men: 64.96 years
Women: 70.79 years

Ethnic composition
Christian Malay 91.5%, Muslim Malay 4%, Chinese 1.5%, other 3%

Religions
Roman Catholic 83%, Protestant 9%, Muslim 5%, Buddhist and other 3%

National languages spoken
Tagalog, English, local languages Cebuano, Ilocan, Hiligaynon or Ilonggo

Literacyrate (over 15 can read and write, 1995 est.) 94.6%
Male: 95%
Female: 94.3%

Singapore

9 Singapore

Malcolm Cook

Section A Economy

Overview

In 2001–02 Singapore was plunged into its sharpest and deepest recession in 36 years. After heady real GDP growth of 10 percent in 2000, real GDP shrank by 2.2 percent in 2001, with 2002 recording only a moderate recovery. While Singapore's unrivaled history of strong economic growth means the economy will survive the 2001 recession intact, it certainly highlighted Singapore's vulnerabilities to volatility in the global IT industry.

The 12.2 percent year-on-year drop in real GDP growth, and repeated growth forecast downgrades in 2001 by the government clearly show Singapore's intense dependence on the global economy and the problems this has caused in effectively planning for 2003–04. With the world's highest trade dependency ratio[1] of about 300 percent, and 36 percent of Singapore's documented exports going to the moribund Japanese and US markets, Singapore's growth in 2002–04 is uncertain.

The Singapore government has aggressively sought to dampen the socio-political impacts of the recession. Aided by decades of budget surpluses and no public foreign debt, the Singapore government issued two supplementary budgets in 2001 totalling S\$13.5 billion in stimulus spending, a 26 percent boost to public spending, worth over 8 percent of GDP. Singapore's fiscal strength with its AAA credit rating make further stimulus packages likely in 2002–04, if the world trade situation does not improve or if Singapore's perceived decline in competitiveness continues.

Since early 2001, Singapore's economic policy-makers have been in overdrive, looking at how to keep Singapore attractive to foreign capital, while shifting the economy towards higher value-added services and away from manufacturing. The 2002 budget release was postponed from the end of February to May 3 to allow the multi-sectoral Economic Review Committee (ERC) headed by Finance Minister and likely next prime minister Brigadier Lee Hsien Loong to begin its revamping of economic policy with reductions in corporate and personal income taxes. The budgets of 2003 and 2004 will provide clearer signs of where the ERC wants to take Singapore. It is likely to recommend more aggressive pursuit of recent diversification policies such as the recruitment of highly-skilled foreign labor, financial sector reform, and more subsidies for 'sunrise industries' like petrochemicals, biotechnology, and health care, while continuing with tax reform.

New openings for foreign investors

The rough regional economic waters since 1997 have accelerated plans to 'modernize' Singapore's economy and firms and move it away from traditional exports and markets. Reflecting on its manufactured exporting success, top leaders like Senior Minister Lee Kuan Yew argue that Singapore must rely on foreign firms to lead its reorientation, suggesting further tax breaks for foreign firms and workers in these 'sunrise industries.'[2]

Ongoing reforms have also opened up new areas for foreign investment with the privatization of government power generating firms from mid 2002. Further openings for foreign banks are also expected with the protagonist of the 1997 drive to liberalize Singapore's financial sector, Deputy Prime Minister Brigadier Lee Hsien Loong, appointed in November 2001 as Finance Minister. Recent stimulus packages and the limitations of the Singapore stock market are likely to further accelerate the government-led development of Singapore's bond market. Offering low but secure yields, this market may be useful for regional risk diversification strategies.

So far, talk of restructuring has not focused on disincentives for traditional areas of foreign investment. Rather, the government-controlled National Wage Council is expected to continue to encourage stable or declining labor costs, while by 2006 corporate income tax will only be 20 percent, down from 26 percent in 1996. Moreover, continued budgetary support packages for the under-performing broad property sector, a long-standing favorite of local and foreign investors, can be expected.

The bottom line: Caution laced with pragmatic opportunism

Investors focusing on traditional export markets and the small domestic market should proceed with caution, given the high level of uncertainty for 2003–04 and Singapore's wavering attraction as a manufacturing exports base. However, with the current low cost of funds, longer-term investors may want to look at being the first movers into the promoted 'sunrise industries' and newly liberalized sectors. Unlike other countries in the region, Singapore's efficient and clean government, its investor-friendly outlook, and well-developed corporate infrastructure offer lower investment risks for all foreign investors, counterbalancing the higher costs of doing business in the territory.

Section B Risks and projections

Macroeconomic performance and risk indicators

- The economy is recovering from recession with real GDP growth flat in 2002, but antici- pated to recover to 4–4.5 percent in 2003. Domestic demand and local private investment is weak. Singaporean banks are shifting money offshore due to low interest rates and a lack of lending opportunities. Singapore's domestic economy and its macroeconomic market risk are very sensitive to the global economy.

Along with Taiwan, the Singaporean economy has been hardest hit by the secular decline of Japan and the slowdown in US economic growth, and dipped into recession in 2001–02 despite having the strongest economic 'fundamentals' in the region. Unemployment figures climbed to 4.7 percent of the labor force by mid 2002, eclipsing 4.3 percent in 1998.[3] With a lack of pick-up in foreign direct investment (FDI) and weak local investment, unemploy- ment figures, by Singapore standards, look grim for 2003–04.

Fortunately, the government sector is uniquely well placed to absorb increased expen- diture and falling revenue projections.

> With no foreign debt, gross international reserves of US$80 billion (the highest in the world per capita, and as a percentage of GDP), and close to negative real interest rates, the 2001–02 budget deficit of S$4 billion and predicted deficit of S$190 million in 2002–03 will have no noticeable effect on the government's fiscal position, interest rates, or the exchange rate.

More worrying for Singapore is increased regional competition in areas where it has long dominated. Singapore's position as the region's premier trading hub and world's busiest port is under some challenge with the Malaysian government focusing on developing the capacity of Port Klang, and Port Tanjung Pelepas (PTP), with PTP already luring major shipping lines such as Maersk, the world's largest shipping fleet, and Evergreen, the world's second largest fleet, to transfer from costlier Singapore. Malaysia is also aiming to challenge Singapore's long-held position as the regional hub for oil refining. With the price-sensitive oil-refining sector making up 12 percent of Singapore's exports any decline here would be worrying indeed.

Private consumption has weakened, tipping Singapore into domestic deflation, like Hong Kong and Japan in late 2001 and early 2002, especially in the domestic supply price index. While this may lower the costs of domestically sourced inputs, if deflation continues in 2003–04 a deflationary spiral is an outside risk. Tourism, worth 5 percent of GDP and hit hard by regional economic difficulties and September 11, is showing signs of recovery in late 2002 with impressive increases in arrivals from China and Hong Kong more than compen- sating for declines in the traditional markets of Japan and the United States. If recovery continues in Southeast Asia, regionally sourced tourism will also likely start to recover to pre-1997 levels by 2003–04.[4]

With external 'fundamentals' still uncertain in 2002, Singapore's macroeconomic picture looks gloomy in the short run, especially on the manufactured export and domestic economy fronts. The knock-on effects of the 2002 budget tax cuts and moves to free up Central Provident Fund (CPF) funds should help the long-suffering broad property sector and local business sector. Unfortunately, the increase in Singapore's GST from 3 to 5 percent and its signaling of a shift from indirect to direct taxation may further dampen consumer confidence, increasing Singapore's already inflated savings rate and cutting into weakened local consumer demand.

Export performance

- The export sector has been at the forefront of Singapore's travails in 2001 and would have suffered more if the economy was not already in the early stages of reorientation. In the short run, domestic exports and entrepôt re-exports (around 40 percent of total exports) will be driven by the fortunes of the developed economies and the global IT and oil industries. China's potential replacement of Southeast Asia as the favorite export platform for multinational companies (MNCs) and Malaysia's nascent challenge to the supremacy of the Singapore port threaten entrepôt re-exports.

After being the driving force behind Singapore's impressive recovery from the 1997–98 regional crisis, non-oil domestic exports (about 44 percent of total exports) have been at the heart of its troubles. Every quarter since 2001 has witnessed a decline in export revenues, climaxing with a fall of 29.9 percent in August and 30.7 percent in September 2001. Reflecting Singapore's intense trade dependence, its overall trade balance has not altered significantly as imports have declined along with exports. Non-oil re-exports have exhibited a more muted downward trajectory reflecting Singapore's hub status in global and regional electronics and IT production networks.

The meltdown in the global IT industry has been the most significant export depressor for Singapore. While semiconductors and disk drive exports 'troughed' in late 2001, declining demand for PC and PC parts, and telecommunications exports were driving the declining export picture in early 2002.[5] While export declines in the broad IT sector have slowed down from 2001, these traditional mainstays of the Singapore export economy are under increasing threat by the plans of MNCs to shift future investment away from Southeast Asia to China. Locally based manufacturers would seem to disagree with this gloomy forecast, as most predict a continued turnaround in late 2002–03, gaining strength in 2004.

> With electronics and IT exports accounting for 66 percent of non-oil domestic exports and 54 percent of total domestic exports, Singapore's export profile is heavily weighted to this single industry. Demand in the sector is extremely price sensitive and subject to rapid change.

Domestic oil exports (17 percent of total domestic exports), buoyed by strong import demand from China, have not declined as much as non-oil exports. But, while troubles in the Middle East boosted world crude oil prices from late 2001 into 2002, moves by Iraq to re-enter the world market and pressure on OPEC to moderate its price manipulation suggest world crude oil prices will decline in 2003–04, cutting into Singapore's export value. While Singapore is under growing threat from refineries in Malaysia and China, oil MNCs in Singapore have indicated keen interest in locating higher-level petrochemical processing plants in Singapore with government support, if regional demand justifies the investment.

One of the major successes of Singapore's moves to reorient itself away from manufactured exports has derived from synergies between the oil and non-oil export sectors. Since the mid 1990s, chemical product exports have been a major new growth area for the Singapore economy. From exports of only S$5.6 billion in 1996 (5.4 percent of total domestic exports), this 'sunrise industry' had expanded to exports of S$12.3 billion in 2000 (9 percent of total domestic exports). Singapore's chemical and biomedical industries are continuing to surge ahead, unlike traditional manufacturing, exemplifying a gradual, effective change to Singapore's industrial balance that should continue in 2003–04. This shift is likely to accelerate when planned local and foreign investment in these industries kick in.

> Despite the current IT related export sector's weakness, Singapore's long-term ability to steadily increase exports across the board, despite the sharp regional appreciation of the Singapore dollar, suggests the underlying export picture is solid.

With oil exports holding up, new export streams developing, and a moderate upturn in the global electronics and IT industry since mid 2002, the outlook will improve in the short run in 2003–04. The longer run is more uncertain, due to the heavy presence of electronics exports, both in Singapore's domestic export and re-export portfolio, and fears that producers may leave Southeast Asia. With the government optimistically predicting that it will take 10 to 15 years to reduce the manufacturing sector from 25 percent to 15 percent of GDP, Singapore may lose its traditional exports quicker than it can capture new markets, aggravating unemployment, capital outflows and social welfare demands on the government.

Currency movements and projections

- Singapore is in a particularly strong position to manage the Singapore dollar due to a savings rate of around 50 percent (most of it funneled through the state-run and low-return Central Provident Fund (CPF)), very low debt service ratio, and the world's highest per capita gross international reserves of around US$80 billion. With recent weakening in the capital and finance accounts and little room for further interest rate cuts, 2003–04 may witness a gradual tightening of the money supply and an appreciation of the Singapore dollar against regional currencies.

The sharp economic downturn in the second half of 2001 combined with growing capital outflows, a product of Singapore's lower interest rates, led the secretive Monetary Authority of Singapore (MAS), to broaden the Singapore dollar–US dollar trading band in the third quarter, to encourage a controlled depreciation of the Singapore dollar. In response, the Singapore dollar reversed its gradual appreciation from July to September and has since fallen from S$1.74 to S$1.84 by the end of 2001. This recent depreciation against the US dollar is congruent with the Singapore dollar's gradual and controlled decline against the US dollar since 1996 when the exchange rate was S$1.40. With the softening of US interest rates from late 2001, in early 2002, the Singapore dollar, has firmed up against the US$, although less so than many of its regional counterparts, reaching S$1.75 by mid 2002.

> The measured depreciation of the Singapore dollar against the US dollar contrasts sharply with the volatile behavior of many regional currencies. Foreign exchange risks are minimal in comparison to those faced by investors in other countries in the region.

Cognizant of MAS's unflappability and believing that the recent depreciation is recession driven, the Singapore dollar six-month forward rate is at a premium to the spot rate, in contrast to other regional forward rates.[6] The indicators for 2003–04 point to a slow but steady appreciation of the Singapore dollar against the US dollar, with temporary, controlled depreciations possible if the Singapore growth picture stays weak or if the US tightens money supply over inflationary fears.

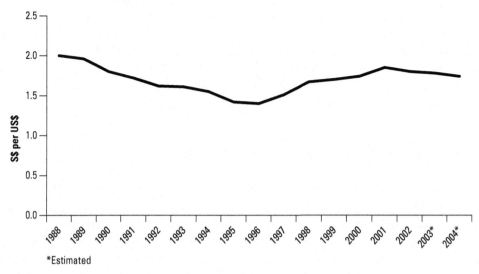

*Estimated

FIGURE 9.1 Exchange rate Singapore dollar to US dollar 1988–2004
Source: Federal Reserve Bank of St. Louis

Singapore's US$80 billion in gross international reserves (over 84 percent of Singapore's 2001 GDP of US$90.3 billion) is a very impressive defence against speculators and evidence of MAS's strong anti-inflationary credentials. Gross international reserves rose steadily from US$30 billion in 1990 to US$80 billion at the end of 2000. The fall-off in reserves in 2001 to 75 billion and the unique way in which this massive sum is managed though has led critics to claim the reserves are under threat and overstated.[7]

A stable currency in a volatile region

While the GIC's secrecy means it is difficult to validate these criticisms, Singapore's very low interest rates (1.06 percent three-month inter-bank rate in March 2002, up from 0.88 percent in October 2001) and the freeing up of state pension plans to invest overseas are the major reasons behind the recent fall-off in reserves. With US$76 billion still in the coffers and now increasing, Singapore's tradition of carefully managing its currency is not at risk and should continue its gradual trade-related appreciation. With recovery expected to begin in 2002–03, interest rates should continue to moderately rise to keep inflation in hand and may slow the longer-term depreciation of the Singapore dollar against the US dollar. Profit repatriations are not at risk, and the Singapore dollar is a good hedge against other more volatile regional currencies.

Financial markets: Performance and developments

- Since 1999 Singapore financial markets have been at the center of the government's plans to reorient the economy and internationalise local firms. The real economy problems of 2001–02 have acted to spur reform of financial markets further. Reforms offer foreign investors new openings and local investors and firms more freedom to expand beyond Singapore.

Singapore has long been the financial hub of Southeast Asia with Asia's largest dollar market and a major offshore banking sector. However, until 1999, Singapore's domestically focused financial markets were staid and underdeveloped. Since 1999, authorities have committed to comprehensively overhaul the long-protected domestic banking sector, moribund bond market, and fund management and insurance industries.

In 1998–99, three major and unexpected steps were taken in domestic banking that were accelerated in 2001–02. In 1999, for the first time since 1971, foreign banks were allowed more room in domestic banking when MAS reformed its licensing system and gave out four new Qualifying Full Bank (QFB) licenses to incumbent foreign banks. These allow holders up to 15 branches (10 real, and five off-branch ATMs) throughout Singapore and to share an ATM network among themselves, set up in 2002. In 2001, two more incumbent foreign banks were upgraded to QFB status, with MAS strongly hinting there is more to come in 2003–04.

> Singapore's domestic banking market may be fully open to foreign banks by as early as 2005. On the downside, MAS will likely force foreign branches to locally incorporate and meet its minimum paid-up capital requirement of S$1.5 billion each.[8]

Second, offshore banks were given more room to operate in 1999, with restrictions on lending in Singapore dollars loosened and offshore banks allowed to engage in Singapore dollar swaps. Plans are afoot to free up the entry of foreign banks into domestic wholesale banking with the goal of attracting them to use Singapore as their Asian banking base.[9]

Third, since 1998, MAS, again under Deputy Prime Minister and Finance Minister, Lee Hsien Loong, and the Singapore government have aggressively pushed Singapore's long-protected and tightly owned local banks to merge. In 1998, Singapore's largest bank, state-controlled State Bank of Singapore (DBS), took over the state-owned Post Office Savings Bank (POS), but local private banks, all family controlled, balked except for insolvent Tat Lee Bank that was bought out by Keppel. In 2001, MAS increased pressure on local banks to merge, and DBS, against Singaporean business custom, launched an unsolicited bid for Overseas Union Bank (OUB), that was countered by privately owned United Overseas Bank (UOB) on the same day, only 10 days after OCBC announced a planned buyout of Keppel Bank. If these mergers pan out, only three large local players will remain, one more than MAS wants. MAS has also opened the door for foreign banks to take a more active role in local banks by scrapping the 40 percent foreign ownership cap but has indicated it will not entertain any attempts by foreigners to take control of local banks; whose consolidation has made them an expensive buy anyway.[10]

New, limited openings, but a mature market

These changes to the domestic banking sector suggest the government is serious about internationalizing Singapore's domestic services sector. However, the lack of foreign bank access to the extensive and advanced ATM network of local banks, linked to the local stock exchange, limits their ability to eat significantly into the local banking market's 62 percent share of local deposits. Moreover, MAS language and their refusal to contemplate foreign buyouts of local banks clearly shows its desire for domestic banking to become more competitive but still under local control.

> Foreign banks entering the domestic market should not expect huge returns; local banks are operationally efficient, loan spreads are very low and competition is fierce.

Singapore banks are a safer bet than most of their regional counterparts as they were much less scarred by the Asian financial crisis and have since reduced their exposure to the region. As a percentage of total assets, Singaporean banks have lowered their exposure to the rest of Southeast Asia from 14.5 percent in September 1998 to less than 10 percent by the mid 2001, with reductions greatest in Indonesia and Thailand.

On the other hand, Singaporean banks, with their desire to expand out of their mature and increasingly competitive market, have bolstered their regional presence by buying into strong regional banks and buying out distressed banks. Reflecting this, loans to the Southeast Asian region have picked up since mid 2001 to climb back to 11.7 percent in 2002, with its share of NPLs slipping from 23.8 percent of total regional loans in March 1999 to only 11.7 percent in 2002. At the moment, these distressed bank buyouts are bleeding after being bought at a premium, but their small size does not threaten Singaporean bank bottom lines significantly and they offer access to higher-profit and expanding banking markets. Reflecting the relative strength of local banks, bank lending to local non-bank customers continued to grow throughout 2001 despite the recession, and picked up again in 2002.

However, these foreign forays and the recession are beginning to be felt as NPLs will reach 11 percent in 2002, up from 6 percent in early 2001. The merger process may also temporarily reduce the quality of local bank capital and their capital adequacy ratios, but these will remain adequate. DBS has seen its shares plummet due to overpaying for its takeover of Hong Kong's Dao Heng Bank, and faces management difficulties with its 20+ percent stake in the Bank of the Philippine Islands. Likewise, UOB's purchase of Westmont Bank in the Philippines is under a legal cloud as the previous local owners, including former Finance Secretary Eduardo Espiritu, are aiming to reclaim the bank after UOB helped to begin to turn it around. Singapore bank shares are not a short-term buy, but for longer-term investors, their discounted price may be worth investigating.

Bonds for the region

Reacting to Singapore's heavy reliance on bank credit and the difficulties of establishing an effective corporate bond market without benchmark government bonds, since 1999 the Singapore government has placed great emphasis on stimulating the local bond market and attracting regional players to raise money through Singapore dollar bonds. So far, regional interest has been muted, and state bodies have been the most active participants in the local bond market. In April 2001, the government introduced a 15-year bond, and Singapore government bonds were added to J.P. Morgan's Global Bond Index with a weighting of 0.33 percent. Buyers and dealers of Singaporean bonds can still access tax rebates that are expected to run out in 2003 but may be extended to help boost the market. Singapore's reliance on MNCs and the family-owned nature of most local private firms suggest that the bond market will remain focused on low-risk, low-return state-linked bonds.

> Singapore's history of low inflation, low interest rates, and currency stability offer investors looking to raise capital in the infant bond market opportunities for low cost finance.

Fund management opportunity

Since 1998, the Singapore authorities have focused on broadening the investor base by funneling state-controlled funds to local and foreign fund managers. MAS, when finished, will farm out S$10 billion and the GIC S$25 billion to kick-start Singapore's desired role as a regional fund management hub. The rules of Singapore's huge state-run savings pool, the CPF (that manages over 80 percent of Singapore's private savings), have been loosened to allow members to invest CPF funds more liberally, releasing S$40 billion to be invested in selected unit trusts, insurance products, and local bonds.

From only S$20 billion in managed funds in 1990, the managed funds industry exploded to more than S$276 billion by the end of 2000. With further loosening of rules for foreign fund managers to enter the local market and state fund managers to invest overseas, fund management will continue to grow and diversify.

The bottom line: Exciting changes, mature market

Together, these regulatory changes have reduced many of the firewalls between Singapore's lightly regulated offshore markets and its cloistered domestic markets. With liberalization affecting all sectors at once, Singapore is truly becoming a financial supermarket backed up by comparatively effective and clean regulation. However, except for fund management, the small size of the Singapore domestic market and the depth and sophistication of Singapore's offshore markets cast doubt on the actual number of new investment opportunities this will create.

Private and public debt: No risks ahead

- Singapore's strong economy and tradition of fiscal prudence means the government has issued no foreign debt since 1985 and its AAA sovereign rating was not lowered throughout the Asian financial crisis. Private sector foreign debt is equally insignificant at about US$9.5 billion and is expected to decline given Singapore's attractive interest rates.

Singapore's intense trade dependence and huge gross international reserves mean that there is virtually no debt-related risk to the economy. The external debt service ratio is negligible at less than 1.5 percent of total exports,[11] while reserves can cover short-term foreign debts more than 20 times over. The NPLs of Singapore banks are declining after a difficult 2001. Similarly, with the government's push to internationalise the domestic economy, large local firms like SingTel and DBS may increase their gearing to purchase regional firms, thus raising their risk profile, but with their implicit state guarantees credit risks remain minimal.

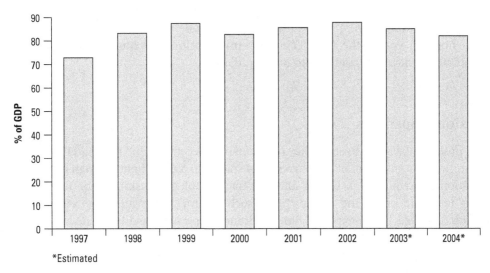

*Estimated

FIGURE 9.2 Public debt, Singapore 1997–2004
Source: Economist Intelligence Unit, Statistics Singapore

The Singapore government's domestic debt is, however, rapidly growing due to moves to energize the local bond market and Singapore's dip into deficit financing. Driven by a budget deficit of S$4 billion, Singapore's public debt to GDP ratio rose from 82.7 percent at the end of 2000 to 85.5 percent by the end of the third quarter of 2001. Due to estimated predicted budget deficit in 2002 of S$190 million, down from an estimate of S$1 billion in 2001, and the government's desire to deepen the bond market, domestic debt will likely continue to rise into 2003–04. However, with government agencies as the major 'captive' purchasers of this debt and its very low interest rates, even this increase should not alarm.

Labor market trends: Foreign labor-led

• The recession's epicenter in export manufacturing has aided Singapore's plan to reduce its dependence on semi-skilled labor. It also has reaffirmed the government's desire to attract highly skilled migrants to Singapore to pioneer its economic reorientation.

Foreign labor accounts for approximately 25 percent of the labor force and is split into two distinct categories: semi-skilled guest workers and highly skilled professionals. Since the mid 1980s, the Ministry of Manpower (MOM) has worked to increase the number of highly skilled migrant professionals and wean the economy of its dependence on semi-skilled guest workers. The recession of 2001–02 and plans to accelerate Singapore's economic reorientation will enhance this dual approach to foreign labor.

A large and flexible pool of foreign labor acts to moderate both wage increases and skill shortages within the local economy. Immigration procedures for short-term expatriate employment continue to be simplified.

Professional openings

Migrant professionals have been the key component in recent productivity and GDP gains in Singapore, and the government has aggressively sought to attract them through greatly eased immigration procedures, tax breaks and fast-tracking of citizenship.[12] For foreign firms planning to set up or expand in Singapore, such pro-migrant regulations reduce staffing difficulties spawned by Singapore's limited domestic pool of highly trained individuals. Recognizing this inherent limitation, Singapore has always tailored education for the labor market and government economic policy goals. Recently, the government has been pouring large funds into science and technology education, with a fresh 970 new tertiary scholarships announced, along with US$1.6 billion in fresh funds for R&D.[13]

Staff turnover ratios have been growing quite rapidly from 1998–2000, with top management's turnover ratio increasing from 4.9 percent in 1998 to 7.1 percent in 2000, and non-sales professionals increasing from 7.2 percent to 12.0 percent.[14] Wage rates for both these key corporate levels also accelerated from 1998–2000. However, the 2001–02 recession and the gradual depreciation of the Singapore dollar have minimized wage rises in 2001–02. With the depreciation of neighboring currencies since 1997 and anemic employment creation in the region, firms in Singapore should continue to attract skilled and

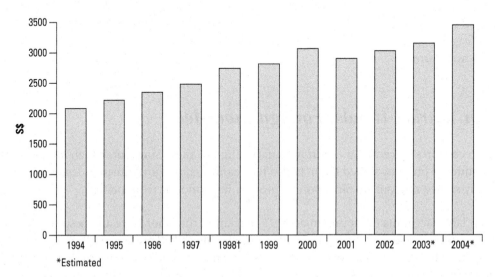

FIGURE 9.3 Monthly wages, Singapore 1994–2004
Source: International Labour Office
† 1998 data not strictly comparable to pre-1998 data

low-cost professionals from these countries. Singapore's close historical ties with South Asia and its large South Asian population (8 percent of the resident population) also make it an attractive market for South Asian professionals.

Low-wage labor support

The 2001–02 recession impacted on low-wage earners hardest, with little sign of an improvement in 2002. With employment in the manufacturing sector lagging behind output falls, rising unemployment can be expected into 2002–03. This lag time meant that productivity declined throughout 2001, especially in manufacturing and wholesale and retail trade. Worryingly, in the fourth quarter of 2001, monthly earnings began to increase across all industries, while productivity continued to decline. The government has responded by hinting at a cut of 2 percent in employer contributions to the CPF for the 2003 budget, after a sharp 4 percent increase in January 2001 (when rapid growth was expected to continue). Employers were disappointed that the 2002 budget offered no such reduction in wage costs. The employer's contribution to the CPF now stands at 20 percent of the covered employee's salary. Similarly, an expected increase in the foreign worker levy has been delayed.

The bottom line: Lower costs in the short run

Growing unemployment and government wage recommendations point to declining or slowing wage growth in Singapore, especially in manufacturing. However, if the forecast global economic is robust, the Singapore government may lift supports for wage moderation among semi-skilled workers. For firms employing professional workers, supply and cost issues will continue to improve as immigration procedures are further streamlined, supported by the lack of Southeast Asian economic dynamism.

Consumer and business confidence

- After recording strongly positive sentiment from 1999 to the first quarter of 2001, consumer and business confidence waned from mid 2001 in accord with the sharpness and severity of the recession. Business confidence has returned to moderately positive levels in 2002, but consumer confidence is likely to be muted due to employment and deflation concerns, and slower economic growth through to mid 2003.

The domestic economy in Singapore is still quite weak and uncertain. The consumer price index has continued to slide from mid 2001 to early 2002, while the domestic supply index is now below 1995 levels and the retail sales index fell again in the first quarter of 2002. This unusual softening of the local economy was reflected in the *Singapore Straits Times* consumer confidence index slipping to its lowest post-1998 reading of 86 in the fourth quarter of 2001. With consumer confidence tied more to local recovery than export recovery, and often lagging behind GDP growth rate recovery, Singapore's disappointing recent retail history is likely to continue into 2003 and possibly 2004.

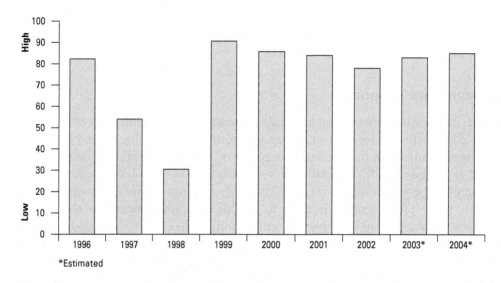

FIGURE 9.4 Business and consumer confidence index, Singapore 1996–2004
Source: MasterIndex Consumer Confidence (MasterCard)

The second and largest supplementary budget in October 2001 of S$11.3 billion, announced just prior to the elections, included a new savings/demand stimulation instrument known as New Singapore Shares (NSS). NSS are interest-rate bearing five-year bonds distributed by the government to mostly low-wage resident workers. The interest rate paid on the bonds will rise with any improvement in the economy. These bonds are tradable and a total of S$2.7 billion in bonds was issued. On top of the temporary 10 percent cut to income tax granted in the 2001 budget (income tax is levied on just 30 percent of the adult population), October pump-priming included further personal tax cuts of about S$650 million. While a reduction in personal income tax from 24.5 percent to 22 percent was announced in the 2002 budget, with a further cut to 20 percent by 2006, suggesting a further boost of disposable income, the increase in the GST announced at the same time from 3 to 5 percent will more than counteract this. With the 2 percent increase in the GST put in place to balance revenue losses from cuts to corporate and personal income tax, more money has been taken out of consumers' pocket, not the government's.

With the recession now seriously biting into employment, Singapore's lack of unemployment insurance, and its population's propensity to save suggest consumer confidence will stay weak and efforts to stimulate demand in 2001–02 will have a limited effect.

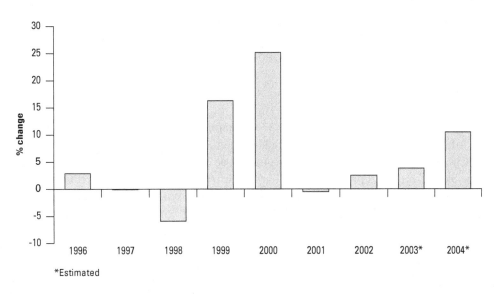

FIGURE 9.5 Retail sales index, Singapore 1996–2004
Source: **Statistics Singapore**

The sharp fall-off in consumer and business confidence in the second half of 2001 is not surprising given the recession and events of September 11. However, the fact that business confidence is recovering in 2002, with a majority of firms predicting higher gross receipts, should be noted, especially for investors looking at short-term buys on the Singapore stock market. However, until the rise in GST is filtered through the economy, employment turns the corner, and consumers regain their taste for shopping, consumer-oriented producers and retailers – except luxury goods retailers – will face tough operating conditions in the next 12 months.

Stock market

- In local currency terms, the Singapore Exchange (SGX) was one of the worst performing exchanges in the region in 2001, though marginal rises were recorded in the final quarter of the year. The number and value of IPOs fell, but with new foreign interest in tapping SGX's liquidity, the number of IPOs will rise in 2002, with further year-on-year increases likely in 2003 and 2004.

From February to mid September 2001, the SGX steadily declined, thereby foreshadowing the coming recession. However, after hitting a low of 1241.25 on September 19, it rose to 1623.6 by year's end, a 31 percent increase, and was above 1730 by May 2002. With leading indicators suggesting that foreign capital is starting to return to the region, Singapore's reputation as a low-risk market should see a significant injection of new capital thereby driving further gains throughout the forthcoming 12 months. However, annual volume in 2001 was down 22 percent from 2000, itself down 12 percent from 1999.[15] A return to the trading volume peaks of 1999 is unlikely before 2004–05.

Regional aspirations

Reflecting the weakness of the SGX, only 37 companies launched IPOs in 2001, 19 of them before June. In comparison, 55 IPOs were launched in 1999, and 83 in 2000. Chinese SME interest in the SGX increased in 2001, giving those at the SGX some cause for optimism. Chinese SMEs from food processing to pharmaceuticals to aviation floated IPOs in 2001 on the second board, with more offerings expected in 2002. With huge demand for capital by Chinese SMEs, the good reputation of the SGX, and Hong Kong's Growth Enterprise Market (GEMs) birthing pains, Chinese firms may be an important new element to the SGX, especially for more risk-tolerant investors. With the poor governance of some bourses in the region and the continued loan aversion of regional banks, other regional firms will also seek a listing on SGX during the forthcoming 12 to 18 months. The SGX is also in the process of expanding its investment options through cross-listing agreements with the Australian ASX and others, and offering Euro-Yen options and the MSCI Japan Index Futures. If these cross-listing and extra-Singapore options continue to expand, the SGX may well position itself, like the Singapore offshore market, as a good regional or global equities base.

Government reforms of the stock market itself and other financial services will also increase SGX's liquidity in the near future. With the government allowing CPF members to increasingly pull out money for housing and approved investment vehicles, more CPF savings and non-CPF savings (earlier consumed by housing) will come into the market. With the reforms to the fund management industry and insurance industries, more demand for stocks is also expected.

To strengthen Singapore's role as a regional stock market, a series of reforms have taken place since 1999. In 1999, the stock exchange was demutualized, with plans for it to be listed by 2004. The SGX and the futures market were also merged. Brokerage fees were gradually liberalized from January to October 2000 with fees falling to 40 to 50 basis points for retail trades and 20 basis points for institutional ones.[16]

The structure of ownership in the Singapore economy, however, limits substantial growth and deepening of the SGX. When Morgan Stanley shifted its global stock indices from weightings based on total market capitalization to freely traded shares, Singapore's weighting was downgraded. The SGX is heavily weighted towards state-controlled firms and large local family-owned firms. In both cases, only a minority of shares in these firms are freely traded and minority shareholders' voices are consequently muted. With no foreseeable change in this market structure, above-average returns on the SGX should not be expected.

Corporate tax: Permanent and temporary relief

• The past three budgets have reduced the across-the-board corporate tax rate from 26 to 22 percent and increased the number of targeted tax incentives for firms. With the government's plan to reorient the economy moving slower than initially forecast, and growing non-tax revenues, the government is likely to further increase the scope of tax incentives available to targeted industries in 2003–04.

The Singapore government's strong fiscal position and significant investment income (16.3 percent of total revenue in 2000) affords a degree of taxation flexibility not available to other governments in the region. From 1997 to 2000, tax revenue averaged just slightly over 50 percent of total revenue. Therefore, the government has great scope to lower taxes during times of slower growth or when it is concerned about economic competitiveness in general or in particular areas. While the CPF is not included as a tax, it is utilised in a similarly flexible manner.

Across-the-board tax rates have declined from 33 percent in 1990 to 22 percent in 2003. On top of the 2002 budget corporate income tax cut from 24.5 to 22 percent and personal income taxes from 26 to 22 percent, in early 2002 the Economic Review Committee (ERC) announced that both corporate and personal income tax rates would decline to 20 percent. On top of across-the-board permanent cuts, selective tax cuts have been made both to favor certain corporate activities and recession-hit industries. The 2001 budget reconfigured the tax system, exempting 75 percent of the first S$10,000 and 50 percent of the next S$90,000 of chargeable income from the new 22 percent rate. This new tiering, while insignificant for large firms, will relieve the tax burden of local and foreign SMEs.

> More significant for locally-incorporated larger firms, the 2002 budget practically removed taxes on dividends and provided for 'group relief' where the losses of one firm can be absorbed by a sister firm, lowering the total tax take for the corporate grouping.

The Singapore government has long used corporate taxation as a tool to achieve its economic goal of industrial restructuring. Firms in preferred sectors like financial services, particularly commodity traders, and firms who use Singapore as an operational headquarters are given tax breaks that mean the effective tax rate may be as low as 10 percent. Similarly, the 2001 budget offered tax exemptions on software payments and better writing-down terms for intellectual property capital expenditures.

Singapore is quickly changing from a high-tax to a low-tax country. For 2003–04, more tax breaks can be expected to help stimulate the economy especially in the sunrise industries and the still moribund property sector.

Residential and commercial property markets

- The real estate sector in Singapore, given the lack of land and the high cost of property, acts as a bellwether to the health of the economy as a whole. Property prices in almost all sectors weakened during 2001. For Grade A commercial and residential properties, the slump looks set to continue throughout 2003–04, but properties outside the CBD are showing signs of recovery.

While Singapore's commercial property sector has offered good returns historically, in 2003 and 2004 this sector is expected to offer negative returns far below its long-term trend line. Market weakness will be further compounded by a number of major new developments, delayed since 2000, that were expected to come online in 2002, thereby inflating already high vacancy rates. In 2002, an estimated 3.55 million square feet of Grade A commercial property will have come online, with demand estimated to only reach 1.8 million square feet.[17] Office space take-up in the third quarter of 2001 of only 151,000 square feet, halved Singapore's historical monthly average of 300,000–500,000 square feet. The fourth quarter of 2001 was even worse with a take-up of –321,000, indicating that real price adjustments will continue for the foreseeable future.

Commercial properties: Increasing supply, stagnant demand

Net monthly rents and annual yields in the CBD are expected to be hardest hit as firms continue to migrate from the CBD to outer regions where office space is newer and much cheaper. Already in 2001, Standard Chartered has shifted many operations out of the CBD, with Exxon Mobil and IBM following suit in 2002. In 2001, office occupancy rates in the non-CBD increased from 80.9 percent to 89.5 percent, while those in the CBD have slipped from 88.5 percent to around 86.5 percent.[18] With most of the new space in 2002 opening up in the CBD, occupancy rates and rents can be expected to fall faster there for 2003–04 compared to non-CBD areas.

> State-owned Jurong Town Corporation, Singapore's largest developer of industrial sites, recently announced a 17 percent cut in factory and industrial land rents.

Residential property: Some signs of recovery, but more problems ahead

In 2001, the Singapore government slashed sales of state-owned land for new residences from 6–7,000 properties to only 4,000 with the rest being held 'in reserve.' With the majority of Singaporeans living in government housing, the residential market has always been more volatile than the commercial property sector, while land scarcity makes condominiums the dominant residential type. The private market is starting to show signs of recovery in the low to medium end of the market, the market most sensitive to interest rates and the opening up of more CPF funds for housing.

Most residential sub-sectors bottomed out in late 2001 and early 2002, with developers cutting prices aggressively, boosting take-up rates. However, with many large condominium projects that were delayed from 2000 expected to come online in 2002–03, and interest rate rises forecast in 2002–03, condominium prices can be expected to fall, and the stock of unsold properties to rise.

Unsold private residential units estimates (by year of completion)

2002	2003	2004	2005	2006
3589	4468	6869	4915	3019

Source: Colliers Jardine Research (Singapore), February 2002

The bottom line: No signs of upturn, good time to move

With so much Grade A office space and condominiums coming online in 2002–03, price growth for both will remain soft, with possible marginal falls. With office occupancy rates rising outside the CBD and most of the new office space located in the CBD, the price gains from moving out of the CBD will decline, but opportunities to move from older to new offices are abound. The government will likely continue to favor the property sector with tax breaks and new supply limitations imposed from 2003–04, especially in the residential sector.

Foreign direct investment

• Equity investment is particularly important for Singapore, accounting for 80 percent of all investment-related capital inflows. It also regularly accounts for more than 30 percent of annual private capital formation, and about two-thirds of manufacturing investment. Since 1997 Singapore has seen both FDI inflows and outflows decline. A significant turn-around in net capital flows is unlikely during 2003–04.

Recent economic troubles have accelerated the declining importance of FDI in Singapore's economy. From 1988–90, FDI inflows accounted for 12.7 percent of GDP (by far the highest of any country); however, from 1998–2000, they only accounted for 2.2 percent, with little growth expected in the short term.[19] Singapore has seen its FDI inflows tail off significantly from 1997 after more than a decade of breakneck growth.

From a total of US$13 billion in 1997, inflows were only US$6.3 billion in 1998, US$7.2 billion in 1999 and US$6.4 billion in 2000. The future pattern of capital flows into the economy looks decidedly negative, when compared to the outlook during the mid 1990s.

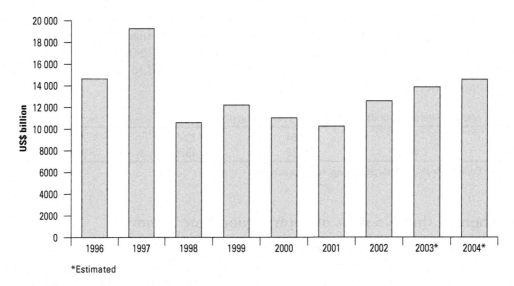

FIGURE 9.6 Foreign direct investment, Singapore 1996–2004
Source: UNCTAD

The China factor

Singapore's FDI woes are a muted microcosm of those facing much of Southeast Asia. Southeast Asia has seen not only its portion of global FDI flows fall but also a sharp decline in the actual value of FDI into the region since 1997. China, on the other hand, has seen its fortunes continue to rise rapidly. In 2001–02, Dutch giant Philips moved its regional headquarters from Singapore to Hong Kong, with rumors persisting that General Motors (GM) may move its regional base to South Korea. At the same time, a number of surveys of business conditions report that Singapore had replaced Hong Kong as the 'best place to do business in Asia,' due to troubled market conditions in Hong Kong. Despite Singapore's better business infrastructure and more efficient government, the lure of China may be too strong.

Outflow blues

From an average FDI outflow of US$1.9 billion (much of it portfolio) from 1989–94, outflows grew to US$6.8 billion in 1996 and US$9.4 billion in 1997 with the mix shifting decidedly towards acquisitions of foreign firms. After falling to only US$0.55 billion in 1998, FDI outflows have recovered to just over US$4.5 billion annually since 1999. Many of Singapore's investments in Southeast Asia and China have been rushed, overpriced, and quickly mired in difficulties, suggesting Singaporean investments overseas will become fewer and more carefully thought out. With very low interest rates and a weakening currency against the US dollar, portfolio and other investment outflows have been increasing recently, causing problems for the balance of payments. The capital account will continue to weaken in 2002–03 before improving in 2003–04 as exports begin to rise again.

The bottom line: Still bright but waning

Singapore still remains a favorite FDI destination for US and European investors but Japanese investors have started to pull back from the island. With China's entry into the World Trade Organization and its continued strong economic growth, Southeast Asia's ability to attract FDI, already weakened, looks set to worsen. With Singapore trying to place itself as a regional headquarters for MNCs, these developments are viewed seriously among Singapore's officials. Singaporean outflows will continue and are likely to recover much of their lost ground, but should be more market savvy in the future, hurting the bottom lines of their large firms less. More generally, the concern of officials will likely presage a more favorable investment climate in Singapore for FDI by way of increased incentives for investors.

Section C Politics

- Singapore's unrivaled political stability continued without a hitch with the People's Action Party (PAP) winning another resounding victory in late 2001. PAP is already grooming new leaders to replace 'the old guard' of Senior Minister Lee Kuan Yew and Prime Minister Goh Chok Tong. Singapore's world-beating business environment of quality infrastructure and low corruption appears rock-solid for 2002–04.

Regime stability

PAP has never come close to losing an election in Singapore, ruling uninterruptedly since separation from Malaysia in 1965. In 2001, PAP took advantage of Singapore's parliamentary system with its flexible election date and called an election early, on November 3, soon after its October S$11.3 billion stimulus package. With PAP candidates unchallenged in more than 50 percent of seats, the party's rule was never threatened.

PAP's large election win amid the economic slowdown and uncertain near-term future clearly showed PAP's unassailable position. PAP won 83 of 85 seats, amassing 75.3 percent of votes cast, its largest win in over two decades. With the next election not due until 2007, few changes in policy direction are expected, and investors can rest assured that Singapore's pro-business climate will be maintained.

The new Cabinet, sworn in on November 23, heralded few surprises, but did supply some strong suggestions for who would be the future leaders of PAP. With Senior Minister Lee Kuan Yew in his twilight years, and Goh Chock Tong expected to retire as Prime Minister prior to 2007, PAP is grooming a new generation of leaders. Deputy Prime Minister and MAS Chairman, Brigadier Lee Hsien Loong was elevated by also being given the finance portfolio. It seems that the Lee family dynasty in Singapore is set to continue with Brigadier Hsien Loong now best positioned to take over as prime minister in or prior to 2007.

Deputy Prime Minister Tony Tan was given the defense portfolio, while Brigadier George Yong-Boon Yeo was given the trade and industry portfolio. This new, second-generation team ties the PAP regime more closely to the powerful Singapore military and the local business elite, given Tony Tan's prior career in OCBC and his very close ties with local business. The already strong ties between PAP, the military and state firm-led Singapore Inc. seem to be tightening.[20]

The bottom line: No need to worry

While succession offers the potential for instability, Singapore is at little or no risk when the first generation of PAP leaders step down. Rather, PAP's resounding win in November 2001, despite Singapore's worst recession in 36 years, and the gelling of the anointed leaders of the next generation of PAP leaders further underline Singapore's political stability.

Leading risk indices: Corruption, stability, governance, risk

Corruption

The seven leading investor risk indices for Singapore show very strong stability with limited volatility, driven by external rather than local factors. Regionally and globally, Singapore's capacity to govern, law and order, political stability and corporate governance are all at the highest end of the scale, while corruption and overall foreign investor risk are very low.

Singapore consistently ranks as the least corrupt business environment in the region, ranking fourth least corrupt (with Iceland) in the world, according to Transparency International's 2002 Corruption Perception Index. Singapore fared worse on the 2000 Bribe Payer's Index ranking a disappointing eleventh, but still on top in Asia.

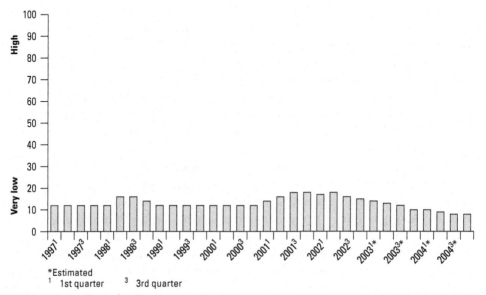

FIGURE 9.7 Corruption index, Singapore 1997–2004
Sources: IMD, Transparency International, PERC, World Bank, Pricewaterhouse Coopers, the Singapore Business Times

Political stability

The political stability index also shows much promise for foreign investors. PAP's stranglehold on elections, the comprehensive and positive role the state plays in the economy, and its strong levers of social control all make the present regime one of the strongest and most stable in the world. These strong levers, along with Singapore's clean judiciary, also mean few if any internal law and order problems exist. The terrorist attacks of September 11 and the discovery of operating terrorist cells in Singapore and its neighbors do present a new threat both to political stability and law and order, but one that is too new to evaluate properly. What is certain is that based on past threats, the Singapore government's response will be swift toward potential terrorists while protection of potential targets will be tight.

Corporate governance

The corporate governance index shows a slow but steady upward trend for both measures. The 1997 crisis and the recession of 2001–02 have bolstered Singapore's propensity to restructure by highlighting the longer-term costs of the status quo and by helping to

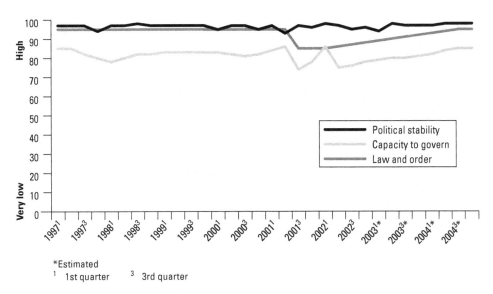

*Estimated
¹ 1st quarter   ³ 3rd quarter

FIGURE 9.8 Political stability index, Singapore 1997–2004

Political stability methodology:
- The capacity-to-govern index is based upon the institutional reach of government defined in terms of its ability to set the political and economic agenda and ensure its legislative program is enacted without significant compromise. This index is adversely affected by legislative opposition, lack of legislative implementation, failure to realize government policy and general political opposition.
- The political stability index measures violent opposition or organized demonstrations, terrorist activities, and popular discontent that adversely affect the institutional and electoral stability of the government.
- The law and order index measures the propensity to civil obedience, and the institutional reach of the rule of law in terms of regulatory compliance and enforcement.

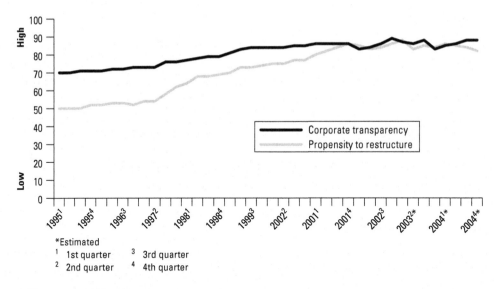

FIGURE 9.9 Corporate governance index, Singapore 1995–2004

Corporate governance index methodology:
- The corporate governance index is a composite index measuring the juridical requirements for corporate disclosure and financial reporting, prudential regime adequacy, prudential compliance enforcement, and the juridical reach of prudential authorities.
- The propensity to restructure index is a composite index based on media releases and reported corporate restructuring as a result of prudential regulation, financial incentives, loan restructuring/re-negotiation, or asset realignment.

promote advocates of reform. Regionally, Singapore's corporate transparency is quite high given the reputation for strictness of the SGX and the MAS. Singapore's intense dependency on MNCs also boosts its transparency scores as they are more likely to work to international best practice than smaller, local firms. Singapore's corporate transparency is slightly muted by the fact that its domestic economy is heavily influenced by government-linked companies (GLCs) and family-owned ones, often with more secretive approaches to corporate information.

Foreign investor risk index

Like political stability, the general foreign investor risk index shows some recent volatility tied to external events and their ramifications for the Singapore economy. Again, the strong pro-business credentials of the Singapore government keep risk generally at a very low level and help mute its sensitivity to outside events. As a result, Singapore should be judged as one of the most competitive locations in the world in which to do business.[21] The risk to foreign investors of adverse changes to the operating environment during 2003 and 2004 is low. Foreign investors' risk will remain stable throughout the forecast period.

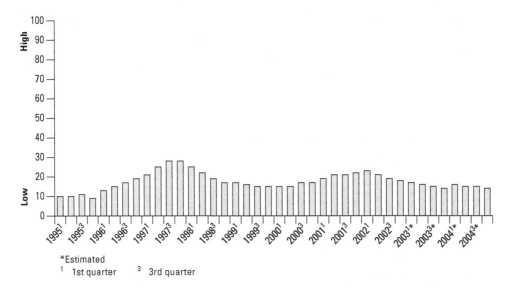

FIGURE 9.10 Foreign investor risk index, Singapore 1995–2004

Foreign investor risk index methodology:
* The foreign investor risk index is a composite index measuring tax burdens, discriminatory regulatory practices, adverse compliance regulations, government policy toward foreign enterprise, receptiveness to issuance of government contracts, foreign enterprise commercial restrictions, and official attitudinal changes to foreign direct investment and foreign commercial operations which impact on operational efficiency. The index also incorporates a nominal measure for market risk and market failure.

Section D Security

* Singapore's internal security situation is strong and stable with no identifiable threats to foreign business. For some investors, September 11 highlighted potential security problems, given Singapore's long-standing function as the regional trading and financial hub, but this should be of little concern to potential investors with internal security maintained at the highest level. Singapore's tradition of stability despite instability in its larger neighbors, and the apparent calming of tensions in Indonesia suggest external security will also remain stable during 2000 and 2004.

Pragmatic diplomacy

Singapore's wealth and its ethnic Chinese majority have helped instill a tradition of diplomatic pragmatism, where Singapore attempts to maintain cordial relations with all countries in the region and with major outside powers like Japan, China and the United States. Singapore has been a strong supporter of ASEAN, and of Western military presence in the region, opening its crowded port to visits from regional and Western navies. With over

50 percent of its fresh water piped in from Malaysia, and much of its fuel coming from Indonesia, Singapore has worked very hard to keep relations with these two prickly neighbors on an even keel.

While there were worries in 2001 that Singapore's close relations with the Suharto regime may poison relations with the more nationalistic President Sukarnoputri, so far relations seem to be harmonious. Similarly, the close consultations between Prime Minister Mahathir and Senior Minister Lee Kuan Yew leading to the Framework Agreement on Bilateral Relations between the two states was a good sign that bilateral tensions, rekindled during the Asian crisis, have subsided, even though both political elites continue to periodically inflame nationalistic feelings among the people of both nations.

> Singapore's difficult bilateral relations with Malaysia and Indonesia may be complicated by the retirement of PAP's first generation of leaders – all of whom have strong ties with the region's political elites.

Economic terrorism

The attacks on the World Trade Center turned Singapore's economic success and impressive skyline of global firms into a security problem overnight. Surveys of foreign investors immediately following the attack showed that Singapore was among the most negatively affected by changed perceptions of security. Worsening the September 11 effect for Singapore was the fact that foreign executives feared that Indonesia and Malaysia, with their large Muslim populations, may become significantly more unstable and belligerent, the longer the war on terror continues.

In December 2001, the Singapore authorities arrested 15 suspected terrorists on suspicion that they were targeting 'Western' business and political interests. With the rapid conclusion of the war against the Taliban, it is doubtful how lasting such fears need be. However, if the US continues to open up multiple fronts in this war, some – Southern Mindanao in the Philippines – may eventually be too close for comfort.

Singapore's long history of no internal threats to security and its pragmatic, risk-averse approach to regional relations will continue, and Singapore should remain one of the safest places in which to invest in the region. Its wealth and centrality suggest it may be a good terrorist target, yet, unlike the United States, the Singapore state has no global diplomatic role, and a muted regional one.

Section E Economic and political risk forecasts

- The extreme macroeconomic volatility of the last three years has clearly underscored Singapore's sensitivity to global trends. With signs of a recovery in the global economy during the first half of 2002, Singapore's economy should improve, lowering FDI and portfolio investment risks. Labor market demand and property sector recoveries are likely to lag significantly. The ability of Singapore to reorient its economic structure from export manufacturing to knowledge services is the key to long-term dynamism. The different investment rationales in knowledge services and China's growing attraction for export manufacturing threaten that Singapore may not be able to make the transition quickly and completely enough to ensure a continuation of the extraordinary growth rates of the past three decades.

Short term forecasts

- The short-term outlook for the economy is improving, but double digit GDP growth seems unlikely to be repeated any time soon. Growth forecasts for 2003–04, using the latest data, see real GDP growth of 2.5 and 5 percent respectively. Unemployment is likely to decline in 2003–04, putting some pressure on wages. Property prices will stay weak due to excess supply in most areas. As the economy recovers, the government should return to a modest budget surplus in 2003–04, but total government debt is likely to increase in order to stimulate the domestic bond market.
- The SGX's recovery since October 2001 will continue with a likely increase in IPOs as firms who waited out the market slump enter the market. The upward pressure on interest rates may, however, quell the rally slightly, but improved fundamentals should support it.
- Singapore's unparalleled business environment in the region faces no foreseeable challenge as the government is accelerating liberalization and corruption remains extremely low.
- Gains for foreign investors from liberalization efforts will be limited due to their focus on the small, mature domestic market.

Short term opportunities

- The weakness of regional currencies compared to the US dollar in contrast to Singapore's managed, slight depreciation offer opportunities to use Singapore dollar instruments as hedges and with very low interest rates, the Singapore market is a cost-effective credit market. With tax breaks on Singapore dollar bonds scheduled to run out by the end of the 2003 financial year, these may offer investors real value in the short term.
- The Singapore government's push into knowledge services and the lack of qualified locals means Singapore is an attractive short-term option for foreign professionals in these areas, especially as there are weak job prospects in other regional economies and an attractive professional lifestyle in Singapore.
- Healthy growth is expected to continue in chemical exports, oil-related exports, insurance and fund management.
- The merger processes and regional purchase problems of Singapore banks and their low share price should be fully worked out by 2003–04, making them a good but weakening contrarian buy.

- The continual need for Singaporean firms to expand beyond Singapore and the problems of earlier acquisitions mean that a new market niche for foreign investment banks and consultancies with experience of regional markets, particularly China, will continue to develop.
- With supply expected to expand much quicker than demand in the private residential and CBD Grade A commercial space, cost savings for corporate relocation and upgrading are abundant, while leasing arrangements are also attractive at present.

Medium to longer term

- In most traditional exports, Singapore's competitive position is expected to decline, both for domestic exports and entrepôt re-exports. With export manufacturing shifting from Southeast Asia to China, Singapore's re-exports and role as a global production and managerial hub will not grow as quickly as previously. Efforts by regional governments to develop business and transport infrastructure, given their lower living and operating cost structures, also threaten Singapore.
- The government's desire to reorient the Singapore economy towards knowledge services opens up new investment opportunities and government subsidies for global firms in these areas. First movers may gain the most from government incentives and in attracting good local and regional talent.
- This reorientation and the lack of local, trained professionals in these areas open up large new opportunities for human resource firms both in job placement and training.
- Singapore's very good business environment and clean and effective government will continue to make Singapore a safe haven for investment.

Overall risk rating

Singapore's risk profile is quite stable with general risk elements such as security, corruption and government attitude towards foreign investment all well-established and very positive. Global instability and competition from China, however, do cast some dark clouds on Singapore's horizon.

Risk: Low and stable to slightly increasing → ↗
Risk Rating (0 = lowest, 10 highest risk) 2.5

Section F Singapore fact sheet*

Geography

Capital
Singapore

Largest city (millions, 2000)
Singapore 3.22

Location
Singapore lies in Southeast Asia, with Peninsular Malaysia to the north, East Malaysia to the east, and Indonesia to the south. The country consists of one main island and 54 islets located approximately 77 miles north of the equator.

Neighboring countries
Malaysia and Indonesia

Terrain
Lowland; gently undulating central plateau contains water catchment area and nature preserve

Land use
2% arable land, 6% permanent crops, 0% permanent pastures, 5% forests and woodlands, 87% other (1993 est.)

Area
647.5 sq km

Economic statistics

Currency
Singapore dollar (SGD)

Exchange rate (2001)
US$1.00 = S$1.7917

Gross Domestic Product (GDP, 2001)
US$98.5 billion

GDP per capita (2001)
US$31,139

GDP per capita – PPP (2000 est.)
$26,500

GDP – composition by sector (2001)
Industry 30%, services 70%

Inflation rate (2001)
1%

Total external debt (2000)
US$9.7 billion

Current account balance (2000)
US$20.8 billion

National unemployment rate (2001)
3.3%

Population below poverty line
N/a

---

* All figures are the latest available except where indicated. All figures are in US dollars. Figures are compiled from national, international and multilateral agencies (United Nations Development Assistance Program, International Monetary Fund, World Bank, World Development Report, UNESCO Statistical Yearbook, International Labour Office, United Nations, Central Intelligence Agency World Fact Book). Gross domestic product (GDP) refers to the value of all goods and services produced in the preceding financial year. GDP per capita, Purchasing Power Parity (GDP per capita – PPP) refers to the indices developed by the World Bank to take account of price differences, cost of living differences, and relative purchasing power of a set basket of goods and services between countries so as to provide a more accurate measure of national wealth.

Labor force (millions, 2000)
2.1

Labor force by occupation (1998)
Financial, business, and other services 38%, manufacturing 21.6%, commerce 21.4%, construction 7%, other 12%

Budget (2000)
Revenues: US$18.5 billion
Expenditure: US$10.48 billion

Industries
Electronics, chemicals, financial services, oil drilling equipment, petroleum refining, rubber processing and rubber products, processed food and beverages, ship repair, entrepôt trade, biotechnology

Major exports (2001)
Machinery, petroleum and petroleum products, chemicals, telecommunications equipment, computer equipment, food and live animals, crude rubber, beverages, tobacco, clothing

Major imports (2001)
Integrated circuits, computer parts, petroleum, semiconductors and printed circuit board assemblies, machinery and transportation equipment, petroleum and petroleum products, crude materials, foodstuffs, tobacco, textiles, iron and steel, aircraft

Major trading partners (exports, 2001)
US 19.8%, Malaysia 15.2%, Hong Kong 8.4%, Japan 6.6%, Taiwan 4.3%, Thailand 3.8%, China 3.7%

Major trading partners (imports, 2001)
Japan 16.7%, Malaysia 15.5%, Thailand 4.8%, China 4.8%, Taiwan 3.8%, Germany 3.4%, Saudi Arabia 3.2%

Televisions (1997)
1.33 million

Televisions per capita (people per color television, 1996)
.03 TVs per capita
3.2 people per television

Telephones (lines in use, 2000)
1.928 million

Telephones (per 100 people, 2000)
48.5

Cellular phones (millions, 2000)
2.333

Cellular phones per capita (cellular phone per 100 people, 2000)
68.3

Registered motor vehicles (private cars, 2001)
115 per 1000

Internet users (2000)
1.74 million

Fiscal year
1 April–31 March

Government and political statistics

Nature of government
Parliamentary republic

Constitution
June 3, 1959 (amended 1965 and 1991).
Independence from Britain: August
9,1965

Structure of government

Executive Branch
President, four-year term. Prime
Minister (head of government)

Legislative Branch
Unicameral 83-member Parliament
(maximum 5-yr. term). Members elected
by popular vote. Cabinet appointed by
the president, responsible to Parliament

President
Sellapan Rama (SR) Nathan

Vice-Presidents
Lee Hsien Loong, Tony Tan Ken Yam

Prime Minister
Goh Chok Tong

Ministers

**Deputy Prime Minister/ Minister of
Defence**
Tony Tan Ken Yam

**Senior Minister, Prime Minister's
Office**
Lee Kuan Yew

Minister of Finance
Lee Hsien Loong

**Minister of Health/ Second Minister
for Finance**
Lim Hng Kiang

Minister of National Development
Mah Bow Tan

**Minister of Foreign Affairs/ Minister
for Law**
Prof. S. Jayakumar

Minister for Manpower
Dr Lee Boon Yang

Minister for Trade and Industry
(NS) George Yeo Yong-Boon

**Minister for Information & the Arts/
Minister for the Environment**
David Lim Tik En

Minister for Home Affairs
Lee Yock Suan

Minister without Portfolio, Prime Minister's Office
Lim Boon Heng and Lee Yock Suan

Minister for Community Development/Minister in charge of Muslim Affairs
Dr Yaacob Ibrahim

Minister for Education/Second Minister for Defence
Teo Chee Hean

Main governing parties and ideological affiliation
People's Action Party or PAP [Nationalist], Young PAP

Main opposition parties
National Solidarity Party, Singapore Democratic Alliances, Singapore Democratic Party, Workers' Party, Singapore People's Party

International memberships
APEC, ARF, AsDB, ASEAN, Australia Group (observer), BIS, C, CCC, CP, ESCAP, G-77, IAEA, IBRD, ICAO, ICC, ICFTU, ICRM, IFC, IFRCS, IHO, ILO, IMF, IMO, Inmarsat, Intelsat, Interpol, IOC, ISO, ITU, NAM, OPCW, PCA, UN, UN Security Council (temporary), UNCTAD, UNIKOM, UNMEE, UNTAET, UPU, WHO, WIPO, WMO, WTO

Business organizations
ARIACO, CASE, SCCCI, SCI, SFCI, Singapore Information Technology Federation, Singapore National Employers' Federation, The Association of Small and Medium Enterprises

Date of UN membership
1965

Social statistics

Population
4,300,419 (July 2001 est.)

Population density (per square km)
6055

Fertility rate (average number of children per woman, 2001 est.)
1.22

Maternal mortality rate (per 100,000 births, 2001 est.)
1.7

Infant mortality rate (2001 est.)
3.62 deaths/1000 live births

Population growth (2001 est.)
3.5%

Life expectancy (2001 est.)
Men: 77.22 years
Women: 83.35 years

Ethnic composition
Chinese 76.7%, Malay 14%, Indian 7.9%,
other 1.4%

Religions
Buddhist (Chinese), Muslim (Malays),
Christian, Hindu, Sikh, Taoist, Confucian

National languages spoken
Chinese (official), Malay (official and
national), Tamil (official), English
(official)

**Literacy rate (over 15 can read and
write, 1999 est.)**
Male: 97%
Female: 89.8%

South Korea

10 South Korea

Terry O'Callaghan

Section A Economy

Overview

South Korea has the third largest economy in the region and the tenth largest in the advanced industrialized world. This is testament to the effectiveness of the export-oriented development strategies initiated during the 1970s. Indeed, exports are the lifeblood of the South Korean economy, constituting some 45 percent of South Korea's GDP. By the mid 1990s, however, it became evident that the South Korean economy had massive structural problems that threatened to undermine its export position.[1] In particular, it became increasingly evident that many South Korean companies had financed their expansion on the back of massive debt build-up, exposing them to the cyclic changes in the global economy. A fall in the price of computer memory chips and capital outflows was enough to precipitate a crisis in the economy in 1997–98.

The government has responded to these difficulties by instigating sweeping reforms in the financial and corporate sectors. These included breaking up the Chaebol, restructuring the financial and banking industry, reducing the regulatory hurdles for foreign investors, attempting to curb corruption, and making the labor market more flexible.[2] On the back of these reform efforts, higher growth returned in 1999 and 2000, but turned downwards again in 2001–02 with the general slowdown in the global economy. In all, the latest shocks to the South Korean economy have affirmed that it continues to be overly susceptible to external economic forces, with its export position deteriorating from March 2001, and continuing to fall for 13 straight months through to March 2002.

While the government has made significant progress in reforming the economy, areas of concern remain.[3] The pace of reforms has slowed, mergers and acquisitions are difficult to accomplish, and labor productivity is substantially lower than in many other OECD countries.[4] The challenge for the government is to avoid reform fatigue and overcome the remaining impediments to foreign investment. However, there is currently no guarantee that the administration will be able to effect further reform, with interest in the reform process sure to be put on the back burner if renewed growth in the global economy serves to mask residual structural problems in the South Korean economy.

The government has two major long-term policy goals. The first is to turn South Korea into a knowledge-based economy. The second is to make it the financial hub of Northeast Asia. Both goals are linked intimately to the likely success of the reform programs, and the ability of the South Korean economy to continue to attract significant amounts of foreign capital. With government leaders now acknowledging that the reforms have not been implemented thoroughly enough, it is doubtful that these goals will be achieved within the time-frame originally identified.

The political scene

Kim Dae-jung, the former leader, proved an unpopular president.[5] Dogged by allegations of economic mismanagement and corruption, and after poor by-election results in the provinces, he stepped down as leader of the ruling Millennium Democratic Party (MDP) in November 2001. In May 2002, he resigned from the party altogether.

The new government has indicated it will not alter course on the reform process or the direction of the economy. Investors need not be concerned about an increase in the level of risk. However, it is unclear how the government will handle North Korea. Kim's 'sunshine policy' has not been popular and will certainly undergo revision in 2003–04.[6]

The situation on the Korean peninsula is extremely fragile.[7] The two Koreas are still technically at war.[8] North Korea is secretive, aggressive, and demanding, and almost certainly has nuclear, chemical and biological weapons. As the missile launch over Japan demonstrated, it also has the capability to deliver warheads, thus placing South Korea (and Japan) at strategic risk.

In June 2001, Kim Dae-jung visited Pyongyang for the first time. The summit resulted in the reunion of hundreds of families separated by the Korean War, and the signing of a series of documents aimed at fostering economic exchanges between the two countries. But further attempts to enhance the relationship have not met with success. After the summit, North Korea's leader, Kim Jong-il, promised to visit Seoul, but this has not yet eventuated. North Korea has given no reason for this.

> Kim Dae-jung's 'sunshine policy' was not solely aimed at improving political relations with North Korea. It was also an economic policy. The North represents a huge untapped commercial market for South Korean companies and foreign investors alike.

Peaceful and well-managed reunification would have long-term benefits for the South Korean economy. New markets would open up for domestic and foreign companies and large infrastructure projects would be needed to develop the North. The Chaebol have been quick to seize on these possibilities. Indeed, they have been pressuring the government for some years now to improve the road and rail linkages and have begun to invest heavily in industrial plants and commercial centers in the North. However, foreign investors should be wary about investing in North Korea. The country could strip companies of their assets without notice or place significant bureaucratic hurdles in their way. And, as many South Korean companies have already found out, it is hard to make a profit in the North. The regulatory environment is extremely poor, markets barely function, with most foreign investors forced to abandon their investments. In all, North Korea remains a high-risk destination for capital.

The bottom line: Good investment potential, but hard work

South Korea is a powerhouse economy, offering investment opportunities in most sectors. But investors will not find South Korea an easy environment to operate in. On-going labor unrest and high-level corruption and bribery continue to pose significant operational problems, and while the regulatory environment has improved dramatically since the 1997–98 crash, inadequate bankruptcy laws, foreign exchange restrictions, and currency controls still pose a number of obstacles to foreign capital.

Investors need also to be cognizant of the potential for domestic and regional instability. The direction of the inter-Korean dialog is likely to change in 2003–04. Opposition to the 'sunshine policy' from within the Grand National Party (GNP) and a souring of relations between the United States and North Korea will undermine the policy's effectiveness. Investors will need to ensure that they are well-informed about changes in policy direction with respect to North Korea.

Section B Risks and projections

Macroeconomic performance and risk indicators

- The South Korean economy slowed during 2001–02. Increased domestic spending and a loosening of monetary policy during 2001 helped the country avoid recession. The economy has begun to improve in 2002, and barring another major international crisis, or a significant hike in oil prices, will gain momentum through 2003–04. Growth rates of around 4.6 percent in 2003 and 5.5 percent in 2004 are likely.[9]

GDP grew by 3 percent in 2001–02.[10] This is substantially less than the 9.3 percent growth rate achieved the previous year. However, the economy has shown signs of recovery in late 2002. Indeed, the short-term macroeconomic outlook for South Korea is good. Unemployment remains low, export performance has been steadily improving, and the interest rate environment is conducive to capital borrowing and investment. Moreover, the country has substantial foreign exchange reserves and its external debt is modest by OECD standards. In all, the economy looks on track to rebound strongly in 2003–04.

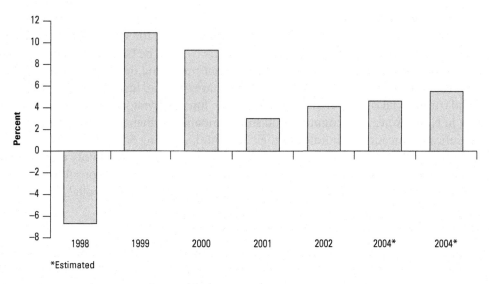

*Estimated

FIGURE 10.1 Gross domestic product, South Korea 1998–2004

Stronger growth prospects are reflected in strong consumer and business sentiment during 2001–02. Consumers, for example, have been purchasing big-ticket items such as automobiles and houses, and a number of large companies have announced substantial profits on the back of a rise in export earnings.

This trend will continue in 2003–04, provided unemployment maintains its downward trajectory. Interest rate rises will begin to dampen consumer confidence in 2003, but real falls in spending will be avoided, boosted by the one-off impact of the World Cup and the Asian Games.

'Korea is well placed to benefit from a global economic upturn, enjoying a diversified economy, a sound structural base, and a low level of non-performing loans.'[11]

Looking ahead to 2003 and 2004, there are a number of issues that investors need to be aware of, each of which has the capacity to dampen South Korea's economic recovery. First, electioneering has slowed the pace of reforms and it will take the new government time to refocus and reinitiate the reform process. Second, inflationary pressures are beginning to creep into the system, threatening the viability of the low interest rate policy. Third, substantial interest rate rises would increase company debt levels and have a negative effect on consumer spending. Finally, should the price of oil increase significantly, it will weaken the country's economic outlook. On balance, however, the short-term outlook for the economy is strong.

Export performance

- The South Korean export sector performed poorly during 2001, driven by falling demand for electronics exports. An early recovery was ruled out in March 2002, when government figures revealed that exports had fallen for the thirteenth straight month. But with an improvement in the US economy and an increase in the price of some computer chips, exports will improve in 2003–04. The major worry for South Korean exporters over the next two years will be the trend toward protectionism and South Korea's reliance on a relatively small number of markets.

The total value of exports for 2001–02 was US$150.5 billion, while imports totaled US$141.09 billion. South Korea's trade surplus for the year was US$9.341 billion dollars. This is the fifth straight annual trade surplus. There is some concern about its dwindling size, however. In 1998, the surplus was US$39.031 billion dollars. Since then, it has dropped by 76 percent. According to the Korean International Trade Association, the poor performance of exports during 2001–02, combined with a depreciating Japanese yen, will see this figure slide to around US$7 billion by December 2002. However, this appears overly conservative. Higher prices for computer chips, liquid crystal displays, and petrochemical products, as well as an improvement in auto sales should push the surplus up over the US$12 billion mark in 2003, possibly reaching US$15 billion in 2004.

With the exception of the iron, steel and shipbuilding industries, the outlook for South Korea's major export industries is positive. Export orders for South Korean automobiles jumped during 2002, and all of South Korea's major car manufacturers have forecast an increase in export sales in 2003–04. Importantly, the electronics and semiconductor industry has also begun to improve, with an increase in export orders from the United States and elsewhere.

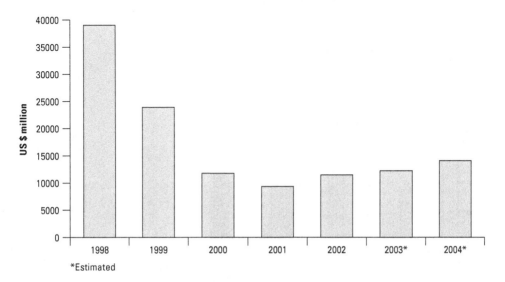

FIGURE 10.2 Trade surplus, South Korea 1998–2004

After two years of restructuring and the completion of new production facilities in 2001, the petrochemical industry is also set to grow by 4 percent in 2002–03, with further solid growth likely in 2003–04. Currently, China is one of the leading destinations for South Korean petrochemical products. China's entry into the World Trade Organization (WTO) will further strengthen South Korea's position as a global leader in petrochemicals.

South Korea is the sixth largest producer of steel in the world. In 2001, it exported over 2 million tons of steel to the United States.[12] The industry will be hard hit by the US decision to increase tariffs on imported steel; a decision that will resonate throughout the South Korean economy. As one South Korean trade official described it, the decision is a 'tragedy' for the country's economy.[13]

In response, South Korea is planning to take the issue to the WTO, but will not proceed with this action until it concludes talks with US officials. Of greatest fear for the South Korean economy is the breakout of a round of tit-for-tat trade sanctions, with countries engaging in protectionist measures to secure their domestic steel industries. The European Union has already threatened to take such action against the United States, and seems likely to do so if discussions with US trade representatives fail to achieve a satisfactory outcome. Moreover, if a retaliatory mentality develops in the global marketplace, there is nothing to stop the scope of tariffs widening to include other products. If either of these events come to pass, it would have a devastating impact on the South Korean steel industry, significantly affecting the overall value of exports and weakening the economy's overall performance.

More generally, South Korea's future export performance is also dependent on how effectively it is able to compete with China. With the Chinese economy growing between 7 percent and 10 percent annually, South Korea's export industries will find it increasingly hard to compete. China is already beginning to challenge both the South Korean shipbuilding

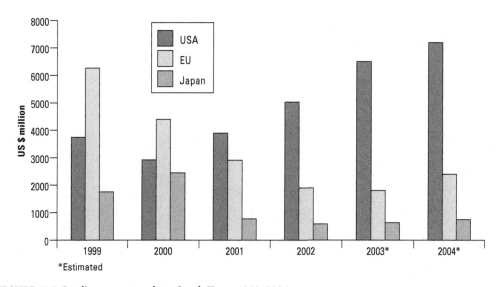

FIGURE 10.3 Leading export markets, South Korea 1999–2004

and the electronics sectors, with cheaper production and labor costs, and is taking the lion's share of the region's foreign direct investment (FDI).

In order to counteract this challenge, the South Korean government is increasing the number of globally competitive products to 220 by the end of 2002.[14] According to the Bank of Korea, 10 major products make up 44.7 percent of the country's total exports, compared with Japan's 36.9 percent.[15] Indeed, this is a timely response, but underscores the fact that the South Korean economy is overly reliant on a few key export markets. The United States, the European Union, and Japan, for example, take the majority of South Korea's exports. South Korean exporters will need to look further afield, especially to transitional economies, if they are to reduce their exposure to the troika.

Also of concern is the appreciating won. If the won appreciates considerably against the US dollar, South Korean export performance will be hurt. Indeed, exporters have already been struggling to compete with a weak yen, albeit that this upward trend is unlikely to continue. More optimistically, however, with a US recovery likely in 2003, the won is likely to depreciate against the dollar and help strengthen the export performance of the South Korean economy.

The bottom line: Mixed messages

The good news is that South Korea's export performance is improving. This trend will continue into 2003–04 and benefit the country's overall economic position. To some degree, economic performance is also being helped along by price rises in some key products, such as DRAM computer chips, improving auto sales in the United States and a general upswing in private consumption. The bad news is that the steel tariffs issue threatens to escalate into something more destructive, possibly exposing the South Korean economy to a round of protectionist measures that would have knock-on effects in the rest of the economy.

Currency movements and projections

• The South Korean won has begun to appreciate after a long period of weakness against the US dollar. In part, this reflects sentiment about the US dollar rather than sudden renewed interest in the won, with most Asian currencies trading upwards since the first quarter of 2002. While this generally reflects a return to longer term trends and weighting averages, it also poses problems for South Korea. Indeed it might well derail its tentative recovery with a higher valued won likely to dampen South Korea's export growth during 2003–04.

South Korea has a floating exchange rate system. Intervention by the Bank of Korea has thus tended to be minimal. At the beginning of the Asian financial crisis, the won bottomed out at 1,810 won to the dollar, constituting a 50 percent depreciation on pre-crisis levels. From late 2000 until January 2002, the won again depreciated after a modest post-crisis recovery.

There were moderately higher valuations in 2002 that are likely to persist into 2003. The won was trading at around 1,223 to the dollar, reaching 1,281.2 won to the dollar in May 2002.[16]

Given the generally positive outlook for the South Korean economy, and the recent rise in interest rates, the won can be expected to appreciate further, tapering off in 2003–04 on the back of a stronger US dollar as economic recovery kicks in and returns the US economy to stronger growth.

One of the significant problems for the won is its lack of tradability on the global markets. This forces domestic banks to send cash overseas so that foreign tourists are able to buy won before they arrive. The government is concerned that the won might become the subject of foreign exchange speculation, similar to that which undermined the Thai baht in 1997. However, the won needs internationalizing if South Korea is to become fully integrated into the world economy.

Foreign exchange control

South Korea still has onerous restrictions governing its foreign exchange market. Consequently, the daily trading volume is lower than many other countries in the region. In response, the government is intending to fully remove these restrictions by 2011. However, as of 2002, no discernible movement signaling some recognition of the urgent need for reform is apparent.

> South Korea still has onerous restrictions governing its foreign exchange market. Officially, these will not be removed until 2011.

Despite this, the administration has announced a three-stage reform process to fully liberalize its exchange market. Over the next three years (2002–05), the first phase of reform will see the government raise the limit on the amount of funds that can be sent overseas without the approval of the Bank of Korea. In addition, the government will also raise the amount of money a non-resident can borrow from South Korean financial institutions, improving the credit provisions to foreign nationals resident in South Korea and helping boost domestic demand. During the second phase of the reform process (scheduled for 2006–08), it will no longer be necessary to seek permission from the Bank of Korea to undertake large foreign exchange transactions. Individuals and companies making foreign exchange transactions will need only to report the transaction. Finally, the third phase of the reform process, slated for 2009–11, will see all foreign exchange restrictions lifted, except where they are necessary to protect the viability of the foreign exchange market itself. What remains unclear at this juncture, however, is how committed the administration is to the longer-term reform process.

The next three years will thus prove critical, and provide investors with their first glimpse of how the reform process will be handled, and of how successful the prudential parameters of the reform process will be. By all accounts, however, the movement toward reform should not be doubted. Indeed, the goal of liberalizing the foreign exchange market is rooted in South Korea's ambition of developing itself into the financial hub of Northeast

Asia by developing primary financial markets for international foreign exchange transactions and trade settlements.

Unfortunately, what might derail this ambition is the excessively long timeframe the government has set to realise the full potential of the proposed reforms. Hong Kong and Singapore, for example, have already relaxed their foreign exchange rules and have much higher daily trading volumes – and might well beat South Korea to the finish line in terms of establishing regional markets and taking the lion's share of trading volumes in Asia. Unless South Korea is prepared to hasten its reform agenda, it is in danger of being bypassed for countries that have more favorable foreign exchange regulations and are already forging profitable associations with various foreign investors in terms of serving their trading and foreign currency needs.[17] Investors need to weigh up their investment options carefully.

Financial markets: Performance and developments

- South Korea's financial markets have showed signs of improvement during 2002. Non-performing loans (NPLs) are now at acceptable levels and the sector has been cleared of most of the heavily indebted companies through either restructuring, merger or downsizing. However, the government still maintains a financial interest in a number of institutions with few signs that it intends to fully divest itself of these stakes any time soon. More generally, financial markets are in need of greater foreign investor involvement to speed up the process of reform, greater transparency, and improvement in prudential regulations. While all this appears to be coming and will likely be realized in various measures during 2005–10, the pace of reform if not quickened threatens to leave South Korea behind in terms of developments elsewhere in the region – especially Singapore.

Reform of the financial services sector was made a pre-condition for the extension of an International Monetary Fund (IMF) assistance package in 1998.[18] The Financial Supervisory Commission (FSC) and the Financial Supervisory Service (FSS) were set up to facilitate the necessary regulatory changes in 1998 and 1999, and assume authority for compliance.[19]

The first phase of the reforms included closing or merging debt-stricken financial companies, capital injection into the sector to deal with NPLs, and generally increasing the level of liquidity to ensure market integrity. In addition, the FSC/FSS began to more rigorously enforce prudential supervision of financial companies.[20] Between January 1998 and March 2001, for example, 532 financial companies were removed from the market.[21] The government also undertook the recapitalization of lending institutions by using public funds to buy out NPLs, instituted a partial deposit insurance system in the banking sector, enacted the Financial Holdings Company Act to ensure greater transparency and regulatory accountability, revised the regulatory environment of the insurance industry and the capital market, instituted measures to raise the liquidity of the bond market, lowered the cost of capital for businesses, and strengthened corporate governance procedures for boards of directors. All this bodes well for South Korea's future, and promises much needed advancement of the depth and regulatory parameters of its financial sector for foreign investors.

Although expensive, these measures have been successful.[22] The level of NPLs has decreased significantly. In December 1999, NPLs stood at 11.3 percent of total bank lending. By 2000, the figure had dropped to 8.1 percent, and continued to decline throughout 2001–02 to around 5.4 percent.[23] Moreover, all the major banks posted substantial profits during 2002, indicating greater capital ability to write-down and provision for NPLs.

In large measure, improvement in the banking sector has been achieved through a low interest rate environment during 2001–02, better asset quality, and higher fees and charges. Stocks in the banking sector have likewise risen on the back of increased profitability. However, the sector is still not globally competitive, with the government still committed to a large financial stake in the banking industry, and as yet no realization in terms of the removal of obtuse regulatory obstacles in the capital markets, or the provision of incentives for securities firms to move into securitization and cross-border financing.[24]

Little significant change is thus forecast for 2002–04.

Public and private debt

- During 2001, and nearly three years ahead of schedule, the South Korean government repaid its IMF loan. This, along with shrinking debt levels in the corporate and financial sectors, saw the year end with the lowest level of external debt since 1994. There will be further falls in the stock of external debt 2003–04. However, private debt is rising, and looks set to continue to do so throughout 2002–04.

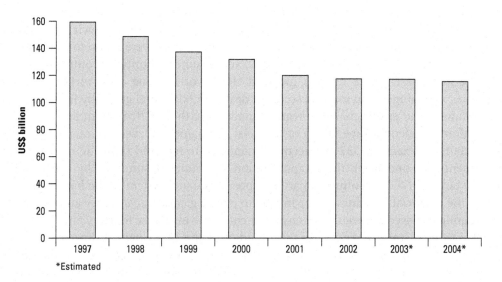

FIGURE 10.4 External debt, South Korea 1997–2004

South Korea has made substantial progress in reducing a crippling foreign debt burden that totaled more than US$160 billion. The latest figures from the Ministry of Finance and Economy put the external debt level at US$119.9 billion for 2001–02. This is the lowest level of external debt since 1994 and is made up of US$81 billion in long-term obligations and US$38.9 billion in short-term liabilities. The ratio of debt to GDP currently stands at 25.5 percent. Consequently, South Korea is now labeled a 'foreign debt-free country' by the World Bank and has an A grade rating from leading ratings agencies. External debt levels will continue to fall in 2003 and 2004, helped primarily by better international receipts from increasing external trade levels, and nominal levels of domestic rationalization.

Private debt

Private household debt increased by 25 percent during 2001 and has continued to climb during 2002, with a further 3.8 percent increase.[25] By 2003, debt levels should begin to plateau as interest rate increases begin to impact on spending and help curb consumer debt and private sector debt.

Labor market trends

- The government's long-term goal is to create a more flexible workforce, and systematically move the economy from an essentially industrial–manufacturing base into a post-industrial, knowledge-based economy. However, this is proving difficult, not least because of stiff opposition from unions concerned about job losses, industrial restructuring, and the problems of labor adaptation. So too, South Korea's level of educational attainment, and education sector restructuring and innovation, will have to be vastly improved if the attainment of a knowledge-based economy is to be realized in the coming years. In all, the immediate short-term move toward industrial restructuring can expect to see a continuation of union intransigence, strike action, and production disruptions during 2002–04.

Labor market reform has been a top priority of the administration since the Asian financial crisis. The aim of these reforms has been to develop a more flexible labor market, one capable of adapting quickly to changes in global production, demand, and export requirements, as well as meet the challenges of a post-industrial knowledge-based economy.

After the Asian financial crisis, and in order to fulfill the IMF's conditions for a bailout loan, the government passed a raft of new legislation and labor laws. These generally opened the market to private labor companies and put in place a number of mechanisms to redeploy labor quickly, avoiding union intransigence and lost value due to slow adaptation. Second, these laws set in place a range of welfare measures to support workers unable to find new employment, thus quelling potential future opposition to labor sector restructuring.[26] These included wage subsidies for companies that retained workers who were technically redundant, re-skilling and vocational training, a widening of the Employment Insurance Scheme (EIS), and expanded public works programs.

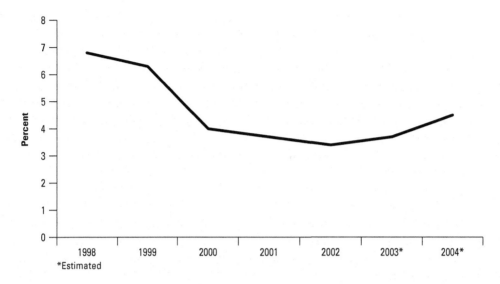

FIGURE 10.5 Unemployment rate, South Korea 1998–2004

However, while labor market conditions have generally improved since the government embarked on its reforms, South Korean labor laws are still restrictive. Companies, for example, are not allowed to downsize their workforce unless, and until, they can demonstrate that they are in financial difficulties.[27] This makes it difficult for corporate flexibility in labor planning, and creates structural disincentives to hire labor in economic upswings due to fears about the ebb and flow of forthcoming market conditions and labor demand requirements. In all, then, South Korean labor laws will have to be further reformed if the ambition of creating a globally competitive economy is to be achieved.

More immediately for South Korea and the health of its economy, the administration is going to have to meet the challenges posed by strong unions. South Korean unions are militant and not afraid to strike or pursue industrial action irrespective of its legality. Violence against the police at such protests is common, with widely varying consequences for production schedules and contractual obligations. Risk from labor disruption thus remains high in South Korea, and will likely remain so during 2002–04.

Unions in Seoul are generally uncooperative, and tend to be more demanding in their dealings with foreign-owned companies than they are with local enterprise. Foreign enterprise generally pay a higher premium in union negotiations than is true for domestic enterprise, adding substantially to operational costs.[28]

In 2001, there were some 208 strikes, amounting to 750,000 lost work days.[29] This figure will rise as the government pushes ahead with plans to sell off state-owned enterprises and restructure state-subsidized industries. Indeed, the strike action during the lead-up to the World Cup demonstrates how powerful South Korean unions are, with blackmail tactics used to gain concessions and compensation in excess of standard labor agreements.

The major concern for foreign investors, however, is the on-going possibility of 'sympathy' strikes. The recent problems at the Korean Electric Power Company and the Korean National Railroad are instructive. Both these strikes were on the verge of becoming national, until a deal was reached with the Korean Confederation of Trade Unions (KCTU). This union represents some 600,000 workers in industries as diverse as shipbuilding, teaching and car manufacturing. A string of national strikes would weaken the South Korean economy and impact on output and profits.

Labor productivity

Labor productivity in South Korea lags behind the advanced economies in the world. Among the 25 OECD countries, South Korea ranks twentieth.[30] In comparative terms, this means that South Korea is less than half as productive as the United States. The most alarming aspect of this, however, is that the gap between South Korea's productivity and countries such as the United States and Japan appears to be widening. In other words, South Korea is becoming less productive. At the same time, wages have been increasing and the imminent introduction of a 40-hour week will further increase costs to companies. Unfortunately, there appears no sense of urgency among government officials to address the problem, or to boost productivity and, by default, economic growth. However, unless significant increases in productivity growth can be achieved, South Korea's longer-term hope of movement toward a knowledge-based economy and substantial improvements in wealth levels, will be severely tested.

The bottom line: Strikes, strikes and more strikes

While reform of the labor market is under way, the lack of flexibility in the market remains a major problem for companies and investors alike. The next two years will be punctuated by strikes and labor discord. The administration will have to do much more if South Korean enterprise is to be more competitive, and risks of labor unrest to foreign enterprise mitigated. Unfortunately, the strength of many unions means little headway can be expected on this issue in the short- to medium-term.[31]

Consumer and business confidence

- Despite the global economic downturn in 2001–02, consumer and business confidence improved steadily throughout the year. With low unemployment and a forecast rise in export growth in 2003 and 2004, confidence will remain high. On the downside, rising interest rates have the potential to dilute the current positive sentiment but are unlikely to rise sharply enough to precipitate a major decline in consumer and business confidence. Continuing positive consumer and business outlook should persist and be complemented by the global economic recovery during 2003–04.

Consumer confidence has been strong throughout 2001–02. The MasterCard MasterIndex survey, for example, puts South Koreans as the second most confident consumers in the Asia-Pacific, achieving a score of 68.1 on the index. Chinese consumers scored 84.4. While lagging behind the Chinese, South Korea's score is nonetheless impressive, and displays a sharp increase in consumer outlook on the previous year, when it scored only a modest 25.9.

The improvement in consumer confidence is affirmed by the government's own Consumer Sentiment Index (CSI), which reveals consumer confidence has risen steadily since October 2001, reaching 106.7 in January 2002.[32] By the end of March, the index had reached 109.7. This is the highest point in over two years, and signals a return to positive short- to medium-term outlooks. Consequently, consumers will maintain current spending patterns, purchasing big-ticket items. Retail markets will also continue to improve.

With the recovery of the South Korean economy well under way, low unemployment along with relatively low interest rates will see consumer confidence remain high well into 2003–04. Indeed, the impact of any interest rate increases will likely be gradual and coincide with overall stronger economic growth, mitigating any adverse consequences on consumer or business sentiment. More generally, the government has also affirmed its commitment to tune monetary and fiscal policy to further stimulate the economy in the advent of continuing sluggish economic performance, providing South Korean consumers with a psychological buffer against the prospect of sudden and deep economic decline. In all, South Korean consumer confidence looks set to persist at strong levels during 2002–04.

Confidence levels among South Korean business are also improving in line with increased export receipts and positive signs in the international economy. In March 2002, for example, the government index hit a high of 141.9.[33] This is the highest level since the index was first formulated in the 1970s. Most companies are positive about the next business cycle, projecting both a growth in external demand and an increase in profits.[34]

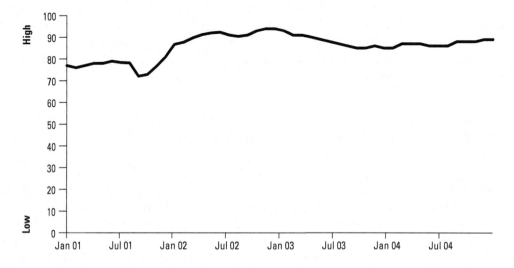

FIGURE 10.6 Consumer sentiment, South Korea, January 2001–July 2004

There are, however, variations across different sectors of the economy. The Korean automotive industry appears particularly positive in its outlook. Production at Daewoo has recommenced, and the deal with GM is likely to go ahead. Hyundai announced a record profit in 2001 of US$894.1 million and expects sales to increase around 10 percent by the end of 2002, with a further double digit increase in sales revenue forecast for 2003. Indeed, all the major car manufacturers announced an increase in profits during 2002.

On the downside, however, heavy industrials like shipbuilding, have remained depressed, with negative returns, signaling a declining industry sector with increasing offshore competition from China. Indeed, many of the old economy, heavy industry business segments have an overall negative outlook, suggesting that regional competition (again from China) is likely to see an absolute reduction in profit margins and volumes and a steady decline in these industry types.

Stock market

- South Korea's stock market rebounded in 2002. Indeed, the market nearly broke through the 1000 point barrier during the first quarter. This strong performance will continue into 2003–04, but it is unlikely that the index will rise much above the 900 point mark. At present, the Korean Stock Market (KSE) is undervalued and there are bargains for astute investors, but the KSE is also renowned for high levels of corruption and lack of transparency.

As a consequence of the September 11 terrorist attacks, the Korean Composite Stock Price Index (KOSPI) fell to its lowest point since 1998. In response, the government initiated regulatory changes to help pump liquidity into the market and preserve the integrity of the bourse. The market rebounded quickly, primarily because of expectations of an early economic recovery both domestically and internationally. As a result, the KOSPI reached a high of 704.50 in early December 2001, then dropped back slightly to end 2001 at 693.70 before rebounding again in 2002 to levels hovering around 810.00.

> Since the September 11 terrorist attacks, the South Korean stock market has fluctuated more severely than other Asian stock markets. In part, this reflects an unstable investment sentiment and concern about sectoral performance in particular market segments. It also reflects the fact that institutional investors, who usually play a supporting role in the market, comprise a lower percentage of participants in the South Korean stock market than in comparable Asian markets, and the fact that the South Korean economy is highly synchronized with US business cycles, and thus prone to wide gyrations.[35]

Despite some fluctuations in the market, stock prices have generally been moving upward since January 2002. By April 2002, for example, the KOSPI had reached 937.61

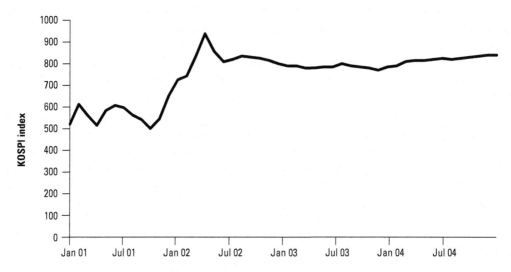

FIGURE 10.7 Stock market, South Korea, January 2001–July 2004

points, almost double the value of the index in late September 2001. Predictions that the index would push up over the 1000 mark have not eventuated, with the bourse tending to hover around the mid 800s for 2002. The KOSDAQ has followed a similar pattern, edging upwards during 2002.[36]

Looking forward to 2003–04, and barring any major global economic shocks, the South Korean stock market will continue to perform strongly. An improving global economic picture, corporate restructuring and strong domestic demand all point to improving market performance, better corporate returns, and thus better yields during 2002–04.

In terms of corporate performance, the best returns have generally been confined to those companies with the highest level of foreign investment, underscoring the importance of Western business practices and productivity incentive structures to corporate health.[37] In terms of specific sectors, the South Korean banks have been performing strongly, and will continue to do so in 2002–04. In addition, the leading insurance companies have made substantial profits during 2001 and 2002 and look set to continue with this trend into the near future.

> South Korea is a market that yields relatively high returns on equity investment and a country that possesses many positive ingredients for the pursuit of successful business.[38]

Also of interest to prospective investors should be the relative lower valuations on the Korean stock exchange, suggesting undervaluation of many South Korean equities. Indeed, the aggregate market value is substantially less than South Korea's GDP, suggesting good longer-term opportunities for foreign portfolio investors.[39] However, the South Korean stock market is not without its risks. Historically known as a 'gambling den' and rating quite low in terms of soundness and transparency, the market has its share of price manipulators, fraudsters and corrupt brokerage firms. While there are harsh penalties for fraudulent and manipulative behavior, the market is still a long way from international best practice standards. As such, risk averse investors should stick to blue chip stocks that have a strong foreign stake in them and transact through brokerage firms that have a solid international reputation.

Corporate tax

- In order to make South Korea a more attractive destination for foreign capital, the government has made significant changes to corporate tax laws as well as attempting to streamline compliance issues and the burden of red tape. Nonetheless, the current tax regime is uncompetitive by regional standards with further reform needed if South Korea is to enjoy successful progress toward the next phase of its developmental growth.

In order to attract foreign investment, the South Korean government offers a range of tax incentives and direct grant systems. Under the 1998 Foreign Investment Promotion Act (FIPA), for example, incentives are given to companies that locate themselves in Free Trade Areas, those that bring new technologies into South Korea, and those companies specified under special presidential decree – at present normally related to technology-based investments, especially bio-technology. Tax liabilities are reduced according to the level of foreign capital invested. If the level of investment is 100 percent, the government will provide a tax break in the first year of an equal amount, and then on a graduated basis for the next six years. If the amount is less than 100 percent, the tax payable is worked out according to a formula which multiplies the income by the ratio of foreign capital. Other tax exemptions are available as well, and normally negotiated prior to start-up. Local governments, for example, are able to offer tax exemptions of between 8 to 15 years.

Recently, the government has expanded the tax incentives for foreign direct investment in special investment zones to include incentives in tourism (hotels and leisure), manufacturing, and logistics. The government is also keen to entice advanced technology or high value-added services that can support the domestic economy.

However, despite a stated desire to improve the tax system to benefit foreign firms operating in South Korea, the corporate tax rate is still high by regional standards.[40] The central problem remains the number of hidden taxes that make estimating the total tax burden difficult. Certainly, business executives want the tax rate lowered so as to make South Korea more competitive regionally. Equally important is the fact that the government's tax incentives are only available to foreign companies investing in a fairly narrow range of goods and services and generally have sunset clauses attached to them.

On the positive side, the new government will not increase the corporate tax rate in 2003–04. GNP officials, for example, have even suggested that they are willing to look at lowering the rate, while the MDP have ruled out any prospective increase in the rate but have been reticient to endorse a lower rate due to what they consider would be the adverse effects on the budget and expenditure options to support those in the lower socio-economic income bracket. Regardless, what is clear is that if the government is serious about attracting foreign investment it is crucial that the taxation system be reviewed as part of its reform package.

Residential and commercial property markets

- By and large, South Korea's real estate market performed strongly in 2001–02 and will continue to do so over the next two years. The sector has been stimulated by the introduction of Real Estate Investment Trusts (REITs) and changes to the laws governing foreign ownership. The commercial office market has been the worst performer in the sector. Structural over-capacity will insure that the commercial office market remains weak in 2002–04.

In order to attract foreign capital, the South Korean government opened up the real estate market to foreign investors in 1998. Foreign investors are now allowed to own property, land, buildings and related assets on the same basis as South Koreans. The new 100 percent ownership rule means that investors can speculate on real estate, develop land and commercial properties, and own multiple properties. The changes in the legislation have been successful, with around 90 percent of all investment in the sector now coming from external investors and amounting to over US$3.5 billion worth of investment to date.

In July 2001, the government made additional changes to the legislation to allow REITs to begin operation. Essentially, REITs are real estate mutual funds. Dividends are paid on sales and on rental returns, providing a secondary market for real estate investment for foreign portfolio investors.

REITs offer a number of benefits to investors. First, they provide an opportunity for small investors to enter indirectly into the South Korean property market, with the ability to invest in a range of real estate products, from large expensive office blocks to commercial and industrial real estate. Second, they are a less risky form of investment and are easy to exit. Third, REITs bring transparency to real estate transactions, and better prudential regulation of the sector. Indeed, overall, REITs show signs of helping to reduce the risks associated with investing in an unfamiliar property market as well as benefiting the domestic economy by adding much needed liquidity.

Land

Land prices in the first quarter of 2002 have risen approximately 33 percent year-on-year figures, indicative of higher consumer sentiment, a willingness to purchase big-ticket items, and a relatively strong business outlook. Within Seoul, land value increases have been as much as 50 percent year-on-year. This rise can be attributed to a number of factors, prime among them the low interest rate environment, the removal of restrictions on development in greenbelt areas like Gijang County near Busan, as well as a generally positive economic forecast for 2003–04. So too, a steady rise in foreign investment in the sector has also served to bolster confidence about the longer-term viability of real estate, with the REITs also adding additional speculative liquidity into the market. More obviously, however, foreign ownership of land has more than tripled since the liberalization of the sector in 1998, and provided a boost to demand. Currently, the level of foreign ownership stands at 137.49 million square meters. Most of this has been purchased by overseas expatriate South Koreans.

While rising interest rates will have some effect on prices during 2002–04, the market is relatively stable and likely to grow by 2 to 3 percent.

The residential market

The price of housing rose steadily during 2002 and will continue to rise during 2003–04. Indeed, a forecast rise of rise of 5.8 percent is likely nationwide, with prices in Seoul rising by as much as 6.8 percent in 2003. The greatest increase will be in Jeonse, where housing prices are forecast to increase by 11 percent.[41] Government attempts to stabilize the market through changes to the capital gains legislation have helped dampen the market slightly, but are unlikely to have much long-term effect on real estate prices. The current shortage of housing, especially Jeonse properties, and good rental returns will continue to see demand outstrip supply and push prices higher in 2003–04.

The condominium market

Condominium prices rose by 9.46 percent during the first quarter of 2002 and will increase by around 7 percent into 2003. The aggregate market value increased by 26.61 trillion won during the quarter, with supply unable to meet demand.[42] Despite this, the second quarter of 2002 saw prices fall slightly as a consequence of government stabilization measures and the imposition of higher taxes on luxury condominiums. However, this was only the first fall in prices after 17 straight months of price increases, indicating persistent demand that is likely to continue in 2003–04. Indeed, the condominium market has been the fastest growing sector in the real estate market and is expected to continue growing between 12 and 15 percent in 2004–05.

The commercial office market

One of the consequences of liberalization has been the rise in the price of office space. Seoul now has some of the most expensive office space in the region. A DTZ Research survey of the Asia–Pacific published in January 2002 rated Seoul as having the sixth most expensive occupancy costs in the region, behind Tokyo (central), Hong Kong, Mumbai, and Taipei.[43]

Unfortunately, the office market has not performed well over the past 12 months, and is not likely to pick up any time soon. According to Colliers Jardine, there is 'a structural oversupply of office space in some parts of the city,' with supply tending to outstrip demand and depressing rental prices.[44] Little immediate change is anticipated for 2002–04.

The bottom line

Taken as a whole, the South Korean real estate market is not without risks. Accurate valuations are sometimes difficult to obtain, as is relevant transaction data. The market is also prone to speculative behavior by brokers. While accountability has improved, the sector is dogged by corruption and a lack of transparency. Undoubtedly, the development of REITs will help improve market transparency, but it is also clear that South Korean authorities will need to introduce new legislation to tighten the sector.

Overall, the South Korean real estate market is strong and will continue to grow in 2003 and 2004. With the exception of the commercial office market, which is burdened with substantial over-capacity, the outlook for the sector is positive.

Foreign direct investment

- The South Korean government has worked hard to increase the level of FDI in the last 5 years. Much of this effort has paid off, with FDI set to increase during 2003–04. However, the longer-term prognosis is less certain. Not only will more FDI be directed into mainland China, but labor instability and inflexibility will undermine investor confidence, and relative declines in South Korea's productivity levels – unless addressed – will make for rising factor costs relative to other potential investment destinations. Much work remains to be done to ensure that South Korea remains attractive to FDI.

The Foreign Capital Inducement Act was overturned in 1998 and replaced by the Foreign Investment Promotion Act (FIPA). At the heart of this new Act is the stated aim of promoting and supporting investment rather than 'controlling and regulating' it. Essentially, the Act has streamlined the procedures for investing, offering a range of tax incentives to investors in the high-tech industry, reduced fees and charges on the lease of government property, establishment of a dedicated agency to facilitate and protect investment, and the establishment of special Foreign Investment Zones in the provinces. The new Act has also reduced the number of sectors that foreigners are prohibited from entering. Similarly, deregulation has occurred in foreign currency trading and South Korean companies are now subject to takeovers by foreign companies.

As a result, there are now only four sectors that are completely closed to investors. They include coastal and inshore fishing, as well as radio and television broadcasting. However, a range of other sectors are partially closed or have foreign investment limits in place. These include telecommunications, transport, publishing, power generation, trust companies, and domestic banking. In addition, there are also investment limits on public companies. Generally, restrictions reflect maximum foreign ownership, ranging from 30 percent to 49 percent. Foreign ownership in Korea Telecom, for example, now stands at 49 percent, while investment in the Korea Gas Corporation is capped at 30 percent. However, there is some recognition by South Korean officials of the need for liberalization in this area, especially in the power generation and energy sectors, which can be expected to translate into reform by 2005–06.

'The global economy is a beauty contest. It does not matter how good you think you are; what matters is how good investors think you are. In a world of mobile capital, investors will take their money out if they are dissatisfied. So for a country like South Korea, with so much at stake in international trade and investment, it is time to shape up or watch investors ship out.'[45]

The bottom line: Heading in the right direction

Beyond these exceptions, the government makes no distinction between local and foreign investors. Foreign investors are now able to trade in the bond and futures markets, option contracts, and commercial paper, operate commercial banking and securities firms, and trade in foreign exchange. They are also able to buy real estate freely and there are no restrictions on ownership in light and heavy industries. While there is still some way to go, South Korea now ranks as one of the more liberalized economies in the region.

Opportunities for investment

There are growing opportunities for investment in South Korea during 2003–05, and beyond. Indeed, the current administration recently announced its fifth Long-term Power Development Plan (LPDP), calling for a doubling of the country's power generation capacity by 2015, and for the external provision of power generating equipment, technology provisioning, and energy supplies. Likewise, demand for allied equipment will also grow, especially in terms of energy/power distribution systems and infrastructure. So too, South

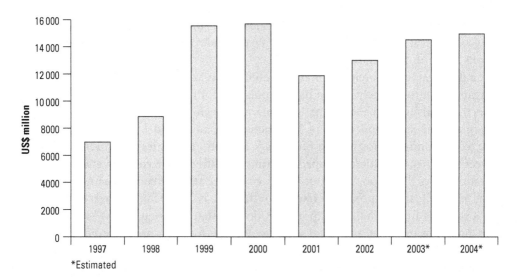

FIGURE 10.8 Foreign direct investment, South Korea 1997–2004

Korea's telecommunications market is growing robustly, with sales in communications equipment set to rise throughout 2002–08. South Korea also has plans to expand its transportation network over the next decade, with opportunities for foreign tendering and allied sales of road construction equipment, project management, and engineering technology.

Other opportunity areas will likely be found in the environmental technologies market, which, in 1999, was worth US$7 billion but will rise to US$12.4 billion in 2003, representing one of the fastest growing industries in South Korea. The government's Green Vision 21, for example, outlines the maintenance of a sufficient supply of clean water, preservation of clean air, the recycling of waste, the creation of an environmentally attuned society, and the establishment of an advanced environmental management system as its key goals. All this signals strong growth in demand for environmental technologies in the coming decade.

'Although South Korea has a highly competent labor force, its relationship with management and tendency to demand excessive pay raises is . . . one of the negative aspects of operating a business in South Korea. Negotiations between labor and management often take the form of demonstrations and strikes rather than an ongoing negotiation process, undermining South Korea's competitiveness in the region.'[46]

South Korea: A difficult place to do business?

South Korea has a highly educated and skilled workforce. Almost 70 percent of the workforce has a university qualification. Transportation facilities, road, and rail links are well developed, as are the country's air and seaports. The country has ample electrical generation capacity and a well-developed telecommunications network. Indeed, South Korea has the cheapest power per kilowatt and the cheapest phone calls in Asia. Equally important is South Korea's geographical location, which provides a gateway for investors seeking to expand their operations in North East Asia and into China.

As a destination for foreign capital, however, South Korea lags well behind Hong Kong and Singapore. Unfortunately, it also has a reputation for being a difficult place for foreign investors to do business. The labor market remains inflexible and strike prone. Variations in the interpretation and application of laws between central and local governments have likewise led to confusion for foreign business.[47] Education facilities for children of foreign employees are generally underdeveloped, catering primarily for US children and not those of other nationalities.[48] So too, corruption and corporate transparency remain a significant concern. And while the corporate tax rate in South Korea is 29.7 percent, lower than Japan or China, it remains higher than Singapore and double that of Hong Kong.[49] Finally, South Koreans have a somewhat parochial attitude toward foreign consumer goods, making market penetration significantly harder to achieve relative to comparable economies in Asia.

Importantly, for foreign investors, investment can often be cumbersome, particularly in the case of merger and acquisitions negotiations that tend to be protracted. The case of AIG is instructive here. The company had been negotiating for a year to buy three of Hyundai's subsidiary companies, but ran into a series of ongoing problems which, in the end, resulted in the venture being abandoned. Likewise, similar stories of South Korean intransigence and protracted, fruitless negotiations can be told by Deutsche Bank and HSBC. In part, the sticking point appears to have been the government's unwillingness to indemnify foreign investors against potential non-transparent debts.[50] However, without this indemnity, companies will continue to be reluctant to enter the market, with consequences for South Korea's economy that desperately needs 'new blood' if it is to become globally competitive. So too, part of the difficulty for foreign companies lies in South Korea's inadequate bankruptcy laws and the level of often non-transparent prudential regulation.[51]

Risks to foreign investors

Commercial factors aside, the major risk for foreign investors remains the tense political relationship with North Korea. North Korea continues to lurch from crisis to crisis, continues to be poverty-stricken, its economy dysfunctional and starved of adequate access to raw materials, and acutely short of sufficient energy to adequately power its limited industrial base. Should the country collapse, it would destabilize the peninsula, lead to the migration of millions of northerners to the south, and dramatically increase the number of job seekers. Indeed, it would cost South Korea billions of dollars to adequately fund unification and place an enormous fiscal and political burden on the South Korean administration.[52] Under this scenario, existing investments would be particularly vulnerable, with foreign interests as exposed to declining internal demand and liquidity as domestic enterprise.

While the implications of a failed North Korean state, and the resultant instability this would cause for South Korea remain of utmost concern, the immediate likelihood of such a collapse is low, in part reflecting the strategic interest China has in supporting the North Korean regime as a security buffer against Western interests due to the common border that China shares with North Korea.

The bottom line

While the South Korean government is working hard to attract more foreign investment through reform and incentive structures, it remains a difficult place for foreign companies to operate successfully. While there are definitely opportunities, and while these are likely to grow significantly in the decade ahead, there are also significant cultural, business practice, political and regulatory hurdles. Unless these can be overcome, and a greater comfort zone for foreign investment interests developed, it remains tenuous how effective the South Korean government's initiatives will be to develop Seoul into a regional headquarters for multinational corporations in Northeast Asia. As the 'hub' of Asia, South Korea still has some way to go, but nonetheless remains well placed geographically, and economically poised to enjoy the shift toward Northeast Asia as the epicenter of investment and wealth generation over the next decade.

Section C Politics

- South Korean domestic politics is aggressive, hostile and unpredictable. This is symptomatic of all young democracies and is not likely to alter in the immediate short term. Fortunately, there is no indication that this will be a concern for foreign investors, albeit that the frequent political factionalism and verbal and physical jousting does create concern about the efficiency of government administration and its longer-term practical stability. Despite this, political interests of all types in South Korea have demonstrated a commitment to attracting foreign investment and to further economic liberalization. Rather, the major issue for investors remains that of corruption, along with the lack of transparency in accounting and management procedures, and the future course of inter-Korean dialog. Political risk is therefore moderate but set to rise slightly in 2003 and 2004 with a new administration whose credentials are yet to be determined.

Kim Dae-jung was elected President in 1997 and took office early in 1998. He came to power on a reform platform and has been responsible for some of the most far-reaching changes to the economy since the Korean War. From a political perspective, however, his presidency has been a turbulent one. Indeed, the price paid for his economic reforms has been an acrimonious and aggressive National Assembly and a less than sympathetic general public. Almost from the moment Kim took office, he has been under siege from the opposition for corruption in his party and in the government, for spending too much time engaging with North Korea during a time of economic hardship, and for political mismanagement. In August and September 2001, both the Minister for Transport and the Minister for Unification were dismissed. Soon after, the entire cabinet resigned, forcing Kim to choose a new one.

'This style of politics, incestuous and factional, does South Korea no favors. Kim Dae-jung of all people, as a lifetime democrat, was expected to change all that. Instead, he has become just another imperial president, whose pointless musical chairs delivers jobs for the same old boys.'[53]

Kim's popularity had been falling steadily since 2001. With the loss of crucial by-elections, he resigned as party head to try and stop the slide. But continued allegations of corruption made against his sons, forced him to quite the party altogether in May 2002.

Kim's legacy has been a mixed one. Because corruption in South Korea is systemic, no president could have single-handedly overcome the practice, with Kim being no exception. Moreover, the inter-Korean dialog has a long and tortuous history, with few opportunities for significant change to the security parameters, despite the fact that they are crucial to South Korea's future wellbeing. Kim, like his predecessors, has not achieved substantial breakthroughs here, but nonetheless did much to help thaw relations and put them on a more amicable footing.

More disappointing was Kim's failure to stabilize South Korean politics and improve the institutional stature of governing institutions. In this regard, the international press have been scathing about Kim, referring to him as a 'lame duck' president and largely ineffectual. To be fair, however, Kim has been responsible for lifting the economy out of the doldrums and pushing forward with economic liberalization. Indeed, the South Korean economy is in much better shape than it was when he came to power.

South Korea will have a new president in 2003. While the GNP are front runners, the outcome is by no means a foregone conclusion. South Korea has a habit of surprising the pundits. For example, no one expected MDP presidential candidate Roh Moo-hyun to win his primary in Gwangju.

Whatever the outcome, and fortunately for investors, there is no indication that a change of leadership will impact negatively on business interests. If Roh wins, he is likely to be a more effective leader than Kim and will continue with the general direction of the reforms. At the same time, the GNP is committed to economic liberalization and free market principles. They also support meaningful restructuring and seek to attract foreign investment. On this, at least, there is little difference between the two parties.

Corruption

South Korea has struggled with corruption for many years. According to Transparency International (TI), South Korea is forty-second in the list of 91 countries surveyed in 2001.[54] Similarly, on TI's recently released Bribe Payers' Index, South Korea languishes near the bottom of the table. Only China, Taiwan, and Russia were regarded as having a worse problem with bribery than South Korea. Perhaps most worrying of all are the results of a 2002 survey conducted by TI's South Korean branch. The survey found that 64 percent of young South Koreans would engage in corruption if the opportunity presented itself.[55] What this suggests is that the practice is deeply rooted in South Korean society.

South Korea's endemic corruption has its genesis in the networks and relationships that have sustained its culture for centuries. In recent years, this has manifested itself in close relations between the Chaebol and the public sector. These large, wealthy, commercial families were able to exercise enormous influence on the government and on public officials. In the aftermath of the Asian financial crisis, the general public tended to link the collapse of the economy with entrenched corruption.

In part, Kim Dae-jung was elected President in 1998 because of his promise to clean up corruption. Unfortunately, his administration has been embroiled in a number of corruption scandals, and his sons also implicated. The latest of these scandals involved his son Kim Hong-gul. Kim has not been implicated in these scandals personally, but repeated allegations against his ministers and family members certainly weakened the legitimacy of his government.

The level of the problem is massive. According to the Ministry of Government Administration and Home Affairs, some 8,200 public officials are known to have accepted bribes.[56] Corruption also takes the form of fake bookkeeping, fraud, price and market manipulation, preferential treatment, money laundering, insider trading, embezzlement, bid fixing, intellectual property theft, and software piracy.

The risks to foreign investors should not be underrated. There are numerous instances where companies have lost large sums of money because of unscrupulous brokers or have been forced to pay bribes to local agents. Some estimates suggest that around 5 to 10 percent of all FDI entering South Korea goes to corrupt public officials. The danger for new foreign investors is that they are unaccustomed to dealing with corruption in their everyday business activities. Entertainment expenses are one example of this phenomenon.[57] Foreign companies have found themselves with huge debts as a consequence of employee extravagance.

However, by far the most corrupt practices exist in and around support businesses servicing the South Korean stock exchange, with foreign investors well advised to deal with established international brokerage firms and understand fully the business culture of South Korean enterprise before committing capital.

> 'Unless such surgical reform is taken, public suspicion about operating mechanisms at the stock market will not go away . . . Stock manipulators are terrorists for innocent investors. The time has come for the government to wage an enduring war against these terrorists.'[58]

Despite these ongoing scandals, some headway against corruption has been made and investors should start to see positive results during 2003–04. For example, the government has enacted a number of new laws, including the Money Laundering Prevention Act and an Anti-Corruption Act. They have also sponsored a number of international conferences, and started the process of domestic acculturation to the nemesis of corruption in terms of how it impacts economic growth and wealth creation for South Korea.

South Korea is also a member of the World Intellectual Property Organisation and the Patent Cooperation Treaty. As a consequence of these efforts, South Korea will improve its ranking in this year's Corruption Perceptions Index. But this will be a modest improvement and is a long way from where South Korea needs to be in order to rank among the least corrupt countries in the world.

Leading risk indices: Corruption, stability, governance, risk

Corruption

The government's anti-corruption legislation is having some success. Over the next two years there will be a slight reduction in the incidence of corruption. But levels are still too high for an advanced industrial society. The government must put more resources into curbing the problem and run a concerted education campaign to ensure that the next generation of South Koreans understand that this practice hurts South Korea's image abroad, weakens the economy, and undermines investor confidence.

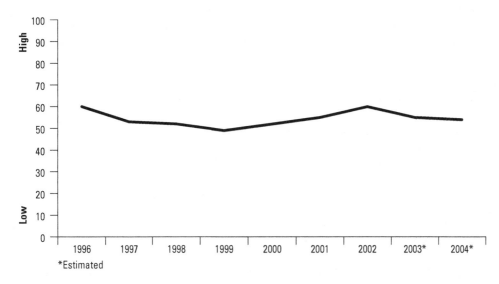

FIGURE 10.9 Corruption index, South Korea, 1996–2004

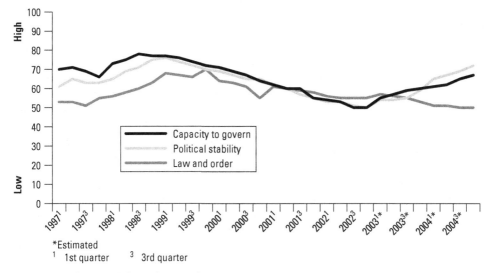

FIGURE 10.10 Political stability index, South Korea 1997–2004

Political stability methodology:
- The capacity-to-govern index is based upon the institutional reach of government defined in terms of its ability to set the political and economic agenda and ensure its legislative program is enacted without significant compromise. This index is adversely affected by legislative opposition, lack of legislative implementation, failure to realize government policy and general political opposition.
- The political stability index measures violent opposition or organized demonstrations, terrorist activities, and popular discontent that adversely affect the institutional and electoral stability of the government.
- The law and order index measures the propensity to civil obedience, and the institutional reach of the rule of law in terms of regulatory compliance and enforcement.

Political stability

While South Korea is relatively stable, there have been worrying signs developing since 1999. Each of the indices records a fall since the beginning of 1999. The fall reflects the internal problems of political mismanagement and corruption that have plagued the government, as well as ongoing problems with labor unions. After the December election, the capacity-to-govern index and the political stability index will stabilize and improve. The law and order index is of most concern, reflecting ongoing problems with labor unions and corruption.

Corporate governance

The corporate governance index is generally positive. Both indices have benefited from a tightening of the regulatory environment, prudential reform, and an improvement in accounting standards.

There has been some leveling out over the past 12 months, however, associated primarily with the slowdown in the number of bankruptcies, reform fatigue, and political campaigning. The trend will continue upwards during 2003–04.

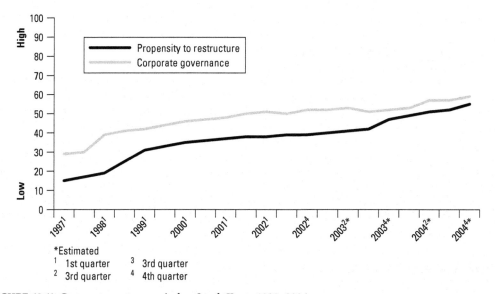

FIGURE 10.11 Corporate governance index, South Korea 1997–2004

Corporate governance index methodology:
- The corporate governance index is a composite index measuring the juridical requirements for corporate disclosure and financial reporting, prudential regime adequacy, prudential compliance enforcement, and the juridical reach of prudential authorities.
- The propensity-to-restructure index is a composite index based on media releases and reported corporate restructuring as a result of prudential regulation, financial incentives, loan restructuring / renegotiation, or asset realignment.

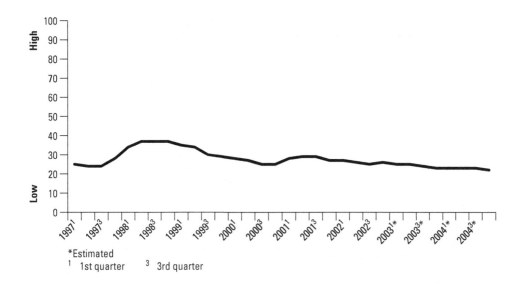

*Estimated
1 1st quarter   3 3rd quarter

FIGURE 10.12 Foreign investor risk index, South Korea 1997–2004

Foreign investor risk index methodology:
• The foreign investor risk index is a composite index measuring tax burdens, discriminatory regulatory practices, adverse compliance regulations, government policy toward foreign enterprise, receptiveness to issuance of government contracts, foreign enterprise commercial restrictions, and official attitudinal changes to foreign direct investment and foreign commercial operations which impact on operational efficiency. The index also incorporates a nominal measure for market risk and market failure.

Foreign investor risk index

The investment climate is improving. Improvements in the regulatory environment, new laws safeguarding foreign investments, and a generally more transparent corporate culture mean that the level of risk is slowly decreasing. The major factor that could alter this is North Korea. Should North Korea experience political instability or the state begin to collapse, foreign and domestic investment would be put at considerable risk. With this caveat, however, and with a cautious appreciation of the dangers of corruption, lost working days through strikes, and Korea's exposure to external shock, investment risk can be regarded as moderate and relatively stable for 2002–04.

Section D Security

• South Korea has generally good relations with its regional neighbors. It is unlikely to be involved in a major military conflict in the near future. The situation on the peninsula, however, is uncertain. North Korea remains a major security concern for South Korea and for the international community more broadly. North Korea is extremely unpredictable and regarded by the United States as part of an 'axis of evil.' However, it is unlikely that war will break out between the two Koreas. A more plausible scenario is that North Korea will experience considerable internal instability, collapse economically, and in a worst case scenario, implode under the weight of its own contradictions and thus force a form of reunification much like that observed in the case of Germany after the fall of the Berlin Wall.

South Korea's only real security threat comes from the North. Since the conclusion of the Korean War, the two countries have been separated by barbed wire and landmines – and technically remain at war. The threat of an invasion from the North has been a constant feature of political life in the South, evidenced by the huge number of armed personnel stationed along the demilitarized zone.

North Korea is a rogue state. It has a reputation for bellicosity, irrationality, and non-conformism, and has spent years trying to develop a nuclear capability and the technical means by which to deliver these weapons long distance.[59] Pyongyang has also been actively pursuing biological weapons.

North Korea is in dire economic straits. It has a chronic energy shortage and is stricken by drought and famine. There is no functioning economy, no financial services sector, and minimal foreign direct investment. The country is, in every sense of the word, dysfunctional and prone to unpredictable behavior.

In recent years, the South Korean government has been trying to reduce the tension between the two countries by pursuing a policy of rapprochement. The policy, colloquially known as the 'sunshine policy', seeks to normalize relations with Pyongyang through a series of confidence-building measures including aid, investment, tourism, family reunions, and high-level diplomacy – perhaps, also, the beginnings of energy-sharing provisions.

The policy has been controversial. Many believe that it has been a failure, with few tangible results to show for the time and money invested. Others have criticised the government's softly softly approach to an aggressive dictatorship. The policy has also had a number of serious setbacks. The unification minister was sacked last year and Kim Jong-il has not embraced inter-Korean dialog with the degree of enthusiasm hoped for by the MDP. However, the most serious blow to the policy has been George Bush's statement that North Korea is part of an 'axis of evil,' effectively setting back prospects for North Korea entering the family of states and the international trading regime any time soon.

Despite these setbacks, South Korea has no alternative but to try to engage in meaningful dialog with the North. Indeed, many of the criticisms of sunshine policy by the GNPs are disingenuous. No South Korean government can afford not to engage with Pyongyang.

There are three broad scenarios for the future of this relationship. The first is that war will break out between the two countries. The second is that North Korea will collapse. The third is peaceful unification. The first of these scenarios is the least likely. Despite the tense character of the relationship, high-level dialog is taking place and there are few signs at present that North Korea is preparing to mount an offensive against the South.

Scenario two is more plausible, given the state of the North Korean economy and the plight of the people. The third is obviously the preferred one, but hardly likely without a catalyst to force the North to reunify – besides, it is unlikely China would welcome or allow such a development.

What remains the most likely outcome, then, is some mix of scenarios two and three. As North Korea slips further into economic backwardness, the North Korean government will likely begin to forge external relationships to preserve its economic viability, which will then implicitly begin a longer-term process of diplomatic engagement and political modernization.

The bottom line

Investors should not be overly concerned about the security risks from investing in South Korea. But they should be cognizant of the fact that reunification, either managed or otherwise, will be a very expensive exercise and, should it be realized, will adversely affect the economy in the short to medium term.

Section E Economic and political risk forecasts

- Economic recovery is under way in South Korea. Export orders are returning to previous levels and the economy will expand by around 5 percent in 2003 and 2004. While reform of the corporate, financial and public sectors helped the economy avoid a debilitating recession in 2001, the scope of the reforms is too narrow to sustain higher growth in 2003–04. Substantial regulatory changes still need to be made to protect investors. In the short to medium term, the risks to foreign investors will come primarily from labor unrest, corruption, and external shocks.

Short-term forecast

- The economy has been recovering in 2002, and will post growth rates of around 5 percent in 2003 and 2004. The recovery will be driven by improved export performance and strong domestic demand.
- The stock market will continue to perform well in 2003–04. It is unlikely to break through the 1000 point barrier. The market continues to be undervalued, although high incidences of fraud and price manipulation are a concern.
- The government will continue the fight bribery and corruption. Over the next two years, the government will see some tangible results for their efforts, and achieve a slightly higher ranking on Transparency International's Corruption Perceptions Index. This will translate into improved investor confidence. However, corruption remains a significant risk to foreign investors.
- Unemployment will rise slightly as the government continues with its plans to sell off its stake in a number of state-owned enterprises. This will lead to an increased incidence of strikes, demonstrations, and political unrest surrounding privatization and downsizing issues.

- Consumer and business confidence will remain positive in 2003–04. While a rise in interest rates will lead to an increase in company debts, this should be compensated for by a general increase in profit levels. Household debt will continue to rise, but will stabilize in late 2003.
- Despite Kim's efforts, a breakthrough in North–South relations is highly unlikely. Indeed, ill-timed comments by George Bush have set back the cause of inter-Korean dialog significantly. No change is evident for 2003–06.

Short-term opportunities

- The government has unveiled a plan to develop Korea into an international business center for the Northeast Asian region. Despite the difficulties of implementing such a vision, the government will need to further expand and upgrade its air and sea ports, transportation facilities, and electronic infrastructure. Foreign companies with expertise in these areas will have significant opportunities for infrastructural provisioning in 2003–06.
- The government is offering considerable incentives (such as tax breaks) to companies that specialize in knowledge-based industries, bio-technology and high valued-added services such as information technology, design, and finance. Given the growth potential of the Northeast Asian region, significant volume and profitability, as well as longer-term market positioning strategies will be available.
- The government plans to develop Jeju Island into an international free city. To facilitate this, new infrastructure will need to be developed, including facilities that meet international standards. Project management and engineering products and services will be in high demand.
- Korea's Green Vision 21 will open up opportunities for companies specializing in environmental technologies. Market size will double between 2002–12.
- Education, especially the provision of English language courses, and distance delivery of content via US and European higher education institutions will see rapid development in the provision of education, training, and delivery systems.
- Reform of the financial services sector since 1998 has opened up considerable investment opportunities, especially in the development of secondary markets and service support for transaction, settlement, and auditing services.

Medium to long term

- China will challenge and possibly surpass South Korean dominance in shipbuilding and petrochemicals. China will also undercut South Korea in light manufacturing industry segments. These industries will likely become sunset industries in the next 10 years, and will see profit levels and volumes diminish.
- The economy will begin to move from a predominantly manufacturing economy to a knowledge-based one, although the pace of transformation will be contingent on the development of education infrastructure and retraining.

- The South Korean government will relax foreign exchange controls to make it easier for companies to move funds in and out of South Korea.
- Corruption and bribery will gradually reduce, although remain high by Western standards.
- North Korea will remain a difficult dialog partner.

Overall risk rating

South Korea's risk profile is improving. Problems of corruption and bribery, labor rigidity, and an overly narrow and unfinished reform agenda mean that foreign investors face a higher degree of risk than in other advanced industrial economies.

Risk: Moderate but stable →
Risk Rating (0 = lowest, 10 highest risk) 5.5 →

Section F South Korea fact sheet*

Geography

Capital
Seoul

Largest city (millions, 2000)
Seoul, 10.373234

Location
Eastern Asia, southern half of the Korean Peninsula bordering the Sea of Japan and the Yellow Sea.

Coordinates
37 00 N, 127 30 E

Adjacent countries
North Korea

Terrain
Mostly hills and mountains; wide coastal plains in west and south

Land use
Arable land 19%, permanent crops 2%, permanent pastures 1%, forests and woodland 65%, other 13%

Climate
Temperate, with rainfall heavier in summer than winter

Area (km²)
Total: 98,480; land 98,190; water 290

* All figures are the latest available except where indicated. All figures are in US dollars. Figures are compiled from national, international and multilateral agencies (United Nations Development Assistance Program, International Monetary Fund, World Bank, World Development Report, UNESCO Statistical Yearbook, International Labour Office, United Nations, Central Intelligence Agency World Fact Book). Gross domestic product (GDP) refers to the value of all goods and services produced in the preceding financial year. GDP per capita, Purchasing Power Parity (GDP per capita – PPP) refers to the indices developed by the World Bank to take account of price differences, cost of living differences, and relative purchasing power of a set basket of goods and services between countries so as to provide a more accurate measure of national wealth.

Natural hazards
Occasional typhoons bring high winds and floods; low-level seismic activity common in southwest

Miscellaneous
Lowest point: Sea of Japan 0 m
Highest point: Halla-san 1,950 m

Economic statistics

Currency
South Korean won (KRW)

Exchange rate (May 2002)
US$1.00 = 1238.6 won

Gross Domestic Product (GDP, 2001)
3%

GDP per capita (2001)
$14,200

GDP per capita – PPP (2000E)
$16,100

GDP – composition by sector
Agriculture 5.6%, industry 41.4%, services 53%

Inflation rate
3%

Foreign debt (2001)
US$119.9 billion

Current account balance (2001, billions)
$10.91

National unemployment rate (February 2002)
3.7%

Labor force
22 million (2000)

Labor force by occupation (2000)
Agriculture 18%, industry 27%, services 56%

Budget
Revenues: $81.8 billion
Expenditure: $94.9 billion, including capital expenditures of $6.1 billion (1999)

Industries
Electronics, automobile production, chemicals, shipbuilding, steel, textiles, clothing, footwear, food processing

Agriculture
Rice, root crops, barley, vegetables, fruit; cattle, pigs, chickens, milk, eggs; fish

Major exports – commodities
Electronic products, machinery and equipment, motor vehicles, steel, ships; textiles, clothing, footwear; fish

Major exports (billions, 2001)
US$150.4

Major imports – commodities
Machinery, electronics and electronic equipment, oil, steel, transport equipment, textiles, organic chemicals, grains

Major imports (billions, 2001)
US$141

Major trading partners (export)
United States, Japan, European Union, China, Hong Kong, Taiwan

Major trading partners (import)
United States, Japan, China, Saudi Arabia, Australia

Income/wealth distribution (household income or consumption by % share)
Lowest 10%
2.9%
Highest 10%
24.3%

Televisions (1997)
15.9 million

Televisions per capita
0.331

Telephones (lines in use, public and private, 1999)
24 million

Telephones per capita
0.501

Cellular phones (June 2000)
27 million

Cellular phones per capita
0.563

Automobiles in use
NA

Internet users (per 10,000 of population, 2000)
15.3

Fiscal year
Calendar year

Government and political statistics

Nature of government
Republic

Constitution
25 February 1988

Structure of government

Political structure
Multi-party system

Executive branch

Chief of state
President Kim Dae-jung (since 25 February 1998)

Head of government
Prime Minister Yi Han-tong (since 23 May 2000) *cabinet* State Council appointed by the president on the prime minister's recommendation

Legislative branch
Unicameral National Assembly or Kukhoe (273 seats total – 227 elected by direct, popular vote; members serve four-year terms)

Chiefs of state and Cabinet members (March 2002)

President
Kim Dae-jung

Prime Minister
Yi Han-tong

Deputy Prime Minister
Chin Nyom

Deputy Prime Minister
Yi Sang-chu

Minister of Agriculture
Kim Tong-t'ae

Minister of Commerce, Industry, and Energy
Sin Kuk-hwan

Minister of Construction and Transportation
Yim In-t'aek

Minister of Culture and Tourism
Namgung Chin

Minister of Education and Human Resources
Yi Sang-chu

Minister of Environment
Kim Myong-cha

Minister of Finance and Economy
Chin Nyom

Minister of Foreign Affairs and Trade
Ch'oe Song-hong

Minister of Gender Equality
Han Myong-sok

Minister of Government Administration
Yi Kun-sik

Minister of Government Policy Coordination
Na Song-Po

Minister of Health and Welfare
Yi T'ae-pok

Minister of Information and Communication
Yang Sung-t'aek

Minister of Justice
Song Chong-ho

Minister of Labor
Pang Yong-sok

Minister of Maritime Affairs and Fisheries
Yu Sam-Nam

Minister of National Defense
Kim Tong-sin

Minister of Planning and Budget
Chang Sung-u

Minister of Science and Technology
Ch'ae Yong-pok

Minister of State for Trade
Hwang Tu-yun

Minister of Unification
Chong Se-hyon

Director, National Intelligence Service
Sin Kon

Director, Government Legislative Agency
Chong Su-po

Governor, Central Bank
Chon Chol-hwan

Main governing parties and ideological affiliation
Millennium Democratic Party or MDP, Grand National Party or GNP, United Liberal Democrats or ULD

International memberships
ADB, APEC, ARF (dialog partner), ASEAN (dialog partner), BIS, FAO, G-77, IAEA, IBRD, ICAO, ICC, ICFTU, ICRM, IDA, IEA (observer), IFAD, IFC, IFRCS, IHO, ILO, IMF, IOC, OECD, OPCW, OSCE (partner), UN, UNCTAD, UNESCO, UNHCR, UNTAET, UPU, WHO, WIPO, WMO, WTO

Number of uniformed soldiers
Males age 15–49: 8,979,778 (2001 est.)

Number of uniformed soldiers by service
Army: 548,000 (8/98), Navy: 60,000, Air force: 52,000, US Troops: 35,910

Percentage of GDP devoted to defense
3.2% (FY98/99)

Social statistics

Population size
47,904,370 (July 2001 est.)

Age structure
0–14 years: 21.59%
15–64 years: 71.14%
65 years and over: 7.27%

Population density (km²)
475.6

Fertility rate (average number of children born by women 15–49 years of age)
1.72 (2001 est.)

Maternal mortality rate (per 100,000 live births)
26

Infant mortality rate (deaths per 1,000 live births, 2001E)
7.71

Population growth (2001E)
0.89%

Life expectancy
Total population: 74.65 years
Male: 70.97 years

Female: 78.74 years (2001 est.)

Ethnic composition
Homogeneous (except for about 20,000 Chinese)

Religion
Christian 49%, Buddhist 47%, Confucian 3%, Shamanist, Chondogyo (Religion of the Heavenly Way), and other 1%

National languages spoken
Korean, English widely taught in junior high and high school

Illiteracy rate (age 15 and over)
Total population: 2 %

Illiteracy rate by gender
Male: 0.7 %
Female: 3.3%

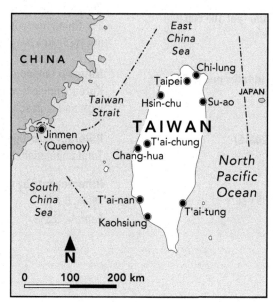

Taiwan

11 Taiwan

Terry O'Callaghan

Section A Economy

Overview

The stunning victory of the Democratic Progressive Party (DPP) in the December 2001 elections will shape the political and economic fortunes of Taiwan over the next three years. This is the first time that the DPP, supported primarily by the Taiwan Solidarity Union (sponsored by former President Lee Teng-hui), will have a working majority in the Legislative Yuan. The Kuomintang (KMT) lost almost half of the seats it held in the old parliament, with voters apparently holding the party responsible for the parlous state of the economy.

The new DPP government is inexperienced and President Chen still has to prove himself as a successful leader. His record on cross-strait relations is poor and he has not been able to deliver on many of the wide-ranging reforms that swept him to power in 2000. Thus, there remain lingering doubts about the ability of the DPP to govern effectively. Moreover, the party cannot govern in its own right. It is reliant on the support of a number of other political groups in the legislature. The challenge for President Chen, then, will be to maintain a consensus between the coalition partners long enough to effect meaningful economic and political change. If consensus breaks down over the course of the next parliament, the legislature will become bogged down in petty squabbles and the country's economic recovery will be put at risk. The political course set by the DPP during 2002–05, will be crucial to Taiwan's long-term economic success.

Taiwan felt the effects of the downturn in the global economy in 2000–01 more acutely than many of its neighbors. Production in the manufacturing and industrial sectors weakened considerably, the stock exchange posted its largest fall on record, export orders slowed, and the New Taiwan dollar slid to a 15 year low. Overall, the economy contracted around 2 percent in 2001–02.[1]

However, forward indicators suggest that the economy is beginning to recover in 2002, and that this should remain the case into 2003–04, assuming a turnaround in the global economy, particularly developments in the US. Evidence for this can be gleaned from the composite index for the economy's overall performance, which reached 104.33 in January 2002. This is the highest number since May 2001, and indicative of an economy that is moving in the right direction. Growth rates of 2 percent in 2002 should show upward trends to around 4–5 percent in 2003–04. However, all is contingent on the much anticipated recovery in the United States, and the avoidance of further instability caused by possible terrorist attacks.[2] On the down side, high levels of corruption and organized crime in Taiwan, strong competition from the mainland and other regional economies, cross-strait tensions, and the need for Taiwan to acquire new engines of growth, coupled with a largely unfinished reform agenda, all pose risks to Taiwan's economic performance in 2003–04.

The bottom line

Taiwan's economy will grow moderately in 2003, with GDP set to rise by 4 percent before rising again in 2004 by 5 percent. But investors should proceed with caution. Taiwan's economy is delicately poised. A great deal depends on the quality of leadership, on the state of cross-strait relations, on Japan's economic performance, and on a strong recovery in the world demand for computer and microelectronic products. Taiwan's economy, then, is subject to as many domestic variables as it is external ones. Most importantly, Taiwan's unstable relationship with mainland China presents investors with a unique set of problems. Those considering long-term investments would be well-advised to incorporate active political risk monitoring. Risk managers should have well-developed exit strategies in case the political climate changes suddenly; for example, due to a sudden deterioration in Taiwan–China relations, or Sino–US relations.

Section B Risks and projections

Macroeconomic performance and risk indicators

- The Taiwanese economy is slowly beginning to recover from its worst contraction on record. Over 2002–04 the economy should return to a strong growth trajectory; however, the recovery will be a muted one and not as robust as the growth trajectory enjoyed prior to the tech-sector meltdown. Despite a relaxation of the rules governing foreign investment in Taiwan, the scrapping of the 'no haste' policy, accession to the WTO, and reform of the banking and financial sector, Taiwan will have difficulty achieving growth rates above 4–5 percent without significant structural reform. There is some doubt about the government's ability to deliver all the reforms necessary to achieve this goal. Investors should be cautious.

Taiwan experienced its first recession in three decades during 2001. A successful recovery will depend on the government's ability to push ahead with its reform agenda, as well as a substantial improvement in global economic performance. Entry into the World Trade Organization (WTO) will help this process, but it will also require a stable political environment with strong political leadership to deliver reform.

While deteriorating, Taiwan has an acceptable level of public debt and huge foreign exchange reserves. With weak domestic demand and lower food prices, and barring a sharp rise in the price of oil, inflation should remain at 2.5–3 percent over 2002–04. Indeed, inflation has been squeezed out of Taiwan through recession, standing at only 0.5 percent in 2002. Slow demand recovery in 2003 should see this trend upwards, but only nominally and within acceptable bands of tolerance.

Despite this, 2003–04 will not be easy for Taiwan's economy. The manufacturing sector, in particular, is facing structural adjustment and likely to remain volatile. As the sector faces increased competition from the mainland, plant closures and downsizings are likely. Indeed, with renewed interest in China as a result of WTO entry, manufacturing infrastructure is already beginning to move offshore. As a result, employment levels will continue to hover around 5 percent for 2003–04.

Likewise, the financial services sector will face increasing competition from foreign companies, with mergers and/or takeovers a distinct possibility. This will present new investment opportunities for foreign banks, fund managers and insurance companies. However, the poor state of the sector will likely mean that returns will be modest in the short term. However, as the reform process begins to kick in, investment returns should show longer-term improvement.

The automotive industry's future is uncertain. First, WTO membership will require that it lower its tariffs and allow more foreign imports into Taiwan. Second, the global trend for car manufacturers is to merge in an effort to exploit economies of scale. This is likely to undermine the viability of the local industry. Indeed, with such a small domestic market, it is doubtful that the industry can be profitable in the longer term. Consequently, the automotive industry will need to follow in the footsteps of South Korea and develop export markets in North America and Western Europe, although the transition time for this could be considerable.

The pharmaceutical industry sector will also be exposed to more competition from foreign companies with both capital and branded patents. However, the industry should benefit from trade liberalization, especially in the manufacture of traditional Chinese medicines. Real estate and construction, however, will remain depressed. Finally, the new 30 percent tariff on steel imported into the United States will hurt the local industry, with 10,000 job losses projected in 2003.

A key growth area is the bio-technology industry. The government intends to spend NT$10 billion annually over 2002–05, and help boost the value of the industry which currently stands at NT$30 billion to NT$67 billion in 2005.[3] In support of this, the administration has also announced plans to spend between 2.5 percent and 3 percent of GDP on research and development over the next decade, thus helping ensure that Taiwan is competitively placed within the region. Despite this, the industry is still in its infancy and cannot expect to make strong inroads into the international bio-technology sector until post 2007 – and then only if government programs are successfully linked with bio-technology industry establishment.

> Increasing competition from regional production centers and a projected new wave of investment into the mainland will make it difficult for Taiwan to achieve its economic goals in the coming years.

The bottom line: Export dependent

The key risk factors affecting Taiwan's economic performance over 2003–04 are cross-strait relations, the slow pace of global economic recovery, and Taiwan's unstable domestic political scene. Unforeseen change in any of these key areas will undermine investor confidence with negative knock-on effects for domestic economic activity.

Export performance

- Computer products make up 25 percent of the total value of exports. Weakening demand for these products in the United States, along with falling margins, constitute the main reasons why Taiwan experienced recession in 2001. The slump highlights a major structural flaw in the mix of Taiwan's export market, which is heavily reliant on technology products and exported predominantly to the United States. Taiwan will have to work hard to diversify its economy, especially its export markets, if it is to reduce external risks in the future and provide a sounder basis for longer-term economic growth.

From January to October 2001, exports fell by 17.1 percent.[4] Export orders in the electronics sector dropped by more than 30 percent. Consequently, many electronics companies had to revise their profit forecasts downwards, a trend that was repeated for 2002. There was one notable exception to this industry-wide trend: Taiwan Semiconductor Manufacturing Co., (TSMC), which managed to increase sales in 2001–02 to register a profit of NT$14,483 million for the year. In part, the single success in the technology sector is explained by TSMC being a world leader in advanced wafer technology, but in any case it masks an otherwise abysmal performance in a sector strategic to Taiwan's economic health. Indeed, even despite TSMC's profit returns, it too has reduced its investment commitments by 25 percent for 2002–03, indicative of outlooks that signal continuing weak sales volumes and profit margins.

> Taiwan is overly reliant on the export of electronic goods. It needs to diversify its export mix or it will find itself at the mercy of an unpredictable market and vulnerable to external demand variations.

Economic recovery in this sector is not likely until the latter half of 2003 and will depend partly on an improvement in the global economic climate and US demand in particular.

More generally, however, the export performance of Taiwan is not simply a matter of waiting for the global recovery to occur. There are also domestic structural impediments that will dampen export performance in 2002–04. First, regional competition in the electronics industry is growing. Both Malaysia and Singapore are seeking to increase their market share of the high-tech industry, with early indications that they will be successful. Second, the price of many computer products has fallen over the past two years. For example, DRAM chips now cost 90 percent less than in January 2000.[5] Third, as industrial migration takes place, some 'hollowing out' of the economy will occur – a problem already experienced in the case of Hong Kong during the 1980s, for example. Fourth, domestic investment in Taiwan is low, which, combined with a high level of non-performing loans (NPLs), creates a reluctance on the part of Taiwan's banks to advance loans in support of new investment. Fifth, large corporations are looking to invest outside of Taiwan. United Microelectronics, for example, recently announced that it will build a new three billion dollar chip factory in Singapore, leaving Taiwan.[6] Finally, the US is Taiwan's largest trading partner, taking almost 25 percent of all Taiwanese exports, while Japan is the second largest trading partner. Without significant improvement in those economies Taiwan's export sector will remain sluggish, and overly reliant on two economies that were under-performing throughout 2000–02.

These factors combined will adversely impact Taiwan's export growth in 2002–04, if not beyond. Indeed, even with an upturn in the US economy, the continuing malaise in the Japanese economy will continue to hurt Taiwan's export sector for some years to come. Only fundamental structural reform of the economy, greater diversity in terms of industrial sectors, and a movement toward the development of alternative and diverse export markets can position Taiwan for stronger and more resilient growth in the future. On the upside, this combination of circumstances presents foreign investors with good credit positions, ample access to finance capital, and some excellent opportunities in the financial services market in 2002–04.

Currency movements and projections

- The Taiwanese dollar has experienced a period of relative weakness during 2001–02, driven by a declining trade balance and net FDI outflows as Taiwanese investors continue the clamor to the mainland. While a sharp recovery leading to a substantial appreciation is unlikely, the Taiwan dollar will begin to appreciate from the end of 2002 into 2003. Unfortunately, this will have some downside for Taiwan's export sector, as well as contribute nominally to higher domestic prices.

Taiwan has a floating exchange rate regime that has been in use since the mid 1980s. The government has a policy of non-interference in the market, except in exceptional circumstances when the currency is under threat. For example, in May 2001 the government stepped in and propped up the New Taiwan dollar to stop it free-falling. Such interventions, however, are rare.

The fall in the New Taiwan dollar since early 2000 reflects the deteriorating character of the Taiwanese economy. During the first quarter of 2000, the New Taiwan dollar rose 2.5 percent against the US dollar. By the second quarter, however, the currency began to lose ground quickly and, following the Japanese yen, traded down to a record low. By May 2001, the currency had hit a 31 month low. This trend has continued throughout 2002, with consistently lower valuations totaling around a 10 percent fall since January 2000.

> Though a declining trade surplus will reduce the capacity of the authorities to manage the currency, 'conservatism' will remain the bedrock of policy decisions.

While the currency has traded downwards during 2000–02, investor fears of a rapid depreciation have been unfounded. The current account balance, though deteriorating, remains in surplus and will stay in surplus for the foreseeable future as falling export demand is offset by falling demand for consumer-related products and intermediate input imports. Second, monetary policy, though more expansionary during the previous two years, remains consistent and transparent. There is no reason to suggest that the central bank's monetary policy committee will abandon what has, to date, been a conservative monetary policy responsible for overseeing currency stability and a low borrowing cost environment for investors. Finally, decades of export success have endowed Taiwan with among the largest foreign exchange reserves (excluding gold) in the world – in absolute terms and per capita. Collectively, these factors combine to act against any sharp movements in the foreign exchange market for the New Taiwan dollar, including a significant depreciation. Indeed, these factors should produce a likely gradual appreciation of the currency against the US dollar and the yen during 2003–04, in the range of 5–10 percent per annum.

Financial markets: Performance and developments

- Taiwan's banking and finance sector suffers from significant structural problems and is in need of reform. Not only does the sector lack the economies of scale necessary for it to compete effectively against foreign banks, but it is also saddled with high levels of non-performing loans (NPLs). While the government is attempting to deal with these problems, it remains doubtful whether the proposed reforms will go far enough.

Prior to 1989, the banking industry in Taiwan was tightly controlled, with most banks owned by the government either directly or through state-controlled agencies. Since the introduction of a new banking law in 1989, the industry has gradually become more liberal-ized with increasing regulatory latitude beyond direct state control. In the early 1990s, 15 new bank licences were issued to bring competition to the industry, with new banks entering the marketplace and kick-starting inter-bank competition for market share.

While the banking sector managed to ride out the Asian financial crisis without severe dislocation, it did suffer from a number of structural difficulties, with these becoming more apparent as the economy slowed in 2000. The most serious of these has been the increasing number of NPLs. Currently, NPLs are in excess of NT$1 trillion, with the farming and fishing cooperatives being the most exposed, with NPL ratios approaching 18 percent of total lending.

NPLs as a proportion of the total loan portfolio for the domestic banking sector are currently estimated at 20 percent in 2002, with only moderate signs of improvement.

> Taiwan's NPLs amount to over NT$1 trillion, or nearly 20 percent of existing loan portfolios.

The poor state of the financial services sector is a direct result of KMT rule, which in 1992 saw the issuance of 16 new banking licences, expanding market entrants at an un-sustainable rate relative to market size. Indeed, there are now 53 commercial banks and 360 credit cooperatives operating in Taiwan. No single bank is able to capture more than a 10 percent market share. Clearly, this is unsustainable in a domestic market of only 23 million people and has led to excessive competition for clients, poor volumes and depressed margins. More generally, the cut-throat competition for market share has fueled irresponsi-ble lending practices, which, for example, saw banks and cooperatives accepting equities as collateral against new loans. Unfortunately, as the stock market fluctuated, absolute col-lateral valuations went down, making many loans technically under-collateralized. More generally, as the economy suffered its worst contraction in 2000–01, business cash flows dried up and with them the debt-servicing capacity of firms.

Successive administrations, including the current one, have been careless in the way they have reacted to the problem. Failure to revamp the industry in the period after the Asian financial crisis has proven to be a major policy error. Indeed, early attempts at reform actually made matters worse. Troublesome banks were kept alive, for example, with injec-tions of cash; the stock market was propped up to keep the value of equities high; and the government directed state-owned banks to roll over bad loans; all of which compounded the problem. Moreover, during the 1990s, government regulations prohibited foreign invest-ment in the sector or mergers among the institutions themselves, depriving them of much needed capital injection. Finally, control of the banking system is spread between three ministries instead of a single entity capable of effectively coordinating the problem.

President Chen promised to restructure the financial services sector as part of his 2000 presidential election campaign. Unfortunately, he immediately became mired in political debate with a KMT-dominated legislature. Nevertheless, he has made some headway. First, legislation has been put in place to allow an independent regulator to oversee the industry and changes to the Financial Holding Company Law will make mergers easier. Second, the government has paved the way for asset management corporations (AMCs) to enter the market and buy up NPLs at a discount rate. Third, the government has set up a fund of NT$140 billion to help the ailing cooperatives. Fourth, foreign ownership restrictions on Taiwanese financial institutions have been lifted. Finally, banks are being cajoled into writing off their bad loans and forced to become more transparent in their reporting practices. This will be reinforced with accession to the WTO, which can be expected to see systematic improvements to regulatory and provisioning practices as well as provide access to international expertise in the design and implementation of prudential measures.

Despite this, however, the government has not gone far enough in its efforts to reform the sector. While the establishment of AMCs is a step in the right direction, the government must also institute wide-ranging amendments to bankruptcy laws and to asset securitization legislation, as well as develop a regulatory framework for effective corporate governance.[7] Without these, the sector will remain dysfunctional, depriving Taiwanese firms and foreign companies of much needed investment capital.

The bottom line

The country's poor economic performance, the relocation of manufacturing to China, and the impact of accession to the WTO will insure that loan quality continues to deteriorate in 2002–03. While the AMCs might provide some attraction to higher-risk foreign investors, most will be disappointed by the sector's under-performance, poor prospects for growth due to market overcrowding, and a less than attractive market segment risk profile. Indeed, even with the substantial reforms on the table, it is still unclear just how successful these might be in the long run. At the very least, it will take 12 to 18 months (2004–05) for the AMCs and mergers to have the desired structural effect.

Private and public debt

- The fiscal position of the government has been deteriorating since late 1999, and continues to do so. As a consequence of escalating expenditure and declining tax revenues, the government's capacity to stimulate the domestic market is weakening. Currently, total tax revenue is equivalent to 12.9 percent of GDP. This is too low to enable the government to undertake effective reform of the financial system. The budget will remain in deficit during 2003–04 with a gradual fall in public sector borrowing requirements likely the following year in 2005.

Over the past few years, Taiwan's fiscal position has been slowly deteriorating. There are a number of reasons for this. First, government expenditure has been steadily climbing, especially in the areas of social welfare payments and medical insurance. Second, the government has been offering tax incentives and other exemptions to lure foreign investment. Third, the government has had to outlay large sums of money in order to rebuild public infrastructure after the September 1999 earthquake, all of which has contributed to substantial expenditure increases and distracted from the fiscal position of the government.

At the same time, tax revenues have been steadily declining. In 1990, revenues amounted to 20.2 percent of GDP. By 1999, this figure had dropped to 12.9 percent. This is a worrying trend but there is little sign that the government has been, or will be able to address the problem any time soon.

'A tax burden of just 12.9 percent calls for serious reconsideration. Taiwan's financial system is unsound enough as it is.'[8]

In an attempt to address this problem, the legislative Yuan has set a ceiling on government debt – a ceiling that is fast approaching its legislative limits. Despite this, the administration has again ruled out revenue increases, and has been forced to engage in a series of amendments to the Public Debt Law and issue new debt instruments. In addition, the administration has embarked on a fire sale of government assets, including divestiture of government equity holdings in state-owned enterprises and public lands. Unfortunately, with the real estate market in a slump, and with state-owned enterprises performing poorly, reliance on capital revenues is a short-term solution.

The revenue position of the government is also compounded by the administration's persistence in offering tax relief to industries. For example, the Council for Economic Planning and Development has recently proposed new tax relief measures to help boost investment in traditional industries and curb industrial migration to the mainland. The measures, similar to those offered to the electronics industry, include a five-year tax holiday.

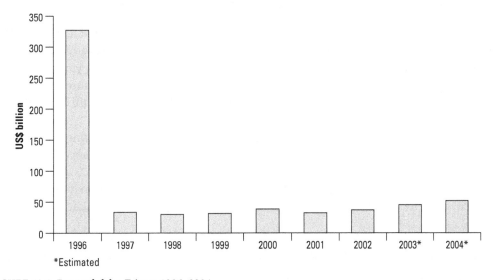

FIGURE 11.1 External debt, Taiwan 1996–2004

Widespread reform of the taxation system is urgently needed. But unless the government's tax policy spreads the burden more evenly it will further distort the tax base and not provide a sound basis for revenue stability into the future. However, neither the KMT nor the DPP appear willing to explore substantial tax reform issues.

> The government will need to increase taxes in order to meet its financial obligations. The longer it delays, the less effective reforms in the financial sector are likely to be.

Despite Taiwan's weak fiscal position, its external public debt is less than US$100 million and its foreign exchange reserves are one of the highest in the world. Currently, the reserves stand at $US116.22 billion. The government believes that it is possible to manage rising debt levels without resorting to new taxes. To be sure, Taiwan has a very high private sector savings rate, standing at slightly over 25 percent in 2002. These funds can be easily tapped by the public sector, an option that is not likely to see a drawn-out fiscal and revenue crisis for the government in 2003–04.

Labor market trends

- The labor market weakened significantly in 2001–02, with job seekers reaching record levels. The drop in export orders, relocation of manufacturing to the mainland, corporate downsizing, and a general weakening of consumer demand are the main reasons behind the rise. It is unlikely that unemployment will drop below 4 percent during 2003, but it will start to trend downwards in 2004 to levels of between 3 and 4 percent.

Industrial migration, plant closures, and the slump in exports pushed the unemployment rate up in 2001–02. While the unemployment figure has been trending upwards since 1996, it remained below 3 percent until 2000. In 2001, the figure rose from 3.66 percent in the first quarter to 5.38 percent in the fourth quarter. This is the highest unemployment rate ever recorded. Trade unions, in particular, have been spooked, attempting to capture public sentiment and the public debate over employment security by suggesting that this figure could reach 8 percent if plant closures continue.

This is unduly pessimistic, however, especially considering the government's initiative to offer tax breaks to traditional industries and forestall the mainland movement of the manufacturing sector. More likely, unemployment has peaked in 2001–02, and will now trend downwards off the back of a modest recovery in the international economy in 2003–04, combined with what is expected to be renewed domestic investment in 2003.

> Trade unions predict that the unemployment rate could go up as high as 8 percent but 4 percent is a more realistic figure.

In response to popular concerns, the administration has taken a number of initiatives to deal with unemployment. In 1999, an unemployment insurance scheme was introduced, as well as retraining programs to assist those made redundant through plant closure and downsizing. A plan to reduce the alien workforce by 15,000 a year has also been put in place. The scheme will compensate employers by NT$10,000 per annum if they replace an alien with a local Taiwanese worker. Pump-priming the economy through increased government expenditure, particularly major construction projects with stipulations on labor employment codes for local workers, has also been a well publicized government response.

The government has had little room to maneuver on unemployment matters, in part reflecting Taiwan's active trade union movement, which in 2001–02, had a total of 3,874 registered unions with a combined membership of 2.8 million members. Indeed, 40 percent of workers are members of unions, making them a significant and very vocal voice in Taiwan's political system. Compared to regional neighbors this makes Taiwan unique; a fact reflected in the Labor Union Law which makes it compulsory for any company with 30 or more employees to form a union and provide representation.

In order to coordinate the excessively large number of unions, the Taiwan Confederation of Trade Unions (TCTU) was formed on May Day 2000. However, since then labor disputes have doubled. This trend is set to continue into 2002–04, as economic restructuring and reform programs are met with popular union resistance, and as plant closures continue amid the general move to the mainland of the manufacturing sector.

By regional standards, Taiwan's minimum wage structure of NT$15,840 per month is high. The government adjusts this rate each year based on negotiations between the Chinese National Federation of Industries and the Chinese Federation of Labor Unions (CFLU).[9] However, reflecting the poor economic conditions of the last few years, no adjustments to this rate have been made. Indeed, in the first quarter of 2001, real wages declined by 1.9 percent. In 2003–04, however, union demands will again be made for an increase in the minimum wage, reflecting a general upswing in economic activity, and the three years of wage stagnation in the face of modest inflation that unions will want to address. Indeed, these negotiations are already underway, with the Council of Labor Affairs and representatives of the business sector tentatively agreeing to lift the minimum monthly salary for workers from NT$15,840 to $NT16,376 in 2002–03.

Labor force skill set

Taiwan's labor force numbers 10 million, and is generally well skilled and educated. Labor shortages are common in semiconductor design, telecommunications and engineering.[10] Skilled managerial shortages are also common, as are high-skilled technical specialists in the financial and banking sector. Foreign investors in these sectors will need to insure that there is an adequate supply of appropriately skilled personnel before committing to particular projects.

As the restructuring process continues, with offshore movement to the mainland of much of the plant and manufacturing sector in Taiwan, there will be an abundance of unskilled labor for prospective start-up ventures.

Consumer and business confidence

- Consumer and business confidence is slowly returning after a dramatic downturn in 2001–02. However, consumer and business sentiment is still fragile, with most consumers continuing to defer expenditure on big-ticket items until trends in the international economy can be discerned. This can be expected to occur mid 2003 and into 2004, when domestic economic conditions should begin to recover from their present doldrums and help boost consumer and business confidence levels. So too, any prospective improvement in confidence levels will depend on the situation across the Taiwan Straits and Taiwan–China relations.

Consumer confidence fell during the first half of 2001 before a notable upswing occurred in the second half of 2001 and into 2002. Indeed, consumer confidence almost doubled between June and December 2001, and has continued to strengthen throughout 2002. These findings confirm research undertaken by the Taiwan Research Institute, indicating that most respondents are now positive about the future of the economy in 2003–04.

However, it is important not to be overly buoyed by this evidence. Consumer confidence will rise and fall in line with the unemployment rate and this will be directly affected by Taiwan's accession to the WTO and consequent plant closures. So too, much depends on the depth and continuity of the international recovery, especially the extent to which IT-related demand returns, a sector especially important to Taiwan. Unfortunately, the latter, in particular, is not assured, with a general consensus forming that a structural shift has occurred in demand patterns for IT-related equipment, consequently representing the end phase of the first IT boom product cycle.

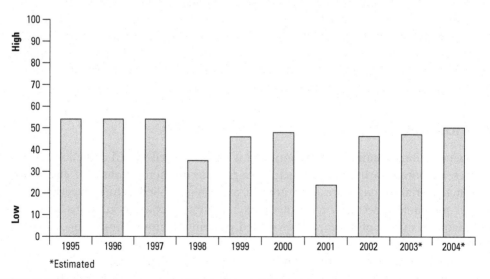

FIGURE 11.2 Business and consumer confidence, Taiwan 1995–2004
Source: MasterCard MasterIndex; Ministry of Economic Affairs

These factors aside, there is also growing evidence to suggest that business sentiment is also recovering. According to the Taiwan Institute for Economic Research, 41 percent of companies held a relatively positive outlook for 2002–03, up from 28.4 percent 12 months previously. More generally, the number of companies with a negative outlook dropped by almost 2 percent on previous figures. Even with the enormous problems faced by the construction sector, increased optimism is also discernible, with a 2.8 percent increase in valuations for construction stock equities – in part, on the back of proposed changes to legislation governing mainland investment in Taiwan. Optimism is also apparent in high-end electronics, new information technology, communications, and bio-technology sectors expecting longer-term upswings around 2005–07. Other sectors remain less optimistic, however, with the future uncertain in the case of the automotive industry, agriculture, steel industry and petrochemicals.

Stock market

- The Taiwan Stock Exchange (TSE) steadily lost ground during 1999–2001, reflecting the deteriorating condition of the domestic economy and following international trends reflecting increased investor caution. However, discernible recovery in late 2001 continued into 2002, prompting speculation that economic recovery is under way. For prospective international investors, the price-to-earnings ratio of many Taiwanese shares is low, indicative of undervaluation. These might provide the more risk-tolerant investor with possible medium-term capital gains.

The TSE has been on a roller-coaster ride since the beginning of 2000, reaching a record high of over 10,000 in March 2000, but from there beginning a long slide for 18 straight months, finishing at 3,500, or just 35 percent of its former market capitalization in December 2001. The trend breaker appears to have been the December 1 elections, which have helped restore stability to the index along with cautious investor optimism that recovery will be ongoing.

An influx of foreign capital from foreign institutional investors keen to take advantage of low equity valuations, and underscored by a relative decline in the valuation of the New Taiwanese dollar, has helped push TSE valuations upward, albeit still trending at relatively low levels compared to previous years. In early 2002, for example, investors poured more than US$1.7 billion into equity funds, with microelectronic sector stocks enjoying the most interest.

Also of importance to the restoration of TSE stability has been the relaxation of previously tight monetary policy by the Central Bank. Record low interest rate yields on bank deposits helped push capital into the stock market.

These trends look set to continue, at least with ongoing pressure on the Taiwanese dollar that should help TSE valuations remain internationally attractive into 2003–04. Interest rate deposit yields should likewise remain low until a tighter monetary policy becomes apparent, although this is not anticipated during 2003–04.

Corporate tax: Targeted incentives available to investors

- Resident companies are subject to corporate income tax on global income. Non-resident companies are taxed on income generated in Taiwan. The tax environment for non-residents is competitive by regional standards, with generous incentives available to companies that invest in priority target areas of the economy. More generally, in the face of offshore mainland movement of large sections of the manufacturing sector, the administration has displayed a commitment to deepen the tax and start-up incentive structures as a means to stem unemployment increases and fend off competition from the mainland.

The Taiwanese government levies taxes on all profit-seeking enterprises. Profit-seeking enterprises include sole proprietorships, partnerships, joint ventures, corporations, and any privately- or government-owned enterprise. This definition is also applied to foreign subsidiaries incorporated under Taiwan's Company Law.

Taxing foreign business: Little change expected

Foreign enterprises operating, but not headquartered, in Taiwan are subject to a 20 percent withholding tax on domestically generated profit. In addition, enterprises must pay an income tax equivalent to 50 percent of the previous year's tax liability, with companies subject to a further 10 percent surcharge on undistributed profits under the government's new imputation system. This is levied in addition to the normal business tax liabilities. Companies are also required to maintain an imputation credit account.

The current administration, while publicly committed to an agenda of tax reform and redressing the incentive structures to attractive foreign venture capital, in reality has not undertaken any concrete steps to realize this. Indeed, given the overall economic situation in Taiwan, there is not likely to be significant movement during 2003–04. What is clear, however, is that the administration remains open to continued development of incentives to business, especially as a means of ensuring employment levels and stemming what is seen as a threatening trend to locate in mainland China.

In 2003–04, investors might look toward a possible relaxation of the currently levied 25 percent company capital tax rule, with rumors circulating that this measure is one of few currently under active consideration by the administration.

> Tax benefits of between 5 percent and 20 percent are available to companies that invest in priority areas such as bio-technology and pharmaceuticals.

For foreign enterprises operating in targeted priority sectors, the range of tax incentives has recently increased, with the administration announcing a range of tax incentives for bio-technology and pharmaceutical industries, aimed at providing accelerated depreciation rates, tax credits on equipment and technology inputs, along with generous write-down allowances for R&D.[11]

Residential and commercial property markets

- While the residential market in Taipei started to improve towards the end of 2001 and into 2002, the commercial sector did not. Prices, rents and occupancy rates have all fallen. On the upside, a low Taiwanese dollar and prospects for medium-term economic turnaround provide foreign investors with cheap acquisition costs. However, rental returns and capital gains yields are likely to remain depressed for 2002–03, if not 2004, with prospective investors well advised to allow sufficient time horizons for profit realization.

All sections of the real estate market performed poorly in 2001–02, with the commercial office rental market performing the worst. In part, this reflects general market sentiments, overall economic slowdown, as well as oversupply, all of which served to push prices down to 10-year lows. Indeed, the Taipei office market posted the first negative absorption in 10 years, indicative of an economy hit hard by external demand contraction and the effect of the technology sector meltdown.

This contraction in economic activity and office rental demand was reflected in an overall price contraction of 7.8 percent in 2001 that continued into the early part of 2002. Office rental values for A grade office space now stand at US$18.40 per square meter, considerably higher than many of its regional neighbors, although still below Tokyo and Singapore levels. A further easing in early 2002 should now give way to stability in this sector, with a return to higher up-take rates in early 2003 in line with better economic performance domestically and internationally.

The residential market: Slighter better prospects

Faring better in 2001–02 was the residential property market which reported an increase in the number of people wanting to buy residential property, in part reflecting the low interest rate environment. This too can be expected to persist into 2003–04 as the economy picks up and interest rates remain low. Indeed, the government will be keen to encourage this demand in residential property, reflecting its desire to pump-prime the economy and provide some much needed relief to the construction industry, traditionally a large employer of unskilled labor.

Not all the news is good, however. While improvement in the residential property market has been discernible since the end of 2001, part of this is due to the overall fall in property values, which have contracted by up to 20 percent year-on-year. In line with this fall, the government was forced to drop the assessed values of properties by 2.39 percent, causing further contraction on its property value tax revenue base.[12] At the same time, the administration help stimulate demand by offering home buyers a grant scheme. In all, then, what little optimism in the residential property market there was during 2002 reflected the overall poor health of the sector rather than organic growth from home buyers.[13]

Regardless, these factors will likely provide the drivers of growth for 2003–04, insuring solid if unspectacular price growth of between 5 and 8 percent during that time, with luxury apartments in Taipei forecast to outperform the residential market average.

The Taipei office market slumped in 2001–02 and will not likely recover until the current excess supply is worked through the system, forecast for early 2003.

New developments

Despite the depressed state of the real estate market, there are two growth areas. The first is warehouse stores such as Carrefour and Price Costco. Indeed, forward estimates suggest that as many as 40 new warehouse stores will open in 2003–04, indicative of strong anticipated demand for storage capacity and hyper-retail stores.

Second, retail shopping outlets are also showing signs of strong growth trends, indicative of the fact that over the past five years the face of retail shopping has changed in Taiwan. Indeed, there has been an explosion of modern retail outlets and specialty shops, modeled along North American delivery systems. Greatest growth has been in shopping mall construction, with 2001 witnessing the opening of Core Pacific, Breeze, and Taichung Tehan malls, with an array of other mega-malls under construction. Over the course of 2002–04, as many as 30 new malls are on the drawing board, with commensurate opportunities for foreign retail and construction companies.

Taiwan is not international enough, the market is too small, cross-strait relations are unclear, with no apparent improvement in the domestic political situation – as well as unattractive rental returns on property investment.[14]

The bottom line

None of the major international real estate companies operating in Taiwan expects the market to pick up dramatically in 2003–04. Indeed, a sense of gloom pervades the industry – apart from mall construction. While much of the negative outlook is attributed to domestic factors associated with the sector itself, much of the gloom also stems from uncertain cross-strait relations, the impact on prices by AMCs, the low rental returns, an unfinished reform agenda, and the relatively small size of the Taiwanese market.

The latter point is important, with Taiwan only a regional bit player for international construction companies with better growth prospects in mainland China. In short, the Taiwanese market is too small, and unlikely to be a sector able to rekindle Taiwan's economic fortunes in 2003–04, at least off the back of domestic demand for commercial and residential property. Rather, stimulus will have to come from foreign investors, leaving two possible scenarios for recovery. First, that businesses from the mainland will expand their operations into Taiwan – albeit for reasons already articulated. This is not likely. The other is that foreign investors will see Taiwan as a strategic launching pad for access to Chinese markets, both in terms of the construction sector and the investment sector generally. This should help see a slow but solid recovery in office and commercial real estate towards the end of 2004 and into 2005.

Until then, the recovery in the property sector is likely to be slow and depend, to a large extent, on two factors: the economic fortunes of mainland China and the development of direct transport links between Taiwan and the mainland.

Opportunities for investors

From an investment point of view, however, there is no better time to buy general real estate or enter into a long-term leasing arrangement. The New Taiwan dollar is weak against the major currencies, and the establishment of asset management companies to deal with NPLs is likely to drive the price of property down still further. Premium A grade properties can be bought at a substantial discount from the level of just a year ago. Moreover, the relaxing of restrictions on foreign ownership and the generally favorable investment climate make Taiwan a buyer's market. But prospective investors must be there for the long term if they intend to derive substantial benefit.

Foreign direct investment

- Taiwan has the lowest rates of foreign direct investment(FDI) in East Asia, indeed, is not a preferred destination for investment. However, the stock of foreign investment has been steadily rising since the government began to liberalize the economy and loosen restrictions on foreign ownership. The current regulatory climate is generally consistent and transparent, with investment opportunities increasingly available in the retail and financial services sector and catering to mainland business operators. Likewise, there are good opportunities for civil and rail contractors, although payments disputes are common.

While FDI into East Asia has grown significantly over 1999–2001, Taiwan has received the smallest share, well behind mainland China and South Korea.[15] There are a number of reasons for this. First, mainland China has the fastest growing economy in the world and offers greater growth opportunities than Taiwan. So too, project start-up costs tend to be lower and the potential domestic market much larger. Second, Hong Kong's well-developed infrastructure and its low tax environment make it a strong competitor. Similarly, commercial property costs in Shanghai are considerably lower than those in Taipei. Third, Taiwan is already substantially developed and large infrastructure projects like those taking place in Shanghai and Beijing are less common.[16] Fourth, FDI into Taiwan is substantially lower than it might otherwise be because of the continuing restrictions on investment by Chinese nationals.[17] Finally, Taiwan's high level of corruption is an important consideration for investors. Some US companies, for example, have complained that their accounts have not been fully paid as a result of unnecessary disputes over sign-off procedures on civil and rail engineering projects.

However, Taiwan has been working to increase levels of FDI over the last few years. During the 1990s, for example, the KMT relaxed ownership laws in the construction industry, real estate, and financial services sector. In 1999, it opened the communications

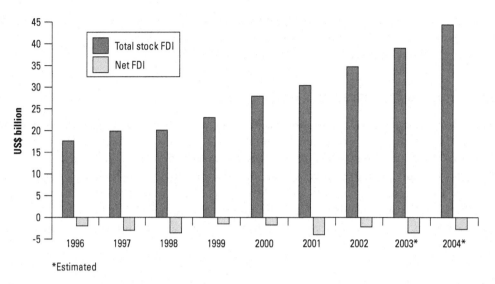

FIGURE 11.3 Foreign direct investment, Taiwan 1996–2004
Source: EIU Country Forecast August 2001

industry to foreign investors, raising the foreign ownership level to 50 percent. In 2000, limits on foreign ownership of companies listed on the TSE and the OTC were also removed. The government has also offered tax incentives to attract foreign investors, especially in priority areas such as bio-technology.

The administration's continuing attempts to attract a greater share of FDI have been successful to the extent that FDI levels were maintained during 2002, with an increase to US$34.72 billion, up from US$30.42 billion in 2001 – and this despite a less than attractive international environment from which to attract capital.

However, perhaps a better picture of foreign capital attraction can be gleaned by looking at net FDI, which rose from US$–1.77 billion to US$–4.00 billion in 2001, albeit trending downward again to US$–2.20 billion in 2002. Much of this can be explained by the circulation of investment funds that travel from the mainland to Taiwan and then directly back to the mainland again so as to be able to claim FDI tax and establishment concessions. Much FDI into Taiwan is thus simply circulated through Taiwan and does not stay there.

Taiwan is not a preferred destination for FDI as a result of restrictions on trade and transport links between Taipei and the mainland. Instead, Taiwanese business has sought to exploit mainland opportunities, so that today Taiwan is among the largest foreign investors in China.

The bottom line

Despite these efforts, Taiwan is unlikely to increase its share of regional FDI significantly in 2003–04. The attraction of China is simply too strong a trend to reverse, or indeed have any significant influence over. The most telling argument to support this conclusion is the fact that Taiwan is one of the largest exporters of FDI in the region, with Taiwanese companies themselves believing that there are better opportunities elsewhere.

Mainland fever or cross-strait risks?

The downturn in the Taiwanese economy has led to an increase in the number of companies wanting to invest in mainland China. Labor costs are lower, as are land and housing costs. Local governments in Shanghai and elsewhere along the coast are offering tax breaks and other incentives to attract investment. However, the long-term impact on the Taiwanese economy is difficult to determine. Since the late 1980s, some 50,000 Taiwanese firms have invested over US$100 billion into the mainland, mainly around the coastal areas. With the recent scrapping of the 'no haste' policy, this figure will rise considerably. But it is not clear if or how this will benefit Taiwan's ailing economy. Some commentators have argued that offshore manufacturers will drive Taiwanese companies out of business by flooding Taiwan with cheap goods. Others have questioned the profitability of investing in the mainland, highlighting the fact that, thus far, there has been very little profit repatriation.

> Taiwan is turning into an economic province of China. Its longer-term economic health looks increasingly to be that of a hopping-off point for FDI investment into China or as a headquarters for Chinese operations. Either way, the prospects signal a fundamental reorientation in regional investment patterns, with China the clear winner.[18]

The business community sees the mainland as the key to Taiwan's economic future. For example, after posting a NT$3.8 billion loss for the first three quarters of 2001, Chunghwa Picture Tubes cut their workforce in Taiwan and moved production offshore.

The most serious risk facing Taiwanese investments on the mainland is not low profitability from mainland investments, but cross-strait tensions. In the event of a crisis, it is likely that investments in the mainland would be compromised as Beijing would try to punish the government of Taiwan. This could include increases in taxation, unfair regulatory changes, special levies, transportation hold-ups, disruption to production schedules, and political harassment, as well as outright expropriation.

This is also a crucial consideration for foreign investors. Companies with their regional headquarters in Taiwan would not be immune from the effects of a political crisis and could be singled out by Beijing for unfair treatment. This would not necessarily be the case with companies headquartered on the mainland. Companies could be excluded from Chinese markets because of commercial relationships they have in Taiwan. US and European defense companies are especially vulnerable. The recent experience of Credit Suisse First Boston (CSFB) is instructive in this regard. Beijing barred CSFB from a multi billion-dollar share sale by China Unicom because the bank held two business conferences that were attended by senior Taiwanese government officials. Similarly, Beijing threatened to ban Japan's Matsushita Communication Industrial Company from selling mobile phones for 12 months because its handsets referred to Taiwan as the Republic of China. This kind of tactic has been used by Beijing on a number of occasions previously and there is no reason to think that they will not use it again.[19] Certainly, accession to the WTO might help to moderate this behavior, but the risk remains a serious one for investors.

Taiwan's accession to the World Trade Organization

Taiwan joined the WTO on 1 January 2002. The country has been working toward this goal for nearly a decade. This is an important milestone for Taiwan, a country that has been excluded from most international forums since being unceremoniously dumped from the United Nations in the early 1970s.[20] Even within this new framework, Taiwan must be referred to as either Chinese Taipei or the Separate Customs Territory of Taiwan, Penghu, Kinmen and Matsu.

To be eligible to join the WTO, Taiwan completed bilateral negotiations with almost all of the membership. As a consequence of these negotiations, many industries have now been opened up to foreign investors, including power generation, oil, telecommunications, transport, and real estate. It has also committed itself to reducing the nominal duty rates on thousands of industrial and agricultural items, as well as making the necessary regulatory changes to protect foreign investments and ensure fair competition.

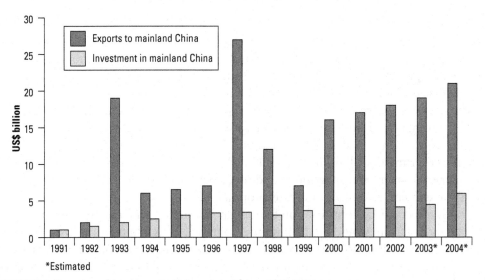

*Estimated

FIGURE 11.4 Exports and investment – Taiwan into China, 1991–2004

Accession to the WTO gives Taiwan a degree of prestige that befits its position as one of the world's largest trading nations. It will also provide an opportunity for Taiwanese firms to further exploit China's markets, and in 2002–05 will see a more liberalized financial services sector open to foreign bank competition. Finally, it will give Taiwan a voice in global economic affairs. Whether it will also help to improve political relations between the two entities is difficult to determine. The WTO's dispute resolution mechanism could serve as a channel for both sides to air their differences.

> Officials estimate that entry into the WTO will cost as many as 20,000 Taiwanese jobs, most of these in agriculture.[21]

The bottom line

Taiwan's comparative advantage lies in the fact that it is developed and Westernized and can cater to the needs of foreign nationals. It has a highly educated workforce, especially in engineering and science, is technologically advanced, and strategically located in the region – especially in relation to China. It is ideally suited to service sector companies, retail outlets, high quality precision manufacturing, and electronic equipment. Accession to the WTO is, on balance, a step forward and will improve the overall economic position of Taiwan in the region, but it will be some time before Taiwan can be considered a secure gateway to the mainland.

Section C Politics

- Taiwan has managed the transition to democracy with relative ease. While not a fully matured liberal democratic state, it continues the process of consolidation and expansion of its institutional base. However, the reform program has not moved along as quickly as most observers would have liked – nor will it do so in 2003–04 – due largely to the KMT's obstruction of legislation during Chen's first year as president and partly as a consequence of Taiwan's poor economic performance during 2000–01. Corruption, too, remains a major problem for the administration and investors alike, with little discernible evidence of proactive policy initiative from the government, or the possibility of establishment of institutionalized means for nurturing anti-corruption measures. In this regard, political risk is moderate to high and will remain so into 2003–04.

The transition from an authoritarian dictatorship to a democratic, multi-party system has gone relatively smoothly. But Taiwan's nascent democracy is marred by well-documented brawls in parliament, vote-buying scandals, and high levels of corruption within all levels of the political system. It has a long way to go before it becomes a mature liberal-democratic country like Australia, New Zealand or the United States.

An evolving democracy

Taiwan's political system is still evolving. Since the founding of the constitution, the country has gone through a number of constitutional amendments. The most important of these occurred in 1997 when the National Assembly sought to better define the relationship between the different branches of the central government. This helped to streamline the regulatory framework, reduce the number of confused and contradictory rulings, and counter excessive levels of corruption in the political system. All this has been to the benefit of investors and helped pave the way for Taiwan's accession to the WTO.

The process of democratisation began in the mid 1980s after martial law was rescinded by Chiang Ching-kuo, the son of Chiang Kai-shek. The first parliamentary elections took place in 1992 and the first presidential election followed in 1996. The turning point in Taiwanese politics occurred in March 2000, when the opposition Democratic Progressive Party won the presidential elections. This was the first time in the island's history that a peaceful transfer of power had occurred.[22] Chen Shui-bian was sworn in as the new president in May 2000. The December 2001 parliamentary elections further undermined the KMT's position as a political force when it lost its majority in the legislative Yuan.

The poor showing of the KMT in the recent elections is the result of a number of factors. First, Lee Teng-hui, the island's first democratically elected president, did not stand for re-election in 2000. Second, Lien Chan, Lee's successor, failed to attract enough votes (23.1 percent) to win government for the KMT. Third, the KMT's longstanding policy on reunification with the mainland is not a popular one among the younger generation of ethnic Taiwanese. Fourth, the KMT has been beset with internal division, factionalism, and bad press associated with its links to organized crime and lack of public accountability. Finally, breakaway parties such as James Soong's People First Party and Lee Teng-hui's sponsored Taiwanese Solidarity Union have watered down the KMT's supporter base. This state of affairs leaves the KMT in a severely weakened position, and indeed it might even see the party disintegrate in the near future.[23] However, while the KMT is in disarray, it remains a disruptive force in the parliament and will continue to be so during 2003–04, likely delaying reform legislation and the reform process generally.

Prospects for reform?

With the KMT now languishing in the political wilderness, the Chen government has an opportunity to push ahead with the reform process. Its success will depend largely on whether it can maintain a political consensus among the various political parties. Two issues have the potential to shatter cooperation. First, Taiwanese politics is beginning to fracture along ethnic lines – between native Taiwanese who generally support independence and mainlanders who support reunification. Should this issue flare up, it is likely that the parliament would become unworkable. Second, a further deterioration in Taiwan's economic position would undermine confidence in the government and lead to political turmoil.

On balance, however, the situation over the life of the next parliament is likely to be much better than during Chen's first 12 months as President. During that period, the KMT sought to have Chen sacked over his cancellation of the island's fourth nuclear power plant, while also blocking a number of important political and economic reform initiatives, including Chen's anti-corruption drive. But with a reduced majority in the legislative Yuan, the KMT's ability to disrupt Chen's ongoing reform agenda is lessened considerably. The period between 2002 and the next presidential elections is likely to offer the government a rare opportunity to bring about meaningful change and push the reform process forward. Investors should not, therefore, be overly concerned about the political climate in Taiwan. Of greater concern are the high levels of corruption and fraud among business and ruling elite.

Corruption

Corruption has been an endemic problem in Taiwan for many years. It takes many forms, but the giving and receiving of bribes, vote-buying, cronyism, the misappropriation of funds and the granting of political and business favors are among the most significant. Transparency International's Bribe-Payers Index ranked Taiwan seventeenth in a list of the 19 most corrupt countries, with South Korea and China languishing at the bottom of the index.

The new DPP government has pledged to do everything in its power to stamp out the so-called 'black gold' politics. There is little to suggest that they will be successful in the short term, primarily because the problem is so deeply entrenched. For example, between July 2000 and May 2001, six legislators, three county commissioners, two city mayors, 29 township chiefs, and 57 representatives of county councils were prosecuted. And, more recently, a number of senior army officials have been jailed on corruption charges. Despite this modest success, the Minister for Justice admits that the task is a formidable one, with at least 10 known gangsters still sitting in the central parliament.

The administration has sought to tackle the problem in a number of ways. For example, it has instituted anti-corruption penal statutes, enacted laws relating to money laundering, encouraged confessions, offered rewards for informing on corrupt officials, and increased the policing powers of the Ministry of Justice. Whether these measures will be enough is open to question. Without absent transparency laws that make it compulsory for government officials to account for the origin of their assets, as well as a raft of new laws to govern the conduct of political parties, corruption will doubtless continue to plague Taiwanese politics.

Of major concern for investors is bid-fixing and court rulings that prejudice foreign investors and contractors. In order to comply with the accession rules for the WTO, the government is working to deal with these problems, although it would be naïve to think this problem will be resolved quickly.

Corporate fraud and transparency

Corporate fraud is also a major problem in Taiwan, with recent efforts aimed at tackling this largely ineffectual. The sector hardest hit has been the microelectronic industry, with well-documented fraud cases of monetary theft, organized plant pilfering, as well as theft of software and hardware designs. Indeed, protecting intellectual property has proven a near impossibility in many technology enterprises, despite concerted efforts.

This has led to a relative boom for foreign security firms, with business looking unfortunately prosperous in 2003–05. Indeed, corporate fraud is increasingly an organized crime activity, with strong indications of connections to the 'Four Seas' and 'United Bamboo' gangs, which, in turn, have links to governing elites, the police force, and the military. Corruption is thus a systemic problem in Taiwan with no early indications that it is being, or can be, successfully challenged.

Protection of intellectual property

Taiwan has had very few bilateral agreements that protect intellectual property. In 1999, the United States put the country on the Special 301 Watch list as one of the least active jurisdictions proactively pursing and enforcing intellectual property. However, since 1999 Taiwan has taken steps to establish an Intellectual Property Office to oversee enforcement efforts. The government has also introduced legislation that specifies music, software, and DVD codification for security assurance of intellectual property content. Despite these initiatives, the situation in Taiwan is far from perfect. The risk of intellectual property theft must be regarded as high.

Leading risk indices: Corruption, stability, governance, risk

Corruption

The problem of corruption continues to be a major deterrent to the inflow and establishment of FDI. Indeed, with the institutionalized nature of corruption, the absence of transparent tendering processes makes it difficult for foreign enterprises to gain a foothold in

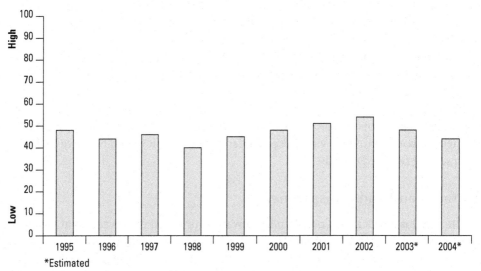

FIGURE 11.5 Corruption index, Taiwan 1995–2004
Source: Transparency International; The Heritage Foundation

the Taiwanese market. Not least, the time, effort, and enormous expense involved in securing political patronage at all levels makes for a less than receptive foreign investor perception, with many investors simply bypassing Taiwan and heading directly to China.

As can be seen from the corruption perceptions index, the figure has risen from 55 in 2000 to 59 in 2001. It rates Taiwan as twenty-seventh out of 91 countries.

Political stability

The obstructionism of the KMT has had a detrimental effect on the first year of the new administration's capacity to govern. This is evidenced by the fall in the index from 2000 to 2001. Nevertheless, there are now clear signs of improvement, in part reflecting the marginalization of the KMT as an effective political opposition. Administrative maturity should also provide Taiwan with better quality management during 2003–04.

The law and order index is also showing signs of upwards movement, but this is probably more related to a steady improvement in the economy, better prospects in 2003–04, and thus a reduction in petty crime and property theft as a result. By Western standards, however, it remains at only middling levels.

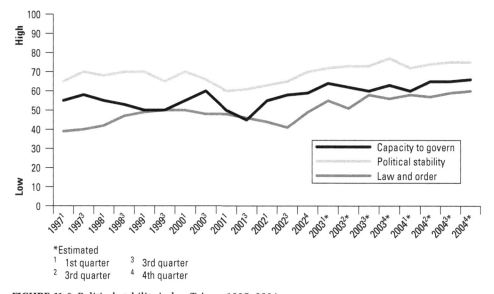

*Estimated
1 1st quarter   3 3rd quarter
2 3rd quarter   4 4th quarter

FIGURE 11.6 Political stability index, Taiwan 1995–2004

Political stability methodology:
- The capacity-to-govern index is based upon the institutional reach of government defined in terms of its ability to set the political and economic agenda and ensure its legislative program is enacted without significant compromise. This index is adversely affected by legislative opposition, lack of legislative implementation, failure to realize government policy and general political opposition.
- The political stability index measures violent opposition or organized demonstrations, terrorist activities, and popular discontent that adversely affect the institutional and electoral stability of the government.
- The law and order index measures the propensity to civil obedience, and the institutional reach of the rule of law in terms of regulatory compliance and enforcement.

More positive is the political stability index, which shows a strong level of stability compared to many regional neighbors, and an upwards trend into 2002–04. This underscores the effective transition to a semi-liberal democratic state, with continued strength in this index likely to grow further as systems of governance and institutions gather more legitimacy.

Corporate governance

The upward trend of both indices of the corporate governance index shows that the government's reform agenda is beginning to bear fruit, not least as it begins to meet the requirements for WTO membership.

The propensity-to-restructure index is also showing an upward trend, indicative of WTO requirements for membership, but also, more importantly, the effects of China on the manufacturing sector which is necessitating industry rationalization. This will deepen in 2003–04.

However, a number of sectors still have a considerable way to go before an adequate level of corporate transparency is reached. This is especially the case with financial sector reform that drags the index down slightly. Reform in this sector is proceeding only slowly. This is partly due to the reluctance of banks and financial institutions to sell down NPLs to AMCs and find suitable merger partners, but also reflects the concern of members of the

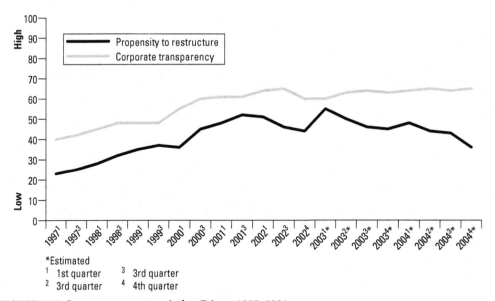

*Estimated
1 1st quarter   3 3rd quarter
2 3rd quarter   4 4th quarter

FIGURE 11.7 Corporate governance index, Taiwan 1997–2004

Corporate governance index methodology
- The corporate governance index is a composite index measuring the juridical requirements for corporate disclosure and financial reporting, prudential regime adequacy, prudential compliance enforcement, and the juridical reach of prudential authorities.
- The propensity to restructure index is a composite index based on media releases and reported corporate restructuring as a result of prudential regulation, financial incentives, loan restructuring / renegotiation, or asset realignment.

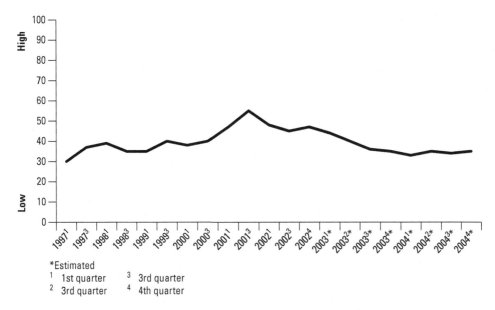

*Estimated
¹ 1st quarter   ³ 3rd quarter
² 3rd quarter   ⁴ 4th quarter

FIGURE 11.8 Foreign investor risk index, Taiwan 1997–2004

Foreign investor risk index methodology:
- The foreign investor risk index is a composite index measuring tax burdens, discriminatory regulatory practices, adverse compliance regulations, government policy toward foreign enterprise, receptiveness to issuance of government contracts, foreign enterprise commercial restrictions, and official attitudinal changes to foreign direct investment and foreign commercial operations which impact on operational efficiency. The index also incorporates a nominal measure for market risk and market failure.

foreign business community about the adequacy of some aspects of the financial sector reforms, particularly the provisions for bankruptcy laws.

Foreign investor risk index

The foreign investor risk index is reflecting both the downturn in the domestic economic situation in Taiwan in 2000–01 and the ongoing tensions across the Taiwan Straits. Without a diplomatic solution to this problem there will be little substantial improvement in this index before early 2003–04. An easing of tensions with China as well as an improvement in the economy, led principally by renewed export growth late in 2002, will see the overall business risk fall in 2003–04.

Section D Security

- The major threat to Taiwanese security comes from China, both directly in the form of political re-incorporation, but also indirectly as a result of collateral risk from Sino–US rivalry in the region. So too, disputes regarding sovereignty issues over the Spratly Islands have the potential to draw Taiwan into a regional conflict. Yet the possibility of conflict breaking out into a hot war is, at this stage, a remote possibility in the short to medium term.

China considers Taiwan a renegade province and openly threatens to invade Taiwan should it pursue formal independence. While China's continued bellicosity is of concern to the Taiwanese government (and the US administration), there are a number of indicators that suggest an invasion from the mainland is unlikely. First, the two economies are becoming more dependent on each other for both goods and services. Second, Taiwanese investment into China is at an all-time high, with this trend likely to continue as Taiwanese companies seek to remain competitive in the global marketplace. Third, both Taiwan and China have recently joined the WTO, an organization that will exert a moderating pattern over their commercial dealings and provide a forum for trade dispute resolution. Indeed, this will have an important stabilizing effect on the cross-strait relationship. Fourth, while Beijing continues to pursue a 'one-China' policy, the new DPP government has backed away from its traditional pro-independence platform, helping to pacify Beijing. In addition, the DPP have begun to revise Lee Teng-hui's 'no haste, be patient policy' governing investment in the mainland. Finally, the number of Taiwanese visiting the mainland is increasing, which, tangentially at least, will help to increase the levels of communication between the two countries and help to promote understanding and tolerance. In fact, this is one of the messages behind the 'three-links' idea of improved trade, transport, and communications.

US–China relations and the Spratly Islands

The Spratly Islands remains one of the most likely sites of the next regional conflict, primarily because of the economic value of the islands, which are rich in resources. Again, however, while the Spratly Islands will likely form the trigger point for any hostility, direct confrontation remains a low possibility in the short to medium term.

Of more concern must be the future of US–China relations, which were strained during 2001. The capture of a US surveillance aircraft by the Chinese, US plans to build a national missile defence shield, the approval of a multi-billion dollar arms package to Taiwan, and a renewed commitment by George W. Bush to defend Taiwan in the event of an attack from China have fueled tensions between the two countries – and continue to do so. There is, however, nothing in the diplomatic statements thus far to suggest that either side is willing to engage in conflict over these issues. Moreover, with the September 11 terrorist attacks, relations have begun to thaw in 2002, and show tentative signs of continuing to do so into 2003–04. Indeed, China too is concerned about the growing Islamic fundamentalists in and around Xingjiang Province, and has openly supported the US stand against terrorism.

Natural disaster and environmental concerns

Taiwan is subject to cyclonic weather patterns during the monsoon season. Earthquakes are also a problem. In 1999, for example, an earthquake measuring 7.6 on the Richter scale killed almost 2,500 people and was estimated to have caused US$9 billion in damage. Anyone investing in Taiwan needs to be insured for public liability, damage to infrastructure and plant, and disruptions to production and delivery systems.

Terrorism

It has been suggested that Osama bin Laden considers Taiwan to be an enemy of Islam. Presumably, this is because of Taiwan's ties with the United States. But these reports have never been substantiated. The island has very few strategic assets that would interest terrorist groups. That aside, Kai Tak airport would be the most likely target, with departing flights possibly targeted by hijackers and flown to targets in the region. Like most airports in East Asia, security needs strengthening. But, in the final analysis, the threat of a direct terrorist attack on Taiwanese soil is extremely low and should not be regarded as an impediment to investment.

Section E Economic and political risk forecasts

- The recession of 2001–02 highlights Taiwan's weak economic position and high level of external dependency. Although the domestic economy will return to positive territory in 2003–04, significant structural weaknesses remain. In the short to medium term the risk to foreign investors comes from an unfinished reform agenda, endemic corruption, and volatility in its relations with the mainland.

Short-term forecasts

- The economy will recover in 2002–04, but the recovery will be modest. GDP growth will be around 3.5 percent in 2002 and just over 4 percent in 2003. Government debt will increase in order to mitigate the impact of entry into the WTO. Incentives schemes and tax breaks for foreign investors will also put pressure on debt levels.
- The stock market will also improve in 2002–04. However, with weak GDP growth, the weighted stock index will not move much above the 7500 mark.
- The government's war against corruption will continue. While funding levels appear adequate, the entrenched nature of the problem will take many years to overcome. Do not expect great inroads into corruption in 2002–04.
- Unless the government can fast-track the merger process and force the banks and cooperatives to rid themselves of their NPLs, the sector will remain uncompetitive and a millstone around the neck of the domestic economy.
- Unemployment will stay between 5 and 6 percent during 2003–04. This is not likely to come down substantially until the latest wave of industrial migration slows. There will also be considerable disruption in agriculture and primary production as these industries lose their protected status.

- As foreign companies begin to take advantage of the new WTO rulings, the automotive, manufacturing and pharmaceutical industries will struggle to remain competitive.
- It is unlikely that there will be any significant breakthrough in cross-strait relations. Beijing's aggressive and uncompromising stand on the issue will continue to be a thorn in the side of the Chen government.

Short-term opportunities

- The low value of the New Taiwan dollar against the US dollar makes real estate affordable for foreign investors. The abolition of limits on foreign ownership will help to stimulate the local market.
- Government plans to spend between 2 percent and 3 percent of GDP on R&D over the next decade will help to establish Taiwan as a knowledge-based economy – with increasing emphasis on bio-technology industries. Good investment opportunities will exist in bio-technology, genetic engineering, advanced telecommunications and information systems.
- The government's global logistics development plan will have important spin-offs for foreign investors and companies already operating in Taiwan. The government is expanding its port and airport cargo facilities, improving commodity inspection procedures, and streamlining the traffic of goods through the various control zones. This will make it easier for companies to do business in Taiwan and use it as a base for regional expansion.
- The government is moving ahead with plans to improve its e-commerce facilities, including electronic payment mechanisms, invoice systems, and new standards for electronic interchange. Companies specializing in these technologies will benefit considerably.
- The government has a vision of turning Taiwan into a 'Green Silicon Island.' Considerable opportunities exist for specialists in environmental management, advanced engineering, and education.

Medium to longer term

- Between 2002–07 the Taiwanese economy will change significantly, moving from a predominantly manufacturing economy to a knowledge-based one.
- Taxes can be expected to rise, and the tax base expanded. With revenues equivalent to only 12.9 percent of GDP, the expenditure commitments of government will not be able to be maintained. Expect an overhaul of the taxation system between 2003–07.
- Growth rates will not return to levels of the 1970s and 1980s. Four percent is achievable in 2004.
- Public opinion in Taiwan is firmly in favor of the country pursuing a separate development path from the mainland. This is unlikely to change in 2003–07. However, increased economic integration, the opening up of direct transport and trade links, and entry into the WTO will affect the long-term political relationship in unforeseen ways.

Overall risk rating

Taiwan's risk profile is improving, but only slightly. The improvement is largely a consequence of the country's entry into the WTO. But the tense state of cross-strait relations, high levels of corruption, and a substantially unfinished reform agenda mean that investor risk remains above average.

Risk: Moderate, relatively stable →
Risk Rating (0 = lowest, 10 highest risk) 5 →

Section F Taiwan fact sheet*

Geography

Capital
Taipei

Largest city (millions)
Taipei, 2.6

Location
East Asia 23 30 N, 121 00 E

Adjacent countries
China, Japan, South Korea

Terrain
Mountain range runs through the center from north to south; foothills and plains. Includes the Penghu Archipelago of 64 small islands

Land Use
Arable land 24%, permanent crops 1%, permanent pastures 5%, forest and woodlands 55%, other 15%

Climate
Tropical; rain during the monsoon season (July to August)

Area (km²)
Total: 35,980
Land: 32,260
Water: 3720 (includes surrounding islands)

Natural hazards
Earthquakes and typhoons

* All figures are the latest available except where indicated. All figures are in US dollars. Figures are compiled from national, international and multilateral agencies (United Nations Development Assistance Program, International Monetary Fund, World Bank, World Development Report, UNESCO Statistical Yearbook, International Labour Office, United Nations, Central Intelligence Agency World Fact Book). Gross domestic product (GDP) refers to the value of all goods and services produced in the preceding financial year. GDP per capita, Purchasing Power Parity (GDP per capita – PPP) refers to the indices developed by the World Bank to take account of price differences, cost of living differences, and relative purchasing power of a set basket of goods and services between countries so as to provide a more accurate measure of national wealth.

Economic Statistics

Currency
1 New Taiwan dollar (NT$) = 100 cents

Exchange rate (May 2002)
US$1.00 = 34.07000 Taiwan dollar

Growth rate
1.9% (2001)

Gross Domestic Product (GDP)
US$310.1 billion (2000)

GDP per capita
US$13,925 (2000)

GDP per capita – PPP
US$22,646 (2000)

GDP – composition by sector
Agriculture 3%, industry 33%, services 64%

Inflation rate
0.8% (average, 1997–2001); 0% (2001, average)

Foreign debt
US$36 million (2001)

Current account balance (billions)
US$7.6 (2001)

National unemployment rate (2001)
3.73%

Adult economic participation rate (by gender)
Male: 68.4%
Female: 46.3%

Labor force
Total: 9.9 million
Employed male: 5.8 million
Employed female: 4 million
Unemployed total: 0.5 million

Labor force by occupation
Agriculture 0.7 million (Feb. 2002), industry 3.3 million (Feb. 2002), services 5.4 million (Feb. 2002)

Budget 2001 (US$ billion)
Revenues: 20.6
Expenditure: 25.9

Industries
Cement, chemicals, electronics, electrical machinery, food processing, footwear, iron and steel, machinery, petroleum refining, textiles, wood products

Agriculture
Beef, corn, fish, fruit, milk, pigs, poultry, rice, soybeans, tea, wheat

Major exports – commodities
Chemicals, electronics, electrical equipment and machinery, metals, plastics, textiles

Major exports (billion)
US$122.8 (end of 2001)

Major imports – commodities
Crude oil, electronics, electrical and machinery equipment, food, iron and steel, plastic and rubber products, precision instruments, textiles, vehicles.

Major imports (billion)
US$107.2 (end of 2001)

Major trading partners (export)
Japan, China, United States, Hong Kong, Netherlands, Germany

Major trading partners (import)
Japan, South Korea, Germany, Malaysia

Average income
US$13,918.00

Televisions
8.8 million (1998)

Televisions per capita
0.39

Telephones (lines in use, public + private)
12.9 million (2001)

Telephones per capita
0.58

Cellular phones
21.6 million (2001)

Cellular phones per capita
0.96

Automobiles in use
4.8 million (2001)

Internet users per 10,000 of population
623 (2001)

Internet domain
tw

Fiscal year
1 July–30 June (up to FY1998/99); 1 July 1999–31 December 2000 for FY2000; calendar year (after FY2000)

Government and political statistics

Nature of government
Multiparty democracy

Constitution
1 January 1947, amended in 1992, 1994, 1997, and 1999

Structure of government

Political structure
Taiwan's unique political structure consists of a president and vice-president directly elected by popular vote, along with five branches of government (known as yuans): the Executive, Legislative, Judicial, Control and Examination Yuans. There is also a National Assembly, the powers of which have recently been reduced. Taiwan's peculiar international status has meant that it has also had parallel government structures on a 'provincial' level. In 1998 a bill was passed to downsize the provincial government and end its autonomous status.

Executive branch

Chief of state:
President Chen Shui-bien (20 May 2000)
and vice President Annette Lu (since 20
May 2000).

Head of government:
Premier (President of the Executive
Yuan) Chang Chun-hsiung (since NA
October 2000) and Vice Premier (Vice
President of the Executive Yuan) Lai
In-jaw (since NA October 2000).
Cabinet: Executive Yuan appointed by
the president

Legislative branch
Unicameral Legislative Yuan
(225 seats – 168 elected by popular
vote, 41 elected on the basis of the
proportion of nationwide votes received
by participating political parties, eight
elected from overseas Chinese
constituencies on the basis of the
proportion of nationwide votes received
by participating political parties, eight
elected by popular vote among the
aboriginal populations; members
serve three-year terms) and
unicameral National Assembly
(300 seats, note – total number of seats
has been reduced from 334 to 300 since
the last election; members are elected
by proportional representation based
on the election of the Legislative Yuan
and serve four-year terms)

Chiefs of State 2001–02

President
Chen, Shui-bian

Vice President
Lu, Annette

Pres., Executive Yuan (Premier)
Chang, Chun-hsiung

Vice Pres., Executive Yuan (Vice Premier)
Lai, In-jaw

Sec. Gen., Executive Yuan
Chiou, I-jen

Pres., Control Yuan
Chien, Fredrick

Pres., Examination Yuan
Hsu, Shui-the

Pres., Judicial Yuan
Weng, Yueh-sheng

Pres., Legislative Yuan
Wang, Jin-ping

Min. of Economic Affairs
Lin, Hsin-yi

Min. of Education
Tseng, Chih-lang

Min. of Finance
Yen, Ching-chang

Min. of Foreign Affairs
Tien, Hung-mao

Min. of Justice
Chen, Ting-nan

Min. of National Defense
Wu, Shih-wen

Min. of Transportation & Communications
Yeh, Chu-lan

Min. without Portfolio
Chang, Yu-hui

Min. without Portfolio
Chen, Ching-huang

Min. without Portfolio
Hu, Chien-biao

Min. without Portfolio
Huang, Jung-tsun

Min. without Portfolio
Lin, Neng-pai

Min. without Portfolio
Tsay, Ching-yen

Chmn., Aborigines Commission
Youharni, Yisicacafute

Chmn., Agricultural Council
Chen, Hsi-huang

Chmn., Atomic Energy Council
Hsia, Teh-yu

Chmn., Central Election Commission
Huang, Hsih-cheng

Chmn., Consumer Protection
Lai, In-jaw

Chmn., Cultural Affairs
Chen, Yu-hsiu

Chmn., Economic Planning & Devpm. Council
Chen, Po-chih

Chmn., Fair Trade Commission
Chao, Yang-ching

Chmn., Labor Affairs Council
Chen, Chu

Chmn., Mainland Affairs Council
Tsai, Ying-wen

Chmn., Mongolian & Tibetan Affairs Comm.
Hsu, Cheng-kuang

Chmn., National Palace Museum
Tu, Cheng-sheng

Chmn., National Science Council
Weng, Cheng-yi

Chmn., National Youth Commission
Lin, Feng-mei

Chmn., Overseas Chinese Affairs Comm.
Chang, Fu-mei

Chmn., Physical Education & Sports Comm.
Hsu, Hsin-yi

Chmn., Public Construction Commission
Lin, Neng-pai

Chmn., Research Devlpm. & Evaluation Comm.
Lin, Chia-cheng

Chmn., Veterans Affairs Commission
Yang, Te-chih

Sec. Gen. of National Security Council
Chiu, I-jen

Dir. Gen., Budget, Accounting & Statistics
Lin, Chuan

Dir. Gen., Central Personnel Administration
Chu, Wu-hsien

Dir. Gen., Department of Health
Lee, Ming-liang

Dir. Gen., Environmental Protection Adm.
Lin, Chun-yi

Dir. Gen., Government Information Office
Chung, Ching

Dir. Gen., National Police Adm.
Wang, Chin-wang

Governor, Central Bank of China
Perng, Fai-nan

Administrative structure of government

Administrative divisions
Since in the past the authorities claimed to be the government of all China, the central administrative divisions include the provinces of Fu-chien (some 20 offshore islands of Fujian Province including Quemoy and Matsu) and Taiwan (the island of Taiwan and the Pescadores islands); note – the more commonly referenced administrative divisions are those of Taiwan Province – 16 counties (hsien, singular and plural), 5 municipalities* (shih, singular and plural), and 2 special municipalities** (Chuan-Shih, singular and plural); Chang-hua, Chia-i, Chia-i*, Chi-lung*, Hsin-chu, Hsin-chu*, Hua-lien, I-lan, Kao-hsiung, Kao-hsiung**, Miao-li, Nan-t'ou, P'eng-hu, P'ing-tung, T'ai-chung, T'ai-chung*, T'ai-nan, T'ai-nan*, T'ai-pei, T'ai-pei**, T'ai-tung, T'ao-yuan, and Yun-lin; the provincial capital is at Chung-hsing-hsin-ts'un
Note: Taiwan uses the Wade-Giles system for romanization

Main governing parties and ideological affiliation
The Democratic Progressive Party (DPP). Perhaps what most distinguishes the DPP from the three other major parties is its tendency to Taiwan independence, or the permanent political separation of Taiwan from China

Main opposition parties
The Kuomintang, the New Party, the Green Party, the People First Party, the Taiwan Solidarity Union

International memberships
APEC, AsDB, BCIE, ICC, ICFTU, IFRCS, IOC, WCL, and WTO

Armed forces

Divisions in the armed forces
Army, Navy (including Marines), Air Force, Coastal Patrol and Defence Command, Armed Forces Reserve Command, Combined Services Forces

Number of uniformed soldiers
(Males aged 15–49): 6,575,689 (2001 est.)

Percentage of GDP devoted to defense
2.8% (FY1998/99)

Social statistics

Population size
22,191,087

Fertility rate (average number of children born to women 15–49 years of age)
1.76

Infant mortality rate (deaths per 1,000 births)
7.06

Population growth
8.3% (2000), 10.5% (2001)

Life expectancy
76.35
Men: 73.62
Women: 79.32

Ethnic composition
Taiwanese (including Hakka) 84%, Mainland Chinese 14%, Indigenous 2%

Religion
Mixture of Buddhism, Confucianism, Taoism 93%, Christian 4.5%, Other 2.5%

National languages spoken
Mandarin Chinese (Official), Taiwanese, Hakka dialects

Illiteracy rate (age 15+)
Total population: 14% (1980 est.); note – illiteracy for the total population has reportedly decreased to 6% (1998 est.)

By Gender
Male: 7% (1980 est.)
Female: 21% (1980 est.)

Thailand

12 Thailand

Darryl S.L. Jarvis

Section A Economy

Overview

The most significant development in Thailand in 2001–02 has been the election of a new government headed by the charismatic businessman and multimillionaire, Thaksin Shinawatra. The election victory was substantial, backed by a large cross-section of Thai society and supported fully by the business community.

The Thaksin administration has been quick to announce new policy directions, signaling a more engaged economic agenda and promising to move Thailand beyond the financial and economic malaise of the post-crisis years. Restoring business confidence, bolstering domestic demand, and providing government fiscal stimulus to the economy are at the heart of the government's economic planning.

Aware of the need for domestic financial reform and restructuring, the new administration has also announced the introduction of a new Thai Asset Management Corporation (TAMC) to help the banking sector restructure non-performing loans (NPLs) and kick-start growth in new bank lending.

The government has also indicated its intentions to work toward a reduction of current interest rate spreads (the difference between the interest banks pay on deposits and interest charged on loans), inject new government spending into rural development (cash grants of B1 million to some 70,000 rural villages) and national infrastructure projects, initiate a new national health system, develop a US$2.19 billion education bond system, provide tax incentives for local business, and increase civil service pay rates.

The spate of new government spending will obviously have deleterious effects on the government's fiscal position, particularly in view of economic slowdown, diminished export performance, increasing external debt and capital outflows, climbing inflation and a falling Thai baht. Meeting popular expectations in a less than robust economic climate will prove increasingly difficult for the new administration during 2003–04.

Most observers, however, are skeptical about the administration's commitment to, and capacity to implement, the reform process. Thailand remains entrapped within a cumbersome bureaucratic system that, by and large, is unresponsive to business and economic pressures. Government reforms to increase the bureaucracy's responsiveness to business needs and reduce the constraints on commercial start-ups and operational effectiveness, will not be realized any time soon. More obviously, many of the government's newly announced spending plans must also be viewed with suspicion, especially since the government's fiscal options will narrow as the fallout of the economic slowdown takes hold.

Potential investors should therefore be cautious, particularly those bidding on national infrastructure projects. Many of these might well be terminated prior to contractual completion, exposing commercial ventures to extensive liabilities.

Growing risks to foreign investment?

More alarming for foreign investors have been Prime Minister Thaksin's overtures of a likely return to protectionism. This will jeopardize future international investment and pose increased risk for international companies currently operating in the Thai economy. The sudden change in policy direction and growing willingness to protect local business from global competition, appears to be modeled on Malaysia's trend of initiating greater control over foreign access and softening the IMF reform recommendations. In the financial sector, for example, the Bank of Thailand's Deputy Governor, Pakorn Malakul Na Ayudhay, has indicated that new measures to defend the Thai baht will be introduced. This might indicate a movement away from the partial capital control measures currently in place to full-blown capital control measures similar to those adopted in Malaysia.

Protectionist sentiments combined with growing levels of public debt, currently standing at almost 60 percent of GDP and likely to blow out to 80 percent with proposed new government spending, would certainly see currency traders short the baht and cause devaluation. Asset and profit redemption is thus at increasing risk if government policy goes protectionist and public debt blows out.

The bottom line: Vigilance, surveillance, caution

Increased investor caution, greater emphasis on feasibility studies, risk analysis and monitoring, along with well-developed risk management and exit strategies will be necessary to manage investment indemnity and secure returns. Risks to operational effectiveness might also face increased impairment as a result of growing protectionist sentiments and stricter licensing and bureaucratic controls.

Section B Risks and projections

Macroeconomic performance and risk indicators

- The economy is stagnant, domestic consumption has fallen, and the slowdown in the US economy is having knock-on effects for the Thai export sector. Attractive investment opportunities catering to domestic market or export ventures are diminishing. Market risk is increasing. Prospects for 2003–04 look marginally better with the anticipated upturn in the US economy. However, this will take time to trickle down and help improve Thai economic performance that, for 2003, is projected to stand at around 2.5–3 percent of GDP growth.

The Thai economy continues to record positive growth rates despite increasing external risks associated with the slowdown in the US economy, fallout from the events of September 11, and continued malaise in the Japanese economy. The revised GDP growth rate for 2002 of 2.5 percent[1] indicates only a nominal improvement on GDP growth for 2001 recorded at 1.8 percent. More generally, the flow-on effects that a slowdown in the US economy represents for Thailand's major export partners (Japan, Singapore, Hong Kong), will further compound external threats, constraining the Thai export sector during 2003, with negative implications for net foreign receipts, employment levels, tax revenues, and the fiscal position of the administration.

Domestic consumption is also slowing with private consumption down more than 5 percent during 2002 (year-on-year). A contracting labor market, declines in farm income, and a dramatic reduction in public construction investment have seen total fixed investment fall from 23 percent for the first half of 2000 to a mere 0.6 percent in 2002. Forward indications also show a dramatic slowdown in the rate of new bank lending despite low interest rates and ample bank liquidity. Little improvement is expected during 2003–04.

There is likely to be an overall contraction in the manufacturing, retail, textile, and intermediate goods sector in 2002–03, albeit within a positive growth environment. Housing and office construction will remain depressed, and national infrastructure construction will suffer from increasing fiscal constraints and the declining fortunes of the Thai baht. The retail and consumer durables sector will generally see a softening in margins and volumes, reflecting a contraction in domestic demand. Tourism, auto assembly and the pharmaceutical sectors will continue to out-perform the rest of the economy.

Export performance

- The export sector has been exposed to declining external demand and longer-term structural changes associated with increased external competition. Year-on-year, exports are down 10 percent. Little discernible benefit from a depreciated baht appears to have transpired. Performance in this sector will remain volatile and dependent on the fortunes of the US technology sector.

While export growth has been the main vehicle propelling Thailand's post-crisis economic recovery, the fragility of the sector has been revealed with trade data that show a B400 million deficit (a 12 percent reduction on figures for January 2000 and the first trade deficit since August 1997), with similar figures repeated for 2001 and 2002.[2] This is important since exports account for 65 percent of Thailand's GDP, with just two countries, the United States and Japan, absorbing 40 percent of Thai exports. Thailand is thus highly sensitive to changes in external demand, and particularly vulnerable to the fortunes of the US and Japanese economies.[3]

> While export volumes have generally risen in the wake of the financial crisis, prices for Asian exports have contracted by 20 percent across the region. Thailand is having to export more just to stand still. Real growth via the export sector will thus become harder unless export values can be increased.

Most at risk have been electronics and computer parts exports which account for 30 percent of Thailand's total export profile. Thailand, like Singapore, Malaysia, and the Philippines, has been one of Asia's chief beneficiaries of the recent IT boom. However, the downturn in demand, principally from the US, is ominous. The price of the industry's standard 64 megabyte random access memory chip, for example, is down 60 percent to levels that are now barely above breakeven point. Industry over-capacity and continued reductions in US and Japanese demand for electronic and computer equipment will thus have prolonged implications for Thai export performance and foreign exchange earnings.

There are also growing indications that the Thai textile industry (traditionally one of the largest employers of non-skilled labor) is undergoing a longer-term structural contraction associated with increased competition from new low-cost market entrants (Vietnam, Bangladesh, Pakistan and China). Similarly, homewares (ceramics, pottery, cutlery, home display items, etc.) previously heavily sourced by US and European chain stores and export-import consortiums, are now increasingly sourced from lower-cost countries like the Philippines, Vietnam and China. Sustained longer-term contraction in both these sectors will have severe employment implications unless movement toward higher value-added processing or service industries can be developed. This, however, is not likely for the foreseeable future due to Thailand's poor education and knowledge infrastructure, and the non-development of secondary financial markets able to offer advanced financial services to Asian economies.

Rapid downsizing in these sectors has been temporarily mitigated by the depreciation of the Thai baht, currently trading at levels against the US dollar not seen since the Asian financial crisis of October 1997 (B45.00). A medium- to longer-term improvement in the Thai baht, or at least a return to less depressed levels, will see a resumption of accelerated decline in these sectors and a loss of international competitiveness.

Foreign direct investment that takes advantage of cheaper asset acquisition, start-up costs and re-export opportunities provided by a low baht currently face the lowest risks. These include sectors like pharmaceuticals, auto and electronic goods assembly, intermediate valued-added goods processing and re-export ventures.

Currency movements and projections

- Asset redemption and profit repatriation will be placed at heightened risk because of the continued poor performance of the Thai baht. On the upside, domestic asset/equity acquisition has never been cheaper, with the Thai baht continuing to hover around levels not seen since the height of the financial crisis.

Of more immediate concern for foreign holders of Thai assets has been deterioration in the value of the Thai baht, already down 15 percent since the beginning of 2000 (and still trading some 33 percent down on its pre-crisis average), but as of late 2002 it has been showing some upward momentum. Continued low real interest rates, slower economic growth, increasing central government debt, and high levels of capital outflows will conspire to maintain a depressed Thai baht (projected ratios between US$1=B40.00–48.00) for the short to medium term.

> The Thai baht is trading downwards around levels not seen since the financial crisis of 1997 – moderate pick-up can be expected in 2003–04.

Also impacting the fortunes of the Thai baht are regional currency trends, particularly the Japanese yen, also suffering relative depreciation as a consequence of investor flight to lower risk, quality equities/bonds in the United States. This has meant overall lower demand for Asian currencies. This trend is not likely to be reversed in the short to medium term, although there are tentative signs that the US dollar might finally be trading downwards with fears about the ability of the US economy to maintain positive recovery during 2003–04.

Recent concerns about Thailand's political stability, especially the indictment and then acquittal of Prime Minister Thaksin on allegations alleging concealment of asset holdings, also depressed confidence in the Thai baht, tending to spook capital and currency markets. Similarly, the recent series of Muslim separatist bombings (probably attributable to either Pattani United Liberation Organization [Pulo] and/or Barisan Revousi Nasional [BRN]) on civilian targets in the south (Songkhla and Yala), along with on-going tensions and firefights with Myanmar rebels on the Thai–Myanmar border, will only add to international investor fears about Thailand's stability as an investment destination.

The Thai baht will also suffer from international jitters should the current administration stray from the IMF-initiated reform process. Statements by Prime Minister Thaksin, for example, blaming commitments to certain international standards for Thailand's financial woes, as well as remarks in an opening address to the Economic Commission for Asia and the Pacific about 'looking inwards,' signal a softening commitment to continue with financial sector reform, banking sector rationalization, greater financial transparency and disclosure laws, and chapter 11 type bankruptcy procedures. Should the economic and/or political predicament of the government deteriorate significantly, increasing pressures to pursue more inward, self-reliant policy directions would have severe implications for international confidence in the Thai baht.

Perhaps the greatest, longer-term structural predicament the Thai baht faces is the continued interest in China, especially with the trading opportunities that will arise as a result of China's entry into the World Trade Organization (WTO). China already accounts for 50 percent of all foreign direct investment into Asia; a figure that will likely increase in the near future. Demand for the Thai baht, along with other regional currencies, will likely remain depressed for the short to medium term and result in continuing soft valuations. Much like Vietnam, Thailand is in danger of being overshadowed as international investors look toward emergent investment opportunities and lower start-up cost structures in China.

Financial markets: Performance and developments

• The financial sector remains weak, vulnerable to high levels of NPLs, poor compliance measures, and a less than stellar performance by the Bank of Thailand (BOT) in terms of regulation and monitoring. Interest rate spreads remain high, bank lending low, and under-capitalization endemic to most banks. Poor provisioning levels for NPL write-downs, BOT tolerance for bank over-valuations of asset holdings, and an arcane accounting standard that allows banks to use backward looking assumptions in provisioning for NPLs, spells high risk for any potential investor.

Thailand's financial markets are still suffering from the fallout of the financial crisis, as well as trepidation associated with the attacks of September 11. Unfortunately, despite repeated governmental announcements concerning 'restructuring,' there is little discernible evidence of substantial progress. Indeed, the poor state of Thailand's financial system is threatening government attempts to pump-prime the economy through a combination of fiscal stimulus, tax concessions, and new government spending programs (education, health, rural development). However, no amount of fiscal stimulus will be able to compensate adequately for poor credit growth and the ongoing malaise in new bank lending. Liquidity in private banks, for example, still exceeds 16 percent of total assets, indicating poor loan demand.

At the root of the problem is the level of NPLs. These are slowly falling from a high of 47.7 percent in 1999, to just on 32 percent or about 22 percent of Thailand's GDP (including those moved to various asset management companies) in 2001–02.[4] However, a more accurate picture of the health of Thailand's banking system is probably gained by looking at total non-performing assets (NPAs), which add NPLs to restructured loans and foreclosed properties. NPAs stand at almost 50 percent of total bank loans plus foreclosed properties. In other words, half of all bank assets are non-performing and will eventually require write-down.

Also of concern is poor banking compliance enforcement and lax BOT monitoring protocols that have seen most bank loans not restructured at all but simply 'rescheduled' (term extension with little net present value reduction). Thus, any continued downturn in the economy will likely see a large portion of these rescheduled loans re-enter bank ledgers in the NPL category as bank grace periods expire and business cash flows contract.

> Restructured debts that relapse back into NPLs are occurring at the rate of 18 billion baht per month in 2001–02. Only a marked pick-up in economic activity during 2003–04 will help alleviate this problem.

Unfortunately for the Thai economy, the endemic problem of NPAs has a direct bearing on growth in new bank lending and credit creation. Interest rate spreads, for example, have remained stubbornly high despite BOT prodding for a reduction on lending margins. Deposit rates, for instance, have dropped to 1.75–2 percent, while medium and long-term loan rates run at 7.5 percent. Banks are using these spreads to help fund NPLs and maintain liquidity levels. The effect, however, is to dampen new bank lending because of the relatively high cost of borrowing money and depress net foreign capital inflow because of low deposit rates and poor bank profits.[5] Government stimulus measures have thus been thwarted and will remain so until a resolution to the NPL problem is achieved.

Few commentators are expecting this to happen any time soon. Some 70 percent of the value of NPLs (some US$50 billion) are concentrated in the corporate sector, representing some of Thailand's largest and most significant corporations who dominate in manufacturing, real estate, wholesale and retail businesses.[6] Restructuring is thus politically sensitive and will involve significant corporate re-engineering, employment downsizing and write-downs, each with far-reaching implications for the performance of the Thai economy. The health of the financial sector is thus tied intimately to the corporate sector, and poorly managed NPL restructuring (orchestrated through the TAMC) could well serve to act like a strong wind on a fragile house of cards.

> Recent surveys suggest that one-third of Thailand's bad loans are now in default because of 'strategic non-repayment.' Despite the fact that loan holders have cash assets, they are refusing to service their debt.

On the upside, the dearth of new bank lending has forced the development of small, secondary financial markets, especially for debt. Reluctant to lend because of high NPL ratios, banks have tended to place growing portions of their liquidity in government and corporate bonds. Likewise, the dearth of domestic capital sources and trepidation to source foreign capital has seen an exponential growth in bond issues by the corporate and governmental sectors. In 1997, for example, government bond issues amounted to some B300 billion but had grown to B1 trillion in 2000. Similarly, corporate bond issues have risen from B200 billion to over B600 billion in the last four years.

But the debt market is fragile and its health rests on how NPL restructuring proceeds relative to growth in new bank lending. If the newly formed TAMC moves too quickly and rapidly absorbs commercial bank NPLs, this could cause a collapse in the bond markets as banks redeem paper debt and move liquidity back into new bank lending.[7] Either way, the financial sector is doomed to a prolonged period of painful restructuring and uncertainty. Any potential investor is well advised to be risk tolerant before entering the market.

> Debt restructuring will not proceed quickly. Only 29 percent of business operators are financially secure enough to go through the process.

The bottom line: Not the time to invest

Despite net losses for the commercial banking sector that in 2001–02 will hover around 86 billion baht, prudential regulation remains weak and reform is slow in coming. All this does not bode well for international investor confidence.[8] As a destination for foreign capital investment, the Thai financial sector has little appeal, with bank balance sheets telling only half the story. Accounting procedures are arcane, meaningful restructuring only half begun, and the small secondary markets that exist are fragile and could easily collapse if NPL problems are not handled carefully.

As a recent World Bank study noted, before foreign private capital will again be attracted to invest in Thai banks, a compelling story will have to be written. Among other things, this will have to include 'full loss recognition on bank balance sheets such that investors can understand what they are buying.'[9] As it presently stands, investing in financial institutions and most financial markets in Thailand means investing blind. Now is not the time to be investing in Thai banks and derivative secondary markets.

Domestic sourcing of capital: A better option?

Good quality foreign business will have few troubles in raising domestic capital in Thailand. But is it worth the effort? Newly announced measures appear to be creating greater administrative and bureaucratic hurdles, suggesting that domestic sourcing of start-up and venture capital by foreign enterprises will face growing uphill battles and increasing compliance measures despite excess bank liquidity.

Foreign borrowings greater than 50 million baht (about US$1.04 million), for example, are required to show proof of underlying commercial transactions and require BOT approval. Inter-bank transactions/settlements are slow and open to abuse. In December 2000, for instance, the BOT was forced to bring Thailand's entire payment system to a halt for a day when it was discovered a rogue trader was making false baht-denominated transactions. The bottom line is that financing and borrowing transactions for foreign corporations in Thailand are increasingly cumbersome. If the protectionist tide grows stronger, which looks increasingly likely, there will be more obstacles in the near future.

Private and public debt: risks ahead[10]

- Central government debt is exploding. With economic growth stagnant, financial markets have real fears about Thailand's debt servicing and pay-down abilities. New government spending will only exacerbate the problem. Expect ratings agencies downgrades unless the situation is reversed. Sovereign bonds will be attracting higher yields as risk increases.

Public sector debt is emerging as one of the key crisis indicators for the Thaksin administration, which is acutely aware that international capital markets are increasingly sensitive to Thailand's climbing debt levels. Since 1996, public debt has risen sharply and currently stands at around 60 percent of GDP or 2.9 trillion baht. In the past four years alone, government debt has more than doubled, with forward estimates suggesting a likely blowout in this figure to around 80 percent of GDP as the economy remains stagnant and government spending increases.

Debt pay-down is also looking unlikely with Prime Minister Thaksin forced to acknowledge in a recent statement that 'debt servicing will be for interest payments' with substantially less devoted to 'principal repayment.'[11]

> Central government debt stood at 15 percent of GDP in 1997. That figure has now blown out to 60 percent and is still rising.

Capital markets will obviously be tested in 2003–04 for their risk tolerance as the government stimulus package attempts to pump-prime the economy and spur growth through public sector debt. The risk, however, is that should the stimulus package fail to push GDP growth to 5.5 percent then the level of public debt will be fiscally unsustainable. Asian Development Bank growth estimates for Thailand in 2003–04, however, have already been revised down to 3 percent.[12] This, combined with the fact that real interest rates are now exceeding the economy's underlying growth rate, mean that the fiscal options of the central government will be severely restricted.

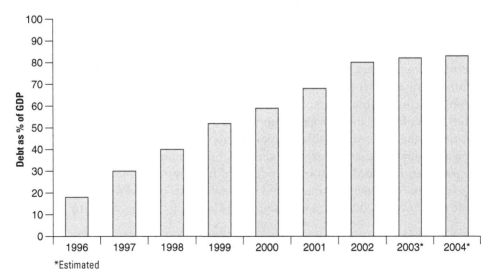

*Estimated

FIGURE 12.1 Debt as percentage of GDP, Thailand 1996–2004
Source: World Bank, Thai Public Debt Management Office

Also of concern are the on-going problems being experienced by the Financial Institutions Development Fund (FIDF), established in the wake of the financial crisis to help ensure commercial bank solvency. Initially costed as some 500 billion baht, the fund is now indebted to the tune of 1.6 trillion baht. The fiscal burden on the Thai taxpayer will be enormous, with Prime Minister Thaksin forced to publicly flag the situation in his recent address to the nation.[13]

If no action is taken to reverse these underlying problems, Thailand is likely to be hit with a series of ratings downgrades that will add a further burden to international debt servicing.

On the upside, total external debt has declined, reflecting an improvement in private external debt due to improved economic conditions in the aftermath of the financial crisis. Short-term private debt, in particular, has tended to be paid down. As of 2001, total external debt stood at around US$78 billion, down from US$80.2 billion in 2000, and US$95.6 billion in 1999.

Sovereign bond issues by the Bank of Thailand and central government will pose increased risks for international investors. Bond issues by public utilities and central government authorities should be evaluated with caution. Ratings downgrades can be expected if the level of public debt continues to blow out.

Labor market trends

- The unskilled labor market is soft. Wage rates are stable but will tend to soften with the persistence of sluggish economic conditions. Much will depend on the length of the US slowdown and the knock-on effects in the export sector. Skilled labor shortages remain acute, with foreign sourcing of skilled labor routine. Moderate employment improvement can be expected if the US economy trends upwards in 2003–04 and export growth is reinvigorated.

The labor market remains soft, with official unemployment levels running at around 4 to 4.5 percent, down from 6.1 percent in 1998 and 5.9 percent in 1999. Despite the downward trend, official unemployment figures do not reveal the extent of labor force underutilization, principally from low reportage and high underemployment.

Most of Thailand's labor force is comprised of unskilled labor, with rural–urban migration providing the majority of this. Unskilled labor has traditionally been absorbed in labor-intensive, low value-added export industries that boomed prior to the financial crisis – textiles, footwear, intermediate goods production, homewares, handicrafts, assembly, etc. Strong post-crisis export performance served to absorb much of this labor, but with a general economic slowdown in 2001–02, a softening in the labor market has been apparent.

Unskilled labor: A buyer's market?

Foreign investment geared to domestic employment and procurement of unskilled labor should experience few problems with adequate labor provisioning during 2003–04. Wage

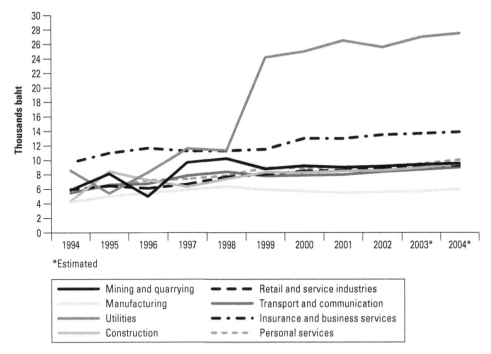

FIGURE 12.2 Average monthly income, Thailand 1994–2004
Source: International Labor Office

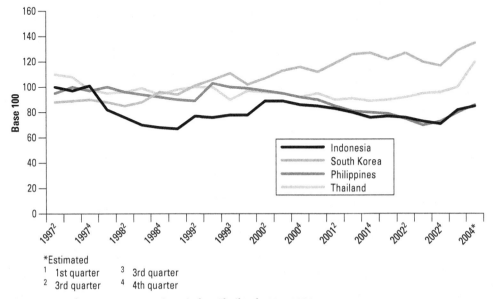

FIGURE 12.3 Real wage rate comparison index, Thailand 1997–2004
Source: Asian Development Bank, Asia Recovery Report, March 2001

labor rates will remain stable and possibly soften in the very short term. A moderate improvement in the export sector and pick-up in the US economy during 2003–04 might exert moderate upward pressure on wage rates, but this will come only after export demand has fed through to the Thai economy. Labor demand during early 2002–03 should remain flat.

Potential employers should be aware, however, that the unskilled labor market in Thailand is finite. Labor shortages during the pre-crisis boom years saw upward pressure on wage rates and an inflationary spiral. The real wage trend over the last seven years has been upwards, largely responsible for the significant decline in competitiveness of the Thai export sector (especially labor intensive sectors like textiles, footwear, homewares, etc.). Start-up ventures in labor-intensive sectors reliant on non-skilled labor thus face a declining competitive environment as real labor costs rise relative to competitor states (Vietnam, China, Indonesia).[14]

Labor laws and corporate downsizing

Foreign business is generally discriminated against when it comes to large scale downsizing, with the Labor and Social Welfare Ministry enacting legislation in 1997 protecting Thai workers against dismissal due to automation or technology-based productivity innovations. Corporate upsizing should thus proceed with a view to the longer term, especially for cyclically sensitive industries. Thailand's cultural norms also make labor retrenchment difficult, with emphasis normally placed on labor reassignment or lateral movement. Surveys of foreign-based employers, for example, reveal significant human resource management problems, and poor margins of maneuverability in terms of dismissal.[15]

Skilled labor shortages

There is an acute skills shortage in Thailand. Poor educational infrastructure and low research productivity have not served the Thai economy well. Secondary school participation rates are particularly low, creating knock-on effects for the tertiary sector. Research innovation has been sparse, and the quality of locally educated PhDs is questionable.

Technical and skill-intensive occupations normally have to be filled by labor importation, creating a large and growing expatriate population (predominantly Bangkok-based). Prospective start-ups or expansion in the service, technology and knowledge-based sectors have been constrained by skilled labor shortages – a problem not likely to be solved any time soon.

Technical sector growth faces similar constraints, with national shortages of suitably qualified personnel in engineering, applied sciences, management sciences, human resources, and technical consulting.

Foreign investment reliant on skilled personnel will invariably be confronted by a tight labor market, and forced to rely on foreign human resource procurement and expatriate labor. Significant time delays and additional start-up costs to procure technical and skilled labor should be appreciated by any foreign enterprise in Thailand.

Consumer and business confidence

• Consumer confidence has shown strong recovery since the financial crisis of 1997, but is again being challenged by continued economic slowdown, employment insecurity, and a soft, unskilled labor market. Business confidence was boosted by the export boom of 1999, but still faces a delayed and protracted period of corporate restructuring. Things could get worse before they get better.

Consumer and business confidence still suffers from the trauma of the financial crisis, and is now haunted by the twin concerns of a poorly performing international economy during 2001–02 and uncertainties in the wake of September 11. Hiring and bank lending practices, as well as business expansion plans have all been negatively affected by poor confidence levels and low business expectations. The robust export market of 1999 went some way to restoring consumer and business confidence, at least in terms of growing expectations about economic turnaround. Again, however, the US slowdown has quashed this, with sluggish economic conditions generally delaying consumer spending until such times as the export sector turns around and a general pick-up in the external environment – especially in the US – is discernible.

    Many of the structural conditions surrounding NPLs also suggest that business confidence will be some time in healing – and may yet face a serious downturn. Many mid- to large-scale corporate businesses still have to deal with their own restructuring and cash management problems. Bank rescheduling has only delayed long-term liquidity problems and issues surrounding corporate downsizing and efficiencies have still not been dealt with.

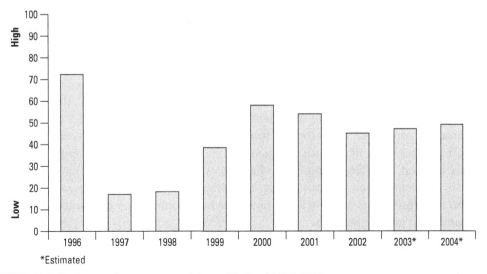

FIGURE 12.4 Business and consumer confidence, Thailand 1996–2004
Source: MasterIndex Consumer Confidence (MasterCard)

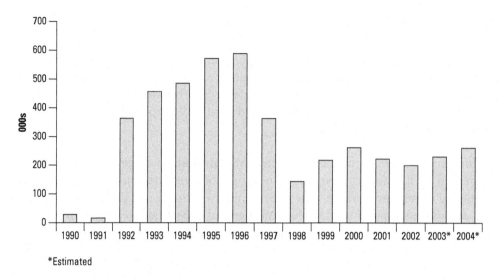

*Estimated

FIGURE 12.5 Total vehicle sales, Thailand 1990–2004
Source: Thailand Automotive Institute

A 2001 Thai Chamber of Commerce survey of senior business executives on the macro-economic outlook for 2002–03 reported a median score of 51.61 (100 signifies normal economic conditions, 200 signifies a boom economy). This represents a gloomy outlook, with respondents pointing out ongoing hindrances to business activity as the major culprits: corruption, government red tape, tough competition, falling prices for agricultural goods, and a poor education system providing poorly qualified employees.[16]

More recently, the MasterCard Consumer MasterIndex for the Asia–Pacific conducted in 2002, showed continued depressed consumer and business confidence, with Thailand the only country in the region to show a marked drop in the index, down to 46.3 (out of 100). Indeed, in all five variables (employment, economy, regular income, stock market, and quality of life) confidence decreased from the previous survey period.[17]

Moderate improvements can be expected during the 2003–04 survey period as a result of improvement in the outlook for the external environment. However, there are not expected to be dramatic changes in sentiment.

Consumer confidence has recovered from the depths of the post-crisis years, but is still tenuous. Big-ticket items like housing are still suffering from dramatic oversupply and low consumer demand. Automobile purchases have rebounded since 1998, but have not recovered to anywhere near their pre-crisis levels. The same is true of white goods, with evidence of general household consumption being postponed due to middling consumer confidence – now running at mid range levels.

Short- to medium-term consumer confidence projections will be contingent on the extent of the economic slowdown and the prospects for a sustained recovery in the US. Again, the events of September 11 have only served to introduce yet more pessimism into business expectations, confirming a generally gloomy business outlook, with consumers steering clear of large consumption items and postponing consumption expenditure. All this bodes ill for the export-sensitive Thai economy. Similarly, employment and income security confidence remain at middling levels and display fragility. Further economic shocks could cause a sharp downturn in confidence and consumer spending levels.

Stock market

- The Stock Exchange of Thailand (SET) lost 50 percent of its value in 2000, regaining 20 percent to the first half of 2001, before enjoying a more significant recovery in 2002. Ongoing concerns about corporate governance and transparency issues, as well as corporate and banking sector reform and capitalization, are keeping investors away from the SET, especially foreign portfolio investment which, prior to the financial crisis, comprised some 40 percent of SET capitalization. Expect moderate turnaround in these conditions during 2003–04.

The SET lost one-half its value during 2000, but through 2002 has improved by around 25 percent, hovering at levels of about 360 on the set composite index. Apart from investor caution post September 11, of major concern holding back investor sentiment has been the underlying structural problems associated with the banking and corporate sector, which accounts for 25 percent of the SET composite index. Fears about slow and inadequate NPL restructuring, and the slowing pace of corporate re-engineering has depressed the SET index.

There are also strong concerns about corporate transparency and governance issues, many of which have yet to be addressed in the wake of the financial crisis. Most analysts predict that downstream corporate downsizing and restructuring will have a deleterious impact on the banking and corporate sector's bottom line, and that earnings downgrades will be inevitable. Much of the fallout from the financial crisis is still to be expressed, posing a longer-term risk for the SET.

The health of the SET will largely rest on the implementation and performance of the Thai Asset Management Company (TAMC) and, in turn, on the realization of significant improvements in the banking and corporate sector's financial health. The prospects for this, however, do not look promising. Recent analysis by Standard and Poors, for example, concluded that the 'AMC concept is not assured' of success, that the problem of corporate sector reform appeared endemic, and that structural problems associated with poor foreclosure, transparency, accounting, and bankruptcy laws might derail any prospective benefits of the TAMC.[18]

While nominal improvement in the SET composite index is indicated, the medium- and longer-term performance of the SET will be tied intimately to reform and governance issues, which, as yet, are not being addressed. Nepotism, price rigging, and corruption issues have featured predominantly in the media, and should send a sharp warning to any prospective investor.

There is also the problem of inadequate capitalization throughout the banking and corporate sector, which poses serious, and in some cases precarious liquidity issues for many institutions. Unfortunately, without sustained and meaningful corporate restructuring, attempts at re-capitalization will be thwarted by a dearth of investor confidence, principally through poor levels of foreign portfolio investment.

Market capitalization might be set for a boost, however, with the newly announced government plan to inject 700 billion baht into the equity market over the next three years. This would involve offering share issues in 18 state enterprises in the hope of fostering renewed interest in Thai equities.

The problem again, however, is the ongoing lack of corporate transparency, poor corporate accounting and reporting procedures, and lack of commitment to corporate restructuring, which will only continue to dampen investor confidence and keep investment away from the equity markets.

Corporate tax: Mixed messages

- The corporate tax rate is likely to be reviewed in the next 12 months, with early indications suggesting a possible reduction. However, for foreign investors, possible changes to the Thai Investment Promotion Act raise concerns about increasing risks and higher establishment/operational costs.

There is mixed speculation about the likelihood of a reduction in the basic corporate tax rate, currently imposed at a flat rate of 30 percent. Government indications have been supportive of speculation that this rate will be reviewed and perhaps reduced as part of the government's stimulus package. Much will depend on the fiscal position of the government vis-à-vis the general economic slowdown and rising government debt. Revenue streams will become increasingly important, especially if the confidence of capital markets is to be maintained in light of the emergent debt crisis.

For international investors, of most concern should be any possible revision of the current Thai Investment Promotion Act (1977; 2000)[19] – particularly in view of the turn towards protectionist measures. The Act currently provides latitude for corporate income tax reduction/exemption (fixed time periods), exemption of import duty on investment inputs and establishment expenditure, as well as a series of generous deductions on infrastructure facilities.

Investment establishment risks will increase with any adverse revisions to the Act. Again, concern over government revenue streams might be the trigger to revising the Act, particularly since the government is tending to take a dim view of much of the foreign direct investment (FDI) arriving in Thailand due to its predominantly low value-adding nature.

Value added at every stage of production is subject to Value Added Tax (VAT), leveled at 10 percent. During the period from 1 April 1999 to 30 September 2001, this was reduced to 7 percent. There are some indications this might be reinstated subject to revenues and the government's desire to stimulate economic activity.[20]

Trepidation should be the first rule for prospective investors, or project deferral until clarification about the Act and government attitudes have emerged. No discernible conclusions can be drawn currently.

Residential and commercial property markets

- The residential and commercial property sector was decimated by the financial crisis, with banks still holding extensive non-performing property assets. While the property market has now bottomed out, recovery is still at the tentative stage. For risk tolerant investors, there are still a great many bargains to be had, especially in view of the depreciated Thai baht that has discounted costs for asset acquisition. Caution is warranted, however, in the case of building quality and construction adequacy.

Residential and commercial property developments came to a virtual standstill in the immediate aftermath of the crisis. In no other sector was the trauma of the crisis so acutely felt, with pre-crisis speculation pushing property prices and new construction to unsustainable levels. Property prices subsequently tumbled and still remain well below their pre-crisis levels, with investors badly hurt and confidence in the sector shattered. Many of the NPLs derive from the crash in the property market, and their continued under-performance has debilitated meaningful restructuring other than through asset write-downs.

However, there are signs of a tentative recovery in the property market, spurred on by low interest rates and new government incentives. Year-on-year, the unsold supply of houses and condominiums has reduced, currently standing at 13,277 (detached houses and townhouses), and approximately a 20 percent unsold/vacancy rate for downtown condominiums.[21]

Vacancy rates for downtown condominiums

1998	1999	2000	2002
50 %	32 %	20 %	18 %

Source: Colliers Jardine/CB Richard Ellis (Thailand) Co.

The luxury condominium market has rebounded with occupancy rates for high-end quality developments reaching 90 percent in 2001–02 compared to 87 percent in the last quarter of 2000. This trend can be expected to continue, subject to economic conditions remaining relatively stable.

Helping the residential market has been the hefty reduction in property fees and taxes under the previous government, and the recently announced assistance packages under the Thaksin administration. Under this program, civil servants and those from lower income brackets can claim a tax allowance of up to B100,000 (US$2,500) spent on buying housing over the next two years (2001–03). More recently, the Government Housing Bank also introduced a new financing package providing 100 percent of the property's collateral value to new borrowers.[22]

On the downside, an increase in housing prices by home builders of between 5 and 10 percent during 2001–02, will likely dampen demand despite lower interest rates. More importantly, bank reluctance to deepen its exposure in the property market means few financing options for prospective buyers and a shortage of liquidity. Growth in this sector will thus be positive but not robust in 2003–04.[23]

The commercial property market is improving

Office and commercial developments have also fared better in 2001–02, bottoming out in 2000. The overall year-end vacancy rate for all grades of offices in Bangkok fell to 35 percent. This is expected to continue to drop into 2002–03 with commensurate increases in rental values. For 2002–03, premium office rental space is expected to increase from US$8 to US$10 per square meter per month, while grade-A office space is projected to increase from US$7 to US$9 per square meter per month.

Little large-scale office construction is anticipated, principally due to financing difficulties and bank reluctance to further property asset exposure.

Hotel property sector: A success story?

Hotel real estate has fared relatively well in the wake of the crisis, with the fall in the baht making Thailand a cheap international tourist destination. Tourism has been one of the few growth areas in the Thai economy and, as a result, hotel occupancy rates have been moderate to good, providing a valuable cash flow to investors in an otherwise crisis-prone economy.

The spate of hotel fire sales anticipated in the wake of the crisis has consequently not materialized. A very proactive Thai Tourism Authority and aggressive international marketing strategies, have provided Thailand with a growing supply of tourists, responsible for about 7 percent of GDP. However, despite an anticipated 7–8 percent growth in tourist arrivals in 2002, the trend during 2000–02 has been growing tourist numbers but decreasing tourist revenues, down 2–3 percent. The revenue prospects for the hotel sector thus look mixed, with average tourist spending declining, suggesting increased price sensitivity to hotel accommodation rates.[24]

The black spot on all this, of course, is the severe drop off in tourist arrivals following the events of September 11. Japanese tourist arrivals, for example, traditionally one of the larger markets for Thailand, dropped precipitously in the months of September, October and November 2001, but have since recovered in 2002.[25] Similar declines in tourist arrivals from destinations such as the United States, Canada, Britain and Germany, have also been evident. This trend has been reversed, however, with increased Asian tourism into Thailand, offsetting the fallout from the events of September 11. Clever marketing strategies by the Tourism Authority of Thailand, promoting Thailand as a safe international destination, have seen international tourist arrivals hit the 10 million mark in 2001–02. Nonetheless, the fact remains that Thai tourist arrivals tend to be from markets with less disposable income, with consequent declines in overall revenues from tourism. The effect on returns on hotel property investments can thus be expected to decline in the immediate short term unless tourist arrivals from prime markets like the United States and Western Europe can be secured. Moderate increases from such markets can be expected assuming there are no further international shocks in 2003–04.

While greater pressure will be exerted on the bottom line of the hotel sector, causing some softening in hotel property prices, these can be expected to stabilize in the intermediate to longer term. On the upside, Thailand has been recently ranked by hotel owners and investors as the fourth most preferred market in Asia (behind Singapore, Hong Kong and Seoul), providing some longer-term prospects for income growth in the sector.

Foreign direct investment

- As a leading indicator of domestic market opportunities and international investor confidence, FDI has proven fickle in the case of Thailand, with institutional investors looking elsewhere for quality equities and higher returns, and domestically orientated FDI becoming jittery over production bottleneck problems and protectionist sentiment. The downward trend in FDI suggests investors are sensing increasing risks, contracting investment opportunities, and better investment markets elsewhere in the region.

FDI has been one of the main vehicles propelling the Thai economy throughout the 1990s. Capital flows, however, have been spotty, influenced strongly by wild gyrations in the domestic fortunes of the Thai economy and frequent jolts to political stability. International business confidence has thus been confronted with a less than stable environment, requiring ongoing monitoring and reappraisal as economic and political conditions change sporadically.

Business investment decisions informed by aggregate FDI data and used as an indicator of international investor confidence and growth trends, should be viewed with suspicion. There are two reasons for this. First, official FDI figures tend to be inflated, and used as a political tool to advance investor confidence and bolster capital inflows.[26] Second, raw FDI data, as with the upward spike in FDI in 1998 (below), does not reveal longer-term trends.

Private capital flows into the Asia–Pacific will fall by nearly 20 percent for 2001–02.[27]

Rather, the 1998 FDI spike was a result of the washout of the financial crisis, especially the dramatic fall in the value of the baht, which made for unusually favorable market conditions. International investors responded to discounted asset acquisition costs and low production costs, almost doubling the level of FDI in 1998 year-on-year.

Short-term shocks aside, the current trend in FDI has been downward, and should serve as an ominous sign to both international investors and Thailand. Thailand is viewed, increasingly, as a less attractive destination for international investment, with risks to capital flows stemming from four principal areas:

1 Lack of corporate and financial sector reform
2 Movement toward protectionism
3 Infrastructure and production bottlenecks
4 Increasing relative wage and production costs.

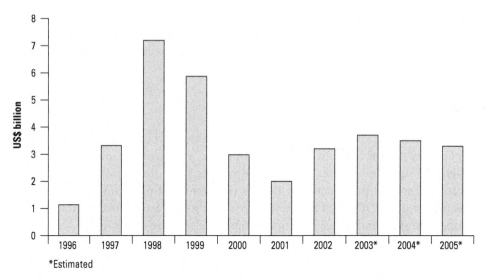

FIGURE 12.6 Net foreign direct investment, Thailand 1996–2004
Source: Bank of Thailand/Asian Development Bank

Unfortunately, the current administration is either not able, or not willing, to speed up the pace of meaningful corporate and financial sector reform, other than through the still-to-be-tested TAMC. Likewise, the political disposition of the current administration, and the political whim of voters, is disposed increasingly toward viewing international investors, globalization, and the internationalization of the Thai economy as a negative trend, harmful to economic development. Popular support for protectionist measures is thus gaining momentum, with growing evidence of discrimination against foreign investment in areas where it impacts domestic enterprise (retail, for example).

With the MSCI emerging market index down 31 percent in the past five years, Thailand will have to do considerably more to attract jittery fund managers now looking for quality stock, solid returns, and low risk. At present, most institutional investors are simply looking elsewhere.

Apart from these concerns, the operational effectiveness of domestically oriented foreign investment is also tested by infrastructural and production bottlenecks, problems otherwise effectively tackled in, for example, Singapore and Malaysia, but ongoing in Thailand. The lack of resolution to these problems reflects a less than responsive government environment and an insular commercial acumen that, from survey evidence, makes commercial practices prone to extensive delays, inefficiencies, and production failures. Some of this can be explained by cultural business practices, others by inefficient bureaucratic administrative procedures, and still others by systemic corruption. Whatever the case, all have proven a hindrance to foreign investment and remain so.

The low level of market capitalization in the SET along with poor corporate transparency have also been responsible for Thailand being largely bypassed by institutional investors. The SET's relatively poor composite index performance, corporate insolvency and slow reform, have not helped international investor confidence, with competitor markets offering lower risks and higher returns. Unfortunately, this story is not likely to be reversed in the near future, with SET performance expected to deteriorate due to increasing external risks, continuing over-capacity in the electronic sector, and the slowdown in the US economy.

> Year-on-year, FDI to Thailand in 2001–02 is down 40 percent.

Of particular concern to international investors should be the fact that, despite the recent downward trend of the baht and thus lower asset acquisition and production costs, FDI has not spiked as in 1998 but, in fact, shows a 40 percent reduction in 2000–02. The explanation for this is two-fold. First, limited domestic opportunities reflecting sluggish demand and excess manufacturing/production capacity, has subsequently depressed demand for new infrastructural investments. Secondly, there have been increasing disincentives relative to competitor markets, ranging from production/supply bottlenecks, operational issues and problems, and increasing relative costs.[28]

> The urgent need for financial sector reform was reinforced when one of the biggest fund mangers in the US, California Public Employees Retirement System, pulled its investments out of Thailand, citing poor stock market performance, poor transparency, and poor investor protection.[29]

On the positive side, export-oriented FDI that takes advantage of cost discounts associated with a depreciated baht, especially in low value-adding industries, will realize competitive advantages. The problem, however, remains with the government which is increasingly prone to view low value-adding FDI with disdain, and might well become proactive in discouraging such investments in the near future.

Section C Politics

- Thailand's economic performance and corporate health have always been a function of political stability and government policy. Nothing has changed with the election of the Thaksin administration. In fact, this relationship has been reinforced, with evidence of increasing political influence in the country's leading statutory bodies, and economic recovery threatened by the ongoing political machinations surrounding allegations of corruption and concealment by the Prime Minister.

Political stability

Of most concern to outside observers have been the political uncertainties surrounding the indictment, trial, and acquittal of Prime Minister Thaksin over allegations of asset conceal-ment, and the repercussions of this for policy continuity. These fears were not realized, however, with the controversial acquittal of the Prime Minister by a slim majority of the Constitutional Court of eight to seven. Instead, what has been raised by the decision of the Constitutional Court paints to more fundamental concerns about the independence of the courts, and of political interference. Some Senate members have already called for an official inquiry, emblematic of concerns that the outright power of Thaksin is creating undue influence and impropriety in the institutional bodies responsible for transparent and impar-tial governance of the Thai economy.

Indeed, this is what should most concern international observers; the extensive and growing political influence of the current administration and extensive popular support enjoyed by Thai Rak Thai are tending to harm the independence of statutory bodies, creating a system of entrenched patronage politics, political appointees, and 'favorite friends,' with implications for the level and extent of soft corruption in political decision-making, awarding of government contracts and business dealings.

The sacking of Mr. Chatu Mongkol Sonakul, Governor of the Bank of Thailand, for example, signals the politicization of the bank. The new appointee, Mr. Pridiyathorn Devakula was hand-selected by Prime Minister Thaksin. BOT independence in determining monetary policy has thus been usurped, signaling a return to older-style Thai politics and a step back from the spirit and intent of the IMF reform recommendations for robust, inde-pendent monetary authorities free of political interference.

Protectionism

Of more concern is the outright predominance of Thai Rak Thai, which has both fueled and fed off nationalistic sentiment, creating increasingly inward-looking policy directions with detrimental effects for international business and investment. The corollary with the nationalistic style of Malaysian Prime Minister Mahathir Mohamad is obvious, rebuking transparency and accountability as 'Western values' detrimental to national interests, and showing little tolerance for dissent.

Thaksin, for example, when addressing the Federation of Thai Industries, noted Thailand would 'cease being a slave to the world' and that his administration would amend laws that 'work against Thai interests.'[30] This inward turn has been reinforced by Thaksin's 'buy Thai' policy directive to government firms and agencies, which are now required to buy locally produced goods and services in an effort to halt a sliding balance of payments. Simi-larly, a 2001 central policy directive to all ministries placed a freeze on the hiring of foreign nationals and the issuing of consulting contracts to foreign firms. To reinforce the point, the government also announced a ten-fold increase in the cost of work permits for foreign nationals.

Taxing foreign business

Most alarming for operators of foreign commercial interests has been the change in regulatory responsibilities for foreign non-government and foreign not-for-profit organizations from the Department of Technical and Economic Cooperation to the Ministry of Labor. The move has resulted in 'unprecedented tax pressure' being placed on such organizations, with a suggested six-fold increase in tax levels under consideration.[31] While no statements have been issued, the revenue crisis in Thailand is likely to see increasing governmental attempts to find revenues from non-Thai sources as a means of securing increased government expenditure. Increased operating costs are thus a distinct possibility for foreign enterprises.

Corruption

Corruption in Thailand is endemic among governmental officials and the civil service (police, military, statutory authorities, government agencies), due to low wages. A recent survey in Thailand, for example, estimated that at least 20 percent of the state budget (160 billion baht annually) ends up in the hands of corrupt officials.[32] Similarly, the Asian Development Bank estimates that up to 30 percent of government procurement expenditure and public investment in Thailand is lost to graft.[33]

The reformist constitution adopted at the height of the financial crisis in 1997, has gone some way to tackling corruption, principally through the empowerment of the National Commission to Counter Corruption (NCCC). The NCCC has had an immediate impact, notably ending the political career of Major-General Sanan Kachornprasart (former Interior Minister and Democrat Party General Secretary) for graft and corruption, as well as indicting the current Prime Minister on corruption and concealment charges.

However, despite some high-profile successes, there is little evidence of corruption curtailment in the vast majority of the Thai economy and polity. A recent survey of Thai businesses, for example, reported that 79 percent of businesses claimed they had to resort to bribing officials to get results, and that these bribes added roughly 20 percent to start-up and business operating costs.

Corporate fraud and transparency

Corruption and lack of accountability extend to the corporate sector in Thailand. Foreign enterprises are the preferred targets for phantom billing practices, financial misappropriation, and white-collar fraud. Appropriate and frequently reviewed financial auditing and accountability, as well as reviews of risk management practices should be standard practice for foreign enterprises operating in Thailand.

Intellectual property fraud is rampant, and employment confidentiality clauses near worthless as a mechanism to control competitor risk and protect commercially sensitive information. Client lists, strategic plans, marketing strategies, and other commercially sensitive documentation, can be bought from corrupt employees of blue-chip companies for

as little as US$100. Enterprises are strongly advised to seek out professional risk manage-
ment advice to protect commercial information.

Corporate transparency is also lacking, with well-documented cases of fraudulent
reporting practices, stock market manipulation, or restricted 'free floats' of shares by 99 of
the 381 companies listed on the Thailand SET. Restricted free floats involve the SET granting
special provision to selected companies, enabling them to release limited amounts of shares,
often less then 10 percent of their overall market capitalization, creating intense speculation
and driving up share prices.[34] Prospective foreign portfolio investment into the SET should
thus proceed with extreme caution.

The slow pace of corporate reform and strong indications that fallout from the financial crisis in terms of private debt restructuring have still to occur in the majority of Thai
corporations, suggests an immediate short-term future fraught with considerable downside.
Prospective acquisition of Thai enterprises by foreign business should proceed only after the
most thorough due diligence processes have been conducted.

Leading risk indices: Corruption, stability, governance, risk

The seven key indices below indicate a period of volatility and, in some cases, retrogression
– especially in terms of corruption. The overall movement of the indices is toward nominally
increasing risk, poorer transparency, and diminishing central government capacity to govern
due to financial constraints and government failure to deliver promised programs.

Corruption

The corruption index indicates an inverse relationship between economic growth and corruption during 1999–2002, with the current economic downturn and economic hardships

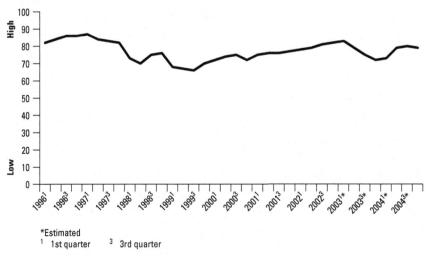

FIGURE 12.7 Corruption index, Thailand 1996–2004
Sources: Transparency International; World Bank; Asian Development Bank; *Bangkok Post; The Nation.*

increasing the likelihood of encountering corruption in business activities (especially soft corruption: pilfering, theft, intellectual property theft, fraudulent activities). The improvement in the corruption index in the immediate aftermath of the financial crisis is attributed to the IMF-sanctioned reform process and good governance measures. This, along with various governance strategies pursued by the World Bank, would now appear to be waning, with the Thaksin administration blaming such measures for Thailand's current economic woes.

On a comparative scale, of the 90 countries ranked Thailand placed in the bottom third at sixtieth place, slightly less corrupt than countries like China, Zimbabwe and Romania.

Stability

While the political stability index suggests mostly continuity, 2003–04 will be tested by popular acceptance or dissatisfaction with the current administration as fiscal limitations restrict government options to deliver pre-election promises. Rural discontent and isolated demonstrations can be expected if the rural development programs are whittled down by Thaksin, or the state-subsidized health system is not delivered and maintained. More important, the state of the economy – especially the government's handling of the debt crisis over the coming years – will determine business confidence toward the administration. This is likely to be tested as economic conditions remain soft, threatening the current administration's capacity to govern and ultimately its electoral stability.

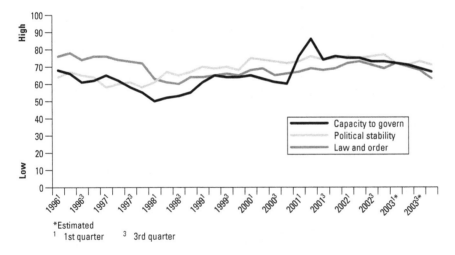

*Estimated
[1] 1st quarter   [3] 3rd quarter

FIGURE 12.8 Political stability index, Thailand 1996–2003

Political stability methodology:
• The capacity-to-govern index is based upon the institutional reach of government defined in terms of its ability to set the political and economic agenda and ensure its legislative program is enacted without significant compromise. This index is adversely affected by legislative opposition, lack of legislative implementation, failure to realize government policy and general political opposition.
• The political stability index measures violent opposition or organized demonstrations, terrorist activities, and popular discontent that adversely affect the institutional and electoral stability of the government.
• The law and order index measures the propensity to civil obedience, and the institutional reach of the rule of law in terms of regulatory compliance and enforcement.

The corporate governance index is also relatively stable, but unfortunately showing no signs of positive increase with much of the fallout from the restructuring process still to occur. Expect short- to medium-term declines in the index, with increasing propensity to poorer governance and transparency until restructuring issues are resolved.

Corporate governance

The foreign investor risk index is showing signs of upward movement, principally as a result of increasing protectionist sentiment, growing evidence of foreign investor discrimination, the distinct possibility of increasing tax regimes for foreign enterprises, and the 'buy Thai' policy and administration directives, which have placed a moratorium on consulting contracts to foreign enterprises. Should the Thaksin administration persist with its inward looking policy initiatives, the index is likely to worsen during 2002–03. Growing investor caution should be practiced. However, there is reason to suppose that improvement can be expected in 2003–04, as the need for foreign capital increases and the administration is forced to modify its external stance.

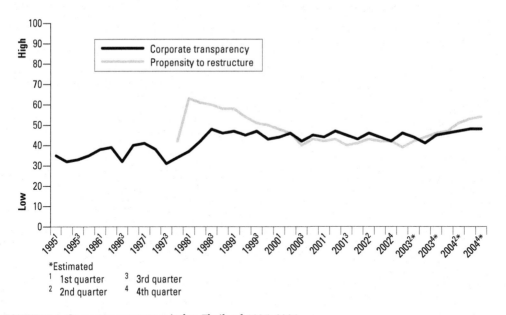

FIGURE 12.9 Corporate governance index, Thailand 1995–2004

Corporate governance index methodology
- The corporate governance index is a composite index measuring the juridical requirements for corporate disclosure and financial reporting, prudential regime adequacy, prudential compliance enforcement, and the juridical reach of prudential authorities.
- The propensity-to-restructure index is a composite index based on media releases and reported corporate restructuring as a result of prudential regulation, financial incentives, loan restructuring/re-negotiation, or asset realignment. In the case of Thailand, it follows closely with the Financial Institutions Development Fund and bank rescheduling practices – and in the future with the newly created TAMC.

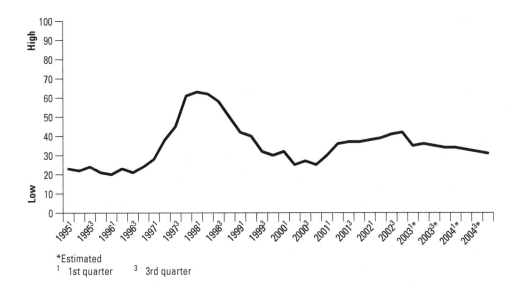

*Estimated
¹ 1st quarter   ³ 3rd quarter

FIGURE 12.10 Foreign investor risk index, Thailand 1995–2004

Foreign investor risk index methodology:
- The foreign investor risk index is a composite index measuring tax burdens, discriminatory regulatory practices, adverse compliance regulations, government policy toward foreign enterprise, receptiveness to issuance of government contracts, foreign enterprise commercial restrictions, and official attitudinal changes to foreign direct investment and foreign commercial operations which impact on operational efficiency. The index also incorporates a nominal measure for market risk and market failure.

Section D Security

- For all the economic risks faced in Thailand, its security situation remains stable. In fact, outside Singapore and Hong Kong, Thailand rates the highest in terms of national and personal security. There are, however, a few problems that, while minor, pose reasons for concern. These should be factored into investment and operational decisions, especially in terms of infrastructure location.

Border problems

The events of September 11 have implications for Thailand as with most other nation-states around the globe. However, they are less pressing than the traditional border problems that have dogged Thailand for the last few decades.

Border tensions, principally with Burma, remain front and center, and have resulted in a series of firefights during 2001–02. Frequent border incursions by Burmese forces pursuing rebel elements have soured Thai–Burma relations and resulted in cancelled senior ministers' meetings. While the Thaksin administration has tended to favor a policy of economic engagement, the frequency of border issues with Burma has slowed prospects for a more interactive relationship and an expansion of trade. However, there are tentative signs that this relationship is warming, with the Thai Foreign Minister, Dr. Surakiart Sathirathai, convening a series of meetings with Burmese officials and promising to begin a process of active engagement. This process will not be easy, however, mainly due to the series of issues that continue to dog the relationship and pose internal security problems for Thai military and paramilitary forces. Cross-border movement of narcotics, for example, along with refugees and illegal labor, have placed considerable pressure on northern border regions, and created extensive illegal networks that undermine any hopes for effective juridical rule in these areas.

Border issues with Laos have tended to be less tense and mainly concerned with trade issues and incidents of goods restriction and confiscation. These are likely to be solved, with Thaksin pursuing a series of negotiations to free up movement of goods between Laos and Thailand.

Internal security

Internal security is mostly stable with only few exceptions. The recent series of bombings in the southern provinces of Songkhla and Yala, while minor in terms of damage, underscore the continuation of Muslim-led separatist movements. These, of course, have become of greater concern with the war against terror, the US bombings of Afghanistan, and Muslim resentment towards the United States and its allies. Importantly, such activities have been confined to mostly rural areas and away from financial and commercial centers with no direct implication for Bangkok, the epicenter of Thailand's economy.

While the Muslim population comprises Thailand's largest religious minority, they tend to be concentrated in the southernmost provinces of Narathiwat, Yala, and Satun, and constitute only some 3.8 percent of the population. Obviously, Thailand, as with other nations, has been forced to reassess its internal security status, increasing surveillance and monitoring of high-risk provinces and certain ethnic/religious minorities. Even before the attacks of September 11, Thai authorities were keen to insure Islamic separatist movements were stamped out, and after the incidents in Songkhla and Yala, embarked upon improved intelligence gathering and a systematic crackdown. There is every reason to suppose this will be largely successful.

Perhaps the most worrying recent trend in Thailand has been the development of business assassination, most often against competitor Thai nationals but more recently also against foreign nationals in Thailand. The recent killing of an Australian auditor, Michael Wansley, for example, was a case in point, particularly since he was involved in the sensitive issues of corporate restructuring. Death threats against foreign auditors and professionals involved in corporate restructuring projects have become more frequent, with the latest involving Mr. Tony Norman, an auditor with the Sydney accounting firm Ferrier Hodgson, engaged by creditor banks to restructure the Thai petrochemical industry. Twenty-four hour bodyguard protection amid numerous death threats and large demonstrations underscore executive safety issues for foreign nationals engaged in the painful process of corporate sector restructuring. All indications suggest these are likely to become more frequent, with the bulk of corporate restructuring still to occur.[35]

Section E Economic and political risk forecasts

- Short- to medium-term risks are increasing in Thailand. As a destination for FDI, Thailand is becoming less attractive with increasing cost disincentives and diminishing domestic market opportunities. Production bottlenecks, a mostly stagnant level of domestic infrastructure, and a predominantly unskilled human resource base with little apparent innovation, limit start-ups and joint ventures to low value-adding export industries. This is increasingly likely to become Thailand's international niche, albeit with the current administration disposed to try and discourage such investment and attract in more high-tech, high value-adding foreign investment. The prospects for this, however, appear bleak in the short term.

Short-term forecasts

- Short-term outlook for the economy is tending downward, with positive GDP growth expected at around 3–3.5 percent in 2003–04, but well below the 7 percent needed to alleviate domestic poverty and provide enough revenues for domestic infrastructure development and debt write-down. Expect debt to increase along with government spending, causing growing concern among international markets about Thailand's debt-servicing abilities and fiscal position.
- Short-term domestically orientated FDI will have diminishing opportunities, with the economy suffering from excess industrial/manufacturing capacity and under-utilization (35 percent).
- The prospects for growing levels of protection and discrimination are already apparent. These are likely to worsen in the short term, especially since Thai Rak Thai sees them as a politically useful tool for electoral support.
- Domestic corporate restructuring is generally being postponed, if not actively avoided, leaving the corporate sector poorly equipped to confront the changing regional circumstances among its competitor states and markets. Little will change in 2003–04.
- Financial sector reform remains stubbornly slow and incomplete. Every indication from the current administration suggests this will continue, especially if there is official disdain for 'international standards' as harmful to Thailand's economic fabric, as currently seems the case.
- The prospects for the privatization of government monopolies and state-owned enterprises (airlines, banks, telecommunications, etc.), while initially foreshadowed under the Thaksin administration, have so far proven fruitless. These look as if they will be more actively contemplated in 2003–04, with indications that the Thai stock market will be privatized.

Short-term opportunities

- The low Thai baht makes asset acquisition attractive, providing substantial discounts for foreign investors. However, regulatory issues and foreign holdings restrictions limit the industry areas where this might be applicable, especially in the case of domestically orientated FDI keen to service Thailand's domestic market. Opportunities thus continue to be largely confined to export-orientated industries, predominantly of a low value-adding category.
- Automobile assembly and re-export is expected to show signs of strong growth, with Volkswagen planning assembly of certain passenger models and Isuzu Motors (49 percent owned by General Motors) planning to transfer its commercial pick-up trucks division from Japan to Thailand for start-up in 2003–04.
- Continued healthy growth is expected in export sectors associated with frozen and canned foods, information technology products, vehicles and parts, tires, pulp and paper, and chemicals and plastics.
- Diminishing opportunities are expected in industry areas reliant on domestic sales, especially in petroleum products, construction, steel products, non-alcoholic drinks and tobacco.
- The computer chip and computer parts sector will undergo fundamental restructuring as a result of the technology downturn in the United States. Competitor risk from Taiwan and South Korea can be expected to marginalize the Thai hi-tech sector which is less equipped to meet the increased competitive challenges ahead.

Medium to longer term

- The competitive position of the Thai economy is set to diminish against the rush toward investment in China and the emergent opportunities provided by China's entry into the WTO. Longer term, unless Thailand can kick-start its economy and recover its dynamic growth, cost competitiveness, and increase its human resource capabilities, then it can expect to see contracting sluggish levels of FDI and increased regional marginalization. Major corporate repositioning and disengagement away from Thailand is thus a distinct possibility.
- Long-term infrastructure needs will present opportunities for the provision of telecommunications infrastructure, power generation and electrification systems, and public works construction in transportation infrastructure: rail, roads, and airports (the latter is already under way – unfortunately under a cloud of corruption and graft allegations, and unfair awarding of contracts)
- Expect continued opportunities in export sectors of the low value-adding category.

Overall risk rating

The risk profile of Thailand is increasing slightly; a combination of poor and stalling levels of financial and corporate sector reform, underdeveloped financial markets, poor regulatory compliance, a cumbersome bureaucracy, inefficient government sector, increasing corruption, increasing real labor costs, and growing protectionism.

Thailand, in short, is heading in all the wrong directions, with competitor states offering markets that are more attractive with better conditions for business investment.

Risk: Increasing ↑

Risk Rating (0 = lowest risk, 10 highest risk) 6 ↑

Section F Thailand fact sheet*

Geography

Capital
Bangkok

Largest city (millions, 1995)
Bangkok, 6.547

Location
15 00 N, 100 00 E

Adjacent countries
Vietnam, Malaysia, Burma, Laos, Cambodia

Terrain
Tropical arable lands, rich, fertile; central plain, Khorat Plateau in the east, mountains elsewhere

Land use
Arable land 34%, permanent crops 6%, permanent pastures 2%, forests and woodland 26%, other 32%

Area (km²)
513,115

Miscellaneous
Controls only land route from Asia to Malaysia and Singapore

Economic statistics

Currency
Baht (B) = 100 satang

Exchange rate (April 2001)
US$1.00 = B47.48

Gross Domestic Product (GDP)
5.2%

GDP per capita
$1,960

GDP per capita – PPP
$5,599

GDP – composition by sector
Agriculture 12%, industry 39%, services 49%

Percentage of the population earning less than US$2.00 per day
28.2

* All figures are the latest available except where indicated. All figures are in US dollars. Figures are compiled from national, international and multilateral agencies (Thailand National Accounts, Thailand Ministry of Finance, International Monetary Fund, World Bank, World Development Report, UNESCO Statistical Yearbook, International Labour Office, United Nations, Central Intelligence Agency World Fact Book). Gross domestic product (GDP) refers to the value of all goods and services produced in the preceding financial year. The Adult Economic Participation rate refers to the percentage of the population aged 15 and over (excluding military personnel) who are economically active. GDP per capita, Purchasing Power Parity (GDP per capita – PPP) refers to the indices developed by the World Bank to take account of price differences, cost of living differences, and relative purchasing power of a set basket of goods and services between countries so as to provide a more accurate measure of national wealth.

Inflation rate
2.2%

Foreign debt (billions)
$70.3

Current account balance (billions)
$11.0

National unemployment rate (1998)
4.5%

**Adult economic participation rate
(by gender, 1998)**
Male: 82%
Female: 66%

Population below poverty line
14%

Labor force (millions)
32.6

Labor force by occupation
Agriculture 54%, industry 15%,
services 31%

Budget (billions)
Revenues: $20
Expenditure: $23

Industries
Tourism, textiles, agricultural
processing, beverages, tobacco,
cement, light manufacturing, jewelry,
electric appliances and components,
computers and parts, furniture, plastics,
silicon, world's second largest tungsten
producer and third largest tin producer

Major exports (billions)
$58.5
Textiles and garments, computers and
computer parts, rice

Major imports (billions)
$45
Capital goods, intermediate goods and
raw materials, consumer goods, fuels

Major trading partners (exports)
United States 22.3%, Japan 13.7%,
Singapore 8.6%, Hong Kong 5.1%,
Netherlands 4.0%, United Kingdom
3.9%, Malaysia 3.3%. China 3.2%,
Taiwan 3.2%, Germany 2.9%

Major trading partners (imports)
Japan 23.6%, US 14.0%, Singapore
5.5%, Malaysia 5.1%, Taiwan 5.2%,
Germany 4.2%, China 4.2%, South Korea
3.5%, Oman 2.6%, Indonesia 2.1%

**Income/wealth distribution (household
income or consumption by % share)**
Lowest 10% of population 2.5%
Highest 10% of population 37.1%

Televisions (1997, millions)
15.19

Televisions per capita
0.24 (people per color television: 4.1)

Telephones (lines in use, millions)
5.4

Telephones per capita
0.10 (people per telephone: 12.1)

Cellular phones (1998, millions)
2.3

Cellular phones per capita (1998)
0.03 (people per cellular phone: 27.3)

Automobiles in use (millions)
1.44

Internet users per 100,000 of population
159.7

Fiscal year
1 October–30 September

Government and political statistics

Nature of government
Constitutional monarchy

Constitution
New constitution enacted by King Phumiphon, 11 October 1997

Structure of government
Executive branch and legislative branch

Executive branch
Headed by the Chief of State: King Phumiphon, Head of Government, Prime Minister Thaksin Shinawatra.

Legislative branch
Bicameral National Assembly (*Rathasapha*) consisting of:

Senate
(*Wuthisapha*): 200 members elected on 6 year terms

House of Representatives
(*Sapha Phuthean Ratsadon*): 500 members elected for 4-year terms)

Cabinet members (as at March 16, 2000)

Prime Minister
Thaksin Shinawatra

Deputy Prime Ministers
Gen. Chavalit Yongchaiyudh
Mr. Suwit Khunkitti
Prof. Dej Boon-long
Mr. Pongpol Adireksarn
Mr. Pitak Intrawitayanunt

Ministers to the Prime Minister's Office
Mr. Chaturon Chaisang
Gen. Thammarak Israngkura Na-Ayutaya
Mr. Somsak Thepsutin
Mr. Krasae Chanawong

Minister of Finance
Mr. Somkid Jatusripitak

Deputy Ministers of Finance
Mr. Varathep Ratanakorn
Mr. Suchat Jaovisidha

Minister of Foreign Affairs
Mr. Surakiart Sathirathai

Minister of Defense
Gen. Chavalit Yongchaiyudh

Deputy Minister of Defense
Gen. Yuthasak Sasiprapha

Minister of Agriculture and Cooperatives
Mr. Shucheep Hansaward

Deputy Ministers of Agriculture and Cooperatives
Mr. Prapat Panyachatirak
Mr. Natee Khlibtong

Minister of Transport and Communications
Mr. Wanmuhamadnoor Matha

Deputy Ministers of Transport and Communications
Mr. Pracha Maleenont
Mr. Pongsakorn Laohavichien

Minister of Commerce
Mr. Adisai Bodharamik

Deputy Ministers of Commerce
Mr. Suvarn Valaisathien

Minister of Interior
Prof. Purachai Piumsombun

Deputy Ministers of Interior
Mr. Sora-at Klinpratoom
Mr. Sombut Uthaisang

Minister of Justice
Mr. Phongthep Thepkanjana

Minister of Labour and Social Welfare
Prof. Dej Boon-long

Deputy Ministers of Labour and Social Welfare
Mrs. Ladawan Wongsriwong

Minister of Science, Technology and Environment
Mr. Sontaya Kunplome

Minister of Education
Mr. Kasem Watanachai

Deputy Ministers of Education
Mr. Jamlong Krutkuntode

Minister of Public Health
Mrs. Sudarat Keyuraphun

Deputy Ministers of Public Health
Mr. Surapong Suebwonglee

Minister of Industry
Mr. Suriya Chungrungruengkit

Deputy Ministers of Industry
Mr. Pichate Satirachaval

Minister of University Affairs
Mr. Suthum Sangpathom

Administrative structure of government
76 administrative divisions (provinces)

Main governing parties and ideological affiliation
Thai Rak Thai Party or TRT (populist, mass based, centrist party, liberal democratic values, appeals to Thai nationalist values, wide appeal among the poor and middle class, ideologically pro business, pro Western and supportive of foreign direct investment)

Main opposition parties
Democratic Party or DP (Prachathipat Party); Liberal Democratic Party or LDP (Seri Tham); Mass Party or MP; National Development Party or NDP; New Aspiration Party or NAP; Phalang Dharma Party or PDP; Social Action Party or SAP; Solidarity Party or SP; Thai Citizen's Party or TCP; Thai Nation Party or TNP

International memberships
Asia-Pacific Economic Cooperation (APEC), Association of South East Asian Nations (ASEAN), Economic and Social Commission for Asian and the Pacific (ESCAP), Food and Agricultural Organization (FAO) World Health Organization (WHO), World Trade Organization (WTO), Group of 77 (G-77), International Monetary Fund (IMF), International Labor Organization (ILO), Non-Aligned Movement (NOM), International Telecommunications Union (ITU), United Nations (UN)

Business organizations
Thai Chamber of Commerce; Marketing Association of Thailand; The Association of Thai Computer Industry; Thailand Board of Investment

Date of UN membership
December 16, 1946

Social statistics

Population size (millions)
62,856,000

Population density (km²)
118

Fertility rate (average number of children born to women 15–49 years of age)
2.14

Maternal mortality rate (per 100,000 births)
200+

Infant mortality rate (per 1,000 births)
31.48

Population growth
1.5%

Life expectancy
69
Men: 65.29
Women: 71.97

Ethnic composition
Thai 75%, Chinese 14%, Other 11%

Religions
Buddhism 95%, Muslim 3.8%, Christianity 0.5%, Hinduism 0.1%, Other 0.6%

National languages spoken
Thai, English (secondary language of the elite), ethnic and religious dialects

Illiteracy rate (age 15+)
2.8%

By gender (ages 25+)
Male: 5.6%
Female: 11.5%

Vietnam

13 Vietnam

Darryl S.L. Jarvis

Section A Economy

Overview

Vietnam continues to push ahead with its series of reforms begun in the late 1980s (*doi moi*) in its attempt to boost exports and economic growth, attract foreign direct investment and modernize its economy. To some degree it has achieved a moderate level of success, evidenced by stable economic growth rates that, since 1996, have hovered between 4.6 and 6 percent. However, starting from such a low point of development these growth rates are not remarkable in themselves, and probably suggest the continuance of a less than perfect investment and business climate.

Of most significance to investors will be President Bush's 8 June 2001 transmission to congress of the request for Normal Trade Relations and the subsequent ratification of the US–Vietnam Free Trade Agreement (3 October 2001).[1] Tariffs on Vietnamese goods now entering the United States have, consequently, fallen from an average of 40 percent to a mere 3 percent. This has re-energized prospects for Vietnamese development and increased the attractiveness of Vietnam as an investment destination for crude manufacturing and product assembly re-export ventures. It also commits Vietnam to a program of economic liberalization and continuing state reform, opening up many of Vietnam's previously protected industry sectors to US investors.

Vietnam's economic prospects were thus significantly brighter at the end of 2001. Unfortunately, this occurred at precisely the same time as the global economic outlook worsened, leaving Vietnam's short-term prospects for 2003–04 somewhat depressed. This highlights the ongoing structural weaknesses of the Vietnamese economy, with its fundamental reliance on foreign investment and exports as the driving dynamics of its growth. Vietnam is particularly sensitive to external economic conditions, with a less than robust internal demand structure able to support economic growth and investment.

High risks for foreign investors

Domestically, the most significant factor at work on the future success of the economy concerns the extent of political commitment to the reform process, and the extent to which market rationalization and privatization will be allowed to continue – and at what pace. To date, the reform process has been deliberately slow, emblematic of the political machinations between the 'government bloc' pro-reformers and the 'party bloc' of conservatives suspicious of marketization and openness. That a significant number of the party political elite are opposed to reform underscores how problematic this process is. This should act as a strong warning to any prospective foreign investor, as well as those currently operating in Vietnam, that such ventures can be fickle, with the regulatory operating environment at the mercy of finely balanced political forces that could change at any moment.

Investment into Vietnam should thus be predicated with the full knowledge that it remains one of Asia's highest risk destinations. Vietnam is not for the faint of heart, with a series of endemic political and economic barriers that make foreign business failure rates the highest in the region. Officially, statistics compiled by international agencies suggest a one in two failure rate (50 percent) for foreign ventures, but more realistically this figure likely runs upwards of 70 percent, except for state-sponsored joint ventures that generally have a better chance of success. In either case, Vietnam remains a tough market, especially for domestically oriented foreign direct investment due to limited market opportunities.

> Foreign investment ventures in Vietnam have the highest failure rate in the region, running between 50 and 70 percent.

On the upside, Vietnam has the ingredients for a robust if not dynamic economy, given the right political environment. The population base is young, with 50 percent being under the age of 35 due to the demographic distortions of war and the postwar baby boom. These postwar baby boomers are also aspirational, many with middle-class, Western values and an eagerness to be modern consumers. If Vietnam maintains its reform agenda and hastens its pace, the market opportunities likely to present themselves will be significant with much pent-up consumer demand likely to see rapid acceptance of Western products and marketing strategies. Again, however, the political environment, the arcane state regulations, and the culture of bureaucratic inertia threaten all of this.[2]

Also of threat is the declining revenue base of the government, with the revenue-to-GDP ratio declining from 19.9 percent in 1998 to 18.3 percent in 1999, and falling again to 15 percent in 2000.[3] This trend will continue into 2003 and beyond. The reasons for this are tied to the structural reforms in the Vietnamese economy. First, the contribution of revenue from state-owned enterprises (SOEs) has fallen dramatically with partial privatization and the adjustment to market systems. Second, income tax has also fallen, and continues to fall, despite significant increases in non-farm incomes. In part, this reflects the government's movement away from an income tax system to a consumption tax system and problems associated with implementation and collection systems. Third, revenues from export duties and tariffs have also fallen significantly as a result of the depressed level of trade following the Asian financial crisis of 1997, and partly as a result of Vietnam's removal of various tariffs under its commitment to the ASEAN Free Trade Area (AFTA).[4]

Of most significance to the falls in government revenue, however, has been the over-reliance on oil, especially production taxes, export duties and import tariffs on oil products. These account for 33 percent of government revenues that, unfortunately, have fallen precipitously with the fall in global oil prices as a result of the world economic slowdown and lower demand for oil. While this is a cyclical problem for Vietnam, it will remain so and deprive Vietnam of fiscal revenue stability unless a more diversified revenue base can be secured.

> Government revenues continue to fall, making precarious the central government's longer-term planning strategies, its ability to commit to long-term infrastructure projects and guarantee hard currency payments.

This should concern potential investors, not least because it raises concerns about the state's ability to make long-term commitments to joint venture operations, adequately provision infrastructure requirements, and meet contractual obligations. Government cash flows or lack thereof, could seriously hinder hard currency payments. Prospective investors should be cautious and employ the full gambit of insurance products available through the World Bank Multilateral Guarantee Agency, and various similar systems operating in Australia, Britain, and Europe, as well as private insurance options.

The bottom line: Look elsewhere

Wage differentials, recent reductions in foreign corporate tax, bilateral trade agreements, and readymade industrial parks have the appearance of making Vietnam an attractive destination for prospective investors. Appearances are deceptive, however, especially so in Vietnam with the highest regional failure rate for start-up foreign ventures. Hidden costs are also substantial, with rampant corruption, structural inefficiencies, and frequent state deafness to urgent foreign business needs. The ledger of business failures from Australian, US, British, and European investors, underscores that Vietnam is no walk in the park. As one executive with a large multinational company specializing in prefabricated steel structures noted of Vietnam, 'It's a great place, as along as you are prepared to lose money!'[5]

Investor caution and a serious commitment to feasibility and risk studies should be standard before the decision is made to proceed to invest in Vietnam. In comparison to other countries in the region, there is little to attract manufacturers or re-export industries that could not be sourced from lower risk countries like Thailand or China.

Section B Risks and projections

Macroeconomic performance and risk indicators

- Economic growth continues to contract, failing to rebound to its mid 1990s highs. Export growth is also contracting, and foreign direct investment (FDI) is only marginally recovering from its falls after the Asian financial crisis. The revenue base of the government is shrinking, decreasing discretionary spending on poverty reduction programs and much needed infrastructure improvements. Modernization programs are geographically specific and mostly limited to Saigon and Hanoi. Domestic demand is being maintained by a combination of increased wages for state employees, low interest rates, and rural subsidies to compensate farmers for falling agricultural prices. Investment opportunities are limited.

The Vietnamese economy continues to enjoy positive economic growth rates despite the global economic slowdown and the fallout from the meltdown in the technology sector. A growth rate of 6.0 percent for 2001 will be maintained during 2002 and into 2003, in part reflecting the government's commitment to fiscal stimulus and continued interest rate cuts aimed at increasing consumer demand.

However, growth in agricultural production, the mainstay of the Vietnamese economy, has slowed from 3.9 percent in 2000 to 3.5 percent in 2001, and has remained static during 2002. Little is expected to change in 2003–04 despite the commitment of substantial foreign aid resources to improve agricultural productivity in the Mekong Delta, a region responsible for over half of Vietnam's agricultural production and fully 30 percent of Vietnam's GDP.[6]

Continuing low world prices for agricultural products have also seen substantial falls in farm incomes with subsequent weakening domestic demand compounding the fall in external demand for exports. However, there has been some resilience in domestic consumption, in part reflecting the continued strong growth in industrial production and the government's commitment to lower interest rates as a stimulatory measure for domestic consumption.

Consumer prices also fell in 2001, reflecting the fall in world agricultural prices and continued depressed prices for oil. However, this trend is likely to be reversed in 2003–04, with a low interest rate policy and a depreciating Vietnamese dong likely to translate into higher prices for imported goods and services. Indeed, recent liberalization of interest rate policy has had the desired effect on currency valuations of the Vietnamese dong, depressing it against the US dollar and cross rates with regional trading partners. This is an intentional government policy aimed at increasing the external competitiveness of Vietnamese exports. However, given that such currency depreciations have been endemic to most Asian economies, it is unlikely this will have a significant impact on Vietnam's longer-term competitive position.[7]

Modest economic growth of 6–7 percent will be maintained during 2003–04 as the global economy picks up. The US–Vietnam Free Trade Agreement will also help boost Vietnamese export earnings, which have remained depressed in the wake of the global economic slowdown.

Domestically, 2003–04 is likely to see continued growth in demand for low-end consumer durables, especially processed food items, alcoholic beverages and carbonated drinks. The increasing fortunes of the small but growing ranks of the middle class will also help foster niche product demand for pharmaceutical and personal hygiene products. However, this is still a very small market with few opportunities for rapid expansion or economies of scale.

Better prospects lie in the expansion of the international tourism market, with Vietnam enjoying significant growth in tourist arrivals since the early 1990s. Again, however, the market segment is small, disproportionately attracting low-end tourists with restricted budgets whose benefit to the local economy, while positive, is not as significant as it is in competitor states.

Export performance

- Export growth continues to contract, falling from 24.1 percent in 1999, to 21.3 percent in 2000, 10.7 percent in 2001, and 8.5 percent in 2002. Falling export revenues from depressed global oil prices, and a general global slowdown in demand for electronic goods will dampen export growth in 2003, with 2004 likely to benefit from the knock-on effects of high global economic growth. Declining prices for rice and coffee have also hit Vietnam's exports hard, with commodity prices likely to continue their fall in 2003. The ongoing fallout from the technology sector meltdown has also depressed the export markets of most of Vietnam's trading partners, with little short- to medium-term relief in sight. Expect export growth to be stagnant in 2003, possibly rebounding in 2004.[8]

Export growth has been vital to the Vietnamese economy, greatly propelling its fortunes and providing necessary stimulus to its industrial expansion and hard currency earnings. Unfortunately, Vietnam's major export markets are a combination of Asia's poorest performing economies or recession-hit western states. Japan, for example, Vietnam's biggest export market, has been in recession for the better part of a decade, with little sign of short-term recovery. China, Vietnam's second largest export market, while enjoying positive growth, has also been hit by declining external demand, and Singapore and the United States, Vietnam's fourth and fifth largest export markets, have both suffered economic downturns, depressing demand for Vietnamese goods. Unfortunately, there is little immediate hope for a dramatic turnaround in the economic fortunes of Vietnam's major export markets, although a slow recovery in the United States during 2003 will go some way to laying the foundations for more robust export growth in 2004.[9]

Greater prospects lie in the recovery of oil prices, which account for around 18 percent of Vietnam's exports, and which have been artificially depressed since September 11. Oil prices are likely to enjoy better returns with a pick-up in global economic activity during 2003–04, with anticipated yields for 2003 projected at US$20 a barrel and for 2004 at US$22 a barrel. Better returns on oil should also help improve the revenue base of government during 2003–04.[10]

Higher oil revenues could be offset, however, by the long-term structural decline in commodity prices. Coffee prices, for example, one of Vietnam's leading commodity exports, have fallen 55 percent since January 1998, with rice prices experiencing a similar trend, down 45 percent since 1998 – albeit experiencing a short-lived price spike in 2001 as a result of the extensive flooding in the Mekong Delta responsible for poorer than expected rice crop yields. True to longer-term trends, however, higher prices for Vietnamese rice exports have not been maintained, falling away again in 2002 from US$175 to US$168 per ton.[11]

> Declining commodity prices continue to depress Vietnam's export performance, and a structural reliance on Japan as Vietnam's principal trading partner will dampen export growth during 2003–04.

Further price falls are also expected, with buyers currently delaying issuing contracts in anticipation of bumper seasonal crops, partly as a result of mineral deposits left after heavy flooding in 2001.[12] Vietnamese rice exports might thus succumb to their own success, with plentiful supplies pushing prices down. On the upside, Vietnam has managed to secure forward rice contracts of 1 million tons with Cuba, Indonesia and Iraq that will help stabilize rice export earnings. Whether this can be replicated in 2003–04 remains to be seen.[13]

Of longer-term importance to Vietnam's export performance is the environmental health of the Mekong Delta region, responsible for 80 percent of Vietnam's rice exports. Problems associated with flooding, drainage, and salinity have forced one-third of farmers in the Mekong region into single crop production rather than the normal two or three crops produced annually. This is obviously depressing production of one of Vietnam's chief commodity exports. Longer-term relief may come though World Bank assistance programs announced in 1999, which aim to improve drainage, salinity and flooding issues, but project realization time for these is still some way off.

> Export growth shrank from 25 percent in 2000 to just 6.5 percent in 2001, moderately recovering in 2002 to 8.5 percent and is projected to pick up markedly in 2003–04 to 12 percent.[14]

More immediately, Vietnam's export performance will be linked intimately to the anticipated pick-up in growth in the United States in 2003–2004, which, combined with the US–Vietnam Free Trade Agreement, is likely to restore Vietnam's export growth to more robust levels.[15] This can be expected in apparel, footwear and marine product exports, albeit that product quality issues, especially in the footwear and garment industry, remain of some concern in terms of US consumer uptake.

There is also reason to suppose that US and European outsourcing of crude homeware products (ceramics in particular) will also see an upward momentum, especially given the increasing positive cost differentials Vietnam enjoys with competitor states like Thailand. On the downside, Vietnam faces increasing competition from China for these same export markets, and remains only a bit player by comparison.

Risks aplenty for foreign investors

For prospective investors, manufacturing and/or processing re-export ventures face not just the fickle demand variations in the global economy, but the multitude of regulatory hurdles imposed by Vietnam's cumbersome bureaucracy. Export licenses, for example, along with foreign exchange licenses (see below), and a litany of constantly changing legal requirements, make Vietnam a compliance-intensive, juridical environment in which to operate. These regulatory issues are compounded by requirements for foreign enterprises to meet Vietnamese legal obligations in terms of accounting standards, as well as grapple with the complex regulations concerning capital and profit repatriation.

In the case of capital repatriation, foreign enterprises must seek the permission of the Ministry of Planning and Investment (MPI) and the provincial People's Committee if the intended repatriation is greater than the original investment. Likewise, profit remittances are only permitted at the end of each financial year and cannot be streamed on a month-by-month or quarterly basis.

Legal problems are also compounded by the tripartite division of the regulatory system. Apart from the various investor licenses required by national government authorities, provincial and local authorities retain a great deal of discretionary authority, evidenced by the frequent need for investors to seek further negotiations with local and provincial authorities, even after export and investor licenses have been granted.[16]

The bottom line: Red tape, paper work, and headaches

Vietnam is still in its infancy in terms of an international investment regime and well off world's best practice standards. Compliance regulations, the multitude of operating permits, licenses and legal instruments needed, together with the ongoing need to monitor taxation laws and changes to the regulatory environment, make Vietnam one of the toughest markets in the region in which to operate.

Currency movements and projections

• The Vietnamese dong has depreciated 25 percent since 1997–98, and has continued to fall since January 2000 despite the post-financial crisis stabilization in other Asian currencies. There is widespread belief that the dong remains overvalued, with continued depreciation anticipated during 2003–04. Despite government announcements that the dong will eventually be allowed to move to a floating exchange rate regime, few anticipate this development in the near future. Currency conversion remains problematic, especially during high demand periods, and investors face regulatory obstacles in terms of profit repatriation.

The Vietnamese dong (VND) continues to exist under a state-managed exchange rate regime and is not fully convertible. In February 1999, the government abolished the practice whereby the State Bank of Vietnam quoted a daily official exchange rate, and replaced it with a managed float system. Under this system, the dong is not allowed to fluctuate more than 0.1 percent beyond the previous day's quoted inter-bank rate. However, in reality the dong's exchange rate has been allowed to reflect market sentiment, albeit closely managed through central bank intervention and tied intimately to Vietnam's macroeconomic policy goals.

Differences in the official exchange rate and those available on the black market for conversion of dong into US dollars, have confirmed widely held perceptions that the dong is overvalued, with consistently softer black market rates compared to official rates. As a consequence, the official exchange rate has been amended downward since 1997 – devalued three times in 1997–98, and since January 2000 has traded downwards by around 12 percent.[17] In all, since 1997, the dong has fallen 25 percent, and on current trends will continue to soften.[18]

> The dong will continue to soften in 2003–04, reflecting continuing sentiment that it is overvalued and needs to be managed downwards if Vietnam is to be returned to a competitive export position.

The dong's softening reflects a combination of market sentiment and government policy to allow it to depreciate against major currencies in order to increase Vietnam's export performance. It also reflects the important role of the black market for US dollars, which acts as a secondary watchdog to check officially quoted rates of exchange. Mindful of this, authorities have not allowed too wide a discrepancy between black market and official rates to develop, with the aim of creating longer-term confidence in the currency through managed intervention to ensure a smooth rate of depreciation. This has also been made necessary in order to ensure wild currency gyrations do not fuel inflation or blow out the debt burden on SOEs.

The dong continues to hover around 15,000 VND to the US dollar, with indications that this will soften to between 15,500–16,500 VND during 2003–04, presenting mild inflationary pressures for Vietnamese authorities through higher import costs.

Watch your dollars

Foreign-owned enterprises are required to be self-supporting with respect to foreign currency requirements, and are technically still required to surrender surplus foreign currency to the State Bank of Vietnam – although this provision has been partially relaxed since 1999. The

Foreign Investment Law (FIL) also requires foreign enterprises to operate foreign currency accounts at Vietnamese banks or foreign banks in Vietnam, to transact all domestic economic activity in dong, and to convert dong into hard currency at the official rate. The latter requires foreign enterprises to have a 'foreign exchange licenses. that technically 'guarantees' conversion. However, such 'guarantees' can be subject to extensive and costly delays, especially at times of peak hard currency demands when shortages are common.

In a sense, however, these provisions remain largely untested; mainly due to the fact that so few foreign enterprises have been profitable in Vietnam that demand for conversion has, unfortunately, been uncommon.

Anecdotal evidence also suggests that these processes are easily, and perhaps frequently, circumvented by Vietnamese authorities who fail to re-issue foreign exchange licenses and/or export licenses once foreign enterprises are operational. Such measures fall outside the normal contractual parameters under which export credit schemes operate and/or insurance products are offered, and can thus pose substantial risks to the viability of an enterprise.

Capital controls are also in force in Vietnam, and limit the amount of hard currency that can be taken out of the country by individuals without a license, currently at US$3,000. Gold too is restricted in terms of export and importation, and currently boasts a lucrative black market economy, estimated to be in the order of 30 tons illegally smuggled into Vietnam each year.[19] Most expatriate workers thus operate offshore accounts to ensure personal income repatriation.

Financial markets: Performance and developments

- Vietnamese financial markets are immature, under-capitalized, only partially governed by market criteria, suffer from state intervention and politically motivated directives, are not transparent, and have few if any prudential parameters to ensure for adequate risk provisioning and regulatory supervision. This, in short, is not a market you want to be in.

Financial markets in Vietnam are in their extreme infancy. The Vietnamese Stock Exchange (VSE) only commenced trading in July 2000, with the number of companies listed rising from a mere 5 to 11 in 2001–02. The combined equity market capitalization of the VSE stands at just over US$100 million, and is experiencing modest growth. As of 1 March 2002 the VSE commenced five consecutive trading sessions per week, up from three during 2001. Volatility, however, has been the hallmark of the VSE, with the index trading upwards of 500 in mid 2001 but falling to 198.44 in 2002.[20]

The trading system is still undergoing evolution, bifurcated between small traders engaged in transactions of less than 10,000 shares who are forced to transact via the Security Trading Centre (STC), and larger traders who can trade directly on the market itself. Either way, the transaction time for settlement of share trading payments remains at a lengthy three trading days (down from four), tending to restrict the liquidity of shares. Furthermore, the price movement of equities is restricted to a 2 percent band of tolerance based on the previous day's closing price.[21]

Not surprisingly, the trading volume on the VSE remains very small and the regulatory requirements of the exchange that govern listing and investor participation are restrictive. For example, there are strict rules governing foreign ownership of listed equities, while foreign companies are not permitted to trade on the VSE and foreign ownership of equitized companies is restricted to a maximum of 20 percent.[22]

> Financial markets in Vietnam are in their extreme infancy, underdeveloped, immature, and high risk. Government regulations are restrictive, and market size is very small compared to regional neighbors.

As a vehicle for portfolio investment, the VSE represents a minuscule market and one whose risk must be rated as extremely high, given both the size and immaturity of the market. However, for the more adventuresome portfolio investors, there are limited opportunities if only because equity values are currently cheap, unlikely to get much cheaper and in the longer term could well appreciate and add considerable value.[23] While average current dividend yields stand at a modest 4 percent, given the considerable liquidity in the Vietnamese economy and the small number of investment instruments currently available, the VSE might prove a viable investment option with the prospects of attracting considerable domestic investor interest and thus capital growth.[24]

There is also an absence of secondary financial markets, with the only substantial market outlet for funds investment being restricted to bond listings carried out under the auspices of the State Bank for Investment and Development of Vietnam and issued via the VSE. Bond trading, however, accounts for only about 6.4 percent of VSE transactions.[25] While a series of moderately capitalized Vietnamese Securities Companies also exist, some of them offshoots of state banks, the opportunities again are limited.

Portfolio or funds investment opportunities have been mostly restricted to the handful of Vietnam-focused specialist investment funds, mostly US and UK registered, and which came into existence after the lifting of the US trade embargo in 1994. However, after an initial flurry of interest, the majority of these funds were trading at an average discount of 50 percent and forced to write down the value of their portfolios.[26] Two of the biggest such funds, Templeton Vietnam and Southeast Asia Fund, for example, were down 75 percent of their value since inception in 1994.[27] More generally, however, many Vietnam-focused funds have been forced to reorient their investment focus due simply because of so few attractive investment opportunities in Vietnam.[28]

Banking on the future?

Vietnam's banking sector is in no better shape, suffering from over-servicing relative to the small size of the market in terms of loans and deposits, but with little prospect for rationalization due to the preponderance of non-market criteria operating in the sector. Four state-owned banks account for 70 percent of all bank lending, with most banks, especially smaller regional banks, severely undercapitalized.[29] There is also a strong cadre of foreign banks now operating in Vietnam (in Hanoi and Saigon), but again in a market that distinguishes itself by smallness of size, restrictive regulations, and less than robust market conditions.

Non-performing loans (NPLs) are officially listed at 13 percent of outstanding loans using Vietnamese accounting standards. In reality, this figure is estimated to be in the order of 30 percent according to accounting staff of the International Monetary Fund (IMF). More importantly, most NPLs are held against SOEs, suggesting that the prospects for performance turnaround or write-down is not high as most of these credit provisions have been made using non-market criteria through state-issued directives. For prospective investors, this should send strong signals, highlighting the role of state intervention and the perversion of market signals as the basis on which Vietnamese business practices are conducted.

Keep your hands in your pockets

At base, the problem with Vietnam's underdeveloped financial markets arises from their gross inefficiency as allocators of financial resources. Public mistrust of official financial institutions, lack of faith in the value of the dong, and poor state management of central and state bank institutions, have translated into a situation where fully 50 percent of personal savings are held as cash (usually US dollars), gold, or other assets *outside* of the banking system.

Foreign currency deposits (FCD), in particular, make effective monetary policy hard to achieve, with estimates that FDC holdings in Vietnam stood at US$5.5. billion in 2001, 80 percent of which were held by ordinary Vietnamese households.[30] This reflects both the lack of faith in the dong and the limited scope of the financial market and the lack of alternative interest-bearing financial instruments available. Indeed, despite the reduction in interest rate spreads between dong and dollar deposits, down from 3 percent and since 2001 and currently averaging 0–0.25 percent, FCDs have continued to increase by an average of 15 percent per annum. This trend is likely to continue, albeit that Vietnamese authorities have attempted to curb this by disallowing foreign banks from offering FCD deposit facilities to Vietnamese.[31]

Foreign banks also face the added strictures of having the interest yields they pay on deposits dictated by central authorities: restricted to 2.5 percent for deposits of less than six months and 3 percent for longer-term deposits. In addition, foreign banks have been faced with increasing financial burdens, especially the increase in the proportion of deposits required to be lodged with the central bank, up from 8 percent to 12 percent.[32]

Despite official hints of market liberalization, little change is expected for 2003–04.

Private and public debt: A growing problem?

- Public sector debt continues to increase, projected to rise to US$20 billion by 2005. However, over half of the debt stock will be raised through concessional lending, easing the debt servicing obligations on Vietnam. The level of government spending in support of debt servicing is increasing, placing burdens on limited fiscal revenues. This is likely to increase during 2003–04. SOE debt levels are also extensive, with little evidence of substantial reform of SOEs or debt reduction. Newly created asset management companies are proving mostly ineffective in recovering the spate of bad loans made during the early 1990s.

Public sector debt continues to increase in Vietnam, standing at US$15.063 billion in 2002, up from US$7.3 billion in 1999, and projected to increase to US$20 billion by 2005. The rate of debt accumulation has been steep, but perhaps not out of line for an economy experiencing strong economic growth in the early to mid 1990s, and also undergoing substantial infrastructure development.[33]

Despite this, the level of debt default, mainly as a result of NPLs held by SOEs stands at US1.3 billion. However, these figures are based on Vietnamese accounting standards which if calculated using international standards blow out to US$4.5 billion.[34] While some attempts have been made to address NPLs, primarily through the creation of an asset management corporation (AMC), the results to date have been poor. Indeed, little substantial debt recovery or restructuring will be able to proceed, mainly due to the fact that most NPLs were made originally in the early to mid 1990s, and most of these without secured collateral to now defunct agricultural cooperatives.[35]

International donors have also lent a further US$2.4 billion to Vietnam during 2002, and anticipate further disbursements from the World Bank and IMF, pushing up Vietnam's total debt stock to around 40 percent of GDP.[36] However, by 2005 approximately half of Vietnam's total debt stock will be concessional debt financing, alleviating any immediate pressures on its external debt servicing ability.

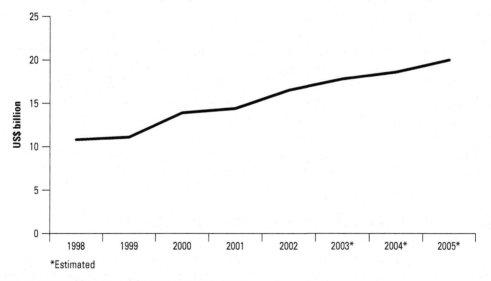

*Estimated

FIGURE 13.1 Public sector debt, Vietnam 1998–2005
Source: David Cohen. et al., (2002), *Selected Issues and Statistical Appendix*, International Monetary Fund, IMF Country Report, January.

What should be of concern, however, is the structural decline in government revenues that, combined with an increase in the total debt stock, pose longer-term problems for Vietnam. The revenue-to-GDP ratio has fallen from 21 percent in 1997, for example, to around 16 percent in 2002, emblematic of poor tax receipt performance as a result of the value added tax (VAT) collection system not operating efficiently.[37]

So too, the composition of government spending suggests the debt burden is beginning to bite, representing 12 percent of government spending in 1997, 17 percent in 2000, and 19 percent in 2002, with this trend set to continue for 2003–04 and beyond. When combined with declining government revenues, the problem is obvious and reflected in Moody's lackluster debt rating of B1 – down from Ba3 in 1999 and showing few prospects of revision upwards.[38]

More immediately, the debt burden on specific SOEs is frequently not counted and/or discounted in official budget estimates, raising the prospects that the debt stock is in fact much greater than official figures suggest. A quick survey of many SOEs, for example, reveal significant debt levels and less then robust performance benchmarks. Unless reform of SOEs is forthcoming and/or the pace of privatization/marketization quickened, the prospects for the longer-term viability of many of the SOEs is in question, adding further dead debt weight to government debt servicing requirements.

While the government is aware of these problems, solutions have not been forthcoming. Attempts to launch a series of bond issues, for example, resulted in poor domestic and international uptake, depriving authorities of a vital source of longer-term debt financing. In part, the problem arises from the fact that bonds are issued in dong denominations, an option not preferred by either domestic or international investors because of convertibility considerations. Unfortunately, there seems little prospect of any significant changes to this policy for 2003–04.

On the upside, there have been discernible signs of liberalization, with the government moving toward market-determined interest rate yields, whereby banks can now set dollar lending rates in line with international market rates. Also of note, since 1 August 2001, the State Bank of Vietnam has liberalized its lending practices, allowing locally-based companies to borrow from overseas lenders.[39]

Labor market trends

- The Vietnamese labor market is soft, a combination of inadequate economic growth levels and a rapidly expanding workforce due to demographic factors. Prospective investors will have few difficulties in recruiting English-speaking employees, especially given the increasingly limited opportunities available for employment in the state sector. Restrictive labor employment codes, however, tend to discriminate against foreign employers, eliciting higher employer contributions than otherwise demanded of local industry.

The labor market remains soft in Vietnam, a combination of uneven development, regional differences, and year-on-year significant numbers of new market entrants. Since 1999 and the fallout from the Asian financial crisis, unemployment has dropped consistently, from 10.1 percent to around 6.5 percent, according to official estimates.[40] However, hidden unemployment and significant levels of underemployment remain unreported.

There is also a wide discrepancy between rural and urban regions, with rural regions suffering from endemic underemployment and large seasonal variations in employment levels, while urban unemployment is frequently higher than the national average due to rural–urban migration, with levels of between 7 percent and 8 percent recorded in 2002.

Demographic age differences are also significant in Vietnam, with 23.8 percent of students graduating from universities and collages unable to find employment, while 24 percent of the graduates who found employment did so in jobs unrelated to their qualifications – typically lower-end, blue collar, entry positions. Youth unemployment also accounts for 63 percent of all rural unemployment. This underscores the uneven level of development in Vietnam and the less than adequate growth in technology, industry, and tertiary sectors able to absorb the rapidly expanding workforce.[41]

> Unemployment continues to hover around 6–7 percent, and is not expected to decline significantly despite a pick-up in economic activity during 2003–04.

This also underscores Vietnam's less than adequate tertiary education system, that tends to stream students into areas favored by state directive or traditional perceptions of social prestige. These problems are particularly acute, since much of the educational infrastructure reflects the old economy, which was previously dominated by SOEs and geared toward the production of graduates to meet their needs. Students thus often find themselves ill-equipped to meet the new growth areas of demand. More generally, cumbersome bureaucracy in educational administration, inattention to market signals, and poor coordination of education curricula planning, means little effective coordination is achieved between the increasing market influences in the economy and graduate training.[42]

Collectively, these problems are likely to become nearly intractable for Vietnam since, in addition to the 2.4 million pool of unemployed, there are an additional 1.4 million new entrants to the labor market each year. The workforce is thus growing at the rate of 3.5 percent annually, placing considerable pressure on authorities to rapidly expand the economy and increase labor utilization.

The rapid growth of the Vietnamese workforce is underscored by the recent trend of exporting excess labor to foreign markets through Vietnam's Labor Overseas Development Corporation. This has grown exponentially, constituting 22,000 workers in 1999, 220,000 workers in 2002, and projected to increase to 500,000 annually by 2005 and 1 million by 2010.[43] Most export labor is destined for other Asian markets, mostly in unskilled construction, retail, and home-help classifications, with some exported to the international shipping industry as deckhands. Remuneration for such workers is typically low, and in 2003–04 will stand around US$280.00 per month, with much of this anticipated to be shipped back to Vietnam to support rural families.

Unskilled labor: Growing abundance

For prospective employers, Vietnamese labor is thus in relatively abundant supply, and tends to be well educated in terms of literacy standards and well disposed to training and adaptability. Local labor also places a premium on securing employment with foreign enterprises, not least because the rates of pay tend to be higher and the social kudos helps with future career development.

While unskilled wage rates vary widely between occupations, global surveys of the textile, clothing and footwear industry (TCF) suggest that Vietnam (and China) is one of the most competitive countries in the world, attracting remuneration in the order of US$0.50 per hour. Indeed, the TCF industry has been one of the few rapid growth areas in the Vietnamese economy, and is increasingly responsible for a large segment of unskilled labor employment. This is expected to continue into 2003–05.[44]

However, on the downside the composite skill-sets of the workforce tend to be restrictive, with poor levels of technical and graduate education compared to other Asian states. Technically specialized occupational requirements will thus be difficult to recruit locally, if not impossible, but given that Vietnam is not currently attracting this type of foreign investment, this should not be an immediate concern.[45]

Wage rates, while stable, will generally suffer from upward pressure during 2003–04, a combination of increasing economic activity, modest export growth, and higher inflation as a result of a lower dong.

While there is some downward pressure on wage rates, reflecting the continuing contraction in employment in the SOE sector, down from 14.7 percent of the labor force in 1991 to 8 percent in 2002, and generally adding to the unemployment pool, this trend is not expected to continue.[46] Expected increases in global demand and modest export growth anticipated as a result of the US–Vietnam Free Trade Agreement, mean wage rates are likely to trend moderately upwards. Compounding this trend will be the effects of a lower dong and increased inflation that will see demands for higher compensation levels.

Skilled labor: A growing expense

While unskilled labor is in abundant supply, the same is not true for skilled labor, especially at the technical and managerial level. Indeed, despite some attractions, labor in Vietnam poses serious problems for foreign enterprises. In part, this stems from the onerous income tax burden, which, at the highest bracket, is imposed at a rate of 80 percent. When combined with Vietnamese legal stipulations, and in order to offer competitive salaries to Vietnamese managers, foreign enterprises thus face a particularly high salaries structure. For example, if an employer wants to recruit a manager and pay them a net salary of US$3,000 per month, the gross cost to the employer runs upwards of US$15,000 per month. Little wonder, then, that most foreign enterprises find it more attractive to employee expatriate labor rather than recruit local managerial talent.[47]

Foreign enterprises will also be challenged by the complexity of the requirements for foreign work permits for expatriate employees, which are usually issued for periods inconsistent with work contracts. This causes great inconvenience, and generally results in additional expenditure of time and money to ensure enterprise compliance to foreign work visa requirements.

Labor laws and foreign enterprises

Labor laws have been enacted (Labor Code of June 1994) and are strongly enforced by Vietnamese authorities. These govern the employment practices, dismissal and minimum wage levels for Vietnamese workers. A number of these codes are quite restrictive, and hinder the latitude of foreign enterprises to engage in employment practices otherwise available in neighboring Asian states.

For example, recruitment practices are mandated by the labor code which stipulates that foreign enterprises must recruit through the local labor office, local labor supply company, or local investment service company, and advertisements to recruit workers from other regions are only allowed after local recruitment drives prove unfruitful. Direct recruitment by foreign enterprises is only permitted if, after 30 days, the local labor office has been unable to fill the required positions.

> Skilled labor is in short supply and reflects poor levels of technical education and the non-responsiveness of the higher education system to market needs. Only 15.52 percent of the workforce has experienced training, and only 11.4 percent have received technical training.[48]

Unfortunately, this has the twin effects of creating long lag times between labor needs and final recruitment and also places primary responsibility for selection procedures in the hands of local labor departments, whose selection processes for candidate placement can often be based on nepotism, favoritism, and not necessarily on merit selection procedures.

A minimum wage code is also in operation, stipulating minimum wages for companies with foreign capital components. These range from US$45 per month in Hanoi and Saigon, to US$40 per month in Can Tho, Da Nang, Hai Phong, Ha Long, Hue, Nha Trang and Vung Tau, to US$35 per month in other regions. More generally, however, skilled labor can demand significantly higher wage levels. In 2002, for example, a secretary/personal assistant working for a foreign enterprise was remunerated between US$200–700 per month, while other professional classifications can run between US$300–1700 per month. This places Vietnamese labor on the higher end of the spectrum compared with many regional neighbors, especially considering that most workers will insist on remuneration in US dollars rather than dong (a requirement mandated in law but since modified [in 1999], allowing foreign enterprises to denominate salaries in dong).

Unions are also strong in Vietnam, and enjoy the state-sanctioned right to strike. Unions also have extensive political clout through their membership in the Communist

Party and typically are cross-appointed to government advisory boards. Indeed, after the well-publicized problems that occurred in 1997 with Nike plants operating in Saigon and employing through sub-contracting agencies over 37,000 workers, the government has been more forthright in regulating foreign enterprise in terms of employment practices and minimum wage levels. Local unions too have been more assertive, and well placed to call upon government authorities to assist in labor code enforcement. Much care should thus be taken in developing management level relationships with union leadership.[49]

Corporate tax

- Foreign corporate tax remains one of the highest in the region, and a spate of secondary taxes imposed on imports, profit remittances, and excess profits, makes for a complex tax system whose transparency is lacking. Foreign enterprises continue to be the object of tax shakedowns, with few rights of appeal. Year-on-year tax assessments also suffer from wide variance, emblematic of the numerous interpretations open to tax officials.

By regional standards, Vietnam's tax burden on foreign enterprise is high and the complexity of the tax system cumbersome, making it easy to fall outside the licensing and compliance regulations imposed by central authorities.

The Corporate Income Tax Law, which came into effect in 1999 and was revised in June 2001, carries a uniform rate of 32 percent, but can be as little as 25 percent or as much as 45 percent depending on the sector in which the enterprise is operating and the incentives granted. In addition, an excess profits tax is also in effect and levied at the rate of 25 percent. This kicks in if a company's after-tax revenue exceeds the value of its registered capital base by more than 20 percent. Exceptions do apply, however. In the case of enterprises enjoying preferential rates of corporate tax granted as part of the setup license, for example, or if companies earn more than 50 percent of their revenue from exports, the excess profits tax is not applicable.

Lower corporate tax rates are in effect for foreign enterprise in construction, transportation, and certain industrial production sectors deemed of national interest, in which case a corporate tax rate of 25 percent applies. In addition, start-up foreign ventures involved in specific production industries are eligible to secure a tax free period of two years and a further two-year 50 percent reduction on the corporate tax rate.

Apart from corporate tax rates, foreign enterprises involved in the importation of materials for processing or as necessary production input, also face a series of import levies of various rates, as well as a 10 percent VAT that has to be paid immediately on the value of goods imported, but which can be reimbursed once the goods have been on-sold. Regardless, this ties up a substantial amount of capital for considerable periods of time, and makes paramount the importance of regulatory compliance to be eligible for VAT refunds.

Vietnam also imposes a remittance tax (see below) on profits repatriated overseas or retained outside of Vietnam. This is levied at the rate of 3 percent for investors contributing above US$10 million, 5 percent on enterprises contributing between US$5–10 million, and 7 percent on enterprises contributing less than US$5 million in realized investment.

Export processing zones and industrial zones

Foreign enterprise is able to produce within export processing zones (EPZ), industrial zones (IZ) or high-tech zones (HTZ). In the case of EPZs and IZs enterprises can take advantage of exemptions from customs duties for equipment, raw materials, and commodities imported into the zones, as well as for finished goods and products exported from the zones. To qualify, EPZ production must be exclusively for export as well as meeting certain other strictures specific to industry and product type, and IZ enterprises may produce for the domestic market but ensure a certain proportion of the output is exported.

The benefits of operating out of either an EPZ or an IZ are that:

- EPZ companies are not required to register for VAT
- no VAT is levied in imports
- no withholding tax is levied on services provided from foreign companies.

Promises versus reality

While the authorities have attempted some modification to the tax burden on foreign investors, gestures have not been followed up by concrete policy modification and implementation. There is, for example, a substantial gap between what senior leadership says and the interpretation and application of tax rulings in terms of its effect on foreign enterprises. The result is a lack of transparency such that tax assessments lack predictability, with corporate calculations at wide variance with official tax assessment and no procedures in place allowing for the right of appeal.

Underlying this is the commonly held view among Vietnamese authorities that foreign enterprises are easy targets, rich and well-heeled and easy to shake down for extra revenue rather than tapping domestic sources. Indeed, the shortfall in government revenue streams, and the declining revenue base relative to GDP, is likely to exert more pressure on such practices and pose increasing burdens for foreign enterprises.[50]

While no immediate changes to the corporate tax regime are anticipated in 2003–04, government fiscal revenue pressures might well witness less willingness to grant preferential tax concessions to foreign enterprises at the time of licensing. Foreign enterprises can also expect a more vigorous interpretation of the tax law by authorities and renewed exuberance at being inventive when it comes to taxing foreign enterprise.

Foreign direct investment

- Since 1995 FDI has generally contracted, only recently recording modest growth and returning it to pre-1996 levels. The US–Vietnam Free Trade Agreement will help rekindle foreign investor interest and provide some growth momentum in 2003–04. However, given the significant obstacles to foreign investment that still persist, this will not be as strong as Vietnamese authorities hope.

Despite an initial spurt of interest and corresponding year-on-year increases in inward flows of FDI during the early 1990s, since 1995 FDI has contracted precipitously; indeed between 1997 and 2001 three consecutive years of decline were recorded.

Vietnam's poor FDI performance reflects two external shocks over which Vietnamese authorities had no control. First, the region-wide contraction in investment as a result of the Asian financial crisis and the general disruption to capital flows due to global economic uncertainty. Second, the technology sector meltdown and contraction in the global economy in 2000–01 have delayed what might otherwise have been a period of consolidation and robust growth in FDI inflows.

Vietnamese authorities have set foreign investment targets of US$25 billion for 2005. However, given current investment levels, a less than enthusiastic international investor response to Vietnam as an investment destination, and the recent withdrawal of a significant number of long-standing foreign enterprises due to unprofitability, this figure would appear to be based on idealistic optimism rather than pragmatic estimation.

However, poor FDI flows also reflect the fact that Vietnam is a tough market, with few foreign enterprises profitable since their entry into the country. As a result, Vietnam has suffered not just from poor external economic circumstances, but a growing realization among foreign investors that it is a less than attractive market. More recently, for example, just as new FDI flows were coming on line, a series of downsizings and closures were announced, with a number of long-standing foreign investors deciding to pull out of Vietnam after five years of unprofitability.[51]

Emblematic of the less than attractive investment climate is the fact that in 2001, Vietnam shipped over US$5 billion offshore, predominantly to Singapore banks as medium-term, interest-yielding deposits. This outflow represents more than the entire sum of FDI for 2001 and 2002 combined. Attracting FDI is thus not in itself the problem, but the absence of attractive investment options and the limited financial instruments available mean Vietnam is constrained by the paucity of its financial markets, investment opportunities, and thus the ability to absorb inflows of FDI.

Creating a sound and attractive business operating environment should thus be the first order of business for Vietnamese authorities. Unfortunately, all too often the attitude to foreign investment has been to fleece it, assuming that foreign enterprise has deep pockets, and that it should be exhorted to offer cash or pay fees at every turn for the privilege of operating in Vietnam. The series of stringent, often contradictory and onerous regulatory laws, fees, and licenses, bear testimony to how Vietnamese authorities have often used foreign enterprise as a source of revenue to fill empty government coffers.

However, Vietnam has tried to renew the interest of FDI and taken at least tacit steps to improve the climate for foreign enterprise. By the end of March 2002, for example, 118 new foreign investment projects had been licensed with a combined capital value of US$228.3 million. The figure marked a 10 per cent increase in the number of projects but a 20 per cent decline in registered capital as against 2001.

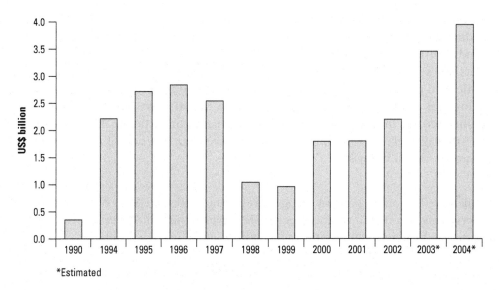

FIGURE 13.2 Foreign direct investment, Vietnam 1990–2004
Source: Asian Development Bank, *Country Economic Review: Socialist Republic of Vietnam.* November, 2000, Manila, Philippines. David Cohen *et al., Vietnam: Selected Issues and Statistical Appendix,* January 2002, International Monetary Fund, Washington, DC.

Changes to the foreign investment law

In large measure, the moderate pick-up in FDI reflected the changes to the Foreign Investment Law and promises of a change in government attitude toward FDI. This occurred in 17 areas, with by far the most important being:

Government guarantees

The Government of Vietnam now offers investment guarantees to foreign investors in infrastructure and other projects deemed of national importance. Before, there was no such legal basis on which to offer investment guarantees. However, the final wording of the legislation is less clear than was first suggested, and it remains to be seen what practical assurances such guarantees really provide to investors.

Licensing

The licensing procedures for foreign enterprises have been simplified and split into two categories: those requiring pre-evaluation before licensing, and those that only require registration. In reality, however, the procedures are still cumbersome, and in the case of the new 'registration category', of limited applicability to most foreign investors. Indeed, depending on the nature, location and scope of the investment, the issuance of licenses still requires three levels of authority to sign off on each project:
• Ministry of Planning and Investment
• Provincial People's Committees

- Board of Management of industrial zones, export-processing zones, and high-technology zones.

Not surprisingly, time delays in the issuance of licenses can still be extensive, and according to anecdotal evidence, usually exceed the 30–45 day turnaround period guaranteed by the government.

> The US–Vietnam Free Trade Agreement should witness renewed interest in Vietnam as an investment destination in 2003–04. However, the limited investment opportunities in Vietnam, the thinness of the financial market, and the considerable hurdles and high tax regime will not secure the growth of investor interest otherwise anticipated by Vietnamese authorities.

Grandfathering

Recognizing that frequent changes to the regulatory environment can adversely impact foreign enterprises, Vietnamese authorities have introduced the grandfathering principle, whereby if a change in law adversely affects the operating interests of a foreign enterprise, the investors are entitled to continued enjoyment of the incentives and regulatory arrangements stipulated in their original investment licenses. So too, should more favorable provisions come into effect as a result of subsequent changes to the law, these will henceforth apply automatically to existing foreign enterprises with operating licenses.

Remittance tax

Remittance tax rates have been lowered from the previous spread rates of 5 percent, 7 percent and 10 percent to 3 percent, 5 percent and 7 percent, thus reducing the tax burden to foreign enterprises. However, the corporate tax rate has been increased in some investment areas to offset the revenue reduction to government of reduced remittance tax (see below).

Obstacles to investment continue

Despite these developments, serious obstacles remain in legal provisions that give minority partners (state enterprises or government entities) veto power in a joint venture. It also remains the case that several government agencies have to approve foreign investment projects and that the approval process continues to be a lengthy one, indeed is arbitrary and tedious by regional standards. Local authorities also continue to have considerable power, and their approval is as necessary as that of central agencies. Even then, disputes over problems such as site clearance, transportation links, and investment placement have caused delays lasting years.[52]

A number of regulations also blow out start-up costs, making Vietnam a high cost start-up environment compared to regional neighbors. For example, land blocks in industrial parks, which cannot be purchased, are subject to 45- to 50-year lease terms, tying up considerable capital for small- and medium-sized foreign enterprises. In addition, the capital used to secure the lease is not then accepted as collateral by local banking authorities for securing loans.

In terms of the operating environment for foreign investors, those engaged in the importation or exportation of goods and services will face a series of constantly changing tariff rates, rules and regulations. The imposition of tariffs can change from customs officer to customs officer; the interpretation of regulatory statutes are enforced randomly and interpreted widely, and corruption is endemic. Tariff and export rates are also high by regional standards, ranging up to 45 percent for export duties, and as much as 50 percent for import duties plus applicable VAT taxes.

Finally, foreign enterprises will find themselves the higher paying consumers of essential services and production inputs, with a dual pricing scheme operating in Vietnam, both official policy and standard practice in business-to-business dealings.

Section C Politics

- Foreign enterprise is at the mercy of Vietnamese authorities, whose non-transparent decision-making processes, wide and varied interpretation of government legal decrees, and penchant for frequent but un-notified changes to tax law, export license law, and excise duties, makes the juridical environment an almost impossible one in which to operate. The risks in Vietnam are thus operationally-based, stemming not so much from policy changes as a result of election cycles or systemic changes to the structure of government, but changes to the legal operating parameters of the enterprise. In this sense, risk remains high in Vietnam.

Political stability in Vietnam is high, ironically one of the highest in the region, and reflects the entrenched legitimacy and hold on power enjoyed by the Communist Party of Vietnam – something not likely to change in the near future. In part, this reflects Vietnam's long and tortuous history, and the central role played by the communists in securing independence, which, to this day, ensures it patronage and respect.

As such, what risk investors face in Vietnam will not come through changes in the political composition of the country, election cycles, or structural changes to the mechanics and operation of government. Vietnam's political machinery is laced with caution, and not prone to sudden reorganization, let alone reform of the tripartite division of political power between local, provincial and central government authorities.

Rather, political risk to foreign enterprise stems from compliance issues and the multitude of legal and regulatory changes issued through government decree and the seemingly endless emendations that follow. This is the norm in Vietnam, with business well advised to keep abreast of these. However, this advice is easier given than followed. This arises from the fact that there exists no official gazette that gathers together the various laws, government ordinances and enforcement regulations.[53]

The political risks faced by foreign enterprise are thus predominantly regulatory in nature and, through a lack of transparency, the inability to foreshadow such changes and devise positioning strategies to mitigate adverse effects on the operational effectiveness of the enterprise. Examples of these risks include:

The legal system and transparency issues

Legal systems in Vietnam are underdeveloped, and their intent is often unclear and not communicated to the various agencies responsible for their implementation and administration. In addition, notification of regulatory changes or the introduction of new laws are often not received until well after the changes take effect, running the risk of placing foreign enterprise outside of the regulatory parameters for legal operation and leaving them open to subsequent fine or penalty.

Where notification of regulatory or legal changes is carried out, over-interpretation by local and provincial authorities can have disruptive effects on business. For example, the 1997 ruling that banned timber exports in order to delimit deforestation in Vietnam, was interpreted by local authorities to include the use of wooden pallets, bringing to a halt the export shipment of all goods that used wooden pallets – the bulk of export manufacturers. Only after lengthy delay did central authorities issue clarifying amendments to customs authorities, who then allowed resumption of export shipments using wooden pallets.

Frequent and random prime ministerial directives can also have far-reaching implications for foreign enterprise. A recent example includes a sudden prime ministerial decision to introduce regulations on felling natural timber and on half-finished wooden products for export, which when implemented proved so cumbersome that the regulation was eventually revoked two years later, but in the interim created havoc for export manufacturers.[54]

License and regulatory revisionism

For export manufacturers, the problems also extend to random changes associated with export tariffs, or the reinterpretation of the original foreign investment operating license. A foreign enterprise that received approval to establish a wood-chip export operation using wood from a cultivated forest, for example, was only subsequently informed after operations commenced that a 10 percent export duty would be levied.[55] This tax did not exist at the time when approval was gained for the project.

Likewise, similar situations resulted for other foreign enterprises whose operating licenses stipulated only the levying of a profit tax, but were subsequently unilaterally amended by Vietnamese authorities to include the levy of a sales tax as well.

It remains to be seen whether the introduction of the 'grandfathering' clause as part of the modifications to the Foreign Investment Law will go any way to solving these problems.

Corruption, corporate fraud and transparency

Corruption is widespread in Vietnam, indeed a way of life. An extensive black market operates for every conceivable product. The enforcement of intellectual property laws, and the adequacy of those laws in the first place, are nowhere apparent. Protection of commercially sensitive information is thus hard to achieve in an operating environment where a few hundred dollars will secure the most detailed company information from willing employees.

Foreign enterprises will also find themselves the object of fraudulent billing practices and should be well prepared to deal with the montage of accountancy practices that can leave them open to financial misappropriation. For example, it is not uncommon for enterprises to be forced to produce three sets of financial statements: those that satisfy

Vietnamese accounting standards; those for taxation authorities who demand intricate accounting details; and those for in-house strategic accounting purposes. This makes ripe conditions for misappropriation, if only through confusion and complexity.

Property theft and pillage of manufactured goods is also commonly reported, with most foreign enterprises forced to employ extensive security protection systems. More generally, insurance to cover such losses is not normally available.

Finally, a well-known problem in Vietnam is that of red-tape corruption, where poorly paid government officials will demand payment for processing rudimentary requests or to issue mandated documentation. This is particularly acute in the case of customs and necessary documentation for the shipment of exports or to process production import requirements. Most enterprises will have to factor this into their cost structures.

The continuation of the reform agenda: Pragmatic, slow and problematic?

Of great risk and concern to existing foreign enterprises already operating in Vietnam is whether the reform process *doi moi* will continue and, more importantly, if it will be reinvigorated. The benefits associated with past reforms are now all but exhausted and further reform is needed if the Vietnamese economy is to enjoy a renewed period of growth and development. While the US–Vietnam Free Trade Agreement indicates a willingness to continue with some degree of economic reform, it nonetheless remains the case that the Communist Party is equally committed to a state-planned economy dominated by SOEs and protected by strong government regulation. There is no indication of outright marketization, a wholesale diminution of the role of SOEs, or that the state will retreat from its central role in economic life.

For international investors expecting a sudden opening up of market opportunities in 2003–04 as a result of the free trade agreement, these expectations will prove misplaced. What can be observed is the pragmatic, but slow response from central authorities to allow some reform when disquiet among domestic constituencies is apparent. Thus, the continuing problem of unemployment, and increasing income disparities between the north and south of the country, and between urban and rural communities, will doubtless push authorities to consider market reforms to quell these problems before they become threatening. Above all, the Vietnamese leadership has been overwhelmingly concerned with maintaining political and economic stability; a concern that, in the end, will ensure the continuation of reform, albeit at a pace that will be much slower than outside observers would view as adequate.

Threatening issues

The Communist Party of Vietnam is faced with a series of current issues, many of which will test the veracity of the party's commitment to the reform process and potentially pose threats to its hold on power. Apart from the growing rural–urban and north–south income disparities, a spate of social problems is also threatening the traditionally conservative nature of Vietnamese society. Drug abuse (mostly smuggled in through adjoining borders with Laos and Cambodia), increasing prostitution, especially in Saigon, as well as increasing levels of HIV infection, have far-reaching social consequences, most of which the party appears bereft of policy to tackle.

In addition, the rule of law, widespread corruption, and declining party membership, are making good governance far more difficult to achieve, and pose longer-term challenges to the power and reach of the Communist Party of Vietnam. There is little indication that leadership renewal will be able to deal with these issues any time soon. Rather, it demonstrates the incongruity between an economy that requires marketization to be viable and a political system that refuses to modernize. Eventually, one of these sectors will suffer from the other's intransigence and lack of reform.

Leading risk indices: Corruption, stability, governance, risk

The seven key indices below suggest mixed results. On the one hand, political stability has declined marginally, reflecting a diminution in both the reach of central authorities and the level of compliance among provincial and local authorities they are able to elicit. On the other hand, while the level of transparency is better than was the case a few years ago – if only because of the development of black letter law – Vietnam continues to score low, especially when compared to other countries in the region. Thus, while some nominal improvement in the various indices can be observed, the bottom line is that Vietnam continues to be a poor place in which to do business.

Corruption

The corruption index indicates at first a perverse positive correlation with market reform. This probably derives from the relative decline in income experienced by state sector

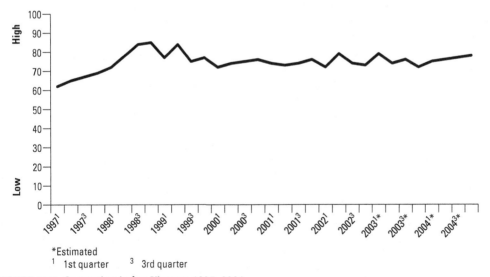

FIGURE 13.3 Corruption index, Vietnam 1997–2004
Source: Transparency International; World Bank; Asian Development Bank.

employees compared to private sector workers and thus the development of an entrepreneurial, albeit illegal set of practices aimed at supplementing state sector wages through red-tape corruption. This can be expected to increase if market reforms continue and income inequalities grow further – both of which look likely.

The corruption index also indicates persistently high and systemic levels of corruption in Vietnam. According to Transparency International's corruption perception index, for example, Vietnam ranks seventy-fifth out of 91 countries surveyed, placing it well behind countries like China, Guatemala, Senegal and Zimbabwe, and scoring a rank indices of only 2.6 out of a possible 10 for transparency.[56]

Political stability

Political stability remains high in Vietnam. On the downside, the capacity-to-govern index remains low, and is declining as provincial and local authorities fail to either fully comply with central government decrees, or as is often the case, demonstrate relative autonomy in terms of local administrative decisions, irrespective of policy decisions made at the party level.

The law and order indices also display downward movement, a result of increasing inequalities in income levels, continuing unemployment and endemic rural poverty.

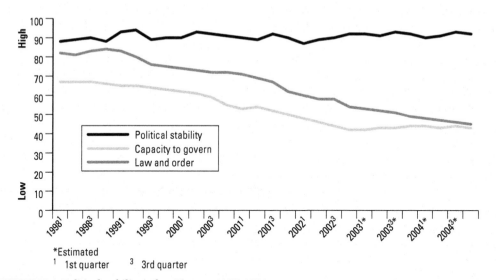

*Estimated
[1] 1st quarter   [3] 3rd quarter

FIGURE 13.4 Political stability index, Vietnam 1998–2004

Political stability methodology
- The capacity-to-govern index is based upon the institutional reach of government defined in terms of its ability to set the political and economic agenda and ensure its legislative program is enacted without significant compromise. This index is adversely affected by legislative opposition, lack of legislative implementation, failure to realize government policy and general political opposition.
- The political stability index measures violent opposition or organized demonstrations, terrorist activities, and popular discontent that adversely affect the institutional and electoral stability of the government.
- The law and order index measures the propensity to civil obedience, and the institutional reach of the rule of law in terms of regulatory compliance and enforcement.

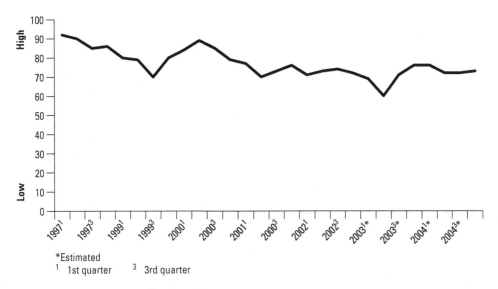

FIGURE 13.5 Foreign investor risk index, Vietnam 1997–2004

Foreign investor risk index methodology
- The foreign investor risk index is a composite index measuring tax burdens, discriminatory regulatory practices, adverse compliance regulations, government policy toward foreign enterprise, receptiveness to issuance of government contracts, foreign enterprise commercial restrictions, and official attitudinal changes to foreign direct investment and foreign commercial operations which impact operational efficiency. The index also incorporates a nominal measure for market risk and market failure.

Foreign investor risk index

The foreign investor risk index indicator, while showing signs of improvement, remains high. Vietnam is still one of the riskiest investment destinations in all of Asia.

Section D Security

- Vietnam enjoys good relations with its neighbors, and has few regional security issues that threaten its stability. Most of its security concerns are internal, reflecting the increase in domestic criminal activity, petty theft, and the growing incidence of drug trafficking and drug addiction, as well as prostitution. On top of this, increasing income inequality and the persistence of endemic poverty have made ripe those conditions that foster crime and corruption. This will be a growing problem for Vietnamese authorities in the years to come.

Internal security is being tested as a result of increasing income inequalities and the continuance of endemic poverty and unemployment. Petty property theft is high, and can be expected to go higher. Much of this is aimed at expatriate workers perceived to be affluent. By and large, however, Vietnam remains a safe place for foreign travelers and business people, at least in terms of personal safety issues, with few reports of serious crime or harm done to expatriate workers.

In part, this reflects Vietnam's harsh rule of law, where the death penalty is still imposed for a total of 33 crimes, in particular: serious corruption, drug trafficking, embezzlement and murder. Indeed, in recent years authorities have used the death penalty more frequently, reflecting the upturn in crime and central government fears about criminal activity and its effects on Vietnam's social fabric – especially the growing incidence of prostitution and drug-taking.

The harsh meting out of Vietnamese justice has itself been an area for increasing international attention, especially the recent treatment of indigenous hill tribes people and their protests against Vietnamese oppression. Central highlands hill tribe people, as well as a vocal minority of Christians, have held a series of protests and civil disobedience campaigns since February 2001. These groups have campaigned for social justice, more government resources to address poverty, illiteracy, and poor housing and health conditions, and have called for autonomous rule of their communities.

Vietnamese authorities have clamped down on such protests, and are suspicious that they are motivated by anti-communist movements and have historical connections with anti-Hanoi groups in the United States. Whatever the case, the treatment of protestors and hill tribe communities has been harsh, with random detentions and widespread reports of torture, including kicking, administration of electric shock, and frequent beatings.[57]

The response of Hanoi to these matters demonstrates a long tradition of disrespect for human rights, and reiterates the fact that Vietnam's justice system is non-transparent and politically based – indeed subservient to the Communist Party, where political denouncement is almost always followed by detention and imprisonment.

A wide number of political prisoners continue to be detained in Vietnam, with the imprisonment of journalists, outspoken anti-government dissidents, and social justice campaigners among them. Two journalists, for example, Le Chi Quang and Tran Khue, were recently detained and imprisoned for publishing anti-government sentiments on the Internet.[58]

Despite the harsh juridical regime in place, corruption and inefficiency in the administration of justice circumvents the effective administration of basic policing in Vietnam and has led to a woefully low apprehension rate. According to Transparency International, for example, of the 14,200 cases of smuggling, illegal trading in goods, and tax avoidance reported in 1999, only 70 cases were brought before the courts.[59]

Crime in Vietnam, then, remains for the most part unrestrained by the rule of law. With such a low rate of apprehension, foreign enterprise should thus conduct its operations with extreme caution, especially business involved in the production of intellectual property where the rule of law will obviously serve as no protection against intellectual property theft.

Legal security issues

Vietnam remains somewhat of an anachronism: one of only five one-party communist states in the world. This poses a series of risks for foreign enterprise not normally encountered in other jurisdictions.

First, the normal series of international memberships, and the juridical reach of international law and legal norms into the legal provisions of Vietnamese law as it relates to the treatment of foreign enterprise and foreign nationals, is not always in evidence. This places foreign assets at greater risk than would be the case in other countries like Malaysia, Singapore, or Thailand, for example.

Second, the Vietnamese legal system is not premised on an English common law ancestry as is true of many countries of the region, so that normal asset, property, and rights-based law is not in operation. Again, this places certain activities of foreign enterprise at heightened risk.

Finally, normal legal appeal mechanisms are also absent, leaving the basis for disputation settlement the preserve of what limited legal apparatus exists or, more generally, the preserve of personal contacts and access to senior decision-makers.

While Vietnam has developed much black letter law as part of its general reform program, the enforcement and administration of these remains problematic. Caution should thus be the order of the day in all contractual and business matters conducted in Vietnam.

Section E Economic and political risk forecasts

- The risk outlook for Vietnam remains steady but still high. Vietnam is now at a crossroads, caught between the need for a second wave of reform if the benefits of increased economic growth and further development are to be realized, but still trapped in a political and economic structure disposed to caution and inherently slow change. The movement toward marketization will need to be increased if efficiencies are to be realized, the SOE sector reformed, NPLs reduced, and interest by foreign investors rekindled. None of this looks to be guaranteed, and much remains problematic about the reform process. Investor caution is warranted and a wait-and-see policy should be the order of the day.

Short-term forecasts

- The short to medium term outlook for the economy is tending upward as a result of the US–Vietnam Free Trade Agreement. This should see some resumption of robust export growth levels and help boost GDP during 2003–04.
- Government debt is increasing, and the level of NPLs is not being addressed. This will increasingly absorb limited government revenues and create fiscal pressure on infrastructure programs needed to boost Vietnam's development.
- FDI is still low by regional standards, and is likely to grow only modestly during 2003–04. This reflects not only the high risk nature of Vietnam but also the limited financial market and investment opportunities available in Vietnam.
- Inflation will tend moderately upward during 2003–04, reflecting a lower dong and attendant increases in import costs. However, inflation will remain at low rates and should not exceed 2–3 percent.

- Reform of the SOE sector has mostly stalled, with many SOEs effectively bankrupt and part of the NPL problem. While employment has been dropping in this sector, there is little indication that central government authorities will move rapidly to implement marketization strategies to increase SOE efficiency.
- Widely held rumors have been circulating that the Vietnamese government is soon to make a major announcement concerning a new reform agenda to address the sorry state of the SOE sector. While some announcements are anticipated, as with most things in Vietnam, the rhetoric will not live up to the reality.
- The dong will continue to depreciate at the behest of government policy to help increase Vietnam's external competitive position. The problems of hard currency conversion will continue in 2003–04.
- Moderate reform of the banking sector can be expected to continue during 2003–04, albeit still dominated by state-owned banks. Dramatic changes in the composition of the banking system are not anticipated, however.
- The stock market will continue to grow in both the number of enterprises admitted to the register and capitalization. However, volatility will remain the hallmark of the index, although the liquidity of shares can be expected to increase with planned reductions in trading payment settlement times. For the adventuresome, the Vietnam Stock Exchange offers some limited growth opportunities.
- Agricultural production (especially rice production) can be expected to witness increased productivity rates as the effects of the Mekong Delta improvement projects come on line and tackle issues of salinity and seasonal flooding.

Short-term opportunities

- The value of imported food has climbed from US$32.5 million in 1996 to US$85 million in 2002. Increased opportunities for food provision will continue to present themselves in 2003–04.
- Supermarket and hypermarket general food merchandising opportunities are growing quickly, with the value of retail food sales increasing from US$2 million when first introduced in 1998 to US$12 million in 2002. Further rapid growth is anticipated in 2003–04.
- Seafood processing and export opportunities continue to be strong, with further growth potential during 2003–04.
- Continued rapid uptake of consumer durables, especially electronics, will continue during 2003–04. However, as with all markets in Vietnam, these do not represent large volumes relative to population size.
- Equity investment opportunities remain limited and high risk. Little is expected to change in the immediate short term.
- There is only moderate growth potential in the services sector.
- Prefabricated steel products will continue to experience relatively strong demand emblematic of the continued developmental needs of Vietnam. However, competition has proved tough.

Medium to longer term

- Long-term opportunities will mostly be tied to Vietnam's infrastructural developmental needs and to the concessional loan and foreign aid funding arrangements negotiated. These are likely to be in the areas of telecommunications infrastructure, power generation and electrical grid systems, bridge and road construction.
- Ongoing opportunities will exist in the oil and gas sector, but expect tough conditions and negotiations from the Vietnamese authorities.

Overall risk rating

While the risk profile for Vietnam remains steady, it nonetheless remains high – one of the highest in the region. The stalled nature of the reform process, continuing lack of transparency in the political, economic and juridical systems of the country, and the culture of fleecing international business in terms of license fees and regulatory obstacles, makes Vietnam a less than attractive location for foreign enterprise.

Despite this, Vietnam has undergone tumultuous change since the beginning of its reform program, *doi moi*, begun in the late 1980s. That Vietnam is attempting to replicate the developmental success of many of its Asian neighbors is no longer in dispute. Governmental reform programs have been implemented in many areas of the economy, attempting to discipline wasteful and inefficiently run state enterprises with the use of market forces. It remains problematic, however, the extent to which these reforms have the wherewithal to change significantly what amounts to a cumbersome bureaucratic structure, macro-structural inefficiencies, and provide an attractive environment for international investors.

Risk: Steady $\rightarrow$
Risk Rating (0 = lowest, 10 highest risk) 7.5

Section F Vietnam fact sheet*

Geography

Capital
Hanoi

Largest city (millions, 1995)
Ho Chi Minh City (Saigon), 3.015473

Location
16 00 N, 106 00 E

Adjacent countries
China, Laos, Cambodia

Terrain
Low with flat deltas in the south and north; central region has highlands with mountainous regions in the far north and northwest

Land use
Arable land 17%, permanent crops 4%, permanent pastures 1%, forests/woodland 30%, other 48%

Area: (km²)
329,560

Miscellaneous
Maritime boundary with Cambodia not defined; involved in a complex dispute over the Spratly Islands with China, Malaysia, Philippines, Taiwan, and possibly Brunei

Economic statistics

Currency
Vietnamese dong (D) = 100 xu

Exchange rate (March 2002)
US$1.00 = D15,126.00

Gross Domestic Product (GDP)
6.7% (2001)

GDP per capita
$396.00 (2000)

GDP per capita – PPP
$1,950 (2000)

GDP – composition by sector
Agriculture 25%, industry 35%, services 40%

Average annual wages (2000)
$240.00

Percentage of population below poverty line
37

Inflation rate
−0.60% (2000)

Foreign debt (billions)
$10.71 (2000)

Current account balance (billions)
$0.642

* All figures are the latest available except where indicated. All figures are in US dollars. Figures are compiled from national, international and multilateral agencies (United Nations Development Assistance Framework for the Socialist Republic of Vietnam 1998–2000, International Monetary Fund, World Bank, World Development Report, UNESCO Statistical Yearbook, International Labour Office, United Nations, Central Intelligence Agency World Fact Book). Gross domestic product (GDP) refers to the value of all goods and services produced in the preceding financial year. GDP per capita, Purchasing Power Parity (GDP per capita – PPP) refers to the indices developed by the World Bank to take account of price differences, cost of living differences, and relative purchasing power of a set basket of goods and services between countries so as to provide a more accurate measure of national wealth.

National unemployment rate (1999)
6.8%

Percentage of the labor force self-employed
80

Population below poverty line
37%

Labor force (millions)
40.6

Labor force by occupation
Agriculture 67%, industry and services 33%

Budget (billions)
Revenues: $5.3
Expenditure: $5.6

Industries
Food processing, garments, shoes, machine building, mining, cement, chemical fertilizer, glass, tires, oil, coal, steel, paper

Major exports (billions)
$1.271
Electronics, crude oil, marine products, garments, footwear, coffee, rice

Major imports (billions)
$1.298
Petroleum, machinery and equipment, leather and garment materials, steel and iron, electronics

Major trading partners (exports)
Japan (15%), Singapore (11%), Taiwan (7.5%), Germany (6.3%), Australia (6.5%), United States (5.9%)

Major trading partners (imports)
Singapore (19%), Japan (12%), South Korea (12.4%), Taiwan (12%), Sweden 6.8%)

Income/wealth distribution (household income or consumption by % share)
Lowest 10% of population 3.5%
Highest 10% of population 29%

Televisions (1997, millions)
3.57

Televisions per capita
0.44 (people per color television: 22.39)

Telephones (lines in use, millions)
2.6 (2000)

Telephones per capita
0.032 (people per telephone: 30.7)

Cellular phones (2000)
730,155

Cellular phones per capita
0.009 (people per cellular phone: 109.4)

Internet users (2000)
121,000

Fiscal year
Calendar year

Government and political statistics

Nature of government
Communist, One Party Rule

Constitution
Communist Political Constitution (amended 1992) administered by the Executive (President, Prime Minister, Communist Party Secretary General), Politburo comprising 15 members (Party Executive), elected by 150 member central committee. (National Legislature)

Structure of government

Executive branch
Communist Party General Secretary
(Nong Duc Manh); Prime Minister (Phan
Van Khai); President (Tran Duc Luong)

Legislative branch
450 member Quoc Hoi (National
Assembly) meets biannually and
elected every 5 years. The Assembly
appoints the president and the cabinet

**Main governing parties and ideological
affiliation**
Communist Party, Writings and
Philosophy of Ho Chi Minh
The Vietnam Fatherland Front

Main opposition parties
None. However, there are divisions
within the Party between the
conservative 'party bloc' who are
concerned with the political and social
consequences of rapid economic
growth and the reformist 'government
bloc' who champion a separation
between the Party and State

Administrative structure of government
58 provinces

Legal system
Combination of Communist legal theory
and French civil law system

International memberships
United Nations, Association of South
East Asian Nations; ASEAN Regional
Forum; Asian Development Bank; Asia
Pacific Economic Cooperation; Customs
Cooperation Council; G77; International
Bank for Reconstruction and
Development; International
Development Association; International
Telecommunications Union; UNESCO;
UNCTAD; World Health Organization;
World Tourism Organization;

Business organizations
Vietnam Chamber of Commerce and
Industry

Date of UN membership
1979

Social statistics

Population size (millions)
79,939,014

Population density (per square km)
237.62

**Fertility rate (average number of
children born to women 15–49 years of
age)**
2.49

**Maternal mortality rate
(per 100,000 births)**
1.1

Infant mortality rate
(deaths per 1,000 births) 30.25

Population growth
1.45%

Life expectancy
69.56
Men: 67.12
Women: 72.19

Ethnic composition
Vietnamese 88%; Chinese 3%; Thai,
Khmer, Hmong, Indigenous 8%

Religions
Buddhism 55%, Roman Catholic 8%,
Muslim 0.25%, Hoa Hoa 2%, Bahnar
0.14%, Other (includes Taos,
Confucians) 34.61%

National languages spoken
Vietnamese, Chinese, Khmer, Cham,
various tribal languages

Illiteracy rate (age 15+)
6.3%

By gender (ages 25+)
Male: 3.5%
Female: 8.8%

Notes

2 Australia

1   Australia's economic history demonstrates a clear relationship between OECD, in particular the US's economic performance and Australia's economic performance. Indeed, the mechanism for transmission is rapid, if poorly understood.
2   *OECD Economic Report*, Australia 2001 p. 1.
3   *ibid* p. 14.
4   *ANZ Industry Brief* June 2001, Manufacturing, p. 1.
5   Australian Financial Review, 'Global Trade Barriers are Set to Tumble' from DFAT, 15 November 2001, p. 10.
6   ANZ Industry Brief November 2001, Tourism, p. 1.
7   *Australian Financial Review*, 'The Secret World of the Australian Dollar,' 17–18 November 2001, p. 55.
8   Westpac, 'Australian Market Insights,' November 2001.
9   *ANZ Economic Outlook*, December quarter 2001.
10 RBA Bulletin, Table F1 and F4 'Interest Rates on Retail Bank Products'. See also ABS cat. no. 5204.0, Australian System of National Accounts, Table 1.19.
11 Evidence gathered from two executives of US and French companies working in Australia, Jan. 2002.
12 AXISS Australia, 'The Regulatory System' at www.axiss.com.au November, 2001 taken from KPMG Financial Institutions Performance Surveys.
13 Standard & Poors, Australia and New Zealand Credit Statistics 2001, June 2001, p. 5.
14 AXISS Australia, op. cit. November 2001.
15 Public or government debt is defined as the stock of recognized direct liabilities of government to the rest of the economy and the world.
16 *OECD Economic Surveys*, Australia 2001, p. 11.
17 *ANZ Economic Outlook*, December Quarter 2001. Bps refers to base points.
18 Swap rates is a term used by financial markets to denote corporate debt rates.
19 ANZ, op. cit. December 2001.
20 ABS, Balance of Payments and International Investment Position, Australia, cat. no. 5302.0, June 2000.
21 Australian Chamber of Commerce, 'Individual Agreements,' May 2001.
22 *Australian Financial Review*, 'Wages Rise as Howard Cautious,' 16 November 2001, p. 16.
23 *Australian Financial Review*, 'A Land of Zero Tolerance, or Mounting Labour Pains?' 24 November 2001, p. 50.
24 ACCI website <www.acci.asn.au/index_surveys> Dec. 2001.
25 *Australian Financial Review* Global Outlook, 'Australia Tipped to Weather Downturn', 21 November 2001.
26 ACCI, op. cit. Dec. 2001.
27 AXISS regulatory system <www.axiss.com.au> Dec. 2001.

28   *ibid.*

29   KPMG, Survey of Australian Capital Markets 2000–01, p. 1.

30   Australian Stock Exchange Monthly Index, at www.axiss.com.au

31   *Andersen Tax Review*, OECD, December 2001.

32   *Price Waterhouse Coopers* <www.asx.com.au> Corporate Tax December 2001.

33   *OECD Economic Surveys*, Australia 2001, p. 13.

34   Colliers Jardine, 'Property Trends,' October 2001.

35   *Australian Financial Review*, 'Australian Hotels Sales Stand Still Amid Turmoil,' 14 December 2001, p. 12.

36   *ibid.*

37   FDI will, for the purposes of this section, include equity flows so as to enable a more accurate picture of foreign investment trends to be developed.

38   Colin White, *Mastering Risk: Environment, Markets and Politics in Australian Economic History*, OUP, South Melbourne, 1992.

39   *Australian Financial Review*, 30 November 2001, p. 10.

40   US State Department Country Commercial Guides, Australia 2001.

41   *ibid.*

42   Foreign Investment Review Board, 'Investment Information,' 1999.

43   Standard & Poors, Australia & New Zealand Electricity Markets, November 2001.

44   Standard & Poors, New Opportunities for Australian Natural Gas Pipelines, November 2001.

45   *Australian Financial Review*, 29 November 2001, p. 8.

46   Ashley Lavalle, 'Native Title and Recent Australian Mineral Exploration Trends', *Journal of Australian Political Economy*, no. 47.

47   Project Finance Magazine, 'PFI to Decline,' December 2001 <www.projectfinance.com>.

48   *ibid.*

49   Glynn, O'Shannessy, *Investing in Australia: A Cultural and Practical Guide*, 2000.

50   *ibid.*

51   *Australian Financial Review*, 'Stepping into the Void,' November 2001, p. 62.

52   Standard & Poors, Corporate Governance Asia–Pacific 100.

53   *Australian Financial Review*, 'Predatory Pricing a Popular Target', 21 November 2001, p. 59.

54   N.B. The figure is exclusive of the one-off effects of the introduction of the GST on 1 July 2000.

3   China

1   *Far Eastern Economic Review*, 18 October 2001, p. 38.

2   This observation is not meant to imply that a liberal free market economy cannot function in the absence of formally democratic traditions.

3   Paul Heytens and Cem Karacadag, 'An Attempt to Profile the Finances of China's Enterprise Sector', *IMF Working Paper, Asia and Pacific Department*, November 2001.

4   World Bank <www.worldbank.org> China Homepage, 15 April 2002.

5   Asian Development Bank, 'Developing Asia and the World,' *Outlook 2002*, April 2002.

6   *ibid.*

7   *ibid.*

8   Economist, Global Agenda, 'In the Red,' <www.economist.com> 4 February 2002.

9   Paul Heytens and Cem Karacadag, op. cit.

10   Neil Gregory and Stoyan Tenev, 'The Financing of Private Enterprise in China,' Finance & Development, March 2001, vol. 38, no. 1.

11   Ministry of Foreign Trade and Economic Cooperation (China) website <http://www.moftec.gov.cn>.

12   Asian Development Bank, April 2002, op. cit.

13   Lanchovichina, E., W. Martin and E. Fukase, 'Assessing the Implications of Merchandise Trade Liberalisation in China Accession to WTO,' *World Bank*, June 2000.

14   Asian Development Bank, April 2002, op. cit.

15   Bruce Gilley, 'People's Republic of Cheats', *Far Eastern Economic Review* pp. 59–60.

16   Asian Development Bank, *Country Economic Review: People's Republic of China*, October 2000.

17   *ibid.*

18   David Murphy, 'A Good Apple,' *Far Eastern Economic Review*, 20 December 2001, p. 34.

19 David Lague, 'A Finger in the Dyke', *Far Eastern Economic Review*, 20 December 2001, p. 30.
20 Public or government debt is defined as the stock of recognized direct liabilities of government to the rest of the economy and the world.
21 *Economist*, 7 March 2002, p. 32.
22 IMF, *People's Republic of China: Staff Report for the 2000 Article IV*, consultation August 2000.
23 Asian Development Bank, October 2000, op. cit.
24 Asian Development Bank, April 2002, op. cit.
25 'The New Frontier', *Far Eastern Economic Review*, December 2001, p. 38.
26 China Briefing, *Far Eastern Economic Review*, 18 October 2001, p. 34.
27 Asian Development Bank, April 2002, op. cit.
28 *Master Index*, 'Survey of 13 Asia-Pacific Countries', 2001.
29 *Far Eastern Economic Review*, 'Special Report: China,' 18 October 2001, p. 51.
30 *ibid*. p. 52.
31 Paul Heytens and Cem Karacadag, op. cit.
32 *ibid*.
33 *Asia Monitor*, China & North East Asia, vol. 9, No. 4 April 2002, p. 5.
34 Sun Gong, Gao Yunzheng, and Xin Li., 'Woguo Qiye Suodeshui Zhidu de Wanshan,' Suiwu Yanjiu 3, 2001. p. 25.
35 Gilley, op. cit. pp. 59–60.
36 Asian Development Bank, op. cit. April 2002.
37 Colliers Jardine, Greater China Residential Property Market, October 2001.
38 Gilley, op. cit
39 *Far Eastern Economic Review*, 'China Briefing,' 22 November 2001, p. 17.
40 *ANZ Country Report*, May 2001.
41 Gilley, op. cit.
42 Gilley, op. cit.
43 *Far Eastern Economic Review*, 'China Briefing,' 12 July 2001, p. 18.
44 *ibid*. p. 36.
45 *Far Eastern Economic Review*, op. cit., 22 November 2001, p. 34.
46 Gilley, op. cit.
47 *Project Finance Magazine* <http://www.projectfinancemagazine.com/public/regions/eastasia/china/briefing/china.html>.
48 Gilley, op. cit. p. 59.
49 *Project Finance Magazine* op. cit.
50 *Economist*, 'Hong Kong and Shanghai: Rivals More than Ever,' 4 April 2002 <www.economist.com>.
51 *ibid*.
52 Susan V. Lawrence, 'The Life of the Party – Beijing,' Far Eastern Economic Review, 18 October 2001.
53 *ibid*.
54 Gilley, op. cit.

4 India

1 International Monetary Fund, *World Economic Outlook*, September 2002. Economist Intelligence Unit Forecasts.
2 Ministry of Finance, Current Fiscal Trends, <www.finmin.nic.in> 2001–02.
3 Asian Development Bank, *Asian Development Outlook*, <www.adb.org> 2001.
4 Ministry of Finance, op. cit. 2001–02.
5 India Infoline, *Indian Economy, Monthly Economy Probe*, 19 March 2002, <www.indiainfoline.com/econ/mosu/laes/es01.html> See also the *Economist Intelligence Unit Country Forecasts*.
6 Reserve Bank of India, Macroeconomic Developments, <www.rbi.org.in> 2001–02.
7 Consensus Economics, <www.consensuseconomics.com> January 2002; Centre for Monitoring the Indian Economy, <www.ccmie.com>, January 2002.
8 Centre for Monitoring the Indian Economy, *National Accounts*, <www.ccmie.com> February 2002.
9 Reserve Bank of India, <www.rbi.org.in> 14 January 2002.
10 Rajagopalan, S, VSNL, IBP to be privatized by March 31: Sinha, <www.hindustantimes.com/nonfram/010202/dleco10.asp> 1 February 2002.

11 Economic Analysis Unit, *India: Old Economy, New Economy*, Department of Foreign Affairs and Trade, AGPS, Canberra, 2001.

12 *ibid.*

13 Asian Development Bank, *Asian Development Outlook*, <www.adb.org> 2001–02.

14 Reserve Bank of India, Bulletin Number 41, 'Foreign Trade', <www.rbi.org.in> unrevised data.

15 Reserve Bank of India, 'Macroeconomic Developments 2001–02', <http://www.rbi.org.in/search/search. asp?sec=0>.

16 Asian Development Bank, *Asian Development Outlook*, <www.adb.org> 2001–02.

17 Indian Ministry of Commerce, <www.commin.nic.in> accessed January 2002.

18 Asian Development Bank, op. cit. 2001–02.

19 Holland, Tom, *Far Eastern Economic Review*, <www.feer.com/articles/2001/0111-29>.

20 —— 'Indian Banking System's Capital Shortfall', *Global Treasury News, Credit Week*, <www. gtnews.com> 6 February 2001.

21 Business Standard, 'India's Banking System Creaking', <www.responservice.com/archives/nov2001_issue1/ business/money.htm> 29 December 2001.

22 Reserve Bank of India, *Annual Report*, <www.rbi.org.in> 2000–01.

23 Reuters, 'Indian Banks to Create Bond Fluctuation Reserve – RBI', <asia.news.yahoo.com> 10 January 2002.

24 — Indian Financial System, www.bankersindia.com> accessed 21 March 2002.

25 Economic Analysis Unit, *India: Old Economy, New Economy*, Australian Department of Foreign Affairs and Trade, AGPS, Canberra, 2001.

26 —— 'Indian Banking System's Capital Shortfall', *Global Treasury News, Credit Week* <www.gtnews.com> February 6, 2001.

27 Ministry of Finance, *Economic Outlook*, <www.finmin.nic.in> Table 6.2 External Debt as a Percentage of GDP, April–December, 2001.

28 Asian Development Bank, *Asian Development Outlook, 2001*; Central Statistical Organisation 'National Income; Consumption Expenditure, Saving and Capital Formation', 1999–2000, January 2001; Reserve Bank of India, Annual Report 1999–2000, <www.rbi.org.in> September 2000; Ministry of Finance, Economic Survey 2000/01, <www.finmin.nic.in> February 2001.

29 Reserve Bank of India, 'External Sector, the Growth Process', <www.rbi.org.in> 2000; Sen, Basudeb, 'Savings and Investment in Competitive Financial Markets', R.S Bhatt, lecture, Industrial Investment Bank of India, 27 October 2001.

30 Ministry of Finance, <www.finmin.nic.in>.

31 Ministry of Finance, *Current Fiscal Trends*, <www.finmin.nic.in> 2001–02.

32 Economic Analysis Unit, India: *Old Economy, New Economy*, Australian Department of Foreign Affairs and Trade, AGPS, Canberra, 2001.

33 Asian Development Bank, *Asian Development Outlook*, <www.adb.org>.

34 Reserve Bank of India, *Macroeconomic Developments*, <www.rbi.org.in>.

35 Centre for Monitoring the Indian Economy, <www.ccmie.com> 2 February 2002.

36 Srinivasan, T.N. *Living Wage in Poor Countries*, February 2001, Dept of Economics, Yale.

37 Reuters, 'RBI sees 2001/02 GDP growth at around 5 percent', <expressindia.com/fullstory/php?newsid=5167>.

38 Shapiro, Andrew & Felder Ellene, *Passage to India*, Deloitte & Touche LLP, July 2001.

39 BBC News, India's Car Giant Slashes Workforce, <news.bbc.co.uk/hi/english/business/newsid_1562000/ 1562789.stm> 25 September 2001.

40 Rao, N, Vasuki, Indian Labor Laws Remain Inflexible, <www.worldroom.com/pages/wrnmb/coverstory2. phtml> accessed January 2002.

41 Das, Guchuran, 'India's Growing Middle Class', The Globalist, 5 November 2001 <www.theglobalist.com/ nor/gdiary/2001/11-05-01.shtml>.

42 Vijaraghaven, Kala, *Economic Times*, 2 February 2001.

43 Confederation of Indian Industry, <www.ciionline.org> 13 October 2001.

44 BBC World Business Report, <www.news.bbc,co,uk/hi/english/world> 4 September 2001.

45 *Far Eastern Economic Review*, Economic Monitor India, August 16, 2001, <www.feer.com/articles/01>.

46 National Council of Applied Economics (NCAER), <www.ncaer.org> 6 November 2001.

47 National Council of Applied Economic Research, <www.ncaer.org> November 2001.

48 —— 'Sensex plunges by 227 pts on Panic Selling, Hits 22-Month Low', The Hindustan Times, 14 March, 2001, <http://www.hindustantimes.com/nonfram/140301/eco.asp>.

49 BBC News, <www.news.bbc,co,uk/hi/english/world> 27 April 2001.

50 Reserve Bank of India, 'Macroeconomic Developments,' <www.rbi.org> 2001–02.

51 Mistry, Sharad, 'Higher FII limits may soften fall in India's weightage in MSCI Index,' *The Financial Express*, 5 October 2001.

52 Economic Intelligence Unit, 'India Country Briefing,' *The Economist*, 16 January 2002, <www.economist.com/countries>.

53 Ministry of Finance, *Economic Outlook*, <www.finmin.nic.in> 2001.

54 Reserve Bank of India, *Annual Report 2000–01*, <www.rbi.org.in>.

55 Frank Knight, India Property Review, <www.knightfrankindia.com> June 2001.

56 Economic Analysis Unit, India: *Old Economy, New Economy*, Australian Department of Foreign Affairs and Trade, AGPS, Canberra, 2001.

57 Frank Knight, op. cit. June 2001.

58 *ibid.*

59 *ibid*; Colliers Jardine, <www.colliersjardine.co.in> November 2001.

60 Colliers Jardine, *ibid* 2001.

61 Reserve Bank of India, *Foreign Investment Inflows* No 46, <www.rbi.org.in> 11 February 2002.

62 *Economist Intelligence Unit Forecasts*.

63 Parry, Sam, Enron's India Disaster, Consortium News.com, 30 December 2001, <www.consortiumnews.com/2001/123001a.html>.

64 — 'Vajpayee Fights Bribery Scandal Damage,' <www.CNN.com> 23 March 2001.

65 Time, 'Indian Government on the Defensive,' <www. Time.com> 17 March 2001.

66 — 'Defensegate: A scandal with a difference,' <www.CNN.com> 21 March 2001.

67 Rashid, Ahmed, 'Hair-trigger Tension Builds Nuclear Fears,' *Australian Financial Review*, 10 January 2002.

68 Bellman, Eric, 'Indo-Chinese Goodwill,' *Australian Financial Review*, 15 January 2002.

5 Indonesia

1 *East Asia Pacific Brief Main Report*, 15 October 2001, p. 4.

2 *Berita Resmi Statistik*, no 6, year V, 1 February 2002, p. 4.

3 Susan V. Lawrence, 'China Investment and Trade: China Business Goes Global.' *Far Eastern Economic Review*, 28 March 2002.

4 *ibid.*

5 Chinese New Year in 2002, for example, saw open displays of Chinese culture, including lion dancing, visits to temples and song contests, unprecedented for decades.

6 Cf. 'Key Performance Indicators of Recapitalized Banks.' IBRA, 21 March 2002, <http://www.bppn.go.id/wp_br_indicators.asp>, accessed 18 April 2002

7 Central Bank of Republic of Indonesia, 'Bank Loan Survey: Quarter 1, 2002' <http://www.bi.go.id/bank_indonesia2/utama/publikasi/upload/bls-q1-02.pdf>.

8 Sadanand Dhume, 'Dumb Deal?' *Far Eastern Economic Review*, 28 March 2002.

9 *EAP Brief Main Report*, 15 October 2001, p. 11.

10 See IBRA *Monthly Report*: January 2002, p. 1.

11 See *Jakarta Post*, 16 April 2002 for further details.

12 Cf. Asep Suryahadi et al., 'Coverage and Targetting in the Indonesian Social Safety Net Programmes.' *ASEAN Economic Bulletin*, v. 18, no. 2, August 2001, pp. 161–75.

13 *Asian Development Outlook 2001 Update: Southeast Asia. Indonesia*. Asian Development Bank, Manila. http://www.adb.org/Documents/Books/ADO/2001/Update/ino_update.asp

14 See *ACNielsen Study Shows Strong Consumer Demand Driving Ad Spend in Indonesia During 2001*, AC Nielsen news release, 26 February 2002, <http://www.acnielsen.co.id/news.asp?newsID=61>.

15 *ibid.*

16 <www.Inweb18.worldbank.org/eap/eap.nsf/attachments/car/File/car.pdf> citing data provided by the Indonesian Automotive Industry Association.

17 Cliff Rees, 'Indonesia Financial Issues', in Guide to *Restructuring in Asia*, White, Pages and ADB, London, 2001, p. 45.

18 Asian Economic Monitor, April 2002 Update: *East Asian Growth and Recovery: A Regional Update*, Asian Recovery Information Centre, ABD, p 10. <http://aric.adb.org/aem/regional_update.pdf>.

[19] *Indonesian Human Development Report 2001. Towards a new consensus: Democracy and human development in Indonesia*, BPS-Statistics Indonesia, BAPPENAS and UNDP, Jakarta, 2001, p 44

[20] See *2001 Investment Climate Statement*, US Embassy, Jakarta, <http://www.usembassyjakarta.org/ econ/investment.html>.

[21] 'Mining Sector Status.' *Miningindo Weekly e-Newsletter*, Issue 02–01, 18 March 2002, citing Price Waterhouse Coopers Survey 2001. See http://www.miningindo.com/e-news/miningindo/enews02-01,2002.htm>.

[22] 'Many Apartments On Hold.' *Properti Indonesia*, December 2001, <www.propertyenet.com/pi/ 200112>.

[23] *Jakarta Office Property Market – 2H 2001*, Colliers Jardine, Jakarta, February 2002, p. 4.

[24] *ibid.*

[25] *ibid*, p. 6.

[26] *Jakarta Retail Property Market. Market conditions at September 2001, forecast to September 2002*, Colliers Jardine Jakarta, p. 3.

[27] *ibid*, p. 4.

[28] 'Beri Kemudahan Investor Individu Asing Beli Properti di Indonesia.' Special Report, *Properti.net*, 1 April 2002 <www.propertyenet.com/berita>.

[29] 'CNOOC buys Indonesian oil fields.' CNN.com/Business, 21 January 2002, <http://www.cnn.com/2002/ BUSINESS/asia/01/21/ind.cnooc/index.html>, accessed 17 April 2002.

[30] 'Indonesia luring international interest again.' CNN.com/Business, 16 April 2002, <http://asia.cnn.com/ 2002/BUSINESS/asia/04/16/indonesia.invest/index.html>.

[31] 'Mining Sector Status.' *Miningindo Weekly e-Newsletter*, Issue 02–01, 18 March 2002, citing Price Waterhouse Coopers Survey 2001. See http://www.miningindo.com/e-news/miningindo/enews02-01,2002.htm>.

[32] Michael Shari, 'Foreign Companies are Thriving Amid Chaos.' *Business Week*, 24 September 2001.

[33] *ibid.*

[34] *ibid.*

[35] 'New Honda Auto Plant Begins Construction in Indonesia.' Honda Corporate news release, 18 January 2002, <http://world.honda.com/news/2002/c020118.html>.

[36] Cf. Gerry van Klinken, 'The Maluku Wars: Bringing Society Back In.' *Indonesia*, 71, April 2001.

[37] *Indonesian Human Development Report 2001*, p. 16.

[38] *Jakarta Post*, 'Megawati Calls on Indonesians to Shed Most Corrupt Asian Nation Tag.' 18 March 2002. Megawati was actually wrong on one count: the survey showed that Indonesia was not perceived to be the most corrupt nation in Asia – that dubious honor went (just) to Vietnam.

[39] Mark Baird, 'Corporate Governance in Indonesia.' *Jakarta Post*, 28 April 2000.

6 Japan

[1] Colliers International (2002), *Asia Pacific Property Trends: Regional Property Forecasts*. Year to Quarter 3, 2003.

7 Malaysia

[1] Asian Development Bank, *Asian Recovery Report*, 2001, p. 67.

[2] *Far Eastern Economic Review* online edition, 8 November 2001.

[3] *Far Eastern Economic Review* online edition, 10 January 2002.

[4] *The Business Times* online edition (Singapore), 4 January 2002.

[5] World Bank, *Malaysia: Social and Structural Review Update*, 2001, p. 5.

[6] Asian Development Bank, *Asia's Growth and Recovery – A Regional Update*, 2001, p. 15.

[7] World Bank, *Malaysia: Macroeconomic Update*, 2001, p. 2.

[8] *The Business Times* online edition (Singapore), 4 January 2002.

[9] Asian Development Bank, op. cit. p. 12.

[10] World Bank, op. cit. p. 3.

[11] Bank Negara Malaysia, *Press Release on Monetary and Financial Developments*, November 2001, pp. 9–11.

[12] Asian Development Bank, op. cit. p. 13.

[13] *Far Eastern Economic Review* online edition, 8 November 2001.

[14] World Bank, op. cit. p. 2.

[15] *ibid.*

16 *Far Eastern Economic Review* online edition, 10 January 2002.

17 *Sydney Morning Herald* online edition, 19 March 2001.

18 See Ministry of Human Resources, Malaysia, *Guidelines on the Implementation of Retrenchment*, <http://www.jaring.my/ksn/gline.htm>.

19 Asiafeatures.com, 'Business Sentiment Worsens in Malaysia.' 26 October 2001.

20 *New Straits Times*, 'Consumer Confidence Turns Cautious', 23 July 2001, p. 24.

21 *ibid.*

22 World Bank, op. cit. p. 5.

23 Asian Development Bank, *Asian Recovery Report*, 2001, pp. 71–2.

24 World Bank, op. cit. p. 5.

25 See *Far Eastern Economic Review*, 14 February 2002, pp. 44–5.

26 See Malaysian Industrial Development Authority (MIDA), <http://www.mida.gov.my/invest.html>.

27 Colliers, Jordan, Jaafar Sdn Bhd, *Colliers Property Review*, third quarter 2001, p. 5.

28 *Economist Intelligence Unit Forecast.*

29 Malaysian International Development Authority, <http://www.mida.gov.my/stats.html>.

30 *The Economist*, 1 December 2000, p. 32.

31 See *Far Eastern Economic Review*, 18 October 2001, pp. 81 and 84 for an interview with Azman Yahya, former head of Danaharta, now head of the Corporate Debt Restructuring Committee.

32 Transparency International, *Corruption Perceptions Index 2001*, <http://www.transparency.org/documents/cpi/2001/cpi2001.html#cpi>.

33 *Sydney Morning Herald*, 22 November 2001, p. 11.

34 Transparency International, *Global Corruption Report 2001*, p. 27.

35 Jomo K.S. and E.T. Gomez, The Malaysian Development Dilemma, in Mushtaq H. Khan and Jomo K.S., eds., *Rents, Rent-Seeking and Economic Development: Theory and Evidence in Asia*, Cambridge University Press, Melbourne, 2000, p. 298.

36 Interview with expatriate managing director, Shah Alam, Malaysia.

37 Asiafeatures.com, 'Malaysia Near Bottom in Corporate Governance.' 30 April 2001, <http://www.asiafeatures.com/businesss/0104,1230,02.html>.

38 *Far Eastern Economic Review*, 29 November 2001, p. 56.

8 Philippines

1 Bangko Sentral ng Pilipinas, 'BOP Surplus in June Mitigates the First Semester, Current Account Continues to be in Surplus' 20 September 2001, <www.bsp.gov.ph/news/2001-09/news-09202001a.htm>; Bangko Sentral ng Pilipinas <www.bsp.gov.ph>, 24 January 2002.

2 Bangko Sentral ng Pilipinas, 'Philippines External Sector', <www.bsp.gov.ph>, 3 April 2002.

3 IMF Public Information Notice on the Philippines No 1/63, 9 July 2001, <www.imf.org/external/np/ssec/ph/2001/pn0163.htm>, accessed on 22 August 2001; Duplito, Salve and Sanchez, Elizabeth, *Businessworld*, <www.bworld.com.ph>, 20 March 2001. *Economist Intelligence Unit Forecasts* 2000–05.

4 *Economist Intelligence Unit Estimates.*

5 *ibid.*

6 National Statistical Coordination Board, <www.nscb.gov.ph>, 30 August 2001.

7 Lucas, Daxim, 'IMF Team to Review Economic Program' *Businessworld*, <www.bworld.com.ph> 26 March 2001.

8 Economist Intelligence Unit op. cit.

9 'Philippines Keeps Interest Rates Unchanged, Fearing Inflation.' 11 April 2002, <http://sg.news.yahoo.com/020411/1/2nu13.html>.

10 Thirlwell, Mark, 'The Philippines' poorly peso', *Australian Export Finance and Insurance Corporation*, <www.efic.gov.au> 26 July 2001.

11 National Statistical Coordination Board, 'First Semester 2001 GNP–Exports', <www.nscb.gov.ph> 31 August 2001.

12 Bangko Sentral ng Pilipinas, 'Balance of Payments', <www.bsp.gov.ph> 23 January 2002. See also Economist Intelligence Unit Forecasts.

13 *Businessworld*, 'New Government Reveals IT Thrust', <www.bworld.com.ph> 30 January 2001.

14 Downer, Alexander, The Hon., 'The Philippines: Beyond the Crisis', Address to the launch of the East Asia Analytical Unit Report on the Philippines, 4 May 1998.

15 — 'A Woman's Work; Rescuing the Philippines', *The Economist*, 24 March 2001 p. 3.

16 — 'Manila Says Off to Good Start to Meet Econ Goals', Reuters, 28 February 2002.

17 This effect might be counterbalanced by a rise in customs duties.

18 Dumlao, Doris, 'Peso to recover to 47', Inquirer News Service, <www.inquirer.net> 29 July 2001.

19 National Australia Bank, *Philippines*, International Economics, December 2001.

20 Asian Development Bank, *Asian Development Outlook 2001*, Pt II, <www.adb.org>.

21 PricewaterhouseCoopers 'Asia Banking and Capital Markets', 2000, <www.pwcglobal.com/ph> March 2001.

22 *ibid.*

23 Country Presentation of the Philippine Panel, *34th ADB Annual Meeting*, 8 May 2001, Hawaii Convention Center, Honolulu. Bangko Sentral ng Pilipinas.

24 Dela Pena, Zinnia, 'The SEC sets new rules' *The Manila Times*, 9 October 2001.

25 Batino, Clarissa, 'RP seen to get $200 million in new World Bank loan' Inquirer News Service, <http://www.inq7.net/bus/2001/aug/02/text/bus_2-1-p.htm>, 1 August 2001.

26 Bangko Sentral ng Pilipinas, 'Foreign Investment', <www.bsp.gov.ph/Statistics> 24 January 2002.

27 Bangko Sentral ng Pilipinas, 'External Sector', <www.bsp.gov.ph/Statistics/sefi/sefip3.htm> 3 April 2002.

28 Bangko Sentral ng Pilipinas, 'Selected Information on the Philippine Banking System.' <www.bsp.gov.ph/statistics/spei/tab23.htm> 2001.

29 Bangko Sentral ng Pilipinas, 'External Sector', <www.bsp.gov.ph> 3 April 2002.

30 This figure could be as much as double if 'stranded assets' are included.

31 Davies, Rob, 'Philippine government ABS: pipe dream? *FinanceAsia*, <www.financeasia.com10> March 2001.

32 Burgonio, Marcel, Ph 2001 Deficit Just Tops Target, *The Manila Times*, <www.manilatimes.net> 26 January 2001.

33 *Far Eastern Economic Review*, <www.feer.com> 31 May 2001.

34 National Statistical Coordination Board, *Sectoral Statistics Labor and Employment*, <www.nscb.gov.ph>.

35 de Vera, Roberto and Lee, Peter, 'Information Technology, e-commerce and the Philippines Economy', Paper Presented to AT10 Researchers' Meeting, February 2000, <www.itmatters.com.ph/features/features_08132001.html>, 13 August 2001.

36 Singapore Ministry of Education , 'Singapore Number One in Mathematics Again in Third International Maths and Science Study', November , 2000, <www1.moe.edu.sg/press/2000/pr06122000.htm>.

37 Tenorio, Arnold, Reforming the Economy to Recovery', *Businessworld*, <www.bworld.com.ph>, 16 February 2001.

38 Cabacungan Jr, 'Massive Layoffs Seen', Inquirer News Service, <www.inq7.net./bus/2001/sep/26/bu_1-1.htm>.

39 Sheehan, Diedre, Economic Monitor: Philippines, *Far Eastern Economic Review*, <www.feer.com>, 21 June 2001.

40 CCTV.Com, 'Ph Growth Reaches 3.4% in 2001', <www.cctv.com/english/news/200s20131/81434.html>, 31 January 2002.

41 *Economist Intelligence Unit Forecasts.*

42 —— '11-month Auto Sales down 9.5%: Uptick in Nov' *Agence France Presse*, 10 December, 2001, <www.inq7.net/brk/2001/dec/10/brkbus_4-1.htm>; *Chamber of Automotive Manufacturers Philippines*, 7 November 2001.

43 Reuters, 'Manila Says Off to Good Start to Meet Econ Goals', <www.reuters.com>, 28 February 2002.

44 The Consulting Group, 'Capital Markets Overview', <http://www.salomonsmithbarney.com/pdf/products_services/consulting_group/capitalmrkts4q01.pdf>.

45 Pricewaterhouse Coopers, 'Asian Handbook.' <Asiabccmhandbook/phil/pwcglobal.com.au> 2001.

46 Ebias, Jun, 'Philippine Central Bank Abandons Aggressive Policy on Rate Cuts', <www.bloomberg.com>, 20 March 2002.

47 *Far Eastern Economic Review*, 'Seeking Bargains and Safe Bets', <www.feer,com> 4 May 2000.

48 *The Manila Times*, 'Manila Off to Good Start to Meet Economic Goals.' <www.manilatimes.net>, 28 February 2002.

49 Burgonio, Marcel, 'Philippines 2001 Deficit Just Beats Target', *The Manila Times*, <www.manilatimes.net> 26 January 2001.

50 Cabacungan, Gil, 'Businessmen Split Over Macapagal's Tax Reform', *Inquirer News Service*, 21 July 2001, <http://www.inq7.net/brk/2001/jul/31/brkpol_3-1.htm>.

51 Batino, Clarissa, 'IMF Bucks Shift in Tax System', 8 August 2001, <www.inq7.net/bus/2001/aug/09/bus_1-1.htm>.

52 Colliers Jardine, *The Knowledge*, The Philippines property market review, July 2001, <www.colliersjardine.com.au>.

53 *ibid.*

54 *ibid.*

55 Ernst and Young, 'Doing Business in the Philippines.' <www.paernstyoung.com.ph/dbiphil.pdf> January 1999.

56 National Statistical Coordination Board, 'First Quarter Foreign Direct Investment', 29 June 2001, <www.nscb.gov.ph/fiis/2001/2q-01/fdiact1.htm>.

57 National Statistical Coordination Board, Approved FDIs by Promotion Agencies, 2nd quarter 2001, <www.nscb.gov.ph/fiis/2001/2q-01/fdiapp1.htm>.

58 Bangko Sentral ng Pilipinas, 'External Sector', <www.bsp.gov.ph/Statistics/spei/tab1.6.htm>, 3 April 2002, *Economist Intelligence Unit Forecasts, 2002.*

59 Downer, Alexander, The Hon, op. cit.

60 Colliers Jardine Philippines, 'Know How: News Clips' August 16–31, 2001, <www.colliersjardine.com>.

61 Government of the Republic of the Philippines, *Profile of the Philippine Economy*, August 2001.

62 —— 'Philippines: After the Gloria Euphoria', *Asiaweek*, 2 February 2001.

63 National Statistical Coordination Board, January 2001, <nscb.gov.ph>.

64 Lugo, Leotes, 'Political Clans Seen Continuing to Dominate Local Politics', *Financial Times* Information Ltd, <www.ft.com>, 14 May 2001.

65 Bhagava, Vinay, 'Combating Corruption', *World Bank*; Bhagava, Vinay , 'Allegations of Corruption Against High Public Officials', Press Release 2000-4 EAP, 17 October 2000.

66 Kawai, Masahiro, 'Corporate and Bank Restructuring in East Asia', World Bank, <www.worldbank.org> 1 November 1999.

67 Bangko Sentral ng Pilipinas, Governor's Speech, 'Briefing on Anti-Money Laundering', Federation of Filipino-Chinese Chamber of Commerce and Industry, Filipino Business Club and Filipino-Chinese General Chamber of Commerce, 6 August 2001, <www.bsp.gov.ph/resources/gov's_speeches/speech_080601.htm>.

68 Luib, Romulo & Payumo, Manolette, '"Investment Flows Follow Fundamentals, Not Politics", says Expert' *Businessworld*, <www.bworld.com.ph>, Manila, 12 January 2001.

69 Sheehan, Deirdre, 'Aid-in-Waiting', *Far Eastern Economic Review*, <www.feer.com>, 7 September 2001.

70 Asian Development Bank, *Poverty Forum 007/01* 7 February 2001.

71 Tenorio, Arnold, 'Reforming the Economy to Recovery', *Businessworld*, <www.bworld.com.ph>, 16 February 2001.

9 Singapore

1 Trade dependency is calculated by adding the value of imports and exports, dividing it by the GDP then multiplying it by 100 percent. Total imports + total exports/GDP* 100%.

2 'SM Lee: Singapore must remake itself.' *The Singapore Business Times*, 16 October 2001.

3 Manpower Research and Statistics Department, 'Labor Market; Second Quarter 2001,' *Ministry of Manpower*, September 2001.

4 *Asia Pulse*, 'Singapore reports 0.8 PCT rise in tourist arrivals in Feb,' 9 April 2002.

5 Statistics Singapore, 'Singapore External Trade 2002,' Press Release, 18 April 2002.

6 'Global conditions and Asian banks: worse to come?' <India Infoline.com> 15 October 2001.

7 'Costly fight for democracy in Singapore' *Nation* (Thailand), 3 March 1999.

8 Deputy Prime Minister, Brigadier Lee Hsien Loong, Chairman of the MAS, 'Consolidation and liberalisation: Building world-class banks', speech at the Association of Banks Annual Dinner, 29 June 2001.

9 For more details on Singapore's plan to make itself a retail banking hub for the region, visit the policy statements window <www.mas.gov.sg>.

10 Deputy Prime Minister, Brigadier Lee Hsien Loong, speech, op. cit.

11 *Barclays Bank*, 'Country report: Singapore,' April 2001.

12 *The Singapore Business Times*, 'MTI: 41 percent of Singapore growth in 90s due to foreigners,' 1 November 2001.

13 *The Star (Kuala Lumpur)*, 'R&D spending doubled over last decade,' 21 September 2001.

14 William M. Mercer, Incorporated October 2000 survey from the *American Chamber of Commerce, Singapore.*

15 *The Star (Kuala Lumpur)*, 'Value of stocks traded down 22 percent last year,' 3 January 2002.

16 *Singapore Selected Issues*, Washington, DC: IMF, 2000, p. 31.

17 *The Singapore Business Times*, 'Grade A office rents fall in Oct. for seventh month,' 15 November 2001.

18 Colliers Jardine, 'Singapore office market overview – 3Q 2001,' October 2001.

19 *World Investment Report 2001: Promoting Linkages*, Annex table A.I.10 'The inward FDI index, 1988–1990 and 1998–2000,' Paris: UNCTAD, p. 254.

[20] Natasha Hamilton-Hart (2000), 'The Singapore state revisited' *The Pacific Review* 13 (2): pp. 195–216.
[21] IMD World Competitiveness Report 2000.

10 South Korea

[1] On the Asian Financial Crisis see Goldstein, M., (1998), *The Asian Financial Crisis: Causes, Cures, and Systemic Implications*. Washington, DC: Institute for International Economics. Noble, G.W., & Ravenhill, J., (2000), *The Asian Financial Crisis and the Architecture of Global Finance*. Melbourne: Cambridge University Press. See also the analysis by the Asian Development Bank.

[2] The term *chaebol* refers to the large family-owned conglomerates that dominate the domestic economy.

[3] In his 2001 New Year's Day address, Kim Dae-jung, the President of the Republic of Korea, apologised to the people of Korea for the incompleteness of the reforms. According to him, the 'direction of reform was right, but we failed to implement it thoroughly.'

[4] American Chamber of Commerce in Korea (2002), *Dynamic Korea: Hub of Asia*, Seoul: American Chamber of Commerce, p. 16.

[5] His approval rating in February 2002 was 20 percent.

[6] This is Kim's policy of engagement with North Korea.

[7] Moreover, the situation is not helped by inflammatory statements by George Bush that North Korea, along with Iran and Iraq, form an 'axis of evil' or that the United States is willing to use nuclear weapons against North Korea.

[8] Calder, K. (1998), *Asia's Deadly Triangle: How Arms, Energy and Growth Threaten to Destabilize Asia-Pacific*. London: Nicholas Brealey Publishing, pp. 25–30.

[9] GDP estimates are from the Economist Intelligence Unit.

[10] Only China fared better during 2001, achieving a growth rate of 7.3 percent.

[11] *Asian Development Outlook 2002*

[12] According to the International Iron and Steel Institute, East Asia accounts for around 43 percent of the global steel output. Together China and Japan produce around 23 million metric tons per month.

[13] Washingtonpost.com, 7 March 2002.

[14] Ministry of Finance and Economy, *Economic Policy Direction for 2002*, p. 14.

[15] *The Korea Herald*, 5 October 2001.

[16] The Bank of Korea, (2002), *Quarterly Bulletin*, p. 4.

[17] Around US$10 billion is traded daily. In comparison, Hong Kong trades around US$67 billion a day.

[18] The loan was for US$58 billion.

[19] The FSC undertakes policy formation for the financial markets and the FSS supervises the industry players. The FSC/FSS are an integrated regulatory body and replace a number of discrete agencies, including the Insurance Supervisory Board and the Securities Supervisory Board.

[20] By extending capital, asset quality, management, earnings, liquidity, and sensitivity (CAMELS) and forward looking criteria (FLC) to the non-banking sector.

[21] This included 11 banks, 26 merchant banks, 359 credit unions, 13 insurance companies, and 10 investment trusts. FSC/FSS, (2001), *Financial Reform and Supervision in Korea*, 2001, p. 9. Currently, there are 1854 companies involved in the sector.

[22] The government has spent more than US$120 billion to repair the financial system. *The Economist*, 1 September, 2001.

[23] *Asia Pulse*, 20 March, 2002. In monetary terms, the total NPLs in 2001 represents 35.1 trillion won.

[24] For a more detailed analysis see FSC/FSS, (2001), *Financial Reform and Supervision in Korea*, 2001, pp. 20–1

[25] *Korea Times*, 22 March 2002.

[26] OECD (2000), *Labour Market Reform and Social Safety Net Policies in Korea*.

[27] American Chamber of Commerce in Korea, (2002) op. cit., p. 12.

[28] *ibid.*

[29] Korea Labor Institute, (2002), *Labor Trends*, p. 5.

[30] Korea Productivity Center, 17 February 2002.

[31] The government has indicated that this is part of the government's economic policy direction for 2002. See Ministry of Finance and Economy, *Economic Policy Direction for 2002*, p. 10.

32 When the index moves above 100, it means that the number of consumers who will spend more in the next six months outweighs the number of consumers who will spend less.

33 This survey was conducted by the Federation of Korean Industries.

34 A similar survey conducted by the Korean Chamber of Commerce that polled over 1400 manufacturers concluded that the economy will improve during 2002.

35 Ministry of Finance and Economy.

36 The KOSDAQ stands for Korea Securities Dealers Automated Quotation System. The market was established to foster small to medium high-tech business ventures.

37 *The Korea Herald*, 14 May 2002.

38 KPMG (2001), *Foreign Direct Investment in Korea*, September.

39 *The Korea Herald*, 24 April 2002.

40 Among the OECD, however, Korea's corporate tax rate of 28.7 percent is one of the most competitive.

41 Korea Research Institute for Human Settlements, December 2001. Under the Jeonse system, tenants pay an upfront lump-sum payment to the owner. They invest this money and retain the interest. At the end of the contract, the initial stake is returned to the tenant.

42 *The Korea Herald*, 2 April 2002.

43 DTZ Research, January 2002, p. 3. In January 2001, a similar survey conducted by CB Richard Ellis rated Seoul as having the eleventh most expensive office space in the world. See CBRE, Global 50 Index, January 2001.

44 Colliers Jardine (2001), *Korea Office Market: Market Conditions at September 2001*.

45 *Far Eastern Economic Review*, 8 February 2001.

46 KPMG (2001), *Foreign Direct Investment in Korea*, September, p. 42.

47 *ibid.* p. 43.

48 *ibid.*

49 American Chamber of Commerce in Korea, op. cit., p. 43.

50 See *Far Eastern Economic Review*, 21 February 2002, p. 46.

51 *ibid.* p. 46.

52 Calder, K. (1999), op. cit., p. 29.

53 Economist Intelligence Unit, *Viewswire*, 31 January 2002.

54 Transparency International, *Corruption Perceptions Index*, 2001.

55 Chosun, 4 January 2002. The survey was conducted by the Korean chapter of Transparency International.

56 ADB/OECD (2001), 'East Asia and the Pacific.' *Global Corruption Report*, p. 13.

57 See *The Korea Times*, 10 October 2001.

58 *The Korea Times*, 26 September 2001.

59 In August 1998, the North Koreans fired a test missile across Japan without warning.

11 Taiwan

1 The political status of Taiwan is problematic. It is not a member of the United Nations, the World Bank, or the International Monetary Fund and it has only observer status at APEC meetings. It does have diplomatic relations with 28 countries, many of which are in Central America. China has consistently lobbied (and cajoled) the international community to deny formal recognition to Taiwan. Moreover, Beijing has warned that if Taiwan formally proclaims independence, it will invade and reclaim the island. To speak of Taiwan as a 'country' here is to acknowledge that while it is not a full member of the international community, it does in all other ways act as a sovereign unit.

2 The poor performance of the Japanese economy has had a marked effect on Taiwan, as it has had on the region as a whole. Japan is one of Taiwan's leading trading partners. Consequently, the Taiwanese recovery is intimately linked to recovery in Japan.

3 A report has suggested that Taiwan is one of five key regional locations for the emerging bio-technology industry, but that China is the country to watch. See *Taipei Times*, 23 November 2001.

4 *Far Eastern Economic Review*, 6 December 2001, p. 73.

5 *Far Eastern Economic Review*, 26 July 2001, p. 49.

6 *Far Eastern Economic Review*, 21 February 2002, p. 49.

7 American Chamber of Commerce, *Topics Magazine Online*, Wednesday 30 January 2002.

8 *Taipei Times*, 21 January 2002.

[9] Prior to the formation of the TCTU, the KMT-controlled Chinese Federation of Trade Unions was the only legal representative of organised labor at the national level. In this sense, the TCTU is more independent of the Taiwanese party system.

[10] Some large companies have been coping with this problem by starting up their own education facilities to train new recruits.

[11] Ministry of Economic Affairs, 'Taiwan's Bio-technology Investor Incentives.'

[12] *Taipei Times*, Wednesday 8 August 2001. The available fund is more than NT$320 billion.

[13] *Taipei Times*, 20 October 2001.

[14] Colliers Jardine Taiwan.

[15] According to the *World Investment Report 2001*, FDI in the region topped US$80 billion in 2000. UNCTAD, *World Investment Report*, 2001, p. 23.

[16] The high speed rail project linking the north and south of the island is an exception to this rule, however. This NT$13.5 billion project is one of the largest of its kind in the world.

[17] According to the *Far Eastern Economic Review*, investment by Chinese nations into Southeast Asia has grown by 50 percent in the last three years. *Far Eastern Economic Review*, 28 March 2002, p. 30.

[18] *Taipei Times*, 21 February, 2002.

[19] Morgan Stanley Dean Witter & Co were stripped of their mandate in 1997 because the Chinese believed that its analysts helped to undermine the Hong Kong stock market. *Taipei Times*, 8 September 2001.

[20] Taiwan has observer status in APEC and is part of the Asian Development Bank under the title Chinese Taipei.

[21] *The Economist*; Ministry for Economic Affairs.

[22] It is important to remember that while the government of the ROC claims to represent the true government of China, it is in fact an imposed political system. Indigenous Taiwanese had no say in who governed them when the Kuomintang fled the mainland.

[23] *The Economist*, 8–14 December 2001, p. 33.

12 Thailand

[1] Asian Development Bank, *Asian Recovery Report* 2002.

[2] *Bangkok Post*, 17 February 2002.

[3] *Far Eastern Economic Review*, 24 May 2001, p. 58.

[4] United Press International, 'Analysis: Trade, debts slow Thai economy.' 28 February 2002.

[5] World Bank: *Country Dialogue Monitor, Thailand*, September 2000, pp. 33–7.

[6] *ibid*. p. 38.

[7] *The Nation*, Bangkok, 11 April 2001, p. B12.

[8] Bank of Thailand forward estimates, 2001.

[9] World Bank, op. cit., 2000, p. 36.

[10] Public or government sector debt is defined as the stock of recognized, direct liabilities of government to the rest of the economy and the world.

[11] *Bangkok Post*, 9 May 2001.

[12] Merrill Lynch has gone further, revising the Asian Development Bank figure down to 2.5 percent for 2003. Growth in government spending is projected by the Ninth Economic and Social Development Plan to be 7.7 percent for 2002 and around 7 percent for 2003.

[13] *Bangkok Post*, 14 May 2001.

[14] Warr, P.G. (1998), 'Thailand.' in McLeod, R.H. & Garnaut, R. (eds.), *East Asia in Crisis: From Being a Miracle to Needing One*. Routledge: London, pp. 49–65.

[15] Labor issues are regulated via the Labor and Social Welfare Ministry. Labor laws are mostly contained in the National Employment Code (NEC) Announcement 103 and the Labor Act of 1975. The Civil and Commercial Code governs termination of employment and related matters.

[16] *Bangkok Post*, 8 February 2001, p. 1.

[17] 'MasterCard International MasterIndex Asia–Pacific Survey.' Asia Pacific News. 7 February 2002. <www.apn.btbtravel.com/s/Editorial-Corporate-Cards.asp?ReportID=32322>.

[18] Nancy Koh, 'Thai National AMC Offers Few Benefits to Banks.' March, 2001. Standard & Poors Financial Institutions Analysis.

[19] Administered by the Thai Board of Investment.

20 Specific business tax is applied to the banking, financial, and insurance business in lieu of the VAT. Depending on the product type this ranges from 2.5 to 3 percent.
21 *Bangkok Post*, 5 February 2001. Colliers Jardine (Thailaind).
22 *Bangkok Post*, 8 February 2001.
23 Colliers Jardine, 8 February 2001
24 Tourism Authority of Thailand.
25 Tourism Authority of Thailand preliminary figures.
26 Identity protected sources at both the Bank of Thailand and the Thai Development Research Institute, for example, informed ARI that it was common practice to inflate FDI figures in order to bolster domestic political support for incumbent administrations and to heighten international investor confidence in Thailand.
27 Institute for International Finance.
28 Bank of Thailand Figures. *The Nation*, 10 April 2001, p. B1.
29 *Project Finance Magazine*.
30 *Far Eastern Economic Review*, 19 April 2001, p. 47.
31 *Far Eastern Economic Review*, 10 May 2001, p. 10.
32 *Bangkok Post*, 9 February 2001, p. 11.
33 'Key Governance Issues in Cambodia, Lao, PDR, Thailand and Viet Nam.' Asian Development Bank, April 2001, pp. 37–45.
34 *Asiawise*, 4 June 2001
35 *Sydney Morning Herald*, 26 May 2001.

13 Vietnam

1 See Mark. E. Manyin, *The Vietnam–US Bilateral Trade Agreement*. Congressional Research Service for Congress, Washington, DC.
2 Steer, A., *et al.*, Vietnam 2010: *Entering the 21st Century: Overview*. Joint Report of the World Bank, Asian Development Bank, United Nations Development Program. World Bank, Washington, 2001, p. 3.
3 Asian Development Bank, *Country Economic Review: Socialist Republic of Viet Nam*. Asian Development Bank, Manila, Philippines, November 2000, p. 10.
4 Cowen, David, et al., *Vietnam: Selected Issues and Statistical Appendix*. International Monetary Fund, Washington, January, 2002, p.5.
5 Conversation with senior executive who preferred to remain anonymous in Hanoi, Sun Hotel, 25 February 2001.
6 World Bank and the International Development Association, '*ISA and Vietnam: Improving Living Conditions*.' URL: http://www.worldbank.org/ida/ida-vietnam.htm.
7 Asian Development Bank Outlook 2001: Update, 'Vietnam.' *Asian Development Bank*, Manila, Philippines, p. 72.
8 Figures complied from Business Monitor International, *Asia Monitor: South East Asia*, Volume 12, No. 12, December 2001, p.14.
9 David Cowen, *Vietnam: Selected Issues and Statistical Appendix*. International Monetary Fund, Washington, DC, pp. 45–48.
10 Business Monitor International, *Asia Monitor, South East Asia*. Volume 13, No. 4, April. 2002, p. 7.See also Margot Cohen, 'Recipe for Change.' *Economic Monitor: Vietnam*. *Far Eastern Economic Review*, December 3, 2001.
11 Matthew Maurer, 'Global Rice Market Review.' *Africa Online*, 25 January 2002. http://www.africaonline.com/site/Articles/1,3,45122.jsp.
12 *ibid.*
13 Business Monitor International, *Asia Monitor, South East Asia*. Volume 13, No. 4, April. 2002, p. 7.
14 *Asian Development Outlook 2002: Economic Trends and Prospects in Developing Asia*. Asian Development Bank, Manila, Philippines.
15 American Embassy, Hanoi (2002), *Vietnam Country Commercial Guide FY2002*. State Department, United States Embassy, Hanoi, p. 5.
16 Foreign Investment Climate, Vietnam, *Countrywatch*. URL: www.countrywatch.com.
17 Onada FX Technical Bid Prices, calculated on 2-year average cross-rate quotes. URL: http://www.oanda.com/products/fxp/playground.shtml.
18 Karl Heinz (2000), 'Vietnam Financial Briefing.' *Project Finance Magazine*, November 20, p. 7.

19 State Bank of Vietnam estimates quoted in Business Monitor International, *Asia Monitor: South East Asia*, Volume 12, No. 12, December 2001, p. 14.

20 'Vietnam' in Asian Development Bank, *Asian Development Outlook 2002: Economic Trends and Prospects in Developing Asia*. Asian Development Bank, Manila, Philippines, pp. 75.

21 Karl Heinz (2000), 'Vietnam Financial Briefing.' *Project Finance Magazine,* November 20, p. 6.

22 United States Embassy, *Vietnam Country Commercial Guides FY2002*. State Department, United States Embassy, Hanoi, p. 69.

23 Gil Baker (2001), 'Small but Perfectly Formed.' *Euromoney Magazine.* February. URL. www.euromoney.com.

24 *ibid.*

25 'Vietnam.' in Asian Development Bank, *Asian Development Outlook 2002: Economic Trends and Prospects in Developing Asia*. Asian Development Bank, Manila, Philippines, p. 75.

26 Christopher Moore (1999) 'What Happened to the Funds?.' *The Vietnam Business Journal,* Volume 7, No. 3, pp. 1–14.

27 Mark Thompson (2001), 'Vietnam's New Generation.' *AsiaWise,* May 2. URL www.asiawise.com.

28 *ibid.* p. 69.

29 The four banks are: Vietnam Bank of Foreign Trade (Vietcombank); The Vietnam Industrial and Commercial Bank (IncomeBank); Bank of Agriculture and Rural Development; Vietnam Investment Bank.

30 David Cohen et al. (2002), *Selected Issues and Statistical Appendix*. International Monetary Fund, IMF Country Report, January, p. 17.

31 *ibid.* p. 20.

32 Gil Baker (2001), 'Small but Perfectly Formed.' *Euromoney Magazine.* February. URL. www.euromoney.com.

33 Karl Heinz (2000), 'Vietnam Financial Briefing.' *Project Finance Magazine,* November 20, p. 4, and World Bank, (2000), *General Statistical Yearbook,* General Statistical Office, World Bank Staff, Washington, DC.

34 'Vietnam Debt Restructuring too Slow, Central Bank.' Reuters News Service, as quoted in Forbes. URL: www.forbes.com/business/newswire.

35 Nayan Chandra (2002), 'Half-hearted Modernity in Vietnam.' *International Herald Tribune.* Tuesday, February 5. See also 'Assessing a Different Approach to Bad Debt.' Vietnam Investment Review, Number 523, 22–28 October 2001.

36 'Vietnam Debt Restructuring Too Slow, Central Bank.' Reuters News Service, as quoted in Forbes. URL: www.forbes.com/business/newswire.

37 Jonathan Haughton (2000), 'Opening the Books: State Budget Reveals Slipping Revenue and Reluctant Transparency.' *The Vietnam Business Journal,* Volume 8, No. 1, February.

38 Defined as 'Generally lack characteristics of desirable investment.' David Levey (2002), *Sovereign Rating History.* January, Moody's Investor Services, Global Credit Research, New York, p. 21.

39 'Vietnam.' in Asian Development Bank, *Asian Development Outlook 2002: Economic Trends and Prospects in Developing Asia*. Asian Development Bank, Manila, Philippines, p. 76.

40 Communist Party of Vietnam, Unemployment estimates. URL: www.cpv.vn/studies.

41 'Vietnam Govt Unveils US$1.5 billion Plan to Cut Jobless Rate.' URL: http://sg.news.yahoo.com/020307/16/2kh6i.html.

42 *ibid.*

43 Nguyen Nam Phuong (2000), '*Asian Crisis: Unemployment Pushes Vietnam to Export Labor.*' Asia Times Online. URL: www.atimes.com/asia-crisis/BG12Db01.html.

44 International Labour Office, *Labour Practices in the Footwear, Leather, Textiles and Clothing Industries.* Report for discussion at the Tripartite Meeting on Labour Practices in the Footwear, Leather, Textiles and Clothing Industries, Geneva, 16–20 October 2000. International Labour Office, Geneva.

45 Even the Vietnamese authorities have recognized the shortage of skilled and technical labor for foreign enterprises in Vietnam, hoping to address this problem by innovating and reforming the educational infrastructure to produce greater numbers of technically skilled graduates. However, despite a commitment of 15% of the national budget to education, there is little discernible evidence of rapid change. See, for example: URL: www.e-my.net.my/kl/izdang/reemployment.htm.

46 'Vietnam Govt Unveils US$1.5 billion Plan to Cut Jobless Rate.' URL: http://sg.news.yahoo.com/020307/16/2kh6i.html.

47 'Vietnam Country Profile.' Mekong Sources. URL: www.mekongresearch.com See also 'Vietnam: Foreign Investment Climate.' Countrywatch. URL: www.countrywatch.com.

48 'Survey on Labor and Employment in Vietnam.' 1 July 2000. URL: www.vietnampanorama.com/labor2000.html.

[49] See, for example, Time Shorrock (1997), 'Vietnam Protects its Labor Force: Foreign Investors Face Fines for Infractions.' URL: www.saigon.com/~nike/news/joc3.htm.

[50] Jonathan Haughton (2000), 'Opening the Books: State Budget Reveals Slipping Revenue and Reluctant Transparency.' *The Vietnam Business Journal*, Volume 8, No. 1, February.

[51] 'Vietnam.' in Asian Development Bank, *Asian Development Outlook 2002: Economic Trends and Prospects in Developing Asia*. Asian Development Bank, Manila, Philippines, p. 75.

[52] Peter Donovan and Adam McCarty, *Vietnam's Integration With ASEAN: The Impact of Foreign Direct Investment*, Report Number 3, August 1997, Department of International Economics Organizations, Office of the Government Van Phong Chinh Phu, and the United Nations Development Program, pp. 91–92.

[53] An English language version of various 'statutes at large' is sold via the Ministry for Planning and Investment, but this is not up-dated frequently, nor is it comprehensive. More generally, it does not interpret the various laws and statues, many of which are less than transparent and open to wide interpretation or over-interpretation by various levels of authority.

[54] Japan Machinery Center for Trade and Investment (2002), *Barriers to Trade and Investment: Vietnam*. Japanese Business Council on Facilitation of Trade and Investment, pp. 1–13.

[55] Name of corporation withheld for confidentiality reasons.

[56] Robin Hodess (2001)(ed.). *Corruption Perceptions index: Global Corruption Report, 2001*. Transparency International, pp. 23–38, 234–236.

[57] Human Rights Watch as quoted by Reuters. URL: www.msnbc.com/news/742308.asp?cp1=1.

[58] John SeSio, (2002), 'Journalists Jailed in Vietnam.' *Asia Observer*, March 25.

[59] Robin Hodess (2001) (ed.). *Corruption Perceptions Index: Global Corruption Report, 2001*. Transparency International, pp. 29.

Index

This index concentrates on bringing together topics across the chapters on each country that comprise the text of the book, which share a common structure. Thus under each country in the index are entries for those topics not found in other chapters. Other topics are found under the common headings such as macroeconomic performance, stock market, etc.